TRANSLATOR AND EDITOR:
Rabbi David Strauss

MANAGING EDITOR:
Baruch Goldberg

EDITOR:
Dr. Edward L. Tepper

ASSOCIATE EDITOR:
Dr. Jeffrey M. Green

COPY EDITOR:
Alec Israel

BOOK DESIGNER:
Ben Gasner

GRAPHIC ARTIST:
Michael Etkin

TECHNICAL STAFF:
Muriel Stein

Random House Staff

PRODUCTION MANAGER:
Richard Elman

ART DIRECTOR:
Bernard Klein

CHIEF COPY EDITOR:
Amy Edelman

THE TALMUD

THE STEINSALTZ EDITION

VOLUME XVIII

TRACTATE SANHEDRIN

PART IV

VOLUME XVIII
TRACTATE SANHEDRIN
PART IV

RANDOM HOUSE
NEW YORK

THE TALMUD

תלמוד בבלי

THE STEINSALTZ EDITION

Commentary by Rabbi Adin Steinsaltz (Even Yisrael)

 Published in the United States by
Random House, Inc., New York, and simultaneously in Canada by
Random House of Canada Limited, Toronto.

This is an English translation of a work originally published
in Hebrew by The Israel Institute for Talmudic Publications,
Jerusalem, Israel.

Library of Congress Cataloging-in-Publication Data
(Revised for volume XVIII)
The Talmud
English, Hebrew, Aramaic.
Includes bibliographical references.
Contents: v. 1. Tractate Bava metzia—
v. 18. Tractate Sanhedrin, pt. 4
Accompanied by a reference guide.
I. Title.
BM499.5.E4 1989 89-842911
ISBN 0-394-57665-9 (guide)
ISBN 0-394-57666-7 (v. 1)
ISBN 0-375-50182-7 (v. 18)

Random House website address: www.randomhouse.com
Printed in the United States of America on acid-free paper

2 4 6 8 9 7 5 3

First Edition

In loving memory of our parents

Johanna and Karl Kann

חנה בת יעקב וקלונימוס בן יהודה הלוי

and

Malwine and Ferdinand Katz

מלכה בת חיים ויוסף בן ברוך הכהן

dedicated by

Margot and Fred Kann

The Steinsaltz Talmud in English

The English edition of the Steinsaltz Talmud is a translation and adaptation of the Hebrew edition. It includes most of the additions and improvements that characterize the Hebrew version, but it has been adapted and expanded especially for the English reader. This edition has been designed to meet the needs of advanced students capable of studying from standard Talmud editions, as well as of beginners, who know little or no Hebrew and have had no prior training in studying the Talmud.

The overall structure of the page is similar to that of the traditional pages in the standard printed editions. The text is placed in the center of the page, and alongside it are the main auxiliary commentaries. At the bottom of the page and in the margins are additions and supplements.

The original Hebrew-Aramaic text, which is framed in the center of each page, is exactly the same as that in the traditional Talmud (although material that was removed by non-Jewish censors has been restored on the basis of manuscripts and old printed editions). The main innovation is that this Hebrew-Aramaic text has been completely vocalized and punctuated, and all the terms usually abbreviated have been fully spelled out. In order to retain the connection with the page numbers of the standard editions, these are indicated at the head of every page.

We have placed a *Literal Translation* on the right-hand side of the page, and its punctuation has been introduced into the Talmud text, further helping the student to orientate himself. The *Literal Translation* is intended to help the student to learn the meaning of specific Hebrew and Aramaic words. By comparing the original text with this translation, the reader develops an understanding of the Talmudic text and can follow the words and sentences in the original. Occasionally, however, it has not been possible to present an exact literal translation of the original text, because it is so different in structure from English. Therefore we have added certain auxiliary words, which are indicated in square brackets. In other cases it would make no sense to offer a literal translation of a Talmudic idiom, so we have provided a close English equivalent of the original meaning, while a note, marked "lit.," explaining the literal meaning of the words, appears in parentheses. Our purpose in presenting this literal translation was to give the student an appreciation of the terse and enigmatic nature of the Talmud itself, before the arguments are opened up by interpretation.

Nevertheless, no one can study the Talmud without the assistance of commentaries. The main aid to understanding the Talmud provided by this edition is the *Translation and Commentary,* appearing on the left side of the page. This is Rabbi Adin Steinsaltz's highly regarded Hebrew interpretation of the Talmud, translated into English, adapted and expanded.

This commentary is not merely an explanation of difficult passages. It is an integrated exposition of the entire text. It includes a full translation of the Talmud text, combined with explanatory remarks. Where the translation in the commentary reflects the literal translation, it has been set off in bold type. It has also been given the same reference numbers that are found both in the original text and in the literal translation. Moreover, each section of the commentary begins with a few words of the Hebrew-Aramaic text. These reference numbers and paragraph headings allow the reader to move from one part of the page to another with ease.

There are some slight variations between the literal translation and the words in bold face appearing in the *Translation and Commentary.* These variations are meant to enhance understanding, for a juxtaposition of the literal translation and the sometimes freer translation in the commentary will give the reader a firmer grasp of the meaning.

The expanded *Translation and Commentary* in the left-hand column is intended to provide a conceptual understanding of the arguments of the Talmud, their form, content, context, and significance. The commentary also brings out the logic of the questions asked by the Sages and the assumptions they made.

Rashi's traditional commentary has been included in the right-hand column, under the *Literal Translation.* We have left this commentary in the traditional "Rashi script," but all quotations of the Talmud text appear in standard square type, the abbreviated expressions have all been printed in full, and Rashi's commentary is fully punctuated.

Since the *Translation and Commentary* cannot remain cogent and still encompass all the complex issues that arise in the Talmudic discussion, we have included a number of other features, which are also found in Rabbi Steinsaltz's Hebrew edition.

At the bottom of the page, under the *Translation and Commentary*, is the *Notes* section, containing additional material on issues raised in the text. These notes deepen understanding of the Talmud in various ways. Some provide a deeper and more profound analysis of the issues discussed in the text, with regard to individual points and to the development of the entire discussion. Others explain Halakhic concepts and the terms of Talmudic discourse.

The *Notes* contain brief summaries of the opinions of many of the major commentators on the Talmud, from the period after the completion of the Talmud to the present. Frequently the *Notes* offer interpretations different from that presented in the commentary, illustrating the richness and depth of Rabbinic thought.

The *Halakhah* section appears below the *Notes.* This provides references to the authoritative legal decisions reached over the centuries by the Rabbis in their discussions of the matters dealt with in the Talmud. It explains what reasons led to these Halakhic decisions and the close connection between the Halakhah today and the Talmud and its various interpreters. It should be noted that the summary of the Halakhah presented here is not meant to serve as a reference source for actual religious practice but to introduce the reader to Halakhic conclusions drawn from the Talmudic text.

English commentary and expanded translation of the text, making it readable and comprehensible

Hebrew/Aramaic text of the Talmud, fully vocalized, and punctuated

TRANSLATION AND COMMENTARY

[1]**and her husband threw her a bill of divorce into her lap or into her basket**, which she was carrying on her head, [2]would you say **here, too,** that **she would not be divorced**? Surely we know that the law is that she *is* divorced in such a case, as the Mishnah (*Gittin* 77a) states explicitly!

אֲמַר לֵיהּ [3]Rav Ashi **said** in reply **to** Ravina: The woman's **basket is** considered to be **at rest, and it is she who walks beneath it.** Thus the basket is considered to be a "stationary courtyard," and the woman acquires whatever is thrown into it.

MISHNAH הָיָה רוֹכֵב [4]If a **person was riding on an animal and he saw an ownerless object** lying on the ground, **and he said to another person** standing nearby, **"Give that object to me,"** [5]if **the other person took** the ownerless object **and said, "I have acquired it for myself,"** [6]he has **acquired it** by lifting it up, even though he was not the first to see it, and the rider has no claim to it. [7]But **if, after he gave** the object **to** the rider, the person who picked it up **said, "I acquired** the object **first,"** [8]**he** in fact **said nothing**. His words are of no effect, and the rider may keep it. Since the person walking showed no intention of acquiring the object when he originally picked it up, he is not now believed when he claims that he acquired it first. Indeed, even if we maintain that when a person picks up an ownerless object on behalf of someone else, the latter does *not* acquire it automatically, here, by *giving* the object to the rider, he makes a gift of it to the rider.

GEMARA תְּנַן הָתָם [9]**We have learned elsewhere** in a Mishnah in tractate *Pe'ah* (4:9): **"Someone who gathered** ***pe'ah*** — produce which by Torah law [Leviticus 23:22] is left unharvested in the corner of a field by the owner of the field, to be gleaned by the poor — **and said, 'Behold, this** ***pe'ah*** which I have gleaned **is** intended **for so-and-so the poor man,'** [10]**Rabbi Eliezer says:** The person who gathered the *pe'ah* **has acquired it**

בִּרְשׁוּת הָרַבִּים [1]וְזָרַק לָהּ גֵּט לְתוֹךְ חֵיקָהּ אוֹ לְתוֹךְ קַלְתָּהּ — [2]הָכָא נַמִי דְּלָא מְגָרְשָׁה? [3]אֲמַר לֵיהּ: קַלְתָּהּ מֵינָח נַיְיחָא, וְאִיהִי דְּקָא מְסַגְּיָא מִתּוּתָהּ.

מִשְׁנָה [4]הָיָה רוֹכֵב עַל גַּבֵּי בְהֵמָה וְרָאָה אֶת הַמְּצִיאָה, וְאָמַר לַחֲבֵירוֹ "תְּנָה לִי", [5]נְטָלָהּ וְאָמַר, "אֲנִי זָכִיתִי בָּהּ", [6]זָכָה בָּהּ. [7]אִם, מִשֶּׁנְּתָנָהּ לוֹ, אָמַר, "אֲנִי זָכִיתִי בָּהּ תְּחִלָּה", [8]לֹא אָמַר כְּלוּם.

גְּמָרָא [9]תְּנַן הָתָם: "מִי שֶׁלִּיקֵּט אֶת הַפֵּאָה וְאָמַר, 'הֲרֵי זוֹ לִפְלוֹנִי עָנִי', [10]רַבִּי אֱלִיעֶזֶר

LITERAL TRANSLATION

in a public thoroughfare [1]and [her husband] threw her a bill of divorce into her lap or into her basket, [2]here, too, would she not be divorced?

[3]He said to him: Her basket is at rest, and it is she who walks beneath it.

MISHNAH [4][If a person] was riding on an animal and he saw a found object, and he said to another person, "Give it to me," [5][and the other person] took it and said, "I have acquired it," [6]he has acquired it. [7]If, after he gave it to him, he said, "I acquired it first," [8]he said nothing.

GEMARA [9]We have learned there: "Someone who gathered *pe'ah* and said, 'Behold this is for so-and-so the poor man,' [10]Rabbi Eliezer says:

Literal translation of the Talmud text into English

RASHI

קלתה – סל שעל ראשה, שנותנת בה כלי מלאכתה וטווי שלה. הכי נמי דלא הוי גיטא – והאנן תנן במסכת גיטין (עז,א): זרק לה גיטה לתוך חיקה או לתוך קלתה – הרי זו מגורשת!

משנה **לא אמר כלום** – דאפילו אמרינן המגביה מציאה לחבירו לא קנה חבירו, כיון דיהבה ליה – קנייה ממה נפשך. אי קנייה קמא דלא מתכוין להקנות לחבירו – הא יהבה ניהליה במתנה. ואי לא קנייה קמא משום דלא היה מתכוין לקנות – הויא ליה הפקר עד דמטא לידיה דהאי, וקנייה האי במאי דעקרה מידיה דקמא לשם קנייה.

גמרא **מי שליקט את הפאה** – אדם בעלמא שאינו בעל שדה. דאי בבעל שדה – לא אמר רבי אליעזר זכה. דליכא למימר "מגו דזכי לנפשיה", דאפילו הוא עני מוזהר הוא שלא ללקט פאה משדה שלו, כדאמר בשחיטת חולין (קלא,ב): "לא תלקט לעני" – להזהיר עני על שלו.

Hebrew commentary of Rashi, the classic explanation that accompanies all editions of the Talmud

REALIA

קַלְתָּה **Her basket**. The source of this word is the Greek κάλαθος, kalathos, and it means a basket with a narrow base.

Illustration from a Greek drawing depicting such a basket of fruit.

CONCEPTS

פֵּאָה ***Pe'ah.*** **One of the presents left for the poor** (מַתְּנוֹת עֲנִיִּים). The Torah forbids harvesting "the corners of your field," so that the produce left standing may be harvested and kept by the poor (Leviticus 19:9).

The Torah did not specify a minimum amount of produce to be left as *pe'ah*. But the Sages stipulated that it must be at least one-sixtieth of the crop.

Pe'ah is set aside only from crops that ripen at one time and are harvested at one time. The poor are allowed to use their own initiative to reap the *pe'ah* left in the fields. But the owner of an orchard must see to it that each of the poor gets a fixed share of the *pe'ah* from places that are difficult to reach. The poor come to collect *pe'ah* three times a day. The laws of *pe'ah* are discussed in detail in tractate *Pe'ah*.

Marginal notes provide essential background information

NOTES

מִי שֶׁלִּיקֵּט אֶת הַפֵּאָה **If a person gathered** ***pe'ah***. According to *Rashi*, the Mishnah must be referring to someone other than the owner of the field. By Torah law the owner of a field is required to separate part of his field as *pe'ah*, even if he himself is poor, and he may not take the *pe'ah* for himself. Therefore the "since" (מגו) argument

HALAKHAH

קַלְתָּה **A woman's basket**. "If a man throws a bill of divorce into a container that his wife is holding, she thereby acquires the bill of divorce and the divorce takes effect." (*Shulḥan Arukh, Even HaEzer* 139:10.)

הַמְלַקֵּט פֵּאָה עֲבוּר אַחֵר **A person who gathered** ***pe'ah*** **for someone else**. "If a poor person, who is himself entitled to collect *pe'ah*, gathered *pe'ah* for another poor person, and said, 'This *pe'ah* is for X, the poor person,' he acquires the *pe'ah* on behalf of that other poor person. But if the person who collected the *peah* was wealthy, he does not acquire the *pe'ah* on behalf of the poor person. He must give it instead to the first poor person who appears in the field," following the opinion of the Sages, as explained by Rabbi Yehoshua ben Levi. (*Rambam, Sefer Zeraim, Hilkhot Mattenot Aniyyim* 2:19.)

Numbers link the three main sections of the page and allow readers to refer rapidly from one to the other

Notes highlight points of interest in the text and expand the discussion by quoting other classical commentaries

On the outer margin of the page, factual information clarifying the meaning of the Talmudic discussion is presented. Entries under the heading *Language* explain unusual terms, often borrowed from Greek, Latin, or Persian. *Sages* gives brief biographies of the major figures whose opinions are presented in the Talmud. *Terminology* explains the terms used in the Talmudic discussion. *Concepts* gives information about fundamental Halakhic principles. *Background* provides historical, geographical, and other information needed to understand the text. *Realia* explains the artifacts mentioned in the text. These notes are sometimes accompanied by illustrations.

The best way of studying the Talmud is the way in which the Talmud itself evolved – a combination of frontal teaching and continuous interaction between teacher and pupil, and between pupils themselves.

This edition is meant for a broad spectrum of users, from those who have considerable prior background and who know how to study the Talmud from any standard edition to those who have never studied the Talmud and do not even know Hebrew.

The division of the page into various sections is designed to enable students of every kind to derive the greatest possible benefit from it.

For those who know how to study the Talmud, the book is intended to be a written Gemara lesson, so that, either alone, with partners, or in groups, they can have the sense of studying with a teacher who explains the difficult passages and deepens their understanding both of the development of the dialectic and also of the various approaches that have been taken by the Rabbis over the centuries in interpreting the material. A student of this kind can start with the Hebrew-Aramaic text, examine Rashi's commentary, and pass on from there to the expanded commentary. Afterwards the student can turn to the Notes section. Study of the *Halakhah* section will clarify the conclusions reached in the course of establishing the Halakhah, and the other items in the margins will be helpful whenever the need arises to clarify a concept or a word or to understand the background of the discussion.

For those who do not possess sufficient knowledge to be able to use a standard edition of the Talmud, but who know how to read Hebrew, a different method is proposed. Such students can begin by reading the Hebrew-Aramaic text and comparing it immediately to the *Literal Translation*. They can then move over to the *Translation and Commentary*, which refers both to the original text and to the *Literal Translation*. Such students would also do well to read through the *Notes* and choose those that explain matters at greater length. They will benefit, too, from the terms explained in the side margins.

The beginner who does not know Hebrew well enough to grapple with the original can start with the *Translation and Commentary*. The inclusion of a translation within the commentary permits the student to ignore the *Literal Translation*, since the commentary includes both the Talmudic text and an interpretation of it. The beginner can also benefit from the *Notes*, and it is important for him to go over the marginal notes on the concepts to improve his awareness of the juridical background and the methods of study characteristic of this text.

Apart from its use as study material, this book can also be useful to those well versed in the Talmud, as a source of additional knowledge in various areas, both for understanding the historical and archeological background and also for an explanation of words and concepts. The general reader, too, who might not plan to study the book from beginning to end, can find a great deal of interesting material in it regarding both the spiritual world of Judaism, practical Jewish law, and the life and customs of the Jewish people during the thousand years (500 B.C.E.–500 C.E.) of the Talmudic period.

Contents

THE TALMUD

THE STEINSALTZ EDITION

VOLUME XVIII

TRACTATE SANHEDRIN

PART IV

Introduction to Chapter Seven

אַרְבַּע מִיתוֹת

The laws regarding execution by stoning, which were clarified in the previous chapter, were part of a general explanation of judicial execution according to Jewish law.

Indeed, execution by stoning is only one of the means of execution assigned to a court, and it is necessary to clarify what the sources are from which we derive the other laws of judicial execution, as well as the way they were actually imposed, and other issues.

Another question that has both theoretical and practical importance is the order of the severity of these means of execution. To clarify this matter, cases in which a person is liable for execution in two different manners for two separate transgressions are very important. Such cases are also used to make the more basic determination of which mode of execution is applicable to each transgression when this is not explicitly stated by the the Torah. However, most of this chapter does not deal with the laws of punishment, but rather with another aspect of criminal law: the laws regarding transgressions punishable by stoning. Some of these transgressions were stated explicitly by the Torah, but regarding most of them the Torah did not state how the transgressor was to be executed, and this is inferred by means of Halakhic Midrash.

The main burden of the discussion concerns the basic meaning of these laws: there is a need to determine both the exact boundaries of each transgression and for which transgressions one actually incurs the death penalty.

Clearly every criminal act has its own pecular aspects and modalities. Transgressions committed in a certain way require execution by stoning, imposed according to Torah law, but in other cases and modalities the transgressor is exempt from punishment. Sometimes this is because the action itself is not prohibited by the Torah, but sometimes the death penalty is not imposed because of the way in which the transgression was committed. Thus every case must be examined individually, to clarify, from the Biblical verses and on the basis of the tradition of the Sages, which specific injunctions apply in each of these many instances.

This is the main concern of this chapter, but since it deals with most of the severe prohibitions of the Torah, several other substantive issues arise, bringing the discussion beyond the narrow subject and extending it to other areas.

TRANSLATION AND COMMENTARY

MISHNAH אַרְבַּע מִיתוֹת [1]**Four** different **methods of execution were given to the court** to punish those found guilty of a capital offense. In the order of decreasing severity, they are: [2]**Stoning, burning,** slaying by **the sword, and strangulation.** This order has practical consequences, for if someone is found guilty of two capital offenses punishable by two different methods of execution, he is put to death with the more severe method. [3]**Rabbi Shimon** disagrees and **says:** The four methods of execution, in order of decreasing severity, are: [4]**Burning, stoning, strangulation, and** slaying by **the sword.** [5]**That** which was taught in the previous chapter elucidates **the obligation regarding those who are liable to death by stoning.** The laws governing the other three modes of judicial execution will be explained in the following Mishnahs.

GEMARA אָמַר רָבָא [6]**Rava said in the name of Rav Seḥora who said in the name of Rav Huna:** [7]**Whenever the Sages taught by way of a list there is no** special **order** to the way that the list was formulated. [8]**The exception** to this rule **is** the Mishnah dealing with **the seven cleaning agents** that must be applied to a stain found on a woman's undergarment to determine whether or not it is blood and could have resulted from menstruation. [9]**For we have learned** in the Mishnah (*Niddah* 61b):

אַרְבַּע

[1]מִיתוֹת נִמְסְרוּ לְבֵית דִּין: [2]סְקִילָה, שְׂרֵיפָה, הֶרֶג, וָחֶנֶק. [3]רַבִּי שִׁמְעוֹן אוֹמֵר: [4]שְׂרֵיפָה, סְקִילָה, חֶנֶק וָהֶרֶג. [5]זוֹ מִצְוַת הַנִּסְקָלִין.

גמרא [6]אָמַר רָבָא אָמַר רַב סְחוֹרָא אָמַר רַב הוּנָא: [7]כָּל מָקוֹם שֶׁשָּׁנוּ חֲכָמִים דֶּרֶךְ מִנְיָין — אֵין מוּקְדָּם וּמְאוּחָר, [8]חוּץ מִשִּׁבְעָה סַמָּנִין. [9]דִּתְנַן: ״שִׁבְעָה

LITERAL TRANSLATION

MISHNAH [1]Four [methods of] execution were given to the court: [2]Stoning, burning, the sword (lit., "slaying"), and strangulation. [3]Rabbi Shimon says: [4]Burning, stoning, strangulation, and the sword. [5]This is the obligation regarding those who are liable to [death by] stoning.

GEMARA [6]Rava said in the name of Rav Seḥora who said in the name of Rav Huna: [7]Whenever the Sages taught by enumeration — there is no fixed order (lit., "before or after"), [8]except for the seven cleaning agents. [9]For we have learned: "Seven

RASHI

משנה ארבע מיתות — סקילה שריפה הרג וחנק. דווקא נקט סידרא, סקילה חמורה משריפה, ושתיהן מהרג, ושלשתן מחנק, ונפקא מינה למתחייב שתי מיתות דקיימא לן לקמן (פא,א) נידון בחמורה. רבי שמעון כו׳ — פלוגתא מפרש בגמרא. זו מצות הנסקלין — שפירשנו בפרקין דלעיל (מה,א): בית הסקילה היה גבוה שתי קומות כו׳, ומשום דבעי למתני מלות הנשרפין והנהרגין והנחנקין כילד, הדר ונקט להאי.
גמרא כל מקום ששנו חכמים דרך מנין — וסידרו דבר אחר דבר. אין מוקדם ומאוחר — לא דקדקו להקדים במשנתן את המוקדם, ולאחר את המאוחר, שיש מקום ששנוי מאוחר במשנה צריך להקדימו במעשה, כגון סדר שמונה בגדים של כהונה גדולה כדמפרש לקמיה דמכנסים קודמין בלבישה, ולא הקדימו לשנותן כסדר לבישתן. ויש מקום שהסדר שנוי כמשפטו לכתחילה, אבל אי אפיך לית לן בה, כגון דברי סדר חליצה כדלקמיה. חוץ מסדר שבעה סממנין — האמורים לענין הכתם של דם, שבהן דיקדקו בסדר משנתן. כל דבר המועיל לחבירו קרי ליה סם לגביה, ואין סם לשון בוסם ולא לשון מרפא, אלא לשון דבר הצריך לתיקון חבירו.

SAGES

רַבִּי שִׁמְעוֹן **Rabbi Shimon** (bar Yoḥai). See *Sanhedrin*, Part I, p. 23.

רָבָא **Rava.** A Babylonian Amora of the fourth generation. See *Bava Metzia*, Part II, pp. 9-10.

רַב סְחוֹרָא **Rav Seḥora.** A Babylonian Amora of the third generation.

רַב הוּנָא **Rav Huna.** A Babylonian Amora of the second generation. See *Sanhedrin*, Part I, p. 61.

NOTES

אַרְבַּע מִיתוֹת **Four methods of execution.** Why was it necessary for the Mishnah to mention the number of methods of execution? It has been suggested that by specifying the number of methods of judicial execution, the Mishnah teaches that each method is counted as a separate commandment. Indeed, *Rambam* in his *Sefer HaMitzvot* counts each method of execution as a separate commandment (*Tosefot Hokhmei Angli'a, Margoliyot HaYam*).

נִמְסְרוּ לְבֵית דִּין **Were given over to the court.** The Jerusalem Talmud derives from this Mishnah that only the court was given all four modes of execution. But the king, who has the prerogative of killing any person disobeying or slandering him, may only put the guilty party to death by way of slaying by the sword. Others suggest that the Mishnah also seeks to limit the number of methods of execution available to the court to four. While we do find

HALAKHAH

אַרְבַּע מִיתוֹת **Four methods of execution.** "Four methods of execution were given to the court to be administered to those found guilty of a capital offense: Stoning, burning, slaying by the sword, and strangulation." (*Rambam, Sefer Shofetim, Hilkhot Sanhedrin* 14:1.)

שִׁבְעָה סַמָּנִין **Seven cleaning agents.** "If a woman found a stain on her garment, and she is in doubt whether it is menstrual blood or not, seven cleaning agents are applied to the stain. If the stain is successfully removed or lightened, we assume that it was menstrual blood. If it remains unchanged, we assume that it is not menstrual blood. The seven cleaning agents must be applied in the following order: Plain saliva, liquified bean grits, fermented urine, Saponaria soap, natron, Cimolian earth, and potash. If the seven cleaning agents are not applied in this order, or if they are applied all at once, the test accomplished nothing. This test is not used today, for we no longer know how to administer it properly." (*Rambam, Sefer Kedushah, Hilkhot Issurei Bi'ah* 9:36-37; *Shulḥan Arukh, Yoreh Deah* 190:31.)

BACKGROUND

סַמָּנִים Cleaning agents. This list of cleaning materials shows that our ancestors used various types of them. Some operated by dissolving the dirt by means of fermentation (plain saliva, barley water); others were mineral materials (Cimonlian earth, natron); and others were made from plants by grinding or burning them, and from their ashes various detergents were made (potash, lixivium).

רוֹק תָּפֵל Plain saliva. Plain saliva is concentrated, because it is not mixed with materials that come from foods and drinks, and it is rich in fermentation, which dissolves various organic materials, and therefore is also useful as a detergent.

LANGUAGE

קְמוּלְיָא Cimolian earth. The word derives from the Greek χιμωλια, *kimulia,* meaning "a kind of white material named after the island Kimolos, where it was used for washing clothes."

אֲשְׁלָג Potash. This word might derive from the Persian اشجال, with the letters reversed. It means "the ashes of plants that are used for laundry." Others claim that the word is derived from the Arabic العلسول, which is one of the soap weeds.

REALIA

אַשְׁלָג Potash (Ice plant).

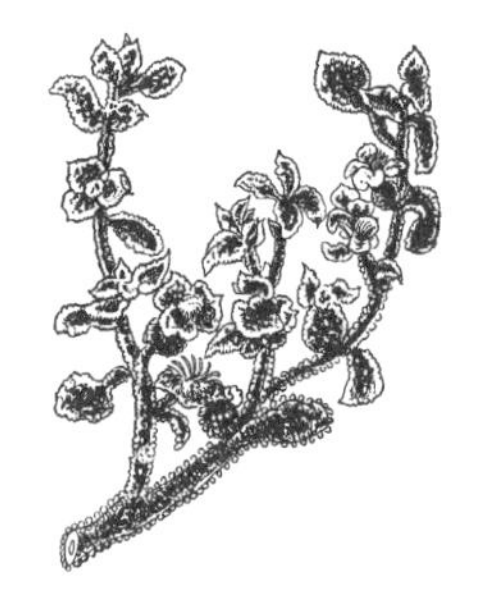

The ice plant (*Mesembryanthemum crystalinum L.*), from the *Aizoaleae* family, grows on the Coastal Plain and in the Sharon on rocks facing the sea. This might be the plant called "potash" or "lixivium."

סַמָּנִין מַעֲבִירִין עַל הַכֶּתֶם: [1]רוֹק תָּפֵל, [2]וּמֵי גְרִיסִין, [3]וּמֵי רַגְלַיִם, וְנֶתֶר, וּבוֹרִית, [4]קְמוּלְיָא, [5]וְאַשְׁלָג״. [6]וְקָתָנֵי סֵיפָא: ״הֶעֱבִירָן שֶׁלֹּא כְּסִידְרָן, [7]אוֹ שֶׁהֶעֱבִירָן שִׁבְעָתָן כְּאֶחָד, [8]לֹא עָשָׂה וְלֹא כְלוּם״.

[9]רַב פַּפָּא סָבָא מִשְּׁמֵיהּ דְּרַב אָמַר: אַף אַרְבַּע מִיתוֹת. [10]מִדְּקָא מַפְלִיג רַבִּי שִׁמְעוֹן, [11]שְׁמַע מִינָּהּ דַּוְקָא קָתָנֵי.

[12]וְאִידָךְ? [13]בִּפְלוּגְתָּא לָא קָא מַיְירֵי.

LITERAL TRANSLATION

cleaning agents are applied to a stain: [1]Plain saliva, [2]liquified grits, [3]urine, natron, Saponaria soap, [4]Cimolian earth, [5]and potash." [6]And the last clause states: "[If] he did not apply them in the order [given], [7]or [if] he applied the seven the same time, [8]he did nothing."

[9]Rav Pappa the Elder said in the name of Rav: Even the four [methods of] execution. [10]Since Rabbi Shimon differs, [11]conclude from this [that] it teaches in precise [order].

[12]And the other one? [13]He does not deal with [enumerations that are the subject of] dispute.

TRANSLATION AND COMMENTARY

"Seven cleaning agents are applied to a stain. If it is successfully removed by those seven agents, we assume that it was indeed blood, and so the woman is regarded as a menstruating woman, and the sanctified food and other items that she has touched are ritually impure. If the stain does not come out, we assume that it is not blood, and so the woman and all that she has touched remain ritually pure. The seven cleaning agents that are applied to a suspected blood stain are: [1]**Plain saliva,** saliva secreted by a person early in the morning, before he has had anything to eat; [2]**liquified grits,** the saliva-containing pap produced by chewing crushed beans; [3]fermented **urine, natron, soap** manufactured from the Saponaria plant; [4]**Cimolian earth;** [5]**and potash."** [6]**And the last clause** of the Mishnah (*Niddah* 62a) **states: "If** the seven cleaning agents **were not applied** to the stain **in the order** given in the Mishnah, [7]**or if the seven** cleaning agents **were applied simultaneously,** [8]**nothing was accomplished** — the test was improperly carried out and nothing may be concluded from its results. Thus the seven agents were listed in a fixed order.

רַב פַּפָּא סָבָא [9]**Rav Pappa the Elder said in the name of Rav: The four methods of execution** mentioned in our Mishnah were given in precise order. [10]**Since Rabbi Shimon disagrees** with the anonymous first Tanna of the Mishnah by arranging the four methods of judicial execution in a different order, [11]it is legitimate to **infer from this that** the four methods of judicial execution **were listed** in the Mishnah **in precise order.**

וְאִידָךְ [12]The Gemara asks: **And** how does **the other** Amora, Rav Seḥora, who said in the name of Rav that only the list in the Mishnah in *Niddah* was arranged in precise order, counter this argument? [13]The Gemara answers: Rav Seḥora did not mention it, because he **was not dealing with enumerations that are the subject of dispute.**

RASHI

מעבירין על הכתם — לבודקו אם דם נדה הוא, ולטמא טהרות שנגע בהן, או צבע הוא והטהרות טהורות. ואם עבר באלו שבע סממנין כשיכבס אותו בהן כסדרן — בידוע שדם היה, ואם לא עבר — בידוע שצבע היה. **רוק תפל** — שלא טעם כלום כל אותו היום. תפל = ריקם ונגוב וחסר כל טעם מאכל, כגון דבר שלא נמלח דמיקרי תפל. **ומי גריסין** — ומי לעיסת גריסין של פול, שלועסין וכוססין אותו ומשפשפין אותו בהן. **ומי רגלים** — שהחמיצו והסריחו. **נתר** — מין אדמה הוא, וקורין לה ניתרא. **ובורית** — עשב הוא ומעביר כתמים, וקורין ליה *אירבנ״ו שבונריי״א. **קמוליא** — התם מפרש לה: שלוף דוץ, ולא ידענא מאי היא. **אשלך** — נמצא בנקבי מרגליות העולות מתוך הים. **לא עשה ולא כלום** — אין זה נסיון, שאם לא עבר בכך אכתי איכא למימר דם הוה, והאי דלא עבר היינו משום דאין גריסין מועילין אלא לאחר הרוק, וכן כולם כסדר. והא דרב סחורה קבועה בהאי גמרא משום דמייתינן להני ארבע מיתות בית דין דמתניתין עלה, כדפליג רב פפא עליה ואמר: אף ארבע מיתות דווקא נשנו, הקודם במשנה קודמת לחברתה אם נתחייב שתי מיתות. **בפלוגתא לא קמיירי** -- רב סחורה נמי אית ליה דמתניתין דווקא תנן, ומיהו כי נקט איהו לא נקט מילי דפלוגתא.

NOTES

that under certain circumstances criminals were put to death in other ways, those modes of execution were not officially given over to the court. Rather they fall under the rule that makes it possible for zealots to kill certain offenders who are caught committing their crimes, or the like (*Maharshashakh*).

מַעֲבִירִין עַל הַכֶּתֶם Are applied to a stain. Our commentary follows *Rashi* and others who understand that the Mishnah is dealing with a stain that might be a blood stain and the seven cleaning agents are applied in order to determine whether its source is blood or something else. *Rabbenu Tam* and *Ran* suggest that the Mishnah is dealing with a stain definitely left by menstrual blood. Even though menstrual blood imparts ritual impurity, whether it is fresh or dry, once a blood-stained garment is laundered with the seven cleaning agents, it no longer imparts ritual impurity, even if it is still visible.

בִּפְלוּגְתָּא לָא קָא מַיְירֵי He does not deal with matters that are the subject of dispute. *Ḥamra Veḥaye* explains this argument as follows: Rav Seḥora did not refer to an explicit disagreement about the order in which a series of laws is to arranged, for then it is clear that the order is significant. Rather Rav Seḥora referred to instances of laws arranged in lists, when it is not evident that the order in which the laws are arranged has significance.

[1]רַב פַּפָּא אָמַר: אַף סֵדֶר יוֹמָא. [2]דִּתְנַן: כָּל מַעֲשֵׂה יוֹם הַכִּפּוּרִים הָאֲמוּרִים עַל הַסֵּדֶר, [3]אִם הִקְדִּים מַעֲשֶׂה לַחֲבֵירוֹ — לֹא עָשָׂה וְלֹא כְלוּם. [4]וְאִידָךְ? [5]הַהוּא חוּמְרָא בְּעָלְמָא. [6]רַב הוּנָא בְּרֵיהּ דְּרַב יְהוֹשֻׁעַ אָמַר: אַף סֵדֶר תָּמִיד, [7]דְּקָתָנֵי עֲלָהּ: ״זֶהוּ סֵדֶר תָּמִיד״. [8]וְאִידָךְ? [9]הַהוּא לְמִצְוָה בְּעָלְמָא. [10]וּלְאַפּוּקֵי מִמִּצְוַת חֲלִיצָה.

LITERAL TRANSLATION

[1]Rav Pappa said: Even the order of Yom Kippur. [2]For we have learned: "All the rites of Yom Kippur that were stated in order — [3]if he performed one rite before the other, he did nothing."

[4]And the other one? [5]That is a mere stringency.

[6]Rav Huna the son of Rav Yehoshua said: Even the order of the daily sacrifice, [7]for it teaches in connection with it: "This is the order of the daily sacrifice."

[8]And the other one? [9]That is merely for the mitzvah.

[10]And to exclude the mitzvah of *halitzah*.

TRANSLATION AND COMMENTARY

רַב פַּפָּא אָמַר [1]**Rav Pappa said: The Yom Kippur service** described in detail in tractate *Yoma* was **also** formulated in precise order. [2]**For we have learned** in the Mishnah (*Yoma* 60a): **"All the rites of Yom Kippur** that are performed in the Temple by the High Priest in his white garments and **were taught in order.** [3]**If** the High Priest **performed one rite before another** rite that was to have preceded it, **he did nothing,** and the rites that had been performed out of order must be repeated."

וְאִידָךְ [4]The Gemara asks: **And** how does **the other** Amora — Rav Seḥora — counter this argument? He agrees that the Yom Kippur service was formulated in precise order, and any deviation from that order disqualifies that service. [5]But **that is merely a stringency** imposed by the holiness of the day. The order in which the Yom Kippur rites must be performed does not reflect any intrinsic difference in the importance or significance of these rites. This list is, therefore, unlike lists in which the items differ in intrinsic severity or importance, like the four methods of judicial execution or the seven cleaning agents.

רַב הוּנָא בְּרֵיהּ דְּרַב יְהוֹשֻׁעַ אָמַר [6]**Rav Huna the son of Rav Yehoshua said: The service** surrounding **the daily sacrifice** described in detail in tractate *Tamid* was **also** formulated in precise order. [7]**For it was taught about** this service (*Tamid* 7:3): **"This is the order of the daily sacrifice,"** implying that the service must be conducted in the precise order that we find in the Mishnah.

וְאִידָךְ [8]The Gemara asks: **And** what does **the other** Amora — Rav Pappa who argued that the Mishnah dealing with the Yom Kippur service is another exception to the rule proposed by Rav Seḥora — say about this? Why did he not mention it? [9]The Gemara explains: Rav Pappa maintains that the order set down in tractate *Tamid* for the daily sacrifice **is merely the preferred rite** for conducting the service. But following that order is not an indispensable condition for fulfilling the obligation of offering the daily sacrifice.

וּלְאַפּוּקֵי [10]The Gemara now notes that Rav Seḥora's intention when he ruled that wherever the Sages taught a series of laws, the order is of no Halakhic significance, he meant **to exclude the mitzvah of *ḥalitzah*** from being invalidated by changing the order given in the Mishnah. A man whose brother died without children is obliged by Torah law to marry his deceased brother's widow or free her from the levirate bond by granting her *ḥalitzah*. During the course of the *ḥalitzah* ceremony, the levir and the widow must make

RASHI

אף סדר יומא — דעבודת יום הכפורים הסדורות במשנה במסכת יומא זו אחר זו, דווקא קתני. **ואידך** — אמר לך: וודאי דוקא קתני, ומיהו חומרא בעלמא הוא שהחמיר הכתוב בעבודת אותו היום, שאם שינה בסידרו — פסול, ולא משום חשיבות דעבודות הוא שתהא זאת חמורה וחשובה מחבירתה, אלא חומר היום שנכתבה חוקה בסידורה לעכב. וכי אמרינן אנן במידי דחשיבותה גרס ליה — כגון ארבע מיתות, דאמרינן לקמן דזו חמורה מזו, וכן בשבע סמנין שצורכו וכחו של כל אחד ואחד גורם לו ליקדם, וכן מכנסיים שחישבן הכתוב להקדימן כדלקמן, אבל יום הכפורים — חומר היום בעלמא הוא שלא לשנות בו ולא כח עבודות. **ואידך** — רב פפא דאיירי נמי בחומרי, אמר לך: ההוא מצוה בעלמא, ואי אפיך לית לן בה. **ולאפוקי ממצות חליצה** — האי כל מקום דקאמר רב סחורא דלא דיקדקו בו — לאפוקי מסדר השנוי במצות חליצה אתא דלא תימא דווקא הוא. ואף על גב דמצותיה הכי כדקא מסדר ואזיל.

SAGES

רַב פַּפָּא Rav Pappa. A Babylonian Amora of the fifth generation. See *Bava Metzia*, Part I, p. 131.

רַב הוּנָא בְּרֵיהּ דְּרַב יְהוֹשֻׁעַ Rav Huna the son of Rav Yehoshua. A Babylonian Amora of the fifth generation. See *Ketubot*, Part II, p. 80.

NOTES

מִצְוַת חֲלִיצָה The mitzvah of *ḥalitzah*. Some of the Rishonim ask: Elsewhere, (*Yevamot* 104a), the Tannaim disagree about whether or not the declarations made by the widow and her husband's brother are indispensable

HALAKHAH

כָּל מַעֲשֵׂה יוֹם הַכִּפּוּרִים All the rites of Yom Kippur. "All the rites which the High Priest performs on Yom Kippur in the sanctuary in his white garments must be performed in the order that they are found in the Mishnah. If he changed the order and performed one rite before another that was to have preceded it, he did nothing." (*Rambam, Sefer Avodah, Hilkhot Avodat Yom HaKippurim* 5:1.)

מִצְוַת חֲלִיצָה The rite of *ḥalitzah*. "If a man dies without children, his widow and brother come before the court, and the court advises the brother whether he should take the

SAGES

רַב יְהוּדָה Rav Yehudah (bar Yeḥezkiel). A Babylonian Amora of the second generation. See *Ketubot*, Part I, p. 8.

TRANSLATION AND COMMENTARY

certain declarations, and the woman must remove a special sandal from her brother-in-law's foot and spit before him, [1]as **we have learned** in the Mishnah (*Yevamot* 106b): [2]**"The mitzvah of *ḥalitzah*** is performed as follows: [3]The levir **and his brother's widow come before the court, and** the levir **is given appropriate advice** as to which option he should choose, levirate marriage or *ḥalitzah*. If, for example, the levir is much older or much younger than his brother's widow, he is advised not to take the woman in levirate marriage, but rather to free her from the levirate bond by way of *ḥalitzah*. [4]This is derived from **the verse** which **states: 'And the elders of his city shall call him, and speak to him.'** [5]If the levir chooses *ḥalitzah*, the woman **declares** (Deuteronomy 25:7): **'My husband's brother refuses** to raise up to his brother a name in Israel.' [6]**He** then stands, and **says** (Deuteronomy 25:8): **'I do not wish to take her.'** [7]And the levir and the widow — **recited** their declarations **in Hebrew,** [8]**'Then shall his brother's wife approach him in the presence of the elders, and loose his shoe from off his foot, and spit in his face** (ibid.).' The words 'in the presence of the elders' is connected to the words 'and spit in his face,' [9]teaching that her **spiting must be visible to the judges.** [10]**'And she shall answer and say, Thus shall it be done to that man** that will not build up his brother's house. **And his name shall be called in Israel,** The house of him that had his shoe loosed (Deuteronomy 25:9-10).'" [11]**And Rav Yehudah said: The mitzvah of *ḥalitzah*** is performed as follows: [12]The widow **makes her declaration,** "My husband refuses...," the levir **makes his declaration,** "I do not wish to take her," [13]**she looses his shoe** from off his foot, **she spits** before him, **and**

[1]דִּתְנַן: [2]״מִצְוַת חֲלִיצָה: [3]בָּא הוּא וִיבִמְתּוֹ לִפְנֵי בֵּית דִּין. [4]הָיוּ נוֹתְנִין לוֹ עֵצָה הַהוֹגֶנֶת לוֹ, [5]שֶׁנֶּאֱמַר: ׳וְקָרְאוּ לוֹ זִקְנֵי עִירוֹ וְדִבְּרוּ אֵלָיו׳. [6]וְהִיא אוֹמֶרֶת: ׳מֵאֵן יְבָמִי וגו׳׳. [7]וְהוּא אוֹמֵר: ׳לֹא חָפַצְתִּי לְקַחְתָּהּ׳. [8]וּבִלְשׁוֹן הַקֹּדֶשׁ הָיוּ אוֹמְרִין. [9]׳וְנִגְּשָׁה יְבִמְתּוֹ אֵלָיו לְעֵינֵי הַזְּקֵנִים וְחָלְצָה נַעֲלוֹ וְיָרְקָה בְּפָנָיו׳ — [10]רוֹק הַנִּרְאֶה לַדַּיָּינִין. [11]׳וְעָנְתָה וְאָמְרָה ״כָּכָה יֵעָשֶׂה לָאִישׁ וגו׳ וְנִקְרָא שְׁמוֹ בְּיִשְׂרָאֵל וגו׳׳״. וְאָמַר רַב יְהוּדָה: מִצְוַת חֲלִיצָה: [12]קוֹרְאָה וְקוֹרֵא, [13]חוֹלֶצֶת

LITERAL TRANSLATION

[1]For we have learned: "The mitzvah of *ḥalitzah*: [2]He and his brother's wife come before the court. [3]They would give him advice that is appropriate for him, [4]as it is written: 'And the elders of his city shall call him, and speak to him.' [5]And she says: 'My husband's brother refuses etc.' [6]And he says: 'I do not wish to take her.' [7]And they would say in Hebrew (lit., 'the holy tongue'). [8]'Then shall his brother's wife approach him in the presence of the elders, and loose his shoe [from off his foot], and spit in his face' — [9]spit that is visible to the judges. [10]'And she shall answer and say, So shall it be done to that man etc. And his name shall be called in Israel etc.'" [11]And Rav Yehudah said: The mitzvah of *ḥalitzah*: [12]She declares, and he declares, [13]she looses [his shoe],

RASHI

היא אומרת — תחילה "מאן יבמי" והוא אומר לה: "לא חפצתי" ואחר כך חולצת, ואחר כך רוקקת, ואחר כך קוראה "ככה יעשה". אפילו הכי — אי אפיך לית לן בה, כדקתני לקמן. **עצה ההוגנת לו** — שאם היה הוא זקן והיא ילדה, הוא ילד והיא זקינה, אומרין לו: כלך אצל שכמותך ולא תכניס קטטה לתוך ביתך. **ובלשון הקודש היו אומרין** — במסכת סוטה יליף לה בפרק "אלו נאמרין בכל לשון" (לב,א). **רוק הנראה** — שיהא בו כדי לראות כשיוצא מפיה, דבעינן "לעיני הזקנים וירקה". **קוראה וקורא חולצת ורוקקת וקוראה** — קוראה "מאן יבמי", וקורא "לא חפצתי", חולצת ורוקקת וקוראה "ככה יעשה לאיש".

NOTES

conditions for the validity of the *ḥalitzah*. Why then was it necessary for Rav Yehudah to say that the *ḥalitzah* is valid, even if its various components were not performed in the order stated in the Mishnah? *Rosh* suggests that our Gemara relates even to the position of Rabbi Eliezer who maintains that the declarations are indispensable conditions for the validity of the *ḥalitzah*. *Ḥamra Veḥaye* suggests that in some cases the total omission of a certain component does not disqualify the act, but the improper execution of that element does disqualify it. For example, a document is invalid if it was signed by disqualified witnesses, even though it could have been valid without the signature of any witnesses.

HALAKHAH

widow as his levirate wife, or grant her *ḥalitzah*." (Today, in most communities the common practice is to grant *ḥalitzah* and not to perform levirate marriage.) (*Shulḥan Arukh, Even HaEzer* 166:1.)

קוֹרְאָה וְקוֹרֵא She reads, and he reads. "The order of the *ḥalitzah* ceremony is as follows: The widow declares in Hebrew: 'My husband refuses, etc.,' and then her husband declares: 'I do not wish to take her.' The woman then looses his shoe from his foot, spits before him on the ground spittle that is visible to the judges, and then declares: 'Thus shall it be done to that man, etc.' If they reversed the order, and the woman first spat before the levir, and only then loosed the shoe from his foot, the *ḥalitzah* is still valid." (*Shulḥan Arukh, Even HaEzer* 169:29, 43.)

וְרוֹקֶקֶת וְקוֹרְאָה. [1]וְהָוֵינַן בָּהּ: מַאי קָא מַשְׁמַע לָן? [2]מַתְנִיתִין הִיא! [3]הָא קָא מַשְׁמַע לָן: מִצְוָה הָכִי, [4]וְאִי אַפֵּיךְ, לֵית לָן בָּהּ.

[5]תַּנְיָא נַמִי הָכִי: בֵּין שֶׁהִקְדִּים חֲלִיצָה לִרְקִיקָה [6]אוֹ רְקִיקָה לַחֲלִיצָה — [7]מַה שֶּׁעָשָׂה עָשׂוּי.

[8]וּלְאַפּוּקֵי מֵהָא, [9]דִּתְנַן: ״כֹּהֵן גָּדוֹל מְשַׁמֵּשׁ בִּשְׁמוֹנָה כֵּלִים, וְהֶדְיוֹט בְּאַרְבָּעָה: [10]בִּכְתוֹנֶת, בְּמִכְנָסַיִם, בְּמִצְנֶפֶת, וְאַבְנֵט. [11]מוֹסִיף עֲלֵיהֶן כֹּהֵן גָּדוֹל: חוֹשֶׁן, וְאֵפוֹד, וּמְעִיל, וָצִיץ.״ [12]וְתַנְיָא: ״מִנַּיִן שֶׁלֹּא יְהֵא דָּבָר קוֹדֵם לְמִכְנָסַיִם? [13]שֶׁנֶּאֱמַר: ׳וּמִכְנְסֵי בַד יִהְיוּ עַל בְּשָׂרוֹ׳.

TRANSLATION AND COMMENTARY

then **she makes** her second **declaration,** "Thus shall it be done to that man...." [1]**And we discussed** Rav Yehudah's comment, asking: **What does** Rav Yehudah intend to **teach us?** [2]He is merely repeating the order of the *ḥalitzah* ceremony stated in **the Mishnah!** [3]Rather, Rav Yehudah comes to **teach us** as follows: This order is the preferred way of performing the *ḥalitzah* ceremony, [4]**but if** the order **was reversed,** and the woman first spat and only then loosed the shoe, **there is no concern,** for the *ḥalitzah* is still valid. This is exactly what Rav Seḥora meant when he said that whenever the Sages taught a series of laws, the order in which the series was arranged is of no Halakhic significance.

תַּנְיָא נַמִי הָכִי [5]**This principle was also taught** in the following Baraita: **"Whether the removal** of the levir's shoe **preceded the spitting,** [6]**or the spitting preceded the removal** of his shoe, [7]**what was done was done,** and the *ḥalitzah* is valid."

וּלְאַפּוּקֵי [8]The Gemara adds that Rav Seḥora's rule **also excludes** the lists of garments worn by priests, which was taught in the Mishnah. Rav Seḥora teaches us that this list does not represent the order in which the priests put on their vestments. [9]**For we have learned** in the Mishnah (*Yoma* 71b): **"The High Priest serves** in the Temple wearing **eight** priestly **garments, and a common priest** serves wearing **four** priestly garments. [10]The four garments worn by the common priest are: **A tunic, trousers, a miter, and a sash.** [11]**The High Priest adds to these** four additional garments that are unique to him, and they are: **The breastplate, the ephod, the robe, and the forehead plate."** Now, this Mishnah might be understood as implying that the tunic should be put on first, for it is listed first among the priestly garments. [12]But **it was taught** otherwise in a Baraita: **"From where do we know that** a priest **should not put on any** other garment **before** his **trousers?** [13]This we learn from **the verse** which **states** (Leviticus 16:4): **'And he shall have linen trousers on his flesh.'"** This implies that when the priest puts on his trousers, there should be no other garment on his flesh." Thus, we see that the order in which the Mishnah lists the priestly garments does not reflect the order in which they are to be put on by the priest, as was argued by Rav Seḥora.

LITERAL TRANSLATION

and she spits, and she declares. [1]And we discussed it: What does he teach us? [2]It is our Mishnah! [3]Thus he teaches us: Thus is the mitzvah, [4]but if he reverses it, we have no concern.

[5]It was also taught thus: "Whether the removal [of the levir's shoe] preceded the spitting, [6]or the spitting [preceded] the removal [of the shoe], [7]what was done was done."

[8]And to exclude that which we have learned: [9]"The High Priest serves with eight garments, and a common priest with four: [10]A tunic, trousers, a miter, and a sash. [11]The High Priest adds to these the breastplate, the ephod, the robe, and the forehead plate." [12]And it was taught: "From where [do we know] that nothing should precede the trousers? [13]As it is said: 'And he shall have linen trousers on his flesh.'"

RASHI

הכי גרסינן: והוינן בה מאי קמשמע לן כו׳ — ומהא דרב יהודה שמעינן דמתניתין לאו דווקא, משום הכי נקט לה הכא. ולאפוקי — מהא דרב סחורה קא מהדר. על בשרו — משמע כשלובשן יהא בשרו מבלי לבוש, דאי לא הא אתא לאשמועינן למה לי על בשרו?

NOTES

כֹּהֵן גָּדוֹל מְשַׁמֵּשׁ בִּשְׁמוֹנָה כֵּלִים **The High Priest serves with eight garments.** Some Rishonim suggest that the Mishnah lists the breastplate, the ephod, and the robe in that order, because that is the way that they are ordered in the Torah (see *Ran*). Others propose that the breastplate and the ephod were listed first in order to mention the robe and

HALAKHAH

כֹּהֵן גָּדוֹל מְשַׁמֵּשׁ בִּשְׁמוֹנָה כֵּלִים **The High Priest serves with eight garments.** "An ordinary priest performs the Temple service wearing four garments: The tunic, trousers, the miter, and the sash. The High Priest wears four additional garments: The robe, the ephod, the breastplate, and the forehead plate." (*Rambam, Sefer Avodah, Hilkhot Kelei HaMikdash* 8:1-2.)

מִנַּיִן שֶׁלֹּא יְהֵא דָּבָר קוֹדֵם לְמִכְנָסַיִם **From where do we derive that nothing should precede the breeches?** "The priest first puts on his trousers, then his tunic, then his sash, and lastly his miter." (*Rambam, Sefer Avodah, Hilkhot Kelei HaMikdash* 10:1.)

[1]וְתַנָּא מַאי טַעְמָא אַקְדְּמֵיהּ לִכְתוֹנֶת? [2]מִשּׁוּם דְּאַקְדְּמֵיהּ קְרָא.
[3]וּקְרָא מַאי טַעְמָא אַקְדְּמֵיהּ? [4]מִשּׁוּם דִּמְכַסְּיָא כּוּלָּהּ גּוּפֵיהּ עֲדִיפָא לֵיהּ.
[5]״סְקִילָה שְׂרֵיפָה כו׳״. [6]סְקִילָה חֲמוּרָה מִשְּׂרֵיפָה — שֶׁכֵּן נִיתְּנָה לַמְגַדֵּף וְלָעוֹבֵד עֲבוֹדָה זָרָה.
[7]מַאי חוּמְרָא? [8]שֶׁכֵּן פּוֹשֵׁט יָדוֹ בָּעִיקָּר.
[9]אַדְּרַבָּה, שְׂרֵיפָה חֲמוּרָה, [10]שֶׁכֵּן נִיתְּנָה לְבַת כֹּהֵן שֶׁזִּינְּתָה.
[11]וּמַאי חוּמְרָא? [12]שֶׁכֵּן מְחַלֶּלֶת אֶת אָבִיהָ!

LITERAL TRANSLATION

[1]And what is the reason that the Tanna mentions the tunic first? [2]Because the verse mentions it first. [3]And what is the reason that the verse mentions it first? [4]Because that which covers his entire body is preferred.

[5]"Stoning, burning, etc." [6]Stoning is more severe than burning, for it was provided for the blasphemer and the whorshiper of idols.

[7]What is the severity? [8]Because he stretches his hand out to the principle.

[9]On the contrary, burning is more severe, [10]for it was given to the daughter of a priest who committed adultery.

[11]And what is the severity? [12]Because she profanes her father.

TRANSLATION AND COMMENTARY

וְתַנָּא [1]The Gemara asks: If indeed the priest is required to put on his trousers first, **what then is the reason that the Tanna** of the Mishnah **mentions the tunic first?** [2]The Gemara explains: The Tanna mentions it first **because the verse mentions it first,** as the verse states (Leviticus 16:4): "He shall put on the holy linen tunic, and linen trousers shall be on his flesh."

וּקְרָא [3]This answer begs the question. But **what is the reason that the verse mentions** the tunic **first?** [4]The Gemara answers: The verse mentions the tunic first, **because it prefers** to mention first **that which covers** the priest's **entire body.**

סְקִילָה שְׂרֵיפָה כו׳ [5]We have learned in the Mishnah: "Four different methods of execution were given to the court to punish those found guilty of a capital offense: **Stoning, burning,** slaying by the sword, and strangulation." [6]**Stoning** is mentioned first, because it **is a more severe** mode of execution **than burning for it was provided to one who blasphemes** God **and to one who worships idols.**

מַאי חוּמְרָא [7]The Gemara asks: **What is the severity** of these two offenses — blasphemy and idol worship that leads you to conclude that the punishment meted out for these transgressions must be the most severe mode of execution? [8]The Gemara answers: These two offenses are so serious, because he who violates either one of them **stretches his hand out to the principle** and denies the basic tenet of Judaism, the belief in one God.

אַדְּרַבָּה [9]The Gemara challenges this line of reasoning: **On the contrary, burning** should be mentioned first, because it **is the more severe** mode of execution, [10]for it was provided for **the daughter of a priest who committed adultery.**

וּמַאי חוּמְרָא [11]The Gemara asks: **And what is the severity** of that offense, that justifies your conclusion that burning must be the most severe mode of execution? The Gemara answers: The adultery committed by the daughter of a priest is regarded as such a severe transgression, [12]**because** she **profanes** not only herself, but also **her father,** as the verse states (Leviticus 21:9): "And the daughter of a priest, if she profane herself by playing the harlot, she profanes her father; she shall be burnt with fire."

RASHI

מאי טעמא אקדמה לכתונת — הואיל ומכנסיים קודמין. **דאקדמיה קרא** — ״כתונת בד קדש ילבש ומכנסי בד וגו׳״ (ויקרא טז). **סקילה חמורה כו׳** — טעמא דמתניתין מהדר לפרושי, מאי טעמא דרבנן דאמרו סקילה קודמת לשריפה, ושריפה להרג, והרג לחנק. **שכן נתנה למגדף** — מברך את השם, והוא בסקילה כדכתיב (שם כד) ״הוצא את המקלל וגו׳״. **ולעבודת כוכבים** — שהן עבירות חמורות. **ומאי חומרא** — דמגדף ועבודת כוכבים דקאמרת דמיתה הניתנה להם ודאי חמורה משאר מיתות — שהרי ניתנה לעבירה חמורה. **שכן מחללת את אביה** — כדקאמרינן לקמן (נב,א) — שאם היו נוהגין בו קדש נוהגין בו חול, אומר: ארור שזו ילד, ארור שזו גידל.

NOTES

the forehead plate together, for those two are made of wool dyed with *tekhelet* (a sky-blue dye). Similarly, in the first list, the sash was mentioned last (unlike the order recorded by *Rambam*), because some maintain that it was made only of linen, like the miter (*Rabbi A.M. Horowitz*). According to *Rambam,* the priest first puts on the breeches, then the tunic, then the sash, and then the miter. Some point out that our passage suggests otherwise, for it implies that with the exception of the breeches which must be put on first, the priest puts on his garments in the order found in the Mishnah (*Tzofnat Pa'aneah*).

שֶׁכֵּן מְחַלֶּלֶת אֶת אָבִיהָ **For she profanes her father.** The question has been raised: How can it be argued that because the priest's daughter profanes not only herself, but

HALAKHAH

סְקִילָה חֲמוּרָה מִשְּׂרֵיפָה **Stoning is more severe than burning.** "Death by way of stoning is a more severe punishment than death by way of burning. Someone who is liable for both modes of execution is put to death by the more severe one." (*Rambam, Sefer Shofetim, Hilkhot Sanhedrin* 14:4.)

[50A] ¹קָסָבְרִי רַבָּנַן: נְשׂוּאָה יוֹצְאָה לִשְׂרֵיפָה וְלֹא אֲרוּסָה. ²וּמִדְּאַפְּקָהּ רַחֲמָנָא לַאֲרוּסָה בִּסְקִילָה, ³שְׁמַע מִינָּהּ סְקִילָה חֲמוּרָה.

⁴סְקִילָה חֲמוּרָה מִסַּיִיף, ⁵שֶׁכֵּן נִיתְּנָה לַמְגַדֵּף וְלָעוֹבֵד עֲבוֹדָה זָרָה. ⁶וּמַאי חוּמְרָא? ⁷כִּדַאֲמָרַן.

LITERAL TRANSLATION

[50A] [1]The Sages maintain: A married woman goes out for burning, but not a betrothed woman. [2]And since the Torah (lit., "the Merciful") set apart (lit., "removed") the betrothed woman for stoning, [3]infer from this that stoning is more severe.

[4]Stoning is more severe than the sword, [5]for it was given to the blasphemer and worshiper of idols.[6]And what is [its] severity? [7]As we said.

TRANSLATION AND COMMENTARY

[50A] קָסָבְרִי רַבָּנַן [1]The Gemara explains: **The Sages** of our Mishnah who say that stoning is a more severe method of execution than burning **maintain** that only if the priest's daughter was **a married woman** when she committed adultery is she executed **by burning, but not** if she was only **a betrothed woman,** for a betrothed woman who commits adultery is always liable to death by stoning whether she is the daughter of a priest or she is the daughter of an ordinary Israelite. [2]**And since the Torah removed the betrothed** daughter of a priest from the rule applying to the married daughter of a priest, imposing upon her the penalty of stoning rather than the penalty of burning, [3]we may **infer from this that stoning is the more severe** mode of execution.

סְקִילָה חֲמוּרָה [4]The Gemara continues: **Stoning** is mentioned in the Mishnah before slaying by the sword, [5]because it **is** a **more severe** mode of execution **than** slaying by **the sword,** since it **is** the punishment **given to one who blasphemes** God **and to one who worships idols.** [6]The Gemara asks: **And what is the severity** of these two offenses — blasphemy and idol worship — that justifies the conclusion that stoning is the more severe mode of execution? [7]And the Gemara answers: **As we said,** because he who violates either one of these two prohibitions denies God.

RASHI

קסברי רבנן — דמתניתין. **נשואה** — בת כהן יוצאה מכלל נשואה בת ישראל מחנק לשריפה, אבל ארוסה דגבי בת ישראל בסקילה לא יצאה בבת כהן מכלל ארוסה בת ישראל. **ומדאפקיה רחמנא לארוסה** — בת כהן מכלל נשואה בת כהן משריפה לסקילה, — **שמע מינה סקילה חמורה,** דעל כרחיך ארוסה חמורה מנשואה שמחללת ומזנה בית אביה, והכתוב החמיר עליה — דהא נשואה בת ישראל בחנק שהיא קלה מכולן, וארוסה בסקילה, לפום ריהטא דסוגיא הכי מיפרשא כדפרישית. ומיהו כי דייקת בה שפיר לא אשכחת קרא לרבנן מנא להו דנשואה יוצאה ולא ארוסה — אלא משום דאית להו סקילה חמורה הוא דקאמרי, על כרחיך לא יצאה ארוסה בת כהן מכלל ארוסה בת ישראל מסקילה לשריפה להקל. ויש להקשות היכי ילפינן מהכא דסקילה חמורה? הא איהי לא קמה להו לרבנן אלא משום דקסברי סקילה חמורה. הלכך על כרחיך האי מדאפקיה רחמנא לארוסה בת כהן בסקילה דנקט הכא, לאו טעמא למילתייהו היא, אלא יתובי מילתא בעלמא, ועיקר טעמייהו מדניתנה למגדף ולעובד עבודה זרה הוא. ודקשיא לך: אדרבה שריפה חמורה שכן ניתנה לבת כהן. **ומאי חומרא** — שכן מחללת את אביה! הכי מתרצה לה כדמתרצינא לקמן גבי מכה אביו ואמו: אפילו הכי פושט ידו בעיקר עדיף. והאי דקאמר דקסברי רבנן נשואה יוצאה לשריפה כו׳, על כרחיך נקט ליה, דלא תימא מדיצאה ארוסה בת כהן מארוסה בת ישראל מסקילה לשריפה — שמע מינה שריפה חמורה. והכי קאמר: לעולם סקילה חמורה דפושט ידו בעיקר עדיף, וגבי בת כהן דאחשבה לשריפה — לאו לגבי סקילה אחשבה, אלא לגבי חנק אחשבה, דנשואה היא דיצאה ולא ארוסה, והאי מדאפקיה רחמנא כו׳ אורך דברים הוא, ונראה בעיני דלא גרסינן לה. **בדאמרן** — שכן פושט ידו בעיקר.

NOTES

also her father, her offense is so heinous? Surely the blasphemer profanes the name of God! It has been suggested that the offense is considered particularly severe because the priest's daughter causes not only to be profaned herself, but also her father, who had no part in the transgression (Leviticus 21:8). However, in the case of the blasphemer, only he himself is profaned, not his family (see *Ran, Ḥamra Veḥaye*).

נְשׂוּאָה יוֹצְאָה לִשְׂרֵיפָה **A married woman goes forth for burning.** *Rashi* asks: How can the Gemara prove from the laws applying to the adulterous daughter of a priest that stoning is a more severe mode of execution than burning? The law that the betrothed young daughter of a priest who committed adultery is liable for death by stoning is based on the assumption that stoning is a more severe mode of execution than burning, which is what we are trying to prove. *Rashi* concludes from this that the Gemara does not mean to use this ruling to prove that stoning is more severe than burning. Rather the Gemara means to say as follows: Stoning is more severe than burning, as the blasphemer and the idol worshiper are liable to death by stoning. As for the argument that burning should be regarded as more severe, because a priest's daughter who committed adultery is liable to death by burning — this is not difficult, for only the married daughter of a priest is liable to death by burning (and not strangulation, the penalty imposed on the daughter of an ordinary Israelite who committed adultery), whereas the betrothed young daughter of a priest who committed adultery is liable to death by stoning. Other Rishonim argue that the law that

HALAKHAH

נְשׂוּאָה יוֹצְאָה לִשְׂרֵיפָה **A married woman goes out for burning.** "The married daughter of a priest who committed adultery is liable to death by burning," following the Sages. (*Rambam, Sefer Shofetim, Hilkhot Sanhedrin* 15:11.)

TRANSLATION AND COMMENTARY

אַדְּרַבָּה [1]The Gemara asks: **On the contrary,** slaying by **the sword** should be mentioned first, for it **is the more severe** mode of execution, [2]since it **is** the punishment **given to the people of a city led astray to idol worship.** Those found guilty of idol worship are ordinarily stoned to death, but if the majority of a city's inhabitants committed the offense, those guilty parties are slain by the sword.

וּמַאי חוּמְרָא [3]The Gemara expands upon this argument, asking: **And what severity** of the offense justifies the conclusion that the punishment of slaying by the sword is more severe than stoning, the punishment imposed upon an individual idolater? [4]The Gemara answers: An individual idolater is put to death, but his property is not touched. But all **the property** in a city led astray **is destroyed,** as a warning to all Israel.

אָמְרַתְּ [5]The Gemara rejects this line of reasoning: **For if you would ask: Which transgression is greater, the transgression committed by the person who leads** others **astray** and incites them to idol worship, **or the transgression** committed **by those people who are led astray** and worship idols? [6]Surely **you would say** that **the transgression** committed **by the person who leads** others **astray** is the more severe of the two. [7]**And it was taught** in a Baraita: **"Those who led the people of a city astray are liable** to death **by stoning."** Thus stoning is a more severe mode of execution than slaying by the sword.

סְקִילָה חֲמוּרָה [8]The Gemara continues: **Stoning,** mentioned in the Mishnah before strangulation, **is** a **more severe** mode of execution **than strangulation,** [9]since it **is** the punishment **given to one who blasphemes** against God **and to one who worships idols.** [10]The Gemara asks: **And what is the severity** of blasphemy and idol worship that allows us to conclude that their punishment must be the more severe mode of execution? [11]And the Gemara answers: **As we said,** because he who violates either one of these two prohibitions denies God.

[1]אַדְּרַבָּה, סַיִיף חָמוּר, [2]שֶׁכֵּן נִיתַּן לְאַנְשֵׁי עִיר הַנִּדַּחַת. [3]וּמַאי חוּמְרָא? [4]שֶׁכֵּן מָמוֹנָן אָבֵד!

[5]אָמְרַתְּ: אֵיזֶה כֹּחַ מְרוּבֶּה — כֹּחַ הַמַּדִּיחַ אוֹ כֹּחַ הַנִּידָּח? [6]הֱוֵי אוֹמֵר: כֹּחַ הַמַּדִּיחַ. [7]וְתַנְיָא: ״מַדִּיחֵי עִיר הַנִּדַּחַת בִּסְקִילָה״.

[8]סְקִילָה חֲמוּרָה מֵחֶנֶק, [9]שֶׁכֵּן נִיתַּן לַמְגַדֵּף וְלָעוֹבֵד עֲבוֹדָה זָרָה. [10]וּמַאי חוּמְרָא? [11]כְּדַאֲמָרַן.

LITERAL TRANSLATION

[1]On the contrary, the sword is more severe, [2]for it was given to the people of a city led astray [to idol worship].

[3]And what is [its] severity? [4]Because their money is destroyed.

[5]You say: Which power is greater — the power of him who leads astray or the power of him who is led astray? [6]You should say: The power of he who leads astray. [7]And it was taught: "Those who led astray [the people of] a city [to idol worship] are liable for stoning."

[8]Stoning is more severe than strangulation, [9]for it was given to the blasphemer and the worshiper of idols. [10]And what is [its] severity? [11]As we said.

RASHI

איזה כח מרובה — כלומר אי זה עון חמור. **מדיחי עיר הנדחת בסקילה** — ב״אלו הן הנחנקין״ (סנהדרין פט,ב) יליף טעמא, ומדמדיח בסקילה ונידחין בסייף — שמע מינה סקילה חמורה.

NOTES

a priest's young daughter who committed adultery is liable to death by stoning and not burning, is not based on the assumption that stoning is a more severe mode of execution than burning. It is based on some other source (such as a *gezerah shavah*). Therefore that law can serve as proof that stoning is a more severe method of execution than burning (see *Ran* and *Rosh*).

סַיִיף חָמוּר **The sword is more severe.** *Tosafot* and others discuss the relationship between the severity of a transgression, and the severity of its punishment. There is no clear symmetry between the two. Sometimes a relatively light mode of execution is imposed on a relatively severe transgression, because special additional penalties are also prescribed. For example, in a city led astray to idolatry, where the transgressors are liable to the relatively light penalty of death by the sword, their property is also destroyed. Thus, conclusions regarding the relative severity of the punishments may only be drawn from very similar cases (such as a priest's daughter who committed adultery and the daughter of an ordinary Israelite who committed that offense) (see *Ran* and *Rosh*).

סְקִילָה חֲמוּרָה מֵחֶנֶק **Stoning is more severe than strangulation.** The Rishonim ask: Some of the proofs recorded here could have been omitted, for we could have arrived at some of the same conclusions by way of a *kal vaḥomer* argument. For example, if burning is more severe than

HALAKHAH

מַדִּיחֵי עִיר הַנִּדַּחַת **Those who lead astray the people of a city to idol worship.** "Someone who leads his fellow townsmen astray to worship idols, so that the place becomes condemned as a city the majority of whose inhabitants are guilty of idol worship, is himself liable to death by stoning." (*Rambam, Sefer Mada, Hilkhot Avodah Zarah* 4:1; 5:2; *Sefer Shofetim, Hilkhot Sanhedrin* 15:10.)

TRANSLATION AND COMMENTARY

אַדְּרַבָּה [1]The Gemara asks: **On the contrary, strangulation** should be mentioned first, for it **is the more severe** mode of execution, [2]since it **is** the punishment **given to one who strikes his father or mother.**

וּמַאי חוּמְרָא [3]The Gemara explains: **And what severity** do we find in the Torah regarding the prohibition of striking ones parents, that justifies the conclusion that it merits a more severe mode of execution? [4]Striking ones parents is a most heinous offense, **because the honor** one must show to ones parents **is comparable to the honor** that one must show **to God.** Regarding ones parents, the verse states (Exodus 20:12): "Honor your father and mother," and regarding God, the verse states (Proverbs 3:9): "Honor the Lord with your substance."

מִדְּאַפְּקֵיהּ [5]The Gemara rejects this argument. Faced with a contradiction of the first proof that stoning is more severe than strangulation, a stronger argument is now suggested: **Since the Torah removed the betrothed** young **daughter of an** ordinary **Israelite from the rule applying to the married daughter of an Israelite,** and changed her punishment for committing adultery **from strangulation to stoning,** [6]we may **infer from this that stoning is the more severe** mode of execution. As the verse states (Deuteronomy 22:23-24): "If a damsel that is a virgin be betrothed unto a husband and a man find her in the city and lie with her....You shall stone them with stones." And since the betrothed young girl was still living with her family, she debases herself and her family, unlike a married woman who is no longer a part of her fathers house.

שְׂרֵיפָה חֲמוּרָה [7]Proving that according to the Sages, stoning is the most severe form of execution, the Gemara continues to discuss the other penalties in our Mishnah. **Burning** is mentioned in the Mishnah before slaying by the sword, because it **is a** more **severe** mode of execution, [8]since it **is** the punishment **given to the**

LITERAL TRANSLATION

[1]On the contrary, strangulation is more severe, [2]for it was given to one who strikes his father or mother.

[3]And what is [its] severity? [4]Because their honor was compared to the honor of God.

[5]Since the Torah (lit., "the Merciful") set apart the betrothed daughter of an Israelite from the rule [applying to] the married daughters of an Israelite from strangulation to stoning, [6]infer from this that stoning is more severe.

[7]Burning is more severe than the sword, [8]for it was given to the daughter of a priest who committed adultery.

[1]אַדְּרַבָּה, חֶנֶק חָמוּר, [2]שֶׁכֵּן נִיתַּן לְמַכֶּה אָבִיו וְאִמּוֹ.
[3]וּמַאי חוּמְרָא? [4]שֶׁכֵּן הוּקַּשׁ כְּבוֹדָן לִכְבוֹד הַמָּקוֹם!
[5]מִדְּאַפְּקֵיהּ רַחֲמָנָא לַאֲרוּסָה בַּת יִשְׂרָאֵל מִכְּלָל נְשׂוּאָה בַּת יִשְׂרָאֵל מֵחֶנֶק לִסְקִילָה, [6]שְׁמַע מִינָּהּ סְקִילָה חֲמוּרָה.
[7]שְׂרֵיפָה חֲמוּרָה מִסַּיִיף, [8]שֶׁכֵּן נִיתְּנָה לְבַת כֹּהֵן שֶׁזִּינְּתָה.

RASHI

מכה אביו ואמו בחנק — דכתיב ביה (שמות כא) "יומת" סתמא, וקיימא לן (סנהדרין נב,ב) כל מיתה האמורה בתורה סתם אינו אלא חנק. **הוקש כבודם לכבוד המקום** — נאמר כאן (שמות כ) "כבד את אביך" ונאמר להלן (משלי ג) "כבד את ה' מהונך". **על כרחיך ארוסה** — חמורה מנשואה, שרעה לשמים ולבריות ולעצמה, שפוגמת כבודה ומשפחתה, ואיכא קלון טפי מנשואה שכבר נפגמה. ומדאפקה רחמנא מכלל "מות יומת הנואף" (ויקרא כ) דהיינו חנק דאף ארוסה היתה בכלל "אשת רעהו" (שם) ואפקה בהדיא לסקילה, כדכתיב (דברים כב) "כי תהיה נערה בתולה מאורסה וגו'" — שמע מינה סקילה חמורה. ואי קשיא לך: למה לי להדורי בתר טעמא בכולהו דתיהוי סקילה חמורה מינייהו? — מכיון דאשכח סקילה חמורה משריפה, ולקמן יליף שריפה חמורה מסייף ממילא ידעינן דסקילה חמורה מסייף! תריץ: משום דלקמן לא קיימא לן שריפה חמורה מסייף — אלא מגזירה שוה מסקילה דאשכחן בה דחמיר מסייף, הלכך מיבעי ליה לאהדורי אטעמא דחמורה סקילה מסייף.

NOTES

strangulation (as follows from the law regarding a priests married daughter who committed adultery), and stoning is more severe than burning (as follows from the law regarding a priest's betrothed young daughter who committed adultery), then surely stoning is more severe than strangulation! *Ramah* suggests that proof brought directly from the Torah is preferred over proof by way of a *kal vaḥomer* argument, no matter how simple that argument is. *Ḥamra Veḥaye* points out that the Gemara could also have adduced other proofs. For example, someone who commits adultery with his father's wife or his son's wife is liable for stoning, and not for strangulation (the usual punishment for adultery with a married woman), proving that stoning is more severe than strangulation.

חֶנֶק חָמוּר שֶׁכֵּן נִיתַּן לְמַכֶּה אָבִיו וְאִמּוֹ **Strangulation is more severe, for it was to one who strikes his father or mother.** It might be asked: Surely one who curses his mother or father is also guilty of humiliating his parents

HALAKHAH

שְׂרֵיפָה חֲמוּרָה מִסַּיִיף **Burning is more severe than the sword.** "Death by way of burning is a more severe punishment than death by way of slaying by the sword. Thus, if those who are liable to death by burning become mixed in among those who are liable to death by the sword, they are put to death by the sword, the less severe of the two punishments." (*Rambam, Sefer Shofetim, Hilkhot Sanhedrin* 14:4.)

TRANSLATION AND COMMENTARY

daughter of a priest who committed adultery. [1]The Gemara asks: **And what is the severity** of that offense, that it merits a more severe mode of execution? [2]And the Gemara answers: The adultery committed by the daughter of a priest is regarded as such a heinous transgression, **because** the woman **profanes** not only herself, but also **her father.**

אַדְּרַבָּה [3]The Gemara asks: **On the contrary,** slaying by **the sword** should be mentioned first, for it **is the more severe** mode of execution, [4]since it **is** the punishment **given to the people of a city led astray** to idol worship. [5]The Gemara expands upon this argument, asking: **And what severity** do we find regarding a city led astray that justifies the conclusion that the punishment imposed upon the guilty parties, slaying by the sword, is more severe than the punishment of burning? [6]All **the property** in a city led astray **is destroyed,** and all the buildings are razed to the ground, a procedure not found in sins punished by burning.

נֶאֱמַר [7]The Gemara rejects this argument. Faced with a contradiction of the first proof that burning is more severe than the sword, the Gemara now suggests a stronger proof: It may be inferred by way of a *gezerah shavah* (a verbal analogy) that burning is a more severe method of execution than slaying by the sword. **Regarding stoning, the verse states** (Deuteronomy 22:21): "And the men of her city shall stone her with stones that she die, because she has perpetrated wantonness in Israel, to play the harlot in her father's house." **And regarding burning, the verse states** (Leviticus 21:9): "And the daughter of a priest, if she profane herself by playing the harlot, she profanes her father; she shall be burnt with fire." Since the same phrase, "her father," appears in both places, we may infer on the basis of a verbal analogy that the same law applies in both cases. [8]**Just as** with respect to the words **"her father" that are said regarding stoning,** [9]we know that **stoning is more severe than the sword,** as was established above, [10]**so too** with respect to the words **"her father" that are said by burning,** [11]it follows that **burning is more severe than the sword.**

שְׂרֵיפָה חֲמוּרָה [12]The Gemara continues: **Burning** is mentioned in the Mishnah before strangulation, because it **is** a **more severe** mode of execution **than strangulation,** [13]since it **is** the punishment **given to the daughter of a priest who committed adultery.** [14]The Gemara asks: **And what is the severity** of that offense? [41]**As we said** above, by committing adultery, the daughter of a priest profanes not only herself, but also her father.

[1]וּמַאי חוּמְרָא? [2]שֶׁכֵּן מְחַלֶּלֶת אֶת אָבִיהָ.

[3]אַדְּרַבָּה, סַיִיף חָמוּר שֶׁכֵּן נִיתַּן לְאַנְשֵׁי עִיר הַנִּדַּחַת. [4]וּמַאי חוּמְרָא? [5]שֶׁכֵּן מָמוֹנָן אָבֵד!

[6]נֶאֱמַר "אָבִיהָ" בִּסְקִילָה, וְנֶאֱמַר "אָבִיהָ" בִּשְׂרֵיפָה. [7]מָה "אָבִיהָ" הָאָמוּר בִּסְקִילָה — [8]סְקִילָה חֲמוּרָה מִסַּיִיף, [9]אַף "אָבִיהָ" הָאָמוּר בִּשְׂרֵיפָה — [10]שְׂרֵיפָה חֲמוּרָה מִסַּיִיף.

[11]שְׂרֵיפָה חֲמוּרָה מֵחֶנֶק, [12]שֶׁכֵּן נִיתְּנָה לְבַת כֹּהֵן שֶׁזִּינְּתָה. [13]וּמַאי חוּמְרָא? [14]כְּדַאֲמָרַן.

LITERAL TRANSLATION

[1]And what is [its] severity? [2]Because she profanes her father.

[3]On the contrary, the sword is more severe for it was given to the people of a city led astray [to idol worship] a majority of whose inhabitants committed idolatry. [4]And what is [its] severity? [5]Because their money is destroyed.

[6]It says "her father" regarding stoning, and it says "her father" regarding burning. [7]Just as "her father" that is said regarding stoning — [8]stoning is more severe than the sword, [9]so too "her father" that is said regarding burning — [10]burning is more severe than the sword.

[11]Burning is more severe than strangulation, [12]for it was given to the daughter of a priest who committed adultery. [13]And what is [its] severity? [14]As we said.

RASHI

נאמר אביה בסקילה — בנערה המאורסה "לזנות בית אביה" (דברים כב). ונאמר אביה בשריפה — בבת כהן "את אביה היא מחללת" (ויקרא כא). סקילה חמורה מסייף — כדיליף טעמא לעיל ממדיחין ונידחין.

NOTES

whom he is obligated to honor, and he is liable to death by stoning! Indeed some commentators suggest that this proves the point. Surely both he who curses his parents and he who strikes them is guilty of humiliating them, but the one who physically attacks his parents is guilty of the more serious offense. He is liable to death by strangulation, which proves that strangulation is a more severe mode of execution even than stoning (*Rabbenu Yonah*).

Why then, according to the Sages, is someone who cursed his parents liable to death by stoning, while someone who struck his parents is liable to death by strangulation, a less, severe mode of execution? Someone who cursed his parents is liable for the more severe mode of execution — stoning — because the same offense can be committed against God. But someone who struck his parents is liable for the less severe mode of execution — strangulation — because there is no comparable offense against God (see *Rabbenu Yonah, Talmidei Rabbenu Peretz*).

[1]אַדְּרַבָּה, חֶנֶק חָמוּר שֶׁכֵּן נִיתַּן לְמַכֵּה אָבִיו וְאִמּוֹ, [2]וּמַאי חוּמְרָא? [3]שֶׁכֵּן הוּקַּשׁ כְּבוֹדָן לִכְבוֹד הַמָּקוֹם!

[4]מִדְּאַפְּקֵיהּ רַחֲמָנָא לִנְשׂוּאָה בַּת כֹּהֵן מִכְּלָל נְשׂוּאָה בַּת יִשְׂרָאֵל מֵחֶנֶק לִשְׂרֵיפָה, [5]שְׁמַע מִינָּהּ שְׂרֵיפָה חֲמוּרָה.

[6]סַיִיף חָמוּר מֵחֶנֶק, [7]שֶׁכֵּן נִיתַּן לְאַנְשֵׁי עִיר הַנִּדַּחַת. [8]וּמַאי חוּמְרָא? — [9]שֶׁכֵּן מָמוֹנָם אָבֵד.

[10]אַדְּרַבָּה, חֶנֶק חָמוּר שֶׁכֵּן נִיתַּן לְמַכֵּה אָבִיו וְאִמּוֹ. [11]וּמַאי חוּמְרָא? [12]שֶׁכֵּן הוּקַּשׁ כו׳!

[13]אֲפִילּוּ הָכִי, פּוֹשֵׁט יָדוֹ בָּעִיקָּר עֲדִיף.

[14]״רַבִּי שִׁמְעוֹן אוֹמֵר כו׳״. [15]שְׂרֵיפָה חֲמוּרָה מִסְּקִילָה, שֶׁכֵּן נִיתְּנָה לְבַת כֹּהֵן שֶׁזִּינְּתָה. [16]וּמַאי חוּמְרָא? [17]שֶׁכֵּן מְחַלֶּלֶת

LITERAL TRANSLATION

[1]On the contrary, strangulation is more severe, for it was given to one who strikes his father or mother. [2]And what is [its] severity? [3]Because their honor was compared to the honor of God!

[4]Since the Torah (lit., "the Merciful") set apart the married daughter of a priest from the rule [applying to] the married daughters of an Israelite from strangulation to burning, [5]infer from this that burning is more severe.

[6]The sword is more severe than strangulation, [7]for it was given to the people of a city led [to idol worship]. [8]And what is [its] severity? [9]Because their money is destroyed.

[10]On the contrary, strangulation is more severe, for it was given to one who strikes his father or mother. [11]And what is [its] severity? [12]Because [their honor] was compared, etc.

[13]Even so, he who stretches his hand out to the principle is more.

[14]"Rabbi Shimon says, etc." [15]Burning is more severe than stoning, for it was given to the daughter of a priest who committed adultery. [16]And what is [its] severity? [17]Because she profanes

TRANSLATION AND COMMENTARY

אַדְּרַבָּה [1]The Gemara asks: **On the contrary, strangulation** should be mentioned first, for it **is the more severe** mode of execution, since it **is** the punishment **given to one who strikes his father or mother.** [2]**And what** is the **severity** found regarding the prohibition of striking one's parents? [3]Striking one's parents is a most henious offense, **because the honor** that must be shown to one's parents **is comparable** to the honor that must be shown to God!

מִדְּאַפְּקֵיהּ [4]The Gemara rejects this argument: **Since the Torah removed the married daughter of a priest from the rule applying to the married daughter of an Israelite,** and changed the penalty in the case of adultery **from strangulation to burning,** [5]we may **infer from this that burning is the more severe** mode of execution, for the offense committed by the priest's daughter is more severe than the comparable offense committed by the daughter of an ordinary Israelite.

סַיִיף חָמוּר [6]The Gemara continues it analysis of the Mishnah: Death by **the sword** is mentioned in the Mishnah before strangulation, because it **is a more severe** method of execution **than strangulation,** [7]since it **is** the punishment **given to the people of a city led astray** to idol worship. [8]**And what severity** do we find regarding a city led astray? [9]All **the property** in the city **is destroyed,** and all the buildings are razed to the ground, a procedure not found in sins punished by strangulation.

אַדְּרַבָּה [10]The Gemara asks: **On the contrary, strangulation** should be mentioned first, for it **is the more severe** mode of execution, since it **is** the punishment **given to one who strikes his father or mother.** [11]**And what** is the **severity** found regarding the prohibition of striking one's parents? Striking one's parents is a most henious offense, [12]**because the honor** that must be shown to one's parents **is comparable** to the honor that must be shown to God!

אֲפִילּוּ הָכִי [13]The Gemara rejects this argument: **Even so, he who stretches his hand out to the principle,** denying the basic tenet of Judaism by blaspheming against God or worshiping idols, **is** guilty of a **more serious** offense, for he detracts from the honor of God Himself.

רַבִּי שִׁמְעוֹן [14]Now that the Gemara has sought to understand the principle behind the order of the punishments stated in the Mishnah, according to the Sages, it turns to Rabbi Shimon's position. We have learned in the Mishnah: "**Rabbi Shimon** disagrees with the anonymous first Tanna of the Mishnah, and **says:** The four methods of execution, in order of decreasing severity, are as follows: Burning, stoning, strangulation, and slaying by the sword." [15]According to Rabbi Shimon, **burning** is mentioned in the Mishnah before stoning, because it **is a more severe** mode of execution **than stoning,** since it **is** the punishment **given to the daughter of a priest who committed adultery.** [16]The Gemara asks: **And what is the severity** of that offense? [17]**Because the**

RASHI

מדאפקיה לנשואה דבת כהן – סתמא כתיב, ארוסה ונשואה משמע. ורבנן הוא דמפקי ארוסה מהיא כלל, ושבקי לה במילתא כדין ישראלית בסקילה משום דאית להו סקילה חמורה שכן ניתנה למגדף, ונשואה מיהת אפקה קרא מדין נשואה ישראלית מחנק

TRANSLATION AND COMMENTARY

daughter of a priest **profanes** not only herself but also **her father.**

אַדְּרַבָּה [1]The Gemara challenges this line of reasoning: **On the contrary, stoning** should be mentioned first, for it **is the more severe** mode of execution, since it **is** the punishment **given to one who blasphemes** against God **and to one who worships idols.** [2]**What is the severity** of these two offenses? [3]Whoever commits them **stretches his hand out to the principle,** denying the basic tenet of Judaism, the belief in one God.

רַבִּי שִׁמְעוֹן [4]The Gemara explains why Rabbi Shimon maintains that burning is more severe than stoning: **Rabbi Shimon follows his own reasoning,** [5]**for he said:** The daughter of a priest who committed adultery, **whether** she was only **betrothed or married, goes out for burning.** [6]**And since the Torah removed the betrothed** young **daughter of a priest from the rule applying to the betrothed** young **daughter of an** ordinary **Israelite,** and changed the penalty in the case of adultery **from stoning to burning,** [7]we may **infer from this that burning is the more severe** mode of execution.

שְׂרֵיפָה חֲמוּרָה [8]The Gemara continues its analysis of the Mishnah: According to Rabbi Shimon, **burning** is mentioned in the Mishnah before strangulation, because it **is** a **more severe** mode of execution **than strangulation,** since it **is** the punishment **given to the daughter of a priest who committed adultery.** [9]The Gemara asks: **And what is the severity** of that offense? [10]**As we said** above, adultery committed by the daughter of a priest profanes not only herself, but also her father.

אַדְּרַבָּה [11]The Gemara asks: **On the contrary, strangulation** should be mentioned first, for it **is the more severe** mode of execution, since it **is** the punishment **given to one who strikes his father or mother.** [12]**And what severity** do we find regarding the prohibition of striking one's parents? [13]Striking one's parents is a most henious, **because the honor** that must be shown to one's parents **is comparable to the honor** that must be shown **to God!**

מִדְּאַפְּקֵיהּ [14]The Gemara rejects this argument: **Since the Torah removed the married daughter of a priest from the rule applying to the married daughter of an** ordinary **Israelite,** and changed the penalty in the case of adultery **from strangulation to burning,** [15]we may **infer from this that burning is the more severe** mode of execution.

שְׂרֵיפָה חֲמוּרָה [16]The Gemara continues its analysis of the Mishnah: According to Rabbi Shimon, **burning** is mentioned in the Mishnah before slaying by the sword, because it **is** a **more severe** mode of execution

---

אֶת אָבִיהָ.
[1]אַדְּרַבָּה, סְקִילָה חֲמוּרָה שֶׁכֵּן נִיתְּנָה לַמְגַדֵּף וְלָעוֹבֵד עֲבוֹדַת כּוֹכָבִים. [2]וּמַאי חוּמְרָא? [3]שֶׁכֵּן פּוֹשֵׁט יָדוֹ בָּעִיקָּר.
[4]רַבִּי שִׁמְעוֹן לְטַעְמֵיהּ, [5]דְּאָמַר: אַחַת אֲרוּסָה וְאַחַת נְשׂוּאָה יָצְאָה לִשְׂרֵיפָה. [6]וּמִדְּאַפְּקֵיהּ רַחֲמָנָא לַאֲרוּסָה בַּת כֹּהֵן מִכְּלָל אֲרוּסָה בַּת יִשְׂרָאֵל מִסְּקִילָה לִשְׂרֵיפָה, [7]שְׁמַע מִינָּהּ שְׂרֵיפָה חֲמוּרָה. [8]שְׂרֵיפָה חֲמוּרָה מֵחֶנֶק, שֶׁכֵּן נִיתְּנָה לְבַת כֹּהֵן שֶׁזִּינְּתָה. [9]וּמַאי חוּמְרָא? [10]כְּדַאֲמָרַן.
[11]אַדְּרַבָּה, חֶנֶק חָמוּר שֶׁכֵּן נִיתַּן לְמַכֵּה אָבִיו וְאִמּוֹ. [12]וּמַאי חוּמְרָא? [13]שֶׁכֵּן הוּקַּשׁ כְּבוֹדָם לִכְבוֹד הַמָּקוֹם!
[14]מִדְּאַפְּקֵיהּ רַחֲמָנָא לִנְשׂוּאָה בַּת כֹּהֵן מִכְּלָל נְשׂוּאָה בַּת יִשְׂרָאֵל מֵחֶנֶק לִשְׂרֵיפָה, [15]שְׁמַע מִינָּהּ שְׂרֵיפָה חֲמוּרָה.
[16]שְׂרֵיפָה חֲמוּרָה מִסַּיִיף, שֶׁכֵּן

LITERAL TRANSLATION

her father.

[1]On the contrary, stoning is more severe, for it was given to the blasphemer and the worshiper of idols (lit., "stars"). [2]And what is [its] severity? [3]Because he stretches his hand out to the principle.

[4]Rabbi Shimon follows his own reasoning, [5]for he said: Both a betrothed woman and a married woman go out for burning. [6]And since the Torah set apart the betrothed daughter of a priest from the rule [applying to] the betrothed daughters of an Israelite from stoning to burning, [7]infer from this that burning is more severe.

[8]Burning is more severe than strangulation, for it was given to the daughter of a priest who committed adultery. [9]And what is [its] severity? [10]As we said.

[11]On the contrary, strangulation is more severe, for it was given to one who strikes his father or his mother. [12]And what is [its] severity? [13]Because their honor was compared to the honor of God!

[14]Since the Torah set apart the married daughter of a priest from the rule [applying to] the married daughters of an Israelite from strangulation to burning, [15]infer from this that burning is more severe.

[16]Burning is more severe than the sword, for

RASHI

לשריפה, אלמא שריפה חמורה, ואף על גב דמלי לאיתויי בגזירה שוה ד"אביה" "אביה" כדאייתיה לסייף — ניחא לאיתויי מגופה. רבי שמעון לטעמיה — לקמן (שם) יליף מקרא דכתיב בת כהן סתמא.

נִיתְּנָה לְבַת כֹּהֵן שֶׁזִּינְּתָה. [1] וּמַאי חוּמְרָא? [2] כְּדַאֲמָרַן. [3] אַדְּרַבָּה, סַיִיף חָמוּר שֶׁכֵּן נִיתַּן לְאַנְשֵׁי עִיר הַנִּדַּחַת. [4] וּמַאי חוּמְרָא? [5] שֶׁכֵּן מָמוֹנָם אָבֵד! [6] אָמַרְתָּ, וְכִי אֵיזֶה כֹּחַ מְרוּבֶּה, [7] כֹּחַ הַמַּדִּיחַ [8] אוֹ כֹּחַ הַנִּידָּח? [50B] [9] הֱוֵי אוֹמֵר כֹּחַ הַמַּדִּיחַ. [10] וְקַל וָחוֹמֶר: וּמַה חֶנֶק שֶׁחָמוּר מִסַּיִיף, שְׂרֵיפָה חֲמוּרָה מִמֶּנּוּ — [11] סַיִיף הַקַּל, לֹא כָּל שֶׁכֵּן. [12] סְקִילָה חֲמוּרָה מֵחֶנֶק, [13] שֶׁכֵּן נִיתְּנָה לַמְגַדֵּף וְלָעוֹבֵד עֲבוֹדָה זָרָה. [14] וּמַאי חוּמְרָא? [15] כְּדַאֲמָרַן. [16] אַדְּרַבָּה, חֶנֶק חָמוּר, [17] שֶׁכֵּן נִיתַּן לְמַכֵּה אָבִיו וְאִמּוֹ. [18] וּמַאי חוּמְרָא? [19] שֶׁכֵּן הוּקַּשׁ כו׳! [20] מִדְּאַפְּקֵיהּ רַחֲמָנָא לַאֲרוּסָה

LITERAL TRANSLATION

it was given to the daughter of a priest who committed adultery. [1] And what is [its] severity? [2] As we said.

[3] On the contrary, the sword is more severe, for it was given to the people of a city led astray [to idol worship]. [4] And what is [its] severity? [5] Because their money is destroyed!

[6] You say: Which power is greater, [7] the power of him who leads astray [8] or the power of him who is led astray? [50B] [9] You should say: The power of his who leads astray. [10] And there is a *kal vaḥomer*: If strangulation which is more severe than the sword, burning is more severe than it — [11] the sword which is lenient, all the more so!

[12] Stoning is more severe than strangulation, [13] for it was given to the blasphemer and the worshiper of idols. [14] And what is the severity? [15] As we said.

[16] On the contrary, strangulation is more severe, [17] for it was given to one who strikes his father or his mother. [18] And what is [its] severity? [19] Because [their honor] was compared, etc.!

[20] Since the Torah (lit., "the Merciful") set apart the betrothed

RASHI

הוי אומר כח המדיח — ורבי שמעון אית ליה מדיחי עיר הנדחת בחנק, ויליף לה מקרא ב״אלו הן הנחנקין״ (פט,ב). ומדמדיחין בחנק ונדחין בסייף — אלמא חנק חמור מסייף, וכבר קיימא לן לעיל דשריפה חמורה מחנק — הלכך כל שכן דחמורה היא מסייף מקל וחומר; מה חנק דחמור מסייף כו׳.

TRANSLATION AND COMMENTARY

than slaying by **the sword,** since burning **is** the punishment **given to the daughter of a priest who committed adultery.** [1] **And what is the severity** of that offense? [2] **As we said** above, adultery committed by the daughter of a priest profanes not only herself, but also her father.

אַדְּרַבָּה [3] The Gemara asks: **On the contrary,** slaying by **the sword** should be mentioned first, for it **is the more severe** mode of execution, since it **is** the punishment **given to the people of a city led astray to idol worship.** [4] **And what severity** do we find in the Torah regarding a city led astray to idol worship? [5] All **the property** in the city **is destroyed,** and all the buildings are razed to the ground.

אָמַרְתָּ [6] The Gemara rejects this line of reasoning: For if you **would ask: Which transgression is greater,** [7] **the transgression** committed **by the person who leads** others **astray** and incites them to idol worship, [8] **or the transgression** committed **by those people who are led astray** and worship idols? [50B] [9] Surely **you should say** that **the transgression** committed **by the person who** leads **others astray** is the more severe of the two. And according to Rabbi Shimon, a person who leads others astray and incites the majority of a city to worship idols is liable for strangulation (see below, 89b). Thus, it follows that strangulation is a more severe mode of execution than slaying by the sword. [10] A *kal vaḥomer* argument can now be proposed: **If strangulation is more severe than** slaying by **the sword** (as we have just established) and **burning is more severe than** strangulation (as was established above), [11] then **all the more so** we should conclude that burning is more severe than slaying by **the sword, which is lenient** in comparison to strangulation.

סְקִילָה חֲמוּרָה [12] The Gemara continues: **Stoning** is mentioned in the Mishnah before strangulation, because it **is** a **more severe** method of execution **than strangulation,** [13] since it **is** the punishment **given to one who blasphemes** against God **and to one who worships idols.** [14] The Gemara asks: **What is the severity** of these two offenses — blasphemy and idol worship — that allows you to conclude that their punishment must be the more severe mode of execution? [15] The Gemara answers: **As we said** above, these two offenses are so serious, because he who violates either one of them denies the basic tenet of Judaism, the belief in one God.

אַדְּרַבָּה [16] The Gemara challenges this argument: **On the contrary, strangulation** should be mentioned first, for it **is the more severe** mode of execution, [17] since it **is** the punishment **given to one who strikes his father or mother.** [18] The Gemara explains: **And what severity** do we find regarding the prohibition of striking one's parents? [19] Striking one's parents is a henious offense, **because the honor** that must be shown to one's parents **is comparable** to the honor that must be shown to God!

מִדְּאַפְּקֵיהּ [20] The Gemara counters this challenge: **Since the Torah removed the betrothed** young **daughter**

בַּת יִשְׂרָאֵל מִכְּלָל נְשׂוּאָה בַּת יִשְׂרָאֵל מֵחֶנֶק לִסְקִילָה, [1]שְׁמַע מִינָּהּ סְקִילָה חֲמוּרָה.

[2]סְקִילָה חֲמוּרָה מִסַּיִף, [3]שֶׁכֵּן נִיתְּנָה לַמְגַדֵּף כו׳.

[4]אַדְּרַבָּה, סַיִף חָמוּר שֶׁכֵּן נִיתַּן לְאַנְשֵׁי עִיר הַנִּדַּחַת. [5]וּמַאי חוּמְרָא? [6]שֶׁכֵּן מָמוֹנָם אָבֵד!

[7]אָמַרְתָּ: וְכִי אֵיזֶה כֹּחַ מְרוּבֶּה — [8]כֹּחַ הַמַּדִּיחַ אוֹ כֹּחַ הַנִּידָּח? [9]הֱוֵי אוֹמֵר: כֹּחַ הַמַּדִּיחַ. [10]וְקַל וָחוֹמֶר: וּמָה חֶנֶק שֶׁחָמוּר מִסַּיִיף, סְקִילָה חֲמוּרָה מִמֶּנּוּ — [11]סַיִיף הַקַּל, לֹא כָּל שֶׁכֵּן.

[12]חֶנֶק חָמוּר מִסַּיִיף, [13]שֶׁכֵּן נִיתַּן לְמַכֵּה אָבִיו וְאִמּוֹ. [14]וּמַאי חוּמְרָא? [15]כִּדְאָמְרַן.

[16]אַדְּרַבָּה, סַיִיף חָמוּר. [17]שֶׁכֵּן נִיתַּן לְאַנְשֵׁי עִיר הַנִּדַּחַת. [18]וּמַאי חוּמְרָא? [19]שֶׁכֵּן מָמוֹנָם אָבֵד!

LITERAL TRANSLATION

daughter of an Israelite from the rule [applying to] the married daughter of an Israelite from strangulation to stoning, [1]infer from this that stoning is more severe.

[2]Stoning is more severe than the sword, [3]for it was given to the blasphemer, etc.

[4]On the contrary, the sword is more severe, for it was given to the people of the city led astray [to idol worship]. [5]And what is the severity? [6]Because their money is destroyed.

[7]You say: Which power is greater — [8]the power of him who leads astray or the power of him who is led astray? [9]You would say: The power of him who leads astray. [10]And there is a *kal vaḥomer*: If strangulation which is more severe than the sword, stoning is more severe than it — [11]the sword which is lenient, all the more so!

[12]Strangulation is more severe than the sword, [13]for it was given to one who strikes his father or mother. [14]And what is [its] severity? [15]As we said.

[16]On the contrary, the sword is more severe, [17]for it was given to the people of a city led astray [to idol worship] [18]And what is]its] severity? [19]Because their money is destroyed.

TRANSLATION AND COMMENTARY

of an ordinary **Israelite from the rule applying to the married daughter of an** ordinary **Israelite,** and changed the punishment for committing adultery **from strangulation to stoning,** [1]we may **infer from this that stoning is the more severe** mode of execution, for the crime committed by the betrothed young woman is more severe than the comparable offense committed by the married woman.

סְקִילָה חֲמוּרָה [2]The Gemara continues: According to Rabbi Shimon, **stoning** is mentioned in the Mishnah before slaying by the sword, because it **is** a **more severe** method of execution **than** slaying by **the sword,** [3]since it **is** the punishment **given to one who blasphemes** God **and to one who worships idols.**

אַדְּרַבָּה [4]The Gemara objects: **On the contrary,** slaying by **the sword** should be mentioned first, for it **is** the **more severe** method of execution, **for** slaying by the sword **is** the punishment **given to the people of the city led astray** to idol worship. [5]The Gemara expands upon this argument, asking: **And what severity** do we find regarding a city led astray? [6]All **the property** of the city **is destroyed,** and all the buildings are razed to the ground.

אָמַרְתָּ [7]The Gemara rejects this line of reasoning: **For if you ask: Which transgression is greater,** [8]**the transgression** committed **by the person who leads** others **astray** and incites them to idol worship, **or the transgression** committed **by those people who are led astray** and worship idols? [9]Surely **you would say** that **the transgression** committed **by the person who leads** others **astray** is the more serious of the two. And according to Rabbi Shimon, a person who leads others astray and incites the majority of a city to worship idols is liable for strangulation (see below, 89b). Thus, it follows that strangulation is a more severe mode of execution than slaying by the sword. [10]**A *kal vaḥomer*** argument can now be proposed: **If strangulation is more severe than** slaying by **the sword** (as was established above) and **stoning is more severe than** strangulation (as we have just established), [11]then **all the more so** we should conclude that stoning is more severe than slaying by **the sword, which is lenient** in comparison to strangulation.

חֶנֶק חָמוּר [12]The Gemara continues: According to Rabbi Shimon, **strangulation** is mentioned in the Mishnah before slaying by the sword, because it **is** a **more severe** method of execution **than** slaying by **the sword,** [13]since it **is** the punishment **given to one who strikes his father or mother.** [14]The Gemara explains: **And what severity** do we find regarding the prohibition of striking one's parents? [15]**As we said** above, the honor that must be shown to one's parents is comparable to the honor that must be shown to God.

אַדְּרַבָּה [16]The Gemara objects: **On the contrary,** slaying by **the sword** should be mentioned first, for it **is** the **more severe** method of execution, [17]**for** slaying by the sword **is** the punishment **given to the people of the city a led astray** to idol worship. [18]The Gemara expands upon this argument, asking: **And what severity** do we find regarding a city led astray? [19]All **the property** in the city **is destroyed,** and all the buildings are razed to the ground.

אָמַרְתְּ: וְכִי אֵיזֶה כֹּחַ מְרוּבֶּה — כֹּחַ הַמַּדִּיחַ אוֹ כֹּחַ הַנִּידָּח? הֱוֵי אוֹמֵר: כֹּחַ הַמַּדִּיחַ. וְתַנְיָא: "מַדִּיחֵי עִיר הַנִּדַּחַת בִּסְקִילָה. רַבִּי שִׁמְעוֹן אוֹמֵר: בְּחֶנֶק.

מַרְגְּלָא בְּפוּמֵיהּ דְּרַבִּי יוֹחָנָן: נַעֲרָה הַמְאוֹרָסָה בַּת כֹּהֵן שֶׁזִּינְּתָה, בִּסְקִילָה. רַבִּי שִׁמְעוֹן אוֹמֵר: בִּשְׂרֵיפָה. זִינְּתָה מֵאָבִיהָ, בִּסְקִילָה. רַבִּי שִׁמְעוֹן אוֹמֵר: בִּשְׂרֵיפָה.

LITERAL TRANSLATION

[1] You say: Which power is greater — [2] the power of him who leads astray or the power of him who is led astray? [3] You would say: The power of him who leads astray. [4] And it was taught: "Those who led astray [the people of] a city [to idol worship] are liable for stoning. [5] Rabbi Shimon says: For strangulation."

[6] Rabbi Yoḥanan was accustomed (lit., "it was regularly in the mouth of") to say: The betrothed [young] daughter of a priest who committed adultery [is liable] for stoning. [7] Rabbi Shimon says: For burning. [8] If she committed adultery with her father, [she is liable] for stoning. [9] Rabbi Shimon says: For burning.

TRANSLATION AND COMMENTARY

אָמַרְתְּ [1] The Gemara rejects this line of reasoning: **For you would ask: Which transgression is greater,** [2] **the transgression** committed **by the person who leads** others **astray** and incites them to idol worship, **or the transgression** committed **by those people who are led astray** and worship idols? [3] Surely **you should say** that **the transgression** committed **by the person who leads** others **astray** is the more severe of the two. [4] **And it was taught** in a Baraita: **"Those who led astray the people of a city to idol worship are liable** to death **by stoning.** [5] **Rabbi Shimon** disagrees and **says:** The inciters are liable to death **by strangulation."** It follows that according to Rabbi Shimon, strangulation is a more severe mode of execution than slaying by the sword.

מַרְגְּלָא בְּפוּמֵיהּ [6] **Rabbi Yoḥanan used to say:** The Sages teach that **the betrothed** young **daughter** (*na'arah*) **of a priest who committed adultery is liable** to death **by stoning,** as they maintain that stoning is a more severe method of execution than burning. A *na'arah* is a young woman between twelve and twelve-and-a-half years old who has reached puberty (as evidenced by her having grown two pubic hairs). Thus, when the Torah says that a priest's daughter who committed adultery is liable to death by burning, it must be referring to his married daughter, and not to a betrothed young daughter (*na'arah*), whose punishment for adultery is stoning (Deuteronomy 22:21). For if it refers even to the priest's betrothed young daughter, it would make her liable for a less severe mode of punishment than the young daughter of an ordinary Israelite who committed the same offense. [7] **Rabbi Shimon** disagrees with this ruling and **says:** The betrothed young daughter of a priest who committed adultery is also liable to death **by burning,** because he maintains that burning is a more severe method of execution than stoning. Therefore, there is no reason to restrict the penalty of burning to the married daughter of a priest, to the exclusion of his betrothed young daughter. [8] Continuing, Rabbi Yoḥanan used to say: **If** the betrothed young daughter of an ordinary Israelite **committed adultery with her father, she is liable** to death **by stoning.** The woman is actually liable for two modes of execution — stoning, for having committed adultery while she was betrothed to another man, and burning, for having cohabited with her father. Someone who is guilty of two capital offenses, which are punishable by two different methods of execution, is put to death by the more severe method of execution. Thus, the woman is executed by stoning, for the Sages maintain that stoning is a more severe method of execution than burning. [9] **Rabbi Shimon** disagrees and **says:** The betrothed young daughter of an ordinary Israelite who committed adultery with her father is liable **for burning,** for burning is the more severe method of execution.

RASHI

מרגלא בפומיה דרבי יוחנן — סדור היה הדבר הזה בפיו, ולא שנאה במשנה וברייתא אלא כך קיבלה שמועה מרבו. בסקילה — דרבנן אית להו דארוסה לא יצאה לשריפה, דאם כן נמצא אתה מיקל בבת כהן. רבי שמעון אומר בשריפה — דשריפה חמורה, הלכך לית לך לאפוקי מכלל סתם בת כהן, דקרא סתמא כתיב. זינתה מאביה — ארוסה בת ישראל שזינתה מאביה, דאיכא שתי מיתות — סקילה משום ארוסה, ושריפה משום דמאביה זינתה, דבשריפה היא כדילפינן ב"אלו הן הנשרפין" (עה,ב). בסקילה — לרבנן דסקילה חמורה. רבי שמעון אומר בשריפה — הא קא משמע לן דלרבנן משום דאית להו סקילה חמורה — סבירא להו דארוסה לא יצאה לשריפה כדמפרש ואזיל וטעמא מאי כו'.

NOTES

מַרְגְּלָא בְּפוּמֵיהּ **It was regularly in his mouth.** *Ramah* understands this phrase to mean: Rabbi Yoḥanan regarded this law like a jewel (מרגלית).

HALAKHAH

נַעֲרָה הַמְאוֹרָסָה בַּת כֹּהֵן שֶׁזִּינְּתָה **The betrothed daughter of a priest who committed adultery.** "The betrothed daughter of a priest who committed adultery is liable to death by stoning," following the Sages. (*Rambam, Sefer Kedushah, Hilkhot Issurei Biah* 3:3; *Sefer Shofetim, Hilkhot Sanhedrin* 15:2.)

TRANSLATION AND COMMENTARY

מַאי קָא מַשְׁמַע לָן ¹The Gemara asks: **What does Rabbi Yoḥanan teach us?** ²The Gemara explains: Rabbi Yoḥanan teaches us that **according to the Sages,** only if the priest's daughter was **married** at the time that she committed adultery does she **go out for burning, but not** if she was **betrothed,** as she would then be stoned. ³And **according to Rabbi Shimon,** whether the priest's daughter was **betrothed or married,** she **goes out for burning.** ⁴**And what is the reasoning** behind each of these positions? ⁵**According to the Sages, stoning is** a **more severe** method of execution than burning. Since an ordinary betrothed young woman who committed adultery is liable to death by stoning, it cannot be that the betrothed young daughter of a priest who committed the same offense should be liable for the more lenient punishment of burning. ⁶**According to Rabbi Shimon, burning is** a **more severe** method of execution than stoning. Therefore, the punishment of burning applies in both cases, whether the priest's daughter was betrothed or married. ⁷Rabbi Yoḥanan teaches that **there is a practical difference** between the positions of the Sages and Rabbi Shimon **regarding someone who is liable for two judicial executions,** ⁸for, as noted, **he is sentenced to the more severe one.** This difference is significant in the case of a betrothed young daughter of an ordinary Israelite who committed adultery with her father.

מַאי רַבִּי שִׁמְעוֹן ⁹The Gemara asks: It was argued above that Rabbi Shimon follows his own reasoning, that the daughter of a priest who committed adultery, whether she was betrothed or married, is punished by burning. **What is** the Tannaitic source regarding this position of **Rabbi Shimon?** ¹⁰The Gemara answers: **For it was taught** in a Baraita: "**Rabbi Shimon says:** ¹¹**Two** rules were stated in the Torah **about the daughter**

LITERAL TRANSLATION

¹What does he teach us? ²According to the Sages, a married woman goes out for burning, but not a betrothed woman. ³According to Rabbi Shimon, both a betrothed woman and a married woman go out for burning. ⁴And what is the reason? ⁵Because according to the Sages, stoning is more severe. ⁶According to Rabbi Shimon, burning is more severe. ⁷[And] there is a practical difference regarding one who is liable for two judicial executions, ⁸[for] he is sentenced to the more severe one. ⁹What is Rabbi Shimon? ¹⁰As it was taught: "Rabbi Shimon says: ¹¹Two

¹מַאי קָא מַשְׁמַע לָן? ²לְרַבָּנַן, נְשׂוּאָה יָצְאָה לִשְׂרֵיפָה, וְלֹא אֲרוּסָה. ³לְרַבִּי שִׁמְעוֹן, אַחַת אֲרוּסָה וְאַחַת נְשׂוּאָה יָצְאָה לִשְׂרֵיפָה. ⁴וְטַעְמָא מַאי? ⁵מִשּׁוּם דִּלְרַבָּנַן סְקִילָה חֲמוּרָה. ⁶לְרַבִּי שִׁמְעוֹן שְׂרֵיפָה חֲמוּרָה. ⁷נָפְקָא מִינָּהּ לְמִי שֶׁנִּתְחַיֵּיב שְׁתֵּי מִיתוֹת בֵּית דִּין, ⁸נִידּוֹן בַּחֲמוּרָה. ⁹מַאי רַבִּי שִׁמְעוֹן? ¹⁰דְּתַנְיָא: "רַבִּי שִׁמְעוֹן אוֹמֵר: ¹¹שְׁנֵי

RASHI

ונפקא מינה — מהא דר' יוחנן דאמר דמשום דלרבנן סקילה חמורה הויא — ארוסה בת כהן בסקילה. ומשום דלר' שמעון שריפה חמורה מוקי לה בשריפה. — שמע מינה המתחייב שתי מיתות נידון בחמורה. דהכא נמי שתי מיתות איכא, סקילה כדין ארוסה, ושריפה כדין בת כהן, הלכך לרבנן על כרחך ארוסה לא יצאה לשריפה, ולרבי שמעון יצאה. מאי רבי שמעון — לעיל מהדר, דאמרן לעיל: רבי שמעון לטעמיה, דאמר: אחת ארוסה ואחת נשואה יצאה לשריפה — היכי שמעינן ליה.

NOTES

וְטַעְמָא מַאי? **And what is the reason?** We noted (see above, 50a) the logic behind the Sages' position that the betrothed young daughter of a priest who committed adultery is liable to death by stoning appears circular, since it is based on the assumption that stoning is a more severe method of execution than burning — the very assumption that it is trying to establish. *Ramban* understands that the Gemara here does not seek here to explain the position of the Sages, as they derive the law that the betrothed young daughter of a priest who committed adultery is liable to death by stoning from the words "the daughter of a priest" (see below). Rather, the Gemara desires to explain the position of Rabbi Yoḥanan. Since the Sages maintain that stoning is a more severe method of execution than burning, it follows that the betrothed young daughter of an Israelite who committed incest with her father is liable to death by stoning. But Rabbi Shimon maintains that she is liable to death by burning, which according to his opinion, is the more serve method of execution.

לְמִי שֶׁנִּתְחַיֵּיב שְׁתֵּי מִיתוֹת **One who is liable for two executions.** It might be asked: What does Rabbi Yoḥanan teach us? The dispute regarding the relative severity of the various methods of execution, as well as the rule that someone who is liable for two different methods of execution is put to death by way of the more severe method, are both stated explicitly in our Mishnah and in the Mishnah below, 81a! *Ḥamra Veḥaye* suggests that Rabbi Yoḥanan wanted to show how it was possible to become liable for two different methods of execution with a single act of intercourse (where the betrothed young daughter

HALAKHAH

נְשׂוּאָה יָצְאָה לִשְׂרֵיפָה **A married woman goes out for burning.** "The married daughter of a priest who committed adultery is liable to death by burning," following the Sages and Rabbi Akiva. (*Rambam, Sefer Kedushah, Hilkhot Issurei Biah* 3:3; *Sefer Shofetim, Hilkhot Sanhedrin* 15:2.)

TRANSLATION AND COMMENTARY

of a priest, one regarding a betrothed young woman and one regarding a married woman. When the Torah stated (Leviticus 20:10): The adulterer and the adulteress shall surely be put to death, teaching that a married woman who committed adultery is liable to death by strangulation (see below, 52b), this law would seem to apply to the daughter of a priest. And when the Torah exempted a betrothed young woman from this rule, and stated that a betrothed woman who committed adultery is liable to death by stoning, here too the law would seem also to apply to the daughter of a priest."

בְּבַת כֹּהֵן [1]The Gemara interrupts its presentation of the Baraita, and asks: Were these two rules stated **about the daughter of a priest, and not about the daughter of an** ordinary **Israelite?**

אֵימָא [2]The Gemara answers: **Say** that the Baraita should be understood as follows: "The two rules regarding adultery were stated **even about the daughter of a priest.** A married woman who committed adultery is liable to death by strangulation, and a betrothed young woman who committed adultery is liable to death by stoning, and the Torah makes no distinction between the daughter of a priest or of an ordinary Israelite."

וְהוֹצִיא הַכָּתוּב [3]The Baraita continues: **"But the verse removed the married** daughter of a priest **from the rule applying to the married** daughter of an ordinary Israelite, changing her punishment from strangulation to burning, [4]**and** it removed **the betrothed** young daughter of a priest **from the rule applying to the betrothed** young daughter of an ordinary Israelite, changing her punishment from stoning to burning, for when the Torah stated that a priest's daughter who committed adultery is liable to death by stoning, it did not distinguish between a married woman and a betrothed woman. Thus, it follows that burning is a more severe method of execution than stoning, [5]for **just as when the verse removed the married** daughter of a priest **from the rule applying to the married** daughter of an ordinary Israelite, **it intended to be stringent,** as all agree that burning is a more severe method of execution than strangulation, [6]**so too when the verse removed the betrothed** daughter of a priest **from the rule applying to the betrothed** daughter of an ordinary Israelite, **it intended to be stringent,** which implies that burning is a more severe method of execution than stoning.

זוֹמְמֵי נְשׂוּאָה [7]The Baraita concludes: "If **witnesses testified falsely against the married daughter of a priest,** claiming that she committed adultery, and they were found to be false, conspiring witnesses, who are generally liable for the punishment which they had sought to inflict on the defendant by their testimony, [8]they **are governed by the rule regarding** witnesses **who testified falsely against the married daughter of an**

כְּלָלוֹת נֶאֶמְרוּ בְּבַת כֹּהֵן״.
[1]בְּבַת כֹּהֵן, וְלֹא בְּבַת יִשְׂרָאֵל?
[2]אֵימָא: ״אַף בְּבַת כֹּהֵן״.
[3]וְהוֹצִיא הַכָּתוּב נְשׂוּאָה מִכְּלָל נְשׂוּאָה, [4]וַאֲרוּסָה מִכְּלָל אֲרוּסָה.
[5]מַה כְּשֶׁהוֹצִיא הַכָּתוּב נְשׂוּאָה מִכְּלָל נְשׂוּאָה, לְהַחְמִיר, [6]אַף כְּשֶׁהוֹצִיא הַכָּתוּב אֲרוּסָה מִכְּלָל אֲרוּסָה, לְהַחְמִיר.
[7]זוֹמְמֵי נְשׂוּאָה בַּת כֹּהֵן [8]בִּכְלָל זוֹמְמֵי נְשׂוּאָה בַּת יִשְׂרָאֵל,

LITERAL TRANSLATION

rules were stated about the daughter of a priest."

[1]About the daughter of a priest, but not about the daughter of an Israelite?

[2]Say: "Even about the daughter of an priest."

[3]"And the verse removed a married woman from the rule [applying to] a married woman, [4]and a betrothed woman from the rule [applying to] a betrothed woman. [5]Just as when the verse removed a married woman from the rule [applying to] a married woman, it was to be stringent, [6]so too when the verse removed a betrothed woman from the rule [applying to] a betrothed woman, it was to be stringent.

[7]"Those who testify falsely against the married daughter of a priest [8]are governed by the rule regarding those who testify falsely against the married daughter of an Israelite.

RASHI

שני כללות נאמר בבת כהן — אחת בארוסה, ואחת בנשואה. כלומר: כשכלל הכתוב באשת איש (ויקרא כ) "מות יומת הנואף והנואפת" — אף בת כהן משמע בחנק, וכשהוציא ארוסה לסקילה אף בת כהן במשמע, היינו כלל שני. ופרכינן **בבת כהן ולא בבת ישראל** — האי קראי סתמא כתיבי. **אימא אף בבת כהן** — והכי קאמר: שתי כללות שנאמרו בתורה בארוסה בסקילה, ובנשואה בחנק, — אף בת כהן היתה תחילה במשמע, ובא הכתוב והוציא לך בת כהן לידון בשריפה, וסתמא כתיבא, ואחת ארוסה ואחת נשואה הוציא לשריפה. **ארוסה בת כהן מכלל ארוסה בת ישראל** — מסקילה לשריפה. **נשואה מכלל נשואה** — מחנק לשריפה. **בא ולמד מיכן ששריפה חמורה** — דמה כשהוציא נשואה מכלל נשואה להחמיר עליה יצאה — דהא שריפה הכל מודים דחמורה מחנק, אף כשהוציא ארוסה מכלל הארוסה — להחמיר עליה הוציאה. **זוממי נשואה בת כהן בכלל זוממי נשואה בת ישראל** — בחנק, שלא הוציא הכתוב אלא אותה לבדה דכתיב (ויקרא כא) "היא באש תשרף" — ולא בועלה ולא זוממיה.

NOTES

of an Israelite committed adultery with her father), and how the disagreement between Rabbi Shimon and the Sages about the relative severity of the various methods of execution applies even in such a case.

¹וְזוֹמְמֵי אֲרוּסָה בַּת כֹּהֵן ²בִּכְלָל זוֹמְמֵי אֲרוּסָה בַּת יִשְׂרָאֵל.
³תָּנוּ רַבָּנַן: ״׳וּבַת אִישׁ כֹּהֵן כִּי תֵחֵל׳, ⁴יָכוֹל אֲפִילּוּ חִלְּלָה אֶת הַשַּׁבָּת. ⁵תַּלְמוּד לוֹמַר: ׳לִזְנוֹת׳ — ⁶בְּחִילּוּלִין שֶׁבִּזְנוּת הַכָּתוּב מְדַבֵּר. ⁷יָכוֹל אֲפִילּוּ פְּנוּיָה. ⁸נֶאֱמַר כָּאן: ׳אָבִיהָ׳, ⁹וְנֶאֱמַר לְהַלָּן: ׳אָבִיהָ׳. ¹⁰מַה לְּהַלָּן: זְנוּת עִם זִיקַּת הַבַּעַל, ¹¹אַף כָּאן זְנוּת עִם זִיקַּת הַבַּעַל. ¹²אוֹ אֵינוֹ אוֹמֵר אָבִיהָ אֶלָּא לְהוֹצִיא אֶת כָּל הָאָדָם? ¹³כְּשֶׁהוּא אוֹמֵר ׳הִיא מְחַלֶּלֶת׳, ¹⁴הֲוֵי כָּל אָדָם אָמוּר. ¹⁵הָא מָה אֲנִי מְקַיֵּים

LITERAL TRANSLATION

[1]And those who testify falsely against the betrothed daughter of a priest [2]are governed by the rule regarding the betrothed daughter of an Israelite." [3]Our Rabbis taught: "'And the daughter of a priest, if she profane herself.' [4]I might have [said] even if she profaned the Sabbath. [5]Therefore the Torah says: 'By playing the harlot' — [6]the verse is talking about profanation by way of harlotry. [7]I might have [said] even an unmarried daughter. [8]It is said here: 'Her father,' [9]and it is said there: 'Her father.' [10]Just as there [it is] harlotry with a bond to her husband, [11]so too here [it is] harlotry with a bond to her husband. [12]Or [perhaps] it states 'her father' only to exclude all [other] people? [13]When it states 'she profanes,' [14]surely all people are mentioned. [15]Then how do I explain

TRANSLATION AND COMMENTARY

ordinary **Israelite.** They are liable to death by strangulation, and not by burning. [1]**And** similarly, if **witnesses testified falsely against the betrothed** young **daughter of a priest,** claiming that she committed adultery, and they were found to be false, conspiring witnesses, [2]they are **governed by the rule regarding** witnesses **who testified falsely against the betrothed daughter of an** ordinary **Israelite.** They are liable to death by stoning, and not by burning. Only the priest's daughter herself was removed from the regular rules governing adultery, but her lover and conspiring witnesses who testified falsely against her are subject to the ordinary rules governing adultery."

תָּנוּ רַבָּנַן [3]**Our Rabbis taught** the following Baraita: "The verse states (Leviticus 21:9): **'And the daughter of a priest, if she profanes herself** by playing the harlot, she profanes her father; she shall be burnt with fire.' Had the verse only stated: 'And the daughter of a priest, if she profanes herself,' [4]**I might have thought** that the penalty of burning applies **even** when a priest's daughter **profanes the Sabbath.** [5]**Therefore the verse states: 'By playing the harlot,'** [6]teaching that **the verse is talking about profanation by way of harlotry.** Had I only had this verse, [7]**I might have thought** that **even an unmarried daughter** of a priest who engages in harlotry is liable to death by burning. But I learn by way of a *gezerah shavah* (a verbal analogy) that this is not the case. [8]**The verse here states:** She profanes ***her father,*** [9]**and the verse there,** regarding a betrothed young women who commits adultery, **states** (Deuteronomy 22:21): To play the harlot in ***her father's*** house. [10]**Just as there,** the verse is dealing with a woman who engaged in **harlotry** while **attached to her husband,** for that verse is dealing with a betrothed woman, [11]**so too here,** the verse is dealing with a woman who was engaged in **harlotry** while **attached to her husband** by betrothal. But an unmarried daughter of a priest engaged in harlotry she would not be liable to death by burning. [12]The Baraita asks: **Perhaps** the words **'her father' were stated** not for a *gezerah shavah,* but **only to exclude all other people?** That is to say, perhaps the words 'her father' teach us that if the priest's daughter committed incest with her father, she is liable to death by burning, but if she committed harlotry with anybody else, she is liable for the same punishment as the daughter of an ordinary Israelite. [13]The Baraita rejects this possibility: **When the verse states 'she profanes** her father,' [14]**surely** it must be **referring** to harlotry with some **person other** than her father. [15]**Then how do I account** for the words **'her father'**? As

RASHI

גבי זוממין גרס בכלל — גרס בכלל ולא גרס מכלל. **בת כהן כי תחל** — אי לא כתב ״לזנות״ משמע אפילו חיללה שבת. **תלמוד לומר לזנות** — ולקמיה פריך חיללה שבת בת סקילה היא! **ונאמר להלן** — בנערה המאורסה, מה להלן שזינתה בשעה שזיקת הבעל עליה, אף כאן זנות בשעה שזיקת הבעל עליה ולא פנויה. והאי דנקט תנא האי לישנא ולא נקט מה להלן ארוסה כו׳ — משום דסופו נמי לאיתויי נשואה לשריפה, כדיליף ואזיל. **או אינו אומר אביה** — לגזירה שוה זו אלא להוציא את כל האדם — שאם זינתה מאביה תידון בשריפה, אבל משאר כל אדם — תידון כבת ישראל. ולקמיה פריך: היכי תיסק אדעתין הא מילתא?! — אם כן מאי איריא בת כהן ואפילו בת ישראל נמי מאביה בשריפה! ב״אלו הן הנשרפין״ (עה,א). **כשהוא אומר היא מחללת** — משמע היא מחללת אותו, ולא הוא מחללה. הרי על כרחיך כשזינתה משאר כל אדם אמור. **הא מה אני מקיים את אביה** — למה לי למיכתביה כלל?! אלא נאמן כאן כו׳, והאי תנא לית ליה האי דרשה דלקמן (נב,א): שאם היו נוהגין בו קודש כו׳, אי נמי אית ליה ליכתוב היא מחללת ולא ליכתוב ״את אביה״ וליהוי משמע אפילו משפחתה, ואביה יותר מכולם.

NOTES

הִיא מְחַלֶּלֶת, הֲוֵי כָּל אָדָם אָמוּר **She profanes, surely all people are mentioned.** *Rashi,* as followed in our commentary, understands the argument as follows: The words, "She profanes her father, imply that the daughter profanes her

'אָבִיהָ'? [1]נֶאֱמַר כָּאן: 'אָבִיהָ', [2]וְנֶאֱמַר לְהַלָּן: 'אָבִיהָ', [3]מַה לְּהַלָּן — זְנוּת עִם זִיקַּת הַבַּעַל, [4]אַף כָּאן זְנוּת עִם זִיקַּת הַבַּעַל. [5]אִי מַה לְּהַלָּן נַעֲרָה וְהִיא אֲרוּסָה, [6]אַף כָּאן נַעֲרָה וְהִיא אֲרוּסָה. [7]נַעֲרָה וְהִיא נְשׂוּאָה, בּוֹגֶרֶת וְהִיא אֲרוּסָה, [8]בּוֹגֶרֶת וְהִיא נְשׂוּאָה, וַאֲפִילּוּ הִזְקִינָה מִנַּיִן? [9]תַּלְמוּד לוֹמַר: 'וּבַת כֹּהֵן' — [10]מִכָּל מָקוֹם. [11]'בַּת כֹּהֵן'. [51A] [12]אֵין לִי אֶלָּא שֶׁנִּיסֵּת לְכֹהֵן. [13]נִיסֵּת לְלֵוִי וּלְיִשְׂרָאֵל, [14]לְכוּתִי, [15]לְחָלָל,

LITERAL TRANSLATION

'her father'? [1]It is said here: 'Her father,' [2]and it is said there: 'Her father.' [3]Just as there [it is] harlotry with a bond to her husband, [4]so too here [it is] harlotry with a bond to her husband. [5]Or [perhaps] just as there [it is] a *na'arah* who is betrothed, [6]so too here [it is] a *na'arah* who is betrothed. [7]A *na'arah* who is married, a *bogeret* who is betrothed, [8]a *bogeret* who is married, and even if she grew old, from where? [9]Therefore the Torah says: 'And the daughter of a priest' — [10]in any case. [11]'The daughter of a priest.' [51A] [12]I have only when she was married to a priest. [13]From where [do I have] one who was married to a Levite, or to an Israelite, [14]to a Cuthean, [15]to a *halal*,

TRANSLATION AND COMMENTARY

was explained above: [1]**The verse here states:** 'She profanes ***her father,'*** [2]**and the verse there states** regarding a betrothed *na'arah* who commits adultery, (Deuteronomy 22:21): 'To play the harlot in ***her father's*** house.' [3]**Just as there,** the verse is dealing with a woman who engaged in **harlotry** while **attached to her husband,** for that verse is dealing with a betrothed woman, [4]**so too here,** the verse is dealing with a woman who engaged in **harlotry** while **attached to her husband** by betrothal. But the unmarried daughter of a priest engaged in harlotry would not be liable to death by burning. [5]The Baraita suggests: **Perhaps** the *gezerah shavah* should be understood differently: **Just as there,** the verse refers to **a betrothed** *na'arah*, [6]**so too here,** the verse is dealing with the daughter of a priest who is **a betrothed** ***na'arah.*** [7]**From where** then do I know that a priests daughter who committed adultery is always liable to death by burning, even if she is **a married young woman,** or **a betrothed** ***bogeret*** — a young woman who reached full maturity at the age of twelve-and-a-half, [8]or **a married** ***bogeret,*** or **even an old** married **woman** (who is not generally referred to as "a daughter"). [9]**Therefore the verse states:** ***And*** **the daughter of a priest** [וּבַת]. The superfluous *vav* in the word וּבַת, *And* the daughter, teaches that the priests daughter is liable to death by burning [10]**in all cases.** [11]The verse states: ***And*** **the daughter of a priest** [וּבַת כֹּהֵן], if she profanes herself. [51A] [12]Had I only had these words, **I would have only known** that a priest's daughter who committed adultery is liable to death by burning if she **was** also **married to a priest** (the Gemara below will explain this assumption). [13]**From where do I know** that a priest's daughter who committed adultery is liable to death by burning even if she **was married to a Levite, or to an** ordinary **Israelite,** [14]or **to a Cuthean** (Samaritan whose Jewish status was a matter of debate among the Sages), [15]or **to a** ***halal*** (a son disqualified from the priesthood by being the son of a priest and a woman to whom a priest is forbidden to marry —

RASHI

נערה — שהביאה שערות ולא הביאה סימני בגרות, במסכת נדה מפרש להו בפרק ["יוצא דופן"] (מז,א): משנתמעך הכף. **תלמוד לומר ובת כהן מכל מקום** — מרבויא דוי"ו קא דריש, וכר' עקיבא סבר לה דדריש לה לקמן (נא,ב) כי האי גוונא. וליכא לפרושי דמדכתיב קרא סתמא יליף טעמא, — דהא אתא גזירה שוה ומפקא ליה מסתמיה. **אין לי אלא שנשאת לכהן** — לקמיה פריך מהיכא תיתי הא אטו משום דניסת ללוי וישראל לאו בת כהן היא? **חלל** — כהן שנשא גרושה או זונה, וילדה לו בן מיקרי חלל מן הכהונה כדכתיב (ויקרא כא) "לא יחלל זרעו". **כותי נתין וממזר** — אף על פי שאסורין לבא בקהל יש להם קידושין, והרי

NOTES

father, but the father does not profane her, which proves that the verse must be dealing with woman who engaged in harlotry with someone else other than her father. *Ramah* suggests that the argument may be understood in a different way: The words, "She profanes her father," imply that the daughter profanes her father, but the father does not profane himself, which proves that her father was not her partner in harlotry.

כּוּתִי **A Cuthean.** The Halakhic status of the Cutheans (otherwise known as Samaritans), was a subject of controversy among the Tannaim, who regarded them as non-Jews who had settled in Samaria and the surrounding territory after the exile of the ten tribes and later converted to Judaism.) Some authorities regarded them as full-fledged converts, who despite differences in their observance of Halakhah, were to be considered as members of the Jewish

HALAKHAH

נִיסֵּת לְלֵוִי וּלְיִשְׂרָאֵל **One who was married to a Levite, or to an Israelite.** "If the daughter of a priest committed adultery, she is liable to death by burning, whether she was married to a priest, or a Levite, or an ordinary Israelite. Even if she was married to a mamzer, or a *natin,* or someone else to whom she is forbidden because of a negative precept, she is liable to death by burning." (*Rambam, Sefer Kedushah, Hilkhot Issurei Bi'ah* 3:3.)

[1]לְמַמְזֵר [2]וּלְנָתִין, מִנַּיִין? [3]תַּלְמוּד לוֹמַר: ׳וּבַת אִישׁ כֹּהֵן׳ — [4]אַף עַל פִּי שֶׁאֵינָהּ כֹּהֶנֶת. [5]׳הִיא׳ בִּשְׂרֵיפָה וְאֵין בּוֹעֲלָהּ בִּשְׂרֵיפָה. [6]׳הִיא׳ בִּשְׂרֵיפָה, [7]וְאֵין זוֹמְמֶיהָ בִּשְׂרֵיפָה. [8]רַבִּי אֱלִיעֶזֶר אוֹמֵר: אֶת אָבִיהָ בִּשְׂרֵיפָה, וְאֶת חָמִיהָ בִּסְקִילָה״.

[9]אָמַר מָר: ״יָכוֹל אֲפִילּוּ חִילְּלָה שַׁבָּת״. [10]חִילְּלָה שַׁבָּת, בַּת סְקִילָה הִיא!

LITERAL TRANSLATION

[1]to a mamzer, [2][or] to a *natin*? [3][Therefore,] the Torah states: 'And the daughter of a man who is a priest' — [4]even though she is not a priestess. [5]'She' [is liable to death] by burning, but her lover is not [liable to death] by burning. [6]'She' [is liable to death] by burning, [7]but her false, conspiring witnesses are not [liable to death] by burning. [8]Rabbi Eliezer says: Her father [is liable to death] by burning, and her father-in-law [is liable to death] by stoning."

[9]The Master said: "I might have said even if she profaned the Sabbath." [10]If she profaned the Sabbath, she is [liable to death] by stoning!

TRANSLATION AND COMMENTARY

a divorcee, for example), [1]or **to a mamzer** (a child born from an incestuous or adulterous relationship), [2]**or to a *natin*** (a descendant of the Gibeonites, a people who had converted to Judaism, but later it was decreed that they should be treated as mamzers)? [3]**Therefore, the Torah states: 'And the daughter of a man who is a priest** [וּבַת אִישׁ כֹּהֵן].' The superfluous term "man [אִישׁ]" comes to teach that an adulterous woman is liable to death by burning if her father is a priest, [4]**even though she** is married to non-priest and **is no** longer regarded as part of the **priestly** family. The verse states: 'She shall be burnt with fire.' [5]The word **'she'** teaches that only the priest's daughter, **is liable** to death **by burning, but her lover is not liable** to death **by burning.** Rather he is liable to death by the same punishment to which he would have been liable had he committed adultery with the daughter of an ordinary Israelite. [6]Furthermore, the word **'she'** teaches that only the priest's daughter herself, **is liable for burning,** [7]**but** if witnesses testified falsely against her, claiming that she committed adultery, and they were found to be **false, conspiring witnesses,** who are generally liable to the punishment that they sought to inflict by their testimony on the defendant, they **are not liable** to death **by burning.** If they testified against the married daughter of a priest, they are governed by the rule regarding witnesses who testified falsely against the married daughter of an ordinary Israelite, and they are liable to death by strangulation. If they testified against the betrothed daughter of a priest, they are governed by the rule regarding witnesses who testified falsely against the betrothed daughter of an ordinary Israelite. [8]**Rabbi Eliezer says: Her father is liable** to death **by burning, and her father-in-law is liable** to death **by stoning** (as will be explained below)."

אָמַר מָר [9]The Gemara now analyzes this Baraita: **It was stated** in the Baraita above: "Had the verse only stated: 'And the daughter of a priest, if she profanes herself,' **I might have said** that the penalty of burning applies **even** to a priest's daughter who **profanes the Sabbath,** a transgression that is referred to as a profanation. Therefore the verse specifies: 'By playing the harlot.'" [10]The Gemara now asks: Surely if the priest's daughter desecrated the Sabbath, **she should be liable** to death **by stoning,** just like anybody else! Why should we subject the daughter of a priest to burning, a less severe method of execution according to the Sages?

RASHI

היא אשת איש דקדושין תופסין בחייבי לאוין, ואף על גב דהאי מתניתין רבי עקיבא דדריש וי״ו ושמעינן ליה דאין קדושין תופסין בחייבי לאוין, איכא תנא ביבמות (סט,א) דאית ליה אליבא דרבי עקיבא, דכי אמר רבי עקיבא אין קדושין תופסין בחייבי לאוין — הני מילי בחייבי לאוין דשאר, אבל בחייבי לאוין גרידי לא אמר, כותי איכא לאו ד״לא תתחתן בם״ (דברים ז) וכן נתין, דהוא מן הגבעונים. **בת איש כהן** — ״איש״ יתירא למה לי — אלא למדרש דאב הוא דבעינן איש כהן, אבל בעל לא בעינן איש כהן, ואף על פי שאינה כהנת — אבת כהן קפיד קרא שתהא בת איש כהן, ולא אשת כהן. **רבי אליעזר אומר כו׳** — לקמן בעי מאי קאמר. **חיללה שבת בת סקילה** — והיכי סלקא דעתך דהקל בה הכתוב משאר בנות ישראל לידון במיתה קלה.

NOTES

people (albeit sinners). Other authorities challenged the validity of their conversion. In the Mishnah the Samaritans are given an intermediate status between Jews and non-Jews. But by the end of the Mishnaic period, the Samaritans had adopted religious practices of their own, and the Sages decreed that they should be treated as non-Jews. From that point on, the Samaritans no longer constituted a separate Halakhic category.

HALAKHAH

וְאֵין בּוֹעֲלָהּ בִּשְׂרֵיפָה **But her lover is not liable to death by burning.** "Even though a priest's daughter who committed adultery is liable to death by burning, her lover is liable to death by strangulation, as if he had committed adultery with the wife of an ordinary Israelite." (*Rambam, Sefer Kedushah, Hilkhot Issurei Bi'ah* 3:3.)

וְאֵין זוֹמְמֶיהָ בִּשְׂרֵיפָה **But her false conspiring witnesses are not liable to death by burning.** "If two witnesses

TRANSLATION AND COMMENTARY

אָמַר רָבָא [1]The Gemara responds: We may understand the issue of Sabbath desecration, according to **Rava** who **said:** In accordance with **whose** viewpoint **was this** Baraita taught? [2]**It** follows the viewpoint of **Rabbi Shimon, who said** that **burning is** a **more severe** method of execution than stoning. Had the verse only stated: "And the daughter of a priest, if she profanes herself," [3]**it might have entered your mind to say** that **since the Torah was more stringent about priests,** [4]and **it imposed additional obligations upon them,** it was also more stringent upon the daughter of a priest, so that if she would profane the Sabbath, **she is liable** to death **by burning,** which according to Rabbi Shimon is the more severe mode of execution. [5]**Therefore,** the verse states: "By playing the harlot, **teaching us** that the punishment of burning is only imposed upon the daughter of a priest for profanation by way of harlotry, but not for her profanation of the Sabbath.

[1]אָמַר רָבָא: הָא מַנִּי? [2]רַבִּי שִׁמְעוֹן הִיא, דְּאָמַר: שְׂרֵיפָה חֲמוּרָה. [3]סָלְקָא דַּעְתָּךְ אָמִינָא: הוֹאִיל וְאַחְמֵיר בְּהוּ רַחֲמָנָא בְּכָהֲנֵי, [4]דְּרַבֵּי בְּהוּ מִצְוֹת יְתֵירוֹת, תִּידוֹן בִּשְׂרֵיפָה. [5]קָא מַשְׁמַע לַן.

[6]מַאי שְׁנָא מִינֵּיהּ דִּידֵיהּ? [7]סָלְקָא דַּעְתָּךְ אָמִינָא: אִיהוּ דְּאִישְׁתְּרַיָא לֵיהּ שַׁבָּת לְגַבֵּי עֲבוֹדָה. [8]הִיא כֵּיוָן דְּלָא אִשְׁתְּרַיָא שַׁבָּת לְגַבָּהּ — [9]אֵימָא תִּידוֹן בִּשְׂרֵיפָה. [10]קָא מַשְׁמַע לַן.

[11]״יָכוֹל אֲפִילּוּ פְּנוּיָה״. [12]הָא

LITERAL TRANSLATION

[1]Rava said: Whose is this? [2]It is Rabbi Shimon, who said: Burning is more severe. [3]You might have thought to say: Since the Torah (lit., "the Merciful") was more stringent about priests, [4]for it added for them additional commandments, she should be [liable to death] by burning. [5]Therefore, it teaches us.

[6]How is it different from him? [7]You might have thought to say: He, because the Sabbath was permitted to him regarding the Temple service. [8]She, since the Sabbath was not permitted for her — [9]say that she should be [liable to death] by burning. [10]Therefore, it teaches us.

[11]"I might have said even an unmarried woman." [12]Surely

RASHI

ומאי שנא מיניה דידיה — לענין שבת למה יחמיר לנו בנקיבות יותר מן הזכרים כהנים? **איהו אשתראי שבת כו׳** — ומשום הכי היכא דלא אשתראי ליה מיהו לא תחמיר עליה.

מַאי שְׁנָא [6]The Gemara asks: **How is** a priest's daughter **different from** the priest himself? Why would we have thought that a priest's daughter who desecrates the Sabbath is liable to death by burning, a more severe method of execution, whereas the priest himself is liable to death by stoning, the less severe method of execution, just like an ordinary Israelite? [7]The Gemara answers: **You might have assumed** that a distinction can be made between a priest and his daughter, for the priest himself **is permitted** to violate certain **Sabbath** prohibitions in order to perform **the Temple service.** Thus, you might have thought that if he violates Sabbath prohibitions that are forbidden to him, the Torah does not relate to him with any more severity than an ordinary Israelite who desecrates the Sabbath. [8]But the priest's daughter **is not permitted** to violate **the Sabbath** prohibitions under these circumstances and is exactly like any other Jewess in this matter. [9]You might then have **said that** when she desecrates the Sabbath, **she should be liable for burning,** a more severe mode of execution, because of the additional obligations imposed upon the priesthood. [10]**Therefore,** the verse states: "By playing the harlot," **teaching us** that the punishment of burning is only imposed upon the priest's daughter for profanation by way of harlotry, but not for profanation of the Sabbath.

יָכוֹל אֲפִילּוּ פְּנוּיָה [11]The Gemara now analyzes the next clause of the Baraita: "Had I only had the verse, 'And the daughter of a priest, if she profanes herself,' **I might have said** that **even an unmarried daughter** of a priest who engages in sexual intercourse is liable to death by burning. But I learn by way of the *gezerah shavah* of 'her father, 'her father,' that this verse refers only to adultery by a married or betrothed woman." [12]The

NOTES

מַאי שְׁנָא מִינֵּיהּ דִּידֵיהּ **How is it different from him.** The same question might be raised regarding adultery: How is a priest's daughter different from the priest himself? Why should a priest's daughter who committed adultery be liable for a more severe penalty than a priest who was found guilty of the same offense? But there is really no difficulty, for the priest's daughter, being a married woman, is absolutely forbidden to any other man other than her

HALAKHAH

testified that the daughter of a priest had committed adultery, and they were found to be false, conspiring witnesses, they are liable to death by strangulation (like the woman's lover), and not to death by burning (like the priest's daughter)." (*Rambam, Sefer Shofetim, Hilkhot Edut* 20:10.)

LANGUAGE (RASHI)

אשוור״א* Apparently this should be written as **אישווייאה**, from the Old French *esviee,* meaning "deviated, strayed from one's path."

TRANSLATION AND COMMENTARY

Gemara asks how: But **surely the** same **verse states: "By playing the harlot** [לִזְנוֹת]." And the term *zenut* does not refer to the promiscuous behaviour of a single woman, but rather to the adulterous relationships of a betrothed or married woman!

כִּדְרַבִּי אֶלְעָזָר, דְּאָמַר [1]The Gemara answers: The Baraita **follows** the position of **Rabbi Elazar, who said:** [2]**If a single man engages in** sexual **intercourse with a single woman not for the sake of marriage, he turns her into a harlot,** so that thereafter she is forbidden to marry a priest. Thus, according to Rabbi Elazar, the term *zenut* can also refer to the promiscuous behaviour of a single woman.

אוֹ [3]The Baraita cited above continues: **"Perhaps** the words **'her father' were stated** not for a *gezerah shavah* to limit the punishment of burning to a woman bound in marriage, but **only to exclude all other people?** And only if the single woman commits incest with her father is she liable to death by burning." [4]The Gemara now explains why this position is unacceptable: According to this interpretation, **what** case **is** the verse dealing with? [5]With a priest's daughter who **committed incest with her** own **father.** [6]But if that is the case, why does the Torah have to **specify that the daughter of a priest,** who commits incest with her father is liable to death by burning, as if she were governed by some special law? [7]**The daughter of an** ordinary **Israelite** who engaged in sexual intercourse with her father is **also** liable to death by burning! [8]**For Rava said: Rav Yitzḥak bar Avudimi said to me:** Regarding one's granddaughter, the verse states (Leviticus 18:10): "The nakedness of your son's daughter, or of your daughter's daughter, their nakedness you shall not uncover; for *they* [*henah*] are your own nakedness." And regarding one's wife's granddaughter, the verse states (Leviticus 18:17): "You shall not uncover the nakedness of a woman and her daughter, neither shall you take her son's daughter, or her daughter's daughter, to uncover her nakedness; for *they* [*henah*] are her near kinswomen: it is *wickedness* [*zimah*]." [9]We **learn** by way of a *gezerah shavah* drawn between the words **"they"** and **"they"** that the same law that applies to one's wife's granddaughter applies to one's own granddaughter. And furthermore just as (in Leviticus 18:17) the law applying to one's wife's daughter is similar to the law applying to her granddaughter, the *gezerah shavah* teaches that the law applying to one's own daughter should be similar to that applying to one's own granddaughter. Moreover, uncovering the nakedness of one's wife's daughter and granddaughter is called "wickedness." And elsewhere, the verse dealing with forbiden sexual intercourse punishable by burning states (Leviticus 20:14): "And if a man takes a wife and her mother, it is wickedness; they shall be burnt with fire,

"לִזְנוֹת" כְּתִיב!

[1]כִּדְרַבִּי אֶלְעָזָר, דְּאָמַר: [2]פָּנוּי הַבָּא עַל הַפְּנוּיָה שֶׁלֹּא לְשׁוּם אִישׁוּת עֲשָׂאָהּ זוֹנָה.

[3]"אוֹ אֵינוֹ אוֹמֵר 'אָבִיהָ' אֶלָּא לְהוֹצִיא אֶת כָּל אָדָם"? [4]אֶלָּא מַאי נִיהוּ? [5]שֶׁזִּינְּתָה מֵאָבִיהָ. [6]מַאי אִירְיָא בַּת כֹּהֵן? [7]אֲפִילּוּ בַּת יִשְׂרָאֵל נַמִּי! [8]דְּאָמַר רָבָא: אָמַר לִי רַב יִצְחָק בַּר אֲבוּדִימִי: [9]אָתְיָא "הֵנָּה" "הֵנָּה",

LITERAL TRANSLATION

it is written: "By playing the harlot."

[1]Like Rabbi Elazar, who said: [2][If] a single man had intercourse with a single woman not for the sake of marriage, he made her into a harlot.

[3]"Or it only states 'her father' to exclude all [other] people?" [4]So what is it? [5]When she committed incest with her father. [6]Why specify the daughter of a priest? [7]Even the daughter of an Israelite also! [8]For Rava said: Rav Yitzḥak bar Avudimi said to me: [9]"They" is derived from "they,"

RASHI

הא לזנות כתיב — ופנויה לאו זונה היא, דאין לשון זונה אלא שזינתה ויצתה מתחת בעלה לאחרים כמו (הושע ט) "כי זנית מעל אלהיך" לשון מורדת ויוצאה מזה לזה = *אשוויר״א בלעז. **כדרבי אליעזר** — במסכת יבמות ב"הבא על יבמתו". **עשאה זונה** — ליפסל מן הכהונה, אלמא זונת מיקרייא. **מאי נינהו** — מאי קאמר לן קרא. **שזינתה מאביה** — בתמיה. **אתיא הנה הנה** — כתיב (ויקרא יח) בבת בנו ובבת בתו "ערות בת בנך או בת בתך וגו'" "כי ערותך הנה" וכתיב (שם) בבת אשתו "שארה הנה זימה היא" — מה באשתו עשה בתה כבת בתה, דכתיב (שם) "ערות אשה ובתה וגו'" אף כאן חייב על בתו כעל

NOTES

husband, and so if she commits adultery, her penalty is especially stringent. But the priest himself, even if he is married, is permitted to other women, and so even if he engages in forbidden intercourse, he is not punished any more severely than an ordinary Israelite (*Rabbenu Yonah*).

זוֹנָה A harlot. The term *zonah* has a precise Halakhic meaning: A woman who has had sexual relations with a man forbidden to her by the Torah and with whom she cannot establish a marital bond (for example, a woman who had relations with a close relative or a non-Jew). A woman is placed in this category whether she engaged in these forbidden relations voluntarily or against her will. In

HALAKHAH

אֲפִילּוּ בַּת יִשְׂרָאֵל נַמִּי Even the daughter of an Israelite. "If a man engaged in sexual intercourse with his daughter, both he and she are liable to death by burning." (*Rambam, Sefer Kedushah, Hilkhot Issurei Bi'ah* 1:5; *Sefer Shofetim, Hilkhot Sanhedrin* 15: 11.)

[1] אָתְיָא ״זִמָּה״ ״זִמָּה״! [2] אִיצְטְרִיךְ. [3] סָלְקָא דַּעְתָּךְ אָמִינָא: קְרָא לְאַפּוֹקֵי מִדְּרָבָא, [4] מִדְּגַלֵּי רַחֲמָנָא בְּבַת כֹּהֵן וְלֹא בְּבַת יִשְׂרָאֵל. [5] קָא מַשְׁמַע לָן. [6] ״׳בַּת כֹּהֵן׳. [7] אֵין לִי אֶלָּא שֶׁנִּיסֵּת לְכֹהֵן. [8] נִיסֵּת לְלֵוִי, לְיִשְׂרָאֵל, וּלְכוּתִי, וּלְחָלָל, לְנָתִין, וּלְמַמְזֵר, מִנַּיִין? [9] תַּלְמוּד לוֹמַר: ׳בַּת אִישׁ כֹּהֵן׳ — [10] אַף עַל פִּי שֶׁאֵינָהּ כֹּהֶנֶת״. [11] מִשּׁוּם דְּאִינַסְבָא לְהוּ לְהָנֵי, [12] לָאו בַּת כֹּהֵן הִיא? [13] וְתוּ, מִידֵּי כֹּהֶנֶת לְכֹהֵן כְּתִיב?

LITERAL TRANSLATION

[1] "wickedness" is derived from "wickedness." [2] It was necessary. [3] You might have thought to say: The verse [comes] to exclude Rava, [4] since the Torah revealed [this] regarding the daughter of a priest, and not regarding the daughter of an Israelite. [5] Therefore, it teaches us.

[6] "'The daughter of a priest.' [7] I have only one who was married to a priest. [8] From where [do I have] one who was married to a Levite, or to an Israelite, to a Cuthean, to a *ḥalal*, to a mamzer, [or] to a *natin*? [9] [Therefore,] the Torah states: 'And the daughter of a man who is a priest' — [10] even though she is not the wife of a priest (lit., 'a priestess')." [11] Because she was married to these, [12] she is not the daughter of a priest? [13] And furthermore, is it written the daughter of a priest (lit., "a priestess") to a priest?

TRANSLATION AND COMMENTARY

both he and they; that there be no *wickedness* [*zimah*] among you." [1] We may **learn** by way of another *gezerah shavah* drawn between the words **"wickedness"** and **"wickedness"** that uncovering the nakedness of one's wife's daughter or granddaughter is also punishable by burning. It, therefore, follows from the first *gezerah shavah* that uncovering the nakedness of one's own daughter or granddaughter is punishable by burning as well. Thus we would have no need for the phrase of "her father" to teach us this!

אִיצְטְרִיךְ [2] The Gemara explains: **It was** nevertheless **necessary** for the verse to state the complete phrase: "She profanes her father," [3] for **otherwise it might have entered your mind to say** that **the verse is meant to negate** the argument put forward by **Rava** in the name of Rav Yitzḥak bar Avudimi that the daughter of an ordinary Israelite who engaged in sexual intercourse with her father is liable to death by burning. For it might have been argued that the words "her father" teach us that if the priest's daughter committed adultery with her father, she is liable to death by burning, but not if she was an ordinary Israelite. [4] And **since the Torah specifies** the punishment of burning **regarding the daughter of a priest, and not regarding the daughter of an** ordinary **Israelite,** it would follow that if the daughter of an Israelite engaged in sexual intercourse with her father, she is not liable to death by burning. [5] It was **therefore** necessary to state: "She profanes her father," and thereby **teach us** that the verse is referring to a priest's daughter who engaged in harlotry with some person other than her father, as explained above.

בַּת כֹּהֵן [6] The Baraita continues: "If the verse would have stated: 'And **the daughter of a priest** [בַּת כֹּהֵן], if she profanes herself,' [7] **I would have only known** that a priest's daughter who committed adultery is liable to death by burning if she **was** also **married to a priest,** retaining her priestly familial status. [8] **How do I know** that she is liable to death by burning even if she lost her priestly status by **being married to a Levite, or to an** ordinary **Israelite,** or **to a Cuthean,** or **to a** ***ḥalal,*** or **to a mamzer, or to a** ***natin?*** [9] **The Torah therefore states: 'And the daughter of a man who is a priest** [בַּת אִישׁ כֹּהֵן].' The superfluous term "man [אִישׁ]" teaches that an adulterous woman is liable to death by burning if her father is a priest, [10] **even though she** herself **is no** longer regarded as having **priestly status."** The Gemara asks: Why was it necessary for the verse to insert the superfluous term "man"? Would not the expression "the daughter of a priest" suffice? [11] Can it be that **because** the priest's daughter **was married to** one of **these people** — a Levite, an ordinary Israelite, a Cuthean, a *ḥalal,* the priesthood, a mamzer, or a *natin* — [12] **she is no** longer regarded as **the daughter of a priest,** about whom the verse states that she is liable to death by burning for committing adultery? [13] **And furthermore, does the verse state** that it is dealing with **the daughter of priest** who is married **to a priest?** The verse speaks about "the daughter of a priest," but says nothing about the identity of her husband?

RASHI

בת בתו, ומן קל וחומר לא תייתיה — דאין עונשין מן הדין, אבל גזרה שוה הוי כאילו מפורש בו, דהא להך דרשה איכתיב "הנה" יתירא. אתיא זימה זימה — לידון בשריפה, כתיב הכא "זימה היא" וכתיב בשריפה זימה (שם כ) "באש ישרפו וגו'". סלקא דעתך אמינא — האי אביה קרא יתירא הוא דגליא שריפה בבת כהן שזינתה מאביה — לאפוקי מגזירה שוה דרבא אתא למימר דלא תידרוש ליה לישראל הבא על בתו בשרפה, דמדגלי רחמנא כו' קא משמע לן "היא מחללת" דזינתה [עם] שאר כל אדם קאמר. לאו בת כהן היא — בתמיה, למה לי "איש" יתירא לריבויי.

NOTES

either case, she is forbidden thereafter to marry a priest or remain married to one (Leviticus 21:7). There is no connection between the Halakhic definition of this term and its everyday usage in the sense of "prostitute."

לְאַפּוֹקֵי מִדְּרָבָא **To exclude Rava.** *Ran* asks: There is a rule that one cannot infer a *gezerah shavah* on one's own. That

SAGES

רַבִּי מֵאִיר Rabbi Meir. See *Sanhedrin,* Part I, pp. 54-5.

LITERAL TRANSLATION

[1]You might have thought to say: The Torah (lit., "the Merciful") states: "If she profanes herself by playing the harlot." [2]These words [apply] when she profanes herself now. [3]But this one, since she was profaned from the outset, [4]for the Master said: "And if a priest's daughter be married to a stranger" — [5]once she had intercourse with someone unfit for her, he disqualifies her. [6]To a Levite and to an Israelite also, "And she returned to her father's house, as in her youth" — [7]implying that while she is with him, she does not eat. [8]Say that she is not [liable to death] by burning. [9]Therefore, it teaches us. [10]And not like Rabbi Meir, for it was taught: [11]"[If] the daughter of a priest was married to an Israelite,

[1]סָלְקָא דַּעֲתָךְ אָמִינָא: ״כִּי תֵחֵל לִזְנוֹת״ אָמַר רַחֲמָנָא. [2]הָנֵי מִילֵּי הֵיכָא דְּקָא מִתַּחַלָּא הָשְׁתָּא. [3]אֲבָל הָא, כֵּיוָן דְּקָא מִתַּחַלָּא וְקָיְימָא מֵעִיקָּרָא, [4]דְּאָמַר מָר: ״וּבַת כֹּהֵן כִּי תִהְיֶה לְאִישׁ זָר״ — [5]כֵּיוָן שֶׁנִּבְעֲלָה לְפָסוּל לָהּ, פְּסָלָהּ. [6]לְלֵוִי וְיִשְׂרָאֵל נַמִי, ״וְשָׁבָה אֶל בֵּית אָבִיהָ כִּנְעוּרֶיהָ״ — [7]מִכְּלָל דְּכִי אִיתֵיהּ גַּבֵּיהּ, לָא אָכְלָה. [8]אֵימָא לֹא תִידּוֹן בִּשְׂרֵיפָה. [9]קָא מַשְׁמַע לָן. [10]וּדְלָא כְּרַבִּי מֵאִיר. דְּתַנְיָא: [11]״בַּת כֹּהֵן שֶׁנִּיסֵּת לְיִשְׂרָאֵל,

TRANSLATION AND COMMENTARY

סָלְקָא דַּעֲתָךְ אָמִינָא [1]The Gemara answers: Had the verse not inserted the superflous word "man," **it might have entered your mind to say** that since **the Torah states: "If she profanes herself by playing the harlot**...she shall be burnt with fire," [2]**this execution applies** if it is only **now** that the priest's daughter **profanes herself** by committing adultery. [3]**But** regarding **this** woman who was married to a *halal,* or a mamzer, or a *natin,* **since she had profaned herself from the outset** when she had entered into marriage with someone who was unfit to marry her, perhaps the law of death by burning does not apply. [4]**For the Master said:** The verse that states (Leviticus 22:12): **"And if a priest's daughter is married to a stranger,** she may not eat of an offering of the holy things," [5]teaches that **once** the daughter of a priest **had** sexual **intercourse with someone who was unfit to** marry her, such as a *mamzer,* or a *natin,* **he** permanently **disqualifies her** from partaking of terumah or marrying a priest. [6]And regarding a priest's daughter who was married **to a Levite or to an** ordinary **Israelite also,** the verse states (Leviticus 22:13): "But if a priest's daughter is a widow, or divorced, and has no child, **and has returned to her father's house, as in her youth,** she shall eat of her father's bread," [7]**implying that while** the priest's daughter **is** still **with** her nonpriestly husband, **she may not eat** terumah. While she is not permanently disqualified from eating terumah, she is now disqualified, and so she too is regarded as having removed herself through marriage from the priestly family. [8]Thus, there is reason to **say that she should not be liable to** death by **by burning** should she commit adultery. [9]**Therefore,** it was necessary for the verse to insert the superfluous word, "man," in order to **teach us** that a priest's daughter who commits adultery is liable to death by burning, even if she is not married to a priest and has no priestly status.

וּדְלָא כְּרַבִּי מֵאִיר [10]The Gemara notes: The Baraita which maintains that a priest's daughter who committed adultery is liable to death by burning, even if she was married to a man unfit to marry her, was **not** taught **in accordance with** the position of **Rabbi Meir, for it was taught** in a Baraita: "By Torah law, an ordinary Jew who inadvertantly eats terumah must pay a priest the value of the terumah, plus an additional fifth. [11]**If the daughter of a priest was married to an** ordinary **Israelite, and she** unwittingly

RASHI

כי תחל לזנות — כשהיא מתחללת על ידי זנות, וזו נתחללה כבר על ידי נשואין שנשאת לחלל לנתין ולממזר — נתחללה מן התרומה, אפילו ימות וזרע אין לה לא תשוב עוד אל בית אביה כנעוריה, ונפסלת נמי מן הכהונה שלא תינשא עוד לכהן, וכולם יליף ביבמות בפרק "אלמנה" (סח,א). **לפסול לה** — כגון נתין וממזר. **פסלה** — עולמית מתרומה ומכהונה. והתם פריך האי מיבעי ליה לגופיה — זר שאינו כהן לא תאכל בתרומה בחייו! ומשני ליה התם, וחלל אף על גב דלא פסיל לה הוא — דהא כשר לבא בקהל, יליף לה בפרק "אלמנה לכהן גדול" (יבמות סט,א) מ"לא יחלל זרעו" מקיש זרעו לו — מה הוא פוסל אף זרעו פוסל, דכהן גדול הבא על האלמנה פוסל מן הכהונה ומן התרומה, דיליף לה מ"לא יחלל" — שני חילולין במשמע — שמחלל אותה ואת הולד. **ללוי וישראל נמי** — אף על פי שאינה מחוללת עולמית, מיהו כל ימי חייו מחוללת מן התרומה, כדכתיב "ושבה וגו'". **דלא כרבי מאיר** — הא דאמרן לעיל בת כהן הנשואה לממזר בקדושתה קיימת ונידונית בשריפה דלא כרבי מאיר.

NOTES

is to say, only a *gezerah shavah* based on a tradition that goes back to Sinai is valid. How then can a verse negate a *gezerah shavah*? If there is a Sinaitic tradition on the matter, the verse cannot negate it, and if there is no Sinaitic tradition, why is such a verse necessary? *Ran* answers that the Gemara does not mean to say that the we might have thought that the verse negates the *gezerah shavah* altogether, but rather that we might have thought that the verse teaches that we may not learn from the *gezerah shavah* that the daughter of an ordinary Israelite woman who engaged in sexual intercourse with her father is liable to death by burning.

וְאָכְלָה תְּרוּמָה, מְשַׁלֶּמֶת אֶת הַקֶּרֶן וְאֵינָהּ מְשַׁלֶּמֶת אֶת הַחוֹמֶשׁ, וּמִיתָתָהּ בִּשְׂרֵיפָה. [1]נִיסֵּת לְאֶחָד מִן הַפְּסוּלִין, מְשַׁלֶּמֶת קֶרֶן וָחוֹמֶשׁ, וּמִיתָתָהּ בְּחֶנֶק. [2]דִּבְרֵי רַבִּי מֵאִיר. [3]וַחֲכָמִים אוֹמְרִים: זוֹ וָזוֹ מְשַׁלְּמוֹת קֶרֶן וְלֹא חוֹמֶשׁ, וּמִיתָתָן בִּשְׂרֵיפָה״.

[4]״רַבִּי אֱלִיעֶזֶר אוֹמֵר: אֶת אָבִיהָ בִּשְׂרֵיפָה, וְאֶת חָמִיהָ בִּסְקִילָה״. [5]מַאי ״אֶת אָבִיהָ״ וְ״אֶת חָמִיהָ״? [6]אִילֵימָא ״אֶת אָבִיהָ״ — מֵאָבִיהָ, וְ״אֶת חָמִיהָ״ — ״מֵחָמִיהָ״, [7]מַאי אִירְיָא בַּת כֹּהֵן? [8]אֲפִילּוּ בַּת יִשְׂרָאֵל נַמִי, בִּתּוֹ בִּשְׂרֵיפָה וְכַלָּתוֹ בִּסְקִילָה! [9]אֶלָּא, ״אֶת אָבִיהָ״ — ״בִּרְשׁוּת אָבִיהָ״, וְ״אֶת חָמִיהָ״ — ״בִּרְשׁוּת

LITERAL TRANSLATION

and she ate terumah, she pays the principal, but she does not pay the fifth, and her execution is by burning. [1][If] she was married to one of those who are disqualified, she pays the principal and the fifth, and her execution is by strangulation. [2][These are] the words of Rabbi Meir. [3]And the Sages say: This one and that one pay the principal, but not the fifth, and their execution is by burning."

[4]"Rabbi Eliezer says: Her father by burning, and her father-in-law by stoning." [5]What is [the meaning of] "her father" and "her father-in-law"? [6]If you say "her father" [means] "with her father," and "her father-in-law" [means] "with her father-in-law," [7]why discuss the daughter of a priest? [8]Even the daughter of an Israelite also, his daughter by burning, and his daughter-in-law by strangulation!

[9]Rather, "her father" [means] "in the domain of her father," and "her father-in-law" [means] "in the domain of

TRANSLATION AND COMMENTARY

ate terumah, she pays the principal, but she does not pay the fifth. She must offer compensation for having taken something to which she is not entitled, but she does not pay the fifth. She is not regarded as a total "stranger" regarding terumah, for if her husband dies, and she has no children, she will once again be entitled to eat terumah. [1]If such a woman committed adultery, **she is executed by burning. If** the priest's daughter **was married to someone who was disqualified** from marrying her and she unwittingly ate terumah, **she pays the principal and** also **the fifth,** for the improper marriag permanently disqualifies her from eating terumah. If such a woman committed adultery, **she is executed by strangulation,** just like the daughter of an ordinary Israelite. [2]**This is the position of Rabbi Meir.** [3]**The Sages** disagree and **say:** Both **this one** — a priest's daughter who was married to an ordinary Israelite — **and that one** — a priest's daughter who was married to someone who was disqualified from marrying her — **pay the principal, but not the fifth,** for neither one is regarded as an absolute stranger. If either one of the two committed adultery, **she is executed by burning."** Our Baraita which maintains that a priest's daughter who committed adultery is liable to death by burning, even if she was married to a person who was disqualified from marrying her, follows the position of the Sages, against Rabbi Meir.

רַבִּי אֱלִיעֶזֶר אוֹמֵר [4]It was taught in the last clause of the Baraita: **"Rabbi Eliezer says: Her father is liable** to death **by burning, and her father-in-law is liable** to death **by stoning."** [5]The Gemara asks: **What** does the Baraita mean when it says **"her father" and "her father-in-law"**? [6]The Gemara proposes an explanation which it immediately rejects: **If you say** that **"her father" means** "if she committed adultery **with her father," and "her father-in-law" means** "if she committed adultery **with her father-in-law,"** [7]**why specify the daughter of a priest,** as if she were governed by some special law? The same law applies to **the daughter of an** ordinary **Israelite.** [8]If an ordinary Israelite engaged in sexual intercourse with **his daughter,** he is liable to death **by burning, and** if he engaged in sexual intercourse with **his daughter-in-law,** he is liable to death **by strangulation!**

אֶלָּא [9]**Rather,** when the Baraita says **"her father,"** it means "while she is still only betrothed and **in the domain of her father,"** and when it says **"her father-in-law,"** it means "after she is married and **in the domain**

RASHI

ואכלה בתרומה בשוגג — דגבי זר איכא חיוב קרן וחומש. **משלמת את הקרן** — דכיון דלא זכי לה רחמנא בגוה גזילה היא אצלה. **ואינה משלמת את החומש** — דלאו זרה היא, הואיל וראויה לחזור אם ימות בעלה וזרע אין לה. **ומיתתה בשריפה** — אם זינתה. **נשאת לאחד מן הפסולים** — שנפסלה עד עולם ונתחללה הרי היא כזרה גמורה. **מאביה** — שזינתה מאביה. **כלתו בסקילה** — במתניתין (נג,א). **ברשות אביה** — ארוסה. **ברשות חמיה** — נשואה.

NOTES

זוֹ וָזוֹ מְשַׁלְּמוֹת קֶרֶן וְלֹא חוֹמֶשׁ This one and that one pay the principal, but not the fifth. *Talmidei Rabbenu Peretz* explain that even though a priest's daughter who was married to someone who was disqualified from marrying her is henceforth disqualified from marrying into the priesthood, she is still regarded as a "priest's daughter."

TRANSLATION AND COMMENTARY

of her father-in-law." Thus, the Baraita teaches that the betrothed daughter of a priest who is liable to death by burning if she committed adultery, and the married daughter of a priest is liable to death by stoning if she committed adultery. [1]The Gemara now wishes to clarify **in accordance with whose** opinion this Baraita was taught: [2]**If** you say that the Baraita was taught **in accordance with** the position of **the Sages** who maintain that stoning is a more severe method of execution than burning, there is a difficulty, [3]for **surely** the Sages **said: The married** daughter of a priest **goes out for burning** if she committed adultery **but not the betrothed** young daughter of a priest, for she is liable to death by stoning for committing adultery. [4]And **if** you say that the Baraita was taught **in accordance with** the position of **Rabbi Shimon,** who maintains that burning is a more severe method of execution than stoning, this too is difficult, for **surely** Rabbi Shimon **said: Both the betrothed** daughter of a priest **and the married** daughter of a priest **go out for burning** if they committed adultery. [5]**And if** you say that the Baraita was taught **in accordance with** the position of **Rabbi Yishmael** (whose viewpoint is presented in a Baraita cited below), this too presents a difficulty, for **surely he said** with regard to adultery: Only **the betrothed** daughter of a priest **goes forth for burning, but not the married** daughter of a priest, for the married daughter of a priest is liable to death by strangulation, just like the married daughter of an ordinary Israelite. [6]According to Rabbi Yishmael, our Baraita should have said that if a priest's daughter committed adultery while she was in **her father-in-law's** domain, she is liable to death **by strangulation!**

שָׁלַח רָבִין [7]**Ravin sent** a ruling **in the name of Rabbi Yose the son of Rabbi Ḥanina:** [8]**This is the structure of** Rabbi Eliezer's **teaching,** as it was taught in the Baraita cited above. [9]And **in fact,** Rabbi Eliezer's viewpoint was taught **in accordance with** the position of **the Sages** who maintain that the married daughter of a priest is liable to death by burning if she committed adultery and the betrothed daughter of a priest is liable to death by stoning for adultery. [10]**And this is what he said: any** ordinary woman **who** commits adultery and **is** liable for a method of execution that is **less** severe **than the** method of **execution** that is imposed if a woman had sexual intercourse with **her father** — [11]**and who is that? The married daughter of an** ordinary **Israelite.** [12]**For the married daughter of an** ordinary **Israelite** who committed adultery **is** liable to death **by strangulation** and if she committed incest with her father she is liable to death by burning,

חָמִיהָ״. [1]מַאן? [2]אִי כְּרַבָּנַן, [3]הָאָמְרִי: נְשׂוּאָה יָצָאת לִשְׂרֵיפָה, וְלֹא אֲרוּסָה. [4]אִי כְּרַבִּי שִׁמְעוֹן, הָאָמַר: אַחַת אֲרוּסָה וְאַחַת נְשׂוּאָה בִּשְׂרֵיפָה. [5]וְאִי כְּרַבִּי יִשְׁמָעֵאל, הָאָמַר: אֲרוּסָה יָצָאת לִשְׂרֵיפָה, וְלֹא נְשׂוּאָה. [6]אֶת חָמִיהָ חֶנֶק הוּא! [7]שָׁלַח רָבִין מִשְּׁמֵיהּ דְּרַבִּי יוֹסֵי בְּרַבִּי חֲנִינָא: [8]כָּךְ הִיא הַצָּעָה שֶׁל מִשְׁנָה: [9]לְעוֹלָם כְּרַבָּנַן, [10]וְהָכִי קָאָמַר: כָּל שֶׁהוּא לְמַטָּה מִמִּיתַת אָבִיהָ, [11]וּמַאי נִיהוּ — נְשׂוּאָה בַּת יִשְׂרָאֵל, [12]דְּאִילּוּ נְשׂוּאָה בַּת יִשְׂרָאֵל בְּחֶנֶק —

LITERAL TRANSLATION

her father-in-law." [1]In accordance with whom? [2]If in accordance with the Sages, [3]surely they said: A married woman goes out for burning, but not a betrothed woman. [4]If in accordance with Rabbi Shimon, surely he said: Both a betrothed woman and a married woman [go out] for burning. [5]And if in accordance with Rabbi Yishmael, surely he said: A betrothed woman goes out for burning, but not a married woman. [6]Her father-in-law is by strangulation!

[7]Ravin sent in the name of Rabbi Yose the son of Rabbi Ḥanina: [8]This is the structure of the Mishnah. [9]In fact, in accordance with the Sages, [10]and this is what it is saying: Whoever is less than the execution of her father, [11]and who is that — the married daughter of an Israelite, [12]for the married daughter of an Israelite is by strangulation —

RASHI

אי כרבנן – דאמרי סקילה חמורה איפכא מיבעי ליה! דהא ארוסה חמורה מנשואה, ולדידהו נשואה יצתה מכלל בת ישראל מחנק לשריפה, ולא ארוסה מסקילה לשריפה. ואי כרבי שמעון – דאית ליה שריפה חמורה מסקילה, הא אמר אחת ארוסה ואחת נשואה יצאו לשריפה. ואי כרבי ישמעאל – הא דאמר שריפה חמורה כרבי ישמעאל דאמר לקמן בשמעתא ארוסה יצאת לשריפה ולא נשואה, דיליף לה מבנין אב דבארוסה הכתוב מדבר. את חמיה חנק הוא – כדין בת ישראל, דהא לא יצתה מכללה. כך הצעה של משנת רבי אליעזר כמו שהיא שנויה ולא תפכה, ולעולם כרבנן דאית להו איפכא: ארוסה בסקילה נשואה בשריפה. ואיהו נמי הכי אמר: כל שהיא בבת ישראל שזינתה מאחר. למטה ממיתת אביה – שריפה, כלומר במיתה שהיא קלה משריפה, כגון נשואה דחנק בעלמא הוא, הכא בבת כהן במיתת אביה כו' כאילו זינתה מאביה – ובשריפה.

SAGES

רַבִּי יִשְׁמָעֵאל **Rabbi Yishmael.** One of the leading Tannaim of the fourth generation, Rabbi Yishmael was taken in captivity to Rome as a child, and was rescued by Rabbi Yehoshua. He became Rabbi Yishmael's first teacher. Other Sages under whom Rabbi Yishmael studied were Rabbi Eliezer and Rabbi Neḥunya ben HaKanah. The Halakhic Midrashim, the Mekhilta, the Sifrei on Numbers and part of the Sifrei on Deuteronomy represent his school of thought, and he is frequently quoted in them. Little is known of his personal life, other than that his two sons died during his lifetime. Rabbi Yishmael died as a martyr at the hands of the Romans.

רָבִין **Ravin.** This is Rabbi Avin, an Amora of the third and fourth generations. He was born in Babylonia and immigrated to Eretz Israel. Ravin was one of Rabbi Yoḥanan's younger students, and also studied under Rabbi Yoḥanan's great disciples. He was apparently a merchant and acted as an "Emmisary of Zion," taking the Torah of Eretz Israel to Babylonia. The Talmud frequently mentions that Ravin's arrival in Babylonia followed that of another emissary, Rav Dimi, and that Ravin's ruling generally determined the Halakhah. Ravin's teachings are also found in the Jerusalem Talmud, where he is called Rabbi Boon.

רַבִּי יוֹסֵי בְּרַבִּי חֲנִינָא **Rabbi Yose the son of Rabbi Ḥanina.** A Palestinian Amora of the second generation. See *Sanhedrin,* Part II, p. 62.

NOTES

Thus she is liable to death by burning if she is found guilty of adultery and she is also exempt from paying the additional fifth if she unwittingly ate terumah.

[1] הָכָא בְּמִיתַת אָבִיהָ, בִּשְׂרֵיפָה. [2] כָּל שֶׁהִיא לְמַעְלָה מִמִּיתַת אָבִיהָ, [3] וּמַאי נִיהוּ — [4] אֲרוּסָה בַּת יִשְׂרָאֵל, דְּאִילּוּ אֲרוּסָה בַּת יִשְׂרָאֵל בְּעָלְמָא בִּסְקִילָה — [5] הָכָא בְּמִיתַת חָמִיהָ, [6] בִּסְקִילָה. [7] מַתְקִיף לָהּ רַבִּי יִרְמְיָה: [8] מִידֵּי ״לְמַעְלָה לְמַטָּה״ קָתָנֵי? [9] אֶלָּא אָמַר רַבִּי יִרְמְיָה: [51B] [10] לְעוֹלָם כְּרַבִּי יִשְׁמָעֵאל. [11] וְהָכִי קָאָמַר: ״אֶת אָבִיהָ״ — ״בִּרְשׁוּת אָבִיהָ״ — בִּשְׂרֵיפָה. [12] וְ״אֶת חָמִיהָ״ — ״מֵחָמִיהָ״, — בִּסְקִילָה. [13] וְכָל אָדָם — בְּחֶנֶק.

[14] אָמַר רָבָא: מַאי שְׁנָא? [15] אוֹ אִידִי וְאִידִי מַמָּשׁ, [16] אוֹ אִידִי וְאִידִי ״רְשׁוּת״.

LITERAL TRANSLATION

[1] here for the execution of her father, by burning. [2] Whoever is more than the execution of her father, [3] and who is that — [4] the betrothed daughter of an Israelite, for the betrothed daughter of an Israelite in general is by stoning — [5] here by the execution of her father-in-law, [6] for stoning.

[7] Rabbi Yirmeyah strongly objected: [8] Does it teach "morer than, less than"?

[9] Rather, Rabbi Yirmeyah said: [51B] [10] In fact, [it is] in accordance with Rabbi Yishmael, [11] and he says as follows: "Her father" [means] "in the domain of her father" — by burning. [12] And "her father-in-law" [means] "with her father-in-law" — by stoning. [13] But [with] all [other] men — by strangulation.

[14] Rava said: Why should there be a difference? [15] Either this and that literally, [16] or this and that "in the domain of."

TRANSLATION AND COMMENTARY

[1] **here** in the parallel case involving the married daughter of a priest who committed adultery, the woman **is liable** to death **by the** method of **execution** that is imposed if a woman had sexual intercourse with **her father.** That is to say, she is liable to death **by burning.** [2] And **any** ordinary woman **who** commits adultery and **is** liable to death by a method of execution that is **more** severe **than the** method of **execution** that is imposed if a woman had sexual intercourse with **her father** — [3] **and who is that?** [4] **The betrothed daughter of an** ordinary **Israelite. For the betrothed daughter of an** ordinary **Israelite is generally** liable to death **by stoning** and if she committed incest with her father she is liable to death by burning — [5] **here** in the parallel case involving the betrothed daughter of a priest who committed adultery, the woman **is liable for the** method of **execution** that is imposed if a woman had sexual intercourse with **her father-in-law.** [6] That is to say, she is liable to death **by stoning.**

מַתְקִיף לָהּ [7] **Rabbi Yirmeyah strongly objected** to this understanding of our Baraita: [8] **Does** the Baraita **state** anything about a method of execution that is **"more** severe **than,"** or **"less** severe **than"** the method of execution imposed if a woman had sexual intercourse with her father? According to Ravin, the most important aspect of Rabbi Eliezer's teaching is missing.

אֶלָּא [9] **Rather, Rabbi Yirmeyah said:** [51B] [10] **In fact,** Rabbi Eliezer's viewpoint is **in accordance with** the position of **Rabbi Yishmael,** who said that only a priest's betrothed daughter who committed adultery is liable to death by burning, but a priest's married daughter who committed adultery is liable to death by strangulation, just like the married daughter of an ordinary Israelite. [11] **And he said as follows: "Her father"** is liable to death by burning — if the priest's daughter committed adultery while she was only betrothed and **in the domain of her father,** she is liable to death **by burning.** [12] But **"her father-in-law"** is liable to death by stoning — if she was married, and she committed adultery **with her father-in-law,** she is liable to death **by stoning,** just like the daughter of an ordinary Israelite, who is liable to death by stoning if she engaged in sexual intercourse with her father-in-law. [13] **And** if she was married, and she committed adultery with **any other man,** she is liable to death **by strangulation,** just like the married daughter of an ordinary Israelite.

אָמַר רָבָא [14] **Rava said: Why is there a difference** between interpreting the two halves of Rabbi Eliezer's statement? If Rabbi Eliezer said that "her father" is liable to death by burning, and "her father-in-law" is liable to death by stoning, [15] then it stands to reason that **either both** terms should be understood **literally,** as adultery with her father or with her father-in-law, [16] **or both** terms should be understood to mean **"in the domain of,"** her father or her father-in-law!

RASHI

כל שהיא — בבת ישראלית, למעלה ממיתת אביה, כגון ארוסה דבסקילה הכא נמי בבת כהן לא יצאת מכלל להקל — ונידונית במיתה חמורה כאלו זנתה מחמיה דבסקילה, והכי קאמר: אביה בשריפה הסמוכה למיתת אביה דנחיתא מינה דרגא — דהיינו נשואה בת ישראל, הכא בבת כהן הוציאה הכתוב להחמיר בשריפה. ושהיא למעלה משריפה — כגון ארוסה את חמיה, דיינין לה כדין כלתו דבסקילה. יש לגמגם אמאי נקיט את חמיה? תיפוק ליה דכן דינה בסקילה אחרי שלא יצאה מן הכלל! ומיהו הא מתקפינן אתקפתא אחריתי ומפקינן ליה מטעמא. **לעולם רבי ישמעאל** — דאמר ארוסה יצתה ולא נשואה. והכי קאמר רבי אליעזר: את אביה ברשות אביה, דהיינו ארוסה — בשריפה. **ואת חמיה** — דהיינו נשואה, אם מחמיה זינתה — בסקילה כבת ישראל, ומכל אדם — בחנק כישראל, דנשואה לא יצתה מן הכלל.

[1]אֶלָּא אָמַר רָבָא: לְעוֹלָם כְּרַבִּי שִׁמְעוֹן, [2]וְקָסָבַר רַבִּי אֱלִיעֶזֶר: נְשׂוּאָה כַּאֲרוּסָה. [3]מָה אֲרוּסָה, חַד דַּרְגָּא מַסְקִינַן לָהּ, מִסְּקִילָה לִשְׂרֵיפָה. [4]אַף נְשׂוּאָה, חַד דַּרְגָּא מַסְקִינַן לָהּ, מֵחֶנֶק לִסְקִילָה.

[5]מַתְקִיף לָהּ רַבִּי חֲנִינָא: [6]הָא אִידִי וְאִידִי רַבִּי שִׁמְעוֹן בִּשְׂרֵיפָה קָאָמַר!

[7]אֶלָּא, אָמַר רָבִינָא: לְעוֹלָם כְּרַבָּנַן, [8]וְאֵיפּוּךְ: אֶת אָבִיהָ —

LITERAL TRANSLATION

[1]Rather, Rava said: In fact, [it is] in accordance with Rabbi Shimon, [2]and Rabbi Eliezer maintains: A married woman is like a betrothed woman. [3]Just as a betrothed woman, we raise her one level from stoning to burning, [4]so too a married woman, we raise her one level from strangulation to stoning.

[5]Rabbi Ḥanina strongly objected to this: [6]But surely Rabbi Shimon said that this and that are by burning!

[7]Rather, Ravina said: In fact, [it is] in accordance with the Sages, [8]and reverse it: Her father —

TRANSLATION AND COMMENTARY

אֶלָּא [1]**Rather, Rava said: In fact,** Rabbi Eliezer's viewpoint was taught **in accordance with** the position of **Rabbi Shimon,** who maintains that burning is a more severe method of execution than stoning. Thus, a priest's betrothed daughter who committed adultery is liable to death by burning, and not stoning as would have been the case with the daughter of an ordinary Israelite. [2]**And Rabbi Eliezer maintains** that **the married** daughter of a priest **is like the betrothed** daughter of a priest. [3]**Just as** with a priest's **betrothed** daughter who committed adultery, **we raise** the severity of **her** mode of execution **one level from from stoning** (the punishment in the case of the daughter of an ordinary Israelite) **to burning,** [4]**so too** with a priest's **married** daughter, **we raise** the severity of **her** mode of execution **one level from strangulation** (the punishment in the case of the daughter of an ordinary Israelite) **to stoning.** And when Rabbi Eliezer spoke of "her father" and "her father-in-law," he was referring to their domain: If the priest's daughter committed adultery while she was betrothed and still in her father's domain, she is liable to death by burning. But if she committed adultery after she was married and in the domain of her father-in-law, she is liable to death by stoning.

מַתְקִיף לָהּ [5]**Rabbi Ḥanina strongly objected** to this understanding of Rabbi Eliezer: [6]**But surely Rabbi Shimon said that both** the betrothed daughter of a priest and the married daughter of a priest **are** liable to death **by burning!** If Rabbi Eliezer agrees with Rabbi Shimon that burning is a more severe mode of execution than stoning, then he should agree with Rabbi Shimon that both the betrothed daughter and the married daughter of a priest are liable to death by burning, or he should say that the betrothed daughter is liable to death by burning, and the married daughter is liable to death by strangulation!

אֶלָּא [7]**Rather, Ravina said: In fact,** Rabbi Eliezer's viewpoint was taught **in accordance with** the position of **the Sages,** who maintain that stoning is a more severe method of execution than burning. Therefore a priest's married daughter who committed adultery is liable to death by burning, but a priest's betrothed daughter who committed adultery is liable to death by stoning, like the betrothed daughter of an Israelite. [8]**And** Rabbi Eliezer's statement should **be reversed,** so that it reads: **Her father is liable** to death **by stoning** — if the priest's daughter committed adultery while she was betrothed and still in her father's domain, she

RASHI

לעולם כרבי שמעון — דאמר שריפה חמורה, הלכך על כרחיך ארוסה יצתה לשריפה, ובנשואה קסבר רבי אליעזר הואיל ובישראל קלה מאד — דבחנק, דיי לך אם תחמיר על בת כהן לדונה בסקילה, דסלקא חד דרגא דלרבי שמעון כך סדרן: שריפה, סקילה, חנק, והרג. ואת אביה ואת חמיה דקאמר — רשות נינהו. **הא אידי ואידי רבי שמעון בשריפה קאמר** — ועל כרחיך לא מצית למימר רבי אליעזר בהא פליג עליה, דמהיכא תיתי? אי לית ליה בנין אב דרבי ישמעאל — על כרחיך כיון דשריפה חמורה וקרא בת כהן סתמא כתיב — שתיהן במשמע! ואי אית ליה בנין אב דבארוסה הכתוב מדבר — נשואה על כרחיך לא יצתה מכלל נשואה בת ישראל, ומי הוציאה לסקילה? אם החמיר הכתוב בארוסה בת כהן מבת ישראל שכן היא חמורה, תחמיר בנשואה שהיא קלה?! איפוך — אידי ואידי רשות, והאי דקאמר "את אביה" ולא נקט לשון ארוסה ולשון נשואה — סירכא נקט אמילתיה דתנא קמא סריך, דאיירי בלישנא דקרא.

SAGES

רַבִּי חֲנִינָא **Rabbi Ḥanina** (bar Ḥama). A Palestinian Amora of the first generation. See *Sanhedrin,* Part I, p. 16.

רָבִינָא **Ravina**. A Babylonian Amora of the fifth and sixth generations. Ravina was actively involved in the editing of the Babylonian Talmud.

NOTES

הָא אִידִי וְאִידִי רַבִּי שִׁמְעוֹן בִּשְׂרֵיפָה קָאָמַר **But surely Rabbi Shimon said that this and that are by burning.** The Rishonim ask: Why not say that Rabbi Eliezer maintains his own position, and that he agrees with Rabbi Shimon about the betrothed daughter of a priest that she is liable to death by burning, and disagrees with him about the married daughter of a priest, saying that she is liable to death by stoning? The Rishonim explain the Gemara's argument as follows: If Rabbi Eliezer maintains that when the Torah speaks of the priest's daughter, it is referring both to his betrothed daughter and to his married daughter, then even the married daughter who committed adultery should be liable to death by burning. And if he maintains that the Torah refers only to the priest's betrothed daughter, then the law regarding his married daughter should be no different than the law applying to the married daughter of an ordinary Israelite, and so the married daughter of priest who committed adultery should also be liable to death by strangulation, and not by stoning.

TRANSLATION AND COMMENTARY

is liable to death by stoning. [1]**And her father-in-law is liable** to death **by burning** — if she committed adultery after she was married and in her father-in-law's domain, she is liable to death by burning. [2]**When** Rabbi Eliezer **spoke of "her father,"** rather than stating explicitly "if she was betrothed," [3]**he was merely using the wording** used earlier in the Baraita (which is itself based on the wording found in the Bible) where the expression of profaning "her father" refers to a betrothed woman in her father's domain (see Deuteronomy 22:21).

אָמַר רַב נַחְמָן [4]The Gemara continues: **Rav Naḥman said in the name of Rabbah bar Avuha who said in the name of Rav:** [5]**The law is** in accordance with what **Ravin sent in the name of Rabbi Yose the son of Rabbi Ḥanina,** as was cited above.

אָמַר רַב יוֹסֵף [6]**Rav Yosef said:** Did Rav come to teach us **a law** which will only be relevant **in the Messianic period?** There is no capital punishment today, and it will not be reinstated until the Messiah comes. Why then did Rav propose a definitive Halakhic ruling?

אָמַר לֵיהּ [7]**Abaye said to** Rav Yosef: **But** according to your line of reasoning, **let us not teach** tractate *Zevaḥim,* which deals with **the slaughter of sacrifices,** [8]for that is surely **law** that will only be relevant **in the Messianic period** when the Temple is restored and the sacrifices are reinstated! [9]**Rather,** regarding the sacrifices, we say: **Expound** the law, **and receive reward** for studying Torah. [10]**Here too,** then, we should say: **Expound** the law, **and receive reward** for studying Torah.

הָכִי קָאָמְרִי [11]Rav Yosef said to Abaye: When I asked my question, **I** meant to **say as follows: Why should it be necessary** to decide whether **the law** is in accordance with Ravin or with Ravina?

בִּסְקִילָה, [1]וְאֶת חָמִיהָ — בִּשְׂרֵיפָה. [2]וְהַאי דְּקָאָמַר "אֶת אָבִיהָ", [3]סִירְכָא בְּעָלְמָא נָקַט.

[4]אָמַר רַב נַחְמָן אָמַר רַבָּה בַּר אֲבוּהּ אָמַר רַב: [5]הֲלָכָה כִּדְשָׁלַח רָבִין מִשְּׁמֵיהּ דְּרַבִּי יוֹסֵי בְּרַבִּי חֲנִינָא.

[6]אָמַר רַב יוֹסֵף: הִלְכְתָא לִמְשִׁיחָא?

[7]אָמַר לֵיהּ אַבַּיֵי: אֶלָּא מֵעַתָּה, שְׁחִיטַת קָדָשִׁים לָא לִיתְנֵי — [8]הִלְכְתָא לִמְשִׁיחָא! [9]אֶלָּא דְּרוֹשׁ וְקַבֵּל שָׂכָר. [10]הָכָא נַמִי, דְּרוֹשׁ וְקַבֵּל שָׂכָר.

[11]הָכִי קָאָמְרִי: הִלְכְתָא לָמָּה לִי?

LITERAL TRANSLATION

by stoning, [1]and her father-in-law — by burning. [2]And that which he said "her father," [3]he merely continued with the same wording (lit., "followed habit").

[4]Rav Naḥman said in the name of Rabbah bar Avuha who said in the name of Rav: [5]The law is as Ravin sent in the name of Rabbi Yose the son of Rabbi Ḥanina.

[6]Rav Yosef said: [Do we fix] a law for the Messianic [period]?

[7]Abaye said to him: But now, let us not teach the slaughter of sacrifices — [8]a law for the Messianic period! [9]Rather, expound and receive reward. [10]Here too, expound and receive reward.

[11]I said as follows: Why do I need the law?

RASHI

הלכתא למשיחא — הלכה זו כשיבאו ימות המשיח אצטריך לנו, שישובו ארבע מיתות בית דין למקומן. **הכי קאמינא הלכה למה לי** סוגיא דשמעתא הלכה קאמר בתמיה, מי שייך למימר הלכה בכי האי מחלוקת שאין בין רבין לרבינא לא חיוב ולא פטור ולא חילוק מיתה, דתרווייהו מפרשי נשואה — בשריפה, ארוסה — בסקילה. ובתיקון לשון הברייתא פליגי, מר מתקן לה ללישנא דלא אצטריך לאפוכה, ומר מפיך לה משום דוחקא דלישנא. ומאי הלכה איכא למימר בסוגיא דשמעתא אחרי שאין אנו למידין ממנה כלום? כשיבא המשיח ויחיה המתים

SAGES

רַב נַחְמָן Rav Naḥman (bar Ya'akov). A Babylonian Amora of the second and third generations. See *Sanhedrin,* Part I, p. 37.

רַבָּה בַּר אֲבוּהּ Rabbah bar Avuha. A Babylonian Amora of the second generation, Rabbah bar Ahuva was a pupil of Rav, and transmitted many teachings in his name. Rabbah bar Ahuva was a member of the Exilarch's family, and Rav Naḥman was his pupil and his son-in-law.

NOTES

סִירְכָא בְּעָלְמָא נָקַט He merely used the common wording. Our commentary follows *Rashi* and others who understand that the Gemara is trying to explain here why Rabbi Eliezer spoke of "her father," rather than stating explicitly "if she was betrothed." *Rabbenu Ḥananel, Tosafot,* and others understand that the Gemara is trying to explain why Rabbi Eliezer made a mistake and said "her father for burning," when he maintains that the betrothed daughter of a priest who committed adultery is liable, not to death by burning, but by stoning. *Rabbenu Ḥananel* explains that the mistake stems from the fact that a daughter who has sexual intercourse with her father is liable to death by burning. *Tosafot* write that it stems from the wording of the verse: "She profanes her father; she shall be burnt with fire. According to *Rabbenu Ḥananel* and *Tosafot,* we understand why this point was noted only according to Ravina's interpretation of the Baraita, for only according to Ravina is there a mistake in the wording of the Baraita. According to *Rashi,* this point is just as relevant to the earlier interpretations of the Baraita, but the Gemara pushed if off and inserted it at the end of the discussion (see *Ḥamra Veḥaye*).

הִלְכְתָא לִמְשִׁיחָא A law for the Messianic period. *Rabbi Ya'akov Emden* notes that all the laws regarding the slaughter of sacrifices, even those regarding the sin-offerings, will be relevant in the Messianic period, as the verse relating to that period says (Isaiah 65:20): "And the *sinner* being a hundred years old shall be deemed accursed."

[1]סוּגְיָא דִשְׁמַעְתָּא הֲלָכָה קָאָמַר? [2]מַאי רַבִּי יִשְׁמָעֵאל? [3]דְּתַנְיָא: ״׳וּבַת [אִישׁ] כֹּהֵן כִּי תֵחֵל לִזְנוֹת׳״ [4]בְּנַעֲרָה וְהִיא אֲרוּסָה הַכָּתוּב מְדַבֵּר. [5]אַתָּה אוֹמֵר בְּנַעֲרָה וְהִיא אֲרוּסָה, [6]אוֹ אֵינוֹ אֶלָּא אֲפִילּוּ נְשׂוּאָה? [7]תַּלְמוּד לוֹמַר: ׳אִישׁ אֲשֶׁר יִנְאַף אֶת אֵשֶׁת רֵעֵהוּ מוֹת יוּמַת הַנֹּאֵף וְהַנֹּאָפֶת׳, [8]הַכֹּל הָיוּ בִּכְלָל הַנּוֹאֵף וְהַנּוֹאֶפֶת, [9]הוֹצִיא הַכָּתוּב בַּת יִשְׂרָאֵל בִּסְקִילָה, [10]וּבַת כֹּהֵן בִּשְׂרֵיפָה. [11]מַה כְּשֶׁהוֹצִיא הַכָּתוּב אֶת בַּת יִשְׂרָאֵל לִסְקִילָה, [12]אֲרוּסָה וְלֹא נְשׂוּאָה, [13]אַף כְּשֶׁהוֹצִיא הַכָּתוּב בַּת כֹּהֵן לִשְׂרֵיפָה, [14]אֲרוּסָה וְלֹא נְשׂוּאָה. [15]זוֹמְמֶיהָ וּבוֹעֲלָהּ

LITERAL TRANSLATION

[1]Did the course of the discussion involve a [dispute of] law?

[2]What is [the source of] Rabbi Yishmael? [3]As it was taught: "'And the daughter of a priest, if she profane herself by playing the harlot.' [4]The verse is speaking of a *na'arah* who is betrothed. [5]You say [it refers] to a *na'arah* who is betrothed, [6]but might it not even be one who is married? [7]Therefore the Torah states: 'And the man who commits adultery with his neighbor's wife, the adulterer and the adulteress shall surely be put to death.' [8]All [women] were in the class of an adulterer and an adulteress. [9]Scripture removed the daughter of an Israelite for stoning, [10]and the daughter of a priest for burning. [11]Just as when Scripture removed the daughter of an Israelite for stoning, [12]she was betrothed, and not married, [13]so too when Scripture removed the daughter of a priest for burning, [14]she was betrothed, and not married. [15]Her false, conspiring witnesses and her lover

TRANSLATION AND COMMENTARY

[1]**Did the course of discussion involve a dispute in law?** Surely, they both agree that according to Rabbi Eliezer, a priest's betrothed daughter who committed adultery is liable to death by stoning, and a priest's married daughter who is guilty of that offense is liable to death by burning? They only disagree about how to interpret his statement, whether to add the words "more than" and "less than," or to reverse the two halves of his ruling? Is it then pertinent to speak **here** about the **law** when there is no difference between Ravina and Rava except in how to understand the wording of the Baraita? When the Messiah arrives and revives the dead, we can go and ask Rabbi Eliezer exactly what he meant, but until then it should not make any difference to us!

מַאי רַבִּי יִשְׁמָעֵאל [2]In the course of the previous discussion, the Gemara alluded to the position of Rabbi Yishmael. The Gemara now asks: **What is** the Tannaitic source in which **Rabbi Yishmael** expressed his position? [3]The Gemara answers: **As it was taught** in the following Baraita: "The verse states (Leviticus 21:9): **'And the daughter of a priest, if she profanes herself by playing the harlot.'** [4]**The verse is speaking of a betrothed** *na'arah* (a young woman between twelve and twelve-and-a-half years old, who has reached puberty, as is evidenced by her having grown at least two pubic hairs. [5]**You say** that the verse is referring to **the betrothed** daughter (*na'arah*) of a priest who committed adultery. [6]**But might it not** refer **even** to his **married** daughter? [7]**Therefore the Torah states** (Leviticus 20:10): **'And the man who commits adultery with his neighbor's wife, the adulterer and the adulteress shall surely be put to death.'** [8]Since the verse makes no distinctions, it includes **all** women **in the rule governing an adulterer and an adulteress,** and so they should all be liable to death by strangulation. For wherever the Torah imposes capital punishment without specifying the mode of execution, the transgressors are put to death by strangulation. [9]But **Scripture removed the daughter** (*na'arah*) **of an** ordinary **Israelite** from this rule, and said that she is liable to death **by stoning,** as the verse states (Deuteronomy 22:21): 'And they shall bring out the girl to the door of her father's house, and the men of her city shall stone her with stones that she die." [10]**And** Scripture also removed **the daughter of a priest** from this ruling, and said that she is liable to death **by burning,** as the verse states (Leviticus 21:9): "She shall be burnt with fire." [11]**Just as when Scripture removed the daughter of an** ordinary **Israelite** from the rule governing adulterous women, and said that she is liable to death **by stoning,** [12]it was dealing with **the betrothed** daughter (*na'arah*) of an ordinary Israelite, **but not** with his **married** daughter, [13]**so too when Scripture removed the daughter of a priest** from the rule governing adulterous women, and said that she is liable to death **by burning,** [14]it was only dealing with **the betrothed** daughter (*na'arah*) of a priest, **and not** with his **married** daughter. [15]**Witnesses who testified falsely against** the

RASHI

נשאל את רבי אליעזר באיזה לשון אמרה. מות יומת הנואף והנואפת — כל מיתה סתם = חנק. הכל היו בכלל הנואף והנואפת — נשואות וארוסות, כהנת וישראלית. הוציא הכתוב — מכלל זה את ארוסה לסקילה כדכתיב (דברים כב) "והוציאו את הנערה" — והוציאו כתוב אחר בת כהן לשריפה, וכתב סתם ולמד סתם מן המפורש: מה כשהוציא בישראל מכלל חנק — ארוסה הוציא, ולא נשואה — אף כשהוציא כו'. זוממיה — בכלל מיתה בועלה. שלא יצא מן הכלל דכתיב (ויקרא כא) "היא" —

LITERAL TRANSLATION

are in the class of 'And you shall do to him, as he had thought to have done, etc.'"

[1][Regarding] her lover, what "as he had thought to have done" is there?

[2]Rather: "Her false conspiring witnesses are in the class of the execution of her lover, [3]for it is said: 'And you shall do to him, as he had thought to have done to his brother' — [4]and not to his sister. [5][These are] the words of Rabbi Yishmael."

[6]"Rabbi Akiva says: Both one who was betrothed and one who was married went out for burning. [7]I might have thought even an unmarried [daughter]. [8]It is said here: 'Her father,' [9]and it is stated there: 'Her father.' [10]Just as there [it is] harlotry with a bond to her husband, [11]so too here [it is] harlotry with a bond to her husband."

[12]"Rabbi Yishmael said to him: [13]Or [perhaps] just as there [it is] a *na'arah* who is betrothed, [14]so too here [it is] a *na'arah* who is betrothed!"

בִּכְלָל 'וַעֲשִׂיתֶם לוֹ כַּאֲשֶׁר זָמַם וגו' '".

[1]בּוֹעֲלָהּ, מַאי "כַּאֲשֶׁר זָמַם" אִיכָּא?

[2]אֶלָּא: "זוֹמְמֶיהָ בִּכְלָל מִיתַת בּוֹעֲלָהּ, [3]מִשּׁוּם שֶׁנֶּאֱמַר: 'וַעֲשִׂיתֶם לוֹ כַּאֲשֶׁר זָמַם לַעֲשׂוֹת לְאָחִיו' — [4]וְלֹא לַאֲחוֹתוֹ. [5]דִּבְרֵי רַבִּי יִשְׁמָעֵאל".

[6]"רַבִּי עֲקִיבָא אוֹמֵר: אַחַת אֲרוּסָה וְאַחַת נְשׂוּאָה יָצְאת לִשְׂרֵיפָה. [7]יָכוֹל אֲפִילּוּ פְּנוּיָה. [8]נֶאֱמַר כָּאן: 'אָבִיהָ', [9]וְנֶאֱמַר לְהַלָּן: 'אָבִיהָ'. [10]מַה לְּהַלָּן זְנוּת עִם זִיקַּת הַבַּעַל, [11]אַף כָּאן זְנוּת עִם זִיקַּת הַבַּעַל".

[12]אָמַר לוֹ רַבִּי יִשְׁמָעֵאל: [13]אִי מַה לְּהַלָּן נַעֲרָה וְהִיא אֲרוּסָה, [14]אַף כָּאן נַעֲרָה וְהִיא אֲרוּסָה!

TRANSLATION AND COMMENTARY

priest's daughter that she was guilty of adultery **and** the priest's daughter's **lover are** included **in the rule** laid down in the verse (Deuteronomy 19:19): **'And you shall do to him, as he had thought to have done** to his brother.'"

בּוֹעֲלָהּ [1]The Gemara interrupts its presentation of the Baraita, and asks in astonishment: **Regarding** the priest's daughter's **lover, what** room **is there** to invoke the rule of "And you shall do to him, **as he had thought to have done** to his brother?"

אֶלָּא [2]**Rather,** explains the Gemara, the Baraita should read as follows: **"Witnesses who testified falsely against** the priest's daughter that she was guilty of adultery **are** included **in the rule governing the execution of the** priest's daughter's **lover.** As is the case with the priest's daughter's lover, they too are liable to death by stoning if the woman was betrothed, and strangulation if she was married, [3]**for the verse states: 'And you shall do to him, as he had thought to have done to his brother.'** When two different punishments might have been imposed for the same testimony, the false, conspiring witness is liable for the punishment that he wished to inflict upon his brother even if less stringent, [4]**and not** the one he wished to inflict **upon his sister.** [5]**This is the position of Rabbi Yishmael."**

רַבִּי עֲקִיבָא אוֹמֵר [6]The Baraita continues: **"Rabbi Akiva says: Whether** the priest's daughter **was betrothed** when she committed adultery, **or she was** already **married,** she **goes out for burning,** as the verse makes no distinctions regarding her "playing the harlot." [7]Therefore, **I might have said even a priest's unmarried daughter** who engaged in promiscuous sexual intercourse is liable to death by burning. However, I derive by way of a *gezerah shavah* that this is not the case. [8]**The verse** regarding a priest's daughter **states** (Leviticus 21:9): 'She profanes ***her father,*'** [9]**and the verse** regarding a betrothed *na'arah* **states** (Deuteronomy 22:21): 'To play the harlot in ***her father's*** house.' [10]**Just as there,** the verse is dealing with a woman who engaged in **harlotry** while **attached to her husband,** for that verse is dealing with a betrothed woman, [11]**so too here,** the verse is dealing with a woman who was **attached to her husband,** either by betrothal or marriage. But if the unmarried daughter of a priest engaged in harlotry she is not liable to death by burning."

אָמַר לוֹ [12]"**Rabbi Yishmael said to** Rabbi Akiva: Since you are ready to invoke the argument of *gezerah shavah,* you should formulate the *gezerah shavah* as follows: [13]**Just as there** the verse is dealing with **a betrothed *na'arah*,** [14]**so too here,** the verse is dealing with **a betrothed *na'arah*.** Thus, the *gezerah shavah* supports my position that only a priest's betrothed daughter is liable to death by burning if she committed adultery, and not his married daughter."

SAGES

רַבִּי עֲקִיבָא **Rabbi Akiva.** A Tanna of the fourth generation. See *Sanhedrin,* Part I, p. 31.

RASHI

ולא בועלה, וזוממיה בכלל מיתת בועליהן דכתיב "כאשר זמם לעשות לאחיו" — ולא לאחותו, במקום שיש חילוק מיתה בעדותן כגון כאן שחייבו לה שריפה ולו סקילה — כדינו נדונין ולא כדינה. אחת ארוסה ואחת נשואה — דקרא סתמא כתיב. אמר לו רבי ישמעאל — הואיל ודורש אתה גזירה שוה, דרוש נמי הא דבארוסה משתעי.

HALAKHAH

זוֹמְמֶיהָ בִּכְלָל מִיתַת בּוֹעֲלָהּ **Her false, conspiring witnesses are in the class of the execution of her lover.** "If two witnesses testified against a man that he committed adultery with the daughter of a priest, and the man was

TRANSLATION AND COMMENTARY

אָמַר לוֹ [1]**"Rabbi Akiva said to** Rabbi Yishmael: **Yishmael, my brother, I expound 'daughter' — *'and* the daughter.'** The verse reads (Leviticus 21:9): 'And the daughter [וּבַת] of a priest, if she profanes herself by playing the harlot.' The extraneous letter vav ("and") in the word וּבַת ("and the daughter"), teaches that even a priest's married daughter who committed adultery is liable for burning."

אָמַר לוֹ [2]"Rabbi Yishmael **said to** Rabbi Akiva: **And because you expound 'daughter'** — ***'and* the daughter,'** [3]**we should** be stringent with the priest's married daughter and **take her out for burning** instead of strangulation? Surely, you are being inconsistent. [4]**If** the verse **implies** that **the married daughter** of a priest should be **included** in the penalty of burning, as against the *gezerah shavah,* then you should **include** also the priest's **unmarried daughter.** [5]**And if** the *gezerah shavah* **implies** that **the unmarried daughter** of a priest should be **excluded** from the penalty of burning, then you should also **exclude** a priest's **married daughter."**

וְרַבִּי עֲקִיבָא [6]The Gemara asks: **And** how does **Rabbi Akiva** counter this argument? The Gemara explains: He can argue as follows: [7]**The *gezerah shavah*** drawn between the two instances of the expression "her father" **serves to exclude the unmarried daughter** of a priest from the penalty of burning. [8]And the extraneous *vav* in **"daughter" — *"and* the daughter" serves to include a** priest's **married daughter** for that punishment.

וְרַבִּי יִשְׁמָעֵאל סָבַר [9]The Gemara now explains Rabbi Yishmael's last objection to Rabbi Akiva: When **Rabbi Yishmael** argued that Rabbi Akiva was being inconsistent, he had **thought** as follows: [10]**Since** Rabbi Akiva **told him** that he derives that the married daughter of a priest is liable for burning from the extraneous vav in **"daughter" — *"and* the daughter,"** [11]**he inferred that** Rabbi Akiva **retracted** his previously stated ***gezerah shavah,*** and that he was inferring his entire position from the amplification implied by the extraneous vav. Therefore, Rabbi Yishmael argued for consistency. If you include the priest's married daughter, include his unmarried daughter too, and if you exclude the priest's unmarried daughter, exclude also his married daughter. But as was explained above, Rabbi Akiva can maintain that the *gezerah shavah* serves to exclude the priest's unmarried daughter, and the extraneous *vav* serves to include his married daughter.

[1]"אָמַר לוֹ רַבִּי עֲקִיבָא: יִשְׁמָעֵאל אָחִי, 'בַּת' — 'וּבַת', אֲנִי דּוֹרֵשׁ. [2]אָמַר לוֹ: וְכִי מִפְּנֵי שֶׁאַתָּה דּוֹרֵשׁ 'בַּת' 'וּבַת' [3]נוֹצִיא זוֹ לִשְׂרֵיפָה? [4]אִם מַשְׁמַע לְהָבִיא אֶת הַנְּשׂוּאָה הֵבִיא אֶת הַפְּנוּיָה. [5]וְאִם מַשְׁמַע לְהוֹצִיא אֶת הַפְּנוּיָה, הוֹצִיא אֶת הַנְּשׂוּאָה".

[6]וְרַבִּי עֲקִיבָא? [7]אַהֲנֵי גְּזֵירָה שָׁוָה לְמַעוּטֵי פְּנוּיָה, [8]וְאַהֲנֵי "בַּת" "וּבַת" לְרַבּוֹת אֶת הַנְּשׂוּאָה.

[9]וְרַבִּי יִשְׁמָעֵאל סָבַר: [10]מִדְּקָאָמַר לֵיהּ "בַּת" "וּבַת" [11]שְׁמַע מִינָּהּ הֲדַר בֵּיהּ מִגְּזֵירָה שָׁוָה.

LITERAL TRANSLATION

[1]"Rabbi Akiva said to him: Yishmael, my brother, I expound 'daughter' — *'and* the daughter.'"

[2]"He said to him: And because you expound 'daughter' — *'and* the daughter,' [3]do we take her out for burning? [4]If it implies to include a married [daughter], include an unmarried [daughter]. [5]And if it implies to exclude an unmarried [daughter], exclude a married [daughter]."

[6]And Rabbi Akiva? [7]The *gezerah shavah* serves to exclude an unmarried [daughter], [8]and "daughter" — *"and* the daughter" serves to include a married [daughter].

[9]And Rabbi Yishmael maintains: [10]Since he said to him: "Daughter" — *"and* the daughter," [11]he concluded from this that he retracted the *gezerah shavah.*

RASHI

בת ובת — וי״ו יתירה לרבות הנשואה. **נוציא זו בשריפה** — ונחמיר עליה ממיתה המפורשת בה דהוי חנק, דאם משמע גזירה שוה להביא את הנשואה הביא נמי את הפנויה, ואם משמע להוציא פנויה הוציא וכו׳. **ורבי ישמעאל** — דפריך ליה אם משמע וכו׳ לא ידע דעתיה דרבי עקיבא, והוה סבירא ליה מדמהדר ליה בת ובת אני דורש — שמע מינה דרבי עקיבא הדר ביה מגזירה שוה, והכי קאמר: ישמעאל אחי אין אני דורש גזירה שוה זו דאתא בת ובת ואפקה, והכי קאמר ליה: אם כן למעוטי פנויה מנא לך.

NOTES

וְכִי מִפְּנֵי שֶׁאַתָּה דּוֹרֵשׁ **And because you expound.** Rabbi Yishmael might not be challenging the validity of a Halakhic inference base on extraneous *vav* (though there are Rishonim who understand that Rabbi Yishmael does not attach Halakhic significance to such a letter), but rather the arbitrariness of the inference, according to which a distinction is made between the married daughter of a priest and his unattached daughter, a distinction which does not follow from the plain meaning of the Biblical text.

HALAKHAH

sentenced to strangulation, and the priest's daughter was sentenced to burning, and the witnesses were then found to be false, conspiring witnesses, the witnesses are liable to death by strangulation, and not by burning." (*Rambam, Sefer Shofetim, Hilkhot Edut* 20:10.)

TRANSLATION AND COMMENTARY

וְרַבִּי יִשְׁמָעֵאל [1]The Gemara now asks: **How does Rabbi Yishmael expound** the extraneous vav in **"daughter"** — **"*and* the daughter"?**

מִיבָּעֵי לֵיהּ [2]The Gemara explains: Rabbi Yishmael **needs** the extraneous vav **for that which was taught** in a Baraita **by the father of Shmuel bar Avin:** [3]**"Since we find that regarding male** priests, **Scripture distinguishes between those with no** physical **blemishes,** who are fit for the Temple service, **and those with** physical **blemishes,** who are unfit for such service, [4]**I might have said that we should make a** similar **distinction regarding** the punishment of **daughters** of such blemished priests who commit harlotry. This would mean that a priest's daughter with no physical blemishes is liable to death by burning if she committed adultery, but a priest's daughter with a physical blemish is treated like the daughter of an ordinary Israelite. [5]**Therefore, the Torah states: 'Daughter' — '*and* the daughter'** — the extraneous vav teaching that even a priest's daughter is liable to death by burning."

וְרַבִּי עֲקִיבָא [6]The Gemara asks: **And** what verse does **Rabbi Akiva** use to show that a priest's daughter who committed adultery is liable to death by burning, even if she has a physical blemish which would disqualify a priest from participating in the Temple service? [7]The Gemara explains: **This follows from** the verse (Leviticus 21:6): "They shall be holy to their God, and not profane the name of their God: for the offerings of the Lord made by fire, and the bread of their God, **they do offer; therefore they shall be holy."** The extraneous words, "therefore they shall be holy," teach that even priests with physical blemishes who are unfit to perform the Temple service are endowed with the special sanctity of the priesthood. Hence even a priest's daughter with a physical blemish is liable to death by burning.

וְרַבִּי יִשְׁמָעֵאל [8]The Gemara asks: So why then does **Rabbi Yishmael** not deduce this law from "therefore they shall be holy"? [9]The Gemara explains: **If from that** verse, **I might have said** that **that rule applies** only **to the priests,** who generally serve in the Temple. The verse teaches that even if a priest has a physical blemish that disqualifies him from this services he must still not defile himself by contact with the dead. [10]**But** regarding **the daughters** of these blemished priests, I might have said that they are treated like the daughters of an ordinary Israelite, and are **not** liable to death by burning if they commit adultery. [11]**Therefore** the Torah **teaches us** with the extraneous vav of "and the daughter" that even a blemished priest's daughter is liable to death by burning.

[1]וְרַבִּי יִשְׁמָעֵאל? הַאי "בַּת" "וּבַת" מַאי דָּרֵישׁ בֵּיהּ? [2]מִיבָּעֵי לֵיהּ לְכִדְתָנֵי אֲבוּהִי דִּשְׁמוּאֵל בַּר אָבִין: [3]לְפִי שֶׁמָּצִינוּ שֶׁחָלַק הַכָּתוּב בִּזְכָרִים בֵּין תְּמִימִים לְבַעֲלֵי מוּמִין, [4]יָכוֹל נַחֲלוֹק בִּבְנוֹתֵיהֶן. [5]תַּלְמוּד לוֹמַר: "בַּת" "וּבַת". [6]וְרַבִּי עֲקִיבָא? [7]מִ"וְהֵם מַקְרִיבִם וְהָיוּ קֹדֶשׁ", נָפְקָא. [8]וְרַבִּי יִשְׁמָעֵאל? [9]אִי מֵהַהִיא, הֲוָה אָמִינָא: הָנֵי מִילֵּי אִינְהוּ, [10]אֲבָל בְּנוֹתֵיהֶן, לָא, [11]קָא מַשְׁמַע לָן.

LITERAL TRANSLATION

[1]And Rabbi Yishmael? How does he expound this "daughter" — "*and* the daughter"?

[2]He needs it for that which the father of Shmuel bar Avin taught: [3]"Since we find that regarding males the Scripture distinguishes between unblemished ones and those with blemishes, [4]I might have said that we should distinguish regarding their daughters. [5][Therefore] the Torah states: 'Daughter' — '*and* the daughter.'"

[6]And Rabbi Akiva? [7]This follows from: "They do offer; therefore they shall be holy."

[8]And Rabbi Yishmael? [9]If from there, I would have said: Those words [apply to] them, [10]but their daughters, not. [11][Therefore] it teaches us [otherwise].

RASHI

בזכרים — בכהנים. **בין תמימים לבעלי מומין** — לענין עבודה. **יכול** אף בנות בעלי מומין יצאו מכלל קדושתן, ויהיה דינם כבנות ישראל אם זנו. **והיו קדש** — לרבות אף בעלי מומין לקדושה. **הני מילי** — דנפקי שאף בעלי מומין בקדושתן מוהיו קדש. **אינהו** — הכהנים עצמן נתרבו לקדושה, שלא תאמר הואיל ופסולין לעבודה יהיו מותרין לטמא למתים.

NOTES

יָכוֹל נַחֲלוֹק בִּבְנוֹתֵיהֶן **I might have said that we should distinguish regarding their daughters.** According to some Rishonim, we might have thought to distinguish between the daughter of priest who has a physical blemish which disqualifies him from serving in the Temple and the daughter of a priest who is free of such blemishes. Others understand that we might have distinguished between a priest's daughter with a physical blemish that would disqualify a male priest from participating in the Temple service and a priest's daughter with no such blemishes (see *Meiri, Ḥamra Veḥaye*).

SAGES

רַב אַשִׁי Rav Ashi. Born in the year that Rava died, he became one of the greatest Amoraim of Babylonia during the sixth generation. He edited the Babylonian Talmud and headed the yeshivah of Mata Meḥasya for sixty years. His main teacher was Rabbi Kahana of Pum Nahara. Rav Ashi's father-in-law was Rami bar Abba, and his son Mar bar Rav Ashi, succeeded to his position. Another of his sons, Rav Sama, was also a Sage.

TRANSLATION AND COMMENTARY

וְרַבִּי יִשְׁמָעֵאל [1]The Gemara asks: **And Rabbi Yishmael** who does not need the expression "her father" for a *gezerah shavah* — [52A] [2]**how does he expound** the words (Leviticus 21:9), **"she profanes her father"?**

מִבָּעֵי לֵיהּ [3]The Gemara explains: Rabbi Yishmael **needs** those words **for that which was taught** in a Baraita: [4]**"Rabbi Meir would say: What does the verse, 'She profanes her father,' teach us?** [5]It teaches us **that if** people **had** previously **treated** her the father **as a holy man, they** now **treat him as an ordinary person,** [6]and if they had previously treated him **with honor, they** now **treat him with scorn.** How so? [7]**They say: Cursed is he who fathered this** daughter who committed adultery, **cursed is he who raised this** daughter who was unfaithful to her husband, **cursed is he from whose loins this** woman **emerged."**

אָמַר רַב אַשִׁי [8]**Rav Ashi said: In accordance with whose** opinion **may we apply the designation "wicked person the son of a wicked person,"** [9]**even to a wicked person who is the son of a righteous person?** [10]**In accordance with whose** position — **in accordance with the** position of **the Tanna,** of the above Baraita, Rabbi Meir, who says that a man's daughter commits adultery, she profanes her father, so that henceforth we relate to him with contempt.

זוֹ מִצְוַת הַנִּסְקָלִין [11]We learned in the last clause of our Mishnah: **"This** elucidates **the obligation regarding those who are liable to death by stoning."** [12]The Gemara asks: **What did** the Tanna of the Mishnah **teach** first **that he teaches** now: [13]**"This** elucidates **the obligation regarding those who are liable to death by stoning"?** Our Mishnah does not deal with the specifics of stoning?

מִשּׁוּם דִּתְנָא [14]The Gemara explains: **Since** the Tanna **taught** in the previous chapter (42b): **"If a verdict was reached** in a capital case, and the defendant was found guilty and sentenced to death by stoning, **he would be taken out to be stoned** on that very day," and also (45a): [15]**"If the place of stoning** from which the condemned party was pushed down to his death **was** a platform **twice the height of an** ordinary **person,"** as well as all the other regulations regarding stoning, [16]**and** now **he wishes to teach** (the next Mishnah): **"That**

[1]וְרַבִּי יִשְׁמָעֵאל? [52A] [2]הַאי "אָבִיהָ הִיא מְחַלֶּלֶת", מַאי דָּרֵישׁ בֵּיהּ?

[3]מִבָּעֵי לֵיהּ לְכִדְתַנְיָא: [4]"הָיָה רַבִּי מֵאִיר אוֹמֵר: מַה תַּלְמוּד לוֹמַר, 'אֶת אָבִיהָ הִיא מְחַלֶּלֶת'. [5]שֶׁאִם הָיוּ נוֹהֲגִין בּוֹ קוֹדֶשׁ, נוֹהֲגִין בּוֹ חוֹל; [6]כָּבוֹד, נוֹהֲגִין בּוֹ בִּזָּיוֹן. [7]אוֹמְרִין: אָרוּר שֶׁזּוֹ יָלַד, אָרוּר שֶׁזּוֹ גִּידֵּל, אָרוּר שֶׁיָּצָא זוֹ מֵחֲלָצָיו".

[8]אָמַר רַב אַשִׁי: כְּמַאן קָרֵינַן "רְשִׁיעָא בַּר רְשִׁיעָא", [9]וַאֲפִילּוּ לִרְשִׁיעָא בַּר צַדִּיקָא? [10]כְּמַאן? כְּהַאי תָּנָא.

[11]"זוֹ מִצְוַת הַנִּסְקָלִין". [12]מַאי תָּנָא דְּקָתָנֵי: [13]"זוֹ מִצְוַת הַנִּסְקָלִין"?

[14]מִשּׁוּם דִּתְנָא: "נִגְמַר הַדִּין, מוֹצִיאִין אוֹתוֹ לְסָקְלוֹ... [15]בֵּית הַסְּקִילָה הָיָה גָּבוֹהַּ שְׁתֵּי קוֹמוֹת", [16]וְאַיְּידֵי דְּקָא בָּעֵי

LITERAL TRANSLATION

[1]And Rabbi Yishmael? [52A] [2]How does he expound this "she profanes her father"?

[3]He needs it for that which was taught: [4]"Rabbi Meir would say: What does the verse, 'She profanes her father,' teach us? [5]That if they had related to him as a holy man, they relate to him as [an] ordinary [person]. [6]With honor, they relate to him with scorn. [7]They say: Cursed is he who fathered her, cursed is he who raised her, cursed is he from whose loins she emerged."

[8]Rav Ashi said: In accordance with whom do we call "wicked person the son of a wicked person," [9]even a wicked person who is the son of a righteous person? [10]In accordance with whom? In accordance with this Tanna.

[11]"This is the obligation regarding those who are liable [to death] by stoning." [12]What did he teach [above] that he [now] teaches: [13]"This is the obligation regarding those who are liable [to death] by stoning"?

[14]Since he taught: "[When] the judgment is concluded, they take him out to stone him.... [15]The place of stoning was twice the height of a man," [16]and since he wishes

RASHI

ורבי ישמעאל – דנפקא ליה במה מלינו, ולא איצטריך גזירה שוה. **האי את אביה** – מאי דריש ביה. **מאי זו** – אהיכא קאי.

NOTES

כְּמַאן קָרֵינַן In accordance with whom do we call. Rav Ashi comes to teach us that if someone calls the father of a sinful child "a wicked person," he is not guilty of speaking ill about a righteous man and his progeny (*Rabbenu Yehonatan*). Some point out that the designation, "wicked person son of a wicked person," may only be applied if the father was known to be a person of only average righteousness. But if the father was known to be a man of extreme righteousness, he may not be scorned or denigrated, even if his child grew up to be a wicked person (*She'eilot U'teshuvot HaMabit*).

TRANSLATION AND COMMENTARY

is the obligation regarding those who are liable to death by burning," [1]**he** first **teaches: "This is the obligation regarding those who are liable to death by stoning,"** and thus summarizes what had been taught up to now.

MISHNAH מִצְוַת הַנִּשְׂרָפִין [2]**The obligation regarding those who are liable to death by burning** would be fulfilled as follows: [3]The condemned criminal **would** first **be sunk in** a pile of **manure** that reached **up to his knees,** to keep him from moving. [4]**A stiff kerchief** which when pulled tight would cause him to open his mouth **would be placed inside a soft** kerchief, **and** the two kerchiefs **would** then **be encircled around his neck.** The two witnesses whose testimony led to the criminal, condemnation would then pull on the ends of the kerchiefs. [5]**One** witness **would pull** the kerchiefs **toward himself, and the other** witness **would pull** the kerchiefs **toward himself, until** the condemned person was forced to **open his mouth.** [6]The executioner **would** then **heat up the strip of metal, and cast it into his mouth, and it would go down to his entrails, scald his bowels,** and cause death.

רַבִּי יְהוּדָה אוֹמֵר [7]**Rabbi Yehudah said:** The condemned person's mouth would not be forced open by way of the kerchiefs, for **if he died at the hands** of those pulling on the kerchiefs, before the strip was cast down his throat, **the obligation of** executing the criminal by way **of burning would not be fulfilled.** He would then have been executed by strangulation. [8]**Rather,** the criminal's **mouth would be forced open with tongs.** The executioner **would** then **heat up the strip, and cast it into his mouth, and**

לְמִיתְנָא "מִצְוַת הַנִּשְׂרָפִין" [1]תָּנָא נַמִי "זוֹ מִצְוַת הַנִּסְקָלִין".

מִשְׁנָה [2]מִצְוַת הַנִּשְׂרָפִין. [3]הָיוּ מְשַׁקְּעִין אוֹתוֹ בַּזֶּבֶל עַד אַרְכּוּבּוֹתָיו, [4]וְנוֹתְנִין סוּדָר קָשָׁה לְתוֹךְ הָרַכָּה, וְכוֹרֵךְ עַל צַוָּארוֹ. [5]זֶה מוֹשֵׁךְ אֶצְלוֹ וְזֶה מוֹשֵׁךְ אֶצְלוֹ עַד שֶׁפּוֹתֵחַ אֶת פִּיו. [6]וּמַדְלִיק אֶת הַפְּתִילָה וְזוֹרְקָהּ לְתוֹךְ פִּיו, וְיוֹרֶדֶת לְתוֹךְ מֵעָיו וְחוֹמֶרֶת אֶת בְּנֵי מֵעָיו. [7]רַבִּי יְהוּדָה אוֹמֵר: אַף הוּא אִם מֵת בְּיָדָם לֹא הָיוּ מְקַיְּימִין בּוֹ מִצְוַת שְׂרֵיפָה. [8]אֶלָּא, פּוֹתֵחַ אֶת פִּיו בִּצְבָת שֶׁלֹּא בְּטוֹבָתוֹ, וּמַדְלִיק אֶת הַפְּתִילָה וְזוֹרְקָהּ

LITERAL TRANSLATION

to teach "The obligation regarding those who are liable [to death] by burning," [1]he taught also "This is the obligation regarding those who are liable [to death] by stoning."

MISHNAH [2]The obligation regarding those who are liable [to death] by burning. [3]They would sink him in manure up to his knees, [4]and place a stiff kerchief inside a soft one, and wrap [it] around his neck. [5]This one would pull to him, and that one would pull to him, until he opens his mouth. [6]Someone would heat up the strip (lit., "light the wick"), and cast it into his mouth, and it would go down to his entrails, and scald his bowels.

[7]Rabbi Yehudah says: If he died thus at their hands, they would not fulfill the obligation of burning. [8]Rather, someone would forcefully open his mouth with tongs, and heat up the strip, and cast it

SAGES

רַב יְהוּדָה **Rav Yehudah.** The name Rav Yehudah without any patronymic in the Gemara refers to Rav Yehudah bar Yeḥezkel, one of the greatest Babylonian Amoraim of the second generation. He was founder of the Pumbedita Yeshivah. According to tradition he was born on the day Rabbi Yehudah HaNasi died.

LANGUAGE (RASHI)

טנליי"ש* Apparently from the Old French *tenayles,* meaning "tongs."

RASHI

משנה משקעין אותו – שלא יתהפך אנה ואנה, ותפול הפתילה על בשרו מבחוץ. קשה לתוך הרכה – כורכין סודר קשה לתוך רכה, מפני שהרכה אינה חונקת לפתוח פיו, והקשה מחבל את גרונו ומנוולתו, לפיכך קשה מבפנים – לחנוק, ורכה מבחוץ – להגין. ומדליק את הפתילה – בגמרא מפרש פתילה של אבר. מדליק – מתיך. וחומרת את בני מעיו – לשון "חמרמרו מעי" (איכה ב) – כוולת. רבי יהודה אומר – אין חונקין אותו בסודרין, דאף הוא אם היה מת בידם על ידי חניקתם קודם זריקת הפתילה, לא היו מקיימין מצות שריפה, "אף הוא" – לישנא בעלמא הוא, כלומר: אם יחניקוהו אף הוא ימות בידם ואין זו שריפה. **בצבת** – *טנליי"ש בלעז.

NOTES

מְשַׁקְּעִין אוֹתוֹ בַּזֶּבֶל **They would sink him in manure.** *Rashi* explains that the condemned criminal would be sunk in a pile of mud that reached up to his knees, so that he would be unable to move about, for if he would be able to move about, the molten lead might fall on his flesh on the outside. *Ramah* points out the difficulties with this explanation: Why is the condemned party sunk in mud, and not in dirt, and why is the same procedure followed in the case of a criminal condemned to death by strangulation? Rather, argues *Ramah,* the condemned criminal would be sunk in a pile of mud that reached up to his knees, so that nobody would notice if he lost control of his bowels, and he would not suffer the additional disgrace of having soiled himself in public. This procedure is followed when the condemned party is executed by burning or by strangulation, for in those cases death does not come immediately, and there is concern that in the meantime the criminal will soil himself. But it is not necessary when the criminal is executed by decapitation, for in that case death is instantaneous.

סוּדָר קָשָׁה **A strong kerchief.** A soft kerchief by itself would not suffice, for it would tear when pulled in opposite directions by the two witnesses (*Ramah*).

פְּתִילָה **The wick.** The piece of lead which would be melted

HALAKHAH

מִצְוַת הַנִּשְׂרָפִין **The obligation regarding those who are liable to death by burning.** "Execution by burning was carried out as follows: The condemned party would be sunk into a pile of mud that reached up to his knees. A stiff

SAGES

רַבִּי אֶלְעָזָר בֶּן צָדוֹק Rabbi Elazar ben Tzadok. See *Sanhedrin*, Part I, pp. 98-9.

רַב מַתְנָה Rav Matenah. A Babylonian Amora of the second generation. Rav Matenah studied with the Amoraim of the first generation in Babylonia, and was a disciple of Shmuel. He also transmitted teachings in the name of Rav. According to a Geonic tradition, he was the son of the great Palestinian Amora, Rabbi Yoḥanan.

TRANSLATION AND COMMENTARY

the red-hot strip **would go down into his entrails, scald his bowels,** and cause death.

¹**Rabbi Elazar ben Tzadok said: It once happened** that **the daughter of a priest committed adultery,** and she was sentenced to death by burning. She was not put to death in the manner described above, but rather **bundles of branches were wrapped around her, and she was set on fire.** ²The Sages **said to him:** That incident proves nothing, **for the court which officiated at that time was not well-versed** in the law and acted improperly.

GEMARA מַאי פְּתִילָה ³**What** does the Mishnah mean when it speaks of a heated strip? ⁴**Rav Matenah said:** The Mishnah refers here to **a strip of lead.** Molten lead would be poured down the criminal's throat, and the burning metal would burn his insides and cause him to die.

מְנָא לָן ⁵**From where do we derive** that someone who is sentenced to burning is executed by that method? ⁶The Gemara answers: The meaning of the expression **"burning"** mentioned with respect to the daughter of a priest who committed adultery **is derived** by a *gezerah shavah* (or verbal analogy) **from** another mention of the expression **"burning"** used regarding **the company of Korah.** Here the verse states (Leviticus 21:9): "She shall be *burnt* with fire," and there the verse states (Numbers 17:4): "Wherewith they that were *burnt* had offered." ⁷**Just as** there regarding the company of Korah, only **their souls were burned, but their bodies remained intact,** ⁸**so too here** regarding the adulterous daughter of a priest, only **her soul is to be burned, but her body is to remain intact.** From here we learn that the condemned party must be burned without destroying his body, by having molten lead poured down his throat.

רַבִּי אֶלְעָזָר אָמַר ⁹**Rabbi Elazar said:** The meaning of the expression **"burning"** with respect to the daughter of a priest who committed adultery **is desired** by a *gezerah shavah* **from** another mention of the expression **"burning"** found in reference to **the sons of Aaron,** Nadab and Abihu. Here the verse states (Leviticus 21:9): "She shall be *burnt* with fire," and below the verse states (Leviticus 10:6): "But let your brethren, the whole

לְתוֹךְ פִּיו, וְיוֹרֶדֶת לְתוֹךְ מֵעָיו וְחוֹמֶרֶת אֶת בְּנֵי מֵעָיו. ¹אָמַר רַבִּי אֶלְעָזָר בֶּן צָדוֹק: מַעֲשֶׂה בְּבַת כֹּהֵן אַחַת שֶׁזִּינְּתָה, וְהִקִּיפוּהָ חֲבִילֵי זְמוֹרוֹת, וּשְׂרָפוּהָ. ²אָמְרוּ לוֹ: מִפְּנֵי שֶׁלֹּא הָיָה בֵּית דִּין שֶׁל אוֹתָהּ שָׁעָה בָּקִי.

גְּמָרָא ³מַאי פְּתִילָה? ⁴אָמַר רַב מַתְנָה: פְּתִילָה שֶׁל אָבָר. ⁵מְנָא לָן? ⁶אָתְיָא "שְׂרֵיפָה" "שְׂרֵיפָה" מֵעֲדַת קֹרַח. ⁷מַה לְּהַלָּן שְׂרֵיפַת נְשָׁמָה וְגוּף קַיָּים, ⁸אַף כָּאן שְׂרֵיפַת נְשָׁמָה וְגוּף קַיָּים.

⁹רַבִּי אֶלְעָזָר אָמַר: אָתְיָא שְׂרֵיפָה שְׂרֵיפָה מִבְּנֵי אַהֲרֹן.

LITERAL TRANSLATION

into his mouth, and it would go down to his entrails, and scald his bowels.

¹Rabbi Elazar ben Tzadok said: It once happened with the daughter of a priest who committed adultery that they wrapped her with bundles of branches, and burned her. ²They said to him: Because the court of that time was not well versed.

GEMARA ³What strip? ⁴Rav Matenah said: A strip of lead. ⁵From where do we derive [this]? ⁶"Burning" is learned (lit., "comes") from "burning" from the company of Korah. ⁷Just as there, by burning of the soul, and the body remaining intact, ⁸so too here, a burning of the soul, and the body remaining intact.

⁹Rabbi Elazar said: "Burning" is learned from "burning" from the sons of Aaron.

RASHI

לא היה בית דין של אותו שעה בקי — לדוקין היו, שאין להם גזירה שוה אלא קרא כמשמעו.

גמרא מנא לן — דכי האי גוונא שריפה היא דקאמר רחמנא? אתיא שריפה שריפה — כתיב הכא (ויקרא כא) "באש תשרף" וכתיב התם (במדבר יז) "אשר הקריבו השרופים" מה להלן גוף קיים, ולקמן פריך: מנא לן? מבני אהרן — דכתיב בהו (ויקרא י) "יבכו את השריפה".

NOTES

and cast into the criminal's mouth would be long and thin like a wick, so that it would melt quickly, and the condemned party would not have to suffer any delay in his execution (*Ramah*).

שֶׁל אָבָר **Of lead.** According to the Jerusalem Talmud, the Mishnah refers here to a string made of lead mixed with tin.

HALAKHAH

kerchief would be placed inside a soft one, and then wrapped around the criminal's neck. The two witnesses would then pull the two ends of the kerchiefs, each witness pulling in the opposite direction, until the condemned party's mouth was forced open. Molten lead was then cast into his mouth, and it would go down to his insides, and scald his bowels," following the Sages in the Mishnah. (*Rambam, Sefer Shofetim, Hilkhot Sanhedrin* 15:3.)

[1]מַה לְהַלָּן שְׂרֵיפַת נְשָׁמָה וְגוּף קַיָּים, [2]אַף כָּאן שְׂרֵיפַת נְשָׁמָה וְגוּף קַיָּים.
[3]מַאן דְּיָלֵיף מֵעֲדַת קֹרַח, מְנָא לֵיהּ? [4]דִּכְתִיב: "וְאֵת מַחְתּוֹת הַחַטָּאִים הָאֵלֶּה בְּנַפְשֹׁתָם" — שֶׁנִּשְׁמָתָן נִשְׂרֶפֶת וְגוּף קַיָּים.
[5]וְאִידָךְ: הַהִיא שְׂרֵיפָה מַמָּשׁ, הִיא. [6]וּמַאי "בְּנַפְשֹׁתָם"? [7]שֶׁנִּתְחַיְּיבוּ שְׂרֵיפָה עַל עִסְקֵי נַפְשׁוֹתָם, כִּדְרֵישׁ לָקִישׁ. [8]דַּאֲמַר רֵישׁ לָקִישׁ: מַאי דִּכְתִיב: "בְּחַנְפֵי לַעֲגֵי מָעוֹג חָרֹק עָלַי שִׁנֵּימוֹ"? [9]בִּשְׁבִיל חֲנוּפָּה שֶׁהֶחֱנִיפוּ לְקֹרַח עַל עִסְקֵי לְגִימָה, [10]חָרַק עֲלֵיהֶן שַׂר שֶׁל גֵּיהִנָּם שִׁנָּיו.
[11]וּמַאן דְּיָלֵיף מִבְּנֵי אַהֲרֹן, מְנָא לֵיהּ? [12]דִּכְתִיב: "וַיָּמֻתוּ לִפְנֵי ה'" — [13]כְּעֵין מִיתָה.
[14]וְאִידָךְ: הַהוּא שְׂרֵיפָה מַמָּשׁ הֲוַאי. [15]וּמַאי דִּכְתִיב: "וַיָּמֻתוּ"? [16]דְּאַתְחֵיל בְּהוּ מִגַּוַּאי, כְּעֵין

LITERAL TRANSLATION

[1]Just as there, by burning of the soul, and the body remaining intact, [2]so too here, by burning of the soul, and the body remaining intact.

[3]He who learned from the company of Korah, from where does he derive [this]? [4]For it is written: "As for the censers of these sinners against their own souls" — their souls were burnt, and their bodies remaining intact.

[5]And the other one: That was actual burning. [6]And what is "against their own souls"? [7]They became liable for burning because of the business of their souls, as Resh Lakish expounded. [8]For Resh Lakish said: What is [meant by] that which is written: "Because of flattery for the eating of food, they grind their teeth against me"? [9]Because of the flattery with which they flattered Korah for the sake of drinking, [10]the angel of Gehinom ground his teeth against them.

[11]And he who learned from the sons of Aaron, from where does he derive this]? [12]For it is written: "And they died before the Lord" — [13]like death.

[14]And the other one: That was actual burning. [15]And what is that which is written: "And they died"? [16]That it started in them from the inside,

TRANSLATION AND COMMENTARY

house of Israel bewail the burning which the Lord has kindled." [1]**Just as there** when Nadab and Abihu were consumed by a divine fire, only **their souls were burned, but their bodies remained intact,** [2]**so too here** regarding the daughter of a priest who committed adultery, only **her soul is to be burned, but her body is to remain intact.**

מַאן דְּיָלֵיף [3]As for the Amora **who derived** the meaning of "burning" **from the company of Korah, from where does he know** that they were burned without destroying their bodies? [4]The Gemara answers: **For the verse states** (Numbers 17:3): **"As for the censers of these sinners against their own souls,"** implying that only **their souls were burned, but their bodies remained intact.**

וְאִידָךְ [5]The Gemara explains: **The other** Amora — Rabbi Elazar — who did not derive the meaning of "burning" from the company of Korah understands that in **that case** the guilty parties were **literally burnt,** and their bodies were consumed by fire. [6]**What** then **is** the meaning of the words **"against their own souls"?** [7]The verse means that the company of Korah **became liable for** the penalty of **burning because of** the flattery which they heaped on Korah when he gave them food and drink for indulging **their souls, as Resh Lakish expounded.** [8]**For Resh Lakish said: What is** the meaning of **the verse which states** (Psalms 35:16): **"Because of flattery for the eating of food, they grind their teeth against me"?** [9]**Because** his company **flattered Korah for the sake of the food** and drink that he offered them, [10]**the angel of** *Gehinnom* **ground his teeth against them.**

וּמַאן דְּיָלֵיף [11]The Gemara asks: As for the Amora **who desired** the meaning of "burning" **from the sons of Aaron, from where does he know** that they were burned without destroying their bodies? [12]The Gemara answers: **For the verse states** (Leviticus 10:2): "And a fire went out from the Lord, and devoured them, **and they died before the Lord."** [13]The words, "And they died," teach that Aaron's sons died in a manner **similar to** ordinary **death,** in which body remains intact.

וְאִידָךְ [14]The Gemara explains: **The other** Amora who did not learn the meaning of "burning" from the sons of Aaron understands that in **that case** those executed suffered **actual burning,** and their bodies were consumed by fire. [15]**What then is** the meaning of **the verse that states: "And they died** before the Lord, which seems to indicate it was similar to an ordinary death"? [16]The Gemara answers: That verse means to teach **that** the fire

SAGES

רֵישׁ לָקִישׁ Resh Lakish. See *Sanhedrin,* Part I, pp. 56-7.

RASHI

מנא לן — דעדת קרח הכי הוו. **בנפשותם** — ולא בגופם. **שריפה ממש** — הלכך על כרחיך לא מצי למילף גוף קיים מהתם. ולקמן פריך: ותהוי שריפה ממש, ולילף שריפת בית דין מיניה ותהוי ממש. **על עסקי נפשותם** — על חנופת אכילה ושתיה הנכנסת בנפשותם. **בחנפי לעגי מעוג** — בשביל חנופת של לגימות מעוג שהאכילם והשקם קרח לעדתו, ונתחברו עמו "חרק עלי וגו'". **מעוג** — לשון דבר הנאכל כדכתיב (מלכים א יז) באלמנה הצרפית שאמרה לאליהו: "חי ה' אלהיך אם יש לי מעוג". **מנא לן** — דגוף קיים בבני אהרן. **שריפה ממש** — אף הגוף, אבל מבפנים התחילה שריפתן ושרפה והלכה עצמות ובשר.

מִיתָה. [1]דְּתַנְיָא: ״אַבָּא יוֹסֵי בֶּן דּוֹסְתַּאי אוֹמֵר: שְׁנֵי חוּטִין שֶׁל אֵשׁ יָצְאוּ מִבֵּית קוֹדֶשׁ הַקֳּדָשִׁים, וְנֶחְלְקוּ לְאַרְבַּע, [2]וְנִכְנְסוּ שְׁנַיִם בְּחוֹטְמוֹ שֶׁל זֶה וּשְׁנַיִם בְּחוֹטְמוֹ שֶׁל זֶה, וּשְׂרָפוּם״.
[3]וְהָכְתִיב: ״וְתֹאכַל אוֹתָם״!
[4]אוֹתָם וְלֹא בִּגְדֵיהֶם.
[5]וְנֵילַף מִפָּרִים הַנִּשְׂרָפִים.
[6]מַה לְהַלָּן שְׂרֵיפָה מַמָּשׁ אַף כָּאן שְׂרֵיפָה מַמָּשׁ!
[7]מִסְתַּבְּרָא, מֵאָדָם הֲוָה לֵיהּ לְמֵילַף, [8]שֶׁכֵּן: אָדָם, חוֹטֵא, נְשָׁמָה, פִּיגּוּל.
[9]אַדְּרַבָּה, מִפָּרִים הַנִּשְׂרָפִים הֲוָה לֵיהּ לְמֵילַף, [10]שֶׁכֵּן: מַכְשִׁיר

LITERAL TRANSLATION

like death. [1]As it was taught: "Abba Yose ben Dostai said: 'Two threads of fire went out from the Holy of Holies, and divided into four, [2]and two went into this one's nostrils and two [went] into that one's nostrils, and burned them.'"
[3]But surely it is written: "And it devoured them!"
[4]Them and not their clothing.
[5]But let us learn from the bulls that are burned. [6]Just as there, actual burning, so too here actual burning.
[7]It stands to reason that he should learn from man, [8]for indeed: Man, a sinner, soul, [and] an offering disqualified by improper intention.
[9]On the contrary, he should learn from the bulls that are burned, [10]for indeed: [An act that] makes fit,

TRANSLATION AND COMMENTARY

started to kill **them from the inside, as** in the case of an ordinary **death.** But then their flesh and bones were also consumed. [1]**As it was taught** in a Baraita: **Abba Yose ben Dostai said:** "**Two threads of fire went out from the Holy of Holies, and divided into four.** [2]Two of the fiery threads **went into** Nadab's **nostrils and two went into** Abihu's **nostrils, and burned them** completely."

וְהָכְתִיב [3]The Gemara raises an objection against the Amora who maintains that Nadab and Abihu suffered actual burning: **But surely the verse states** (Leviticus 10:2): "And a fire went out from the Lord, **and devoured them.**" The word "them [אוֹתָם]" is a restrictive term, implying that the fire devoured them, but not something else. Now if the bodies of Nadab and Abihu were entirely consumed by fire, what does the verse comes to exclude?

אוֹתָם [4]The Gemara answers: The fire burned **them, and not their clothing.**

וְנֵילַף [5]The Gemara asks: **But let us desire** the meaning of the expression "burning" mentioned with respect to a priest's daughter of a priest who committed adultery by a *gezerah shavah* **from** another use of the expression "burning" found regarding **the bulls that are burned,** a special class of sin offerings the meat of which is not eaten by the priests, but rather it is burned outside Jerusalem. Regarding the bulls that are burned the Torah states (Leviticus 4:12): "And he shall carry the whole bullock outside the camp to the a clean place, where the ashes are poured out, and *burn* it on the wood with fire,' and (Leviticus 4:21): "And he shall carry the bullock outside the camp, and *burn* it as he burned the first bullock." [6]**Just as there** the Torah refers to **actual burning, so too here** we should say that the priest's daughter should be put to death by way of **actual burning.**

מִסְתַּבְּרָא [7]The Gemara answers: **It stands to reason that we should derive** the nature of the punishment of burning **from** what the Torah says about burning in connection with **man.** [8]**For indeed,** the sinner who is liable to death by burning and the company of Korah or the sons of Aaron all involve **persons,** not bulls. They refer to **sinners,** not bulls, which did no wrong. They also involve the taking of **life,** which is not so regarding the bulls, which are slaughtered before burning. And regarding punishment by burning, there is no concept that it can, like **an offering, be disqualified by improper intention.** That is not the case regarding the bulls, for they can indeed become disqualified if the priest, while bringing the sacrifice, *expresses* the intention of sprinkling the blood of the sacrifice, or burning it on the altar, or eating if after the appropriate time.

אַדְּרַבָּה [9]**On the contrary,** argues the Gemara, **we could well derive** the nature of the penalty of execution by burning **from** what the Torah says about **the bulls that are to be burned,** [10]**for indeed** there are a number of features that are common to the two. In both cases, the burning **fulfills a religious obligation.** The burning fulfills a mitzvah — the mitzvah of executing a person liable to death by capital punishment, and the mitzvah of offering the bull that is to be burned. However, this w is not the case regarding the company of Korah or the sons of Aaron, for God is under no obligation to fulfill commandments. Moreover, regarding both execution and the bulls, the burning is a matter that applies **for all generations,** for it is a fixed law, which

RASHI

והא כתיב ותאכל אותם — דמשמע מיעוט אותם ולא דבר אחר, ואם הכל נשרף מאי קא ממעט? ומשני: אותם ולא בגדיהם. **שכן אדם חוטא נשמה פיגול** — אדם מאדם, חוטא מחוטא, נטילת נשמה מנטילת נשמה. אבל שריפת פרים אין בהם נטילת נשמה — שכבר הן נשחטין. פיגול — דבר שאין בו פיגול מדבר שאין בו פיגול. **מכשיר** — שריפת בית דין מכשיר הכשר מצות המקום, וכן פרים הנשרפים. אבל שריפה דהני לאו בידי אדם הוה שיקיימו בהם מצות המקום.

לְדוֹרוֹת.
[1]הָנָךְ נְפִישִׁין.
[2]מַאן דְּיָלֵיף מֵעֲדַת קֹרַח, [3]מַאי טַעְמָא לָא יָלֵיף מִבְּנֵי אַהֲרֹן?
[4]הַהוּא שְׂרֵיפָה מַמָּשׁ הֲוַאי.
[5]וְנֵילַף מִינָּהּ!
[6]אָמַר רַב נַחְמָן אָמַר רַבָּה בַּר אֲבוּהּ: אָמַר קְרָא: "וְאָהַבְתָּ לְרֵעֲךָ כָּמוֹךָ" — [7]בְּרוֹר לוֹ מִיתָה יָפָה.
[8]וְכִי מֵאַחַר דְּאִיכָּא דְּרַב נַחְמָן, [9]גְּזֵירָה שָׁוָה לָמָּה לִי?
[10]אִי לָאו גְּזֵירָה שָׁוָה, [11]הֲוָה אָמִינָא: שְׂרֵיפַת נְשָׁמָה וְגוּף קַיָּים לָאו שְׂרֵיפָה הִיא כְּלָל. [12]וְאִי מִשּׁוּם "וְאָהַבְתָּ לְרֵעֲךָ כָּמוֹךָ", [13]לַפֵּישׁ לֵיהּ חֲבִילֵי זְמוֹרוֹת כִּי הֵיכִי דְּלִישְׁרוֹף לַעֲגָל. [14]קָא מַשְׁמַע לָן.

LITERAL TRANSLATION

[and] for generations.
[1]These are many.
[2]He who learned from the company of Korah, [3]what is the reason that he did not learn from the sons of Aaron? [4]That was actual burning. [5]Then learn from it!
[6]Rav Naḥman said in the name of Rabbah bar Avuha. The verse states: "Love your neighbor as yourself" — [7]select for him a humane (lit., "beautiful") death.
[8]And since there is that of Rav Naḥman, [9]why do I need a *gezerah shavah*?
[10]If there were no *gezerah shavah*, [11]I might have said [that] burning the soul with the body remaining intact is not burning at all. [12]And if because of "Love your neighbor as yourself," [13]let him add bundles of branches so that he burns quickly. [14]Therefore, it teaches us.

TRANSLATION AND COMMENTARY

is not the case regarding the divine burning of the company of Korah or the sons of Aaron.

הָנָךְ נְפִישִׁין [1]The Gemara answers: The similarities between execution by burning and the burning of the company of Korah or the sons of Aaron **are** nevertheless **more numerous** than the similarities between execution by burning and the burning of the bullocks. Thus it is more reasonable to derive the nature of that mode of execution from what we find in the Torah regarding the burning of Korah's company or Aaron's sons.

מַאן דְּיָלֵיף [2]The Gemara asks: The Amora **who learned** the meaning of "burning" by way of a *gezerah shavah* **from the company of Korah,** [3]**what is the reason that he did not learn** the meaning of that term **from the sons of Aaron?** [4]As we explained above, that Amora maintains that the sons of Aaron suffered **actual burning,** and their bodies were consumed by fire. [5]We should then **derive from** them that the punishment of burning to be imposed in later generations is actual burning, and not pouring molten lead down the criminal's throat.

אָמַר רַב נַחְמָן [6]**Rav Naḥman said in the name of Rabbah bar Avuha: The verse** which **states** (Leviticus 19:18), **"Love your neighbor as yourself,"** [7]applies even to the condemned criminal, whom we must love by **selecting for him the** most **humane death** possible. And certainly the mode of execution described in our Mishnah is a more humane mode of execution — both less painful and quicker — than actually setting afire the criminal's body.

וְכִי מֵאַחַר [8]The Gemara asks: **Now that we know** the rule of **Rav Naḥman,** that the law of loving your neighbor applies even to a condemned criminal, [9]**why do we need the *gezerah shavah*** to teach us that a person who is liable for death by burning must be put to death so that his soul is burned, but his body remains intact? Even without the *gezerah shavah,* we would know that the criminal must be put to death by a more humane mode of execution!

אִי לָאו [10]The Gemara answers: **If there were no *gezerah shavah*,** [11]**we might have thought that burning the soul while leaving the body intact is not** considered **burning at all.** And surely if a certain crime is punishable by burning, the offender cannot be put to death in another way. [12]**And if** you say that we should execute the criminal by pouring molten lead down his throat **because of** the requirement of **"Love your neighbor as yourself,"** this is no argument, [13]we can fulfill that requirement by **adding** more **bundles of branches** around him **so that he should burn** and die more **quickly.** [14]**Therefore,** the Torah **teaches us** by way of a *gezerah shavah* that burning the soul while leaving the body intact is still regarded as burning. Since the obligation of loving your neighbor as yourself applies even to a condemned criminal, that is the proper mode of execution for someone liable to death by burning.

RASHI

ולדורות — דבר הנוהג לדורות מדבר הנוהג לדורות. ופרכינן: מאי דיליף מעדת קרח, מאי טעמא לא יליף מבני אהרן — משום דקסבר שריפה ממש הואי. ותהוי שריפה ממש ונילף שריפת בית דין מיניה לשריפה ממש, דהוה ליה אדם מאדם, וחוטא מחוטא, ונשמה, ופיגול. לאו שריפה היא — ובבית דין שריפה כתיב, ואי אתה רשאי לברור לו זו שאינה קרויה שריפה. ואי בעי לקיומי ואהבת לרעך כמוך — אפיש ליה חבילי זמורות. לעגל — מהר. קא משמע לן — גזירה שוה דמיקריא נמי שריפה, והשתא דאיהי מיקריא שריפה — ברור אותה לו מדרב נחמן.

[1]וּכְבָר הָיוּ מֹשֶׁה וְאַהֲרֹן מְהַלְּכִין בַּדֶּרֶךְ וְנָדָב וַאֲבִיהוּא מְהַלְּכִין אַחֲרֵיהֶן וְכָל יִשְׂרָאֵל אַחֲרֵיהֶן. [2]אָמַר לוֹ נָדָב לַאֲבִיהוּא: אֵימָתַי יָמוּתוּ שְׁנֵי זְקֵנִים הַלָּלוּ וַאֲנִי וְאַתָּה נַנְהִיג אֶת הַדּוֹר? [3]אָמַר לָהֶן הַקָּדוֹשׁ בָּרוּךְ הוּא: ״הַנִּרְאֶה מִי קוֹבֵר אֶת מִי״. [4]אָמַר רַב פַּפָּא: הַיְינוּ דְּאָמְרִי אֱינָשֵׁי: נְפִישִׁי גַּמְלֵי סָבֵי דִּטְעִינִי מַשְׁכֵי דְהוּגְנֵי. [5]אָמַר רַבִּי אֱלִיעֶזֶר: [52B] [6]לְמַה תַּלְמִיד חָכָם דּוֹמֶה לִפְנֵי עַם הָאָרֶץ? [7]בַּתְּחִלָּה דּוֹמֶה לְקִיתוֹן שֶׁל זָהָב. [8]סִיפֵּר הֵימֶנּוּ, דּוֹמֶה לְקִיתוֹן שֶׁל כֶּסֶף. [9]נֶהֱנָה מִמֶּנּוּ, דּוֹמֶה לְקִיתוֹן שֶׁל חֶרֶשׂ, כֵּיוָן שֶׁנִּשְׁבַּר, שׁוּב אֵין לוֹ תַּקָּנָה. [10]אִימְרָתָא בַּת טָלֵי בַּת כֹּהֵן

LITERAL TRANSLATION

[1]And Moses and Aaron were already walking on their way, and Nadab and Abihu were walking after them, and all of Israel were after them. [2]Nadab said to Abihu: "When will those two old men die, so that you and I will lead the generation?" [3]The Holy One, blessed is He, said to them: "We shall see who buries whom."

[4]Rav Pappa said: This is what people say: Many old camels are laden with the hides of the young ones.

[5]Rabbi Elazar said: [52B] [6]How does a Torah scholar appear to an ignorant man (lit., "people of the land")? [7]At first he appears like a golden flask. [8][If] he converses with him, he appears like a silver flask. [9][If] he benefits from him, he appears like a earthenware flask, which once broken, cannot be repaired.

[10]Imrata, the daughter of Talei, was a priest's daughter

TRANSLATION AND COMMENTARY

וּכְבָר הָיוּ [1]Having referred to the death of Aaron's sons, Nadab and Abihu, the Gemara now tells a story about them. **Moses and Aaron were already walking on their way to Mount Sinai, and Nadab and Abihu were walking after them, and all of Israel were** walking **after them.** [2]**Nadab said to Abihu: "When will those two old men,** Moses and Aaron, **die, so that you and I will lead the generation?"** [3]**The Holy One, blessed is He, said to them:** "**Let us see who buries whom.**" Shortly thereafter, Nadab and Abihu died, because of their desire to supplant their elders.

אָמַר רַב פַּפָּא [4]**Rav Pappa said: This is** the meaning of **the popular adage: Many old camels are laden with the hides of young** camels, that is to say, many old people survive the young.

אָמַר רַבִּי אֱלִיעֶזֶר [5]Resh Lakish above connected the downfall of Korah's company — who were all Torah scholars, as the verse states (Numbers 16: 2); "Princes of the assembly, regularly summoned to the congregation, men of renown" — to their having accepted Korah's entertainments. The Gemara now develops a similar idea, citing that which **Rabbi Elazar said:** [52B] [6]**How does a Torah scholar appear to an uneducated person?** [7]**At first,** when the Torah scholar keeps a dignified distance from the uneducated person, **he appears** to him **like a golden flask.** [8]**If** the Torah scholar **engages in** idle **conversation with** the uneducated person, **he** lowers himself and **appears** to him **like a silver flask.** [9]**If** the Torah scholar **benefits from** the uneducated person, and takes food and drink at his table, **he** lowers himself even further **and he appears** to him **like an earthenware flask, which once broken, cannot** ever **be repaired.** So too regarding Korah and his company.

אִימְרָתָא בַּת טָלֵי [10]It was related that **Imrata, the daughter of Talei, was a priest's daughter who**

LANGUAGE

הוּגְנֵי A Young camel. Similar to the Arabic, هجن, which also means "a young camel."

קִיתוֹן Flask.

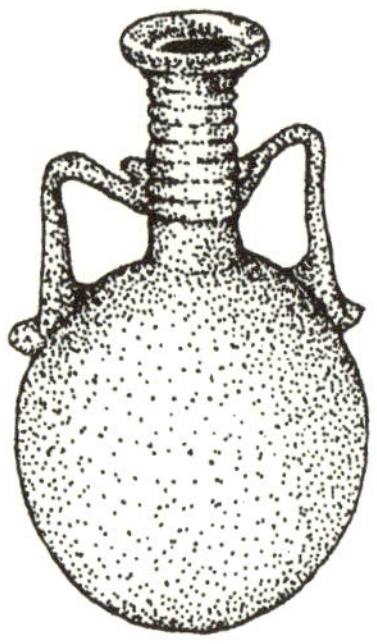

This word is derived from the Greek χωθων, *kiton*, meaning "a vessel for drinking."

RASHI

וכבר היו — אידי דאיירי בבני אהרן תני ליה הכא לאשמועינן, דבשביל שהיו מבקשים שררה ורבנות מתו. **נפישי גמלי סבי דטעיני משכי דהוגני** — הרבה גמלים זקנים שטעונים עורות גמלים יונקין שמתו, בכרי מדין ועיפה (ישעיה ס) ומתרגמינן הוגני, ״בכרה קלה״ (ירמיה ב) היינו גמלא נערה ויונקה, שהיא קלה, ועסקיה רעים מחמת שלא הורגלה לטעון משאוי. **האי את אביה** — מאי דריש ביה. **מאי זו** — אהיכא קאי. **למה תלמיד וכו׳** — משום דאיירי בעדת קרח נקט לה, שהיו תלמידי חכמים כדכתיב (במדבר טז) ״נשיאי עדה קריאי מועד אנשי שם״, ועל שם שפיתם אותו רשע כשנהנו ממומונו הקלו בעיניו להשיאם ולהחזיק ידו במחלוקת ולמרוד בהקדוש ברוך הוא. **בתחלה** — בעודו מתנהג בכבודו שאין צריך לו, הוא יקר בעיניו.

NOTES

וּכְבָר הָיוּ מֹשֶׁה וְאַהֲרֹן And Moses and Aaron were already. *Maharsha* understands that the Gemara cites this Midrash in order to explain the position, according to which the sons of Aaron suffered actual burning. Elsewhere, it is taught that the sons of Aaron were liable either for having served in the Tabernacle while under the influence of wine, or else for having issued a Halakhic ruling in the presence of their master. In either case, their bodies should not have been consumed by fire, for both of these offenses are punishable by death at the hand of God, i.e., death in a manner which leaves the body intact. Thus, the Gemara explains that the sons of Aaron were guilty of another offense, their envy of Moses and Aaron, whose deaths they were awaiting, so that they could assume the leadership of the people of Israel. It was because of this offense that their bodies were also consumed by the fire, as the verse states (Proverbs 14:30): "But envy is the rottenness of the bones."

TRANSLATION AND COMMENTARY

committed adultery. [1]**Rav Ḥama bar Toviyah** administered her death sentence by **wrapping her with bundles of twigs, and burning her,** rather than in the manner described in our Mishnah.

אָמַר רַב יוֹסֵף [2]**Rav Yosef said:** Rav Ḥama bar Toviyah **erred about two** points of law. [3]First, **he erred about** the law established by **Rav Matenah,** who ruled above that the punishment of burning is carried out by pouring molten lead down the criminal's throat. [4]**And** second, **he erred about what was taught** in the following Baraita: "The verse states (Deuteronomy 17:9): **"And you shall come to the priests the Levites, and the judge that shall be in those days."** [5]This verse teaches that **when there is a priest** serving in the Temple, **judgment is rendered** in capital cases; but **when the Temple has been destroyed, and there is no priest** serving there, **judgment is not rendered** in capital cases." Thus, the adulterous daughter of the priest should never have been tried and sentenced, and she certainly should not have been burned at the stake.

אָמַר [6]We have learned in the Mishnah: **"Rabbi Elazar ben Tzadok said: It once happened** that **the daughter of a priest committed adultery,** and she was sentenced to death by burning. Bundles of branches were wrapped around her, and she was set on fire. The Sages said to him: That incident proves nothing, for the court which officiated at that time was not well-versed in the law, and so it acted improperly." [7]**Rav Yosef said:** That ruling **was** issued by **a court** composed **of Sadducees,** a heterodox sect during the Second Temple period, that did not accept the Oral Law, and therefore interpreted the Written Torah in their own way.

שֶׁזִּינְּתָה הֲוַאי. [1]אַקְּפָהּ רַב חָמָא בַּר טוֹבִיָּה חֲבִילֵי זְמוֹרוֹת וּשְׂרָפָהּ.

[2]אָמַר רַב יוֹסֵף: טָעָה בִּתַרְתֵּי. [3]טָעָה בִּדְרַב מַתְנָה. [4]וְטָעָה בִּדְתַנְיָא: "וּבָאתָ אֶל הַכֹּהֲנִים הַלְוִיִּם וְאֶל הַשֹּׁפֵט אֲשֶׁר יִהְיֶה בַּיָּמִים הָהֵם". [5]בִּזְמָן שֶׁיֵּשׁ כֹּהֵן, יֵשׁ מִשְׁפָּט; בִּזְמַן שֶׁאֵין כֹּהֵן, אֵין מִשְׁפָּט.

[6]"אָמַר רַבִּי אֶלְעָזָר בְּרַבִּי צָדוֹק: מַעֲשֶׂה בְּבַת כֹּהֵן שֶׁזִּינְּתָה וכו׳". [7]אָמַר רַב יוֹסֵף: בֵּית דִּין שֶׁל צְדוֹקִים הֲוָה.

LITERAL TRANSLATION

who committed adultery. [1]Rav Ḥama bar Toviyah wrapped her with bundles of twigs and burned her. [2]Rav Yosef said: He erred about two [matters]. [3]He erred about Rav Matenah. [4]And he erred about what was taught: "And you shall come to the priests the Levites, and the judge who shall be in those days." [5]When there is a priest, there is judgment; when there is no priest, there is no judgment."

[6]"Rabbi Elazar ben Tzadok said: It once happened with a priest's daughter who committed adultery, etc." [7]Rav Yosef said: It was a court of Sadducees.

RASHI

רב חמא – בדורות האחרונים היה, כשאר האמוראים. טעה בדרב מתנה – דאמר לעיל: שריפת בית דין – פתילה של אבר היא. וטעה בדתניא – שאין בית דין ממיתין אלא בזמן לשכת הגזית, בעוד סנהדרין נוהגת בלשכת הגזית נוהגת אף בחוץ לארץ, כדאמרינן במסכת מכות (ז,א). של צדוקין – שדורשין מקרא ככתבו.

NOTES

אַקְּפָהּ חֲבִילֵי זְמוֹרוֹת וּשְׂרָפָהּ He wrapped her with bundles of vine-shoots and burned her. Even though the Gemara finds fault with Rav Ḥama bar Toviyah's sentencing of the priest's daughter to death by burning, *Maharshal* argues that his ruling may in fact be justified. Rav Ḥama bar Toviyah did not mean to suggest that he was acting in accordance with Torah law, but rather in accordance with the authority given to the court to inflict punishments — even corporal and capital punishments — that are not mandated by the Torah whenever it considers that the imposition of such punishments are necessary in order to uphold the authority and enforce the observance of the law. He had her wrapped in bundles of twigs and burned, rather than executed in the manner described in our Mishnah, in order to demonstrate that this was an extralegal punishment imposed because of the needs of the hour (see also *Ram Arak, Ra'ayah*). It has been argued that Rav Ḥama bar Toviyah was still in error, for the court is only authorized to impose such a punishment in order to erect a fence around the Torah regarding an issue that is subject to frequent violation. But the infrequent offense of adultery that was committed by the priest's daughter did not call for such a drastic measure (*Ri*).

טָעָה בִּדְרַב מַתְנָה He erred about Rav Matenah. The Rishonim ask: Why does the Gemara not say that Rav Ḥama bar Toviyah erred about the Mishnah, for the Mishnah itself states that a person who is sentenced to death by burning is put to death by having a strip of molten lead cast down his throat? *Ran* explains that the Mishnah by itself does not prove that Rav Ḥama bar Toviyah was in error, for he might have followed the position cited by Rabbi Elazar ben Tzadok. *Maharam* explains that when the Gemara states that Rav Ḥama bar Toviyah erred about Rav Matenah, it means that he did not know what kind of metal to heat up so that it could be cast down the criminal's throat and burn his insides, and because of his doubt, he wrapped the priest's daughter in bundles of twigs, and burned her.

HALAKHAH

בִּזְמָן שֶׁיֵּשׁ כֹּהֵן When there is a priest. "Capital cases are only adjudicated at a time when the Temple stands, and when the Great Sanhedrin convenes in its appointed place in one of the Temple's chambers," following the Baraita. (*Rambam, Sefer Shofetim, Hilkhot Sanhedrin* 14:11.)

TRANSLATION AND COMMENTARY

הָכִי אֲמַר [1]The Gemara asks: **Is this what** Rabbi Elazar ben Tzadok really **said to** the Sages, **and is this what** the Sages **answered him?** [2]**But surely it was taught** otherwise in the following Baraita: **"Rabbi Elazar the son of Rabbi Tzadok said:** [3]**I remember** that **when I was a child and rode on my father's shoulder, a priest's daughter who committed adultery was brought** for execution, **bundles of twigs were wrapped around her, and she was set on fire.** [4]After hearing this report, the Sages **said to him:** According to your account **you were a minor** at the time of the incident, [5]**and** there is a rule that **we do not bring proof from** that which was seen by **a minor,** despite his reporting about it as an adult." There seems to be a contradiction between what we learned in our Mishnah and what was taught in the Baraita both with respect to Rabbi Elazar ben Tzadok's reporting of the incident, and with respect to the Sages' response.

שְׁנֵי מַעֲשִׂים הֲווּ [6]The Gemara explains: **There were two** separate **incidents.** Rabbi Elazar ben Tzadok reported both of them to the Sages, and they responded differently in each case.

הֵי אֲמַר [7]The Gemara asks: **Which** incident **did** Rabbi Elazar ben Tzadok **report to** the Sages **first?** [8]**If you say** that **first he reported to them the** incident which is cited in our Mishnah, there is a difficulty, [9]for **if he** first **reported** to them **what happened when he was an adult, and they did not pay him** any **heed,** claiming that the court must not have been well-versed in the law — [10]**when he** later **reports** to them **what happened when he was** only **a minor, would they pay him** any **heed?** [11]**Rather,** Rabbi Elazar ben Tzadok must **first** have **reported to** the Sages **this** incident which is cited in the Baraita, **and they said to him:** We cannot accept your report, for at the time of the incident **you were** only **a minor.** [12]**And** later **he reported** to them **what happened when he was an adult, and they said to him:** [13]That incident proves nothing, **for the court** which officiated **at that time was not well-versed** in the law.

MISHNAH מִצְוַת הַנֶּהֱרָגִין [14]**The obligation regarding those who were liable to death by** the sword would be fulfilled as follows: The executioners **would shear off** the condemned criminal's **head with a sword, in the**

[1]הָכִי אֲמַר לְהוּ וְהָכִי אַהַדְרוּ לֵיהּ? [2]וְהָתַנְיָא: "אָמַר רַבִּי אֶלְעָזָר בְּרַבִּי צָדוֹק: [3]זְכוּרַנִי כְּשֶׁהָיִיתִי תִּינוֹק וּמוּרְכָּב עַל כְּתֵיפוֹ שֶׁל אַבָּא, וְהֵבִיאוּ בַּת כֹּהֵן שֶׁזִּינְּתָה, וְהִקִּיפוּהָ חֲבִילֵי זְמוֹרוֹת וּשְׂרָפוּהָ! [4]אָמְרוּ לוֹ: קָטָן הָיִיתָ, [5]וְאֵין מְבִיאִין רְאָיָה מִן הַקָּטָן".

[6]שְׁנֵי מַעֲשִׂים הֲווּ.

[7]הֵי אֲמַר לְהוּ בְּרֵישָׁא? [8]אִילֵימָא הָא קַמַּיְיתָא אֲמַר לְהוּ בְּרֵישָׁא, [9]אֲמַר לֵיהּ כְּשֶׁהוּא גָּדוֹל וְלָא אַשְׁגַּחוּ בֵּיהּ, [10]אֲמַר לְהוּ כְּשֶׁהוּא קָטָן וְאַשְׁגְּחוּ בֵּיהּ? [11]אֶלָּא, הָא אֲמַר לְהוּ בְּרֵישָׁא, וְאָמְרוּ לֵיהּ: קָטָן הָיִיתָ. [12]וַאֲמַרוּ לְהוּ כְּשֶׁהוּא גָּדוֹל. וַאֲמַרוּ לֵיהּ: [13]מִפְּנֵי שֶׁלֹּא הָיָה בֵּית דִּין שֶׁל אוֹתָהּ שָׁעָה בָּקִי.

משנה [14]מִצְוַת הַנֶּהֱרָגִין: הָיוּ מַתִּיזִין אֶת רֹאשׁוֹ בְּסַיִיף,

LITERAL TRANSLATION

[1]Is this what he said to them, and is this what they answered him? [2]But surely it was taught: "Rabbi Elazar the son of Rabbi Tzadok said: [3]I remember when I was a child and rode on my father's shoulder, and they brought a priest's daughter who committed adultery, and they wrapped her with bundles of twigs, and burned her. [4]They said to him: You were a minor, [5]and we do not bring proof from a minor."

[6]There were two incidents.

[7]Which one did the report to them first? [8]If you say the first one reported to them first — [9]if he told them [what happened] when he was an adult, and they did not pay him heed, [10]when he reports [what happened] when he was a minor, they should pay him heed? [11]Rather, this one reported to them first, and they said to him: You were a minor. [12]And he reported [what happened] when he was an adult, and they said to him: [13]Because the court at that time was not well-versed.

MISHNAH [14]The obligation regarding those who are liable [to death] by the sword (lit., "slaying"): They would shear off his head with a sword,

RASHI

הכי קאמר — רבי אלעזר לחכמים, בתמיה, כדאמרינן במתניתין דמשמע שראה מעשה זה משגדל. והכי אהדרו ליה: לא היה בית דין בקי. **והתניא** — דאין מביאין ראיה מן הקטן אהדרו ליה. **אמר להו כשהוא גדול** — מעשה שראה בגדלו ולא אשגחו ביה, דאמרו ליה: לא היה בית דין של אותה וכו׳, והדר אמרו להו, מעשה שראה בקטנו.

HALAKHAH

מִצְוַת הַנֶּהֱרָגִין **The obligation regarding those who are liable to death by the sword.** "Execution by slaying was carried out as follows: The head of the condemned party would be chopped off with a sword." (*Rambam, Sefer Shofetim, Hilkhot Sanhedrin* 15:4.)

TRANSLATION AND COMMENTARY

way practiced by the Roman **authorities.** [1]**Rabbi Yehudah** disagreed and **said: This** mode of execution **is a disgrace to** the criminal. [2]**Rather,** the executioners **would place** the criminal's **head on a** wooden chopping **block and cut it off with a hatchet** that butchers use to cut up a slaughtered animal. [3]The Sages **said to** Rabbi Yehudah: **There is no** mode of **execution more disgraceful than that,** for it treats the offender like an animal. Thus, it is preferable to perform executions by decapitation with a sword.

GEMARA תַּנְיָא [4]**It was taught** in a Baraita: **"Rabbi Yehudah said to the Sages:** [5]**I too know that** what I have proposed **is a mode of execution that disgraces** the criminal, **but what can I do?** [6]**The Torah states** (Leviticus 18:3): **'And you shall not walk in their statutes.'** Decapitating the criminal with a sword contravenes this injunction, for that is the way that the Roman government executes its criminals."

וְרַבָּנַן [7]The Gemara asks: **And** how do **the Sages** who disagree with Rabbi Yehudah counter this argument? [8]The Gemara explains: While it is true that the Roman government practices decapitation by the sword, **since the Torah** itself **mentions** decapitation by **the sword,** [9]**we are not deducing** the method of decapitation **from** the Romans, but rather from the Torah. Thus, there is no contravention of the injunction, "And you shall not walk in their statutes." [10]This argument must be valid, **for if you do not say this,** then how can we understand **that which was taught** in a Baraita: "Royal garments and utensils **may be burned** as a sign of mourning **for** the passing of a Jewish **king, and this is not** regarded as **an Amorite custom,** a superstitious rite practiced by non-Jews that may not be emulated." [11]**How are we permitted to burn** the king's garments and utensils? [12]That is a non-Jewish custom, and **surely the verse states: "And you shall not**

LITERAL TRANSLATION

the way the authorities do. [1]Rabbi Yehudah says: This is a disgrace for him. [2]Rather, they would place his head on a block and chop it off with a hatchet. [3]They said to him: There is no execution more disgraceful than that.

GEMARA [4]It was taught: "Rabbi Yehudah said to the Sages: [5]I too know that this is a disgraceful [mode of] execution, but what can I do, [6]for the Torah said: 'And you shall not walk in their statutes.'"

[7]And the Sages? [8]Since [execution by] the sword is written in the Torah, [9]we do not deduce [it] from them. [10]For if you do not say this, regarding that which was taught: "We burn for kings, and this is not an Amorite practice," [11]how may we burn? [12]Surely, it is written:

כְּדֶרֶךְ שֶׁהַמַּלְכוּת עוֹשָׂה. [1]רַבִּי יְהוּדָה אוֹמֵר: נִיווּל הוּא לוֹ. [2]אֶלָּא מַנִּיחִין אֶת רֹאשׁוֹ עַל הַסַּדָּן וְקוֹצֵץ בְּקוֹפִיץ. [3]אָמְרוּ לוֹ: אֵין מִיתָה מְנוּוֶּלֶת מִזּוֹ.

גמרא [4]תַּנְיָא: "אָמַר לָהֶן רַבִּי יְהוּדָה לַחֲכָמִים: [5]אַף אֲנִי יוֹדֵעַ שֶׁמִּיתָה מְנוּוֶּלֶת הִיא, אֲבָל מָה אֶעֱשֶׂה, [6]שֶׁהֲרֵי אָמְרָה תּוֹרָה: 'וּבְחֻקֹּתֵיהֶם לֹא תֵלֵכוּ'"!

[7]וְרַבָּנַן? [8]כֵּיוָן דִּכְתִיב סַיִיף בְּאוֹרַיְיתָא, [9]לָא מִינַּיְיהוּ קָא גָּמְרִינַן. [10]דְּאִי לָא תֵּימָא הָכִי, הָא דְּתַנְיָא: "שׂוֹרְפִין עַל הַמְּלָכִים וְלֹא מִדַּרְכֵי הָאֱמוֹרִי", [11]הֵיכִי שָׂרְפִינַן? [12]וְהָכְתִיב:

RASHI

משנה ניוול הוא זה — השתא משמע מפני שהרגו מעומד ונופל. על סדן — עץ עבה תקוע בארץ כמו של נפחים.

גמרא שורפין על המלכים — מטתו, מטתן וכלי תשמישן, ואין בהן משום דרכי האמורי.

LANGUAGE

קוֹפִיץ A hatchet. This is derived from the Greek κοπίς, *kopis*, meaning "a large knife used to chop or cut things."

BACKGROUND

קוֹפִיץ A hatchet.

A chopping knife being used to chop meat, from a Greek drawing.

This kind of chopping knife was usually large, with a slightly curved blade, used for cutting and chopping.

NOTES

אֵין מִיתָה מְנוּוֶּלֶת מִזּוֹ There is no execution more disgraceful than that. Some understand that there is no mode of execution more disgraceful than placing the criminal's head on a chopping block and cutting if off with a hatchet, because that is the way that an animal is slaughtered. Decapitation by the sword is less disgraceful, because only human beings are put to death in that manner. Others suggest that placing the head on a chopping block and cutting it off with a hatchet is most disgusting, because the hatchet mangles the surrounding flesh. Decapitation by the sword is less disgracing, because its sharp edge effects a clean cut (*Ramah*).

לָא מִינַּיְיהוּ קָא גָּמְרִינַן We do not learn it from them. *Meiri* explains that the prohibition against "walking in their statutes" only applies to practices that are somehow related to idol worship. But the Sages expanded the prohibition so that any non-Jewish custom which has no legitimate rationale is forbidden (for if the practice is adopted for some reasonable purpose, it is not regarded as an emulation of a non-Jewish rite). As for the Gemara's statement that death by the sword is mentioned in the Torah, some understand that this proves that the Jewish law precedes the non-Jewish custom. But the Gemara probably means to say that since the matter is found in the Torah, we are not concerned if the custom is also practiced by non-Jews.

HALAKHAH

שׂוֹרְפִין עַל הַמְּלָכִים We burn for kings. "If a Jewish king or Nasi died, his personal effects may be burned. This practice is not regarded as a violation of the prohibition against destroying things of value, nor that of adopting Amorite customs, for the practice is based on a Biblical source." (*Rambam, Sefer Shofetim, Hilkhot Evel* 14:26; *Shulḥan Arukh, Yoreh Deah* 348:1.)

TRANSLATION AND COMMENTARY

walk in their statutes." [1]**Rather,** it must be that **since the Scripture mentions burning** the king's garments and utensils — **for the verse states** (Jeremiah 34:5): "You shall die in peace, **and with the burnings of your fathers,** the former kings which were before you, so shall they make a burning for you,' — [2]**we are not deducing** this practice **from** the non-Jews, but rather from our own sources. [3]**Here too,** then, **since the Torah mentions** decapitation by **the sword, we are not deducing** that practice **from** the Romans, but rather from our own sources.

וְהָא דִּתְנַן [4]The Gemara continues: **And this is what we have learned in another chapter** in our tractate (*Sanhedrin* 76b): [5]**"These are** the offenders who are **liable to death by the sword: The murderer, and the inhabitants of a city led astray** to idol worship."

בִּשְׁלָמָא [6]The Gemara asks: **Granted** that the inhabitants of **a city led astray** to idol worship are liable to death by the sword, **for the verse states about them** (Deuteronomy 13:16): "You shall surely smite the inhabitants of that city **with the edge of the sword."** [7]**But from where do we know** that also **a murderer** is liable to death by the sword?

דְּתַנְיָא [8]The Gemara answers: **As it was taught** in a Baraita: "Regarding the murder of a non-Jewish slave by his master, the verse states (Exodus 21:20): 'And if a man smite his slave...**he shall surely be avenged.'** [9]Had I only had this verse, **I would not have known** the meaning **of** the term **'avenging.'** [10]But **since the verse states** elsewhere (Leviticus 26:25): **'And I will bring a sword upon you, that shall avenge my covenant,'** thus teaching that God avenges by the sword, [11]I therefore **say that the 'avenging'** mentioned with respect to the murder of a non-Jewish slave **is** likewise **by the sword."**

וְאֵימָא [12]The Gemara asks: Granted that the murderer and the inhabitants of a subverted city are put to death by the sword. How do we know that they are decapitated? **Say that** the executioners **stab them!**

לְפִי חָרֶב [13]The Gemara answers: **The verse states:** "You shall surely smite the inhabitants of that city **with the edge of the sword"** — with its edge, and not with its point.

"וּבְחֻקֹּתֵיהֶם לֹא תֵלֵכוּ"! [1]אֶלָּא, כֵּיוָן דִּכְתִיב שְׂרֵיפָה בְּאוֹרַיְיתָא, דִּכְתִיב: "וּבְמִשְׂרְפוֹת אֲבוֹתֶיךָ וגו'", [2]לָאו מִינַּיְיהוּ קָא גָּמְרִינַן. [3]וְהָכָא נַמִי, כֵּיוָן דִּכְתִיב סַיִיף בְּאוֹרַיְיתָא, לָאו מִינַּיְיהוּ קָא גָּמְרִינַן.

[4]וְהָא דִּתְנַן בְּאִידָךְ פִּירְקִין: [5]"אֵלּוּ הֵן הַנֶּהֱרָגִין: הָרוֹצֵחַ וְאַנְשֵׁי עִיר הַנִּדַּחַת".

[6]בִּשְׁלָמָא עִיר הַנִּדַּחַת, כְּתִיב בְּהוּ: "לְפִי חָרֶב". [7]אֶלָּא רוֹצֵחַ מְנָלַן?

[8]דְּתַנְיָא: "'נָקֹם יִנָּקֵם'. [9]'נְקִימָה' זוֹ אֵינִי יוֹדֵעַ מַה הוּא. [10]כְּשֶׁהוּא אוֹמֵר: 'וְהֵבֵאתִי עֲלֵיכֶם חֶרֶב נֹקֶמֶת נְקַם בְּרִית' [11]הֱוֵי אוֹמֵר נְקִימָה זוֹ סַיִיף.

[12]וְאֵימָא דְּבָרֵיז לֵיהּ מִיבְרַז! [13]"לְפִי חָרֶב" כְּתִיב.

LITERAL TRANSLATION

"And you shall not walk in their statutes." [1]Rather, since burning is written in the Torah, for it is written: "And with the burnings of your fathers," [2]we do not deduce [it] from them. [3]And here too, since [execution by] the sword is written in the Torah, we do not learn [it] from them.

[4]And this is what we have learned [later] in our other chapter: [5]"These are liable [to death] by the sword (lit., "slaying"): The murderer, and the people of a city led astray [to idol worship]."

[6]Granted the city led astray, it is written about them: "With the edge of the sword." [7]But from where do we [know about] a murderer?

[8]As it was taught: "'He shall surely be avenged.' [9]I do not know what this 'avenging' is. [10]When it says: 'And I will bring a sword upon you, that shall avenge my covenant,' [11]say that avenging is by the sword.

[12]Say that he stabs him!

[13]It is written: "With the edge of the sword."

RASHI

אלא משום דכתיב הך שריפה בדאורייתא — שנאמר בצדקיהו "בשלום תמות ובמשרפות אבותיך המלכים הראשונים כן ישרפו לך וגו'". נקם ינקם — במכה עבדו כנעני ומת תחת ידו, דהוי במיתת בית דין — משום דעבד שייך במצות שהאשה נוהגת בהן. דבריז ליה מיבריז — תוקעה בבטנו או בגרונו, כמו ברזא דחביתא. לפי חרב כתיב = פיפיות של חרב, שני צדדין מכאן ומכאן, דכתיב (תהלים קמט) "חרב פיפיות" אלמא תרי נינהו.

NOTES

לְפִי חָרֶב **With the edge of the sword.** *Ramah* explains that since the Torah speaks about smiting the inhabitants of the city with the *peh* of the sword [לְפִי חָרֶב], it must be referring to decapitation with the edge of the sword, and not piercing the body with the sword's point, for elsewhere the verse speaks about more than one *peh* to a sword, proving that the term must be referring to the sword's edge (for a sword has two edges), and not to its point. Alternatively, since the verse speaks about smiting with the *peh* (in the singular) of the sword, it must be referring to decapitation with one of the sword's edges, and not to piercing the body with the sword's point, in which the flesh is cut with the sword's two edges.

[1] וְאֵימָא דְּעָבֵיד לֵיהּ גִּיסְטְרָא! [2] אָמַר רַב נַחְמָן אָמַר רַבָּה בַּר אֲבוּהּ: אָמַר קְרָא: "וְאָהַבְתָּ לְרֵעֲךָ כָּמוֹךָ" — [3] בְּרוֹר לוֹ מִיתָה יָפָה.
[4] אַשְׁכְּחַן דְּקָטַל עַבְדָּא. [5] בַּר חוֹרִין מְנָא לַן?
[6] וְלָאו קַל וָחוֹמֶר הוּא? [7] קָטַל עַבְדָּא — בְּסַיִיף, בַּר חוֹרִין בְּחֶנֶק?
[8] הָנִיחָא לְמַאן דְּאָמַר חֶנֶק קַל. [9] אֶלָּא לְמַאן דְּאָמַר חֶנֶק חָמוּר, [10] מַאי אִיכָּא לְמֵימַר?
[11] נָפְקָא לֵיהּ מִדְּתַנְיָא: [12] "'וְאַתָּה תְּבַעֵר הַדָּם הַנָּקִי מִקִּרְבֶּךָ' — [13] הוּקְשׁוּ כָּל שׁוֹפְכֵי דָמִים לְעֶגְלָה עֲרוּפָה. [14] מָה לְהַלָּן בְּסַיִיף וּמִן הַצַּוָּאר, [15] אַף כָּאן בְּסַיִיף וּמִן הַצַּוָּאר".

LITERAL TRANSLATION

[1] Say that he cuts him in half!
[2] Rav Naḥman said in the name of Rabbah the son of Avuha: The verse states: "Love your neighbor as yourself" — [3] select for him a humane (lit., "beautiful") death.
[4] We have found regarding one who murdered a slave. [5] From where [do we know about one who murdered] a free man?
[6] Is it not a *kal vaḥomer*: [7] [If] he killed a slave, [execution is] by the sword, [could murdering] a free man be [punished] by strangulation?
[8] This is well according to the one who says strangulation is [more] lenient. [9] But according to the one who says strangulation is [more] severe, [10] what is there to say?
[11] He derives it from what was taught: [12] "'And you shall put away the [guilt of] innocent blood from among you' — [13] all those who shed blood are compared to a heifer whose neck is broken. [14] Just as below, by a sword and the neck, [15] so too here, by a sword and the neck."

TRANSLATION AND COMMENTARY

וְאֵימָא [1] The Gemara asks: The question still remains: How do we know that the condemned parties are decapitated? **Say that** the executioners **cut them in half** lengthwise!

אָמַר רַב נַחְמָן [2] **Rav Naḥman said in the name of Rabbah the son of Avuha: The verse** that **states** (Leviticus 19:18), **"Love your neighbor as yourself,"** applies even to a condemned criminal, [3] whom we must love by **selecting for him the** most **humane death** possible.

אַשְׁכְּחַן [4] The Gemara asks: **We have found** proof **that** a man **who murdered** his non-Jewish **slave** is liable to death by decapitation. [5] **But from where do we know that the murderer of a free man** is also liable to death by decapitation? Perhaps he is liable to death by strangulation, for regarding an ordinary murderer, the Torah does not use the term "avenging," but only states that "he shall surely die" (Exodus 21:12), and there is a general rule that wherever the Torah speaks of capital punishment without specifying the punishment, the offender is liable to death by strangulation.

וְלָאו [6] The Gemara answers: **Does it not** follow from **a *kal vaḥomer*** (*a fortiori*) argument: [7] **If** someone **killed** his **slave,** he is liable to death **by the sword,** is it possible that if he killed **a free man,** he should only be liable to death **by strangulation?**

הָנִיחָא [8] The Gemara asks: **This** argument is **acceptable according to** the anonymous Tanna of the Mishnah (49b) **who says** that **strangulation is a** more **lenient** method of execution than slaying by the sword. [9] **But according to** Rabbi Shimon **who says** that **strangulation is a** more **severe** method of execution than slaying by the sword, [10] **what is there to say?** If the murderer of a slave is liable for death by the sword, the murderer of a free man might indeed be liable for the more severe punishment of death by strangulation!

נָפְקָא לֵיהּ [11] The Gemara answers: **Rabbi Shimon derives** that the murderer of a free man is executed by the sword from the Baraita **that was taught** regarding the heifer whose neck is broken when a corpse is found outside a town and the murderer could not be found (see Deuteronomy 21:1-9): "The verse states (Deuteronomy 21:9): [12] **'And you shall put away the guilt of innocent blood from among you,'** [13] thereby **comparing all those who shed** innocent **blood to the heifer whose neck is broken.** [14] **Just as there,** regarding the heifer, they cut off its head **with a sword at the neck,** [15] **so too here,** regarding murderers, they are executed **with a sword at the neck."**

LANGUAGE

גִּיסְטְרָא **Cuts in half.** This appears to be derived from the Greek γαστρα, *gastra*, meaning the lower part, or belly, of a clay pot. This word is used by the Sages to refer to the fragile, lower part of a clay pot. That is apparently why it is used by extension to refer to cutting something in two parts, especially in the middle of the body.

RASHI

גיסטרא – חולקו לאורכו לשנים. **קטל בר חורין** – דלא כתיב ביה אלא מיתה סתם, וכל מיתה סתם חנק הוא. **מנלן** – בסייף. **מן הצואר** – גרון.

NOTES

"וְאָהַבְתָּ לְרֵעֲךָ כָּמוֹךָ" **"Love your neighbor as yourself."** The simple meaning of this Midrash is that the obligation to love your neighbor as yourself applies at all times and to all members of the people of Israel, even to a criminal who is condemned to death and whom we must love by selecting for him the most humane death possible. Some add that the obligation to love your neighbor as yourself cannot be fulfilled completely during the neighbor's lifetime, when the opposing principle of "your own life takes precedence" applies. The opportunity to fulfill the obligation in its fullest only presents itself when the neighbor is being put to death. *Ramah* suggests that according to this

TRANSLATION AND COMMENTARY

אִי מַה [1]The Gemara asks: **Or** perhaps we should say that **just as there,** regarding the heifer, they cut off its head **with a hatchet** which is used to butcher slaughtered animals **and at the continuation of the neck,** meaning at the back of the head, rather than on the back of the neck itself, [2]**so too here,** regarding murderers, they should be executed **with a hatchet and at the continuation of the neck?**

אָמַר רַב נַחְמָן [3]**Rav Naḥman said in the name of Rabbah bar Avuha: The verse** which **states: "Love your neighbor as yourself,"** [4]teaches that we must **select the** most **humane death** possible **for** the condemned criminal. Thus, while we learn from the heifer whose neck is broken that the murderer of a free man is executed by decapitation, the instrument by which his head is removed, and the point at which it is cut off are determined by the rule that the condemned criminal must be put to death in the most humane manner possible, meaning decapitation with a sword and at the neck.

MISHNAH מִצְוַת הַנֶּחֱנָקִין [5]**The obligation regarding those who are liable to death by strangulation** would be fulfilled as follows: [6]The condemned criminal **would** first **be sunk in** a pile of **manure** that reached **up to his knees.** [7]**A stiff kerchief would be placed inside a soft** kerchief, **and** the two kerchiefs **would be encircled around** the criminal's **neck.** The two witnesses on the basis of whose testimony the criminal was convicted would then pull on the two ends of the kerchiefs. [8]**One** witness **would pull** the kerchiefs **toward himself, and the other** witness **would pull** the kerchiefs **toward himself.** [9]They would continue to pull **until** the condemned party's **soul would depart.**

GEMARA תָּנוּ רַבָּנַן [10]**Our Rabbis taught** the following Baraita: "The verse states (Leviticus 20:10): 'And the man who commits adultery with another man's wife, who commits adultery with his neighbor's wife, the adulterer and the adulteress shall surely be put to death.' [11]The words, **'And the man,'** teach that only a grown man who committed adultery is put to death, **to the exclusion of a minor.** [12]The words, **'who commits**

[1]אִי מַה לְהַלָּן, בְּקוֹפִיץ וּמִמּוּל עוֹרֶף, [2]אַף כָּאן בְּקוֹפִיץ וּמִמּוּל עוֹרֶף?

[3]אָמַר רַב נַחְמָן אָמַר רַבָּה בַּר אֲבוּהּ: אָמַר קְרָא "וְאָהַבְתָּ לְרֵעֲךָ כָּמוֹךָ" — [4]בְּרוֹר לוֹ מִיתָה יָפָה.

משנה [5]מִצְוַת הַנֶּחֱנָקִין: [6]הָיוּ מְשַׁקְּעִין אוֹתוֹ בַּזֶּבֶל עַד אַרְכּוּבּוֹתָיו, [7]וְנוֹתֵן סוּדָר קָשָׁה לְתוֹךְ הָרַכָּה, וְכוֹרֵךְ עַל צַוָּארוֹ, זֶה מוֹשֵׁךְ אֶצְלוֹ [8]וְזֶה מוֹשֵׁךְ אֶצְלוֹ, [9]עַד שֶׁנַּפְשׁוֹ יוֹצֵאת.

גמרא [10]תָּנוּ רַבָּנַן: [11]"'אִישׁ' — פְּרָט לְקָטָן. [12]'אֲשֶׁר יִנְאַף אֶת

LITERAL TRANSLATION

[1]Or just as below, by a hatchet and at the continuation of the neck, [2]so too here by a hatchet and at the continuation of the neck?

[3]Rav Naḥman said in the name of Rabbah bar Avuha: The verse states: "Love your neighbor as yourself" — [4]select for him a humane death.

MISHNAH [5]The obligation regarding those who are liable [to death] by strangulation: [6]They would sink him in manure up to his knees, [7]and he places a stiff kerchief inside a soft one, and wraps [it] around his neck. [8]This one would pull toward himself, and that one would pull toward himself, [9]until his soul departs.

GEMARA [10]Our Rabbis taught: [11]"'And the man' — to exclude a minor. [12]'Who commits adultery with

RASHI

ממול עורף — מאחרי הפנים, דכתיב (דברים כא) "וערפו" לשון עורף מול הרואה את העורף, דהיינו אחורי צואר שרואין את העורף, ועורף הוא *קטרי"ל שכנגד הפנים דכתיב (ירמיה לב) "ויפנו אלי עורף ולא פנים" אלמא עורף להדי פנים.

NOTES

midrash, the word רֵעֲךָ, literally "your neighbor," is understood as "the wicked [הרעים] among you," and so the verse teaches that even the wicked who are condemned to death must be loved and pitied.

פְּרָט לְקָטָן — 'אִישׁ' **'Man' — to the exclusion of a minor.** The question has been raised: Why does a minor have to be excluded? A minor is always exempt from liability for a transgression! *Talmidei Rabbenu Peretz* suggest that since the verse regarding sexual sins says (Leviticus 18:29): "And the persons [הַנְּפָשׁוֹת] that commit them shall be cut off from among their people," we might have thought that even minors are included, for they too are included under the category of *nefashot,* "persons." Alternatively, we might have thought that a minor is put to death just like an animal with whom a person engaged in bestiality is put to death (*Hagahot Ri Berlin*). Or else, we might have thought that the minor is put to death after he reaches adulthood (*Tzafnat Pa'aneaḥ*).

HALAKHAH

מִצְוַת הַנֶּחֱנָקִין **The obligation regarding those who are liable to death by strangulation.** "Execution by strangulation was carried out as follows: The condemned party would be sunk into a pile of manure that reached up to his knees. A stiff kerchief would be placed inside a soft one, and then wrapped around the criminal's neck. The two witnesses would then pull on the two ends of the kerchiefs, each witness pulling in the opposite direction, until the condemned party died," following the Mishnah (*Rambam, Sefer Shofetim, Hilkhot Sanhedrin* 15:5.)

פְּרָט לְקָטָן **To the exclusion of a child.** "If an adult woman engaged in intercourse with a minor over nine years old,

אֵשֶׁת אִישׁ׳ — פְּרָט לְאֵשֶׁת קָטָן. [1]׳אֵשֶׁת רֵעֵהוּ׳ — פְּרָט לְאֵשֶׁת אֲחֵרִים. [2]׳מוֹת יוּמָת׳ — בְּחֶנֶק. [3]אַתָּה אוֹמֵר בְּחֶנֶק. [4]אוֹ אֵינוֹ אֶלָּא בְּאַחַת מִכָּל מִיתוֹת הָאֲמוּרוֹת בַּתּוֹרָה? [5]אָמַרְתָּ: כָּל מָקוֹם שֶׁנֶּאֱמַר מִיתָה בַּתּוֹרָה סְתָם, [6]אֵין אַתָּה רַשַּׁאי לְמוֹשְׁכָהּ לְהַחְמִיר עָלֶיהָ, [7]אֶלָּא לְהָקֵל עָלֶיהָ. [8]דִּבְרֵי רַבִּי יֹאשִׁיָּה. [9]רַבִּי יוֹנָתָן אוֹמֵר: לֹא מִפְּנֵי שֶׁהִיא קַלָּה, [10]אֶלָּא כָּל מִיתָה הָאֲמוּרָה בַּתּוֹרָה סְתָם אֵינָהּ אֶלָּא חֶנֶק. [11]רַבִּי אוֹמֵר: נֶאֱמַר מִיתָה בִּידֵי שָׁמַיִם, [12]וְנֶאֱמַר מִיתָה בִּידֵי אָדָם. [13]מַה מִּיתָה הָאֲמוּרָה בִּידֵי שָׁמַיִם, מִיתָה שֶׁאֵין בָּהּ רוֹשֶׁם, [14]אַף

LITERAL TRANSLATION

another man's wife' — to exclude the wife of a minor. [1]'His neighbor's wife' — to exclude the wife of a non-Jew (lit., 'others'). [2]'They shall surely be put to death' — by strangulation. [3]You say by strangulation. [4]But might it not be by anyone of the deaths mentioned in the Torah? [5]Say: Wherever the Torah speaks of execution without specifying, [6]you are not permitted to explain it (lit. "draw it towards") in a strict [manner], [7]but rather in a lenient [manner]. [8][These are] the words of Rabbi Yoshiyah. [9]Rabbi Yonatan says: [It is] Not because it is lenient, [10]but [because] any execution mentioned in the Torah without specification is strangulation. [11]Rabbi says: Execution at the hand of Heaven is mentioned, [12]and execution at the hand of man is mentioned. [13]Just as the execution at the hand of Heaven is an execution that leaves no mark, [14]so too

TRANSLATION AND COMMENTARY

adultery with another man's wife,' teach that a man is only liable for adultery if he had sexual intercourse with the wife of a grown man, **to the exclusion of the wife of a minor,** for the marriage of a minor has no validity in Torah law. [1]The words, **'his neighbor's wife,'** teach that a man is only liable for adultery if he had sexual intercourse with the wife of a fellow Jew, **to the exclusion of the wife of a non-Jew** who is not considered a 'neighbor,' for the marriage of a Jewess to a non-Jew has no Halachic validity. [2]The words, **'they shall surely be put to death,'** teach that the adulterer and the adulteress are put to death **by strangulation.** [3]**You say** that they are put to death **by strangulation.** [4]**But might it not be** that they are put to death **by one of the** other **modes of execution mentioned in the Torah?** [5]**Say that wherever the Torah speaks of execution without specifying** the mode of execution, [6]**you are not permitted to explain it in a strict manner,** and may not impose one of the more severe modes of execution, [7]**but rather** you must lean **towards leniency,** and impose the most lenient mode of execution. Since strangulation is the most lenient of the four modes of execution, wherever the Torah imposes capital punishment without specifying the manner of execution, the criminal is executed by strangulation. [8]**This is the position of Rabbi Yoshiyah.** [9]**Rabbi Yonatan says:** The adulterer and the adulteress are liable to death by strangulation, **not because** that mode of execution **is** the most **lenient** method, for strangulation is in fact more severe than slaying by the sword, [10]**but** rather **because whenever the Torah speaks of execution without specifying** the mode of execution, it **is** referring to **strangulation.** [11]**Rabbi** Yehudah HaNasi explains the viewpoint of Rabbi Yonatan and **says:** The Torah **speaks** in different places **of execution at the hands of Heaven** without specifying the mode of execution, such as Genesis 38:7: "And the Lord slew him," [12]**and** it also **speaks of execution at the hand of man** without specifying the mode of execution. [13]**Just as the execution at the hand of Heaven is an execution that leaves no** external **mark** on the body of the executed person, [14]**so too the execution at**

RASHI

פרט לאשת קטן — אשמועינן דקטן אין לו קדושין. **לאשת אחרים** — נכרים, אשמועינן שאין קידושין לנכרי. ומהכא תיפוק לן בכל דוכתא. **אלא להקל עליה** — ולקמן מפרש דארבע מיתות כסידרן גמרא גמיר להו רבי יאשיה מסיני, וכיון דחנק קלה מכולם על כרחיך נתנה לחייבי מיתות הסתומין, שהרי אין לך כח להחמיר עליהם, שמנין לך לדונם בחמורה שמא לא נתחייב בה. **לא מפני שהיא קלה** — דסבירא ליה כרבי שמעון דאמר (לעיל מט,ב) חנק והרג. **אינה אלא חנק** — ורבי מפרש לה לדרבי יונתן. **נאמר מיתה בידי שמים** — "וימת גם אותו" (בראשית לח) ונאמרה מיתה סתם בידי אדם. **אין בה רושם** — אין בה חבורה וסימן.

SAGES

רַבִּי Rabbi (Yehudah HaNasi). See *Sanhedrin,* Part I, pp. 27-8.

HALAKHAH

she is liable for the same punishment as if she had intercourse with an adult, but the child is exempt. If she engaged in intercourse with a child under the age of nine, both the woman and the child are exempt." (*Rambam, Sefer Kedushah, Hilkhot Issurei Bi'ah* 1:13.)

פְּרָט לְאֵשֶׁת קָטָן To the exclusion of the wife of a minor. "If a man had intercourse with the wife of a minor, he is not liable, for the marriage of a minor has no validity." (*Rambam, Sefer Kedushah, Hilkhot Issurei Bi'ah* 3:1.)

׳מוֹת יוּמָת׳ — בְּחֶנֶק They shall surely die — by strangulation. "If a married woman committed adultery, she and her lover are liable for death by strangulation," following the Baraita. (*Rambam, Sefer Kedushah, Hilkhot Issurei Bi'ah* 1:6; *Sefer Shofetim, Hilkhot Sanhedrin* 14:1.)

TRANSLATION AND COMMENTARY

the hand of man is an execution that leaves no external **mark** on the body of the executed person. Thus, it follows that wherever the Torah speaks of execution without specifying the method, it must be referring to strangulation which leaves no external mark on the body."

וְאֵימָא שְׂרֵיפָה [1]The Gemara raises an objection: **But say** that unspecified execution is **burning,** for burning also leaves no external mark on the body of the executed person!

מִדַּאֲמַר [2]The Gemara answers: **Since the Torah said that the daughter of a priest** who committed adultery **is** liable **for burning,** [3]**it follows that this one** — the daughter of an ordinary Israelite who committed adultery — **is not liable to death by burning.** If the daughter of an ordinary Israelite were also liable to death by burning, there would be no reason to single out the daughter of a priest. Thus, when the Torah states: "The adulterer and the adulteress shall surely be put to death," without specifying the mode of execution, it must be referring to strangulation, a mode of execution that also leaves no mark on the body.

[53A] בִּשְׁלָמָא [4]The Gemara asks: **Granted** that we understand the position of **Rabbi Yonatan, as Rabbi** Yehudah HaNasi **explains** the **reason** why whenever the Torah speaks of execution without specifying the mode of execution, it must be referring to strangulation. This is deduced a *gezerah shavah* that the Torah must be referring to a mode of execution which leaves no external mark, and as explained by the Gemara, cannot be burning. [5]**But according to Rabbi Yoshiyah,** there is a difficulty, for **how does he know that strangulation exists** as one of the modes of judicial execution? [6]Why not **say** that there are only three modes of capital punishment, and that wherever the Torah speaks of execution without specifying the mode, it is referring to the most lenient of the three, slaying **by the sword?**

אָמַר רָבָא [7]**Rava said: It was learned by tradition that there are four modes of execution** — stoning, burning, slaying by the sword, and strangulation. Since the Torah does not state explicitly that any particular transgression is punishable by strangulation, that must be the most lenient mode of execution, and therefore administered whenever the Torah speaks of capital punishment without specifying the mode of execution.

מַאי [8]The Gemara asks: **What** did Rabbi Yonatan mean when he said that the adulterer and the adulteress are liable to be executed by strangulation, but **not because** strangulation **is** the most **lenient** mode of execution? [9]The Gemara explains: This teaches us that Rabbi Yonatan and Rabbi Yoshiyah **disagree about the matter in dispute between Rabbi Shimon and the Sages,** the anonymous Tanna of the Mishnah (49b). Rabbi Yoshiyah agrees with the Sages that strangulation is the most lenient mode of execution, and Rabbi Yonatan agrees with Rabbi Shimon that the most lenient mode of execution is slaying by the sword.

אָמַר לֵיהּ רַבִּי זֵירָא [10]**Rabbi Zera said to Abaye:** The Torah states explicitly that certain offenders are liable to be executed by stoning: An idolater, someone who has sexual intercourse with the betrothed daughter (*na'arah*) of an ordinary Israelite, a Sabbath desecrater, a medium, a wizard, and a blasphemer.

מִיתָה הָאֲמוּרָה בִּידֵי אָדָם, מִיתָה שֶׁאֵין בָּהּ רוֹשֶׁם. [1]וְאֵימָא שְׂרֵיפָה! [2]מִדַּאֲמַר רַחֲמָנָא בַּת כֹּהֵן בִּשְׂרֵיפָה, [3]מִכְּלָל דְּהָא לָאו בַּת שְׂרֵיפָה הִיא. [53A] [4]בִּשְׁלָמָא לְרַבִּי יוֹנָתָן, כִּדְקָא מְפָרֵשׁ רַבִּי טַעְמָא. [5]אֶלָּא לְרַבִּי יֹאשִׁיָּה, מִמַּאי דְּאִיכָּא חֶנֶק בָּעוֹלָם? [6]אֵימָא סַיִיף! [7]אָמַר רָבָא: אַרְבַּע מִיתוֹת גְּמָרָא גְּמִירִי לְהוּ. [8]מַאי "לֹא מִפְּנֵי שֶׁהִיא קַלָּה"? [9]קָמִיפַּלְגִי בִּפְלוּגְתָּא דְּרַבִּי שִׁמְעוֹן וְרַבָּנַן. [10]אָמַר לֵיהּ רַבִּי זֵירָא לְאַבַּיֵי:

LITERAL TRANSLATION

the execution at the hand of man is an execution that leaves no mark."

[1]But say [it is by] burning!

[2]Since the Torah (lit., "the Merciful") said that the daughter of a priest is by burning, [3]this implies that this one is not liable [to death] by burning.

[53A] [4]Granted according to Rabbi Yonatan, as Rabbi explains the reason. [5]But according to Rabbi Yoshiyah, from where [does he know] that there is strangulation in the Torah (lit., "world")? [6]Say by the sword!

[7]Rava said: They learned by tradition that there are four [modes of] execution.

[8]What is [the meaning of] "not because it is lenient"? [9]They disagree about [the matter] in dispute between Rabbi Shimon and the Sages.

[10]Rabbi Zera said to Abaye:

RASHI

מדקאמר רחמנא בת כהן שזינתה בשריפה — מכלל דבת ישראל לאו בשריפה, הלכך "מות יומת הנואף" על כרחיך חנק הוא. הכי גרסינן — **בשלמא לרבי יונתן כדמפרש רבי טעמא.** **ממאי דאיכא חנק בעולם** — במיתת בית דין, דילמא אין מיתות בית דין אלא שלש! קלה שבהן סייף. **ארבע מיתות** — בשמן הנקוב להן, וכיון שלא פירש למי נתן חנק על כרחיך קלה היא מכולן, והניחה לסתומיה שאינו רשאי למשכה להחמיר עליה אלא להקל עליה, לפיכך לא הוצרך לפרש.

SAGES

רַבִּי יֹאשִׁיָּה Rabbi Yoshiyah. Also known as Rabbi Yoshiyah Rabbah (the Great), to distinguish him from the Amora of the same name. Rabbi Yoshiyah lived in the generation prior to the completion of the Mishnah. He came from the city of Hutzal in Babylonia and emigrated to Eretz Israel to study with Rabbi Yishmael. He and his colleague Rabbi Yonatan were Rabbi Yishmael's closest disciples. He generally appears in the Talmud in association with Rabbi Yonatan, with whom he disagrees about certain basic issues of Halakhic Midrash. He seems to have returned to Babylonia to study with Rabbi Yehudah ben Betera. Rabbi Aḥai, Rabbi Yoshiyah's son, was also an important Sage, and also lived in Hutzal.

רַבִּי יוֹנָתָן Rabbi Yonatan. A Tanna who lived in the generation prior to the completion of the Mishnah, Rabbi Yonatan was a disciple of Rabbi Yishmael and a colleague of Rabbi Yoshiyah, with whom he differed on many issues of Halakhic Midrash. It is likely that he emigrated from Eretz Israel to Babylonia, and this may be the reason why his name does not appear in the Mishnah.

[1] שְׁאָר הַנִּסְקָלִין דְּלָא כְּתִיב בְּהוּ סְקִילָה, [2] דְּגָמְרִי מֵאוֹב וְיִדְּעוֹנִי, [3] בְּמַאי גָּמְרִי? [4] בְּ"מוֹת יוּמְתוּ" גָּמְרִי, [5] אוֹ בִּ"דְמֵיהֶם בָּם" גָּמְרִי?

[6] אָמַר לֵיהּ: בִּ"דְמֵיהֶם" "דְּמֵיהֶם בָּם" גָּמְרִי. [7] דְּאִי בְּ"מוֹת יוּמְתוּ" גָּמְרִי, [8] "דְּמֵיהֶם" "דְּמֵיהֶם" לָמָּה לִי?

[9] אֶלָּא מַאי — בִּ"דְמֵיהֶם" "דְּמֵיהֶם" גָּמְרִי, [10] "מוֹת יוּמְתוּ" לָמָּה לִי?

[11] כִּדְתַנְיָא: "'מוֹת יוּמַת הַמַּכֶּה רֹצֵחַ הוּא', [12] אֵין לִי אֶלָּא בְּמִיתָה הַכְּתוּבָה בּוֹ, [13] מִנַּיִין שֶׁאִם אִי אַתָּה יָכוֹל לַהֲמִיתוֹ בְּמִיתָה הַכְּתוּבָה בּוֹ [14] שֶׁאַתָּה מְמִיתוֹ בְּכָל מִיתָה שֶׁאַתָּה יָכוֹל

LITERAL TRANSLATION

[1] The rest of those liable [to death] by stoning, regarding whom stoning is not written, [2] [and] who are learned from a medium and a wizard, [3] how are they learned? [4] Are they learned from "they shall surely be put to death," [5] or are they learned from "their blood shall be upon them"?

[6] He said to him: They are learned from "their blood [shall be upon them]," "their blood shall be upon them." [7] For if they are learned from "they shall surely die," [8] why do I need "their blood," "their blood"?

[9] Rather, what — they are learned from "their blood," "their blood." [10] Why do I need "they shall surely be put to death"?

[11] As it was taught: "'He that smote him shall surely be put to death.' [12] I have only the [mode of] execution that is written regarding him. [13] From where [do I know] that if you cannot put him to death with the [mode of] execution that is written regarding him, [14] you put him to death with any [mode of] execution with which you can put

RASHI

שאר הנסקלין – דלאו עבודה זרה, ונערה המאורסה, וחלול שבת, ואוב וידעוני, ומגדף, דהנך כתיבי בהו סקילה – וכולהו שאר הנסקלין לא כתיבא בהו סקילה בהדיא, וגמרינן להו לקמן בגזירה שוה דאוב וידעוני. במאי גמרי – איזו תיבה מופנית לגזירה שוה, "דמיהם בם" או "מות יומתו".

TRANSLATION AND COMMENTARY

[1] As for **the rest of those liable to die by stoning, about whom it is not written** explicitly in the Torah that they are put to death with **stoning,** [2] their liability to death by stoning **is derived** by a *gezerah shavah* **from a medium and a wizard,** about whom the verse states (Leviticus 20:27): "A man also or a woman that is a medium or a wizard, shall surely be put to death; they shall stone them with stones; their blood shall be upon them." [3] **How** precisely **is it learned** that the other offenders are also liable to be executed by stoning? [4] **Is it derived from "they shall surely be put to death,"** [5] **or is it derived from "their blood shall be upon them"?** In order to base a ruling on a *gezerah shavah,* an expression in the verse must be redundant. Which expression in the verse relating to a medium and wizard is unnecessary in its context, so that it can be used to apply the punishment to other capital offenders regarding whom the same expression is used?

אָמַר לֵיהּ [6] Abaye **said to** Rabbi Zera: **This is** deduced from the expressions **"their blood** shall be upon them" and **"their blood shall be upon them"** found in the two verses. [7] Know that this is true, **for if this is derived with** a *gezerah shavah* based on the expressions **"they shall surely be put to death,"** [8] **why do I need** the words **"their blood** shall be upon them" and **"their blood** shall be upon them"?

אֶלָּא מַאי [9] The Gemara asks: **Rather, what** are you claiming? That the ruling that the other offenders are also liable to be executed by stoning is **derived** with a *gezerah shavah* based on the words **"their blood** shall be upon them" and **"their blood** shall be upon them." But if this is true, a similar question may be raised: If the *gezerah shavah* is based on the words "their blood shall be upon them," [10] **why do I need "they shall surely be put to death"?**

כִּדְתַנְיָא [11] The Gemara answers: "They shall surely be put to death" is necessary **for that which was taught** in a Baraita: "The verse regarding a murderer states (Numbers 35:21): "'**He that smote him shall surely be put to death** [מוֹת יוּמַת].' Had the verse not used the double verb form and merely stated, 'He shall be put to death [יוּמַת],' [12] **I would only know** that the murderer may be put to death by decapitation, **the mode of execution that is** specifically **written regarding him.** [13] **From where do I know that if** for some reason, such as his escape, **he cannot be put to death by way of the mode of execution that is** prescribed **for him,** [14] **he may be put to death**

NOTES

מוֹת יוּמַת הַמַּכֶּה **He that smote him shall surely be put to death.** Regarding the law that if the condemned criminal cannot be put to death by the mode of execution specified in his regard, he may be put to death by any possible mode of execution, *Meiri* distinguishes between a murderer and other criminals who are liable to be executed. The murderer may be put to death by any possible mode of execution by any person, but the other criminals may only be put to death by those other means by the witnesses who testified against them.

SAGES

רַב אַחָא מִדִּפְתִּי Rav Aḥa of Difti. A Babylonian Amora of the sixth and seventh generation. Rav Aḥa of Difti was the outstanding pupil of Ravina, and frequently raises objections to Ravina's teachings. He is mentioned as a colleague of Mar bar Rav Ashi, and he was the preferred canidate to become the head of the great Yeshiva of Sura.

He is named after his place of birth, to distinguish him from many other Sages who were named Rav Aḥa. Difti was apparently a large city on the Euphrates in the district of Sura.

TRANSLATION AND COMMENTARY

by way of any possible method of execution? [1]That is derived from **the verse that states: 'He shall surely be put to death** [מוֹת יוּמַת].' The double-verb form teaches that, when necessary, **any method** of execution may be employed." Similarly, whenever the Torah uses the expression, "they [or he] shall surely be put to death," it means that, if necessary, the criminal may be put to death by any possible mode of execution.

אָמַר לֵיהּ [2]The later Amoraim discuss now the interchange that took place between Rabbi Zera and Abaye. **Rav Aḥa of Difti said to Ravina:** Why was Rabbi Zera interested in clarifying which expression found in the verse of the medium and the wizard is the basis of the *gezerah shavah*? What difference does it make which expression is used? [3]**If** in fact **the** punishment of stoning **would have been derived from** the words **"they shall surely be put to death," what** is Rabbi Zera's **difficulty?** [4]**You might say** that **he has difficulty with** the law applying to **a married woman** who committed adultery. If the *gezerah shavah* would be based on the words "they shall surely be put to death," [5]then why may we not **learn from a medium and a wizard** that a married woman who committed adultery is also liable to be executed by stoning? For regarding a married woman who committed adultery, the verse states (Leviticus 20:10): "And the man who commits adultery with another man's wife, who commits adultery with his neighbor's wife, the adulterer and the adulteress shall surely be put to death." [6]The *gezerah shavah* would then teach that **just as there,** the medium and the wizard are liable to be executed **by stoning,** [7]**so too here** the married woman who committed adultery should be liable to death **by stoning.** But since we know that a married woman who committed adultery is liable to death by strangulation, "they shall surely be put to death" cannot be the basis of the *gezerah shavah*. But this is really not an objection. [8]**Since the Torah said that a betrothed woman** who committed adultery **is** liable to death **by stoning,** [9]**it follows that a married woman** who committed adultery **is not liable** to death **by stoning,** but rather a less severe mode of execution. Thus a married woman is explicitly excluded from the teaching of the *gezerah shavah*, which still can be applied to other cases. What then was Rabbi Zera's difficulty with deriving stoning from the phrase, "they shall surely be put to death"?

וְאֶלָּא [10]**Rather,** continues Rav Aḥa of Difti, it must be that Rabbi Zera **would have difficulty with** the law applying to **someone who strikes his father or mother.** For if we learn that the other offenders are liable for stoning from a *gezerah shavah* based on the words "they shall surely be put to death," [11]then why not say that we should **learn from a medium and a wizard** that also someone who smote his father or mother is liable to death by stoning? For regarding such a person, the verse states (Exodus 21:16): "And he that strikes his father, or his mother, shall surely be put to death." We should have argued on the basis of the *gezerah shavah* that just as the medium and the wizard are liable to death by stoning, so too someone who strikes his father or mother should be liable to death by stoning. Why then does the Mishnah (*Sanhedrin* 84b) say that such a person is liable to be executed by strangulation? But this too is not difficult. [12]**Instead of deriving** the punishment to be imposed upon someone who strikes his father or mother **from a medium and a wizard,**

לַהֲמִיתוֹ? [1]תַּלְמוּד לוֹמַר: ׳מוֹת יוּמַת הַמַּכֶּה׳ — מִכָּל מָקוֹם״. [2]אָמַר לֵיהּ רַב אַחָא מִדִּפְתִּי לְרָבִינָא: [3]וְאִי בְּ״מוֹת יוּמְתוּ״ גָּמְרִי, מַאי קָא קַשְׁיָא לֵיהּ? [4]אִילֵימָא אֵשֶׁת אִישׁ קָא קַשְׁיָא לֵיהּ, [5]לְמֵיתֵי וּלְמִיגְמַר ״מוֹת יוּמַת״ מֵאוֹב וְיִדְּעוֹנִי: [6]מַה לְּהַלָּן בִּסְקִילָה, [7]אַף כָּאן בִּסְקִילָה! [8]מִדְּאָמַר רַחֲמָנָא אֲרוּסָה בִּסְקִילָה, [9]מִכְּלָל דִּנְשׂוּאָה לָאו בִּסְקִילָה. [10]וְאֶלָּא מַכֵּה אָבִיו וְאִמּוֹ קָא קַשְׁיָא לֵיהּ, [11]לְמֵיתֵי וּלְמִיגְמַר מֵאוֹב וְיִדְּעוֹנִי! [12]עַד דְּגָמְרִי

LITERAL TRANSLATION

him to death? [1]The verse states: 'He shall surely be put to death' — any [mode]."

[2]Rav Aḥa of Difti said to Ravina: [3]And if they are learned from "they shall surely be put to death," what is his difficulty? [4]If you say he has a difficulty with a married woman — [5]come and learn "he shall surely be put to death" from a medium and a wizard: [6]Just as below by stoning, [7]so too here by stoning! [8]Since the Torah (lit., "the Merciful") said that a betrothed woman is by stoning, [9]this implies that a married woman is not by stoning.

[10]Rather, he has a difficulty with one who strikes his father or mother — [11]come and learn from a medium and a wizard! [12]Instead of learning

RASHI

אמר ליה רב אחא מדפתי לרבינא – הא דאמר רבי זירא לאביי: במאי גמרי? מאי הוה קשיא ליה לרבי זירא, אי הוה גמרי ב״מות יומתו״. **אי נימא אשת איש קא קשיא ליה** – אמאי קרי ליה מיתה סתם ובחנק, תיגמר מינה גזירה שוה מאוב וידעוני כי היכי דגמרינן כל הנסקלין דלא כתיב בהו אלא ״מות יומתו״ סתמא, וגמרינן להו מהתם. **מכה אביו ואמו** – אמרינן לקמן דמיתתו בחנק ב״אלו הן הנחנקין״ (פד,ב), וקשיא ליה: לגמריה לסקילה מאוב וידעוני, ומאי קשיא ליה? אדגמר מאוב וידעוני לגמריה מאשת איש דהכי שפיר, דכיון דאיכא למיגמר קלה ואיכא למגמר חמורה, אי אתה רשאי למשכה להחמיר.

TRANSLATION AND COMMENTARY

[1]we should **learn** his punishment **from a married woman** who committed adultery. Just as a married woman who committed adultery is liable for strangulation, so too someone who smote his father or his mother should be liable to death by strangulation. It is preferable to make use of this *gezerah shavah,* [2]**for** whenever there is any doubt about which mode of execution to administer, **we are not permitted to lean toward severity,** [3]**but rather** we must lean **toward leniency,** and strangulation is a more lenient mode of execution than stoning. What then would be Rabbi Zera's difficulty if we deduced that the other offenders are liable to death by stoning from the words "they shall surely be put to death"?

אָמַר לֵיהּ [4]Ravina **said to** Rav Aḥa of Difti: In such a case, Rabbi Zera **would have difficulty with the rest of those liable** to death **by stoning.** [5]**If we** had **deduced** that the other offenders are liable to death by stoning with a *gezerah shavah* based on the words **"they shall surely be put to death,"** [6]**instead of deducing** the punishment imposed upon those other offenders by way of a *gezerah shavah* **from a medium and a wizard,** [7]we should have **deduced** their punishment by way of a *gezerah shavah* **from a married woman** who committed adultery. We would conclude that just as a married woman who committed adultery is liable to death by strangulation, so too those other offenders should be liable to death by strangulation. It would have been preferable to deduce this *gezerah shavah,* for whenever there is doubt about which mode of execution to administer, we are not permitted to lean toward severity, but rather we must lean towards leniency, and strangulation is a more lenient mode of execution than stoning. Therefore, Rabbi Zera wished to emphasize that we learn that the other offenders are liable to death by stoning using a *gezerah shavah* based on the words, "their blood shall be upon them," an expression that appears regarding a medium and a wizard, but not regarding a married woman who committed adultery (see Leviticus 20:10).

MISHNAH אֵלּוּ הֵן הַנִּסְקָלִין [8]From here until the end of the eighth chapter of the tractate, the Mishnah discusses the offenses which are punishable by stoning. The Mishnah first lists those offenses, and then discusses each in greater detail. Regarding some of the offenders who are liable to be executed by stoning, the Torah states explicitly that they are liable to death by that punishment. Regarding others, their liability to death by stoning is learned with a *gezerah shavah* from the words "their blood shall be upon them" found in reference to a medium and a wizard, as discussed above. **These are** the offenders who are **liable** to death **by stoning:** (1) **Someone who has** sexual **intercourse with his mother, or** (2) **with his father's wife,** even if she

מֵאוֹב וְיִדְּעוֹנִי [1]לִיגְמְרוּ מֵאֵשֶׁת אִישׁ, [2]דְּאִי אַתָּה רַשַּׁאי לְמוֹשְׁכָהּ לְהַחְמִיר עָלֶיהָ [3]אֶלָּא לְהָקֵל עָלֶיהָ!

[4]אָמַר לֵיהּ: שְׁאָר הַנִּסְקָלִין גּוּפַיְיהוּ קָא קַשְׁיָא לֵיהּ, [5]דְּאִי בְּ"מוֹת יוּמָת" גָּמְרִי, [6]עַד דְּגָמְרִי מֵאוֹב וְיִדְּעוֹנִי, [7]לִיגְמְרוּ מֵאֵשֶׁת אִישׁ.

מִשְׁנָה [8]אֵלּוּ הֵן הַנִּסְקָלִין: הַבָּא עַל הָאֵם, וְעַל אֵשֶׁת

LITERAL TRANSLATION

from a medium and a wizard, [1]learn from a married woman, [2]for you are not permitted to explain it (lit., "draw it towards") in a strict [manner], [3]but rather in a lenient [manner]!

[4]He said to him: He has a difficulty with the rest of those liable for stoning themselves, [5]for if they are learned from "they shall surely be put to death," [6]instead of learning from a medium and a wizard, [7]learn from a married woman.

MISHNAH [8]These are stoned: Someone who has intercourse with [his] mother, or with [his] father's wife,

RASHI

לגמרו מאשת איש – כדאמרינן דאינה רשאי למושכה להחמיר, הלכך בדמיהם בם גמרי.

משנה אלו הן הנסקלין – דכתיב בהו סקילה הא כתיב ביה, ולא כתיב ביה סקילה כתיב בהו "דמיהם בם" – וגמירי מאוב וידעוני.

NOTES

אֵלּוּ הֵן הַנִּסְקָלִין **These are stoned.** Various explanations have been offered regarding the order in which the criminals who are liable to death by stoning are listed. *Rabbi Yehonatan* says that the criminals are grouped in categories: The Mishnah opens with sexual sins, continues with sins involving heresy, and concludes with all the other offenses that are punishable by stoning. *Tosafot Yom Tov* demonstrates that the order in which the criminals are listed in the Mishnah is related to the order in which they are mentioned in the Torah, and accounts thereby for some of the apparent oddities in the Mishnah. For example, a man who had intercourse with a betrothed girl is found toward the end of the list apart from all the other sexual offenders, because all the other sexual offenses are listed together in the Book of Leviticus, whereas the prohibition against intercourse with a betrothed girl is recorded separately in the Book of Deuteronomy. *Kelei Ḥemdah* adds that beginning with the person who cursed his father or his

HALAKHAH

הַבָּא עַל הָאֵם וכו׳ **He who has intercourse with his mother, etc.** "A man who has intercourse with his mother or with another of his father's wives or with his son's wife or with another man, or if another man has intercourse with him,

TRANSLATION AND COMMENTARY

is not his mother, [1]**or** (3) **with his daughter-in-law, or** (4) **with a man, or** (5) **with an animal,** (6) [2]**a woman who has** sexual **intercourse with an animal,** (7) **someone who blasphemes** God, (8) **an idol worshipper,** (9) [3]**someone who offers his seed to Molech,** the fire-God of the Canaanites, (10) **a medium,** (11) **a wizard,** (12) **a Sabbath desecrater,** (13) [4]**someone who curses his father or his mother,** (14) **someone who has** sexual **intercourse with a betrothed *na'arah*,** (15) [5]**someone who incites an individual to worship idols,** (16) **someone who incites a community to worship idols,** (17) [6]**a warlock, and** (18) **a stubborn and rebellious son.**

הַבָּא עַל הָאֵם [7]**Someone who** unwittingly **engages in** sexual **intercourse with his mother** who was also his father's wife **is liable for** two sin-offerings — one

הָאָב, [1]וְעַל הַכַּלָּה, וְעַל הַזָּכוּר, וְעַל הַבְּהֵמָה, [2]וְהָאִשָּׁה הַמְּבִיאָה אֶת הַבְּהֵמָה, וְהַמְגַדֵּף, וְהָעוֹבֵד עֲבוֹדָה זָרָה, [3]וְהַנּוֹתֵן מִזַּרְעוֹ לַמּוֹלֶךְ, וּבַעַל אוֹב וְיִדְעוֹנִי, וְהַמְחַלֵּל אֶת הַשַּׁבָּת, [4]וְהַמְקַלֵּל אָבִיו וְאִמּוֹ, וְהַבָּא עַל נַעֲרָה הַמְאוֹרָסָה, [5]וְהַמֵּסִית, וְהַמַּדִּיחַ, [6]וְהַמְכַשֵּׁף, וּבֵן סוֹרֵר וּמוֹרֶה.

[7]הַבָּא עַל הָאֵם חַיָּיב עָלֶיהָ

LITERAL TRANSLATION

[1]or with [his] daughter-in-law, or with a man, or with an animal, [2]and a woman who has intercourse with an animal, and a blasphemer, an idol worshipper, [3]and someone who offers his seed to Molech, and a medium, and a wizard, and someone who desecrates the Sabbath, [4]and someone who curses his father or his mother, and someone who has intercourse with a betrothed *na'arah*, [5]and someone who incites [an individual to worship idols], and someone who incites [a community to worship idols], [6]and a warlock, and a stubborn and rebellious son.

[7]Someone who has intercourse with [his] mother is liable

RASHI

והאשה המביאה את הבהמה – עליה. **והנותן מזרעו למולך** – קסבר האי תנא מולך לאו עבודה זרה הוא, מדתנן עבודה זרה ותנא מולך, אלא חק העבודה זרה בעלמא הוא, ורחמנא חייב עליה סקילה והכי אמרינן בגמרא. **אוב וידעוני** – במתניתין לקמן (סה,א) מפרש להו. **והמקלל אביו ואמו** – החמיר מבמכה, משום דאיכא תרתי: קלון אביו ואמו, ומוציא שם שמים לבטלה. **והמסית** – את היחידים. **והמדיח** – עיר הנדחת, לקמן באלו הן הנחנקין (פט,ב) מפרש לה מנא לן דבסקילה. **מכשף** – בגמרא (סז,א) יליף לה מנא לן דבסקילה. **הבא על האם** – בשוגג חייב עליה שתי חטאות, דבכולהו עריות כתיב בהו כרת, וכתיב בהו חלוק חטאות ואפילו בגוף אחד, כדאמרינן בפרק בתרא דמסכת מכות (יד,א) לחייבו על אחותו שתים, שהיא אחותו מאביו ואחותו מאמו, והכא נמי כתיב בהו חלוק לרבנן, כדמפרש בגמרא.

NOTES

mother, the Mishnah lists offenders who are liable to death by stoning, but not excision. This explains why some of the offenders mentioned toward the end of the list are not mentioned earlier, as one might have expected in light of the nature of their offenses.

HALAKHAH

or if he has intercourse with an animal, or a woman with whom an animal has intercourse — all of these are executed by stoning." (*Rambam, Sefer Kedushah, Hilkhot Issurei Bi'ah* 1:4; Ibid., *Sefer Shofetim, Hilkhot Sanhedrin* 15:10.)

הַמְגַדֵּף **He who blasphemes God.** "Whoever blasphemes God and worships idols is to be executed by stoning." (*Rambam, Sefer Mada, Hilkhot Avodah Zarah* 2:6; Ibid., *Sefer Shofetim, Hilkhot Sanhedrin* 15:10.)

הַנּוֹתֵן מִזַּרְעוֹ לַמּוֹלֶךְ **He who offers of his seed to Molech.** "Whoever offers his semen to Molech is to be stoned." (*Rambam, Sefer Mada, Hilkhot Avodah Zarah* 6:3; Ibid., *Sefer Shofetim, Hilkhot Sanhedrin* 15:10.)

בַּעַל אוֹב וְיִדְעוֹנִי **A conjurer of spirits and a medium.** "A conjurer of spirits and a medium is executed by stoning." (*Rambam, Sefer Mada, Hilkhot Avodah Zarah* 6:1; Ibid., *Sefer Shofetim, Hilkhot Sanhedrin* 15:10.)

מְחַלֵּל אֶת הַשַּׁבָּת **A violator of the Sabbath.** "Whoever violates the Sabbath is executed by stoning." (*Rambam, Sefer HaZemanim, Hilkhot Shabbat* 1:1; Ibid., *Sefer Shofetim, Hilkhot Sanhedrin* 15:10.)

מְקַלֵּל אָבִיו וְאִמּוֹ **Who curses his father and mother.** "A person who curses his father and mother is executed by stoning." (*Rambam, Sefer Shofetim, Hilkhot Sanhedrin* 15:10; Ibid., *Sefer Shofetim, Hilkhot Memarim* 5:1.)

הַבָּא עַל נַעֲרָה הַמְאוֹרָסָה **He who has intercourse with a betrothed *na'arah*.** "A man who has intercourse with a betrothed *na'arah* is executed by stoning." (*Rambam, Sefer Shofetim, Hilkhot Sanhedrin* 15:10; Ibid., *Sefer Kedushah, Hilkhot Issurei Bi'ah* 1:6.)

הַמֵּסִית, וְהַמַּדִּיחַ **Whoever incites to apostasy.** "Whoever incites an individual to idol worship or whoever incites an entire city to idol worship is executed by stoning." (*Rambam, Sefer Shofetim, Hilkhot Sanhedrin* 15:10; Ibid., *Sefer Mada, Hilkhot Avodah Zarah* 5:2..)

הַמְכַשֵּׁף **The Sorcerer.** "A sorcerer is executed by stoning." (*Rambam, Sefer Shofetim, Hilkhot Sanhedrin* 15:10; Ibid., *Sefer Mada, Hilkhot Avodah Zarah* 11:15.)

בֵּן סוֹרֵר וּמוֹרֶה **A rebellious son.** "A rebellious son is executed by stoning." (*Rambam, Sefer Shofetim, Hilkhot Sanhedrin* 15:10; Ibid., *Sefer Shofetim, Hilkhot Memarim* 7:1.)

אִמּוֹ שֶׁהִיא אֵשֶׁת אָב **His mother who is his father's wife.** "A man who has intercourse with his mother while she is married to his father is liable both because she is his

מִשּׁוּם אֵם וּמִשּׁוּם אֵשֶׁת אָב. [1]רַבִּי יְהוּדָה אוֹמֵר: אֵינוֹ חַיָּיב אֶלָּא מִשּׁוּם הָאֵם בִּלְבַד. [2]הַבָּא עַל אֵשֶׁת אָב חַיָּיב מִשּׁוּם אֵשֶׁת אָב וּמִשּׁוּם אֵשֶׁת אִישׁ, [3]בֵּין בְּחַיֵּי אָבִיו בֵּין לְאַחַר מִיתַת אָבִיו, [4]בֵּין מִן הָאֵירוּסִין בֵּין מִן הַנִּישּׂוּאִין. [5]הַבָּא עַל כַּלָּתוֹ חַיָּיב עָלֶיהָ מִשּׁוּם כַּלָּתוֹ, וּמִשּׁוּם אֵשֶׁת אִישׁ, [6]בֵּין בְּחַיֵּי בְנוֹ בֵּין לְאַחַר מִיתַת בְּנוֹ, [7]בֵּין מִן הָאֵירוּסִין בֵּין מִן הַנִּישּׂוּאִין.

LITERAL TRANSLATION

for [his] mother and for [his] father's wife. [1]Rabbi Yehudah says: He is only liable for [his] mother. [2]Someone who has intercourse with [his] father's wife is liable for [his] father's wife and for a married woman, [3]both during his father's lifetime, and after his father's death, [4]whether from betrothal, or from marriage. [5]Someone who has intercourse with his daughter-in-law is liable for his daughter-in-law and for a married woman, [6]both during his son's lifetime, and after his son's death, [7]whether from betrothal, or from marriage.

TRANSLATION AND COMMENTARY

for the unwitting violation of the prohibition against intercourse with **his mother** (Leviticus 18:7: "The nakedness of your mother, you shall not uncover"), **and** one for the unwitting violation of the prohibition against intercourse with **his father's wife,** even if she were not his mother (Leviticus 18:8: "The nakedness of your father's wife you shall not uncover"). [1]**Rabbi Yehudah** disagrees and **says: He is only liable for** one sin-offering, for having unwittingly violated the prohibition against intercourse with **his mother.**

הַבָּא עַל אֵשֶׁת אָב [2]**Someone** who unwittingly **engages in** sexual **intercourse with his father's wife** who was not his mother **is liable for** two sin-offerings — one for the unwitting violation of the prohibition against intercourse with **his father's wife, and** one **for** the unwitting violation of the prohibition against intercourse with **a married woman.** A person is liable for the violation of the prohibition against intercourse with his father's wife, [3]**both during his father's lifetime, and** also **after his father's death,** but he is only liable for the violation of the prohibition against intercourse with a married woman while his father is alive and married to the woman. A person is liable for the violation of these prohibitions, [4]**whether** his father only **betrothed** the woman, **or** he **married her,** for the marital tie is created at the time of betrothal, and from that point on she is regarded as a married woman.

הַבָּא עַל כַּלָּתוֹ [5]**Someone who** unwittingly **engages in** sexual **intercourse with his daughter-in-law is liable for** two sin-offerings — one for the violation of the prohibition against intercourse with **his daughter-in-law** (Leviticus 18:15: "You shall not uncover the nakedness of your daughter-in-law"), **and** one **for** the violation of the prohibition against intercourse with **a married woman.** A man is liable for the violation of the prohibition against intercourse with his daughter-in-law, [6]**both during his son's lifetime, and** also **after his son's death.** A man is liable for the violation of these prohibitions, [7]**whether** his son only **betrothed** the woman, **or he married her.**

RASHI

משום אשת אב – אם נתקדשה לאביו – שלא ילדתו בזנות, או נתקדשה לו אחרי כן. **אלא משום אם** – וטעמא מפרש בגמרא. **בין לאחר מיתת אביו** – אחיוב דאשת אב קאי, דמרבה ליה קרא אף לאחר מיתה כדמפרש בגמרא, אבל משום אשת איש לאחר מיתה לא קאמרי. **בין מן האירוסין** – דכיון דקדשה אשתו היא, דכתיב (דברים כד) "כי יקח איש אשה" משעת לקיחה נקראת אשתו, והך קיחה קידושין היא, דגמרינן "קיחה" "קיחה" משדה עפרון.

NOTES

אֵינוֹ חַיָּיב אֶלָּא מִשּׁוּם הָאֵם **He is only liable for his mother.** It would appear that Rabbi Yehudah only disagrees with the Sages about a man who unwittingly had intercourse with his father's wife who was also his mother. But he agrees with them about a man who unwittingly had intercourse with his father's wife, who was also a married woman, that the offender is liable for two sin-offerings, because incest and adultery are two separate categories of offenses (*Talmidei Rabbenu Yonah*).

מִשּׁוּם אֵשֶׁת אִישׁ...בֵּין לְאַחַר מִיתַת בְּנוֹ **For a married woman...and after his son's death.** It is clear that if a man engaged in sexual intercourse with his daughter-in-law after his son's death, he is not liable for having had intercourse with a married woman, for she is no longer a married woman. Rather, the Mishnah teaches us that if the woman remarried, he is liable not only for having violated the prohibition against intercourse with a married woman, but also for having violated the prohibition against intercourse with his daughter-in-law. Even though she has remarried, she is still considered his daughter-in-law (*Ran*).

HALAKHAH

mother and also because she is his father's wife, both during his father's lifetime and also after his death," in accordance with the anonymous Mishnah. (*Rambam, Sefer Kedushah, Hilkhot Issurei Bi'ah* 2:2.)

אֵשֶׁת אָב **His father's wife.** "A man who has intercourse with his father's wife while she is married to him is liable both because she is his father's wife and also because she is a married woman. Even after his father's death, he is liable because she is his father's wife." (*Rambam, Sefer Kedushah, Hilkhot Issurei Bi'ah* 2:1.)

גמרא [1]תַּנְיָא: [2]"רַבִּי יְהוּדָה אוֹמֵר: אִם לֹא הָיְתָה אִמּוֹ רְאוּיָה לְאָבִיו, [3]אֵינוֹ חַיָּיב אֶלָּא מִשּׁוּם הָאֵם בִּלְבַד". [4]מַאי "אֵינָהּ רְאוּיָה לוֹ"? [5]אִילֵימָא חַיָּיבֵי כְרִיתוּת [6]וְחַיָּיבֵי מִיתוֹת בֵּית דִּין, [7]מִכְּלָל דְּרַבָּנַן סָבְרִי: אַף עַל גַּב דְּאֵינָהּ רְאוּיָה לוֹ? [8]הָא לֵית לֵיהּ קִידּוּשִׁין בְּגַוָּוהּ! [9]אֶלָּא: חַיָּיבֵי לָאוִין. [10]וְרַבִּי יְהוּדָה סָבַר לַהּ כְּרַבִּי עֲקִיבָא, [11]דְּאָמַר: אֵין קִידּוּשִׁין תּוֹפְסִין בְּחַיָּיבֵי לָאוִין.

LITERAL TRANSLATION

GEMARA [1]It was taught: [2]"Rabbi Yehudah says: If his mother was not fit for his father, [3]he is only liable for his mother."

[4]What is "not fit for his father"? [5]If you say those liable for excision [6]or those liable for execution by the court, [7]does this imply that the Sages maintain: Even if she was not fit for him? [8]Surely he does not have a betrothal with her!

[9]Rather, those who are forbidden to him by a negative precept. [10]And Rabbi Yehudah agrees with Rabbi Akiva, [11]who said: Betrothal takes no effect with those forbidden by a negative precept.

TRANSLATION AND COMMENTARY

GEMARA תַּנְיָא [1]A slightly different version of Rabbi Yehudah's position **was taught** in a Baraita: [2]**"Rabbi Yehudah says: If** someone unwittingly engaged in sexual intercourse with **his mother,** and she **was not fit for his father,** meaning that she was forbidden to him in marriage, [3]**he is only liable for** a single sin-offering for the violation of the prohibition against intercourse with **his mother,** and not a second sin-offering for the violation of the prohibition against intercourse with his father's wife."

מַאי [4]The Gemara wishes to clarify the meaning of this Baraita. **What** does the Baraita mean here when it states that his mother was **"not fit for his father"**? [5]**If you say** that we are dealing here with **a** severely prohibited forbidden **relationship that is punishable by excision,** [6]**or** with **an** even more severely prohibited forbidden **relationship that is** also **punishable by execution by the court,** there is a difficulty, [7]for **does this** not **imply that the Sages** who disagree with Rabbi Yehudah **maintain** that the son is liable for a second sin-offering violating the prohibition against intercourse with his father's wife, **even if** his mother **was not fit for** his father? [8]**Surely** everybody agrees that if a man betrothes a woman who is forbidden to him by such a prohibition, **the betrothal is not valid,** and so she can never be considered his legal wife!

אֶלָּא [9]**Rather,** the Baraita must be dealing with a woman who **is forbidden to** her husband **by a negative precept** that is not punishable by excision or judicial execution, but only by lashes. [10]**And Rabbi Yehudah agrees with Rabbi Akiva,** [11]**who said** that **betrothal does not take effect with** women **who are forbidden to** a man **by a negative precept.** Thus, he maintains that if someone unwittingly engaged in sexual intercourse with his mother, and she was forbidden to his father by a negative precept that is punishable by lashes, he is not liable for a sin-offering for the violation of the prohibition against intercourse with his father's wife, for his mother is not his father's legal wife. The Sages who disagree with Rabbi Yehudah maintain that the son is liable for a second sin-offering, for they argue with Rabbi Akiva and maintain that if a man betrothes a woman who is forbidden to him by a negative precept, the betrothal is in fact valid, and she is regarded as his legal wife.

RASHI

גמרא תניא רבי יהודה אומר וכו׳ – האי תנא פליג אתנא דידן דלא מפליג לדרבי יהודה בין ראויה לשאינה ראויה, והאי תנא אית ליה, דהיינו טעמא דרבי יהודה דלא היה לו לאביו אישות בה – הלכך לא קרינא ביה אשת אב. **חייבי כריתות** – שאסורין עליו באיסור כרת, דקיימא לן בקדושין בפרק שלישי (סז,א) דלא תפסי בהו קדושין. **מכלל דרבנן וכו׳** – בתמיה. **אלא בחייבי לאוין** – כגון ממזרת ונתינה, או אלמנה לכהן גדול, דקיימא לן (קידושין סח,א) דתפסי בהו קדושי מ"האשת אהובה" ו"האחת שנואה", וטעמא דרבי עקיבא התם מפרש מ"לא יקח איש את אשת אביו" וסבר דבאנוסת אביו הכתוב מדבר, דלאו ד"לא יגלה כנף אביו" – כנף שראה אביו הוא דאיכא, וקאמר רחמנא דלא יקח – אין לו לקוחין בה.

NOTES

אֵין קִידּוּשִׁין תּוֹפְסִין **Betrothal takes no effect.** Jewish law distinguishes between two types of forbidden marriages — marriages that are prohibited and void, and marriages that are prohibited but valid. When intercourse between the two parties is punishable by excision or capital punishment, marriage between the two parties is not only prohibited, but also void. Even if the parties conducted a wedding ceremony, the marriage has no legal validity. For example, if a man married his sister, he is not regarded as her husband, and she is not considered a married woman. When intercourse between the two parties is forbidden by a less stringent prohibition, marriage between the two parties is forbidden, but valid. Despite the prohibition, the marriage takes effect, and the woman is considered a married woman. Since the marriage remains prohibited, its dissolution by divorce can generally be compelled. Rabbi Akiva disagrees with the Sages and says that even if a woman is forbidden to her husband by an ordinary negative precept that is not punishable by excision or capital punishment, but only by lashes, the marriage is void.

[1] מְתִיב רַב אוֹשַׁעְיָא: [2] ״אִיסּוּר מִצְוָה וְאִיסּוּר קְדוּשָּׁה — [3] חוֹלְצוֹת וְלֹא מִתְיַיבְּמוֹת.

[53B] [4] ״׳אִיסּוּר מִצְוָה׳ — [5] שְׁנִיּוֹת מִדִּבְרֵי סוֹפְרִים״.

[6] וְאַמַּאי קָרוּ לְהוּ ״אִיסּוּר מִצְוָה״? [7] שֶׁמִּצְוָה לִשְׁמוֹעַ דִּבְרֵי חֲכָמִים.

[8] ״׳אִיסּוּר קְדוּשָּׁה׳ — [9] אַלְמָנָה לְכֹהֵן גָּדוֹל, גְּרוּשָׁה וַחֲלוּצָה לְכֹהֵן הֶדְיוֹט״.

LITERAL TRANSLATION

[1] Rav Osha'aya objected: [2] "[A woman who is forbidden because of] a prohibition stemming from a commandment and [a woman who is forbidden because of] a prohibition stemming from holiness — [3] perform *ḥalitzah*, and may not be taken in levirate marriage.

[53B] [4] "'A prohibition stemming from a commandment' — [5] secondary relationships by the words of the Sages."

[6] And why do they call them "a prohibition stemming from a commandment"? [7] Because there is a commandment to listen to the words of the Sages.

[8] "'A prohibition stemming from holiness' — a widow to a High Priest, [9] a divorcee or a *ḥalutzah* to an ordinary priest."

TRANSLATION AND COMMENTARY

מְתִיב רַב אוֹשַׁעְיָא [1] **Rav Oshaya raised an objection** to this explanation of the Baraita from a Mishnah (*Yevamot* 20a): "If a man died without children, his brother is obligated by Torah law to take his deceased brother's widow in levirate marriage or free the woman from the levirate tie by granting her *ḥalitzah*. If the widow was forbidden to her brother-in-law by a severe prohibition that is punishable by excision or judicial execution, she may not be taken in levirate marriage, and she is free to marry another man without having been granted *ḥalitzah*. [2] But if **the woman is forbidden** to her brother-in-law **because of a prohibition stemming from a commandment or because of a prohibition stemming from holiness** (these two categories of prohibitions will be explained immediately), [3] she **must perform *ḥalitzah*, but she may not be taken in levirate marriage.** She may not be taken in levirate marriage, because she is forbidden to her brother-in-law. But she cannot remarry without *ḥalitzah*, because she is bound to her brother-in-law by the levirate bond, from which she cannot be released without *ḥalitzah*.

[53B] ׳אִיסּוּר מִצְוָה׳ [4] And the Mishnah continues: "The expression, **'a prohibition stemming from a commandment,'** [5] refers to the **secondary relationships** that were forbidden as incestuous **by Rabbinic decree.** In addition to those sexual relationships that are specifically forbidden by the Torah (see Leviticus, chapters 18 and 20), there are additional relationships of a secondary degree that are forbidden by Rabbinic law, such as those between a man and his grandmother, and the wife of his grandfather. Should one's brother marry one of these women and die without children, the woman must be released from the levirate bond through the *ḥalitzah* ceremony."

וְאַמַּאי [6] The Gemara interrupts its presentation of the Mishnah, and asks: **And why are** these forbidden relationships **called "prohibitions stemming from a commandment"?** [7] The Gemara explains: **Because there is a** Torah **commandment to listen to the words of the Sages** (Deuteronomy 17:11): "You shall not deviate from the sentence which they shall tell you, to the right, or to the left."

אִיסּוּר קְדוּשָּׁה [8] The Mishnah continues: "The expression, **'a prohibition stemming from holiness,'** refers to relationships that are forbidden not because of the family relationsip between the parties, but because of the husband's sanctified status. [9] These include the marriage of **a widow to a High Priest,** or the marriage of **a divorcee or a *ḥalutzah*** (a woman who underwent the ceremony of *ḥalitzah*) **to an ordinary priest.** Should the husband of one of these women die without children, she must be released from the levirate bond through the *ḥalitzah* ceremony."

RASHI

איסור מצוה כו׳ — יבמה שנפלה לפני יבם והיא אסורה עליו משום מצוה או משום קדושה, — חולצת ואינה יוצאה בלא כלום, אף על גב דגבי חייבי כריתות קיימא לן בפרק קמא דיבמות (ג,ב) מגזרה שוה ד״עליה״ דיוצאה הימנו בלא כלום — בלא חליצה, התם הוא דאסורה ליה איסור חמור דלא תפסי ביה קדושי, אבל איסור מצוה או קדושה דבנות קדושין נינהו מרבינן התם (כ,א) מ״יבמתו״ ״יבמתו״ יש לך אחרת שעולה השערה לחלוץ ואינה עולה ליבום, ואיזו? — זו חייבי לאוין. **ולא מתייבמת** — דהא אסירא ליה, וכי תימא: תיתי עשה ותדחה לא תעשה גזירה ביאה ראשונה שמקיים בה ״יבמה יבא עליה״ (דברים כה) אטו ביאה שניה שאין בה מצות עשה. **איסור מצוה שניות מדברי סופרים** — תנא גופיה קתני לה במשנה הכי. **ואמאי קרי לה וכו׳** — פירוש אמוראים נינהו.

HALAKHAH

אִיסּוּר מִצְוָה וְאִיסּוּר קְדוּשָּׁה **A prohibition because of a positive commandment and a prohibition because of sancitity.** "Women who are prohibited to a man because of a prohibition because of a positive commandment (those who are of the second degree with respect to incest, such as his father's or mother's mother), and also those who are forbidden because of sanctity (such as a divorced woman and a priest), if one such woman had been the wife of his half-brother on his father's side, and if that half-brother died childless, she is not permitted to remarry unless she performs *ḥalitzah*. He is not allowed marry her through levirate marriage." (*Shulkhan Arukh, Even HaEzer* 174:4)

TERMINOLOGY

וְתַנְיָא עֲלָהּ And it was taught about it, meaning, the following Baraita was taught in reference to the Mishnah. This term is used to introduce a Baraita which explains the Mishnah under discussion and in effect forms an integral part of it.

TRANSLATION AND COMMENTARY

וְאַמַּאי [1]The Gemara asks: **And why are** these forbidden relationships **called "prohibitions stemming from holiness"?** [2]And the Gemara answers: **Because the verse** regarding the priests **states** (Leviticus 21:6): **"They shall be holy to their God."**

וְתַנְיָא עֲלָהּ [3]Rav Oshaya continues with his objection: **And** a Baraita **was taught with respect to** this Mishnah: **"Rabbi Yehudah reverses** the two categories." According to Rabbi Yehudah, the expression, "a prohibition stemming from a commandment," refers to the prohibition of a widow to a High Priest, or a divorcee or a *halutzah* to a common priest. They are called prohibitions stemming from a commandment, because the concluding verse of Leviticus which follows all of the special priestly laws reads (Leviticus 27:34): "These are the commandments which the Lord commanded Moses." And the expression, "a prohibition stemming from holiness," refers to the secondary relationships which were forbidden as incestuous by Rabbinic decree. They are called prohibitions stemming from holiness, because the Rabbis said that a person should make himself holy by abstaining from that which is permitted to him by Torah law, to avoid violating explicit prohibitions ordained by the Torah. [4]Now, Rabbi Yehudah **reverses** the two categories mentioned in the Mishnah, **but** he seems to agree with what was taught there that if a woman was forbidden to her brother-in-law, because, for example, she was a widow and her brother-in-law was the High Priest, she may not enter into levirate marriage with him, but ***halitzah* is** nevertheless **required.** [5]**"And if you think that Rabbi Yehudah agrees with Rabbi Akiva,** who said that betrothal does not take effect with women who are forbidden to a man by a negative precept, [6]**surely according to Rabbi Akiva, those** women **who are forbidden to a man by a negative precept**, such as a widow to a High Priest, **are** just **like those** women **with whom** sexual intercourse is **punishable by excision,** [7]**and those** women **with whom** sexual intercourse is **punishable by excision are not obligated in *halitzah* or levirate marriage,** as they were never married to the dead brother! If Rabbi Yehudah maintains that a widow requires *halitzah,* even if she is forbidden to her late husband's brother because of the negative precept prohibiting a widow to a High Priest, it must be that he maintains that if the High Priest betrothed the widow, the betrothal would take effect, against Rabbi Akiva!

לְדְבָרָיו [8]The Gemara responds: In fact, Rabbi Yehudah agrees with Rabbi Akiva that betrothal does not take effect with those women who are forbidden to a man by a negative precept. And when Rabbi Yehudah commented on the two categories mentioned in the Mishnah in *Yevamot*, "prohibitions stemming from a commandment," and "prohibition stemming from holiness," **he was talking according to the position of the** anonymous **first Tanna.** He argues that the anonymous first Tanna, who maintains that a widow requires *halitzah,* even if she was forbidden to her brother-in-law because he was the High Priest, should not include such a woman under the category of "prohibitions stemming from holiness," but rather under the category of "prohibitions stemming from a commandment." [9]**But** Rabbi Yehudah **does not agree with him,** for he maintains that a widow who is forbidden to her brother-in-law by a negative precept is free to remarry even without having been granted *halitzah.*

[1]וְאַמַּאי קָרוּ לְהוּ ״אִיסּוּר קְדוּשָּׁה״? [2]דִּכְתִיב: ״קְדֹשִׁים יִהְיוּ לֵאלֹהֵיהֶם״.
[3]וְתַנְיָא עֲלָהּ: ״רַבִּי יְהוּדָה מַחֲלִיף״. [4]חֲלוּפֵי הוּא דְּמַחֲלִיף — הָא חֲלִיצָה בָּעֲיָא. [5]וְאִי סָלְקָא דַּעְתָּךְ רַבִּי יְהוּדָה כְּרַבִּי עֲקִיבָא סְבִירָא לֵיהּ, [6]מִכְּדִי חַיָּיבֵי לָאוִין לְרַבִּי עֲקִיבָא כְּחַיָּיבֵי כְרִיתוֹת דָּמֵי, [7]וְחַיָּיבֵי כְרִיתוֹת לָאו בְּנֵי חֲלִיצָה וְיִבּוּם נִינְהוּ! [8]לִדְבָרָיו דְּתַנָּא קַמָּא קָאָמַר, [9]וְלֵיהּ לָא סְבִירָא לֵיהּ.

LITERAL TRANSLATION

[1]And why do they call them "a prohibition stemming from holiness"? [2]Because it is written: "They shall be holy to their God."
[3]And it was taught about it: "Rabbi Yehudah reverses [them]." [4]He reverses them — but *halitzah* is required. [5]But if it enters your mind that Rabbi Yehudah agrees with Rabbi Akiva, [6]surely according to Rabbi Akiva, those who are forbidden to him by a negative precept are like those for whom he is liable for excision, [7]and those for whom he is liable for excision are not obligated in *halitzah* or levirate marriage! [8]He said according to the words of the first Tanna, [9]but he does not agree with him.

RASHI

רבי יהודה מחליף — שהיה שונה ומפרש: איסור מצוה — אלמנה לכהן גדול, דכתיב (ויקרא כז) בסוף ספר ויקרא כשהשלים כל מצות כהונה אלה המצות. איסור קדושה — שניות מדברי סופרים, כגון אם אמו ואם אביו. ואמאי קרי ליה איסור קדושה — שאמרו לו חכמים: קדש עצמך במותר לך, להתרחק אף מזו המותר כדי שלא תכשל באיסורא, אבל חליצה בעיא. חייבי לאוין — דקתני אלמנה. כחייבי כריתות — משוי להו דלא תפסי בהו קדושי. וחייבי כריתות לאו בני חליצה ויבום נינהו — וכן חייבי לאוין לרבי עקיבא, מה חייבי כריתות אינן בתורת קדושין ואין בהן חליצה ויבום — אף אלו הואיל ואינן בתורת קדושין — אין בהן חליצה ויבום. לדבריו דתנא קמא — דמחייב אלמנה בחליצה

TRANSLATION AND COMMENTARY

כִּי אֲתָא [1]The Gemara continues: **When Rabbi Yitzḥak came, he taught** a Baraita that is similar in formulation to what **we have learned** in our Mishnah: [2]**"Rabbi Yehudah says:** If someone unwittingly engaged in sexual intercourse with his mother who was also his father's wife, he **is only liable for** one sin-offering, for violating the prohibition against intercourse with **his mother.** But he is not liable for a second sin-offering for violating the prohibition against intercourse with his father's wife, even if his mother was fit for his father."

וְטַעְמָא מַאי [3]The Gemara asks: **What is the reason** that the son is not liable for the second sin-offering? [4]**Abaye said: Because the verse states** (Leviticus 18:7): "The nakedness of your father, or the nakedness of your mother, shall you not uncover; **she is your mother,** you shall not uncover her nakedness." The extraneous words, "she is your mother," teach that if a person had sexual intercourse with a woman who is both his mother and also his father's wife, [5]**you may find him liable** for a sin-offering **on account of** his violation of the prohibition against intercourse with **his mother,** [6]**but you may not find him liable** for a second sin-offering **on account of** his violation of the prohibition against intercourse with **his father's wife.**

אֶלָּא מֵעַתָּה [7]The Gemara asks: **If** this is **so,** then the verse (Leviticus 18:8): **"The nakedness of your father's wife shall you not uncover; she is your father's nakedness,"** should also be interpreted in this fashion. That is to say that the extraneous words, "she is your father's nakedness," should be understood as teaching that if a man had sexual intercourse with a woman who is both his father's wife, and also his mother, [8]**you may find him liable** for a sin-offering **on account of** his violation of the prohibition against intercourse with **his father's wife,** [9]**but you may not find him liable for** a second sin-offering **on account of** his violation of the prohibition against intercourse with **his mother.** [10]But **if** this is **so,** then regarding a man's **mother who is** also **his father's wife** — [11]**if you stand there,**

[1]כִּי אֲתָא רַבִּי יִצְחָק תָּנֵי כִּדְתְנַן: [2]״רַבִּי יְהוּדָה אוֹמֵר: אֵינוֹ חַיָּיב אֶלָּא מִשּׁוּם הָאֵם בִּלְבַד״.

[3]וְטַעְמָא מַאי? [4]אָמַר אַבַּיֵי: דְּאָמַר קְרָא: ״אִמְּךָ הִיא״ — [5]מִשּׁוּם אִמּוֹ אַתָּה מְחַיְּיבוֹ, [6]וְאִי אַתָּה מְחַיְּיבוֹ מִשּׁוּם אֵשֶׁת אָב. [7]אֶלָּא מֵעַתָּה, ״עֶרְוַת אֵשֶׁת אָבִיךָ לֹא תְגַלֵּה עֶרְוַת אָבִיךָ הִיא״, [8]מִשּׁוּם אֵשֶׁת אָב אַתָּה מְחַיְּיבוֹ, [9]וְאִי אַתָּה מְחַיְּיבוֹ מִשּׁוּם אִמּוֹ? [10]אֶלָּא, אִמּוֹ שֶׁהִיא אֵשֶׁת אָבִיו, [11]קָאֵי הָכָא

LITERAL TRANSLATION

[1]When Rabbi Yitzhak came he taught as we have learned: [2]Rabbi Yehudah says: He is only liable for [his] mother."

[3]And what is the reason? [4]Abaye said: Because the verse states: "She is your mother" — [5]you find him liable because of his mother, [6]and you do not find him liable because of [his] father's wife.

[7]But now, "The nakedness of your father's wife shall you not uncover; she is your father's nakedness" — [8]you find him liable because of [his] father's wife, [9]and you do not find him liable because of his mother. [10]If so, his mother who is his father's wife — [11]if you stand

RASHI

קאמר רבי יהודה: לדבריך דמחייבת ליה בחלילה — אין לך לקרותה איסור קדושה, אלא איסור מלוה. תני כדתנן — אייתי מתניתא בידיה דתני בה דרבי יהודה אומר: אף בראויה לאביו קאמר דאינו חייב אלא משום אם בלבד, וכדתנן במתניתין. אמך היא — "ערות אביך וערות אמך לא תגלה אמך היא" למה לי "אמך היא"? אלא לומר לך שאם יש בה שני שמות: אם, ואשת אב, אינך חייב אלא משום אמו. אלא מעתה — דדרשת אמך היא למעוטי. ערות אביך היא — דכתיב גבי אשת אב, תדרשיה נמי למעוטי שֵם אֵם מינה, ונימא דהכי קאמר: הך ערות אשת אב דרישא דקרא, אם יש עוד עליה שם אחר, כגון: שהיא אמך, לא תתחייב אלא משום אשת אב. אלא אמו שהיא אשת אביו — בתמיה, כלומר: לדבריך קאי הכא ומעיט לה מאיסור אם, קאי הכא ומעיט לה מאיסור אשת אב, אם כן על כרחיך לגמרי מיעטה! דקראי אהדדי לא נימא דסתרי. ותמיהה לי אמאי לא אקשי ליה לרבי יהודה גופיה, דהא משום אֵם מודה ליה דחייב, ואי איכא למדרשיה להאי "היא" למיעוטא הכי דרשינן, ובכי האי גוונא מתרלי, דהכי קאמר: אם אמך לבד היא — לא תגלה ערותה, אבל אם יש שֵם אחר עליה — אינך מוזהר עליה. ו"היא" דערות אביך הכי נמי מדרים: ערות אשת אביך לא תגלה — אם ערות אביך לבד היא. אבל אם יש שם אחר עליה אינך מוזהר עליה. והשתא יש לומר: אמו שאינה אשת אביו ואשת אביו שאינה אמו — חייב, אשת אביו שהיא אמו לא ליחייב. ולי נראה דהשתא אמו שאינה אשת אביו וכו' לישנא יתירא הוא, והכי גרסינן: קאי הכא וממעט לה, קאי הכא וממעט לה, ותו לא מידי. והכי קא קשיא ליה: אם כן קשו קראי אהדדי, הא מיחייב ליה באמו וממעט ליה מאשת אב, והאי ממעט ליה מאמו, ומחייב באשת אב.

TERMINOLOGY

תָּנֵי כִּדְתְנַן **He taught as we have learned.** The readings of the Mishnah are generally regarded as authoritative, whereas the readings found in the various Baraitot are generally considered less reliable. But we do find that when a Mishnah is difficult to understand or when it gives rise to Halakhic problems, we rely on alternative readings found in the Baraitot to emend the Mishnah or to interpret the Mishnah in a manner different from the plain meaning of the text. In our case (and as we find elsewhere in the Talmud), an Amora cites a Baraita which supports the reading of our Mishnah, and thus compels the other Sages to interpret the Mishnah in accordance with its plain sense, and not in accordance with the Baraita that had been cited earlier in the discussion.

NOTES

אִמּוֹ שֶׁהִיא אֵשֶׁת אָבִיו **His mother who is his father's wife.** The Rishonim note that the Sages often make great efforts to prove matters that appear to be self-evident. For example, they try to prove that the prohibition against intercourse with one's sister applies not only in the case of a half-sister from his father's side, or in the case of a half-sister from his mother's side, but even in the case of a full sister from both parents' sides. Here, too, the Gemara

— וּמְמַעֵט לָהּ, [1]קָאֵי הָכָא — וּמְמַעֵט לָהּ. [2]הָשְׁתָּא אִמּוֹ שֶׁאֵינָהּ אֵשֶׁת אָבִיו — מִיחַיַּיב, [3]אֵשֶׁת אָבִיו שֶׁאֵינָהּ אִמּוֹ — מִיחַיַּיב, [4]אִמּוֹ שֶׁהִיא אֵשֶׁת אָבִיו, לֹא מִיחַיַּיב כְּלָל? [5]וְתוּ: לְרַבָּנַן נַמִי הָכְתִיב ״אִמְּךָ הִיא״! [6]אֶלָּא, הַהוּא מִיבָּעֵי לֵיהּ לְכִדְרַב שֵׁישָׁא בְּרֵיהּ דְּרַב אִידִי. [7]לְרַבִּי יְהוּדָה נַמִי, הַהוּא מִיבָּעֵי לֵיהּ לְכִדְרַב שֵׁישָׁא בְּרֵיהּ דְּרַב אִידִי!

[8]אֶלָּא אָמַר רַב אַחָא בְּרֵיהּ דְּרַב אִיקָא: אָמַר קְרָא: ״עֶרְוָתָהּ״. [9]מִשּׁוּם עֶרְוָה אַחַת אַתָּה מְחַיְּיבוֹ, וְאִי אַתָּה מְחַיְּיבוֹ

TRANSLATION AND COMMENTARY

in the verse relating to his mother, [1]**you exclude her** that he should not be liable on account of the prohibition against intercourse with his father's wife, [2]**and if you stand there,** in the verse relating to his father's wife, **you exclude her** that he should not be liable on account of the prohibition against intercourse with his mother. [3]**Now,** if the verses are not to contradict each other, we must say that the verse "she is your mother" teaches that if someone has sexual intercourse with **his mother who is not** also **his father's wife, he is liable** for a single sin-offering, but if she is also his father's wife, there is no liability. [4]And the verse "she is your father's nakedness" teaches that if he has sexual intercourse with **his father's wife who is not his mother, he is liable** for a single sin-offering, but if she is also his mother, there is no liability. [5]And thus it follows that if he had sexual intercourse with **his mother who is** also **his father's wife, he is not liable at all,** not for having violated the prohibition against intercourse with his mother, and not for having violated the prohibition againt intercourse with his father's wife. But how can it possibly be that he is liable for his mother who is not his father's wife, and for his father's wife who is not his mother, but he is not liable for his mother who is also his father's wife? [6]**And furthermore, according to the Sages** who disagree with Rabbi Yehudah and say that if a man has intercourse with a woman who is both his mother and his father's wife, he is liable for two sin-offerings. **Surely the verse states: "She is your mother"**! How do they interpert this verse? [7]**Rather,** we must say that according to the Sages, **that** verse **is needed for that** which was taught **by Rav Shesha the son of Rav Idi** (below, 54a). [8]Thus, we should say that **for Rabbi Yehudah as well, that** verse **is needed for that** which was taught **by Rav Shesha the son of Rav Idi.** And so the question remains: What is the Biblical source for Rabbi Yehudah's position that if a man has intercourse with a woman who is both his mother and his father's wife, he is only liable for one sin-offering, on account of having violated the prohibition against having sexual intercourse with his mother?

אֶלָּא [9]**Rather, Rav Aḥa the son of Rav Ika said:** This is derived from **the verse** that states (Leviticus 18:7: "The nakedness of your father, or the nakedness of your mother, shall you not uncover; she is your mother, you shall not uncover **her nakedness."** The singular form of the expression "her nakedness" teaches that if a man has intercourse with his mother, [10]**you may find him liable because of one forbidden sexual relationship,**

LITERAL TRANSLATION

here, [1]you exclude her, [2][and] if you stand there, you exclude her. [3]Now, [for] his mother who is not his father's wife, he is liable; [4][and for] his father's wife who is not his mother, he is liable; [5][and for] his mother who is his father's wife, he is not liable at all? [6]And furthermore, according to the Sages also, surely it is written, "She is your mother"! [7]Rather, that is needed for that of Rav Shesha the son of Rav Idi. [8]For Rabbi Yehudah too, that is needed for that of Rav Shesha the son of Rav Idi. [9]Rather, Rav Aḥa the son of Rav Ika said: The verse states: "Her nakedness." [10]You find him liable because of one nakedness, and you do not find him liable

RASHI

ותו — אי איכא למדרשיה להאי ״היא״ למיעוטא, כי האי גוונא רבנן מאי עבדי ליה?! אלא על כרחיך לא משמע מ״היא״ מיעוטא למימר דאיסור זה לבדו עליה ולא אחר, וכי משמע ״היא״ מיעוטא, הכי משמע: ״אמך היא״ — ואין אחרת אמך, והאי ״היא״ דלא מצית למדרשה הכי על כרחך לאו למיעוטא אתא אלא לדרשה אחרינא אתא, לכדרב שישא בריה דרב אידי בשלהי שמעתין, לעונש דאמו שאינה אשת אביו דלא כתיב בה ״דמיהם בם״, דבאשת אביו כתיב ״דמיהם בם״ ומשמע בין אשת אביו שאינה אמו, בין שהיא אמו. אבל אמו שאינה אשת אביו, אזהרה כתיב בה (ויקרא יח) ״ערות אמך לא תגלה״ ומשמע אף על פי שאינה אשת אביו, אבל עונש לא כתיב בה, ויליף לה מ״אמך היא״ — בהוייתה תהא, כל לדדיה שוין, דכי היכי דאמך שהיא אשת אביך ענש בה — כך אמך שאינה אשת אביך ענש בה, והכי נמי לרבי יהודה להכי מבעי ליה, וכן ״היא״ דערות אביך לדרשה אחרינא — לחייב עליה אפילו לאחר מיתת אביו, כלומר בהוייתה תהא לעולם, כדלקמן בשמעתין, ולאו למעוטי מאיסורא אתי, מן אלא מעתה עד לכדרב שישא בריה דרב אידי חדא אתקפתא היא. אמר קרא — ״ערות אמך היא לא תגלה ערותה״.

NOTES

considers the possibility that a man maybe liable for having sexual intercourse with his mother who is not his father's wife, and for his father's wife who is not his mother, but he is not liable for having intercourse with his mother who is also his father's wife (see *Rabbenu Yonah, Tosafot*).

SAGES

רַב שֵׁישָׁא בְּרֵיהּ דְּרַב אִידִי **Rav Shesha the son of Rav Idi.** A Babylonian Amora of the fourth and fifth generations. Rav Shesha (or, as he is sometimes called, Rav Sheshet) was the son of the Sage Rav Idi bar Avin, who belonged to the third generation of Babylonian Amoraim. Rav Shesha discusses Halakhic issues with Abaye and Rava and also with the greatest of their students.

רַב אַחָא בְּרֵיהּ דְּרַב אִיקָא **Rav Aḥa the son of Rav Ika.** A Babylonian Amora of the fifth generation. See *Sanhedrin,* Part I, p. 18

TRANSLATION AND COMMENTARY

but you may not find him liable because of two forbidden sexual relationships, even if his mother is also his father's wife.

אֶלָּא מֵעַתָּה [1]The Gemara asks: **If this is so,** then the verse (Leviticus 18:15): **"You shall not uncover the nakedness of your daughter-in-law: she is your son's wife; you shall not uncover her nakedness,"** should also be interpreted in this fashion. [2]**So too** we should say that the singular form of the expression, "her nakedness," teaches that if a man has intercourse with his daughter-in-law, **you may find him liable because of one forbidden sexual relationship,** sexual relations with one's daughter-in-law, [3]**but you may not find him liable because of a second forbidden sexual relationship,** sexual relations with a married woman. [4]**But surely we have learned** otherwise in our Mishnah, for our Mishnah teaches: **"Someone who** unwittingly **engaged in** sexual **intercourse with his daughter-in-law is liable for** two sin-offerings — one for intercourse with **his daughter-in-law, and** one **for** intercourse with **a married woman.** [5]A man is liable for the violation of the prohibition against intercourse with his daughter-in-law, **both during his son's lifetime, and** also **after his son's death."** [6]**And** regarding that ruling **Rabbi Yehudah does not disagree.** [7]**Rather,** you must understand the singular form of the expression "her nakedness" as follows: **Since** the transgressions are committed with **one body** — the woman who is both his daughter-in-law and also a married woman — **even though** the transgressions **are two** separate **prohibitions, the verse uses** the singular expression, **"her nakedness."** [8]**Here too,** then, regarding the intercouse with one's mother, you should understand the singular form of the expression "her nakedness" as follows: **Since** the transgressions are committed **with one body** — the woman who is both his mother and also his father's wife — **even though** the transgressions **are two** separate **prohibitions** — **the verse uses** the singular expression, **"her nakedness."** And so we come back to the question: What is the Biblical source for Rabbi Yehudah's position that a man who has intercourse with a woman who is both his mother and his father's wife is only liable for one sin-offering, for intercourse with his mother?

אֶלָּא [9]**Rather, Rava said: Rabbi Yehudah maintains** as follows: When the verse states (Leviticus 18:7): **"The**

מִשּׁוּם שְׁתֵּי עֲרָוֹת.

[1]אֶלָּא מֵעַתָּה, ״עֶרְוַת כַּלָּתְךָ לֹא תְגַלֵּה אֵשֶׁת בִּנְךָ הִיא לֹא תְגַלֵּה עֶרְוָתָהּ״, [2]הָכִי נַמִי, מִשּׁוּם עֶרְוָה אַחַת אַתָּה מְחַיְּיבוֹ, [3]וְאִי אַתָּה מְחַיְּיבוֹ מִשּׁוּם שְׁתֵּי עֲרָוֹת? [4]וְהָתְנַן: ״הַבָּא עַל כַּלָּתוֹ חַיָּיב עָלֶיהָ מִשּׁוּם כַּלָּתוֹ, וּמִשּׁוּם אֵשֶׁת אִישׁ, [5]בֵּין בְּחַיֵּי בְּנוֹ בֵּין לְאַחַר מִיתַת בְּנוֹ״, [6]וְלָא פָּלֵיג רַבִּי יְהוּדָה! [7]אֶלָּא, כֵּיוָן דְּחַד גּוּפָא הוּא, אַף עַל גַּב דִּתְרֵי אִיסּוּרֵי נִינְהוּ, כְּתִיב ״עֶרְוָתָהּ״. [8]הָכָא נַמִי, כֵּיוָן דְּחַד גּוּפָא הוּא, אַף עַל גַּב דִּתְרֵי אִיסּוּרֵי נִינְהוּ, כְּתִיב ״עֶרְוָתָהּ״.

[9]אֶלָּא אָמַר רָבָא: קָסָבַר רַבִּי

LITERAL TRANSLATION

because of two nakednesses.

[1]But now, "You shall not uncover the nakedness of your daughter-in-law: she is your son's wife; you shall not uncover her nakedness." [2]So too, you find him liable because of one nakedness, [3]and you do not find him liable because of two nakednesses? [4]But surely we have learned: "Someone who has intercourse with his daughter-in-law is liable for his daughter-in-law and for a married woman, [5]both during his son's lifetime, and after his son's death." [6]And Rabbi Yehudah does not disagree. [7]Rather, since it is one body, even though they are two prohibitions, it is written "her nakedness." [8]Here too, since it is one body, even though they are two prohibitions, it is written "her nakedness."

[9]Rather, Rava said: Rabbi

RASHI

אלא אמר רבא — לעולם מקרא קמא ד״היא״ בערות אמך מיעוטא משמע, כדהוה דרשינן מעיקרא, ומיהו ״היא״ דערות אביך דקשיא לך: דממעט ליה נמי מאיסור אם, לאו פירכא היא דהא רישא דקרא ד״ערות אביך״ שם אשת אב הוא דאדכר, ולא משום אסור אם, ומייתי לה בגזירה שוה כדלקמן: נאמר כאן ״ערות אביך לא תגלה״ ונאמר להלן ״ערות אביו גלה״ מה להלן באישות הכתוב מדבר, אף כאן באישות הכתוב מדבר. ומשמע לן איסורא בין אשת אביו שהיא אמו, ובין אשת אביו שאינה אמו, דחייב עליה משום איסור אשת אב. הלכך כי הדר כתיב בסיפא דאידך קרא ״ערות אביך היא״ — לאו למדרש מיניה משום אב ולא משום אם, דהא רישא דקרא ערות אביך נמי משום אשת אב הוא דחייביה, בין אינה אמו בין היא אמו, הלכך לרבי יהודה ״ערות אביך היא״ למעוטי משום אשת איש מוקים לה לקמן, דלא תימא שם אשת איש לא נפיק מכלל אשת אב דרישא דקרא דהא אביו נמי עמיתו הוא — וקרי נמי ביה ״ואל אשת עמיתך לא תתן שכבתך וגו׳״ (שם) ״וערות אשת אביך היא״ דרישא מוקי לאזהרת אשת אב לאחר מיתה, אבל ״היא״ דגבי אמך, לרבי יהודה למעוטי מאיסור אשת אב אתא, דהא נפקא ליה מרישא דקרא דלחייב עליה משום אשת אב כשהיא אמו, ואשת אביו דקסבר רבי יהודה ״ערות אביך״ דרישא דקרא זו אשת אביך, ולא אביך במשכב זכור ממש, דיליף לה בגזירה שוה כדלקמן, ומשמע אף כשהיא אמו חייב עליה באיסור אשת אב, ו״ערות אמך״ להביא אמו אנוסה, והדר כתיב ״אמך היא״ — לאפוקי ממשמעותיה דרישא, ולמימרא דמשום אמו אתה מחייבו וכו׳, ולדרב שישא בריה דרב אידי לא מיבעי

TRANSLATION AND COMMENTARY

nakedness of your father...shall you not uncover," it means that a man may not engage in intercourse with **his father's wife.** [1]This **he learns with a *gezerah shavah*:** Here the verse states: "The nakedness of your father shall you not uncover." And the verse below states (Leviticus 20:11): "And the man that lies with his father's wife has uncovered his father's nakedness." Just as there "his father's nakedness" refers to his father's wife, so too here "the nakedness of your father" refers to his father's wife. [2]**And** that verse **implies** that intercourse between a man and her father's wife is forbidden **whether his father's wife is his mother, or his father's wife is not his mother.** [3]**From where does he know** that a man is also forbidden to have intercourse with **his mother who is not** also **his father's wife?** [4]This is derived from **the verse** which **states** (Leviticus 18:7): **"The nakedness of your mother shall you not uncover."** [5]The verse continues: **"She is your mother."** These extraneous words negate the implication of the beginning of the verse, that a man is also liable for having violated the prohibition against intercourse with one's father's wife, even if she is his mother. The words, "she is your mother," teach that if someone has intercourse with his father's wife who is also his mother, **he is only liable** for a sin-offering **on account of** his violation of the prohibition against intercourse with **his mother,** [6]**but he is not liable** for a second sin-offering **on account of** his violation of the prohibition against having intercourse with **his father's wife.**

[54A] תַּנְיָא כְּוָותֵיהּ [7]A Baraita **was taught in accordance with Rava:** "The verse states (Leviticus 20:11): 'And the man that lies with his father's wife has uncovered his father's nakedness: both of them shall surely be put to death; their blood is upon them.' The words, **'And the man,'** teach that only a grown man who has intercourse with his father's wife is put to death, [8]**to the exclusion of a minor.** [9]The words, **'that lies with his father's wife,'** [10]**imply that** a man who has intercourse with his father's wife is put to death, **whether his father's wife was** also **his mother,** [11]**or his father's wife was not** also **his mother.** [12]**From where do we know** that a man is put to death for having intercourse with **his mother who was not** also **his father's wife?** [13]This is derived from that which **the Torah states: 'He has uncovered his father's nakedness.'** [14]These words are **free,** unnecessary in their own context, and therefore we may justifiably assume that they were included **for the purpose of inferring a *gezerah shavah*.** They teach that a man is also put to death for having intercourse with his mother who was not his father's wife, as will be explained below.

יְהוּדָה: "עֶרְוַת אָבִיךָ" — זוֹ אֵשֶׁת אָבִיךָ. [1]וּמַיְיתֵי לַהּ בִּגְזֵירָה שָׁוָה. [2]וּמַשְׁמַע בֵּין אֵשֶׁת אָבִיו שֶׁהִיא אִמּוֹ בֵּין אֵשֶׁת אָבִיו שֶׁאֵינָהּ אִמּוֹ. [3]אִמּוֹ שֶׁאֵינָהּ אֵשֶׁת אָבִיו מִנַּיִין? [4]תַּלְמוּד לוֹמַר: "עֶרְוַת אִמְּךָ לֹא תְגַלֵּה". [5]"אִמְּךָ הִיא" — מִשּׁוּם אִמּוֹ אַתָּה מְחַיְּיבוֹ, [6]וְאִי אַתָּה מְחַיְּיבוֹ מִשּׁוּם אֵשֶׁת אָבִיו.

[54A] [7]תַּנְיָא כְּוָותֵיהּ דְּרָבָא: "'אִישׁ' — [8]פְּרָט לְקָטָן. [9]'אֲשֶׁר יִשְׁכַּב אֶת אֵשֶׁת אָבִיו' — [10]מַשְׁמַע בֵּין אֵשֶׁת אָבִיו שֶׁהִיא אִמּוֹ, [11]וּבֵין אֵשֶׁת אָבִיו שֶׁלֹּא אִמּוֹ. [12]אִמּוֹ שֶׁאֵינָהּ אֵשֶׁת אָבִיו מִנַּיִין? [13]תַּלְמוּד לוֹמַר: 'עֶרְוַת אָבִיו גִּלָּה'. [14]מוּפְנֶה לְהַקִּישׁ וְלָדוּן מִמֶּנּוּ גְּזֵרָה שָׁוָה.

LITERAL TRANSLATION

Yehudah maintains: "The nakedness of your father" — this is your father's wife. [1]And he learns it with a *gezerah shavah.* [2]And it implies both his father's wife who is his mother, and his father's wife who is not his mother. [3]From where [does he know about] his mother who is not his father's wife? [4]The verse states: "The nakedness of your mother shall you not uncover." [5]"She is your mother" — you find her liable because of his mother, [6]and you do not find him liable for his father's wife.

[54A] [7]It was taught in accordance with Rava: "'And the man' — [8]to the exclusion of a minor. [9]'That lies with his father's wife' — [10]this implies both his father's wife who is his mother, [11]and his father's wife who is not his mother. [12]From where [do we know] his mother who is not his father's wife? [13]The Torah states: 'He has uncovered his father's nakedness.' [14][This is] free to compare and learn from it a *gezerah shavah.*

RASHI

ליה לרבי יהודה, דכיון דאית ליה האי גזירה שוה דלקמן מיניה נפקא ליה נמי עונש לאמו שאינה אשת אביו, דלרבנן דלית להו גזירה שוה נפקא להו מהאי קרא ד"אמך היא" — הא דרב שישא בריה דרב אידי, ולמעוטי באיסור אשת אב לא משתמע להו לרבנן, משום דקא סברי האי "ערות אביך" דרישא דקרא במשכב זכור ממש קאמר, כדלקמן, ולאו באיסור אשת אב איירי מידי, הלכך לא אתא סיפא למעוטי מידי דלא דמי ליה. **תניא כוותיה** — בתורת כהנים. דסתם ספרא רבי יהודה, דערות אביך לרבי יהודה זו אשת אביך, ואית ליה גזירה שוה למילף מיניה עונש לאמו שאינה אשת אביו, ואייתר ליה "אמך היא" להאי דרשה. **תלמוד לומר ערות אביו גלה** — ומשמעות לא משמע אנוסה, דהאי לאו ערות אביך היא — אלא מופנה הוא לגזירה שוה, כדדריש בסופה, ומההיא תיפוק לן עונש לאמו אנוסה, כדמפרש בסופה.

TRANSLATION AND COMMENTARY

[1]The words, **'both of them shall surely be put to death,'** teach that the offending pair are executed **by stoning.** [2]**You say** that the verse refers to death **by stoning, but might it not be** that the verse refers to **one of the** other modes of **execution mentioned in the Torah?** The meaning of 'they shall surely be put to death' is learned by a *gezerah shavah:* [3]**Here the verse states: 'Their blood shall be upon them,'** [4]**and regarding a medium and a wizard, the verse states** (Leviticus 20:27): **'Their blood shall be upon them.'** [5]**Just as there,** the medium and the wizard are liable to death **by stoning,** as the verse states explicitly: 'They shall stone them with stones,' [6]**so too here,** the offending pair are liable to death **by stoning.** [7]**We have heard the punishment** that is imposed upon a man who engaged in intercourse with his father's wife. [8]But **where is the warning** teaching that the act is prohibited? There is a rule that an act is not a punishable criminal offense unless it was forbidden explicitly in the Bible. Where then does the Torah state it is forbidden for a man to have intercourse with his father's wife? [9]This is learned from **the verse** which **states** (Leviticus 18:7): **'The nakedness of your father,** or the nakedness of your mother, **shall you not uncover.'** [10]**'The nakedness of your father'** refers to **your father's wife.** [11]**You say** that 'the nakedness of your father,' refers to **your father's wife.** [12]**But might it might it not be** that those words refers to **your father's nakedness, literally,** and that the verse prohibits homosexual intercourse with one's father? The meaning of 'the nakedness of your father' is learned by a *gezerah shavah:* [13]**Here the verse states: 'The nakedness of your father shall you not uncover.'** [14]**And the verse below states** (Leviticus 20:11): 'And the man that lies with his father's wife **has uncovered his father's nakedness.'** [15]**Just as there the verse speaks of** his father's nakedness in return to **marriage,** i.e., forbidden intercourse with a woman who was married to his father, [16]**so too here the verse speaks of** his father's nakedness by way of a **marriage.** This verse, 'the nakedness of your father shall you not uncover,' [17]**implies** that intercourse with a man's father's wife is forbidden **whether his father's wife is** also **his mother,** [18]**or his father's wife is not** also **his mother.** [19]**From where do we know** that a man is also forbidden to have intercourse with **his mother who is not** also **his father's wife?** [20]This is derived from **the verse** which **states** (Leviticus 18:7): **'The nakedness of your mother shall you not uncover.'** [21]**I only know regarding the warning that the Torah equates** a person's **mother who is not his father's wife with his mother**

[1]'מוֹת יוּמְתוּ' — בִּסְקִילָה. [2]אַתָּה אוֹמֵר בִּסְקִילָה, אוֹ אֵינוֹ אֶלָּא בְּאַחַת מִכָּל מִיתוֹת הָאֲמוּרוֹת בַּתּוֹרָה? [3]נֶאֱמַר כָּאן: 'דְּמֵיהֶם בָּם'. [4]וְנֶאֱמַר בְּאוֹב וְיִדְּעוֹנִי: 'דְּמֵיהֶם בָּם'. [5]מַה לְהַלָּן — בִּסְקִילָה, [6]אַף כָּאן — בִּסְקִילָה. [7]עוֹנֶשׁ שָׁמַעְנוּ. [8]אַזְהָרָה מִנַּיִן? — [9]תַּלְמוּד לוֹמַר: 'עֶרְוַת אָבִיךָ לֹא תְגַלֵּה'. [10]'עֶרְוַת אָבִיךָ' — זוֹ אֵשֶׁת אָבִיךָ. [11]אַתָּה אוֹמֵר אֵשֶׁת אָבִיךָ, [12]אוֹ אֵינוֹ אֶלָּא עֶרְוַת אָבִיךָ מַמָּשׁ? [13]נֶאֱמַר כָּאן: 'עֶרְוַת אָבִיךָ לֹא תְגַלֵּה'. [14]וְנֶאֱמַר לְהַלָּן: 'עֶרְוַת אָבִיו גִּלָּה'. [15]מַה לְהַלָּן בְּאִישׁוּת הַכָּתוּב מְדַבֵּר, [16]אַף כָּאן בְּאִישׁוּת הַכָּתוּב מְדַבֵּר. [17]וּמַשְׁמַע בֵּין אֵשֶׁת אָבִיו שֶׁהִיא אִמּוֹ [18]בֵּין אֵשֶׁת אָבִיו שֶׁאֵינָהּ אִמּוֹ. [19]אִמּוֹ שֶׁאֵינָהּ אֵשֶׁת אָבִיו מִנַּיִן? [20]תַּלְמוּד לוֹמַר: 'עֶרְוַת אִמְּךָ לֹא תְגַלֵּה'. [21]אֵין לִי אֶלָּא בְּאַזְהָרָה, שֶׁעָשָׂה הַכָּתוּב אִמּוֹ שֶׁאֵינָהּ אֵשֶׁת אָבִיו כְּאִמּוֹ

LITERAL TRANSLATION

[1]'[Both of them] shall surely be put to death' — by stoning. [2]You say by stoning, but might it not be by one of all the executions mentioned in the Torah? [3]It is stated here: 'Their blood shall be upon them.' [4]And it is stated regarding a medium and a wizard: 'Their blood shall be upon them.' [5]Just as there — by stoning, [6]so too here — by stoning. [7]We have heard the punishment. [8]From where the warning? [9]The verse states: [10]'The nakedness of your father shall you not uncover.' 'The nakedness of your father' — this is your father's wife. [11]You say your father's wife, [12]but might it might it not be your father's nakedness, literally? [13]It is stated here: 'The nakedness of your father shall you not uncover.' [14]And it is stated below: 'He has uncovered his father's nakedness.' [15]Just as there the verse speaks of marriage, [16]here too the verse speaks of marriage. [17]And it implies both his father's wife who is his mother, [18]and his father's wife who is not his mother. [19]From where [do we know] his mother who is not his father's wife? [20]The Torah states: 'The nakedness of your mother shall you not uncover.' [21]I only have by the warning that the verse made his mother who is not his father's wife like his mother

RASHI

מה להלן באישות הכתוב מדבר — דהא רישא דקרא "איש אשר ישכב את אשת אביו" כתיב, ומשמע בין אשת אביו וכו׳, וחייב עליה משום אשת אב, עד דאתא "אמך היא" דסופה, ומיעטה ואוקמה לרישא דקרא על כרחיך באשת אביו שאינה אמו.

TRANSLATION AND COMMENTARY

who is his father's wife. [1]**From where** do I know that regarding **the punishment** as well the Torah equates a person's mother who is not his father's wife with his mother who is his father's wife? The Baraita now explains the *gezerah shavah* which it alluded to above: [2]**Here the verse states** (Leviticus 18:7): **'Your father's nakedness shall you not uncover.'** [3]**And the verse below states** (Leviticus 20:11): **'He has uncovered his father's nakedness.'** [4]**Just as regarding the warning, the Torah equates** a man's **mother who is not** also **his father's wife with his mother who is** also **his father's wife,** [5]**so too regarding the punishment, the Torah equates** a man's **mother who is not his father's wife with his mother who is his father's wife.** The verse which teaches that intercourse with your father's wife is prohibited continues: [6]**'She is your mother.'** The extraneous words, 'she is your mother,' negate the implication of the beginning of the verse that a man is liable for violating the prohibition against intercourse with his father's wife, even if she is also his mother. Those words teach that if a man had intercourse with his father's wife, who is also his mother, [7]**he is liable** for a sin-offering **on account of** his violation of the prohibition against intercourse with **his mother,** [8]**but he is not liable** for a second sin-offering **on account of** his violation of the prohibition against intercourse with **his father's wife."**

LITERAL TRANSLATION

who is his father's wife. [1]From where the punishment? [2]It is stated here: 'Your father's nakedness shall you not uncover.' [3]And it is stated below: 'He has uncovered his father's nakedness.' [4]Just as regarding the warning, the verse made his mother who is not his father's wife like his mother who is his father's wife, [5]so too regarding the punishment, the verse made his mother who is not his father's wife like his mother who is his father's wife. [6]'She is your mother.' [7]Because of his mother you find him liable, [8]but you do not find him liable because of his father's wife."

[9]And the Rabbis — "The nakedness of your father," literally.

[10]That is learned from "With a man."

[11]To obligate him twice, [12]and in accordance with Rabbi Yehudah, [13]for Rabbi Yehudah said: [If] a non-Jew had intercourse with his father, he is liable

שֶׁהִיא אֵשֶׁת אָבִיו. [1]עוֹנֶשׁ מִנַּיִין? [2]נֶאֱמַר כָּאן: ׳עֶרְוַת אָבִיךָ לֹא תְגַלֵּה׳. [3]וְנֶאֱמַר לְהַלָּן: ׳עֶרְוַת אָבִיו גִּלָּה׳, [4]מַה בְּאַזְהָרָה — עָשָׂה הַכָּתוּב אִמּוֹ שֶׁאֵינָהּ אֵשֶׁת אָבִיו כְּאִמּוֹ שֶׁהִיא אֵשֶׁת אָבִיו, [5]אַף בְּעוֹנֶשׁ — עָשָׂה הַכָּתוּב אִמּוֹ שֶׁאֵינָהּ אֵשֶׁת אָבִיו כְּאִמּוֹ שֶׁהִיא אֵשֶׁת אָבִיו. [6]׳אִמְּךָ הִיא׳. [7]מִשּׁוּם אִמּוֹ אַתָּה מְחַיְּיבוֹ, [8]וְאִי אַתָּה מְחַיְּיבוֹ מִשּׁוּם אֵשֶׁת אָב״.

[9]וְרַבָּנַן, ״עֶרְוַת אָבִיךָ״ מַמָּשׁ.

[10]הַאי מִ״וְאֶת זָכָר״ נָפְקָא!

[11]לְחַיֵּיב עָלָיו שְׁתַּיִם, [12]וְכִדְרַב יְהוּדָה, [13]דְּאָמַר רַב יְהוּדָה: נָכְרִי הַבָּא עַל אָבִיו, חַיָּיב

RASHI

בעונש מניין — היינו הך דאתחיל בה לעיל ושבקה. **אמך היא** — ארישא דקרא מהדר לאפוקי ממשמעותיה, והיכא דאשת אביו הויא אמו אינו חייב עליה משום אשת אב, אלא משום אם. **ערות אביך ממש** — אבל אשת אב לא רמיזא הכא, הלכך לא אתיא ״אמך היא״ למעוטי, ולדרשה אחרינא אתא כדלקמן. **נכרי הבא על אביו** — מפרש ליה רבא דישראל קאמר, והא דנקט נכרי — לישנא מעליא.

וְרַבָּנַן [9]The Gemara asks: **The Rabbis** who disagree with Rabbi Yehudah and say that a man who had intercourse with his mother who is also his father's wife is liable for two sin-offerings, one for violating the prohibition against intercourse with one's mother, and a second one for violating the prohibition against intercourse with one's father's wife — how do they interpret these verses? The Gemara explains: The Rabbis understand **"the nakedness of your father," literally,** meaning that the verse prohibits homosexual intercourse with one's father. Since the verse is not dealing with the prohibition against intercourse with one's father's wife, the words "she is your mother" cannot mean that if a man has intercourse with his father's wife who was also his mother, he is only liable for a sin-offering for violating of the prohibition against intercourse with his mother. Rather they come to teach us something else, as will be explained below.

הַאי [10]The Gemara asks: Surely the prohibition against homosexual intercourse with one's father **is learned from** the verse (Leviticus 18:22): "You shall not lie **with a man** as one lies with a woman"!

לְחַיֵּיב עָלָיו [11]The Gemara answers: The verse, "The nakedness of your father shall you not uncover," **makes** a man who engaged in homosexual intercourse with his father **liable for two** transgressions, "You shall not lie with a man as one lies with a woman,y" and "The nakedness of your father shall you not uncover." [12]This is **in accordance with** the position of **Rabbi Yehudah,** [13]**for Rabbi Yehudah said: If a non-Jew had intercourse with his father, he is liable for two** transgressions, "You shall not lie with a man as one lies

HALAKHAH

הַבָּא עַל אָבִיו אוֹ אֲחִי אָבִיו **A man had intercourse with his father, or with his father's brother.** "If a man had

TRANSLATION AND COMMENTARY

with a woman," and "The nakedness of your father shall you not uncover." [1]And similarly, **if he had intercourse with his father's brother, he is liable for two** transgressions, "You shall not lie with a man as one lies with a woman," and (Leviticus 18:14): "You shall not uncover the nakedness of your father's brother." [2]And **Rava said: It stands to reason that Rabbi Yehudah's statement relates to a Jew who unwittingly** had intercourse with his father or his father's brother, **and to the sin-offering** that he must now bring. If a Jew unwittingly had intercourse with his father or his father's brother, he is liable for two sin-offerings, one for his violation of the general prohibition against homosexual intercourse, and a second sin-offering for his violation of the specific prohibition against homosexual intercourse with one's father or with one's father's brother. [3]**And that which** Rabbi Yehudah **said:** "If **a non-Jew** had intercourse with his father or with his father's brother," that **was merely a euphemism.** Rabbi Yehudah spoke of a non-Jew, rather than of a Jew, for he did not want to speak of a Jew committing such an offense. [4]Know that this is true, **for if you think** that he was referring to **a non-Jew, literally,** there is a difficulty. [5]For **what is the law** regarding a non-Jew who engages in homosexual intercourse? He is liable for **execution,** even if he sinned unwittingly. [6]But **can** the non-Jew **be executed with two executions?** Rather, Rabbi Yehudah must be referring to a Jew who unwittingly had intercourse with his father or with his father's brother, and he ruled that he is liable for two sin-offerings.

תַּנְיָא נַמִי הָכִי [7]**The same thing was also taught** in a Baraita: **"If someone** unwittingly **had** homosexual **intercourse with his father, he is liable for two** sin-offerings. [8]And similarly, **if someone** unwittingly **had** homosexual **intercourse with his father's brother, he is liable for two** sin-offerings."

אִיכָּא דְּאָמְרִי [9]**There are those** authorities **who say** that this Baraita was **not** taught **in accordance with** the position of **Rabbi Yehudah**, for according to Rabbi Yehudah, the verse, "The nakedness of your father shall you not uncover," forbids intercourse with one's father's wife, and not homosexual intercourse with one's father. Thus, a man who had intercourse with his father is liable for only one sin-offering for his violation of the general prohibition against homosexual intercourse.

אִיכָּא דְּאָמְרִי [10]**There are** other authorities **who** disagree and **say** that **you can even say** that this Baraita was taught in accordance with the position of **Rabbi Yehudah.** Even though Rabbi Yehudah maintains that the verse, "The nakedness of your father shall you not uncover," refers to intercourse with one's father's wife, and not homosexual intercourse with one's father, he agrees that the verse (Leviticus 18:14) , "You shall not uncover the nakedness of your father's brother," refers to homosexual intercourse with one's uncle,

שְׁתַּיִם. [1]הַבָּא עַל אֲחִי אָבִיו, חַיָּיב שְׁתַּיִם. [2]אָמַר רָבָא: מִסְתַּבְּרָא מִילְּתָא דְּרַב יְהוּדָה בְּיִשְׂרָאֵל, בְּשׁוֹגֵג, וּבְקָרְבָּן. [3]וְהַאי דְּקָאָמַר "נָכְרִי" לִישָּׁנָא מְעַלְּיָא הוּא. [4]דְּאִי סָלְקָא דַּעֲתָךְ נָכְרִי מַמָּשׁ, [5]דִּינוֹ מַאי נִיהוּ — קְטָלָא, [6]בִּתְרֵי קְטָלֵי קָטְלַתְּ לֵיהּ?

[7]תַּנְיָא נַמִי הָכִי: "הַבָּא עַל אָבִיו, חַיָּיב שְׁתַּיִם. [8]הַבָּא עַל אֲחִי אָבִיו, חַיָּיב שְׁתַּיִם.

[9]אִיכָּא דְּאָמְרִי: דְּלָא כְּרַבִּי יְהוּדָה.

[10]וְאִיכָּא דְּאָמְרִי: אֲפִילּוּ תֵּימָא

LITERAL TRANSLATION

for two. [1][If] he had intercourse with his father's brother, he is liable for two. [2]Rava said: It stands to reason that Rabbi Yehudah's statement [relates to] a Jew [who transgressed] unwittingly, and regarding the [sin-]offering. [3]And that which he said "a non-Jew" was a mere euphemism. [4]For if it enters your mind a non-Jew, literally, [5]what is his law — execution. [6]Do you execute him with two executions?

[7]It was also taught thus: "[If] someone had intercourse with his father, he is liable for two. [8][If] someone had intercourse with his father's brother, he is liable for two."

[9]There are [those] who say: Not like Rabbi Yehudah.

[10]And there are [those] who say: You can even say

RASHI

חייב שתים — מ"ואת זכר" ו"ערות אביך". **על אחי אביו** — מ"ואת זכר" ו"ערות אחי אביך לא תגלה" דמשמע ליה ממש. **בשוגג ולקרבן** — דכיון דאיכא שני לאוין חלוק חטאות ביניהם, אף על גב דכרת אחת היא דנפקא לן במסכת מכות ב"אלו הן הלוקין" (יד,ב) ברישיה, דדרשינן "אחותו" יתירא לחלק כרת למפטם וסך, דכתיב ביה שני לאוין וכרת אחת, והוא הדין לכל שני לאוין וכרת אחת. **דינו מאי ניהו קטלא** — ואפילו שוגג, דקאמר לקמן (נז,ב) בהאי פירקא אזהרה שלהם זו היא מיתתם. **דלא כרבי יהודה** — דהא לא משמע "ערות אביך" ממש, דאתיא גזירה שוה ואפיקתיה ממשמעותיה.

HALAKHAH

intercourse with his father, he is liable for two transgressions, homosexual intercourse, and intercourse with father. If he had intercourse with his father's brother, he is also liable for two transgressions, homosexual intercourse, and intercourse with his uncle." (*Rambam, Sefer Korbanot, Hilkhot Shegagot* 4:1.)

TRANSLATION AND COMMENTARY

for intercourse with the wife of one's father's brother is explicitly forbidden by the continuation of that verse, "You shall not approach to his wife; she is your aunt." [1]**And** Rabbi Yehudah **learns** that there is a specific prohibition forbidding homosexual intercourse with one's father **by a *kal vaḥomer*** argument **from** the specific prohibition forbidding homosexual intercourse with **one's father's brother.** [2]**If regarding one's father's brother, who is** only **a relative of his father,** a man **is liable for two** sin-offerings, one for the general prohibition against homosexual intercourse, and one for the specific prohibition against intercourse with one's uncle, [3]then **all the more so regarding one's father,** a person should be liable for two sin-offerings, one for the general prohibition against homosexual intercourse, and one for the specific prohibition against intercourse with one's father.

וְקָמִיפַּלְגִי [4]The Gemara notes that these two sets of authorities **disagree about a matter** that is **in dispute between Abaye and Rava.** Elsewhere Abaye and Rava disagree as to whether it is possible to inflict punishment on the basis of a law that was inferred through a *kal vaḥomer* argument, but not explicitly stated in the Torah. [5]**The one** Amora — Abaye — **maintains: We punish on the basis of a *kal vaḥomer* argument.** [6]**And the other** Amora — Rava — **maintains: We do not punish on the basis of a *kal vaḥomer* argument.** Those who say that even according to Rabbi Yehudah, a man who had intercourse with his father is liable for two sin-offerings, agree with Abaye that a punishment — in this case, a sin-offering — may indeed be inflicted on the basis of a *kal vaḥomer* argument. And those who say that according to Rabbi Yehudah, a man who had intercourse with his father is liable for only one sin-offering, agree with Rava that a punishment may not be inflicted on the basis of a *kal vaḥomer* argument.

וְרַבָּנַן [7]The Gemara asks: **From where do the Rabbis** who disagree with Rabbi Yehudah **derive a warning regarding one's father's wife?** If the verse, "The nakedness of your father shall you not uncover," refers to homosexual intercourse with one's father, where is the verse forbidding intercourse with one's father's wife? [8]The Gemara explains: The Rabbis **derive this from** the verse (Leviticus 18:8): **"The nakedness of your father's wife shall you not uncover."**

וְרַבִּי יְהוּדָה [9]The Gemara asks: **And** what does **Rabbi Yehudah** derive from that verse? He already knows that intercourse with one's father's wife is forbidden from the previous verse (Leviticus 18:7: "The nakedness of your father shall you not uncover"! [10]The Gemara answers: Rabbi Yehudah **needs that** second verse **for a warning** teaching that intercourse with **one's father's wife** is prohibited even **after** the father's **death.**

וְרַבָּנַן [11]The Gemara asks: **And** from where do **the Rabbis** learn that a person is forbidden to have intercourse with his father's wife even after the father's death? [12]The Gemara explains: **That is derived from** the extraneous words found at **the end of that** very same **verse: "She is your father's nakedness."**

וְרַבִּי יְהוּדָה [13]The Gemara asks: **And** what does **Rabbi Yehudah** derive from those extraneous words? [14]The Gemara answers: Rabbi Yehudah **needs those** words **for** the law that if a man had intercourse with his

רַבִּי יְהוּדָה, [1]וּמַיְיתִי לָהּ בְּקַל וָחוֹמֶר מֵאֲחִי אָבִיו. [2]וּמָה אֲחִי אָבִיו, דִּקוּרְבָה דְּאָבִיו הוּא, חַיָּיב שְׁתַּיִם, [3]אָבִיו לֹא כָּל שֶׁכֵּן.

[4]וְקָמִיפַּלְגִי בִּפְלוּגְתָּא דְּאַבַּיֵי וְרָבָא. [5]מָר סָבַר: עוֹנְשִׁין מִן הַדִּין. [6]וּמָר סָבַר: אֵין עוֹנְשִׁין מִן הַדִּין.

[7]וְרַבָּנַן, אַזְהָרָה לְאֵשֶׁת אָבִיו מְנָא לְהוּ? [8]נָפְקָא לְהוּ מֵ"עֶרְוַת אֵשֶׁת אָבִיךָ לֹא תְגַלֵּה".

[9]וְרַבִּי יְהוּדָה? [10]הַהוּא מִיבָּעֵי לֵיהּ לְאַזְהָרָה לְאֵשֶׁת אָבִיו לְאַחַר מִיתָה.

[11]וְרַבָּנַן? [12]הַהוּא מִסֵּיפָא דִּקְרָא נָפְקָא "עֶרְוַת אָבִיךָ הִיא".

[13]וְרַבִּי יְהוּדָה? [14]הַהוּא מִיבָּעֵי לֵיהּ: מִשּׁוּם אֵשֶׁת אָב אַתָּה

LITERAL TRANSLATION

Rabbi Yehudah, [1]and he learns it with a *kal vaḥomer* from his father's brother. [2]If regarding his father's brother, who is a relative of his father, he is liable for two, [3]all the more so regarding his father.

[4]And they disagree about the [matter in] dispute between Abaye and Rava. [5]The one maintains: We punish on the basis of a *kal vaḥomer* argument. [6]And the other one maintains: We do not punish on the basis of a *kal vaḥomer* argument.

[7]And from where do the Rabbis [derive] a warning regarding his father's wife? [8]They derive this from "The nakedness of your father's wife shall you not uncover."

[9]And Rabbi Yehudah? [10]That he needs for a warning for his father's wife after death.

[11]And the Rabbis? [12]That is derived from the end of the verse: "She is your father's nakedness."

[13]And Rabbi Yehudah? [14]That he needs for: You find him liable him because of [his] father's wife,

RASHI

מאחי אביו — דההוא ודאי משמע ליה ממש, דכתיב בגופיה "אל אשתו לא תקרב". פלוגתא דאביי ורבא — בעונשין מן הדין, "באלו הן הנשרפין".

[1] מְחַיְּיבוֹ, וְאִי אַתָּה מְחַיְּיבוֹ מִשּׁוּם אֵשֶׁת אִישׁ.

[2] וְהָאֲנַן תְּנַן: "הַבָּא עַל אֵשֶׁת אָב" חַיָּיב עָלֶיהָ מִשּׁוּם אֵשֶׁת אָב, [3] וּמִשּׁוּם אֵשֶׁת אִישׁ, [4] "בֵּין בְּחַיֵּי אָבִיו בֵּין לְאַחַר מִיתַת אָבִיו". [5] וְלָא פְּלִיג רַבִּי יְהוּדָה!

[6] אָמַר אַבַּיֵי: פְּלִיג בְּבָרַיְיתָא.

[7] וְרַבָּנַן, עוֹנֶשׁ דְּאֵשֶׁת אָבִיו לְאַחַר מִיתָה מְנָא לְהוּ? [8] בִּשְׁלָמָא רַבִּי יְהוּדָה, מַיְיתֵי לָהּ בִּגְזֵירָה שָׁוָה. [9] אֶלָּא רַבָּנַן מְנָא לְהוּ?

[10] אָמְרִי לָךְ: הַהוּא "עֶרְוַת אָבִיו גִּלָּה" [11] דְּמַפֵּיק לָהּ רַבִּי יְהוּדָה לִגְזֵירָה שָׁוָה, [12] מַפְּקֵי לֵיהּ אִינְהוּ לְעוֹנֶשׁ דְּאֵשֶׁת אָבִיו לְאַחַר מִיתָה.

[13] וְרַבָּנַן, עוֹנֶשׁ לְאִמּוֹ שֶׁאֵינָהּ אֵשֶׁת אָבִיו מְנָא לְהוּ?

LITERAL TRANSLATION

[1] and you do not find him liable because of a married woman.

[2] But surely we have learned: "Someone who has intercourse with [his] father's wife is liable for [his] father's wife [3] and for a married woman, [4] both during his father's lifetime, and after his father's death." [5] And Rabbi Yehudah does not disagree!

[6] Abaye said: He disagreed in the Baraita.

[7] And from where do the Rabbis [derive] the punishment for one's father's wife after death? [8] Granted according to Rabbi Yehudah, he learns it through a *gezerah shavah.* [9] But from where do the Rabbis [learn it]?

[10] They can say to you: That "He has uncovered his father's nakedness" [11] which Rabbi Yehudah uses for a *gezerah shavah,* [12] they use for the punishment for one's father's wife after death.

[13] And from where do the Rabbis [derive] the punishment for his mother who is not his father's wife?

TRANSLATION AND COMMENTARY

father's wife, **he is liable** for a sin-offering for his violation of the prohibition against intercourse with **his father's wife,** [1] **but he is not liable** for a second sin-offering for his violation of the prohibition against intercourse with **a married woman.**

וְהָאֲנַן תְּנַן [2] The Gemara raises an objection: **But surely we have learned** otherwise in our Mishnah: **"A man who** unwittingly **engaged in** sexual **intercourse with his father's wife** who is not also his mother **is liable for** two sin-offerings — one for the unwitting violation of the prohibition against intercourse with **his father's wife,** [3] **and** one **for** the unwitting violation of the prohibition against intercourse with **a married woman.** A man is liable for violating the prohibition against having intercourse with his father's wife, [4] **both during his father's lifetime, and** also **after his father's death,** but he is only liable for violating the prohibition against intercourse with a married woman while his father is alive and married to the woman." [5] **And** while **Rabbi Yehudah** disagrees with the previous ruling of the Rabbis regarding a man who had intercourse with his mother who was also his father's wife, he **does not** appear to **disagree** with this ruling! How then can you say that in such a case Rabbi Yehudah maintains that the offending son is liable for only a single sin-offering?

אָמַר [6] **Abaye said:** Though the Mishnah fails to mention that Rabbi Yehudah disagrees with the Rabbis about this second matter, we find **in a Baraita that he does** indeed **disagree** with them on this point as well.

וְרַבָּנַן [7] The Gemara asks: We have seen how both Rabbi Yehudah and the Rabbis derive from the verses that a man is forbidden to have intercourse with his father's wife, even after his death. But **from where do the Rabbis** who disagree with Rabbi Yehudah **derive the punishment** that is imposed upon a man for having intercourse with **his father's wife after** his **death?** [8] **Granted according to Rabbi Yehudah, he learns** the punishment that is imposed in such a case **by way of a *gezerah shavah,*** for as we saw above, Rabbi Yehudah draws a *gezerah shavah* between the verse containing the warning and the verse containing the punishment. [9] **But from where do the Rabbis learn** the punishment that is imposed?

אָמְרִי לָךְ [10] The Gemara answers: The Rabbis **can say to you:** The words, **"He has uncovered his father's nakedness,"** [11] which appear in the verse which teaches the punishment for intercourse with one's father's wife and **which Rabbi Yehudah uses for** his *gezerah shavah,* [12] the Rabbis **use** as the source **for the punishment** imposed upon a man for having intercourse with **his father's wife after** the father's **death.**

וְרַבָּנַן [13] The Gemara asks: **From where do the Rabbis** who disagree with Rabbi Yehudah **derive the punishment** that is imposed upon a man who had intercourse with **his mother who is not** also **his father's wife?** Granted according to Rabbi Yehudah, he learns the punishment that is imposed in such a case by a *gezerah shavah.* But from where do the Rabbis learn the punishment that is imposed?

RASHI

ואי אתה מחייבו משום אשת איש — דכיון דמחייב עליה רישא דקרא משום אשת אב, משמע נמי אשת איש, ואתא "היא" ואפקיה. **ורבנן עונש באשת אב לאחר מיתה מנא להו** — אבל אזהרה כתוב בה, כדדרשינן מדרשה למר ולמר. **בשלמא לרבי יהודה** — דיליף עונש מאזהרה בגזירה שוה, מייתי לה נמי בגזירה שוה, אלא לרבנן מנא להו? **ערות אביו גלה** — גבי עונש כתיב. **עונש באמו**

[1]אָמַר רַב שֵׁישָׁא בְּרֵיהּ דְּרַב אִידִי: [2]אָמַר קְרָא: ״אִמְּךָ הִיא״. [3]עֲשָׂאָהּ הַכָּתוּב לְאִמּוֹ שֶׁאֵינָהּ אֵשֶׁת אָבִיו כְּאִמּוֹ שֶׁהִיא אֵשֶׁת אָבִיו.

[4]״הַבָּא עַל כַּלָּתוֹ כו׳״. [5]וְלִחַיֵּיב נַמִי מִשּׁוּם אֵשֶׁת בְּנוֹ!

[6]אָמַר אַבַּיֵי: פָּתַח הַכָּתוּב בְּכַלָּתוֹ, [7]וְסִיֵּים בְּאֵשֶׁת בְּנוֹ, [8]לוֹמַר לְךָ: זוֹ הִיא כַּלָּתוֹ, זוֹ הִיא אֵשֶׁת בְּנוֹ.

מִשְׁנָה [9]הַבָּא עַל הַזָּכוּר וְעַל הַבְּהֵמָה, [10]וְהָאִשָּׁה הַמְּבִיאָה אֶת הַבְּהֵמָה — בִּסְקִילָה. [11]אִם אָדָם חָטָא, בְּהֵמָה מֶה חָטְאָה? [12]אֶלָּא, לְפִי

LITERAL TRANSLATION

[1]Rabbi Shesha the son of Rav Idi said: [2]The verse states: "She is your mother." [3]The verse made his mother who is not his father's wife like his mother who is his father's wife.

[4]"Someone who has intercourse with his daughter-in-law, etc." [5]And let him also be liable for his son's wife!

[6]Abaye said: The verse opened with his daughter-in-law, [7]and concluded with his son's wife, [8]to teach you: This is his daughter-in-law, this is his son's wife.

MISHNAH [9]A man who has intercourse with a man, or with an animal, [10]and a woman who allowed herself to be coupled with an animal — by stoning. [11]If the person sinned, did the animal sin? [12]Rather, because

TRANSLATION AND COMMENTARY

אָמַר [1]**Rabbi Shesha the son of Rav Idi said:** [2]This is derived from **the verse** which **states** (Leviticus 18:7): **"She is your mother."** [3]The extraneous words, "She is your mother," teach that **the Torah equates** a man's **mother who is not** also **his father's wife with his mother who is** also **his father's wife.** In all cases, she is your mother, and therefore governed by the same regulations.

הַבָּא עַל כַּלָּתוֹ [4]We have learned in our Mishnah: **"A man who** unwittingly **engaged in** sexual **intercourse with his daughter-in-law** is liable for two sin-offerings — one for having intercourse with his daughter-in-law, and one for having intercourse with a married woman." [5]The Gemara asks: **But let him also be liable for** violating the prohibition against intercourse with **his son's wife!** For the verse states (Leviticus 18:15): "You shall not uncover the nakedness of your daughter-in-law: she is your son's wife; you shall not uncover her nakedness," implying that there are two separate prohibitions, one against intercourse with one's daughter-in-law, and one against intercourse with one's son's wife.

אָמַר אַבַּיֵי [6]**Abaye said: The verse opens with his daughter-in-law** — "You shall not uncover the nakedness of your daughter-in-law" — [7]**and concludes with his son's wife** — "She is your son's wife." The verse does not mean to say that there are two separate prohibitions, [8]but rather it **teaches you** that when the Torah speaks of a man's **daughter-in-law,** it is referring to **his son's wife.**

MISHNAH הַבָּא עַל הַזָּכוּר [9]**A man who engaged in intercourse with** another **man, and** a man who coupled **with an animal,** [10]**and a woman who allowed herself to be coupled with an animal** are all put to death **by stoning,** and so too the animal involved in the offense is put to death by stoning. [11]The Mishnah asks: **If the person sinned, did the animal sin?** Surely an animal does not bear criminal liability! Why then is it put to death if a human being engaged in sexual relations with it? [12]The Mishnah explains: **Since a person**

RASHI

לא כתיב, אלא באשת אב הוא דכתיב. אמך היא — בהוויתה היא, כל לדדין שוין בה, בין שהיא אשת אב, בין שאינה אשת אביו. **ונחייב נמי משום אשת בנו** — דהא שני לאוין ושני שמות הן, ״ערות כלתך לא תגלה אשת בנך היא לא תגלה ערותה״ (ויקרא יח). **וסיים באשת בנו** — דכתיב ״היא״ ומשמע היא האמורה ברישא דקרא. והאי דהדר וכתביה — לחייב עליה אף לאחר מיתה.

NOTES

פָּתַח הַכָּתוּב בְּכַלָּתוֹ **The verse opened with his daughter-in-law.** *Ramban* understands this as follows: The verse opens with the word *kallah,* and concludes with the expression "your son's wife," in order to teach that the word *kallah* means "your son's wife." Other Rishonim object that this is difficult, for surely we know from other verses that the word *kallah* means "daughter-in-law." *Ran* suggests that *Ramban* means to say that the verse concludes with the expression "your son's wife," for otherwise we might have mistakenly thought that the term *kallah* refers here to a bride during the days of her wedding celebration.

הַבָּא עַל הַזָּכוּר **A man who had intercourse with a man.** The Rishonim ask: Why does the Mishnah repeat here what was stated in the previous Mishnah that a man who

HALAKHAH

הַבָּא עַל הַזָּכוּר **A man who had intercourse with a man.** "If a man engaged in homosexual intercourse with another man, he is liable for stoning." (*Rambam, Sefer Shofetim, Hilkhot Sanhedrin* 15:10.)

וְעַל הַבְּהֵמָה **Or with an animal.** "A man who coupled with an animal and a woman who was the object of coupling with an animal are liable for stoning." (*Rambam, Sefer Shofetim, Hilkhot Sanhedrin* 15:10.)

TRANSLATION AND COMMENTARY

came to an offense through the animal, [1]**therefore the Torah said that** the animal **should be stoned,** to prevent others from committing a similar offense. [2]The Mishnah offers **another explanation:** The animal is put to death, **so that it not pass through the market, [3]and people say: "This is** the animal **on account of which so-and-so was stoned,"** bringing further disgrace to the executed party.

GEMARA זָכָר מְנָא לַן [4]The Gemara asks: **From where do we know** the punishment imposed upon **a man who had intercourse with** another **man?** [5]The Gemara explains: **As our Rabbis taught** in a Baraita: "The verse states (Leviticus 20:13): 'And if a man lies with a man, as one lies with a woman, both of them have committed an abomination: they shall surely be put to death; their blood shall be upon them.' The words, **'And if a man,'** teach that only a grown man who perpetrated an act of sodomy is put to death, **to the exclusion of a minor.** [6]The words, **'Lies with a man,'** teach that an adult who perpetrated an act of sodomy is put to death, **whether** the subject of the act of sodomy was **an adult or a minor.** Regarding the perpetrator of the act, the verse uses the word אִישׁ, 'man,' teaching that he is only liable if he is an adult. But regarding the object of the act, the verse uses the word זָכָר, literally, 'male,' teaching that the perpetrator is liable even if the object of the act is only a minor. The verse continues with the words, [7]**'As one lies with a woman'** — מִשְׁכְּבֵי אִשָּׁה, literally, 'lyings with a woman.' By using the plural term "lyings," [8]**the verse teaches you that there are two manners of lying with a woman,** 'natural' (vaginal) intercourse, and 'unnatural' (anal) intercourse. If a man engaged in sexual intercourse with a woman who is forbidden to him, he and she are liable whichever of the two ways he penetrated her.

שֶׁבָּאָה לָאָדָם תַּקָּלָה עַל יָדָהּ, [1]לְפִיכָךְ אָמַר הַכָּתוּב תִּסָּקֵל. [2]דָּבָר אַחֵר: שֶׁלֹּא תְּהֵא בְּהֵמָה עוֹבֶרֶת בַּשּׁוּק, [3]וְיֹאמְרוּ: זוֹ הִיא שֶׁנִּסְקַל פְּלוֹנִי עַל יָדָהּ.

גמרא [4]זָכָר מְנָא לַן? [5]דְּתָנוּ רַבָּנַן: ״׳אִישׁ׳ — פְּרָט לְקָטָן, [6]׳אֲשֶׁר יִשְׁכַּב אֶת זָכָר׳ — בֵּין גָּדוֹל בֵּין קָטָן. [7]׳מִשְׁכְּבֵי אִשָּׁה׳ — [8]מַגִּיד לְךָ הַכָּתוּב שֶׁשְּׁנֵי מִשְׁכָּבוֹת בָּאִשָּׁה.

LITERAL TRANSLATION

the person came to an offense through it, [1]therefore the verse said it should be stoned. [2]Another explanation: So that the animal will not pass through the market, [3]and [people] say: This is one for which So-and-so was stoned.

GEMARA [4]From where do we [know about a man who had intercourse with] a man? [5]For our Rabbis taught: "'And if a man' — to the exclusion of a minor. [6]'Lie with a man' — whether an adult or a minor. [7]'As one lies with a woman' — [8]the verse teaches you that there are two manners of lying with a woman.

RASHI

משנה תקלה – מכשול, עון.

גמרא אשר ישכב את זכר – מדלא כתיב איש – לא חלק בנשכבים בין גדול בין קטן להתחייב השוכב עליה, ואשמעינן דלא בעינן תרוייהו בני עונשין, ומינה נמי ילפינן דאי הוה נשכב גדול ושוכב קטן, כגון: בן תשע שנים ויום אחד, דביאתו ביאה ולאו (בני) עונשין הוא, ומחייב נשכב. משכבי אשה – שתי משכבות יש באשה שוין זה לזה לחייב בכל עריות, כדרכה ושלא כדרכה.

NOTES

engaged in homosexual intercourse is put to death by stoning? *Melekhet Shelomo* suggests that the Mishnah teaches that even though we stone an animal which was used sexually, because it brought a person to a capital offense, we do not inflict a similar punishment upon a minor who was used for homosexual intercourse. Most Rishonim understand that since this and the later Mishnahs clarify what was taught in the previous Mishnah, they mention each of the offenders listed above even if there is nothing to add about that particular type of criminal (*Ramah*; see also *Meiri, Tosefot Yom Tov,* and *Rashash*).

שֶׁשְּׁנֵי מִשְׁכָּבוֹת בָּאִשָּׁה There are two manners of lying with a woman. According to *Ran,* this is not derived from the plural term "lyings," but rather from the very fact that the Torah imposes liability on homosexual intercourse, which is always "unnatural (anal) intercourse." Nevertheless, the phrase, "as one lies with a woman," also applies to anal intercourse. A man is liable for having sexual relations with a woman who is forbidden to him, even if he penetrated her in an "unnatural manner."

HALAKHAH

קָטָן אֲשֶׁר יִשְׁכַּב אֶת זָכָר A minor who had homosexual intercourse with a man. "If two adult men over the age of thirteen engaged in homosexual intercourse, they are both liable for stoning. If one of the parties was a child over the age of nine, the adult party is liable for stoning, and the child is exempt. If an adult engaged in intercourse with a child under the age of nine, they are both exempt, but the adult should be given Rabbinically-ordained lashes." (*Rambam, Sefer Kedushah, Hilkhot Issurei Bi'ah* 1:14.)

שְׁנֵי מִשְׁכָּבוֹת בָּאִשָּׁה Two manners of lying with a woman. "With regard to all the prohibitions against sexual intercourse, the offending parties are liable for both vaginal ('natural') intercourse and anal ('unnatural') intercourse." (*Rambam, Sefer Kedushah, Hilkhot Issurei Bi'ah* 1:10.)

[1]אָמַר רַבִּי יִשְׁמָעֵאל: הֲרֵי זֶה בָּא לְלַמֵּד וְנִמְצָא לָמֵד. [2]׳מוֹת יוּמְתוּ׳ — בִּסְקִילָה. [3]אַתָּה אוֹמֵר בִּסְקִילָה, [4]אוֹ אֵינוֹ אֶלָּא בְּאַחַת מִכָּל מִיתוֹת הָאֲמוּרוֹת בַּתּוֹרָה? [5]נֶאֱמַר כָּאן: ׳דְּמֵיהֶם בָּם׳. [6]וְנֶאֱמַר בְּאוֹב וְיִדְּעוֹנִי: ״דְּמֵיהֶם בָּם״. [7]מַה לְּהַלָּן בִּסְקִילָה — [8]אַף כָּאן בִּסְקִילָה. [54B] [9]עוֹנֶשׁ שָׁמַעְנוּ. [10]אַזְהָרָה מִנַּיִן? [11]תַּלְמוּד לוֹמַר: ׳וְאֶת זָכָר לֹא תִשְׁכַּב מִשְׁכְּבֵי אִשָּׁה תּוֹעֵבָה הִיא׳. [12]לָמַדְנוּ אַזְהָרָה לַשּׁוֹכֵב, [13]אַזְהָרָה לַנִּשְׁכָּב מִנַּיִן? [14]תַּלְמוּד לוֹמַר: ׳לֹא יִהְיֶה קָדֵשׁ מִבְּנֵי יִשְׂרָאֵל׳. [15]וְאוֹמֵר: ׳וְגַם קָדֵשׁ הָיָה בָאָרֶץ עָשׂוּ כְּכֹל הַתּוֹעֵבֹת הַגּוֹיִם אֲשֶׁר הוֹרִישׁ וגו׳׳.

LITERAL TRANSLATION

[1]Rabbi Yishmael said: This came to teach [about something else], and ultimately it taught [about itself]. [2]'They shall surely be put to death' — by stoning. [3]You say by stoning, [4]but might it not be by one of all the executions mentioned in the Torah? [5]It is stated here: 'Their blood shall be upon them.' [6]And it is stated regardomg a medium and a wizard: 'Their blood shall be upon them.' [7]Just as there by stoning, [8]so too here — by stoning.

[54B] [9]We have heard the punishment. [10]From where the warning? [11]The verse states: 'You shall not lie with a man in the manner of a woman; it is abomination.' [12]We have learned a warning for the perpetrator of the sodomy. [13]From where the warning for the object of the sodomy? [14]The verse states: 'Nor shall there be a male prostitute of the sons of Israel.' [15]And it states: 'And there was also prostitution in the land; and they did according to all the abominations of the nations which [the Lord] cast out, etc.'

TRANSLATION AND COMMENTARY

[1]**Rabbi Yishmael said: These** words, 'Lyings with a woman,' **came to teach** that a man is liable for anal intercourse with another man, **but ultimately** those words also **taught** about heterosexual intercourse. It was unnecessary to speak about homosexual relations, for in that case the Torah must be referring to anal intercourse. Rather, the verse teaches about heterosexual relations, that a man is liable for intercourse with a woman who is forbidden to him, whether he engaged in vaginal or anal intercourse. [2]The words, **'They shall surely be put to death,'** teach that the offending pair are executed **by stoning.** [3]**You say** that the verse refers to death **by stoning,** [4]**but might it not be** that the verse refers to **one of the** other modes of **execution mentioned in the Torah?** The meaning of "they shall surely be put to death" is learned by a *gezerah shavah*: [5]**Here the verse states: 'Their blood shall be upon them,'** [6]**and regarding a medium and a wizard, the verse states** (Leviticus 20:27): **'Their blood shall be upon them.'** [7]**Just as there,** the medium and the wizard are liable for death **by stoning,** as the verse states explicitly: 'They shall stone them with stones,' [8]**so too here,** the offending pair are liable for death **by stoning.**

[54B] עוֹנֶשׁ שָׁמַעְנוּ [9]**We have heard the punishment** that is imposed for homosexual intercourse. [10]**But where is the warning** teaching that the act is prohibited? [11]This is learned from **the verse** which **states** (Leviticus 18:23): **'You shall not lie with a man in the manner of a woman; it is abomination.'** [12]**We have learned** from this verse **a warning for the perpetrator of the** act of **sodomy.** [13]**But where is the warning for the object of the sodomy?** [14]This is learned from **the verse** which **states** (Deuteronomy 23:18): **'Nor shall there be a male prostitute of the sons of Israel.'** [15]**And** elsewhere the verse **states** (I Kings 14:24): **'And there was also prostitution in the land; and they did according to all the abominations of the nations which the**

RASHI

הרי זה בא ללמד — על זכר שחייב אפילו שלא כדרכה. **ונמצא למד** — למשכב זכור לא איצטריך קרא, דפשיטא לן דכל משכב זכר שלא כדרכו הוא, אלא האי "משכבי" לאשמועינן אתא דהבא על אשה בין כדרכה בין שלא כדרכה — חייב. **וגם קדש היה בארץ** — מה קדש האמור כאן יש בו תועבה, אף ב"לא יהיה קדש" יש בו תועבה. והדר גמרינן תועבה האמור ב"לא יהיה קדש" מתועבה האמור במשכב זכור, דכתיב "אשר ישכב את זכר משכבי אשה תועבה עשו שניהם דמיהם בם", מה תועבה האמור שם אף נשכב במשמע. **וגם קדש היה בארץ** — לשון זנות, דכתיב "כתועבות הגוים" ומשכב זכור תועבה היא.

NOTES

בָּא לְלַמֵּד וְנִמְצָא לָמֵד This came to teach about something else, and ultimately it taught about itself. The Rishonim point out that this expression usually means that the verse teaches about something else, and ultimately taught both about something else and about it itself. What then does the expression, "lyings with a woman," teach about homosexual intercourse? *Talmidei Rabbenu Peretz* suggest that it teaches that one is liable for the first stage of intercourse, genital contact, not only in heterosexual intercourse, but also in homosexual intercourse. *Rabbenu Yonah* explains that it teaches about the case of an *androgynos*, a person with both male and female reproductive organs. There too a man is liable whichever way the *androgynos* was penetrated.

וְאוֹמֵר: וְגַם קָדֵשׁ And it states: "And there was also prostitution." Even though this verse is not found in the

[1]דִּבְרֵי רַבִּי יִשְׁמָעֵאל. [2]רַבִּי עֲקִיבָא אוֹמֵר: אֵינוֹ צָרִיךְ. [3]הֲרֵי הוּא אוֹמֵר: ׳וְאֶת זָכָר לֹא תִשְׁכַּב מִשְׁכְּבֵי אִשָּׁה׳. [4]קְרִי בֵּיהּ: ׳לֹא תִשָּׁכֵב׳״.

[5]בְּהֵמָה מְנָא לָן? [6]דְּתָנוּ רַבָּנַן: ״׳אִישׁ׳ — פְּרָט לְקָטָן. [7]׳אֲשֶׁר יִתֵּן שְׁכָבְתּוֹ בִּבְהֵמָה׳ — בֵּין גְּדוֹלָה בֵּין קְטַנָּה. [8]׳מוֹת יוּמָת׳ — בִּסְקִילָה. [9]אַתָּה אוֹמֵר בִּסְקִילָה, אוֹ אֵינוֹ אֶלָּא בְּאַחַת מִכָּל מִיתוֹת הָאֲמוּרוֹת בַּתּוֹרָה? [10]נֶאֱמַר כָּאן: ׳תַּהֲרֹגוּ׳. [11]וְנֶאֱמַר לְהַלָּן: ׳כִּי הָרֹג תַּהַרְגֶנּוּ׳,

LITERAL TRANSLATION

[1][These are] the words of Rabbi Yishmael. [2]Rabbi Akiva says: There is no need. [3]Surely it states: 'You shall not lie with a man in the manner of a woman.' [4]"Read: 'You shall not be sodomized.'"

[5]From where do we [know about someone who coupled with] an animal? [6]For our Rabbis taught: "'A man' — to the exclusion of a minor. [7]'Lie with a beast' — whether full-grown or young. [8]'He shall surely be put to death' — by stoning. [9]You say by stoning, but might it not be by one of all the executions mentioned in the Torah? [10]It is stated here: 'You shall kill it.' [11]And it is stated below: 'But you shall surely kill him.'

TRANSLATION AND COMMENTARY

Lord cast out before the children of Israel.' Just as the prostitution mentioned in the book of Kings is an abomination, so too the prostitution mentioned in the book of Deuteronomy is an abomination. And the meaning of the verse in Deuteronomy that forbids male prostitution which is an abomination is learned from the verse in Leviticus which refers to homosexual intercourse as an abomination (Leviticus 20:13): 'And if a man lie with a man, as one lies with a woman, both of them have committed an abomination; they shall surely be put to death.' And just as that verse refers also to the object of the act of sodomy ('both of them'), so too the verse, 'Nor shall there be a male prostitute,' serves as a warning for the object of the act of sodomy. [1]This is **the position of Rabbi Yishmael.** [2]**Rabbi Akiva says: There is no need** to learn the warning for the object of the act of sodomy from the verse, 'Nor shall there be a male prostitute.' [3]For **surely** the verse **states: 'You shall not lie** [לֹא תִשְׁכַּב] **with a man in the manner of a woman.'** According to the Mesorah, the words לא תשכב are read *lo tishkav,* 'You shall not lie,' referring to the perpetrator of the sodomy. [4]But the words can also be **read** as *lo tishakhev* (in the *nif'al* form), **"You shall not allow sodomy,'** referring to the object of the act of sodomy."

בְּהֵמָה מְנָא לָן [5]The Gemara now proceeds to discuss the next prohibition mentioned in the Mishnah: **From where do we know** the punishment imposed **upon someone who coupled with an animal?** [6]The Gemara explains: **For our Rabbis taught** in a Baraita: "The verse states (Leviticus 20:15): 'And if a man lies with a beast, he shall surely be put to death; and you shall kill the beast.' The words, 'And if **a man,'** teach that only a grown man who coupled with an animal is put to death, **to the exclusion of a minor.** [7]The words, **'Lie with a beast,'** teach that an adult who coupled with an animal is liable for his transgression, **whether** the animal was **full-grown or** still **young.** [8]The words, **'He shall surely be put to death,'** teach that the offense is punishable by death, **by stoning.** [9]**You say** that the verse refers to death **by stoning, but might it not be** that the verse refers to death **by one of the** other modes of **execution mentioned in the Torah?** The meaning of 'He shall surely be put to death' is learned by way of a *gezerah shavah.* [10]**Here the verse states: 'You shall kill** the beast.' [11]**And below the verse states** with respect to one who incites others to worship idols (Deuteronomy 13:10): **'But you shall surely kill him.'**

RASHI

לא תשכב — קרי ביה נמי לא תשכב.
ונאמר להלן במסית — דכתיב "וסקלתו באבנים".

NOTES

Torah, but only in the Book of Kings, and there is a rule that exegetical inferences concerning the Torah cannot be drawn from the Prophets or the Hagiographa, the Sages said that exegetical inferences that are only based on allusion, or that "merely reveal something" may in fact be derived even from the Prophets and the Hagiographa.

קְרִי בֵּיהּ לֹא תִשָּׁכֵב **Read: "You shall not allow sodomy."** *Ran* argues that Rabbi Akiva does not mean to say that we should read the words *lo tishkav* as *lo tishakhev,* for Rabbi Akiva himself maintains that the vocalized text of the Torah, and not its consonantal text, is authoritative. In his view we follow the vocalized text of the Torah for purposes of Halakhic Midrash. Rather, Rabbi Akiva's interpretation is based on an extension of the meaning of the word שְׁכִיבָה, so that it refers not only to the perpetrator of the act of sodomy, but also to the subject of the act of sodomy, similar to what we find regarding the daughters of Lot (Genesis 19:34): "Behold, I lay [שָׁכַבְתִּי] last night with my father."

HALAKHAH

מִשְׁכַּב בְּהֵמָה **Sexual intercourse with an animal.** "If a man coupled with an animal, or he was the object of coupling with an animal, he is liable to death by stoning." (*Rambam, Sefer Kedushah, Hilkhot Issurei Bi'ah* 1:16.)

TRANSLATION AND COMMENTARY

[1] **Just as there,** the inciter is liable to death **by stoning**, as the next verse states explicitly (Deuteronomy 13:11): 'And you shall stone him with stones,' **so too here,** the person who coupled with an animal, as well as the animal itself, are liable to death **by stoning.** [2] **We have learned** from this verse **the punishment** imposed upon **someone who coupled with an animal.** [3] But **from where** do we know the punishment imposed upon **someone who allowed himself to be coupled with an animal?** [4] **The verse states** (Exodus 22:18): **'Whoever couples with a beast shall surely be put to death.'** [5] **Since** that verse **is not needed for someone who coupled with an animal,** for his punishment is already stated elsewhere, as we saw above, it is legitimate to **refer** the verse **to someone who allowed himself to be coupled with an animal.** [6] Thus, **we have learned the punishment** that is imposed **both** upon **someone who coupled with an animal and** upon **someone who allowed himself to be coupled with an animal.** [7] But **where is the warning** teaching that the act is prohibited? [8] This is learned from **the verse** which states (Leviticus 18:23): **'Neither shall you lie with any beast to defile yourself with it.'** [9] **We have learned** from this verse **the warning for someone who couples with an animal.** [10] But **where is the warning for someone who allows himself to be coupled with an animal?** [11] This is learned from **the verse** which **states** (Deuteronomy 23:18): **'Nor shall there be a male prostitute of the sons of Israel.'** [12] **And** elsewhere the verse **states** (I Kings 14:24): **'And there was also prostitution in the land;** and they did according to all the abominations of the nations which the Lord cast out before the children of Israel." Having animals couple with men was one of the abominations practiced by the nations which were cast out of the Land of Israel. [13] This is **the position of Rabbi Yishmael.** [14] **Rabbi Akiva says: There is no need** to learn the warning for someone who allows himself to be coupled with an animal from the verse, "Nor shall there be a male prostitute." [15] For **surely** the verse **states: 'Neither shall you lie** [לֹא תִתֵּן שְׁכָבְתְּךָ] with any beast to defile yourself with it.' According to the Mesorah, the words לֹא תִתֵּן שְׁכָבְתְּךָ read *lo titen shekhavtekha,* 'Neither shall you lie.' [16] But the words can also be read as לֹא תִתֵּן שְׁכִיבָתְךָ, *lo titen shekhivatkha,* **'Neither shall you give your being lain with,' meaning, to let an animal couple with you.'"**

[1] מַה לְהַלָּן בִּסְקִילָה, אַף כָּאן בִּסְקִילָה. [2] לָמַדְנוּ עוֹנֶשׁ לַשּׁוֹכֵב, [3] עוֹנֶשׁ לַנִּשְׁכָּב מְנָלַן? [4] תַּלְמוּד לוֹמַר: ׳כָּל שֹׁכֵב עִם בְּהֵמָה מוֹת יוּמָת׳. [5] אִם אֵינוֹ עִנְיָן לַשּׁוֹכֵב, תְּנֵיהוּ עִנְיָן לַנִּשְׁכָּב. [6] לָמַדְנוּ עוֹנֶשׁ בֵּין לַשּׁוֹכֵב בֵּין לַנִּשְׁכָּב, [7] אַזְהָרָה מִנַּיִין? [8] תַּלְמוּד לוֹמַר: ׳וּבְכָל בְּהֵמָה לֹא תִתֵּן שְׁכָבְתְּךָ לְטָמְאָה בָהּ׳. [9] לָמַדְנוּ אַזְהָרָה לַשּׁוֹכֵב, [10] לַנִּשְׁכָּב מִנַּיִין? [11] תַּלְמוּד לוֹמַר: ״לֹא יִהְיֶה קָדֵשׁ מִבְּנֵי יִשְׂרָאֵל״, [12] וְאוֹמֵר: ״וְגַם קָדֵשׁ הָיָה בָאָרֶץ וגו׳״, [13] דִּבְרֵי רַבִּי יִשְׁמָעֵאל. [14] רַבִּי עֲקִיבָא אוֹמֵר: אֵינוֹ צָרִיךְ. [15] הֲרֵי הוּא אוֹמֵר: ׳לֹא תִתֵּן שְׁכָבְתְּךָ׳ — [16] ׳לֹא תִתֵּן שְׁכִיבָתְךָ׳״.

LITERAL TRANSLATION

[1] Just as there — by stoning, so too here — by stoning. [2] We have learned the punishment for someone who coupled [with an animal]. [3] From where the punishment for someone who allowed himself to be coupled [with an animal]? [4] The verse states: 'Whoever couples with a beast shall surely be put to death.' [5] If it is not relevant to someone who coupled [with an animal], refer it to someone who allowed himself to be coupled [with an animal]. [6] We have learned the punishment both for someone who coupled [with an animal] and someone who allowed himself to be coupled [with an animal]. [7] From where the warning? [8] The verse states: 'Neither shall you lie with any beast to defile yourself with it.' [9] We have learned the warning for someone who couples [with an animal]. [10] From where the warning for someone who allows himself to be coupled [with an animal]? [11] The verse states: 'Nor shall there be a male prostitute of the sons of Israel.' [12] And it states: 'And there was also prostitution in the land, etc.". [13] [These are] the words of Rabbi Yishmael. [14] Rabbi Akiva says: There is no need. [15] Surely it states: 'Neither shall you lie' — [16] neither shall you give your lying.'"

RASHI

לנשכב מניין — זכר שנרבע לבהמה. **אזהרה מניין** — בשוכב בהדיא כתיב "ובכל בהמה לא תתן שכבתך", אבל נשכב בזכר לא כתיב. **כתועבות הגוים** — האי נמי מתועבותיהם הוא, דכתיב בפרשת עריות (ויקרא יח) "כי את כל התועבות האלה עשו אנשי הארץ".

NOTES

תְּנֵיהוּ עִנְיָן לַנִּשְׁכָּב **Refer it to someone who allowed himself to be coupled.** According to this, the word שׁוֹכֵב refers not to the act of copulation, but to mating, as if the verse said: Whoever mates with a beast shall surely be put to death, whether he perpetrated the act of bestiality or he allowed himself to be the subject of bestiality (*Ḥayyim Shenayim Yeshalem*).

TRANSLATION AND COMMENTARY

הַבָּא עַל הַזָּכוּר [1]The Gemara draws certain conclusions from what was stated above: If **someone** unwittingly **perpetrated sodomy upon a man, and** also **allowed himself to be sodomized by a man.** [2]**Rabbi Abbahu said** that the law is as follows: **According to Rabbi Yishmael,** the offender **is liable for two sin-offerings,** [3]**one** sin-offering **for** violating the prohibition of **"You shall not lie** with a man in the manner of a woman," [4]**and a second** sin-offering **for** violating the prohibition of **"Nor shall there be a male prostitute** of the sons of Israel." These are two separate prohibitions derived from two different verses, and so a person who violated the two prohibitions is liable for two sin-offerings. [5]**According to Rabbi Akiva,** the offender **is only liable for one sin-offering.** [6]**"You shall not lie** with a man in the manner of a woman" **and** [7]**"You shall not allow sodomy** with a man in the manner of a woman" **are** two different readings of **one** and the same verse, and therefore a single prohibition obligating a single sin-offering.

הַבָּא עַל הַבְּהֵמָה [8]The Gemara continues: Similarly, if **someone** unwittingly **coupled with an animal, and** also **allowed an animal to couple with him,** [9]**Rabbi Abbahu said** that the law is as follows: **According to Rabbi Yishmael,** the offender **is liable for two sin-offerings,** [10]**one** sin-offering **for** violating the prohibition of **"Neither shall you lie** with any beast to defile yourself with it," [11]**and a second** sin-offering **for** violating the prohibition of **"Nor shall there be a male prostitute** of the sons of Israel." These are two separate prohibitions derived from two different verses, and so a person who violated the two prohibitions is liable for two sin-offerings. [12]**According to Rabbi Akiva,** the offender **is only liable for one sin-offering.** [13]"Neither **shall you lie**" **and** "Neither shall you give **your lying**" **are** two different readings of **one** and the same verse, and therefore a single prohibition obligating a single sin-offering.

[1]הַבָּא עַל הַזָּכוּר, וְהֵבִיא עָלָיו זָכָר, [2]אָמַר רַבִּי אַבָּהוּ: לְדִבְרֵי רַבִּי יִשְׁמָעֵאל חַיָּיב שְׁתַּיִם, [3]חֲדָא מִ״לֹא תִשְׁכַּב״, [4]וַחֲדָא מִ״לֹא יִהְיֶה קָדֵשׁ״. [5]לְדִבְרֵי רַבִּי עֲקִיבָא — אֵינוֹ חַיָּיב אֶלָּא אַחַת. [6]״לֹא תִשְׁכַּב״ [7]״לֹא תִשָּׁכֵב״ חֲדָא הִיא.

[8]הַבָּא עַל הַבְּהֵמָה וְהֵבִיא בְּהֵמָה עָלָיו, [9]אָמַר רַבִּי אַבָּהוּ: לְדִבְרֵי רַבִּי יִשְׁמָעֵאל חַיָּיב שְׁתַּיִם: [10]חֲדָא מִ״לֹא תִתֵּן שְׁכָבְתְּךָ״, [11]וַחֲדָא מִ״לֹא יִהְיֶה קָדֵשׁ״. [12]לְדִבְרֵי רַבִּי עֲקִיבָא אֵינוֹ חַיָּיב אֶלָּא אַחַת, [13]״שְׁכָבְתְּךָ״ ״וּשְׁכִיבָתְךָ״ חֲדָא הִיא.

LITERAL TRANSLATION

[1]A man who perpetrated sodomy upon a man, and allowed himself to be sodomized by a man — [2]Rabbi Abbahu said: According to the words of Rabbi Yishmael, he is liable for two [sin-offerings], [3]one for "You shall not lie," [4]and one for "Nor shall there be a male prostitute." [5]According to the words of Rabbi Akiva, he is only liable for one sin-offering. [6]"You shall not lie" [and] [7]"You shall not be sodomized" are one.

[8]A man who coupled with an animal, and allowed himself to be coupled with an animal — [9]Rabbi Abbahu said: According to the words of Rabbi Yishmael, he is liable for two [sin-offerings], [10]one for "Neither shall you lie," [11]and one for "Nor shall there be a male prostitute." [12]According to the words of Rabbi Akiva, he is only liable for one [sin-offering]. [13]"You lying" [and] "Your being kin with" are one.

RASHI

הבא על הזכור והביא זכר עליו — בהעלם אחת. **חייב שתים** — דשני לאוין הם, דמתרי קראי אתו, לפיכך חלוק חטאות ביניהם, והביא זכר עליו גרסינן, ולא גרסינן זכור, דלא מקרי זכור אלא נקב המשכב. **לדברי רבי עקיבא אינו חייב אלא אחת** — דכיון דמחד קרא נפקי אין חלוק חטאות ביניהם.

NOTES

הַבָּא עַל הַזָּכוּר וְהֵבִיא עָלָיו זָכָר **A man who perpetrated sodomy upon a man, and allowed himself to be the subject of sodomy with a man.** According to some Rishonim, we are dealing here with a case where someone unwittingly perpetrated sodomy upon a certain man, and also allowed himself to be the subject of sodomy with some

HALAKHAH

הַבָּא עַל הַזָּכוּר וְהֵבִיא עָלָיו זָכָר **Someone who perpetrated sodomy upon a man, and allowed himself to be the object of sodomy with a man.** "If a man unwittingly perpetrated sodomy upon another man, and also allowed himself to be the object of sodomy with another man, all in a single "period of unawareness" (meaning that he committed the second offense before realizing that he had sinned the first time), he is only liable for a single sin-offering," following Rabbi Akiva. (*Rambam, Sefer Korbanot, Hilkhot Shegagot* 4:1.)

הַבָּא עַל הַבְּהֵמָה וְהֵבִיא בְּהֵמָה עָלָיו **Someone who coupled with an animal, and allowed himself to be coupled with an animal.** "If someone unwittingly coupled with an animal, and also allowed himself to be coupled with by an

SAGES

רַבִּי אַבָּהוּ **Rabbi Abbahu.** A Palestinian Amora of the third generation. See *Sanhedrin,* Part I, pp. 13-14.

[1]אַבַּיֵי אָמַר: אֲפִילּוּ לְדִבְרֵי רַבִּי יִשְׁמָעֵאל נַמִי אֵינוֹ חַיָּיב אֶלָּא אַחַת, [2]דְּכִי כְּתִיב: ״לֹא יִהְיֶה קָדֵשׁ״, בְּגַבְרֵי כְּתִיב.
[3]אֶלָּא לְרַבִּי יִשְׁמָעֵאל אַזְהָרָה לַנִּשְׁכָּב מְנָא לֵיהּ? [4]נָפְקָא לֵיהּ מִ״כָּל שֹׁכֵב עִם בְּהֵמָה מוֹת יוּמָת״. [5]אִם אֵינוֹ עִנְיָן לַשּׁוֹכֵב, [6]תְּנֵיהוּ עִנְיָן לַנִּשְׁכָּב. [7]וְאַפְּקֵיהּ רַחֲמָנָא לַנִּשְׁכָּב בִּלְשׁוֹן שׁוֹכֵב, [8]מַה שּׁוֹכֵב — [9]עָנַשׁ וְהִזְהִיר, [10]אַף נִשְׁכָּב — עָנַשׁ וְהִזְהִיר.
[11]הַנִּרְבָּע לַזָּכָר וְהַנִּרְבָּע לַבְּהֵמָה, [12]אָמַר רַבִּי אַבָּהוּ: לְדִבְרֵי רַבִּי עֲקִיבָא — חַיָּיב שְׁתַּיִם,

LITERAL TRANSLATION

[1]Abaye said: Even according to the words of Rabbi Yishmael, he is only liable for one, [2]for when it was written: "Nor shall there be a male prostitute," it was written about men.

[3]Then according to Rabbi Yishmael, from where does he have a warning for someone who allows himself to be coupled [with an animal]? [4]He learns it from "Whoever couples with a beast shall surely be put to death." [5]If it is not relevant to someone who coupled [with an animal], [6]refer it to someone who allowed himself to be coupled [with an animal]. [7]And the Torah (lit., "the Merciful") referred to someone who allowed himself to be coupled in terms of someone who coupled [with an animal]. [8]Just as [regarding] someone who coupled [with an animal], [9]it punished and warned, [10]so too [regarding] someone who allowed himself to be coupled, it punished and warned.

[11]Someone who was the object of sodomy with a man and the object of bestiality with an animal — [12]Rabbi Abbahu said: According to the words of Rabbi Akiva, he is liable for two [sin-offerings],

TRANSLATION AND COMMENTARY

אַבַּיֵי אָמַר [1]**Abaye** disagreed with Rabbi Abbahu, and **said: Even according to Rabbi Yishmael,** someone who unwittingly coupled with an animal and also allowed an animal to couple with him **is only liable for one** sin-offering, for violating the prohibition of "Neither shall you lie with any beast to defile yourself with it." [2]He is not liable for a second sin-offering for his having violated the prohibition of **"Nor shall there be a male prostitute** of the sons of Israel," **for when the Torah stated** that prohibition, **it was referring to** homosexual intercourse with a **man,** and not to bestiality with an animal.

אֶלָּא [3]The Gemara asks: If the verse, "Nor shall there be a male prostitute of the sons of Israel," refers only to homosexual intercourse, and not to bestiality, **then according to Rabbi Yishmael, where is the warning for someone who allows himself to be coupled with an animal?** [4]The Gemara explains: **He learns this from** the verse (Exodus 22:18): **"Whoever couples with a beast shall surely be put to death."** [5]**Since** that verse **is not needed for a man who coupled with an animal,** for his punishment is already stated elsewhere, [6]it is legitimate to **refer** the verse **to a man who allowed an animal to couple with him.** [7]Thus, we see that **the Torah refers to someone who allowed an animal to couple with him in terms of someone who coupled with an animal.** [8]This teaches us that **just as regarding someone who coupled with an animal,** [9]the Torah **stated the punishment** that is to be imposed upon him, **and** also issued **a warning** that the act is forbidden, [10]**so too regarding someone who allowed an himself to be coupled with him,** the Torah **stated the punishment** that is to be imposed upon him, **and** also issued **a warning** that the act is forbidden.

הַנִּרְבָּע לַזָּכָר [11]The Gemara continues: If **someone was** the unwitting **subject of sodomy with** another **man, and also** the unwitting **subject of bestiality with an animal,** [12]**Rabbi Abbahu said** that the law is as follows: **According to Rabbi Akiva,** the offender **is liable for two sin-offerings,**

RASHI

דכי כתיב לא יהיה קדש — בזנות דגברי כתיב, אבל לבהמה אין זנות — כדילפינן ביבמות (נט,ב) מ״אתנן זונה ומחיר כלב״ ולא שייך בה לשון קדשות, והאי דתנייה תנא לעיל ״לא יהיה קדש״ — לרווחא דמילתא, אבל עיקר אזהרה לאו מהתם. אלא מנא לן נפקא ליה מכל שוכב — דאפיקתיה לעונש לנשכב בלשון שוכב, נילפיה משוכב לאזהרה, הלכך אזהרה לשוכב ונשכב מלאו ד״לא תתן שכבתך״ הוא, חד במשמעותיה וחד מדאיתקש לחבריה, וכיון דחד לאו לתרוייהו — אין חלוק חטאות ביניהם.

NOTES

other man. Others argue that in such a case all agree that he is liable for two sin-offerings, even if perpetrating sodomy and being the subject of sodomy are regarded as a single prohibition, and even if the two transgressions were committed "within the same period of unawareness," for each transgression was committed with a different person. Rather, here someone unwittingly perpetrated sodomy upon a certain man, and also allowed himself to be the subject of sodomy with that same man (see *Meiri*).

HALAKHAH

animal, all in a single 'period of unawareness,' he is only liable for a single sin-offering," following Rabbi Akiva. (*Rambam, Sefer Korbanot, Hilkhot Shegagot* 4:1.)

[1]חֲדָא מִ״לֹּא תִשְׁכַּב״ [2]וַחֲדָא מִ״לֹּא תִתֵּן שְׁכָבְתְּךָ״, [3]לְדִבְרֵי רַבִּי יִשְׁמָעֵאל, אֵינוֹ חַיָּיב אֶלָּא אַחַת, [4]אִידִי וְאִידִי ״לֹא יִהְיֶה קָדֵשׁ״ הוּא.

[5]אַבַּיֵי אָמַר: אֲפִילּוּ לְדִבְרֵי רַבִּי יִשְׁמָעֵאל נַמִּי חַיָּיב שְׁתַּיִם, [6]דִּכְתִיב: ״כָּל שֹׁכֵב עִם בְּהֵמָה מוֹת יוּמָת״. [7]אִם אֵינוֹ עִנְיָן לַשּׁוֹכֵב תְּנֵיהוּ עִנְיָן לַנִּשְׁכָּב, [8]וְאַפְּקֵיהּ רַחֲמָנָא לַנִּשְׁכָּב בִּלְשׁוֹן שׁוֹכֵב, [9]מַה שׁוֹכֵב עָנַשׁ וְהִזְהִיר — [10]אַף נִשְׁכָּב עָנַשׁ וְהִזְהִיר.

[11]אֲבָל הַבָּא עַל הַזָּכוּר וְהֵבִיא זָכָר עָלָיו, [12]הַבָּא עַל הַבְּהֵמָה וְהֵבִיא בְּהֵמָה עָלָיו, [13]בֵּין לְרַבִּי אַבָּהוּ בֵּין לְאַבַּיֵי — [14]לְרַבִּי יִשְׁמָעֵאל חַיָּיב שָׁלֹשׁ,

LITERAL TRANSLATION

[1]one for "You shall not lie" [2]and one for "Neither shall give your lying." [3]According to the words of Rabbi Yishmael, he is only liable for one [sin-offering]. [4]This and that — "Nor shall there be a male prostitute."

[5]Abaye said: Even according to the words of Rabbi Yishmael, he is liable for two sin-offerings, [6]for it is written: "Whoever couples with a beast shall surely be put to death." [7]If it is not relevant to someone who coupled [with an animal], refer it to someone who allowed himself to be coupled [with an animal]. [8]And the Torah referred to someone who allowed himself to be coupled [with an animal] in terms of someone who coupled. [9]Just as it punished and warned [regarding] someone who coupled [with an animal], [10]so too [regarding] someone who allowed himself to be coupled [with an animal], it punished and warned.

[11]But a man who perpetrated sodomy upon a man, and allowed himself to be sodomized by a man, [12]and coupled with an animal, and allowed himself to be coupled with an animal, [13]both according to Rabbi Abbahu and according to Abaye — [14]according to Rabbi Yishmael, he is liable for three [sin-offerings];

TRANSLATION AND COMMENTARY

[1]**one** sin-offering **for** his having violated the prohibition of **"You shall not lie** with a man in the manner of a woman," which, according to Rabbi Akiva, can also be read as "You shall not submit to sodomy with a man in the manner of a woman," [2]**and a second** sin-offering **for** violating the prohibition of **"Neither shall you lie** with any beast to defile yourself with it," which, according to Rabbi Akiva, can also be read as "Neither shall you give your lying to any beast." [3]**According to Rabbi Yishmael,** the offender **is only liable for one sin-offering,** [4]for he maintains that **both** sodomized by a man **and** having an animal couple with a man are forbidden by the same prohibition, **"Nor shall there be a male prostitute** of the sons of Israel."

אַבַּיֵי [5]**Abaye** disagreed with Rabbi Abbahu, and **said: Even according to Rabbi Yishmael,** someone who was the unwitting object of sodomy and also the unwitting object of bestiality **is liable for two sin-offerings,** one sin-offering for violating the prohibition of "Nor shall there be a male prostitute of the sons of Israel" by being the object of sodomy, and a second sin-offering for being the object of bestiality, and thus violating the prohibition of "Neither shall you lie with any beast to defile yourself with it." [6]**For the verse states** (Exodus 22:18): **"Whoever couples with a beast shall surely be put to death."** [7]**Since** that verse **is not relevant to a man who coupled with an animal,** for his punishment is already stated elsewhere, it is legitimate to **refer** the verse **to someone who allowed an animal to couple with him.** [8]Thus, we see that **the Torah refers to someone who allowed an animal to couple with him in terms of someone who coupled with an animal.** [9]This teaches us that **just as regarding a man who coupled with an animal,** the Torah **stated the punishment** that is to be imposed upon him, **and** also issued **a warning** that the act is forbidden, [10]**so too regarding a man who allowed himself to be coupled with an animal couple,** the Torah **stated the punishment** that is to be imposed upon him, **and** also issued **a warning** that the act is forbidden.

אֲבָל [11]The Gemara concludes this discussion with a final case: **But** if **someone** unwittingly **perpetrated sodomy upon a man, and** also **allowed himself to be sodomized by a man,** [12]**and** also **coupled with an animal,** and also **an animal to couple with him,** [13]**both according to Rabbi Abbahu and according to Abaye,** the law is as follows: [14]**According to Rabbi Yishmael,** the offender **is liable for three sin-offerings.** According to Rabbi

RASHI

אביי אמר אף לדברי רבי ישמעאל חייב שתים — דכי כתיב ״לא יהיה קדש״ בגברי הוא דכתיב, כדאמרן לעיל. ונרבע לבהמה לאו מיניה יליף אלא מדאפקיה בלשון שוכב, ואיכא לאו ד״לא תתן שכבתך״. **בין לרבי אבהו בין לאביי לרבי ישמעאל חייב שלש** — לרבי אבהו בא על הזכור מ״לא תשכב״, הביא זכר עליו מ״לא יהיה קדש״, בא על הבהמה מ״לא תתן שכבתך״. אבל משום נרבע לבהמה לא מחייב בהדיא הביא זכר עליו דמחד קרא נפקי. ולאביי, בא על הזכור והביאו עליו תרי נינהו, ״ואת זכר לא תשכב״ ו״לא יהיה קדש״. בא על הבהמה והביאה עליו מ״לא תתן שכבתך״, אבל משום נרבע לבהמה לא מחייב, דכיון דחזינן נרבע מהאי קרא ״וכל שוכב עם בהמה״, מדאפקיה רחמנא בלשון שוכב לא מחייב אלא אחת, כיון שאינן חלוקין בלאוין.

TRANSLATION AND COMMENTARY

Abbahu, he is liable for one sin-offering for sodomy with a man, thus violating the prohibition of "You shall not lie with a man in the manner of a woman"; and he is liable for a second sin-offering, for allowing a man to sodomize him, thus violating the prohibition of "Nor shall there be a male prostitute"; and he is liable for a third sin-offering, for coupling with an animal, thus violating the prohibition of "Neither shall you lie with any beast to defile it." But he is not liable for a fourth sin-offering, for allowing an animal to couple with him, for that is also forbidden by the prohibition, "Nor shall there be a male prostitute." According to Abaye, he is liable for the same three offenses, and for having violated the same three prohibitions. He is not liable for a fourth sin-offering, for allowing an animal to couple with him, for that is also forbidden by the prohibition, "Neither shall you lie with any beast to defile it." [1]**According to Rabbi Akiva,** the offender **is liable for two sin-offerings,** one sin-offering for sodomy with a man and being sodomized by a man, thus violating the prohibition of "You shall not lie with a man in the manner of a woman; and a second sin-offering for coupling with an animal, and allowing an animal to couple with him, thus violating the prohibition of "Neither shall you lie with any beast to defile it."

תָּנוּ רַבָּנַן [2]**Our Rabbis taught** the following Baraita: "Regarding the **male** object of homosexual intercourse, **a minor is not treated like an adult.** Even though we learn from the words, 'And if a man lies with a man,' that an adult who committed sodomy is liable to the death penalty, whether he did so with an adult or a minor, this only means that the object of the act of sodomy need not be an adult, but he must still have passed some minimum age (as will be explained below). [3]But regarding the **animal** who is the object of bestiality, **a young animal is treated like a fully-grown one,** so that the person who perpetrated the act of bestiality is always liable for the death penalty."

מַאי [4]The Gemara asks: **What** did the Baraita mean when it said that regarding the male partner in homosexual intercourse, **"a minor is not treated like an adult"?** [5]The Amoraim disagree about the matter: **Rav said:** This means that homosexual **intercourse with a child less than nine years old is not treated like** homosexual intercourse **with a child over nine years old,** so that a man who engaged in homosexual intercourse with a child under nine years old is not liable for punishment. [6]**Shmuel** disagreed and **said:** This means that homosexual **intercourse with a child less than three years old is not treated like** homosexual intercourse **with a child over three years old** so that a man who had homosexual intercourse with a child less than three years old is not liable for punishment.

[1]לְרַבִּי עֲקִיבָא חַיָּיב שְׁתַּיִם. [2]תָּנוּ רַבָּנַן: זָכוּר לֹא עָשׂוּ בּוֹ קָטָן כְּגָדוֹל, [3]בְּהֵמָה עָשׂוּ בָּהּ קְטַנָּה כִּגְדוֹלָה. [4]מַאי "לֹא עָשׂוּ בּוֹ קָטָן כְּגָדוֹל"? [5]אָמַר רַב: לֹא עָשׂוּ בִּיאַת פָּחוֹת מִבֶּן תֵּשַׁע שָׁנִים כְּבֶן תֵּשַׁע שָׁנִים. [6]וּשְׁמוּאֵל אָמַר: לֹא עָשׂוּ בִּיאַת פָּחוֹת מִבֶּן שָׁלֹשׁ שָׁנִים כְּבֵן שָׁלֹשׁ שָׁנִים.

LITERAL TRANSLATION

[1]according to Rabbi Akiva, he is liable for two [sin-offerings].

[2]Our Rabbis taught: "A man — they did not make a minor like an adult. [3]An animal — they made a young animal like a fully-grown one."

[4]What is [the meaning of] "they did not make a minor like an adult"? [5]Rav said: They did not make intercourse with [a child] less than nine years old like [that with a child] nine years old. [6]And Shmuel said: They did not make intercourse with [a child] less than three years old like [that with a child] three years old.

RASHI

זכור לא עשה בו קטן בגדול – בנשכב מיירי, והכי קאמר: ליחייב שוכבו כדאמרינן לעיל "אשר ישכב את זכר" – בין גדול בין קטן, ואשמעינן הכא דלאו בכל קטנים קאמר, אלא דלא בעינן בני עונשין לחייב שוכבו. אבל גדול קאת בעינן, ולקמן פריך: מאי היא? **בהמה עשה בה גדולה בקטנה** – לחייב את הרובעה. **מאי לא עשו בו קטן בגדול** – איזהו קטן פטור שוכבו, ואיזהו דקרית ליה גדול לחייב שוכבו? דהא פשיטא לן דלאו גדול ממש ובר עונשין בעי, דהא "את זכר" כתיב, בין גדול בין קטן. **לא עשו בו ביאת פחות מבן תשע וכו'** – אם בא על פחות מבן תשע – פטור. ולקמן מפרש טעמא.

HALAKHAH

בְּהֵמָה — עָשׂוּ בָּהּ קְטַנָּה כִּגְדוֹלָה **An animal — they made a young animal like a fully-grown one.** "A person who engaged in bestiality is liable to death by stoning, whether the animal was a day old or fully grown." (*Rambam, Sefer Kedushah, Hilkhot Issurei Bi'ah* 1:16.)

לֹא עָשׂוּ בִּיאַת פָּחוֹת מִבֶּן שָׁלֹשׁ שָׁנִים **They did not make the intercourse with a child less than nine years old.** "If an adult engaged in intercourse with a child under the age of nine, they are both exempt, but the adult should be given Rabbinically-ordained lashes." (*Rambam, Sefer Kedushah, Hilkhot Issurei Bi'ah* 1:14.)

[1]בְּמַאי קָמִיפַּלְגִי? [2]רַב סָבַר: כָּל דְּאִיתֵיהּ בְּשׁוֹכֵב אִיתֵיהּ בְּנִשְׁכָּב, [3]וְכָל דְּלֵיתֵיהּ בְּשׁוֹכֵב לֵיתֵיהּ בְּנִשְׁכָּב. [4]וּשְׁמוּאֵל סָבַר: ״מִשְׁכְּבֵי אִשָּׁה״ כְּתִיב.

[5]תַּנְיָא כְּוָותֵיהּ דְּרַב: זָכָר בֶּן תֵּשַׁע שָׁנִים וְיוֹם אֶחָד. [55A] [6]הַבָּא עַל הַבְּהֵמָה, בֵּין כְּדַרְכָּהּ בֵּין שֶׁלֹּא כְּדַרְכָּהּ [7]וְהָאִשָּׁה הַמְּבִיאָה אֶת הַבְּהֵמָה עָלֶיהָ, בֵּין כְּדַרְכָּהּ בֵּין שֶׁלֹּא כְּדַרְכָּהּ — חַיָּיב״.

[8]דָּרַשׁ רַב נַחְמָן בַּר רַב חִסְדָּא: בְּאִשָּׁה שְׁנֵי מִשְׁכָּבוֹת. [9]וּבִבְהֵמָה מִשְׁכָּב אֶחָד.

LITERAL TRANSLATION

[1]About what do they disagree? [2]Rav maintains: Whoever can perpetrate sodomy can be sodomized. [3]And whoever cannot perpetrate sodomy cannot be sodomized. [4]And Shmuel maintains: It is written: "As one lies with a woman."

[5]It was taught in accordance with Rav: "A male, nine years and one day old. [55A] [6]A man who had intercourse with an animal, whether in a natural manner or in an unnatural manner, [7]or a woman who allowed herself to be coupled with an animal, whether in a natural manner or in an unnatural manner, is liable."

[8]Rav Naḥman bar Rav Ḥisda expounded: Regarding a woman, two manners of lying; [9]and regarding an animal, one manner of lying.

TRANSLATION AND COMMENTARY

בְּמַאי קָמִיפַּלְגִי [1]The Gemara asks: **About what** point **do** Rav and Shmuel **disagree?** [2]**Rav maintains** that **whoever can perpetrate sodomy can** also **be the object of sodomy.** [3]**And whoever cannot perpetrate sodomy can** also **not be the object of sodomy.** If a boy under the age of nine perpetrated sodomy upon an adult, the adult is not liable for punishment, for the intercourse of a boy under nine years of age is not legally an act of intercourse. Since a child less than nine years old cannot commit sodomy, he can also not be the object of sodomy. [4]**And Shmuel maintains** that since **the verse states:** "And if a man lies with a man, **as one lies with a woman,**" we learn that the law regarding the male object of sodomy is like that of a woman. Intercourse with a girl three years of age is legally considered to be intercourse, so that if someone to whom she is forbidden had intercourse with her, he is liable for punishment. Hence intercourse with a boy three years of age should be legally considered an act of intercourse, and if an adult had homosexual intercourse with him, he should be liable for sodomy.

תַּנְיָא כְּוָותֵיהּ [5]A Baraita **was taught in accordance with** the position of **Rav:** "If a man engaged in homosexual intercourse with another **male nine years and one day old,** he is liable. [55A] [6]If **a man engaged in** sexual **intercourse with an animal, whether** he penetrated the animal **in a natural manner,** by way of vaginal intercourse, **or in an unnatural manner,** by way of anal intercourse, [7]or if **a woman allowed an animal** to couple with her, **whether in a natural manner or in an unnatural manner,** he or she **is liable.**" This Baraita supports Rav, for it teaches that if a man engaged in homosexual intercourse with a child under the age of nine, he is exempt from liability.

דָּרַשׁ [8]**Rav Naḥman bar Rav Ḥisda expounded: Regarding a woman** who allowed an animal to couple with her, she is liable for **two manners of lying:** For natural (vaginal) intercourse, and for unnatural (anal) intercourse. [9]**But regarding** a man who coupled with **an animal,** he is only liable for **one manner of lying,** for natural (vaginal) intercourse. The verse (Leviticus. 20:13): "And if a man lies with a man, as one lies with a woman [מִשְׁכְּבֵי אִשָּׁה, literally, 'layings with a woman']," teaches that there are two manners of lying with a woman. Rav Naḥman bar Rav Ḥisda understands that there are also two manners in which an animal lies with a woman. But there is no similar verse regarding an animal, and so a man who engaged in bestiality is only liable for one manner of lying, natural (vaginal) intercourse.

RASHI

רב סבר — הואיל ואזהרת נשכב משוכב אתא, כדרבי עקיבא, כל דליתיה בשוכב — ליתיה בנשכב, ושוכב פחות מבן תשע הבא על הזכור גדול וכר עונשין — אינו מחייבו מיתה, דהא לאו ביאה היא, כדאמרינן במסכת נדה (מה,א) ולקמן מייתי לה בשמעתין בן תשע שנים ויום אחד הבא על יבמתו וכו׳, הלכך, נשכב פחות מבן תשע נמי אינו מחייב את שוכבו. **ושמואל סבר משכבי אשה כתיב** — בזכר. ואשה בת שלש שנים ראויה לביאה, ומחייב שוכבה מיתה, וזכר נשכב נמי לא שנא. **תניא נמי הכי וכו׳** — בן תשע שנים ויום אחד הוי זכור. הא פחות מכן — לא הוי זכור. ובנשכב קאמר, דאילו בשוכב לא קאמר זכו., ועוד: אי בשוכב קאמר ולחייב את הנשכב גדול קאמר, מאי שנא זכור דנקט? כל עריות נמי לא ניחייבו על ידי ביאת קטן פחות מבן תשע. **הבא על הבהמה בין כדרכה בין שלא כדרכה** — מקרי רובע, ומילי מילי קתני לה. **באשה שני משכבות** — כדכתיב בה ״משכבי״. **ובהמה משכב אחד** — דהא לא כתיב בה ״משכבי״. ולענין רביעה קאמר דהאשה הנרבעת לבהמה מתחייב אף שלא כדרכה, כדרך שהיא מתחייבת בבעילת אדם, דאילו בבעילת אדם לא איצטריך לרב נחמן למימר דקראי טובא ומתניתין איכא, ורב פפא נמי לא מלי למימר איפכא.

[1]מַתְקִיף לָהּ רַב פַּפָּא: [2]אַדְּרַבָּה, אִשָּׁה דְּאוֹרְחָהּ הִיא, [3]אַמִּשְׁכָּב — מִיחַיָּיב, [4]אַמִּידַּעַם אַחֲרִינָא — לָא מִיחַיָּיב. [5]בְּהֵמָה דְּלָאו אוֹרְחָא הִיא — לִחַיֵּיב עֲלָהּ עַל כָּל נֶקֶב וָנֶקֶב.

[6]תַּנְיָא (דְּלָא כְּתַרְוַיְיהוּ): [7]״זָכָר בֶּן תֵּשַׁע שָׁנִים וְיוֹם אֶחָד, [8]הַבָּא עַל הַבְּהֵמָה, בֵּין כְּדַרְכָּהּ בֵּין שֶׁלֹּא כְּדַרְכָּהּ, [9]וְהָאִשָּׁה הַמְּבִיאָה אֶת הַבְּהֵמָה עָלֶיהָ בֵּין כְּדַרְכָּהּ בֵּין שֶׁלֹּא כְּדַרְכָּהּ — חַיָּיב״.

[10]אָמַר לֵיהּ רָבִינָא לְרָבָא: הַמְעָרֶה בְּזָכוּר מַהוּ? [11]הַמְעָרֶה בְּזָכוּר? [12]״מִשְׁכְּבֵי אִשָּׁה״ כְּתִיב בֵּיהּ!

LITERAL TRANSLATION

[1]Rav Pappa strongly objected: [2]On the contrary, a woman with whom it is natural, [3]for lying she is liable, [4]for something else, she is not liable. [5]An animal, with which it is unnatural, let him be liable for each and every orifice.

[6]It was taught not in accordance with either of them: [7]"A male nine years and one day old, [8]A man who had intercourse with an animal, whether in a natural manner or in an unnatural manner, [9]or a woman who allowed herself to be coupled with an animal, whether in a natural manner or in an unnatural manner, is liable."

[10]Ravina said to Rava: Someone who engages in the first stage of sexual intercourse with a male, what [is the law]? [11]Someone who engages in the first stage of sexual intercourse with a male? [12]It is written: "As one lies with a woman"!

TRANSLATION AND COMMENTARY

מַתְקִיף לָהּ [1]**Rav Pappa strongly objected** to Rav Nahman bar Rav Ḥisda's position: [2]**On the contrary,** it stands to reason that **a woman, with whom it is natural** for a man to engage in sexual intercourse, [3]**should be liable for lying** with an animal in the "natural" manner, [4]but **for** lying with an animal in **some other manner, she should not be liable.** [5]But as for a man's relations with **an animal, with which it is unnatural** for him to engage in sexual intercourse of any kind, a man **should be liable for** sexual intercourse by way of **any orifice,** whether in a "natural" manner or in an "unnatural" manner.

תַּנְיָא [6]The Gemara notes that the Baraita which **was taught** above is **not in accordance with either** view, neither the position of Rav Naḥman bar Rav Ḥisda nor with that of Rav Pappa: [7]"If a man engaged in homosexual intercourse with another **male nine years and one day old,** he is liable. [8]If **a man engaged in** sexual **intercourse with an animal, whether** he penetrated the animal **in a natural manner,** by way of vaginal intercourse, **or in an unnatural manner,** by way of anal intercourse, [9]**or** if **a woman allowed** an animal **to couple with** her, **whether in a natural manner or in an unnatural manner,** he or she **is liable."** The Baraita implies that no distinction is made between a woman who allows an animal to couple with her, and a man who couples with an animal, for in both cases the offending party is liable, whether intercourse took place in a natural manner or in an unnatural manner.

אָמַר לֵיהּ [10]**Ravina asked Rava: What is the law** regarding **a man who engaged in the first stage of sexual intercourse with** another man? Regarding most forbidden sexual relations, no differentiation is made between the first stage of sexual intercourse and the completion of the sexual act, punishment being imposed even if the offending parties only reached the first stage of intercourse and did not complete the act. (The precise definition of "the first stage of sexual intercourse" is, however, the subject of Talmudic debate. According to one opinion, physical contact between the two parties' sexual organs suffices. According to another opinion, a measure of penetration is required.) What is the law on this matter regarding homosexual intercourse?

הַמְעָרֶה בְּזָכוּר [11]The Gemara asks in astonishment: Can there be any question regarding **a man who engaged in the first stage of sexual intercourse with** another **man?** [12]Surely **the verse states** (Leviticus 20:13): "And if a man lies with a man, **as one lies with a woman,"** which teaches that any act that constitutes

RASHI

מתקיף לה רב פפא אדרבה אשה דאורחא — בבעילה, אמידעם דאורחא היא מחייב אמידעם אחרינא, דהיינו שלא כדרכה, לא דאין אורחה, דאין הנאתה מרובה. **בהמה דלאו אורחא** — לבא עליה, ביאת שניהם שוין. **(תניא דלא כתרווייהו). המערה** — שלא גמר ביאתו, איכא למאן דאמר (יבמות נה,ב) זו נשיקת אבר על הנקב, ואיכא למאן דאמר הערא זו הכנסת עטרה דהוא דבר מועט אבל יותר הוא על נשיקה, מיהו גבי עריות קיימא לן (שם) הערא כגמר ביאה, דכתיב בנדה "את מקורה הערה" וילפינן (שם ח,א) שאר עריות מנדה בהקישא דרבי יונה "כי את כל אשר יעשה מכל התועבות האל" הוקשו כולן זה לזה, הכא מאי. **משכבי אשה כתב ביה** — בזכר, ומאי קא מבעיא ליה כל דמחייב באשה מחייב נמי ביה.

HALAKHAH

הַמְעָרֶה בְּזָכוּר **Someone who engages in the first stage of sexual intercourse with a male.** "In homosexual intercourse one is liable for genital contact just as one is liable for full intercourse," following Rava. (*Rambam, Sefer Kedushah, Hilkhot Issurei Bi'ah* 1:14.)

TRANSLATION AND COMMENTARY

intercourse with a woman is punishable in the case of intercourse with a man! Thus a man who engaged in the first stage of sexual intercourse with another man should indeed be liable for homosexual intercourse.

אֶלָּא [1]**Rather,** Ravina asked Rava as follows: **What is the law** regarding **someone who engaged in the first stage of sexual intercourse with an animal?** The Torah does not say that one may not lie with an animal, "as one lies with a woman." The question therefore arises whether the first stage of sexual intercourse with an animal is a punishable action, or whether the sexual act must be completed?

אָמַר לֵיהּ [2]Rava **said to** Ravina: Liability for the first stage of sexual intercourse is learned from the verse regarding the prohibition of intercourse with a menstruating woman which states (Leviticus 20:18): "And if a man shall lie with a woman during her menstrual sickness, and shall uncover her nakedness, he has made naked [הערה] her flow." The word הערה is understood as a reference to העראה, "the first stage of sexual intercourse," teaching that the first stage of sexual intercourse is a punishable action just like the completion of the sexual act. This law is extended to all other forbidden sexual relationships by an analogy based on the verse (Leviticus 18:29): "For whoever shall commit any of these abominations," which compares all of the forbidden sexual relationships one to the other. In addition, the verse forbidding intercourse with one's aunt states (Leviticus 20:19): "And you shall not uncover the nakedness of your mothers' sister, nor of your father's sister: for he uncovers [הערה] his near kin; they shall bear their iniquity," the word הערה referring once again to the first stage of sexual intercourse. [3]Now **since** that word **is not relevant to the first stage of sexual intercourse with respect to the sister of one's father or mother — as it would have been unnecessary** for the Torah to specify that, [4]**because** we already know it from **the analogy to the first stage of sexual intercourse with a menstruating woman,** [5]it is legitimate to **refer** that word **to the first stage of sexual intercourse with an animal,** teaching that it, too, is a punishable act.

מִכְּדֵי בְּהֵמָה [6]The Gemara asks: But **surely** intercourse with **an animal is** a transgression **that is punishable,** not only by excision, but also **by judicial execution.** [7]**Why** then **is** the allusion to the prohibition regarding **the first stage of sexual intercourse with** an animal **written** in the context of a passage dealing **with** a transgression **that is** only **punishable by excision,** the prohibition against intercourse with one's aunt? [8]The Torah **should have written** the allusion to the first stage of sexual intercourse in the context of a passage dealing **with** a transgression **that is punishable by judicial execution,** [9]**and** then **we could have learned** the prohibition regarding the first stage of intercourse with an animal, a transgression **that is punishable by judicial execution,** from that other transgression **that is** also **punishable by judicial execution!**

[1]אֶלָּא: הַמְעָרֶה בִּבְהֵמָה מַהוּ? [2]אָמַר לֵיהּ: [3]אִם אֵינוֹ עִנְיָן לְהַעֲרָאָה דִּכְתִיבָא גַּבֵּי אֲחוֹת אָבִיו וַאֲחוֹת אִמּוֹ, דְּלָא צְרִיכָא, [4]דְּהָא אִיתְקַשׁ לְהַעֲרָאָה דְּנִדָּה — [5]תְּנֵיהוּ עִנְיָן לְהַעֲרָאָה דִּבְהֵמָה.

[6]מִכְּדִי בְּהֵמָה מֵחַיָּיבֵי מִיתוֹת בֵּית דִּין הִיא, [7]לָמָּה לִי דִּכְתִיב לְהַעֲרָאָה דִּידָהּ גַּבֵּי חַיָּיבֵי כְּרִיתוֹת? [8]לִכְתְּבֵיהּ גַּבֵּי חַיָּיבֵי מִיתוֹת בֵּית דִּין, [9]וְלִיגְמוֹר חַיָּיבֵי מִיתוֹת בֵּית דִּין מֵחַיָּיבֵי מִיתוֹת בֵּית דִּין?

LITERAL TRANSLATION

[1]Rather, someone who engages in the first stage of sexual intercourse with an animal, what [is the law]?

[2]He said to him: [3]If it is not relevant to the first stage of sexual intercourse which is written regarding the sister of one's father or the sister of one's mother, for it is not necessary, [4]for surely it was compared to the first stage of sexual intercourse with a menstruating woman — [5]refer it to the first stage of sexual intercourse with an animal.

[6]Surely an animal is among those who are liable for execution by the court. [7]Why is the first stage of sexual intercourse with it written with those who are liable for excision? [8]Let it write it with those who are liable for execution by the court, [9]and let him infer those who are liable for execution by the court from those who are liable for execution by the court!

RASHI

אם אינו ענין — להך העראה דכתיבא גבי אחות אמו ואחות אביו, דכתיב בהו (ויקרא כ) "כי את שארו הערה" אם אינו עניין לגופיה דהא אתיא בהקש דנדה ככל שאר עריות כדפרישית, תנהו ענין לבהמה. **למה לי למכתביה להעראה דידה גבי חייבי כריתות** — אחות אב ואחות אם אין בהם מיתה. **לכתבה גבי** — חד מעריות של חיוב מיתה.

HALAKHAH

הַמְעָרֶה בִּבְהֵמָה **Someone who engages in the first stage of sexual intercourse with an animal.** "In sexual intercourse with an animal, one is liable for genital contact just as one is liable for full intercourse," following Rava. (*Rambam, Sefer Kedushah, Hilkhot Issurei Bi'ah* 1:16.)

¹הוֹאִיל וְכוּלֵּיהּ קְרָא לִדְרָשָׁא הוּא דְּאָתֵי, ²כְּתִיבָא נַמִי מִילְּתָא דִּדְרָשָׁא.

³בְּעָא מִינֵּיהּ רַב אַחַדְבוֹי בַּר אַמִי מֵרַב שֵׁשֶׁת: הַמְעָרֶה בְּעַצְמוֹ, מַהוּ?

⁴אָמַר לֵיהּ: קְבַסְתָּן!

⁵אָמַר רַב אַשִׁי: מַאי תִּיבָּעֵי לָךְ? ⁶בְּקוֹשִׁי, לָא מַשְׁכַּחַת לָהּ. ⁷כִּי מַשְׁכַּחַת לָהּ — בִּמְשַׁמֵּשׁ מֵת. ⁸לְמַאן דְּאָמַר מְשַׁמֵּשׁ מֵת בָּעֲרָיוֹת פָּטוּר, ⁹הָכָא פָּטוּר. ¹⁰וּלְמַאן דְּאָמַר חַיָּיב, הָכָא מִיחַיַּיב תַּרְתֵּי. ¹¹מִיחַיַּיב אַשּׁוֹכֵב ¹²וּמִיחַיַּיב אַנִּשְׁכָּב.

¹³בָּעוּ מִינֵּיהּ מֵרַב שֵׁשֶׁת: נָכְרִי הַבָּא עַל הַבְּהֵמָה מַהוּ?

LITERAL TRANSLATION

[1]Since the entire verse comes for interpretation, [2][this] matter is also written for interpretation.

[3]Rav Aḥadboi bar Ammi asked Rav Sheshet: Someone who engaged in the first stage of sexual intercourse with himself, what [is the law]?

[4]He said to him: You disgust us!

[5]Rav Ashi said: What do you ask? [6]With an erection, you cannot find it. [7]Where can you find it — where he has intercourse without an erection. [8]According to the one who says [that] someone who has intercourse without an erection with a woman who is forbidden to him is exempt, [9]here he is exempt. [10]And according to the one who says he is liable, here he is liable on two [counts]. [11]He is liable for lying [12]and he is liable for being the subject of lying.

[13]They asked Rav Sheshet: [If] a non-Jew had intercourse with an animal, what [is the law]?

TRANSLATION AND COMMENTARY

הוֹאִיל [1]The Gemara answers: **Since the entire verse comes for interpretation,** [2]**this word** הערה **was also written for interpretation.** The prohibitions themselves against intercourse with one's father's sister and one's mother's sister were already recorded separately in an earlier passage (see Leviticus 18:12-13). Therefore we know that this verse was written in the Torah in order to be read closely as the basis for other judgments. Among other things, the word הערה is used to derive the law regarding the first stage of sexual intercourse with an animal, even though that law should perhaps have been written in a different context.

בְּעָא מִינֵּיהּ [3]**Rav Aḥadboi bar Ammi asked Rav Sheshet: What is the law** regarding **someone who engaged in the first stage of sexual intercourse with himself?** Is such a person liable for homosexual intercourse?

אָמַר לֵיהּ [4]Rav Sheshet **said** to Rav Aḥadboi bar Ammi: **You disgust us** with your question!

אָמַר רַב אַשִׁי [5]**Rav Ashi said: What is your question?** [6]If you are asking about a person who was engaged in his autoerotic behavior **while he had an erection, you cannot find** such a case, for it is physically impossible. [7]**Where can you find such a case — when** a person **was engaged in** his **autoerotic behavior without an erection.** And in such a case, his liability is dependent upon the Amoraic dispute regarding sexual intercourse without an erection. [8]**According to the** authority **who says that** if **someone engaged in incestuous intercourse without an erection,** he **is exempt** from liability, [9]**here** too **he is exempt** from liability. [10]**And according to the** authority **who says** that if someone engaged in incestuous intercourse without an erection, he **is liable, here he is liable on two counts.** [11]**He is liable for perpetrating** homosexual **intercourse** upon himself, [12]**and he is liable for** allowing himself to **be the object of** homosexual **intercourse** with himself.

בָּעוּ מִינֵּיהּ [13]**Rav Sheshet was asked** by his disciples the following question: **If a non-Jew engaged in** sexual **intercourse with an animal, what is the law** regarding putting the animal to death? The Gemara

RASHI

אידי דכולי קרא — דעריות, אחות אמך, ואחות אביך "כי את שארו הערה וגו'" (שם). לדרשא אתא — ביבמות בפרק "הבא על יבמתו" (נד,ב). דהא כתיבא בכל חד וחד באנפי נפשיה בפרשת עריות ב"אחרי מות", והדר כתיב בקדושים תהיו. קבסתן = צערתני, ששאלתני דבר שאי אפשר. בקושי — בקשיו של אבר. לא משכחת — שיוכל לכופו לעצמו. משמש מת — באבר מת, בלא קושי. למאן דאמר משמש מת בעריות וכו' — פלוגתא היא בשבועות בשלהי "ידיעות הטומאה" (יח,א). מחייב אשוכב ואנשכב — דתרווייהו איתנהו ביה. נכרי הבא על הבהמה מהו — שתסקל הבהמה על ידו, גבי ישראל פרשינן במתניתין תרי טעמי: לפי שבאת לאדם תקלה על ידה, ושלא תהא עוברת בשוק לאחר זמן ויאמרו וכו', דהיינו קלון, וגבי נכרי תקלה איכא דבני נח הוזהרו על העריות, לקמן בפרקין (נו,א).

NOTES

קְבַסְתָּן **You disgust us.** According to *Arukh,* this term means: You anger us. *Rabbenu Ḥananel* suggests that it means: You deceive us by posing a question which appears to be valid, but which in fact is not a real question. According

HALAKHAH

מְשַׁמֵּשׁ מֵת **Intercourse without an erection.** "If a man committed a forbidden act of sexual intercourse without an erection, he is not liable, not for excision, nor for flogging, and certainly not for judicial excision," following the opinion of Rava in tractate *Makkot.* (*Rambam, Sefer Kedushah, Hilkhot Issurei Bi'ah* 1:11; *Tur, Even HaEzer* 7).

נָכְרִי הַבָּא עַל הַבְּהֵמָה **If a non-Jew had intercourse with an animal.** "If a non-Jew had intercourse with an animal,

TRANSLATION AND COMMENTARY

explains the two sides of the question: We learned in the Mishnah that the animal with which a Jew engaged in sexual intercourse is put to death for two reasons: First, because it was a stumbling-block which had brought the person to his offense, and second, because if it continued to live, it would bring further disgrace to the executed offender, for people would be reminded of his crime every time they saw the animal. [1]Do we say that in order to put the animal to death, **it is necessary** for the animal to be **a stumbling-block, and** also to threaten the executed party with further **disgrace?** [2]**Here** then in the case of a non-Jew who engaged in sexual intercourse with an animal, the animal had served as **a stumbling-block,** for even a non-Jew is forbidden by Torah law to engage in bestiality. [3]**But there is no** concern of **disgrace,** for non-Jews are not disgraced by bestiality, since bestiality was not uncommon among them. Thus the animal should not be put to death. [4]**Or perhaps,** a single factor suffices. Since the animal is **a stumbling-block, even though there is no** concern of **disgrace,** it should indeed be put to death.

אָמַר רַב שֵׁשֶׁת [5]**Rav Sheshet said** to his disciples: **You have** already **learned** a Tannaitic source which answers your question: [6]**"If regarding trees** worshipped as part of idolatrous rites, **which do not eat or drink or smell, the Torah said: Destroy, burn, and** totally **consume** them, as the verse states (Deuteronomy 12:3): 'And you shall burn their asherot with fire,' [7]all **because a person came to** commit **an offense on account of them** (non-Jews are also forbidden by Torah law to practice idolatry) — [8]**he who causes another person to stray from the paths of life to the paths of death, all the more so** must they be put to death." We see from here that whatever served as a stumbling-block and brought a person to commit a capital offense must be destroyed. Hence an animal with which a non-Jew engaged in bestiality must be put to death.

אֶלָּא מֵעַתָּה [9]The Gemara asks: **If** it so that a stumbling-block must be destroyed, even if there is no concern about disgrace, then it follows that **if a non-Jew bowed** in worship **to his animal, it should be forbidden** for benefit **and put to death!** But we know that this is not true, for living creatures that are worshipped do not become forbidden for benefit, and they certainly do not have to be put to death!

[1]תַּקָּלָה וְקָלוֹן בָּעֵינַן, [2]וְהָכָא תַּקָּלָה אִיכָּא, [3]קָלוֹן לֵיכָּא. [4]אוֹ דִּילְמָא, תַּקָּלָה אַף עַל פִּי שֶׁאֵין קָלוֹן?

[5]אָמַר רַב שֵׁשֶׁת, תְּנִיתוּהָ: [6]"מָה אִילָנוֹת שֶׁאֵין אוֹכְלִין וְאֵין שׁוֹתִין וְאֵין מְרִיחִין, אָמְרָה תּוֹרָה: הַשְׁחֵת שְׂרוֹף וְכַלֵּה, [7]הוֹאִיל וּבָא לָאָדָם תַּקָּלָה עַל יָדָן, [8]הַמַּתְעֶה אֶת חֲבֵירוֹ מִדַּרְכֵי חַיִּים לְדַרְכֵי מִיתָה, עַל אַחַת כַּמָּה וְכַמָּה.

[9]אֶלָּא מֵעַתָּה נָכְרִי הַמִּשְׁתַּחֲוֶה לִבְהֶמְתּוֹ תִּיתְּסַר וּמִקְטְלָא?

LITERAL TRANSLATION

[1]We need a stumbling-block and disgrace, [2]and here there is a stumbling-block, [3][but] there is no disgrace. [4]Or perhaps, a stumbling-block even if there is no disgrace.

[5]Rav Sheshet said: You have learned it: [6]"If [regarding] trees, which do not eat or drink or smell, the Torah said: Destroy, burn, and consume, [7]because a person came to an offense on account of them, [8]he who causes his fellow to stray from the paths of life to the paths of death, all the more so."

[9]But now, if a non-Jew bowed to his animal, it should be forbidden and put to death!

RASHI

קלון ליכא — דרכן בכך ואין מתביישין. ועוד: דאקלון דידהו לא חס רחמנא. אילנות — של אשירה דכתיב בהו (דברים יב) "תשרפון באש" אמרה תורה וכו' אלמא תקלה אף על פי שאין קלון, דהא אשירה לנכרי אינה קלון אלא תקלה, שאף הם הוזהרו על עבודה זרה. אלא מעתה — דמשום תקלה לחודה נסקלת. נכרי המשתחוה לבהמתו — דאיכא תקלה שהוא נהרג על ידה, תתסר הבהמה לישראל בהנאה ונקטלה לבהמה.

TERMINOLOGY

תְּנִיתוּהָ **You have learned it.** Sometimes an Amora may answer a question by noting that the answer is already found in a Tannaitic source. This term was often used by Rav Sheshet, and the sources which it introduces were usually well known.

SAGES

רַב שֵׁשֶׁת **Rav Sheshet.** A Babylonian Amora of the second and third generations. See *Sanhedrin,* Part I, p. 49.

NOTES

to this, the word קבסתן is related to the word קוביוסטוס, "gambler, cheat." The Geonim understand the word as: You disgust us, you nauseate us.

אילָנוֹת הוֹאִיל וּבָא לָאָדָם תַּקָּלָה **Trees, because a person came to an offense.** *Ramah* explains that only regarding an animal do we say that its continued existence will bring further disgrace to the executed party, but not regarding a tree, for the animal passes through the market-place reminding people of the executed party's crime, but the tree remains stationary.

HALAKHAH

he alone is liable for execution, but the animal is not put to death," for the problem posed before Rav Sheshet was not resolved, and the animal cannot be put to death when the matter is in doubt (*Kesef Mishneh*). (*Rambam, Sefer Shofetim, Hilkhot Melakhim* 9:6.)

TRANSLATION AND COMMENTARY

מִי אִיכָּא מִידֵּי [1]The Gemara answers: **Is there something that** is **not forbidden to a Jew, but** is **forbidden to a non-Jew?** Surely if a Jew bowed in worship to his animal, it does not become forbidden for benefit, nor must it be put to death, and so it cannot be that if a non-Jew did the same, his animal should become forbidden for benefit, and be put to death.

יִשְׂרָאֵל [2]The Gemara asks: This itself is difficult. **Regarding a Jew himself,** if he bowed in worship to his animal, **it should become forbidden** for benefit, and be put to death, **just as** the animal would be put to death **if the** Jew **coupled with it!**

אָמַר אַבַּיֵי [3]**Abaye said:** A distinction may be drawn between the two cases: **In the** case of sexual intercourse with an animal, he committed a transgression whose **disgrace is great, but in the** case of bowing to his animal, he committed a transgression whose **disgrace is small.** Bestiality is an even more heinous offense than idolatry, and so the Torah was more stringent about bestiality, and commanded that the animal be put to death.

וַהֲרֵי אִילָנוֹת [4]The Gemara asks: **But surely,** regarding **trees** that were worshipped as part of idolatrous rites, the **disgrace** of the transgression committed through them **is not great,** [5]**and** nevertheless **the Torah said: Destroy, burn, and** totally **consume** them!

בְּבַעֲלֵי חַיִּים [6]The Gemara answers: When we said that if the disgrace of a transgression is small, we do not kill the animal that acted as the stumbling-block that brought a person to commit a capital offense, **we were talking about living creatures, for which the Torah has compassion.** Only in the case of the most serious offenses, such as in the case of bestiality, does the Torah command that the animal be put to death. But trees and other inanimate objects that brought a person to commit a capital offense must be destroyed, even if the disgrace of the transgression that had been committed is small.

רָבָא אָמַר [7]**Rava said** that there is another reason to differentiate between an animal which was the object of bestiality and an animal which was worshipped: **The Torah said** that since **the animal which** was the object of bestiality **derived enjoyment from** having participated in **the transgression,** it must be **put to death.** But the animal which was worshipped derived no enjoyment from the transgression, and so there is no obligation to kill it.

[1]מִי אִיכָּא מִידֵּי דְּלְיִשְׂרָאֵל לָא אָסַר, וּלְנָכְרִי אָסַר?

[2]יִשְׂרָאֵל גּוּפֵיהּ לִיתַּסַר, מִידֵּי דַּהֲוָה אַרְבִּיעָה.

[3]אָמַר אַבַּיֵי: זֶה קְלוֹנוֹ מְרוּבֶּה, וְזֶה קְלוֹנוֹ מוּעָט.

[4]וַהֲרֵי אִילָנוֹת, דְּאֵין קְלוֹנָן מְרוּבֶּה, [5]וְאָמְרָה תּוֹרָה: הַשְׁחֵת שָׂרוֹף וְכַלֵּה!

[6]בְּבַעֲלֵי חַיִּים קָאָמְרִינַן, דְּחַס רַחֲמָנָא עֲלַיְיהוּ.

[7]רָבָא אָמַר: אָמְרָה תּוֹרָה: בְּהֵמָה נֶהֱנֵית מֵעֲבֵירָה תֵּיהָרֵג.

LITERAL TRANSLATION

[1]Is there something that was not forbidden to a Jew, but was forbidden to a non-Jew?

[2][Regarding] a Jew himself it should be forbidden, just like with coupling!

[3]Abaye said: This one, his disgrace is great; but this one, his disgrace is small.

[4]But surely, trees, whose disgrace is not great, [5]and the Torah said: Destroy, burn, and consume!

[6]We were talking about living creatures, for the Torah (lit., "the Merciful") has compassion for them.

[7]Rava said: The Torah said: The animal which enjoyed the transgression is put to death.

RASHI

איכא מידי דלישראל לא מיתסר – בהמתו בהשתחואתו, דקיימא לן (תמורה כט,א) בעלי חיים אין נאסרין מפני עבודה זרה, דמדאיצטריך קרא למיסר נעבד לקרבן גבוה – מכלל דלהדיוט שרי. **לישראל נמי תתסר מידי דהוה ארביעה** – דאסרינן לה ומקטלא, וכי איצטריך למיסר נעבד לגבוה כגון נעבד על פי עד אחד או על פי הבעלים דגברא לא מקטיל ואיהי נמי לא מקטלא, דהא רובע ונרבע אסר להו קרא לגבוה, וקשיא לן: למה לי קרא, "ממשקה ישראל" כתיב, מן המותר לישראל ואוקים נרבע על פי עד אחד, או על פי הבעלים דגברא לא מקטיל ואיהי נמי לא מקטלא, בפרק שני דתמורה (שם). **אמר אביי זה קלונו מרובה** – שיש כאן קלון שעבר על מצות קונו, וקלון שגינה עצמו בדבר מגונה. **וזה קלונו** – דנכרי מועט, וסבירא ליה לאביי תקלה וקלון בעינן, דלית ליה דרב ששת. אי נמי סבירא ליה כותיה דמתוך שקלונו מרובה – איכא קלון ואפילו מנכרי, ומיהו מאילנות לא גמר לה. **בבעלי חיים קא אמרינן** – דלא מתסרי במלתא זוטרתא. **דהא חס רחמנא** – שהצריך להם בית דין של עשרים ושלשה והעדאת עדים. **רבא אמר** – להכי לא ילפינן נעבד מנרבע, משום דלא נהנית הבהמה מעבירה. וגבי נכרי הבא על הבהמה כרב ששת סבירא ליה דהא איתהניא מעבירה.

NOTES

מִי אִיכָּא מִידֵּי דְּלְיִשְׂרָאֵל לָא אָסַר **Is there something that was not forbidden to a Jew.** The Rishonim note that the Gemara's formulation here is not precise. The argument, "Is there something that was not forbidden to a Jew, but was forbidden to a non-Jew," is generally used to deny that a certain act is forbidden to a non-Jew, but permitted to a Jew. Here we are not dealing with the permissibility or prohibition of bowing down to an animal, but rather with the question of whether or not the animal that was worshipped is henceforth forbidden for benefit. Thus the Gemara means: If a Jew, with whom the Torah was more stringent, does not cause the animal which he worshipped

[1] וַהֲרֵי אִילָנוֹת, דְּאֵין נֶהֱנִין מֵעֲבֵירָה, וְאָמְרָה תּוֹרָה: הַשְׁחֵת שְׂרוֹף וְכַלֵּה! [2] בְּבַעֲלֵי חַיִּים קָאָמְרִינַן, דְּחַס רַחֲמָנָא עֲלַיְיהוּ.
[3] תָּא שְׁמַע: [4] ״דָּבָר אַחֵר: שֶׁלֹּא תְּהֵא בְּהֵמָה עוֹבֶרֶת בַּשּׁוּק וְיֹאמְרוּ: [5] זוֹ הִיא שֶׁנִּסְקַל פְּלוֹנִי עַל יָדָהּ״. [6] מַאי לָאו [55B] מִדְּסֵיפָא תַּקָּלָה וְקָלוֹן, [7] רֵישָׁא תַּקָּלָה בְּלֹא קָלוֹן. [8] וְהֵיכִי דָּמֵי? [9] נָכְרִי הַבָּא עַל הַבְּהֵמָה!
[10] לָא, סֵיפָא תַּקָּלָה וְקָלוֹן. [11] רֵישָׁא — הָא קָא מַשְׁמַע לָן

LITERAL TRANSLATION

[1] But surely, trees do not enjoy the transgression, and the Torah said: Destroy, burn, and consume! [2] We were talking about living creatures, for the Torah has compassion for them.

[3] Come [and] hear: [4] "Another explanation: So that the animal not pass through the marketplace, and [people] say: [5] This is it on account of which So-and-so was stoned." [6] Is it not [55B] that since [in] the last clause [there is] a stumbling-block and disgrace, [7] [in] the first clause [there is] a stumbling-block without disgrace? [8] And what is it like? [9] A non-Jew who had intercourse with an animal.

[10] No, [in] the last clause [there is] a stumbling-block and disgrace. [11] The first clause — this it teaches us

TRANSLATION AND COMMENTARY

וַהֲרֵי אִילָנוֹת [1] The Gemara asks: **But surely, trees** that are worshipped as part of idolatrous rites **do not enjoy the transgression** committed through them, **and** nevertheless **the Torah said: Destroy, burn, and** totally **consume** them!

בְּבַעֲלֵי חַיִּים [2] The Gemara answers: When we said that an animal that had served as a stumbling-block that brought a person to commit a capital offense is not put to death unless the animal itself derived enjoyment from the transgression, **we were talking about living creatures, for which the Torah has compassion.** Only in a case where the animal itself derived enjoyment from the transgression, such as when it was the subject of bestiality, does the Torah command that the animal must be put to death. But trees and other inanimate objects that brought a person to commit a capital offense must be destroyed, even though they did not derive any enjoyment from the offense.

תָּא שְׁמַע [3] The Gemara now tries to prove from our Mishnah that an animal that served as a stumbling-block must indeed be put to death, even when there is no concern of disgrace. **Come and hear** what we have learned in the last clause of our Mishnah: [4] "The Mishnah offers **another explanation** as to why an animal that was the object of bestiality must be put to death: **So that it not pass through the market, and people say:** [5] **'This is** the animal **on account of which So-and-so was stoned,'** bringing further disgrace to the executed party." [6] **Does it not follow** [55B] **that since the last clause** implies that in order to put the animal to death, both factors must be present — the animal must have been both **a stumbling-block, and** it must threaten the executed party with further **disgrace** — [7] **the first clause** must be understood as implying that the animal is put to death, even if the animal was only **a stumbling-block, but** there is **no** concern of **disgrace.** Otherwise the first clause would be extraneous. [8] **And how can we visualize** such a case? [9] When **a non-Jew engaged in** sexual **intercourse with an animal,** for then the animal acted as a stumbling-block that brought the person to commit a capital offense, but there is no concern of disgrace, as was explained above.

לָא [10] The Gemara rejects this argument: **No, the last clause** indeed implies that in order to put the animal to death, the animal must both have acted as **a stumbling-block, and** it must also threaten the executed party with further **disgrace.** [11] And **the first clause teaches us** that even if the animal only threatens the

RASHI

תא שמע — דתקלה בלא קלון מקטיל, מדקתני במתניתין תרי בבי והויא רישא משנה יתירא, דקתני סיפא דבר אחר וכו׳ ומהך סיפא משמע דתרווייהו איכא, דקתני, ויאמרו זו היא — היינו קלון, ושנסקל — היינו תקלת עבירה, ומדתנא לרישא שמע מינה תקלה גרידתא דוקא נקט בלא קלון, כגון נכרי, דהא ליכא למימר תנא רישא תקלה וסיפא קלון למימרא דתרווייהו בעינן — דהא מדסיפא שמע מינה. הכי גרסינן — לא סיפא תקלה וקלון ורישא הא קא משמע לן וכו׳. סיפא — ודאי תרווייהו איכא, ואימא לך דכולה מתניתין בישראל קא איירי, ואשמועינן רישא דאף על גב דליכא אלא חדא: קלון בלא תקלה, כגון ישראל שוגג כסבור מותר, דאיכא קלון — שגינה עצמו בדבר מגונה, ותקלה ליכא, ומאי תקלה דקתני שבאת לאדם תקלה — על ידי תקלת קלון קאמר, וניחא לאוקמה הכי ולא תוקמא רישא בעובד כוכבים וסיפא בישראל.

NOTES

to be forbidden for benefit, all the more so a non-Jew, with whom the Torah was less stringent, should not cause the animal which he worshipped to be forbidden for benefit (*Ramban*).

הַשְׁחֵת שְׂרוֹף וְכַלֵּה **Destroy, burn, and consume.** It has been suggested that the apparent redundancy in the expression, "Destroy, burn, and consume," be understood as follows: "Destroy," refers to an idol worshipped by a non-Jew, which becomes permitted for benefit if it is subsequently defaced by the non-Jew; "Burn" — refers to an *asherah,* a tree which was worshipped, and must be burnt; "Consume" — refers to an idol worshipped by a Jew, which has no remedy, but rather must be totally consumed (*Rabbi E. M. Horowitz*).

דַּאֲפִילּוּ קָלוֹן בְּלֹא תַּקָּלָה, נַמִי מְחַיְּיבִי. [1]וְהֵיכִי דָּמֵי? [2]יִשְׂרָאֵל הַבָּא עַל הַבְּהֵמָה בְּשׁוֹגֵג, וְכִדְבָעֵי רַב הַמְנוּנָא.
[3]דִּבְעֵי רַב הַמְנוּנָא: יִשְׂרָאֵל הַבָּא עַל הַבְּהֵמָה בְּשׁוֹגֵג, מַהוּ? [4]תַּקָּלָה וְקָלוֹן בָּעֵינַן, [5]וְהָכָא קָלוֹן אִיכָּא, [6]תַּקָּלָה לֵיכָּא. [7]אוֹ דִּילְמָא, קָלוֹן אַף עַל פִּי שֶׁאֵין תַּקָּלָה?
[8]אָמַר רַב יוֹסֵף: תָּא שְׁמַע: [9]״בַּת שָׁלֹשׁ שָׁנִים וְיוֹם אֶחָד

LITERAL TRANSLATION

that even [if there is] disgrace without a stumbling-block, so too they are obligated. [1]And what is it like? [2]A Jew who unwittingly had intercourse with an animal, and as Rav Hamnuna asked.

[3]For Rav Hamnuna asked: [If] a Jew unwittingly had intercourse with an animal, what [is the law]? [4]We need a stumbling-block and disgrace, [5]and here there is disgrace, [6][but] there is no stumbling-block. [7]Or perhaps, disgrace even if there is no stumbling-block?

[8]Rav Yosef said: Come [and] hear: [9]"A girl three years and one day old

TRANSLATION AND COMMENTARY

offending party with further **disgrace, but** did **not** act as **a stumbling-block** that led to his execution, **we are obligated** to put the animal to death (according to this, the word תַּקָּלָה in the first clause refers not to the stumbling-block of an offense, but to the stumbling-block of disgrace). [1]**And how can we visualize** such a case? [2]We find this in a case **where a Jew unwittingly engaged in** sexual **intercourse with an animal,** a case which **Rav Hamnuna inquired** about below. In such a case, the animal did not act as a stumbling-block, for the unwitting violation of the prohibition against bestiality is not punishable by execution, but the animal will still bring the offender disgrace, and so it must be put to death. But when the animal acted as a stumbling-block that brought a person to commit a crime punishable by execution, but there is no concern about the animal bringing the executed party further disgracc, there might be no obligation to put the animal to death.

דִּבְעֵי רַב הַמְנוּנָא [3]The Gemara now explains that **Rav Hamnuna asked: If a Jew unwittingly engaged in** sexual **intercourse with an animal, what is the law** regarding putting the animal to death? The Gemara explains the two sides of the question: We learned in the Mishnah that the animal with which a Jew had willfully engaged in sexual intercourse is put to death for two reasons: First, because it had acted as a stumbling-block which had brought the person to his offense, and second, because if it would continue to live, it would bring further disgrace to the executed party, for people would be reminded of his crime every time they saw the animal pass by in the market-place. [4]Do we say that **it is necessary** that the animal was both **a stumbling-block and** also threatened the executed party with further **disgrace?** [5]If so, **here,** if a Jew unwittingly engaged in sexual intercourse with an animal, the animal threatens the offending party with **disgrace,** [6]**but** it did **not** serve as **a stumbling-block,** and so the animal should not be put to death. [7]**Or perhaps,** since the animal threatens the offending party with further **disgrace, even though it** was **not a stumbling-block,** the animal should indeed be put to death.

אָמַר רַב יוֹסֵף [8]**Rav Yosef said: Come and hear** an answer to this question from what we have learned in the following Mishnah (*Niddah* 42b): "Sexual intercourse with a girl over three years old is regarded as sexual intercourse for all purposes. [9]Therefore, **a girl three years and one day** given away in betrothal by

RASHI

בת שלש שנים ויום אחד – קיס להו לרבנן דשוב אין בתוליה חוזרין, ומאז היא ראויה לביאה.

NOTES

יִשְׂרָאֵל הַבָּא עַל הַבְּהֵמָה **If a Jew unwittingly had intercourse with an animal.** Although it is theoretically possible to say that we are dealing here with a man who had intercourse with an animal without realizing what he was doing, it stands to reason that we are dealing with man who had intercourse with an animal thinking that the act was permitted. Depending upon the circumstances, his transgression is regarded either as a *shegagah,* an unintentional sin, or *ones,* a violation of law resulting from circumstances over which a person has no control.

HALAKHAH

יִשְׂרָאֵל הַבָּא עַל הַבְּהֵמָה **If a Jew unwittingly had intercourse with an animal.** "If a man or a woman unwittingly engaged in intercourse with an animal, the animal is not put to death, for the question posed by Rav Hamnuna was not answered, and in a case of doubt the animal is not stoned." (*Rambam, Sefer Kedushah, Hilkhot Issurei Bi'ah* 1:18.)

בַּת שָׁלֹשׁ שָׁנִים וְיוֹם אֶחָד מִתְקַדֶּשֶׁת בְּבִיאָה **A girl three years and one day old may be betrothed through intercourse.** "A girl three years and one day old may be given away in betrothal by her father by way of sexual intercourse with her bridegroom. But if she is less than three years old, the act is not regarded as sexual intercourse." (*Shulhan Arukh, Even HaEzer* 37:1.)

TRANSLATION AND COMMENTARY

her father **may be betrothed by** way of sexual **intercourse** with her bridegroom. [1]**If** her husband died without children, and **his brother engaged in** sexual **intercourse with her, he acquired her** as his levirate wife, so that she is regarded as his wife for all purposes. If she was given away in betrothal by her father, and a man other than her husband engaged in intercourse with her, [2]**he is liable to** the death penalty **on account of** having had intercourse with **a married woman.** [3]If she was menstruating, **she imparts ritual impurity to the man with whom she has intercourse, so that** he is ritually impure for seven days, [4]and **he renders the object upon which he lies ritually impure,** that object conveying the same level of ritual impurity **as the cover over** a man suffering from gonorrhea. The object upon which he lies has the status of 'first degree ritual impurity,' and so it renders food and drink ritually impure, but not people or utensils. [5]**If she** is the daughter of an ordinary Israelite and **was married off** by her father **to a priest, she** is permitted to **eat terumah.** [6]**If someone of unfit status had intercourse with her,** such as a non-Jew, or a son born to a priest and a woman whom the priest is forbidden to marry, **she becomes disqualified from**

מִתְקַדֶּשֶׁת בְּבִיאָה. [1]וְאִם בָּא עָלֶיהָ יָבָם, קְנָאָהּ. [2]וְחַיָּיבִין עָלֶיהָ מִשּׁוּם אֵשֶׁת אִישׁ. [3]וּמְטַמְּאָה אֶת בּוֹעֲלָהּ [4]לְטַמֵּא מִשְׁכָּב תַּחְתּוֹן כְּעֶלְיוֹן. [5]נִישֵּׂאת לַכֹּהֵן, אוֹכֶלֶת בִּתְרוּמָה. [6]בָּא עָלֶיהָ אֶחָד מִן הַפְּסוּלִים, פְּסָלָהּ

LITERAL TRANSLATION

may be betrothed through intercourse. [1]And if the levir had intercourse with her, he acquires her. [2]And they are liable for her on account of a married woman. [3]And she imparts ritual impurity to the man who has intercourse with her [4]so that he renders the object upon which he lies ritually impure like the cover over [a man suffering from gonorrhea]. [5][If] she marries a priest, she eats terumah. [6][If] one of those who are disqualified had intercourse with her, she is disqualified

RASHI

מתקדשת בביאה — על ידי אביה אם מסרה אביה לאחר לבא עליה לשום קדושין, דהאב זכאי בבתו בקדושיה דכתיב (דברים כב) "את בתי נתתי לאיש הזה". אבל היא עצמה ואמה ואחיה כשהיא יתומה אין בה קדושי תורה אלא רבנן הוא דתקון, ולא הצריכוה גט אלא מיאון בעלמא. **ואם בא עליה יבם קנאה** — וילאה ידי יבום, ומתגרשת הימנו בגט ומקבלו אביה ואינה צריכה חליצה, דהא בביאת יבם תלה רחמנא, דכיון שלקחה נעשית כאשתו לכל דבר — שמגרשה בגט, וזה הרי בא [עליה], אבל פחות משלש שנים אינה ביאה ואינה נקנית לו, ואם בא לגרשה בגט אינו יכול, אלא ימתין עד שתהא בת שלש שנים ויום אחד ויבעול, או עד שתביא שתי שערות — ותחלוץ. **וחייבין עליה** — אם קבל אביה קידושין ובא עליה אחר, חייב עליה משום אשת איש, דביאה היא. אבל פחות מבת שלש נהי דקדושי כסף שלה קדושין הן לחייב עליה לאחר שלש, אבל הבא עליה בתוך שלש לא נתחייב אף על פי שהיא אשת איש — דלאו ביאה היא. **ומטמאה את בועלה** — בנדותה, דקיימא לן (נדה לב,א) מרבויא דוי"ו "ואשה כי תהיה זבה" — לרבות תינוקת בת יום אחד שמטמאה בנדתה. ומיהו כי מטמאה בנדה, במגע ובמדרס הוא דמטמאה טהרות ואדם וכלים כשאר נדה, אבל בא עליה בתוך שלש אינה מטמאתו טומאת שבעה כבועל נדה דכתיב ביה (ויקרא טו) "ותהי נדתה עליו" — אלא הרי הוא כנוגע בעלמא לטומאת ערב, משום דלאו ביאה היא, אבל בת שלש מטמאתו כדין בועל נדה. **לטמא משכב התחתון בעליון** — שהבועל נדה מטמא משכב התחתון משום משכב אפילו לא נגע בו, כעליון של זב, הכי מפורש במסכת נדה בפרק "בנות כותים" (לג,ב) שאין משכבו של בועל נדה חמור כמשכב נדה וכמשכב זב שנעשים אב הטומאה לטמא אדם וכלים, דכתיב בהו "וכל אשר יגע במשכבה" אלא הרי הוא כעליונו של זב, בגד שנישא על גבי הזב שאינו אלא ראשון לטומאה ואינו מטמא אדם וכלים — אלא אוכלין ומקראי ילפינן לה התם. **נשאת לכהן** — על ידי קדושי אביה. **אוכלת בתרומה** — אבל פחות מבת שלש אף על פי שקידושיה קידושין על ידי אביה — הואיל ואין ביאתה ביאה, אין חופתה חופה, והויא לה כארוסה. דאף על גב דקנין כספו הוא — אמרו רבנן: אין האשה אוכלת בתרומה עד שתכנס לחופה. **בא עליה אחד מן הפסולין** — כגון נכרי, או חלל, או נתין וממזר, פסלה מן התרומה דהא ביאתה ביאה, וביבמות (סח,א) ובקדושין בפרק בתרא (סט,ב) ילפי לה מהאי קרא "ובת כהן כי תהיה לאיש זר וגו'" כיון שנבעלה לפסול לה פסלה עולמית, מהתם יליף לה שפיר ולוויה וישראלית מרבו מרבויא דבת ובת.

NOTES

מִשּׁוּם אֵשֶׁת אִישׁ **On account of a married woman.** *Ramah* notes that the Mishnah says that the man is liable to the death penalty for having intercourse with a married woman, and not for having intercourse with a betrothed girl. This comes to teach us that if a man betrothed a woman by sexual intercourse, and then another man had intercourse with her, that man is liable to death by strangulation, as if the groom had already married his bride, and not death by stoning, the penalty for intercourse with a betrothed girl. Alternatively, the Mishnah refers to the case of a father who gave his three-year-old daughter away in betrothal, and afterwards had her enter the bridal chamber with her husband. The Mishnah comes to teach us that she is henceforth regarded as a married woman, for the marriage is legally fit for consummation.

HALAKHAH

וְאִם בָּא עָלֶיהָ יָבָם, קְנָאָהּ **And if the levir had intercourse with her, he acquires her.** "If the levir had intercourse with his brother's widow, and she was three years and one day old, he acquired her as his levirate wife." (*Shulḥan Arukh, Even HaEzer* 167:4.)

וְחַיָּיבִין עָלֶיהָ מִשּׁוּם אֵשֶׁת אִישׁ **And they are liable for her on account of a marries woman.** "If a man had intercourse with a minor girl who had been married off by her father, he is liable for death by strangulation," following the Mishnah. (*Rambam, Sefer Kedushah, Hilkhot Issurei Bi'ah* 3:2.)

TRANSLATION AND COMMENTARY

marrying into **the priesthood,** and if she is the daughter of a priest, she becomes disqualified from eating terumah in her father's house. [1]**And if one of those whom the Torah says is forbidden to her,** such as her father, **had intercourse with her,** [2]**he is put to death on account of her, but she is exempt** from punishment, for a minor bears no liability." [3]Now, when the Mishnah speaks of **"one of those** whom the Torah says is **forbidden to her,"** surely it is referring **even** to **an animal.** [4]**And here** the animal threatens the girl with **disgrace,** [5]**but** it did **not** serve as **a stumbling-block,** for the girl is not liable for execution. [6]**And** nevertheless, the Mishnah **states** that the animal **is put to death on account of her.** Thus, it follows that if a Jew unwittingly engaged in sexual intercourse with an animal, the animal must be put to death, for there too the animal threatens the offending party with further disgrace, even though it did not act as a stumbling-block.

כֵּיוָן דִּמְזִידָה הִיא [7]The Gemara rejects this proof: **Since** the girl **sinned intentionally** (for otherwise there would have been no reason for the Mishnah to have mentioned that she is exempt), she should indeed be liable for execution. Thus, the animal with whom she had intercourse did **indeed** act as **a stumbling-block** that brought a person to be liable for capital punishment. [8]The girl herself is not put to death, because **the Torah had compassion for her** on account of her age. [9]However, it was only **for her** that **it had compassion,** [10]but **it did not have compassion for the animal.** Hence, the Mishnah cannot tell us anything about a Jew who unwittingly engaged in sexual intercourse with an animal, for in that case the animal did not act as a stumbling-block that brought a person to liability for capital punishment.

אָמַר רָבָא [11]**Rava said: Come and hear** a solution to the question raised by Rav Hamnuna from the very next Mishnah in *Niddah* (47a): "The sexual intercourse of a boy over nine years old is regarded as sexual intercourse for all purposes. [12]Therefore, **a boy nine years and one day old who has intercourse with his** late **brother's wife acquires her** as his levirate wife, so that he takes possession of his late brother's estate, and she requires a bill of divorce to sever the marital tie. [13]**But he may not give her a bill of divorce until he reaches adulthood** at the age of thirteen, since he is still only a minor, and his bill of divorce cannot cancel the betrothal which had been effected by his brother. [14]If he has intercourse with a menstruating woman,

מִן הַכְּהוּנָּה. [1]וְאִם בָּא עָלֶיהָ אֶחָד מִכָּל הָעֲרָיוֹת הָאֲמוּרוֹת בַּתּוֹרָה, [2]מוּמָתִין עַל יָדָהּ, וְהִיא פְּטוּרָה". [3]"אֶחָד מִכָּל עֲרָיוֹת — וַאֲפִילּוּ בְּהֵמָה", [4]וְהָא הָכָא דְּקָלוֹן אִיכָּא, [5]תַּקָּלָה לֵיכָּא, [6]וְקָתָנֵי: "מוּמָתִין עַל יָדָהּ"! [7]כֵּיוָן דִּמְזִידָה הִיא — תַּקָּלָה נַמִי אִיכָּא, [8]וְרַחֲמָנָא הוּא דְּחַס עֲלָהּ. [9]עֲלָהּ דִּידָהּ חַס, [10]אַבְּהֵמָה לֹא חַס.

[11]אָמַר רָבָא: תָּא שְׁמַע: [12]"בֶּן תֵּשַׁע שָׁנִים וְיוֹם אֶחָד הַבָּא עַל יְבִמְתּוֹ קְנָאָהּ. [13]וְאֵינוֹ נוֹתֵן גֵּט עַד שֶׁיַּגְדִּיל. [14]וּמְטַמֵּא כְּנִדָּה

LITERAL TRANSLATION

from the priesthood. [1]And if one of all those forbidden to her that are mentioned in the Torah had intercourse with her, [2]they are put to death on account of her, and she is exempt." [3]One of all those forbidden to her — and even an animal. [4]And surely here there is disgrace, [5][but] there is no stumbling-block. [6]And it states: "They are put to death on account of her!" [7]Since she sinned intentionally, there is also a stumbling-block, [8]and it is the Torah that had compassion for her. [9]For her it had compassion; [10]for an animal it did not have compassion.

[11]Rava said: Come [and] hear: [12]"A boy nine years and one day old who had intercourse with his brother's widow acquires her. [13]And he may not give her a bill of divorce until he reaches adulthood. [14]And he imparts ritual impurity like a menstruating woman

RASHI

מומתין על ידה — אם מחייבי מיתות הן, דהא ביאתה ביאה. **והיא פטורה** — דלאו בת עונשין היא. **תקלה ליכא** — דלאו בת עונשין היא, והרי היא בכלל שוגג. **קנאה** — ליורשה, ושלא תפטר עוד בחליצה אלא בגט. **ואינו נותן גט עד שיגדיל** — שהרי על ידי קדושי אחיו גדול נאסרה, וגירושין של זה אין חשובין להפקיע קדושי אחיו, דקטן הוא ואינו בן דעת. **ומטמא כנדה** — כבועל נדה, ולא כנוגע.

HALAKHAH

בֶּן תֵּשַׁע שָׁנִים וְיוֹם אֶחָד הַבָּא עַל יְבִמְתּוֹ קְנָאָהּ A boy nine years and one day old who had intercourse with his brother's widow acquires her. "If a boy younger than nine years and one day old had intercourse with his late brother's widow, he did not acquire her as his levirate wife. But if he was more than nine years old, he acquired her as his levirate wife." (*Shulḥan Arukh, Even HaEzer* 167:1.)

וְאֵינוֹ נוֹתֵן גֵּט עַד שֶׁיַּגְדִּיל And he may not give her a bill of divorce until he reaches adulthood. "If a boy older than nine years and one day had intercourse with his brother's widow, he may not divorce her with a bill of divorce until he reaches majority. If he did not have intercourse with her after he had reached majority, he must also grant her *ḥalitzah*." (*Shulḥan Arukh, Even HaEzer* 167:2.)

וּמְטַמֵּא כְּנִדָּה And he imparts ritual impurity like a menstruating woman. "If a minor older than nine years

[1] לְטַמֵּא מִשְׁכָּב תַּחְתּוֹן כְּעֶלְיוֹן. [2] פּוֹסֵל, [3] וְאֵינוֹ מַאֲכִיל. [4] וּפוֹסֵל אֶת הַבְּהֵמָה מֵעַל גַּבֵּי הַמִּזְבֵּחַ. [5] וְנִסְקֶלֶת עַל יָדוֹ. [6] וְאִם בָּא עַל אַחַת מִכָּל הָעֲרָיוֹת הָאֲמוּרוֹת בַּתּוֹרָה, [7] מוּמָתִים עַל יָדוֹ״. [8] וְהָא הָכָא קָלוֹן אִיכָּא, [9] תַּקָּלָה לֵיכָּא, [10] וְקָתָנֵי: ״נִסְקֶלֶת עַל יָדוֹ״!

[11] כֵּיוָן דְּמֵזִיד הוּא, תַּקָּלָה נַמִי

LITERAL TRANSLATION

[1] so that he renders the object upon which he lies ritually impure like the cover over [a man suffering from gonorrhea]. [2] He disqualifies [from eating terumah], [3] but does not qualify to eat [terumah]. [4] And he disqualifies an animal from the altar. [5] And it is stoned on account of him. [6] And if he had intercourse with one of all those forbidden to him that are mentioned in the Torah, [7] they are put to death on account of him." [8] And surely here there is disgrace, [9] [but] there is no stumbling-block. [10] And it states: "It is stoned on account of him!"

[11] Since he sinned intentionally, there is also a stumbling-block,

TRANSLATION AND COMMENTARY

he imparts ritual impurity like a menstruating woman, [1] **so that he renders the object upon which he lies ritually impure,** that object conveying the same level of ritual impurity **as the cover** over a man suffering from gonorrhea. The object upon which he lies has the status of 'first degree ritual impurity,' and so it renders food and drink ritually impure, but not people or utensils. If he is of unfit status, such as a non-Jew or the son born to a priest and a woman whom the priest is forbidden to marry, and he has intercourse with the daughter of a priest, [2] **he disqualifies** her from eating terumah in her father's house. [3] **But** if he is a priest, and he marries the daughter of an ordinary Israelite, **he does not qualify her to eat terumah.** Even though his sexual intercourse is regarded legally as sexual intercourse, his acquisition of the woman is incomplete. [4] If he has intercourse with an animal, and there is only a single witness to the offense, **he disqualifies the animal from** being sacrificed on **the altar.** [5] If there are two witnesses to the offense, the animal **is stoned on account of him,** but he himself is exempt from punishment, for a minor bears no liability. [6] And similarly, **if he has intercourse with one of those whom the Torah says is forbidden to him,** such as his mother, [7] **she is put to death on account of him,** but he himself is exempt from punishment." [8] **Here** if a boy has intercourse with an animal, the animal threatens the boy with further **disgrace,** [9] **but** it did **not** serve as **a stumbling-block,** for the boy is not liable for execution. [10] **And** nevertheless, the Mishnah **states** that the animal **is put to death on account of him.** Thus, it follows that if a Jew unwittingly engaged in sexual intercourse with an animal, the animal must be put to death, for there too the animal threatens the offending party with further disgrace, even though it did not act as a stumbling-block leading to his execution.

כֵּיוָן דְּמֵזִיד הוּא [11] The Gemara rejects this proof just as it rejected the previous proof: **Since** the boy **sinned intentionally,** he should indeed be liable for execution. Thus, the animal with which he had intercourse did **indeed** act as **a stumbling-block** that brought a person to be liable for capital punishment.

RASHI

לטמא משכב — שלו, התחתון כעליונו של זב, אבל פחות מבן תשע אינו אלא כנוגע בנדה לטומאת ערב. **ופוסל** — את האשה בביאתו מן התרומה אם הוא אחד מן הפסולין. **ואינו מאכיל** — אם הוא כהן ובא עליה לשם קדושין אינו מאכילה בתרומה, דקטן אף על גב דביאתו ביאה אין קניינו קנין, ולא קרינא ביה ״קנין כספו״. **ופוסל את הבהמה מעל המזבח** — משום נרבע, כגון על פי עד אחד או על פי הבעלים, שאינה נסקלת ואינה נאסרת להדיוט. **ונסקלת על ידו** — אם יש עדים, דאין שור ובהמה נסקלין אלא על ידי עדים וסנהדרין, כדאמר בפרק קמא (ב,א): כמיתת בעל כך מיתת השור.

HALAKHAH

and a day had intercourse with a menstruating woman, he imparts ritual impurity like someone who had intercourse with a menstruating woman. If he was less than nine, he imparts ritual impurity like someone who came into physical contact with a menstruating woman." (*Rambam, Sefer Taharah, Hilkhot Metam'ei Mishkav u'Moshav* 3:3.)

פּוֹסֵל, וְאֵינוֹ מַאֲכִיל **He disqualifies from eating terumah, but does not qualify to eat terumah.** "If a woman had sexual intercourse with a minor who is forbidden to her, and he is older than nine years and a day, she is disqualified from marrying into the priesthood, and if she is the daughter of a priest, she is disqualified from eating terumah. But if the daughter of an ordinary Israelite married a nine-year-old priest, he does not qualify her to eat terumah, for he does not fully acquire her as his wife until he reaches majority." (*Rambam, Sefer Zeraim, Hilkhot Terumot* 8:11.)

וּפוֹסֵל אֶת הַבְּהֵמָה מֵעַל גַּבֵּי הַמִּזְבֵּחַ **He disqualifies an animal from the altar.** "If a minor over the age of nine years and a day engaged in bestiality with an animal, the animal is disqualified from use as a sacrifice." (*Rambam, Sefer Avodah, Hilkhot Issurei Mizbe'aḥ* 4:3.)

וְנִסְקֶלֶת עַל יָדוֹ **It is stoned on account of him.** "If a boy older than nine years and a day or a girl older than three years and a day engaged in bestiality with an animal, the animal is stoned, and they are exempt from liability. If the boy was under nine years old or the girl was under three years old, the animal is not stoned." (*Rambam, Sefer Kedushah, Hilkhot Issurei Bi'ah* 1:17.)

אִם בָּא עַל אַחַת מִכָּל הָעֲרָיוֹת **If he had intercourse with one of all those forbidden to him.** "If an adult woman engaged in sexual intercourse with a boy who was forbidden

איכָּא, [1]וְרַחֲמָנָא הוּא דְּחַס עִילָּוֵיהּ. [2]עֲלֵיהּ דִּידֵיהּ חַס רַחֲמָנָא; [3]אַבְּהֵמָה לֹא חַס רַחֲמָנָא.

[4]תָּא שְׁמַע: [5]״דָּבָר אַחֵר: [6]שֶׁלֹּא תְּהֵא בְּהֵמָה עוֹבֶרֶת בַּשּׁוּק וְיֹאמְרוּ: [7]זוֹ הִיא שֶׁנִּסְקַל פְּלוֹנִי עַל יָדָהּ״. [8]מַאי לָאו, מִדְּסֵיפָא תַּקָּלָה וְקָלוֹן, [9]רֵישָׁא קָלוֹן בְּלֹא תַּקָּלָה. [10]וְהֵיכִי דָּמֵי? [11]יִשְׂרָאֵל הַבָּא עַל הַבְּהֵמָה בְּשׁוֹגֵג!

[12]לֹא, סֵיפָא — תַּקָּלָה וְקָלוֹן, [13]רֵישָׁא תַּקָּלָה בְּלֹא קָלוֹן. [14]וְהֵיכִי דָּמֵי? [15]נָכְרִי הַבָּא עַל הַבְּהֵמָה, [16]וְכִדְבָעוּ מִינֵּיהּ מֵרַב שֵׁשֶׁת.

מִשְׁנָה [17]הַמְגַדֵּף אֵינוֹ חַיָּיב

LITERAL TRANSLATION

[1]and it is the Torah that had compassion for him. [2]For him it had compassion; [3]for an animal it did not have compassion.

[4]Come [and] hear: [5]"Another explanation (lit., "word"): [6]So that the animal not pass through the market, and [people] say: [7]This is it on account of which so-and-so was stoned." [8]Is it not that since [in] the last clause [there is] a stumbling-block and disgrace, [9][in] the first clause [there is] disgrace without a stumbling-block? [10]And what is it like? [11]A Jew who unwittingly had intercourse with an animal.

[12]No, [in] the last clause [there is] a stumbling-block and disgrace, [13][and in] the first clause [there is] a stumbling-block without disgrace. [14]And what is it like? [15]A non-Jew who had intercourse with an animal, [16]and as they asked Rav Sheshet.

MISHNAH [17]A blasphemer is not liable

TRANSLATION AND COMMENTARY

[1]The boy himself is not put to death, because **the Torah had compassion for him** on account of his age. [2]However, it was only **for him** that **it had compassion,** [3]**but it did not have compassion for the animal,** and so the animal must indeed be put to death. Thus, the Mishnah teaches us nothing about the case where a Jew unwittingly engaged in sexual intercourse with an animal, for in that case the animal did not act as a stumbling-block that brought a person to liability for capital punishment.

תָּא שְׁמַע [4]The Gemara suggests one last proof: **Come and hear** what we have learned in the last clause of our Mishnah: [5]"The Mishnah offers **another explanation** as to why an animal that was used for sex must be put to death: [6]**So that it not pass through the market, and people say:** [7]**'This is** the animal **on account of which So-and-so was stoned,'** bringing further disgrace to the executed person." [8]**Does it not** follow **that since the last clause** implies that the animal must have been both **a stumbling-block, and** it must also threaten the executed party with further **disgrace,** [9]**the first clause** must therefore imply that the animal is put to death, even if the animal only threatens further **disgrace, but** did **not** act as **a stumbling-block.** Otherwise the first clause would be extraneous. [10]**And how can we visualize** such a case? [11]When **a Jew unwittingly engaged in** sexual **intercourse with an animal,** for then there is concern of disgrace, but the animal was not a stumbling-block.

לֹא [12]The Gemara rejects this argument: **No, the last clause** indeed implies that in order to put the animal to death, the animal must have acted as **a stumbling-block, and** it must threaten the executed party with further **disgrace.** [13]And **the first clause** teaches us that the animal is put to death, even if the animal only acted as **a stumbling-block, but** there is **no** concern of **disgrace.** [14]**And how can we visualize** such a case? [15]When **a non-Jew engaged in** sexual **intercourse with an animal,** [16]the case that **Rav Sheshet was asked about** above. Although there is no concern about disgrace, the animal was a stumbling-block that brought a person to liability for capital punishment. Therefore it must be put to death. But when there is a concern regarding disgrace, and the animal did not act as a stumbling-block, as when a Jew unwittingly engaged in sexual intercourse with an animal, there might be no obligation to put the animal to death.

MISHNAH הַמְגַדֵּף [17]The next Mishnah clarifies the regulations applying to the blasphemer, who was listed in the previous Mishnah (53a) among those liable to death by stoning. **Someone who blasphemes** God

RASHI

מאי לאו מדסיפא תקלה וקלון – דהא קתני: יאמרו ״זו היא״ – היינו קלון, וקתני: שנסקל – היינו תקלה, משנה יתירה דרישא לאיתויי קלון בלא תקלת אדם, ומאי תקלה דקתני בה – תקלת קלון, דאילו לאתויי תקלת עבירה בלא קלון בהכי לא מצית לאוקומא, דבישראל תקלת עבירה בבהמה בלא קלון לא משכחת לן, וקא סלקא דעתך דכולה בישראל קא איירי.

NOTES

הַמְגַדֵּף **A blasphemer.** The term *megadef,* blasphemer, is found in Numbers 15:30, but according to the plain sense

HALAKHAH

to her, and he was older than nine years and a day, she is subject to the punishment entailed by that transgression, and he is exempt. If he was younger than nine years old, both of them are exempt." (*Rambam, Sefer Kedushah, Hilkhot Issurei Bi'ah* 1:13.)

הַמְגַדֵּף **A blasphemer.** "A person who blasphemes God is

TRANSLATION AND COMMENTARY

is not liable to death by stoning **unless he utters God's name explicitly** and curses it. [1]**Rabbi Yehoshua ben Korḥah said:** [56A] [2]**Whenever** the judges **examined the witnesses** in a case involving blasphemy, they would discuss the matter with them using **a substitute word.** [3]The witnesses would testify that the blasphemer said: **'May Yose strike Yose,'** substituting the name Yose for the Divine Name. [4]**If the judgment was concluded** and the judges agreed on a guilty verdict, **they could not send** the condemned party out **for execution on the basis** of the testimony that they had heard which used **the substitute word.** [5]**Rather,** the judges **would remove everybody** from the courtroom, so that the blasphemy would not be repeated before the general public. [6]They would then **question the senior** witness, **and say to him:** [7]**'Tell us precisely what you heard** the blasphemer say.' [7]The witness **would** then **repeat** what he had heard, using the blasphemer's own words. [8]Upon hearing the actual blasphemy, **the judges would stand on their feet, rend their garments** in mourning over the desecration of God's

עַד שֶׁיְּפָרֵשׁ הַשֵּׁם. [1]אָמַר רַבִּי יְהוֹשֻׁעַ בֶּן קָרְחָה: [56A] [2]בְּכָל יוֹם דָּנִין אֶת הָעֵדִים בְּכִינּוּי, [3]״יַכֶּה יוֹסֵי אֶת יוֹסֵי״. [4]נִגְמַר הַדִּין לֹא הוֹרְגִין בְּכִינּוּי. [5]אֶלָּא מוֹצִיאִין כָּל אָדָם לַחוּץ, שׁוֹאֲלִין אֶת הַגָּדוֹל שֶׁבֵּינֵיהֶן, וְאוֹמֵר לוֹ: [6]״אֱמוֹר מַה שֶּׁשָּׁמַעְתָּ בְּפֵירוּשׁ״. [7]וְהוּא אוֹמֵר, [8]וְהַדַּיָּינִין עוֹמְדִין עַל רַגְלֵיהֶן וְקוֹרְעִין, וְלֹא מְאַחִין.

LITERAL TRANSLATION

unless he utters the [divine] name explicitly. [1]Rabbi Yehoshua ben Korḥah said: [56A] [2]Every day they would examine the witnesses with a substitute word. [3]"May Yose strike Yose." [4]If the judgment was concluded, they would not execute on the basis of a substitute word. [5]Rather, they would take everybody out, [and] ask the senior among them, and say to him: "State precisely what you heard." [6]And he would state [what he heard], [7]and the judges would stand on their feet, and rend [their garments], and not mend [them].

SAGES

רַבִּי יְהוֹשֻׁעַ בֶּן קָרְחָה **Rabbi Yehoshua ben Korḥah.** See *Sanhedrin*, Part I, p. 54.

RASHI

משנה עד שיפרש את השם — שיזכור את השם. אבל אם לא הוציא שם מפיו, אלא שמע שם יוצא מפי אחר וברכו — פטור. **בכל יום** — כל זמן שהיו נושאין ונותנין בבדיקת עדים היו דנין אותן בכינוי, כלומר: היו דנין עמהן ובודקין אותם בכינוי, היאך אמר? כך אמר: ״יכה יוסי את יוסי״, האי כינוי לאו כינוי השם קאמר, אלא בית דין מכנין בדבריהם הקללה כלפי אחרים. כל מי שמהפך דבריו ומדבר כאדם זה שמדבר ומקלל ותולה באחר קרי ליה כינוי בלשון חכמים, ויש לו חבר בשבועות (לה,א), וגם בלשון המקרא ״ואל אדם לא אכנה כי לא ידעתי אכנה״ (איוב לב) ולהכי נקט יוסי את יוסי, דארבע אותיות איכא כשם בן ארבע אותיות דאינו חייב אלא על שם המיוחד, דהיינו שם בן ארבע אותיות. ומשום דחשבונו של יוסי כחשבונו של אלהים, ולהכי נקט יכה זה את זה, דילפינן לקמן דאינו חייב עד שיברך שם בשם. **נגמר הדין** — ובאו לומר חייב הוא, לא היו יכולין להרגו על פי עדות ששמעו, שהרי לא שמעו מפיהם אלא קללת כינוי. **אלא מוציאין את כל אדם לחוץ** — דגנאי הוא להשמיע ברכת השם לרבים. **וקורעין** — בגדיהם. **ולא מאחין** — עולמית, וטעמא מפורש בגמרא.

NOTES

of that text, the verse does not refer to someone who cursed God. Elsewhere (*Keritut* 7b), the Tannaim disagree about whether that verse is referring to idol worship, or to the cursing of God. Our Mishnah adopts the view of the Sages that the term *megadef* refers to someone who cursed God, because it prefers to use the more ambiguous term *megadef*, "blasphemer," rather than the more explicit term *mekalel*, "curser" (*Ran*).

יַכֶּה יוֹסֵי אֶת יוֹסֵי **May Yose strike Yose.** The Rishonim offer several suggestions as to why the name Yose was chosen to substitute for the Divine Name. *Rashi* says that Yose was chosen because it is a Four-Letter name, and its numerical value is 86, just like the Divine Name *Elohim*. *Ramah* cites the explanation that the name Yose — yod, vav, samekh, yod — is made up of three letters (the two yods and the vav) whose numerical value is 26, the numerical value of the Tetragrammaton (the name spelled yod, heh, vav, heh), and the letter samekh, which stands for *siman*, "sign." He also cites another reading: Yosah — yod, vav, samekh, heh — which, as he points out, is made up of most of the letters of the Tetragrammaton.

לֹא הוֹרְגִין בְּכִינּוּי **They would not execute on the basis of a substitute word.** *Torat Kohanim* derives this law from Leviticus 24:11, which uses the word וַיְקַלֵּל, "And he cursed," and not the euphemism וַיְבָרֵךְ, "And he blessed," as we find in the story regarding Nabot. This teaches us that the court cannot send the blasphemer to his death unless the witnesses report exactly what they heard, without using euphemisms or substitute names.

אֱמוֹר מַה שֶּׁשָּׁמַעְתָּ **State what you heard.** The Jerusalem Talmud explains that the witness would not repeat exactly what he had heard from the blasphemer, but rather he

HALAKHAH

not liable to death by stoning unless he explicitly mentioned the Four-Letter Name of God and cursed it with one of the other names of God which may not be erased. According to *Rambam*, he is liable to death by stoning, both for the name spelled alef, dalet, nun, yod, and for the name spelled yod, heh, vav, heh. According to others, he is only liable for the name spelled yod, heh, vav, heh. If he cursed one of the other Divine Names, he is not liable to death by stoning, but merely subject to flogging." (*Rambam, Sefer Mada, Hilkhot Avodat Kokhavim* 2:7.)

בְּכָל יוֹם דָּנִין אֶת הָעֵדִים **Every day they would examine the witnesses.** "When the judges would interrogate the witnesses in a case involving blasphemy, they would discuss the matter substituting another word for the divine

TRANSLATION AND COMMENTARY

name, **and never mend them.** [1]**The second** witness **would** then **say: 'I also** heard just **like** the first witness,' without repeating the blasphemer's actual words. [2]If there was **a third** witness, he too **would say: 'I also** heard just **like him.'** After hearing this testimony, the judges would issue their ruling, and send the blasphemer out for execution.

GEMARA תָּנָא [3]**A Tanna taught** a related Baraita: "Someone who blasphemed God is not liable for stoning **unless he cursed** one divine **name with** another divine **name,** saying, for example, 'May the Lord strike the Lord.'"

מְנָהָנֵי מִילֵּי [4]The Gemara asks: **From where is this law learned?** [5]**Shmuel said:** This is derived **from the verse** which **states** (Leviticus 24:16): **"And he who blasphemes the name** of the Lord, shall surely be put to death, and all the congregation shall certainly stone him: both the stranger, and he that is born in the land, **when he blasphemes the name** of the Lord, **he shall be put to death."** The verse repeats the words "blasphemes the name of the Lord," to teach that the blasphemer is only liable if he cursed one divine name with another divine name.

מִמַּאי דְּהַאי [6]The Gemara asks: **How do we know that this** verb ***"nokev"*** (translated here as "blasphemes") **is used** here in **the sense of cursing?** [7]The Gemara explains: This we learn from **the verse** in which Bileam **states** (Numbers 23:8): **"How shall I curse** [*ekav*], **whom God has not cursed** [*kaboh*]." [8]**And the warning** that cursing God is prohibited is learned **from here** (Exodus 22:27): **"You shall not curse God."**

וְאֵימָא [9]The Gemara asks: **But say that** the word *nokev* **is used** here in the sense of **piercing, as the verse states** (II Kings 12:10): **"And he bored** [*vayikov*] **a hole in its lid."** Thus the verse would refer not to blasphemy but to piercing God's name that was written on a piece of parchment. [10]**And the warning** that such an action is forbidden is learned from here (Deuteronomy 12:3-4): **"And you shall destroy their name** out of that place. **This you shall not do to the Lord your God."**

[1]וְהַשֵּׁנִי אוֹמֵר: ״אַף אֲנִי כָּמוֹהוּ״. [2]וְהַשְּׁלִישִׁי אוֹמֵר: ״אַף אֲנִי כָּמוֹהוּ״.

גמרא [3]תָּנָא: ״עַד שֶׁיְּבָרֵךְ שֵׁם בְּשֵׁם״.

[4]מְנָהָנֵי מִילֵּי? [5]אָמַר שְׁמוּאֵל: דְּאָמַר קְרָא: ״וְנוֹקֵב שֵׁם וגו׳ בְּנָקְבוֹ שֵׁם יוּמָת״.

[6]מִמַּאי דְּהַאי נוֹקֵב לִישָּׁנָא דְבָרוֹכֵי הוּא? [7]״מָה אֶקֹּב לֹא קַבֹּה אֵל״. [8]וְאַזְהָרְתֵיהּ מֵהָכָא: ״אֱלֹהִים לֹא תְקַלֵּל״.

[9]וְאֵימָא מִיבְרַז הוּא, דִּכְתִיב: ״וַיִּקֹּב חֹר בְּדַלְתּוֹ״. [10]וְאַזְהָרְתֵיהּ מֵהָכָא: ״וְאִבַּדְתֶּם אֶת שְׁמָם.... לֹא תַעֲשׂוּן כֵּן לַה׳ אֱלֹהֵיכֶם״.

LITERAL TRANSLATION

[1]And the second one would say: "I too like him." [2]And the third one would say: "I too like him."

GEMARA [3][A Tanna] taught: "Until he curses (lit., 'blesses') a name with a name."

[4]From where are these things [derived]? [5]Shmuel said: For the verse states: "And he who blasphemes the name...when he blasphemes the name, he shall be put to death."

[6]From where [do we know] that this *nokev* is a term of cursing? [7]For it is written: "How shall I curse, whom God has not cursed." [8]And its warning from here: "You shall not curse God."

[9]But say that it is piercing, as it is written: "And he bored a hole in its lid." [10]And its warning from here: "And you shall destroy their name....This you shall not do to the Lord your God."

RASHI

אף אני – שמעתי כמוהו, ואין צריך לחזור ולהזכיר ברכת השם. **גמרא שם בשם** – כגון: יכה פלוני את פלוני, או: יקלל שם פלוני את שם פלוני. **ונוקב שם בנקבו שם** – להכי אהדריה בהאי קרא, לומר לך עד שיקוב שם בשם. **וממאי דהאי ונוקב שם וגו׳** – עד לא תעשון לשון קושיא הוא, דאין תירוץ בינתים. **מברז** – שלא לתחוב סכין לדקור נקב נקב בשם הכתוב בקלף. **ואזהרתיה מהכא ואבדתם את שמם** – וסמיך ליה ״לא תעשון כן לה׳ אלהיכם״.

NOTES

would state the Divine Name which the blasphemer had used, and then he would continue: The name which I have just mentioned, the blasphemer cursed as follows.

וְהַשְּׁלִישִׁי אוֹמֵר: אַף אֲנִי כָּמוֹהוּ **And the third one would say: I too like him.** The Mishnah had to say that the third witness would also say: "I also heard just like him," because had it mentioned only the second witness, we might have thought that only the second witness can testify in that manner, because his testimony follows immediately after the testimony of the first witness. But regarding the

HALAKHAH

name. That is to say, they would ask the witnesses whether the blasphemer had said: 'May Yose strike Yose.' If the judges reached a guilty verdict, they would clear out the courtroom, and ask the senior witness to repeat exactly what he had heard the blasphemer say. The witness would testify as to what he heard, and the judges then rise to their feet, rend their clothes, and never mend them. The second witness would say: 'I heard the same thing.' If there were additional witnesses, they would each say: 'I heard the same thing.'" (*Rambam, Sefer Mada, Hilkhot Avodah Zarah* 2:8.)

וְאַזְהָרְתֵיהּ מֵהָכָא **And its warning from here.** "The warning teaching that cursing God is forbidden is found in the verse, 'You shall not curse God.'" (*Rambam, Sefer Mada, Hilkhot Avodah Zarah* 2:8.)

TRANSLATION AND COMMENTARY

בָּעֵינָא שֵׁם [1]The Gemara rejects this argument: Whatever action is prohibited by this verse **must be** done to **one** divine **name with** another divine **name,** as we learned in the Baraita cited above, **and there is no** possibility of such a thing if the action prohibited here is piercing a piece of parchment containing God's name.

וְאֵימָא [2]The Gemara asks: **But say that** such a thing is indeed possible if the person **places two** divine **names** written on two pieces of parchment **one on** top of **another and tears** through **them** both.

הַהוּא נוֹקֵב [3]The Gemara answers: **That would be piercing** God's name once **and** then **piercing** God's name once **again,** and not piercing one divine name with another.

וְאֵימָא [4]The Gemara asks: **But say that** such a thing is indeed possible if the person **engraves a** divine **name on the blade of a knife, and** then **cuts with** the knife through God's name written on a piece of parchment.

וְהַהוּא חוּרְפָּא [5]The Gemara answers: In that case, **it is the sharp edge of the knife,** and not the name of God engraved on the blade, **which cuts** through the divine name on the parchment.

וְאֵימָא [6]The Gemara now proposes another interpretation of the prohibition: **Say that** the word *nokev* **is** used here in the sense of **uttering a name, as the verse states** (Numbers 1:17): **"And Moses and Aaron took these men whom they pointed out** [*nikvu*] **by their name."** According to this, the verse refers not to blasphemy, but to uttering God's name in vain. [7]**And the warning** teaching that such an action is forbidden is learned **from here** (Deuteronomy 6:13): **"You shall fear the Lord your God,** and serve him, and shall swear by his name," which teaches that one is forbidden to utter God's name in vain.

חֲדָא [8]The Gemara counters with two arguments: **First,** whatever action is prohibited by this verse **must be** done to **one** divine name **with** another divine **name,** as we learned in the Baraita cited above, **and there is no** possibility of such a thing if the action prohibited here is uttering God's name in vain. [9]**And furthermore,** the warning, "You shall fear the Lord," **is a warning** to fulfill **a positive commandment,** the fear of God, [10]**and a warning** to fulfill **a positive commandment is not regarded as a warning** that can make a person liable for judicial execution.

וְאִיבָּעֵית אֵימָא [11]The Gemara continues: **And if you wish,** you can **say** that the word *nokev* must refer to blasphemy for the following reason: **The verse states** (Leviticus 24:11): **"And** the Israelite woman's son **blasphemed** (*vayikov*) the name of the Lord, **and cursed,"** [12]which **teaches** us **that** the word ***nokev* means curse.**

[1]בָּעֵינָא שֵׁם בְּשֵׁם, וְלֵיכָּא. [2]וְאֵימָא דְּמַנַּח שְׁנֵי שֵׁמוֹת אַהֲדָדֵי וּבָזַע לְהוּ! [3]הַהוּא נוֹקֵב וְחוֹזֵר וְנוֹקֵב הוּא. [4]וְאֵימָא דְּחָיֵיק שֵׁם אַפּוּמָא דְסַכִּינָא, וּבָזַע בָּהּ? [5]וְהַהוּא חוּרְפָּא דְסַכִּינָא הוּא דְּקָא בָּזַע. [6]אֵימָא פָּרוֹשֵׁי שְׁמֵיהּ הוּא, דִּכְתִיב: "וַיִּקַּח מֹשֶׁה וְאַהֲרֹן אֵת הָאֲנָשִׁים הָאֵלֶּה אֲשֶׁר נִקְּבוּ בְּשֵׁמוֹת". [7]וְאַזְהָרָתֵיהּ מֵהָכָא "אֶת ה׳ אֱלֹהֶיךָ תִּירָא"! [8]חֲדָא, דְּבָעֵינָא שֵׁם בְּשֵׁם, וְלֵיכָּא. [9]וְעוֹד, הָוְיָא לֵיהּ אַזְהָרַת עֲשֵׂה, [10]וְאַזְהָרַת עֲשֵׂה לֹא שְׁמָהּ אַזְהָרָה. [11]וְאִיבָּעֵית אֵימָא: אָמַר קְרָא: "וַיִּקֹּב וַיְקַלֵּל", [12]לְמֵימְרָא דְּנוֹקֵב קְלָלָה הוּא.

LITERAL TRANSLATION

[1]We need a name with a name, and there is not.

[2]But say that he places two names one on another and tears them!

[3]That is piercing and again piercing.

[4]But say that he engraves a name on the blade of a knife, and cuts with it.

[5]It is the sharp edge of the knife which cuts.

[6]Say that it is uttering the name, as it is written: "And Moses and Aaron took these men who were pointed out by their name." [7]And its warning from here: "You shall fear the Lord your God."

[8]First, we need a name with a name, and there is not. [9]And furthermore, it is a warning from a positive commandment, and a warning from a positive commandment is not regarded as a warning.

[10]And if you wish, say: The verse says: "And he blasphemed...and cursed," [11]to indicate that *nokev* means curse.

RASHI

בעינן שם בשם – כדיליף לעיל, ובנקיבה לא משכחת שם בשם שינקוב את חבירו. **שני שמות אהדדי** – כתובים בשתי חתיכות קלף ויתנם זה על זה. **נוקב וחוזר ונוקב** – בסכין הוא ואין שם נוקב את שם חבירו, דלאחר שינקוב העליון ינקוב התחתון. **פרושי** – באותיותיו ופירושיה. **לא שמה אזהרה** – ולא ענש עליה מיתה.

NOTES

third witness whose testimony is separated from that of the first witness by the testimony of the second witness, we might have thought that he is required to state explicitly what he had heard from the blasphemer (*Kos Yeshuot*).

TRANSLATION AND COMMENTARY

וְדִילְמָא [1]The Gemara asks: **But perhaps** someone who blasphemed God is not liable unless **he committed both** offenses, uttering God's name in vain and blaspheming Him. And the verse just cited should be understood as follows: "And the Israelite woman's son uttered the name of the Lord in vain, and cursed."

לָא סָלְקָא דַּעְתָּךְ [2]The Gemara rejects this situation: **This cannot enter your mind, for the verse states** (Leviticus 24:14): **"Bring forth him that has cursed,"** [3]**and it does not state: "Bring forth him that has uttered** God's name in vain **and has cursed."** [4]Therefore it is legitimate to **infer from this that** the blasphemer committed only **one** offense, blaspheming God.

תָּנוּ רַבָּנַן [5]**Our Rabbis taught** the following Baraita: "The verse states (Leviticus 24:15): '**Any man** who curses his God shall bear his sin.' [6]The words **'any man'** (literally, "man, man" [*ish ish*]) are used **to include non-Jews** in the prohibition, meaning **that they are forbidden to curse God just like Jews.** [7]**But** unlike Jewish transgressors of this prohibition, who are liable to death by stoning, non-Jewish violators **are put to death by decapitation,** [8]**for wherever execution is mentioned** in the Torah **with respect to non-Jews,** it refers to **decapitation."**

וְהָא מֵהָכָא [9]The Gemara asks: **But is** it **from here** that we **learn** that non-Jews are also forbidden to curse God? [10]Surely **it is learned from** a verse found **elsewhere,** for the verse states (Genesis 2:16): "And the Lord God commanded the man, saying." [11]As the Gemara will explain below, the words, **'The Lord,'** refer to the prohibition against **cursing God,** which applies even to non-Jews.

[1]וְדִילְמָא עַד דְּעָבֵד תַּרְוַיְיהוּ? [2]לָא סָלְקָא דַּעְתָּךְ, דִּכְתִיב: "הוֹצֵא אֶת הַמְקַלֵּל", [3]וְלָא כְּתִיב: "הוֹצֵא אֶת הַנֹּקֵב וְהַמְקַלֵּל". [4]שְׁמַע מִינָּהּ חֲדָא הִיא.

[5]תָּנוּ רַבָּנַן: "'אִישׁ' מַה תַּלְמוּד לוֹמַר? [6]'אִישׁ אִישׁ' — לְרַבּוֹת אֶת הַנָּכְרִים, שֶׁמּוּזְהָרִין עַל בִּרְכַּת הַשֵּׁם כְּיִשְׂרָאֵל. [7]וְאֵינָן נֶהֱרָגִין אֶלָּא בְּסַיִיף, [8]שֶׁכָּל מִיתָה הָאֲמוּרָה בִּבְנֵי נֹחַ אֵינָהּ אֶלָּא בְּסַיִיף".

[9]וְהָא מֵהָכָא נָפְקָא? [10]מֵהָתָם נָפְקָא: [11]"ה'" — זוֹ בִּרְכַּת הַשֵּׁם!

LITERAL TRANSLATION

[1]But perhaps until he does both of them?

[2]This cannot enter your mind, for it is written: "Bring forth him that has cursed," [3]and it is not written: "Bring forth him that has uttered [God's name in vain], and has cursed." [4]Infer from this [that] it is one.

[5]Our Rabbis taught: "'Any man' what does this teach? [6]'Any man' — to include non-Jews, that they are warned against cursing God like Jews. [7]But they are slain only with a sword, [8]for every execution stated with respect to non-Jews (lit., 'descendants of Noah') is only by the sword."

[9]But is this learned from here? [10]It is learned from there: [11]"The Lord" — this is cursing the [divine] name.

RASHI

תרווייהו – פרושי וברוכי, ובחדא לא מחייב. איש איש – בברכת השם כתוב "איש איש כי יקלל אלהיו וגו'" (ויקרא כד). אינה אלא סייף – דכתיב בהו (בראשית ט) "באדם דמו ישפך", ומיתה אחרת לא הוזכרה בהם. והא מהכא נפקא – דנכרים מוזהרין על ברכת השם. ה' זו ברכת השם – לקמיה דרשינן "ויצו ה' אלהים וגו'".

NOTES

כָּל מִיתָה הָאֲמוּרָה בִּבְנֵי נֹחַ אֵינָהּ אֶלָּא בְּסַיִיף **Every execution stated with respect to non-Jews is by the sword.** It may be asked: How can it be argued that wherever execution is mentioned in the Torah with respect to the descendants of Noah, it refers to decapitation? But surely Judah said about Tamar (Genesis 38:25): "Bring her out and let her be burnt"! *Tosafot* answer that Tamar was not actually liable for the death sentence, according to the laws that apply to the descendants of Noah, nor according to the laws that apply to Jews. But rather they were stringent with her, and treated her like a woman who had committed adultery while bound by the levirate tie. They sentenced her to burning, the mode of execution that applies to the daughter of a priest, because she was a descendant of Shem. *Ba'alei HaTosafot* on the Torah explain that Judah did not mean to say that Tamar should be burnt to death, but rather that she should burned on the face, in the manner that promiscuous women are punished.

HALAKHAH

לְרַבּוֹת אֶת הַנָּכְרִים **To include non-Jews.** "If a non-Jew cursed God, whether he referred to God by His proper name, the Tetragrammaton, or he referred to Him by one of His other names, he is liable to the death penalty," following Rav Meyasha who maintains that even the Sages also hold non-Jews liable for cursing with one of God's substitute names. (*Rambam, Sefer Shofetim, Hilkhot Melakhim* 9:3.).

כָּל מִיתָה הָאֲמוּרָה בִּבְנֵי נֹחַ **Every execution stated with respect to non-Jews.** "If a non-Jew violated one of the seven Noachide laws, he is liable to death by decapitation," following the Baraita. (*Rambam, Sefer Shofetim, Hilkhot Melakhim* 9:14.)

[1]אָמַר רַבִּי יִצְחָק נַפָּחָא: לֹא נִצְרְכָא אֶלָּא לְרַבּוֹת אֶת הַכִּינּוּיִין, [2]וְאַלִּיבָּא דְּרַבִּי מֵאִיר. [3]דְּתַנְיָא: ״׳אִישׁ אִישׁ כִּי יְקַלֵּל אֱלֹהָיו וְנָשָׂא חֶטְאוֹ׳, [4]מַה תַּלְמוּד לוֹמַר? [5]וַהֲלֹא כְּבָר נֶאֱמַר: ׳וְנֹקֵב שֵׁם ה׳ מוֹת יוּמָת׳, [6]לְפִי שֶׁנֶּאֱמַר, ׳וְנֹקֵב שֵׁם מוֹת יוּמָת׳, [7]יָכוֹל לֹא יְהֵא חַיָּיב אֶלָּא עַל שֵׁם הַמְיוּחָד בִּלְבַד. [8]מִנַּיִין לְרַבּוֹת כָּל הַכִּינּוּיִין? [9]תַּלְמוּד לוֹמַר: ׳אִישׁ כִּי יְקַלֵּל אֱלֹהָיו׳, [10]מִכׇּל מָקוֹם. [11]דִּבְרֵי רַבִּי מֵאִיר. [12]וַחֲכָמִים אוֹמְרִים: עַל שֵׁם הַמְיוּחָד, בְּמִיתָה, [13]וְעַל הַכִּינּוּיִין, בְּאַזְהָרָה״. [14]וּפְלִיגָא דְּרַבִּי מְיָישָׁא, [15]דְּאָמַר

LITERAL TRANSLATION

[1]Rabbi Yitzḥak Nappaḥa said: It was only needed to include substitute names, [2]and according to Rabbi Meir. [3]For it was taught: "'Any man who curses his God shall bear his sin.' [4]What does the verse teach? [5]But surely it was already stated: 'And he who blasphemes the name of the Lord, shall surely be put to death.' [6]Since it is stated, 'And he who blasphemes the name, shall surely be put to death,' [7]I might have thought that he is only liable for the special [divine] name. [8]From where [do I know] to include all the substitute names? [9]The verse states: 'Any man who curses his God,' [10]in any case. [11][These are] the words of Rabbi Meir. [12]And the Sages say: For the special [divine] name, with execution; [13]and for the substitute names, with a warning."
[14]And this is in disagreement with Rabbi Meyasha, [15]for Rabbi

TRANSLATION AND COMMENTARY

אָמַר רַבִּי יִצְחָק נַפָּחָא [1]**Rabbi Yitzḥak Nappaḥa said:** The words, "Any man," **were only needed to include substitute names** for God in the prohibition. A non-Jew is put to death, not only for cursing God while referring to Him by His proper name, the Tetragrammaton, but also for cursing God while referring to Him by one of His other names. Had we only had the verse, "And the Lord God commanded the man," we would only have known that a non-Jew is liable for cursing the Tetragrammaton. "Any man" teaches that a non-Jew is liable even for a substitute name, just like a Jew. [2]This is all **according to Rabbi Meir,** who maintains that a Jew is liable for blasphemy, even if he only used one of God's substitute names. [3]**For it was taught** in a Baraita: "The verse states (Leviticus 24:15): **'Any man who curses his God shall bear his sin.'** [4]**What does this verse teach?** [5]**Surely** another **verse already stated** (Leviticus 24:16): **'And he who blasphemes the name of the Lord, shall surely be put to death,** and all the congregation shall certainly stone him: both the stranger, and the native, when he blasphemes the name of the Lord, he shall be put to death.' [6]**Since the verse states: 'And he who blasphemes the name, shall surely be put to death,'** [7]**I might have thought that** a person **is only liable** for execution if he cursed God using **the special divine name,** the Tetragrammaton. [8]**From where do I know to include all the** other **substitute names** as well? [9]Therefore, **the verse states: 'Any man who curses his God** shall bear his sin,' [10]which teaches that the blasphemer is liable for execution **in any case,** no matter which of the divine names he used. [11]This is **the position of Rabbi Meir.** [12]**The Sages** disagree and **say:** If the blasphemer cursed God using **the special name,** the Tetragrammaton, he is liable **for execution** by stoning, as the verse states: 'And he who blasphemes the name of the Lord, shall surely be put to death.' [13]But if he cursed God using one of **the substitute names,** he has violated the **prohibition** (Exodus 22:27): 'You shall not curse God," but he is not liable for execution."

וּפְלִיגָא [14]The Gemara notes: Rabbi Yitzḥak Nappaḥa said that according to Rabbi Meir, who maintains that a Jew is liable for execution for blasphemy even if he only cursed God with one of His substitute names, the words, "Any man," teach that a non-Jew is also put to death for cursing God with one of His substitute names. This implies that according to the Sages, who disagree with Rabbi Meir, and say that a Jew is only liable for execution if he cursed God using His proper name, a non-Jew is also not liable for execution if he cursed God with one of the substitute names. Regarding **this** point, Rabbi Yitzḥak Nappaḥa **is in disagreement with Rabbi Meyasha,** [15]**for Rabbi Meyasha said:** If **a non-Jew cursed God**

RASHI

לא נצרכה — האי ״איש איש״ אלא לרבות את הכנויים, שיהו הנכרים מוזהרים על ברכתו כישראל. דאי מהתם הוה אמינא שם המיוחד דוקא — דכתיב ה׳, דהאי אלהים דההוא קרא לאזהרת עבודה זרה דרשינן ליה לקמן. **ואליבא דרבי מאיר** — מתוקמא דמחייב ישראל על הכנויין מהאי קרא, ואתא ״איש איש״ להשוות נכרים וישראל בכל הני כנויים, כגון אלהים, שדי, צבאות, ולא דמו לכנויים דמתניתין דקתני: יכה יוסי את יוסי דכנוי דקתני מתניתין דנין את העדים בכינוי — לאו כנוי השם הוא כדפרשינן לעיל. **על שם המיוחד** — דהא כתיב ה׳ והיינו שם מיוחד, דכתיב ״זה שמי לעולם״ (שמות ג). **כי יקלל אלהיו** — דהיינו כנוי דלאו שם המיוחד, וסמיך ליה מיתה ״ונוקב שם ה׳ מות יומת״, וקאי נמי א״כי יקלל אלהיו״. **וחכמים אומרים על שם המיוחד במיתה** — כדכתיב ״ונוקב שם ה׳ וגו׳״, והאי ״ונשא חטאו״ לא מיתה, אלא ונשא חטאו דכרת. **ועל הכנויין באזהרה** — ״אלהים לא תקלל״ אף על הכנויין נוהר. ושם המיוחד נמי בהא אזהרה נפיק, דכל אלהים לשון שררה כמו (שם ז) ״נתתיך אלהים״. **ופליגא דרבי מיישא** — הא דאמר רבי יצחק נפחא לרבות את הכנויים

SAGES

רַבִּי יִצְחָק נַפָּחָא Rabbi Yitzḥak Nappaḥa. A Palestinian Amora of the second and third generations. He was a disciple of Rabbi Yoḥanan, and often presents teachings in the latter's name. He spent part of his life in Babylonia, where he was an important source of information about the teachings and customs of Eretz Israel.

רַבִּי מְיָישָׁא: בֶּן נֹחַ שֶׁבֵּירַךְ אֶת הַשֵּׁם בְּכִינּוּיִים, לְרַבָּנַן חַיָּיב. [1]מַאי טַעְמָא? [2]דְּאָמַר קְרָא: ״כַּגֵּר כָּאֶזְרָח״ — [3]גֵּר וְאֶזְרָח הוּא דְּבָעֵינַן ״בְּנׇקְבוֹ שֵׁם״, [4]אֲבָל נׇכְרִי, אֲפִילּוּ בְּכִינּוּי.

[5]וְרַבִּי מֵאִיר, הַאי ״כַּגֵּר כָּאֶזְרָח״ מַאי עָבֵיד לֵיהּ? [6]גֵּר וְאֶזְרָח, בִּסְקִילָה, [7]אֲבָל נׇכְרִי, בְּסַיִיף. [8]סָלְקָא דַּעְתָּךְ אָמִינָא: [9]הוֹאִיל וְאִיתְרַבּוּ, אִיתְרַבּוּ. [10]קָא מַשְׁמַע לָן.

[11]וְרַבִּי יִצְחָק נַפָּחָא אַלִּיבָּא דְּרַבָּנַן, [12]הַאי ״כַּגֵּר כָּאֶזְרָח״, מַאי עָבֵיד לֵיהּ? [13]גֵּר וְאֶזְרָח, [14]הוּא דְּבָעֵינַן שֵׁם בְּשֵׁם, [15]אֲבָל נׇכְרִי, לָא בָּעֵינַן שֵׁם בְּשֵׁם. [16]״אִישׁ אִישׁ״ לָמָּה לִי?

LITERAL TRANSLATION

Meyasha said: A non-Jew who cursed God with substitute names, according to the Sages, is liable. [1]What is the reason? For the verse states: "Both the stranger, and the native" — [2][regarding] a stranger and the native we need "when he blasphemes the name," [3]but a non-Jew, even with a substitute name.

[4]And Rabbi Meir, what does he do with this "Both the stranger, and the native"? [5]The stranger and the native, with stoning, [6]but a non-Jew, with the sword. [7]It might have entered your mind to say: [8]Since they were included, they were included. [9][Therefore,] it teaches us.

[10]And Rabbi Yitzhak Nappaha according to the Sages, [11]what does he do with this "Both the stranger, and the native"? [Regarding] a stranger and a native, [12]we need a name with a name, [13]but [regarding] a non-Jew, we do not need a name with a name.

[14]Why do I need "Any man"?

TRANSLATION AND COMMENTARY

with one of His **substitute names,** then even **according to the Sages,** he **is liable** for execution. [1]**What is the reason** that a non-Jew is liable in such a case, when a Jew is not? [2]This is learned from **the verse** which **states** (Leviticus 24:16): **"Both the stranger, and the native,** when he blasphemes the name of the Lord, he shall surely be put to death." [3]**Regarding a stranger and the native** who are both members of the Jewish people, **it is necessary** that **"he blaspheme the name** of the Lord." Unless, he curses God using His proper name, he is not put to death. [4]**But a non-Jew** is put to death, **even** if he cursed God using one of his **substitute names.**

וְרַבִּי מֵאִיר [5]The Gemara asks: **Rabbi Meir** who says that a non-Jew who cursed God using one of His substitute names is liable for execution just like a Jew — **what does he do with** the words, **"Both the stranger, and the native"?** Surely those words seem to differentiate between non-Jews and Jews! [6]The Gemara explains: Those words teach that both **the stranger and the native** who blasphemed God are liable to death **by stoning.** [7]**But a non-Jew** who is guilty of blasphemy is liable to death **by decapitation,** the usual punishment for a non-Jew who violated a prohibition that he is obligated to observe. [8]**You might have thought** otherwise, that **since** non-Jews **are included** by the words "Any man" in the prohibition against cursing God with one of His substitute names, **they are** also **included** in the punishment of stoning. [9]**Therefore,** the verse **teaches us** that this is not so.

וְרַבִּי יִצְחָק נַפָּחָא [10]The Gemara asks: **Rabbi Yitzhak Nappaha** who says that **according to the Sages,** a non-Jew is not liable for execution if he cursed God using one of His substitute names — [11]**what does he do with** the words, **"Both the stranger, and the native"?** Surely those words differentiate between a non-Jew and a Jew. Granted according to Rabbi Meir, they exclude a non-Jew from the punishment of stoning. But according to the Sages, that is not necessary, for there would have been no reason to think that a non-Jew is included in the punishment of stoning. [12]The Gemara explains: Those words teach that **regarding the stranger and the native,** [13]**it is necessary** that he curse one divine **name with** another **name,** as was explained above, or else he is not liable for execution. [14]**But regarding a non-Jew, it is not necessary** that he curse one divine **name with** another divine **name.**

אִישׁ אִישׁ [15]The Gemara asks: According to the Sages, **why do I need** the words **"Any man"?** Granted according to Rabbi Meir, they teach that even a non-Jew is liable for execution, if he cursed God with one of His substitute names. But according to the Sages who maintain that a Jew is not liable if he cursed God with a substitute name, what do the words "Any man," teach?

RASHI

ואליבא דרבי מאיר — דמשמע הא לרבנן פטור בן נח על הכנויין, פליגא דרבי מיישא דאיהו סבר אף על גב דאמרי רבנן על הכנויין באזהרה בישראל, מיהו נכרי חייב מיתה מ״כגר וכאזרח״ — מדכתיב גר ואזרח יתירה שמע מינה לחיובי נכרים בכנוי. ורבי מאיר — דאמר גר ואזרח חייבין בכנוי, ונכרים אתרבו מ״איש איש״ — ממאי קא ממעט גר ואזרח לבני נח? הואיל ואיתרבו — להאי פרשתא לכנויין, איתרבו אף לכל האמור בפרשה — ובסקילה. ורבי יצחק נפחא אליבא דרבנן — כיון דאמרי רבנן נכרים פטורין מן הכנוי כישראל, גר ואזרח מאי קא ממעטי? אי למעוטינהו מסקילה — לא איצטריך, דמהיכא תיתי הא לא אתרבו בהא פרשתא! דבשלמא לרבי מאיר סלקא דעתך אמינא הואיל ואיתרבי איתרבי. איש איש למה לי — בין לרבי מיישא בין לרבי יצחק נפחא אליבא דרבנן ברכת השם מ״ויצו ה׳ אלהים״ נפקא כנויים מגר ואזרח נפקי לרבי מיישא ואי לרבי יצחק נפחא הא אמר לרבנן פטורין.

TRANSLATION AND COMMENTARY

דִּיבְּרָה תּוֹרָה [1]The Gemara answers: **The Torah speaks in the** ordinary **language of people,** and the doubling of the word *ish,* "man," in the expression *ish ish,* "any man," is purely stylistic, with no special Halakhic significance.

תָּנוּ רַבָּנַן [2]Having mentioned that non-Jews are bound by the prohibition against blasphemy, the Gemara now begins an extensive discussion regarding the Halakhic obligations enjoined by the Bible upon all human beings — "the seven Noachide laws." It opens with a Baraita in which **our Rabbis taught: "Non-Jews are commanded about seven commandments:** [3]The injunction to establish a system of **laws,** and the prohibitions against **blasphemy, idolatry, incest and adultery, bloodshed, robbery, and** eating **a limb from a living animal.**

[56B] רַבִּי חֲנַנְיָה בֶּן גַּמְלָא [4]**Rabbi Ḥananyah ben Gamla says**: Non-Jews are also bound by the prohibition against eating **the blood of a living animal.** [5]**Rabbi Ḥidka says:** They are **also** bound by the prohibition against **castrating** human beings or animals. [6]**Rabbi Shimon says:** They are **also** bound by the prohibition against **sorcery.** [7]**Rabbi Yose says**: All the magical practices **that are listed in the** Torah **section regarding sorcery are forbidden** also **to a non-Jew**. This is what the Torah meant when it stated (Deuteronomy 18;10-12): [8]**'There must not be found among you anyone that passes his son or his daughter**

[1]דִּיבְּרָה תּוֹרָה כִּלְשׁוֹן בְּנֵי אָדָם. [2]תָּנוּ רַבָּנַן: ״שֶׁבַע מִצְוֹת נִצְטַוּוּ בְּנֵי נֹחַ: [3]דִּינִין, וּבִרְכַּת הַשֵּׁם, עֲבוֹדָה זָרָה, גִּילּוּי עֲרָיוֹת, וּשְׁפִיכוּת דָּמִים, וְגָזֵל, וְאֵבֶר מִן הַחַי.

[56B] [4]רַבִּי חֲנַנְיָה בֶּן גַּמְלָא אוֹמֵר: אַף עַל הַדָּם מִן הַחַי. [5]רַבִּי חִידְקָא אוֹמֵר: אַף עַל הַסֵּירוּס. [6]רַבִּי שִׁמְעוֹן אוֹמֵר: אַף עַל הַכִּישּׁוּף. [7]רַבִּי יוֹסֵי אוֹמֵר: כָּל הָאָמוּר בְּפָרָשַׁת כִּישּׁוּף בֶּן נֹחַ מוּזְהַר עָלָיו. [8]׳לֹא יִמָּצֵא בְךָ מַעֲבִיר בְּנוֹ

LITERAL TRANSLATION

[1]The Torah spoke in the language of men.

[2]Our Rabbis taught: "Non-Jews (lit., "the descendants of Noah") were commanded about seven commandments: [3]Laws, cursing God, idol worship, incest and adultery, and bloodshed, and robbery, and a limb from a living animal.

[56B] [4]Rabbi Ḥananyah ben Gamla says: Also for the blood of a living animal. [5]Rabbi Ḥidka says: Also for castration. [6]Rabbi Shimon says: Also for sorcery. [7]Rabbi Yose says: Whatever is stated in the section regarding sorcery — a non-Jew is warned about it. [8]'There must not be found among you anyone who passes his son

SAGES

רַבִּי חִידְקָא **Rabbi Ḥidka.** Rabbi Ḥidka was a Tanna whose teachings do not appear in the Mishnah but only in Baraitot presented in the Gemara and in Halakhic and Aggadic Midrashim. He was apparently one of the senior disciples of Rabbi Akiva, and his teachings, both Halakhic and Aggadic, are mentioned in the Talmud and other sources.

RASHI

שבע מצות – יליף לה לקמן. **וגלוי עריות** – כולן חוץ מנערה המאורסה, כדכתיב (בראשית כ) גבי אבימלך ״הנך מת על האשה אשר לקחת והיא בעולת בעל״, בעולת בעל – יש להם, נערה המאורסה – אין להם. **אף על הדם מן החי** – כולהו יליף טעמייהו לקמן. **בפרשת מכשף** – זו היא שמזכיר והולך ״לא ימצא בך ובגלל התועבות האלה וגו׳״ ומדנענשו עליהם – שמע מינה הוזהרו על כולם דלא ענש אלא אם כן הזהיר.

NOTES

אֵבֶר מִן הַחַי **A limb from a living animal.** According to some authorities, Adam himself was only commanded to observe six commandments, for he was not permitted to eat meat (see below, 59b), and so the prohibition against eating the limb of a living animal did not apply to him. Others understand that while Adam was not bound by the prohibition against eating the limb of a living animal, he too was commanded to observe seven commandments, for he was bound by the additional prohibition against eating meat. When the descendants of Noah were granted permission to eat meat, that prohibition was replaced by the ban against eating the limb of a living animal (see *Margoliyot HaYam*).

שֶׁבַע מִצְוֹת **Seven commandments.** It has been pointed out that in addition to the derivations mentioned in our passage, there are allusions to the Noachide laws in other verses. For example, the prohibition against idolatry is mentioned in Job 31:26-28; the prohibition against bloodshed follows from Cain's punishment for killing his brother; the prohibition against sexual sins follows from Abimelech's punishment for his advances towards Sarah; the prohibition against robbery follows from the punishment of the generation of the flood for that offense; and the prohibition against eating a limb from an animal was given to Noah (*Lekaḥ Tov*).

אַף עַל הַסֵּירוּס **Also for castration.** *Meiri* suggests that castration is forbidden, because it is similar to eating a limb from a living animal.

אַף עַל הַכִּישּׁוּף **Also for sorcery.** Sorcery is forbidden because it leads to idol worship, for both sorcery and idolatry are based on the same principles (*Meiri*).

HALAKHAH

שֶׁבַע מִצְוֹת נִצְטַוּוּ בְּנֵי נֹחַ **Non-Jews were commanded about seven commandments.** "Adam was given six commandments: The prohibitions against idol worship, blasphemy, bloodshed, sexual sins, and robbery, and the injunction to establish a system of laws. A seventh commandment was given to Noah, the prohibition against eating the limb of a living animal. According to some authorities (*Rashi, Tosafot*), already Adam was given the prohibition against eating the limb of a living animal." (*Rambam, Sefer Shofetim, Hilkhot Melakhim* 9:1.)

TRANSLATION AND COMMENTARY

through the fire, or that uses divination, a soothsayer, or an enchanter, or a witch, or a charmer, or a medium, or a wizard, or a necromancer. For all that do these things are an abomination to the Lord, **and because of these abominations the Lord your God drives them out from before you**.' The verse says that God drove the Canaanite nations out of Eretz Israel because they practiced magic. [1] **And since** God **does not administer punishment** for a misdeed **unless He** first **issued a warning** against it, all the magical practices mentioned in that section must be forbidden to a non-Jew. [2] **Rabbi Elazar says**: Non-Jews are **also** bound by the prohibition against **forbidden mixtures**. How so? [3] **Non-Jews are permitted to wear** garments containing **a mixture of wool and linen**, and they are also permitted to **plant diverse kinds** in one area of the same field. [4] They **are only forbidden to crossbreed** different species of **animals, and graft** different species of **trees** onto one another."

מְנָהָנֵי מִילֵּי [5] The Gemara asks: **From where are all these laws derived?** Which Biblical verse is the source of all these prohibitions? [6] **Rabbi Yoḥanan said**: The seven Noachide laws listed by the anonymous first Tanna of the Baraita are derived from **the verse** containing God's instructions to Adam which **states** (Genesis 2:16-17): [7] **"And the Lord God commanded the man, saying, Of every tree of the garden you may freely eat."** Rabbi Yoḥanan now pins a different Noachide law to each word in this verse. He does so by citing other verses where each word appears. [8] **"And the Lord God commanded" — this is** a reference to the injunction to establish a system of **laws**. [9] **And similarly** the verse regarding Abraham **states** (Genesis 18:19): **"For I know him, that he will command his children** and his household after him, and they shall keep the way of the Lord, to do justice and judgment." [10] "And **the Lord** God commanded"— **this is** a reference to the prohibition against **cursing God**. [11] **And similarly** the verse **states** (Leviticus 16:24): **"And he who blasphemes the name of the Lord, shall surely be put to death."** [12] "And the Lord **God** commanded" — **this** refers to the prohibition against **idolatry**. [13] **And similarly** the verse

וּבִתּוֹ בָּאֵשׁ קֹסֵם קְסָמִים מְעוֹנֵן וּמְנַחֵשׁ וּמְכַשֵּׁף וְחֹבֵר חָבֶר וְשֹׁאֵל אוֹב וְיִדְּעֹנִי וְדֹרֵשׁ אֶל הַמֵּתִים וגו׳ וּבִגְלַל הַתּוֹעֵבֹת הָאֵלֶּה ה׳ אֱלֹהֶיךָ מוֹרִישׁ אוֹתָם מִפָּנֶיךָ׳, [1] וְלֹא עָנַשׁ אֶלָּא אִם כֵּן הִזְהִיר. [2] רַבִּי אֶלְעָזָר אוֹמֵר: אַף עַל הַכִּלְאַיִם. [3] מוּתָּרִין בְּנֵי נֹחַ לִלְבּוֹשׁ כִּלְאַיִם, וְלִזְרוֹעַ כִּלְאַיִם, [4] וְאֵין אֲסוּרִין אֶלָּא בְּהַרְבָּעַת בְּהֵמָה וּבְהַרְכָּבַת הָאִילָן.

[5] מְנָהָנֵי מִילֵּי? [6] אָמַר רַבִּי יוֹחָנָן: דְּאָמַר קְרָא: [7] ״וַיְצַו ה׳ אֱלֹהִים עַל הָאָדָם לֵאמֹר מִכֹּל עֵץ הַגָּן אָכֹל תֹּאכֵל״. [8] ״וַיְצַו״ — אֵלּוּ הַדִּינִין. [9] וְכֵן הוּא אוֹמֵר: ״כִּי יְדַעְתִּיו לְמַעַן אֲשֶׁר יְצַוֶּה אֶת בָּנָיו וגו׳״. [10] ״ה׳״ — זוֹ בִּרְכַּת הַשֵּׁם. [11] וְכֵן הוּא אוֹמֵר: ״וְנֹקֵב שֵׁם ה׳ מוֹת יוּמָת״. [12] ״אֱלֹהִים״ — זוֹ עֲבוֹדָה זָרָה. [13] וְכֵן הוּא

LITERAL TRANSLATION

or his daughter through fire, or that uses divination, a soothsayer, or an enchanter, or a witch, or a charmer, or a medium, or a wizard, or a necromancer....And because of these abominations the Lord your God drives them out from before you.' [1] And He did not punish unless He warned. [2] Rabbi Elazar says: Also for forbidden mixtures. [3] Non-Jews are permitted to wear mixtures of wool and linen, and plant diverse kinds, [4] and are only forbidden to crossbreed animals, and graft trees."

[5] From where are these things [derived]? [6] Rabbi Yoḥanan said: For the verse states: [7] "And the Lord God commanded the man, saying, Of every tree of the garden you may freely eat." [8] "And [the Lord God] commanded" — this is laws. [9] And similarly it states: "For I know him, that he will command his children, etc." [10] "The Lord" — this is cursing the [divine] name. [11] And similarly it states: "And he who blasphemes the name of the Lord, shall surely be put to death." [12] "God" — this is idol worship. [13] And similarly it

RASHI

מותרין בני נח וכו׳ — סיפא דמילתא דרבי אלעזר הוא, וכוליה מפרש לקמן.

NOTES

לְמַעַן אֲשֶׁר יְצַוֶּה **That he will command.** The proof-text cited here reads (Genesis 18:19): "For I know him, that he will command his children and his household after him, and they shall keep the way of the Lord, to do justice (צְדָקָה) and judgment (מִשְׁפָּט)." The Rishonim disagree about the meaning of the word *tzedakah* (translated here as

HALAKHAH

אַף עַל הַכִּלְאַיִם **Also for forbidden mixtures.** "Non-Jews are forbidden to crossbreed animals of different species, and they are also forbidden to graft trees of different species onto one another." (*Rambam, Sefer Shofetim, Hilkhot Melakhim* 10:6.)

עֲבוֹדָה זָרָה **Idolatry.** "If a non-Jew worshipped an idol in the manner in which it is usually served, he is liable for execution. If a non-Jew committed an idolatrous act for

LITERAL TRANSLATION

states: "You shall have no other gods [besides me]." [1]"The man" — this is bloodshed. [2]And similarly it states: "Whoever sheds man's blood, etc." [3]"Saying"— this is incest and adultery. [4]And similarly it states: "It was said, If a man puts away his wife, and she goes from him, and become another man's." [5]"Of every tree of the garden" — [6]and not that which was stolen. [7]"You may freely eat" — [8]and not a limb from a living animal.

[9]When Rabbi Yitzhak came he taught the reverse: [10]"'And [the Lord God] commanded' — this is idol worship. [11]'God' — this is laws."

[12]Granted that "God" is laws, [13]for it is written: "And the master of the house shall be brought to the judges." [14]But "And [the Lord God] commanded"— this is idol worship, [15]what is the meaning?

אוֹמֵר: ״לֹא יִהְיֶה לְךָ אֱלֹהִים אֲחֵרִים״. [1]״עַל הָאָדָם״ — זוֹ שְׁפִיכוּת דָּמִים. [2]וְכֵן הוּא אוֹמֵר: ״שֹׁפֵךְ דַּם הָאָדָם וגו׳״. [3]״לֵאמֹר״ — זוֹ גִּילּוּי עֲרָיוֹת, [4]וְכֵן הוּא אוֹמֵר: ״לֵאמֹר הֵן יְשַׁלַּח אִישׁ אֶת אִשְׁתּוֹ וְהָלְכָה מֵאִתּוֹ וְהָיְתָה לְאִישׁ אַחֵר״. [5]״מִכֹּל עֵץ הַגָּן״ — [6]וְלֹא גָּזֵל. [7]״אָכֹל תֹּאכֵל״ — [8]וְלֹא אֵבֶר מִן הַחַי.

[9]כִּי אֲתָא רַבִּי יִצְחָק תָּנֵי אִיפְּכָא: [10]״׳וַיְצַו׳ — זוֹ עֲבוֹדָה זָרָה, [11]׳אֱלֹהִים׳ — זוֹ דִּינִין״.

[12]בִּשְׁלָמָא ״אֱלֹהִים״ זוּ דִּינִין, [13]דִּכְתִיב: ״וְנִקְרַב בַּעַל הַבַּיִת אֶל הָאֱלֹהִים״. [14]אֶלָּא ״וַיְצַו״ — זוֹ עֲבוֹדָה זָרָה, [15]מַאי מַשְׁמַע?

RASHI

מכל עץ הגן ולא גזל — מדאיצטריך למישרי ליה ולהפקיר לו עצי הגן — שמע מינה שאינו מופקר לו נאסר לו. **אכול תאכל** — העומד לאכילה, ולא תאכל אבר מן החי דבהמה בחייה אינה עומדת לאכילה אלא לגדל ולדות.

TRANSLATION AND COMMENTARY

states (Exodus 20:3): **"You shall have no other gods besides me."** [1]"And the Lord God commanded **the man**"— **this** refers to the prohibition against **bloodshed**. [2]**And similarly** the verse **states** (Genesis 9:6): **"Whoso sheds man's blood** by man shall his blood be shed." [3]"And the Lord God commanded the man **saying**"— **this is** a reference to **incest and adultery**. [4]**And similarly** the verse **states** (Jeremiah 3:1): "**It was said**, **If a man put away his wife, and she go from him, and become another man's,** shall he return to her again? shall not that land be greatly polluted? but you have played the harlot with many lovers, and will you yet return again to me? says the Lord." [5]**"Of every tree of the garden** you may freely eat" — you may eat of the trees that have been permitted to you, [6]**but** you may **not** eat of **that which was stolen** and does not belong to you. [7]"Of every tree of the garden **you may freely eat**" — you may freely eat of that which is meant to be eaten, [8]**but** you may **not** eat **a limb from a living animal**, for a living animal is not meant to be eaten.

כִּי אֲתָא [9]**When Rabbi Yitzḥak came** from Eretz Israel to Babylonia, **he taught** a Baraita **which reversed** the derivations: "The verse states: 'And the Lord God commanded.' [10]**'And the Lord God commanded'— this is** a reference to the prohibition against **idolatry**. [11]'And the Lord **God** commanded' — **this is** a reference to the injunction to establish a system of **laws."**

בִּשְׁלָמָא [12]The Gemara asks: **Granted that** the word **"God** [*Elohim*]" can be understood as a reference to the injunction to establish a system of **laws**, [13]**for** the verse **states** (Exodus 22:7): **"And the master of the house shall be brought to the judges** [*Elohim*]." [14]**But** as for the second derivation, according to which **"And the Lord God commanded" is** a reference to the prohibition against **idolatry**, [15]**what is the** basis for this **interpretation?**

NOTES

"justice," but which can also mean "charity") in this context, and whether it constitutes a separate obligation that was imposed upon the descendants of Noah. According to *Ramah,* the word *tzedakah* refers here to compromise reached by arbitration, and as such is included in the injunction to establish a system of civil law. Others (*Ran*) argue that non-Jews are bound by the obligation to give charity, and that they are punished if they fail to fulfill this obligation, as the verse states (Ezekiel 16:49): "And she did not strengthen the hand of the poor and needy."

לֵאמֹר הֵן יְשַׁלַּח It was said, If a man put away. The derivation of the prohibition against sexual sins from the word לֵאמֹר is based on the fact that in the verse in Jeremiah 3:1, the word לֵאמֹר appears in an unusual position at the beginning of the verse. Thus, the word may be understood as an allusion to marriage (like the Talmudic term מַאֲמָר) (*Margoliyot HaYam*).

אָכֹל תֹּאכֵל — וְלֹא אֵבֶר מִן הַחַי You may freely eat — and not a limb from a living animal. The Rishonim disagree about the relationship between the prohibition imposed upon Adam against eating meat (see below, 59b), and the Noachide prohibition against eating the limb of a living

HALAKHAH

which a Jew would be sentenced to death, he too is liable for the death penalty. And if he committed an idolatrous act for which the Jew would not be sentenced to death, he too is not liable for the death penalty, but the act is nevertheless forbidden to him." (*Rambam, Sefer Shofetim, Hilkhot Melakhim* 9:2.)

TRANSLATION AND COMMENTARY

רַב חִסְדָּא [1]**Rav Ḥisda and Rav Yitzḥak bar Avidimi** disagreed about the matter: [2]**One** of these Sages **said:** The connection between "command" and idolatry is learned from the verse which states (Exodus 32:8): **"They have turned aside quickly out of the way which I commanded them; they have made them** a molten calf, and have worshipped it, and have sacrificed to it, and said, These are your gods, O Israel, which have brought you up out of the land of Egypt." [3]**And the other** Sage **said:** The connection between the two is learned from the verse which states (Hosea 5:11): **"Ephraim is oppressed and crushed in judgment, because he willingly walked after the command"** of the false prophets who worshipped idols.

מַאי בֵּינַיְיהוּ [4]The Gemara asks: **What is** the practical **difference between** these two derivations? [5]The Gemara explains: **There is** a practical difference **between** the two regarding **a non-Jew who made an idol, but did not bow down to it.** [6]**According to the** Amora **who said** that the prohibition against idolatry for a non-Jew is derived from the verse which states: [7]**"They have made them** a molten calf," the non-Jew **is liable** for his transgression **from the time that he made** the idol, before worshiping it. [8]But **according to** the Amora **who said** that the prohibition against idolatry for a non-Jew is derived from the verse which states: [9]**"Because he willingly walked after** the command," the non-Jew is not liable **unless he went after** the idol **and** actually worshipped it.

אָמַר רָבָא [10]**Rava said: Is there** really **someone who says that if a non-Jew made an idol, but did not bow down to it,** he **is liable** for execution? [11]**But surely it was taught** otherwise in the following Baraita: **"Regarding idolatry,** transgressions **for which a Jewish court would execute** a Jew, **a non-Jew is prohibited** from doing. [12]But transgressions for which a **Jewish court would not execute** a Jew, even though they are forbidden to the Jew, **a non-Jew is not prohibited** from doing." [13]**What** does this Baraita **exclude?**

LITERAL TRANSLATION

[1]Rav Ḥisda and Rav Yitzḥak bar Avidimi: [2]One said: "They have turned aside quickly out of the way which I commanded them; they have made them, etc." [3]And one said: "Ephraim is oppressed and crushed in judgment, because he willingly walked after the command."

[4]What is [the difference] between them? [5]There is between them a non-Jew who made an idol, but did not bow down to it. [6]According to the one who said "they made them," [7]he is liable from the time of making. [8]According to the one who said: "Because he willingly walked after," [9]until he goes after it and worships it.

[10]Rava said: And is there one who says [that] a non-Jew who made an idol, but did not bow down to it, is liable? [11]But surely it was taught: "Regarding idol worship, things for which a Jewish court executes, a non-Jew is warned about. [12][Things for which] a Jewish court does not execute, a non-Jew is not warned about." [13]To exclude

[1]רַב חִסְדָּא וְרַב יִצְחָק בַּר אַבְדִּימִי: [2]חַד אָמַר: ״סָרוּ מַהֵר מִן הַדֶּרֶךְ אֲשֶׁר צִוִּיתִם עָשׂוּ לָהֶם וגו׳״. [3]וְחַד אָמַר: ״עָשׁוּק אֶפְרַיִם רְצוּץ מִשְׁפָּט כִּי הוֹאִיל הָלַךְ אַחֲרֵי צַו״.

[4]מַאי בֵּינַיְיהוּ? [5]אִיכָּא בֵּינַיְיהוּ נָכְרִי שֶׁעָשָׂה עֲבוֹדָה זָרָה, וְלֹא הִשְׁתַּחֲוָה לָהּ. [6]לְמַאן דְּאָמַר ״עָשׂוּ״, [7]מִשְּׁעַת עֲשִׂיָּיה מִחַיַּיב. [8]לְמַאן דְּאָמַר: ״כִּי הוֹאִיל הָלַךְ״, [9]עַד דְּאָזֵיל בַּתְרָהּ וּפָלַח לָהּ.

[10]אָמַר רָבָא: וּמִי אִיכָּא לְמַאן דְּאָמַר נָכְרִי שֶׁעֲשָׂאָהּ עֲבוֹדָה זָרָה וְלֹא הִשְׁתַּחֲוָה לָהּ חַיָּיב? [11]וְהָתַנְיָא: ״בַּעֲבוֹדָה זָרָה, דְּבָרִים שֶׁבֵּית דִּין שֶׁל יִשְׂרָאֵל מְמִיתִין עֲלֵיהֶן, בֶּן נֹחַ מוּזְהָר עֲלֵיהֶן. [12]אֵין בֵּית דִּין שֶׁל יִשְׂרָאֵל מְמִיתִין עֲלֵיהֶן, אֵין בֶּן נֹחַ מוּזְהָר עֲלֵיהֶן״. [13]לְמַעוּטֵי

RASHI

עשוק אפרים — מיד שונאיו ״ורצוץ משפט״ רצוץ על ידי שפטיו של הקדוש ברוך הוא. **כי הואיל הלך אחרי צו** — מפני שנתרצה ללכת אחרי צווי של נביאי הבעל.

NOTES

animal. According to *Tosafot,* Adam was also bound by the prohibition against eating the limb of a living animal. The prohibition against eating meat only forbade him to kill an animal for its meat, but if an animal died a natural death, he was permitted to eat it. But he was forbidden to eat the limb of a living animal, even if the limb became detached from the animal's body by itself. According to *Ran,* Adam was not bound by the prohibition against eating the limb of a living animal, and the verse, "Of every tree of the garden you may freely eat," forbade Adam to eat meat. When meat was later permitted to the descendants of Noah, the verse, "You may freely eat," assumed a narrower meaning, prohibiting the descendants of Noah to eat the limb of a living animal. Alternatively, from the outset, the verse, "You may freely eat," alluded to the prohibition against eating the limb of a living animal, which would apply in future generations.

TRANSLATION AND COMMENTARY

[1]**Does it not come to exclude a non-Jew who made an idol, but did not bow down to it?** A Jew is forbidden to make an idol, as the verse states (Exodus 20:4): "You shall not make for yourself any carved idol, or any likeness," but he is not liable for execution unless he actually worships the idol. Thus, it follows from the Baraita that a non-Jew is not prohibited from making an idol.

אָמַר רַב פַּפָּא [2]**Rav Pappa said: No,** a non-Jew who made an idol but did not bow down to it is in fact liable for execution, even though a Jew would not be put to death for such an offense. [3]And the Baraita comes **to exclude embracing and kissing** the idol. If a Jew embraces or kisses an idol, he violates the prohibition (Exodus 20:5): "You shall not serve them," but he is not liable for execution. The Baraita teaches us that a non-Jew is not prohibited from embracing or kissing an idol.

גִּיפּוּף וְנִישּׁוּק [4]The Gemara clarifies this matter: To **what** kind of **embracing and kissing** an idol is the Baraita referring? [5]**If you say** that **the usual manner** of worshipping that particular idol is through embraces and kisses, a Jew who embraced or kissed the idol **is** indeed **liable** to death **by execution,** since serving an idol the way in which other idolaters worship it is always a capital offense. [6]**Rather** the Baraita must come **to exclude** embracing and kissing the idol when it is **not the usual manner** in which other idolaters worship it. Since a Jew would not be liable for execution if he embraced or kissed the idol, a non-Jew is not prohibited from serving the idol in that manner.

דִּינִין בְּנֵי נֹחַ [7]The Gemara raises a question regarding the Baraita's list of Noachide laws: **Are non-Jews** really **enjoined** to establish **a legal system?** [8]**But surely it was taught** otherwise in the following Baraita: "The people of **Israel were commanded about the ten commandments** when they camped **in Marah** — [9]**the seven** obligations **which the non-Jews had** previously **accepted upon themselves,** [10]**and to these** seven **were added** another three obligations: Establishing a system of **laws,** observing **the Sabbath, and honoring one's father and mother.**" [11]The Gemara adds: From where do we know about those three additional obligations? As for establishing **a legal system,** [12]**the verse** describing the events at Marah **states** (Exodus 15:25): **"There he made for them a statute and an ordinance."** Satutes and ordinances refer to a system of laws. [13]As for observing **the Sabbath and honoring one's father and mother,** [14]**the verses state** (Deuteronomy 5:12): "Keep the Sabbath day to sanctify it, **as the Lord your God has commanded you**"; and (Deuteronomy 5:16): "Honor your father and you mother, as the Lord your God has commanded you." [15]**And Rav Yehudah said:** What is meant here by the words, **"As the Lord your God has commanded you"?**

מַאי? [1]לָאו לְמַעוּטֵי נָכְרִי שֶׁעָשָׂה עֲבוֹדָה זָרָה, וְלֹא הִשְׁתַּחֲוָה לָהּ?

[2]אָמַר רַב פַּפָּא: לָא, [3]לְמַעוּטֵי גִּיפּוּף וְנִישּׁוּק.

[4]גִּיפּוּף וְנִישּׁוּק דְּמַאי? [5]אִילֵימָא כְּדַרְכָּהּ — בַּר קְטָלָא הוּא. [6]אֶלָּא לְמַעוּטֵי שֶׁלֹּא כְּדַרְכָּהּ.

[7]דִּינִין בְּנֵי נֹחַ אִיפְּקוּד? [8]וְהָתַנְיָא: "עֶשֶׂר מִצְוֹת נִצְטַוּוּ יִשְׂרָאֵל בְּמָרָה, [9]שֶׁבַע שֶׁקִּיבְּלוּ עֲלֵיהֶן בְּנֵי נֹחַ, [10]וְהוֹסִיפוּ עֲלֵיהֶן: דִּינִין, וְשַׁבָּת, וְכִיבּוּד אָב וָאֵם. [11]דִּינִין, [12]דִּכְתִיב: "שָׁם שָׂם לוֹ חֹק וּמִשְׁפָּט". [13]שַׁבָּת וְכִיבּוּד אָב וָאֵם, [14]דִּכְתִיב: "כַּאֲשֶׁר צִוְּךָ ה׳ אֱלֹהֶיךָ". [15]וְאָמַר רַב יְהוּדָה:

LITERAL TRANSLATION

what? [1]Is it not to exclude a non-Jew who made an idol, but did not bow down to it?

[2]Rav Pappa said: No, [3]to exclude embracing and kissing.

[4]Embracing and kissing what? [5]If you say in its usual manner — he is liable for execution. [6]Rather to exclude not in its usual manner.

[7]Are non-Jews commanded about laws? [8]But surely it was taught: "Israel was commanded about the ten commandments in Marah, [9]seven which the non-Jews accepted upon themselves, [10]and they added to them: Laws, the Sabbath, and honoring one's father and mother. [11]Laws, [12]as it is written: "There he made for them a statute and an ordinance" [13]The Sabbath and honoring one's father and mother, [14]as it is written: "As the Lord your God has commanded you." [15]And Rav Yehudah said:

RASHI

למעוטי גיפוף ונישוק — אבל עשה אתרבי מ״וילו״ אף על גב דבית דין של ישראל אין ממיתין. **מגפף ומנשק** — אמרינן במתניתין (סנהדרין ס,ב) דגבי ישראל אינו נהרג. **בבדרכה** — שדרך עבודתה בכך, ישראל נמי כל עבודה שדרך עבודתה בכך ישראל חייב עליה ואפילו הוא דרך בזיון כגון פוער לפעור וזורק אבן למרקולים, כדאמר במתניתין (שם) וילפינן מקראי, וכל שכן כשהוא דרך כבוד, דכולהו כדרכן נפקי מ״איכה יעבדו הגוים האלה את אלהיהם וגו׳״. **כאשר צוך ה׳ אלהיך** — כתיב בדברות האחרונות, גבי שבת וכבוד אב ואם, והיכן צוך? הא ליכא למימר דמשה הוה אמר להו בערבות מואב, ״כאשר צוך בסיני״, דמשה לאו מאליו היה שונה להם משנה תורה ומזהירם על מצותיה אלא כמו שקבלה הוא, והיה חוזר ומגיד להם, וכל מה שכתוב בדברות האחרונות היה כתוב בלוחות וכן שמע בסיני.

LITERAL TRANSLATION

"As [the Lord your God] has commanded you" — [1]at Marah.

[2]Rav Naḥman said in the name of Rabbah bar Avuha: [3]It was only needed for a congregation, and witnesses, [4]and a warning.

[5]If so, what is [meant by] "they added to them laws"?

[6]Rather, Rava said: [7]It was only needed for the laws of fines.

[8]Still, it should have [stated]: "They added with regard to the laws"!

[9]Rather, Rav Aḥa bar Yaakov said: [10]It was only needed to establish a court in each and every province, and in each and every city.

[11]But about this non-Jews were not commanded?

"כַּאֲשֶׁר צִוְּךָ" — [1]בְּמָרָה.

[2]אָמַר רַב נַחְמָן אָמַר רַבָּה בַּר אֲבוּהּ: [3]לָא נִצְרְכָה אֶלָּא לְעֵדָה, וְעֵדִים, [4]וְהַתְרָאָה.

[5]אִי הָכִי, מַאי "וְהוֹסִיפוּ עֲלֵיהֶן דִּינִין"?

[6]אֶלָּא אָמַר רָבָא: [7]לָא נִצְרְכָה אֶלָּא לְדִינֵי קְנָסוֹת.

[8]אַכַּתִּי: "וְהוֹסִיפוּ בְּדִינִין" מִיבָּעֵי לֵיהּ!

[9]אֶלָּא אָמַר רַב אַחָא בַּר יַעֲקֹב: [10]לָא נִצְרְכָה אֶלָּא לְהוֹשִׁיב בֵּית דִּין בְּכָל פֶּלֶךְ וּפֶלֶךְ וּבְכָל עִיר וָעִיר.

[11]וְהָא בְּנֵי נֹחַ לֹא אִיפְּקוּד?

RASHI

לעדה ועדים והתראה — וכן נלטוו ישראל במרה להיות דנין בסנהדרין של עשרים ושלשה, כדאמרינן (סנהדרין ב,א): עדה שופטת ועדה מצלת, דנכרים לא איפקוד בהכי, כדילפינן לקמן (נז,ב) מקראי דבן נח נהרג בעד אחד ובדיין אחד. אי הכי מאי הוסיפו עליהן דינין — אין אלו דינין אלא מצות דיינין. דיני קנסות — הוסיפו במרה, דבני נח לא הוזהרו עליהן דכתיב "ויצו", וגמרינן לה מ"אשר יצוה" דהתם צדקה ומשפט כתיב, דהיינו דין ופשרה, אבל קנסות לאו משפט נינהו — דקנסינן ליה טפי מדיניה. בדינין מבעי ליה — דניהוי משמע שהוסיפו להם בהלכות דינין שנלטוו עליהם כבר, אבל השתא דקתני הוסיפו עליהם דינין, משמע כל הלכות דינין הוסיפו. כל פלך — מדינה.

TRANSLATION AND COMMENTARY

Where had God commanded Israel about the Sabbath and honoring one's parents before then? [1]He commanded them about these matters **at Marah**. This Baraita implies that establishing a system of **laws** is not included among the seven Noachide laws, but rather that obligation was given to Israel, and to Israel alone, when they were at Marah.

אָמַר רַב נַחְמָן [2]**Rav Naḥman said in the name of Rabbah bar Avuha:** Establishing a legal system is in fact included among the seven Noachide laws. The Baraita said that the obligation of establishing a legal system was given to Israel at Marah, [3]only because **that was necessary** for certain details regarding the judicial system: That capital cases must be tried before a Lesser Sanhedrin, a court composed of twenty-three judges; that punishments may only be administered on the basis of the testimony of two **witnesses;** [4]**and** that punishments may only be administered if the transgressor was properly **warned.**

אִי הָכִי [5]The Gemara asks: **If so, what did** the Baraita mean when it said: "To these seven Noachide laws, **were added** the obligation of establishing a system of **laws,** and two other obligations"?

אֶלָּא אָמַר רָבָא [6]**Rather, Rava said:** Establishing a legal system is in fact included among the seven Noachide laws. When the Baraita said that the obligation of establishing a system of laws was added at Marah, [7]**that was only necessary regarding the laws of fines.** Non-Jews were commanded to establish a legal system and execute justice, but they were not commanded to impose punitive fines upon wrongdoers. At Marah Israel was commanded about the laws of fines which go beyond the execution of justice.

אַכַּתִּי [8]The Gemara asks: A difficulty **still** remains, for rather than stating: "They added to them the obligation of establishing a system of laws," which implies that the entire obligation of establishing a system of laws was given at Marah, the Baraita **should have stated: "They added with regard to the** obligation of establishing a system of **laws,"** which would imply that the basic obligation of establishing a system of laws already existed!

אֶלָּא [9]**Rather, Rav Aḥa bar Ya'akov said:** Establishing a legal system is in fact included among the seven Noachide laws. [10]The Baraita, **was only necessary** for the additional obligation **to establish a court in each and every province, and in each and every city,** that obligation being incumbent upon Israel, but not upon others.

וְהָא בְּנֵי נֹחַ [11]The Gemara asks: [73]**But** is it really true that **non-Jews were not commanded** to establish a

SAGES

רַב אַחָא בַּר יַעֲקֹב Rav Aḥa bar Ya'akov. A Babylonian Amora of the third and fourth generations, Rav Aḥa bar Ya'akov was a disciple of Rav Huna and must have lived to a great age, for he also discusses the Halakhah with Abaye and Rava. Rav Aḥa bar Ya'akov lived in the city of Papunya (sometimes he is named "Papuna'i," after his place of residence). He was the leading Sage of that city and instituted various regulations.

In addition to his eminence as a Torah scholar — he was praised by Rava as a great man, and Rav Naḥman, too, acknowledged his intelligence. He was one of the most saintly members of his generation and a worker of miracles. Several of the Sages of the following generation studied under him.

His son, Ya'akov, is mentioned in tractate *Kiddushin,* and we also know of a nephew, Rav Aḥa bar Rav Ika.

NOTES

מַאי וְהוֹסִיפוּ What is meant by "they added." Some Rishonim explain this query as follows: The Baraita says that establishing a system of laws was added for Israel at Marah. If this refers to the regulations regarding a Lesser Sanhedrin, two witnesses, and a warning, there is a difficulty, for this is not an "addition," but rather a restriction of the authority of the court (*Ramah, Ra'avad*).

TRANSLATION AND COMMENTARY

court in every province and city? [1]**But surely it was taught** otherwise in a Baraita: **"Just as Israel was commanded to establish courts in each and every province, and in each and every city,** as the verse states (Deuteronomy 16:18): 'Judges and officers shall you make you in all your gates, which the Lord your God gives you, throughout your tribes,' [2]**so too non-Jews were commanded to establish courts in each and every province, and in each and every city,** for that same verse continues: 'And they shall judge the people with righteous judgment,' and non-Jews are commanded to execute judgment."

אֶלָּא אָמַר רָבָא [3]**Rather, Rava said: The Tanna** of this Baraita who maintains that only Jews are obligated to establish a legal system **is the Tanna of the School of Menashe, who removed** from the list of seven Noachide laws the obligation of establishing a legal system and the prohibition against blasphemy (in Hebrew *d"kh, dinin* and *birkhat hashem*), [4]**and replaced them with** the prohibitions against **castration and forbidden mixtures** (in Hebrew, *s"kh, sirus* and *kilayim*). [5]**For a Tanna of the School of Menashe taught** the following Baraita: **"Non-Jews are commanded about seven commandments:** [6]The prohibitions against **idolatry, incest and adultery, bloodshed, robbery,** eating **a limb from a living animal, castrating** a human being or an animal, **and prohibited mixtures,** (but they are not forbidden to curse God nor are they obligated to establish a system of laws). [7]**Rabbi Yehudah says: The first man was only commanded about** the prohibition against **idol worship,** [8]**as the verse states** (Genesis 2:16): **'And the Lord God commanded the man'** — the Lord imposed His Godhood upon the man, forbidding him to make himself another god. [9]**Rabbi Yehudah ben Betera says:** The first man was **also** prohibited from **cursing God,** as the verse states: 'And the Lord God commanded the man' — the Lord imposed His Godhood upon the man, forbidding him to curse Him. **And there are those who say:** The first man was **also** commanded to establish a system of **laws,** as the verse states: 'And the Lord God commanded the man' — the Lord imposed His Godhood upon the man, instructing him to fear Him alone, and no other man, for if he fears other men, he will pervert justice."

[1]וְהָתַנְיָא: "כְּשֵׁם שֶׁנִּצְטַוּוּ יִשְׂרָאֵל לְהוֹשִׁיב בָּתֵּי דִינִין בְּכָל פֶּלֶךְ וּפֶלֶךְ, וּבְכָל עִיר וָעִיר, [2]כָּךְ נִצְטַוּוּ בְּנֵי נֹחַ לְהוֹשִׁיב בָּתֵּי דִינִין בְּכָל פֶּלֶךְ וּפֶלֶךְ, וּבְכָל עִיר וָעִיר! [3]אֶלָּא אָמַר רָבָא: הַאי תָּנָא דְּבֵי מְנַשֶּׁה הוּא, [4]דְּמַפֵּיק ד"ך וְעַיֵּיל ס"ך. [5]דְּתָנָא דְּבֵי מְנַשֶּׁה: שֶׁבַע מִצְוֹת נִצְטַוּוּ בְּנֵי נֹחַ: [6]עֲבוֹדָה זָרָה, וְגִילּוּי עֲרָיוֹת, וּשְׁפִיכוּת דָּמִים, גָּזֵל, וְאֵבֶר מִן הַחַי, סֵירוּס, וְכִלְאַיִם. [7]רַבִּי יְהוּדָה אוֹמֵר: אָדָם הָרִאשׁוֹן לֹא נִצְטַוָּוה אֶלָּא עַל עֲבוֹדָה זָרָה בִּלְבַד, [8]שֶׁנֶּאֱמַר: 'וַיְצַו ה' אֱלֹהִים עַל הָאָדָם'. [9]רַבִּי יְהוּדָה בֶּן בְּתֵירָה אוֹמֵר: אַף עַל בִּרְכַּת הַשֵּׁם. [10]וְיֵשׁ אוֹמְרִים: אַף עַל הַדִּינִים".

LITERAL TRANSLATION

[1]But surely it was taught: "Just as Israel was commanded to establish courts in each and every province, and in each and every city, [2]so too non-Jews were commanded to establish courts in each and every province, and in each and every city."

[3]Rather, Rava said: This Tanna is the Tanna of the School of Menashe, [4]who takes out *d"kh,* and puts in *s"kh,* [5]for [a Tanna] of the School of Menashe taught: "Non-Jews were commanded about seven commandments: [6]Idol worship, and incest and adultery, and bloodshed, and robbery, and a limb from a living animal, and castration, and forbidden mixtures. [7]Rabbi Yehudah says: The first man was only commanded about idol worship, [8]as it is stated: 'And the Lord God commanded the man.' [9]Rabbi Yehudah ben Betera says: Also for cursing God. [10]And there are those who say: Also for laws."

RASHI

ישראל נצטוו להושיב — דיינין בכל עיר ועיר, כדכתיב (דברים יז) "תתן לך בכל שעריך". **כך נצטוו נכרים** — דהא משפט כתיב ביה, והכא נמי כתיב (שם) "ושפטו את העם משפט צדק". **האי תנא** — דברייתא דלעיל דקתני — הוסיפו עליהן דינין, דמשמע דבני נח לא נצטוו עליהם — תנא דבי מנשה הוא. **ד"ך** — דינין וברכת השם. **ס"ך** — סירוס וכלאים. **שבע מצות וכו'** — לקמן מפרש דתנא דבי מנשה לא דריש "ויצו". והני כל חדא באנפי נפשיה כתיב בהו. **אדם הראשון לא נצטווה אלא על עבודה זרה בלבד שנאמר ויצו ה' אלהים** — את אלהותו צוה עליו על האדם שלא ימירהו באחר. **אף על ברכת השם** — דנפקא ליה נמי מ"אלהים" אלהותו צוה עליו שלא יקללהו, כדכתיב (שמות כב) "אלהים לא תקלל". **אף הדינין** — מ"אלהים" נמי נפקא, יהא אלהותי עליך להיות מוראי עליך, ולהיות מוראי בלבך ולא מורא בשר ודם להטות משפט, "כי המשפט לאלהים הוא" כדמפרש רב ואזיל.

SAGES

רַבִּי יְהוּדָה בֶּן בְּתֵירָה Rabbi Yehudah ben Betera. The Ben Betera family produced renowned Sages over a number of generations. Some members of the family served as Nasi during the time of Hillel, but transferred the position to him.

It is almost certain that there were two Sages named Yehudah ben Betera. The second may have been the grandson of the first. Both lived in the city of Netzivin (Nisibis) in Babylonia — one while the Temple was still standing, and the second at the end of the Tannaitic period.

HALAKHAH

נִצְטַוּוּ יִשְׂרָאֵל לְהוֹשִׁיב בֵּית דִּינִין בְּכָל פֶּלֶךְ וּפֶלֶךְ Israel was commanded to establish courts in each and every province. "There is a positive commandment by Torah law to appoint judges and court officers in every city and every province," following the Baraita. (*Rambam, Sefer Shofetim, Hilkhot Sanhedrin* 1:1.)

כָּךְ נִצְטַוּוּ בְּנֵי נֹחַ לְהוֹשִׁיב בֵּית דִּינִין בְּכָל פֶּלֶךְ וּפֶלֶךְ So too non-Jews were commanded to establish courts in each and every province. "Non-Jews are obligated to appoint judges in every province in order to judge cases involving

[1]כְּמַאן אָזְלָא הָא דְּאָמַר רַב יְהוּדָה אָמַר רַב: [2]אֱלֹהִים אֲנִי — לֹא תְקַלְּלוּנִי, [3]אֱלֹהִים אֲנִי — לֹא תְמִירוּנִי, [4]אֱלֹהִים אֲנִי — יְהֵא מוֹרָאִי עֲלֵיכֶם. [5]כְּמַאן? [6]כְּיֵשׁ אוֹמְרִים.

[7]תָּנָא דְּבֵי מְנַשֶּׁה — [8]אִי דָּרֵישׁ ״וַיְצַו״, [9]אֲפִילּוּ הָנָךְ נַמִי. [10]אִי לָא דָּרֵישׁ ״וַיְצַו״, [11]הָנֵי מְנָא לֵיהּ?

[12]לְעוֹלָם, לָא דָּרֵישׁ ״וַיְצַו״. [13]הָנֵי — כָּל חֲדָא וַחֲדָא בְּאַפֵּי נַפְשֵׁיהּ כְּתִיבָא. [14]עֲבוֹדָה זָרָה וְגִילּוּי עֲרָיוֹת — [57A] [15]דִּכְתִיב: ״וַתִּשָּׁחֵת הָאָרֶץ לִפְנֵי הָאֱלֹהִים״. [16]וְתָנָא דְּבֵי רַבִּי יִשְׁמָעֵאל: ״בְּכָל מָקוֹם שֶׁנֶּאֱמַר: ׳הַשְׁחָתָה׳ אֵינוֹ אֶלָּא דְּבַר עֶרְוָה וַעֲבוֹדָה זָרָה. [17]דְּבַר עֶרְוָה, שֶׁנֶּאֱמַר: ׳כִּי הִשְׁחִית

LITERAL TRANSLATION

[1]In accordance with whom goes that which Rav Yehudah said in the name of Rav: [2]I am God — do not curse me. [3]I am God — do not exchange me. [4]I am God — let my fear be upon you. [5]In accordance with whom? [6]In accordance with those who say.

[7]The Tanna of the School of Menashe — [8]if he interprets "And He commanded," [9]even those too. [10]If he does not interpret "And He commanded," [11]from where does he know these?

[12]In fact, he does not interpret "And He commanded." [13]These — each and every one is written separately. [14]Idol worship and incest and adultery [57A] [15]as it is written: "The earth also was corrupt before God." [16]And [the Sage] of the School of Rabbi Yishmael taught: "Wherever 'corruption' is stated it refers only to sexual matters and idol worship. [17]Sexual matters, as it is stated: 'For all flesh had

TRANSLATION AND COMMENTARY

כְּמַאן אָזְלָא [1]The Gemara asks: **In accordance with** the position of **which** Tanna **did Rav Yehudah say in the name of Rav:** God said to the first man: [2]**"I am God"** — therefore do not curse me. [3]**"I am God"** — therefore **do not exchange me** for another god. [4]**"I am God"** — therefore **let my fear be upon you,** and not the fear of other men, lest you come to pervert justice. [5]The Gemara answers: **In accordance with** the position of **which** Tanna was this statement made? [6]**In accordance with** the position of **those who said** in the Baraita cited above that the verse "And the Lord commanded the man" alludes to three commandments, the prohibitions against idolatry and blasphemy, and the obligation to establish a legal system.

תָּנָא דְּבֵי מְנַשֶּׁה [7]The Gemara asks about the position of the **Tanna of the School of Menashe:** [8]**If he interprets** the verse, **"And** the Lord God **commanded** the man," as alluding to the universal obligations imposed upon non-Jews, [9]then he should say they were **also** commanded **to obey the other** two commandments: The prohibition against blasphemy and the obligation to establish a legal system. [10]And **if he does not interpret** the verse, **"And** the Lord God **commanded** the man," in that manner, [11]then **from where does he know** anything about the Noachide laws?

לְעוֹלָם [12]The Gemara explains: **In fact,** the Tanna of the School of Menashe **does not interpret** the verse, **"And** the Lord God **commanded** the man," as alluding to the universal obligations imposed upon non-Jews. [13]In his list of Noachide laws, **each commandment is alluded to separately** in the Torah. [14]The prohibitions against **idolatry, incest and adultery** [57A] are alluded to by [15]**the verse** which **states** (Genesis 6:11): **"The earth also was corrupt before God,** and the earth was filled with violence." Since God punished Noah's generation for its "corruption," it must be that "corruption" is forbidden. [16]**And the Sage of the School of Rabbi Yishmael taught** the following Baraita: **"Wherever** the Torah **speaks of 'corruption,' it refers to** transgressions involving **sexual matters and idol worship.** [17]'Corruption' refers to **sexual matters, as the verse states** (Genesis 5:12): 'And God looked upon the earth, and behold it was corrupt; **for all**

RASHI

אלהים אני — נאמר לאדם הראשון. **אל תמירני** — כדאמרינן ״לא יהיה לך אלהים אחרים על פני״ זולתי. **לא תקללוני** — כדאמרינן ״אלהים לא תקלל״. **יהא מוראי עליכם** — כדאמרינן אלהים לשון שררה ורבנות, כמו ״נתתיך אלהים לפרעה״ (שמות ז) — יהא מוראי עליך ולא מורא בשר ודם, ״לא תגורו מפני איש כי המשפט לאלהים הוא״ (דברים א) דהיינו דינין. **כיש אומרים** — דמרבי לכולהו. **אפילו הנך נמי** — דינין וברכת השם. **ותשחת הארץ** — מדאיענש עלייהו — שמע מינה איפקוד עלייהו. **כי השחית כל בשר את דרכו על הארץ** — גלוי עריות, דכתיב (משלי ל) ״דרך גבר בעלמה״, ודור

NOTES

יְהֵא מוֹרָאִי עֲלֵיכֶם Let My fear be upon you. This is an allusion to the obligation to establish a judicial system, for if the judges fulfill their duties, correcting injustices and punishing the wrongdoers, the fear of God will be instilled in the hearts of men, and they will refrain from sinning (*Ran*).

HALAKHAH

the six Noachide prohibitions, and rebuke the people to act properly." (*Rambam, Sefer Shofetim, Hilkhot Melakhim* 9:14.)

כָּל בָּשָׂר אֶת דַּרְכּוֹ׳. [1]עֲבוֹדָה זָרָה, דִּכְתִיב: ׳פֶּן תַּשְׁחִתוּן וַעֲשִׂיתֶם וגו׳׳״.
[2]וְאִידָךְ? [3]אוֹרְחַיְיהוּ דְּקָא מְגַלֵּי.
[4]שְׁפִיכוּת דָּמִים, דִּכְתִיב: ״שֹׁפֵךְ דַּם הָאָדָם וגו׳״.
[5]וְאִידָךְ? [6]קְטָלַיְיהוּ הוּא דְּקָמְגַלֵּי.
[7]גָּזֵל, דִּכְתִיב: ״כְּיֶרֶק עֵשֶׂב נָתַתִּי לָכֶם אֶת כֹּל״. [8]וְאָמַר רַבִּי לֵוִי: ״כְּיֶרֶק עֵשֶׂב״, [9]וְלֹא כְּיַרַק גִּנָּה.
[10]וְאִידָךְ? [11]הַהוּא לְמִישְׁרֵי בָּשָׂר הוּא דַּאֲתָא.

LITERAL TRANSLATION

corrupted its way.' [1]Idol worship, as it is stated: 'Lest you become corrupt, and make, etc.'"
[2]And the other one? [3]It reveals their ways.
[4]Bloodshed, as it is written: "Whoever sheds man's blood, etc."
[5]And the other one? [6]It reveals their death.
[7]Robbery, as it is written: "Even as the green herb have I given you all things." [8]And Rabbi Levi said: "As the green herb," [9]and not the green of the garden.
[10]And the other one? [11]That came to permit meat.

TRANSLATION AND COMMENTARY

flesh had corrupted its way,' the word 'its way' alluding to sexual intercourse. [1]And 'corruption' refers to **idol worship, as the verse states** (Deuteronomy 4:16): '**Lest you become corrupt, and make** a carved idol, the similitude of any figure.'"

וְאִידָךְ [2]The Gemara asks: **The other** Sage who derives the prohibitions against forbidden sexual relations and idolatry from the verse "And the Lord God commanded the man" — what does he learn from this verse? [3]The Gemara explains: This verse merely **reveals** the wicked **ways** of Noah's generation, the sins for which they were punished with the great flood.

שְׁפִיכוּת דָּמִים [4]The Gemara continues: The prohibition against **bloodshed** is inferred from **the verse** which **states** (Genesis 9:6): "**Whoever sheds man's blood** by man shall his blood be shed."

וְאִידָךְ [5]The Gemara asks: And the **other** Sage, who derives the prohibition against bloodshed from a different verse, what does he infer from this verse? The Gemara explains: According to that Sage, the prohibition against bloodshed is derived from the verse, "And the Lord God commanded the man," [6]and the verse cited here **teaches** the punishment for that crime: those who are guilty of bloodshed are put to **death.**

גָּזֵל [7]The Gemara continues: The prohibition against **robbery** is derived from **the verse** which **states** (Genesis 9:3): "Every moving thing that lives shall be food for you; **even as the green herb have I given you all things.**" [8]And as **Rabbi Levi said: "As the green herb** have I given you all things" — [9]but you may **not** eat the **green of** someone's private **garden.**

וְאִידָךְ [10]The Gemara asks: And what does the **other** Sage learn from this verse? [11]The Gemara answers: **This** verse **permits meat** to be eaten, as is taught by Rav later in the chapter (59b). Adam was forbidden to eat meat, as the verses state (Genesis 1:29-30): "And God said, Behold I have given you every herb bearing seed, which is upon the face of all the earth, and every tree, on which is the fruit yielding seed; to you it shall be for food. And to every beast of the earth, and to every bird of the air, and to everything that creeps on the earth, wherein there is life, I have given every herb of food." God gave man the green herbs, but He did not give him the beasts of the earth. But after Noah and his family left the ark, God permitted them to eat meat, as the verse states (Genesis 9:3): "Every moving thing that lives shall be food for you; even as the green herb have I given you all things."

RASHI

המבול על העריות נענשו כדכתיב (בראשית ו) "ויראו בני האלהים את בנות האדם כי טובות הנה". ואידך — מאי דריש "ויצו" אמר לך: אזהרה מ"ויצו" הוזהר אדם הראשון, וגבי דור המבול אורחייהו מגלי להודיעך על מה נענשו. קטלייהו קאי מגלי — באיזו מיתה ימיתם, ולעולם הוזהרו מ"ויצו". כירק עשב — עשב קרי עשב השדה, וכל הגדל מאליו שאין בו טורח לחרוש ולזרוע. למישרי בשר הוא דאתא — כדאמר לקמן בפרקין (נט,ב): אדם הראשון לא הותר לו בשר באכילה אלא עשבים ואילנות דכתיב "הנה נתתי לכם את כל עשב זורע זרע לכם יהיה לאכלה ולחית הארץ" — העשבים והאילנות תאכלו אתם וחית הארץ. ולא חית הארץ לכם והוזהרו על אבר מן החי מ"אכול תאכלו". וללמדך דאפילו אינך ממיתה אלא שנפל ממנה אבר מאליו לא תאכלנו, ובאו בני נח והתיר להם להמית ולאכול, ולאו למדרש מינה ולא כירק גנה אתא, דלגופיה אצטריך, לפי שירק עשב הותר לאדם הראשון תלה להו לבני נח בהמות וחיות כירק עשב.

TERMINOLOGY

וְאִידָךְ? **And the other one?** I.e., what does the other scholar, holding the conflicting opinion, say to this argument? This expression is used to clarify differences of opinion between scholars, with the Gemara asking each in turn how he will answer the argument brought by the other.

NOTES

כְּיֶרֶק עֵשֶׂב **As the green herb.** The prohibition against robbery could not have been derived from what the Torah says about the generation of the flood, for it could have been argued that the Torah wishes to reveal the wicked ways of Noah's generation for which they were punished by the great flood, and not to teach the prohibition against robbery. *Ḥamra Veḥaye* adds that the verse regarding Noah's generation would only teach about robbery, but the verse, "As the green herb," implies that not only robbery but also theft is forbidden.

[1]אֵבֶר מִן הַחַי, דִּכְתִיב: [2]"אַךְ בָּשָׂר בְּנַפְשׁוֹ דָמוֹ לֹא תֹאכֵלוּ". [3]וְאִידָךְ? [4]הַהוּא לְמִישְׁרֵי שְׁרָצִים הוּא דַּאֲתָא. [5]סֵירוּס, דִּכְתִיב: [6]"שִׁרְצוּ בָאָרֶץ וּרְבוּ בָהּ". [7]וְאִידָךְ? [8]לִבְרָכָה בְּעָלְמָא. [9]כִּלְאַיִם, דִּכְתִיב: [10]"מֵהָעוֹף לְמִינֵהוּ". [11]וְאִידָךְ? [12]הַהוּא לְצַוְתָא בְּעָלְמָא. [13]אָמַר רַב יוֹסֵף: אָמְרִי בֵּי רַב: [14]עַל שָׁלֹשׁ מִצְוֹת בֶּן נֹחַ נֶהֱרָג: [15](גֶּשֶׁ"ר סִימָן). [16]עַל גִּילּוּי עֲרָיוֹת, וְעַל שְׁפִיכוּת דָּמִים, וְעַל בִּרְכַּת הַשֵּׁם. [17]מַתְקִיף לָהּ רַב שֵׁשֶׁת:

TRANSLATION AND COMMENTARY

אֵבֶר מִן הַחַי [1]The Gemara proceeds to discuss the next of the Noachide laws: The prohibition against eating **a limb from a living animal** is derived from **the verse** which **states** (Genesis 9:4): [2]**"But flesh with its life, which is its blood, you shall not eat,"** meaning that you may not eat the flesh of an animal while it is still alive.

וְאִידָךְ [3]The Gemara asks: **And** how does **the other** Sage interpret this verse? [4]The Gemara answers: **This** verse **comes to permit** a non-Jew to eat the limb of a **crawling creature**, as will be explained later in the chapter (see 59b).

סֵירוּס [5]The Gemara continues: The Noachide law prohibiting **castration** is derived from **the verse** which **states** (Genesis 9:7): [6]"And as for you, be fruitful, and multiply; **bring forth abundantly in the earth, and multiply in it."** This implies that one is forbidden to prevent human beings and animals from multiplying.

וְאִידָךְ [7]The Gemara asks: **And** how does **the other** Sage understand this verse? [8]The Gemara explains: According to the other Sage, the verse was not meant to be understood as a commandment, but **merely as a blessing.** God blessed Noah and his family that they would be fruitful and multiply, but He did not command them to do so, nor did He forbid them from taking steps that would interfere with their multiplication..

כִּלְאַיִם [9]The Gemara continues: The prohibition against **mixing species** is alluded to in **the verses** which **state** (Genesis 6:19-20): "And of every living thing of all flesh, two of every sort shall you bring into the ark, to keep them alive with you; they shall be male and female. [10]**Of birds after their kind,** and of cattle after their kind, of every creeping thing of the earth after its kind." The fact that God commanded Noah to bring two of each species into the ark rather than allow the animals to crossbreed, implies that crossbreeding animals is forbidden.

וְאִידָךְ [11]The Gemara asks: **And** how does **the other** Sage interpret this verse? [12]The Gemara explains: **This** verse does not forbid crossbreeding, but rather it was **merely** meant as advice to Noah that he bring two of each species into the ark **for company's sake.**

אָמַר רַב יוֹסֵף [13]**Rav Yosef said: The Sages of the school of Rabbi** Yehudah HaNasi **said:** [14]Even though a non-Jew is commanded to obey seven commandments, he **is** only **put to death** for the violation of **three** of those **commandments** — the prohibitions against forbidden sexual relations, bloodshed, and blasphemy, as will be explained below. [15]**(A mneumonic device** by which to remember which prohibitions are punishable by the death sentence is *Gshr* — [16]an acronym for ***gillui arayot*** [**forbidden sexual relations**], ***shefikhut damim*** [**bloodshed**], and ***birkat hashem*** [**blasphemy**]).

מַתְקִיף לָהּ [17]**Rav Sheshet strongly objected** to this ruling: **Granted** that a non-Jew is executed for

LITERAL TRANSLATION

[1]A limb from a living animal, as it is written: [2]"But flesh with its life, which is its blood, you shall not eat."

[3]And the other one? [4]That came to permit crawling creatures.

[5]Castration, as it is written: [6]"Bring forth abundantly in the earth, and multiply in it."

[7]And the other one? [8]Merely for a blessing.

[9]Forbidden mixtures, as it is written: [10]"Of birds after their kind."

[11]And the other one? [12]That is merely for company's sake.

[13]Rav Yosef said: [The Sages] of the school of Rabbi said: [14]A non-Jew is put to death for three commandments: [15](A sign: *Gshr*). [16]Forbidden sexual relations, bloodshed, and cursing God.

[17]Rav Sheshet strongly objected:

RASHI

בשר בנפשו דמו — בעוד שהוא הבשר בנפשו, דהיא דמו — לא תאכלו הבשר. **למישרא שרצים הוא דאתא** — משום שהוזהרו באבר מן החי מ"אכול תאכל" אתא האי קרא למשרא אבר מן החי בשרצים, והכי דרשינן לקמן בפרקין (נט,ב): אותו בשר שקרוי דמו בנפש, והבשר קרוי בשר דהיינו דמו חלוק מבשרו אסרנא לכו באבר מן החי, ולא בשרצים שאין דמו קרוי נפש אלא הרי הוא כבשרו, דאילו בישראל לא מחייבי עליה כרת כדאמר בכריתות (כא,א) דלית ביה אלא לאו, דדם דשרצים כבשר. **לברכה בעלמא** — לא לפרות ולא לרבות צוום, אלא ברכם בפריה ורביה. **מן העוף למינהו** — מדנצטווה להביא זכר ונקבה לתיבה מכל מין ולא שיזדווג לו מין אחר — שמע מינה אסורין להרביע כלאים. **ואידך** — לאו משום איסור כלאים אלא לצוות בעלמא, שכל אחד ואחד נוח לו לצוות מינו מלצוות מין אחר. **על שלש מצות בן נח נהרג** — ואף על פי שנצטוו בשבע אין נהרגין אלא על שלש, כדפירש להו רב ששת דבשפיכות דמים כתיבא בהדיא "דמו ישפך" וגלוי עריות וברכת השם כתיב גבי ישראל "איש איש" ודרשינן להו לרבות את הכותים להיות במיתה כישראל.

TRANSLATION AND COMMENTARY

bloodshed, [1]**for the verse** explicitly states (Genesis 9:6): **"Whoever sheds man's blood** by man shall his blood be shed." [2]**But** as for **those** other two prohibitions — sexual sins and blasphemy, **from where do** the Sages of the school of Rabbi Yehudah HaNasi **know** that they carry a death sentence? [3]**If they learned** this by an analogy **from** the punishment imposed in a case of **bloodshed,** then they should have learned by that same analogy that the death sentence should [4]**also** be imposed for the violation of **all the other** prohibitions that apply to a non-Jew. [5]And **if** the death sentence in the case of those two prohibitions **is derived** from the expression, ***"ish ish,"*** [6]then a death sentence in the case of **idol worship should also be derived from** the expression ***"ish ish"***! Regarding forbidden sexual relations, the verse states (Leviticus 18:6): "No man [*ish ish*] shall approach to any that is near of kin to him, to uncover her nakedness." And regarding blasphemy, the verse states (Leviticus 24:15): "Any man [*ish ish*] who curses his God shall bear his sin." In each of those cases, the doubling of the word *"ish* [man]" in the expression *"ish ish"* is understood as teaching that every man, even a non-Jew, is included in the prohibition, and liable for execution for its violation. But that same expression is found regarding the prohibition against idol worship, as the verse states (Leviticus 20:2): "Any man *[ish ish]* of the children of Israel, or of the strangers that sojourn in Israel, that gives of his seed to Molech, he shall surely be put to death." Thus, a non-Jew should also be included in that prohibition, and liable for execution for its violation.

אֶלָּא [7]**Rather, Rav Sheshet said: The Sages of the school of Rav said** as follows: Even though a non-Jew is commanded to obey seven commandments, [8]he **is** only **put to death** for the violation of **four** of those **commandments** — the prohibitions against forbidden sexual relations, bloodshed, blasphemy, and idolatry. The punishment in the case of bloodshed is stated explicitly in the verse, and the punishment in the other three cases is learned from the expression *ish ish.* [9]The Gemara asks: **Is a non-Jew** really **put to death** for the violation of the prohibition against **idol worship**? [10]**But surely it was taught** otherwise in a Baraita: **"Regarding idolatry,** transgressions **for which a Jewish court would execute** a Jew, [11]**a non-Jew is prohibited** from doing." A careful reading of the Baraita leads to the following conclusion: [12]A non-Jew is **indeed** governed by the **prohibition** against idol worship, [13]but, unlike a Jew, he is **not** liable for **execution** for its violation!

אָמַר [14]**Rav Naḥman bar Yitzḥak said:** The fact that the Baraita speaks only of a prohibition does not mean that the transgression is not punishable by execution, for whenever the Torah imposed a **prohibition** on non-Jews, the punishment for violating the prohibition **is execution.**

בִּשְׁלָמָא שְׁפִיכוּת דָּמִים, [1]דִּכְתִיב: "שֹׁפֵךְ דַּם הָאָדָם וגו׳". [2]אֶלָּא הָנָךְ, מְנָא לְהוּ? [3]אִי גָּמַר מִשְּׁפִיכוּת דָּמִים, [4]אֲפִילּוּ כּוּלְּהוּ נַמִי. [5]אִי מִשּׁוּם דְּאִיתְרַבַּאי מֵ"אִישׁ אִישׁ", [6]עֲבוֹדָה זָרָה נַמִי אִיתְרַבֵּי מֵ"אִישׁ אִישׁ"!

[7]אֶלָּא, אָמַר רַב שֵׁשֶׁת: אָמְרִי בֵּי רַב: [8]עַל אַרְבַּע מִצְוֹת בֶּן נֹחַ נֶהֱרָג. [9]וְעַל עֲבוֹדָה זָרָה בֶּן נֹחַ נֶהֱרָג? [10]וְהָתַנְיָא: "בַּעֲבוֹדָה זָרָה, דְּבָרִים שֶׁבֵּית דִּין שֶׁל יִשְׂרָאֵל מְמִיתִין עֲלֵיהֶן, [11]בֶּן נֹחַ מוּזְהַר עֲלֵיהֶן". [12]אַזְהָרָה — אִין, [13]מִיתָה — לָא!

[14]אָמַר רַב נַחְמָן בַּר יִצְחָק: אַזְהָרָה שֶׁלָּהֶן זוֹ הִיא מִיתָתָן.

LITERAL TRANSLATION

Granted bloodshed, [1]for it is written: "Whoever sheds man's blood, etc." [2]But those, from where do they [know]? [3]If he learns from bloodshed, [4]even all of them also. [5]If because they were included by *"ish ish,"* [6]idol worship was also included by *"ish ish"*!

[7]Rather, Rav Sheshet said: [The Sages] of the school of Rav said: [8]A non-Jew is put to death for four commandments. [9]And for idol worship a non-Jew is put to death? [10]But surely it was taught: "Regarding idol worship, things for which a Jewish court executes, [11]a non-Jew is warned about." [12]A warning — yes; [13]execution — no!

[14]Rav Naḥman bar Yitzḥak said: Their warning is their execution.

RASHI

בעבודה זרה נמי — כתיב גבי מולך "איש איש" ב"קדושים תהיו". על ארבע מצות — עבודה זרה הוסיף עמהם. בעבודה זרה דברים שבית דין ישראל וכו׳ — הכי קאמר: באיסור עבודה זרה אותם דברים שבית דין ישראל ממיתין עליהם, כגון כל עבודות שדרכה של עבודה זרה בכך, וזבוח וקיטור אפילו שלא כדרכה, כדלקמן בפירקין (ס,ב). אזהרה שלהם — כלומר כל אזהרה דתנא תנא גבי בני נח זו היא מיתה שלהם, דלא דייק בהו תנא למיתני מיתה גבי חייבי מיתות, ואזהרה — בשאין בהן מיתה כלגבי ישראל.

NOTES

אַזְהָרָה שֶׁלָּהֶן זוֹ הִיא מִיתָתָן **Their warning is their execution.** Various interpretations have been offered for this statement. Some understand that this means that whenever the Torah imposed a prohibition on non-Jews, the punishment for violating the prohibition is execution. Others understand that this means that non-Jews are liable for the death

TRANSLATION AND COMMENTARY

רַב הוּנָא [1]**Rav Huna, Rav Yehudah, and all the disciples of Rav said: A non-Jew is put to death** for the violation of any one of the seven **commandments** that apply to him. [2]**The Torah taught** the punishment **regarding one** prohibition — bloodshed — **but the same law applies to all** the rest **of the** prohibitions as well.

וְעַל הַגָּזֵל [3]The Gemara asks: **Is a non-Jew** really **put to death** for the violation of the prohibition against **robbery?** [4]**But surely it was taught** otherwise in the following Baraita: **"Regarding robbery, if he stole** something **or robbed** somebody, **and similarly** if he took **a beautiful woman** as his prisoner of war (which is a robbery of sorts), [5]**and similarly** if he did **something else that is like** one of **these** acts, the following distinction applies: [6]Regarding **a non-Jew** stealing **from** another **non-Jew, or a non-Jew** stealing **from a Jew,** the act **is forbidden.** [7]**And** regarding **a Jew** stealing **from a non-Jew,** the act **is permitted,** for the verse states (Leviticus 19:13): 'You shall not steal from your neighbor' — from your neighbor you shall not steal, but you may steal from a non-Jew." [8]**And if it is** so that a non-Jew is put to death for violating the prohibition against robbery, **let** the Baraita **teach explicitly** that if a non-Jew steals from another non-Jew, or from a Jew, **he is liable** for execution!

מִשּׁוּם [9]The Gemara answers: A non-Jew is in fact put to death for robbery. The Baraita does not speak of his liability, because the first part of the Baraita was formulated under the stylistic influence of the last part of the Baraita. Since the Baraita **wanted to teach in the last clause:** [10]"Regarding **a Jew** stealing **from a non-Jew,** the act is **permitted,"** [11]**it taught in the first clause:** "Regarding a non-Jew stealing from another non-Jew, or from a Jew, the act **is forbidden."** Had the Baraita stated in the first clause that the non-Jew is liable for execution for robbery, it would have had to state in the next clause that if a Jew steals from a non-Jew, he is exempt from punishment. But this would have implied that the Jew is only exempt from punishment, but the act itself is forbidden, which is not the case.

[1]רַב הוּנָא וְרַב יְהוּדָה וְכוּלְּהוּ תַּלְמִידֵי דְּרַב אָמְרִי: עַל שֶׁבַע מִצְוֹת בֶּן נֹחַ נֶהֱרָג. [2]גַּלֵּי רַחֲמָנָא בַּחֲדָא, וְהוּא הַדִּין לְכוּלְּהוּ.
[3]וְעַל הַגָּזֵל בֶּן נֹחַ נֶהֱרָג? [4]וְהָתַנְיָא: ״עַל הַגָּזֵל, גָּנַב וְגָזַל, וְכֵן יְפַת תּוֹאַר, [5]וְכֵן כַּיּוֹצֵא בָּהֶן — [6]נָכְרִי בְּנָכְרִי וְנָכְרִי בְּיִשְׂרָאֵל, אָסוּר; [7]וְיִשְׂרָאֵל בְּנָכְרִי, מוּתָּר״. [8]וְאִם אִיתָא, נִיתְנֵי: חַיָּיב!
[9]מִשּׁוּם דְּקָבָעֵי לְמִיתְנֵי סֵיפָא: [10]״יִשְׂרָאֵל בְּנָכְרִי, מוּתָּר״, [11]תָּנָא רֵישָׁא: ״אָסוּר״.

LITERAL TRANSLATION

[1]Rav Huna and Rav Yehudah and all the disciples of Rav said: A non-Jew is put to death for seven commandments. [2]The Torah (lit., "the Merciful") revealed about one, and the same law applies to all of them.

[3]And for robbery a non-Jew is put to death? [4]But surely it was taught: "For robbery, [if] he stole or he robbed, and similarly a woman of beautiful appearance, [5]and similarly that which is like them — [6]a non-Jew from a non-Jew, and a non-Jew from a Jew, he is forbidden; [7]and a Jew from a non-Jew, he is permitted." [8]And if it is, let it teach: He is liable!

[9]Since it wanted to teach in the last clause: [10]"A Jew from a non-Jew, he is permitted," [11]it taught in the first clause: "He is forbidden."

RASHI

גלי רחמנא בחדא – בשפיכות דמים. על הגזל – כך הוא מצות בני נח, גנב וגזל וכן יפת תואר דהוי נמי גזל שגוזלין את אשתו במלחמה. וכן כיוצא בהן – שאינן ממש גזל אלא דומין להם, ולקמן מפרש להו. ישראל בנכרי מותר – ד"לא תעשוק את רעך" כתיב (ויקרא יט) ולא נכרי, ומדרבנן איכא למאן דאסר משום חילול השם ב"הגוזל" בתרא (בבא קמא קיג,א). משום דקבעי למיתנא סיפא ישראל בנכרי מותר – ואי תנא גבי נכרי בנכרי חייב, הוה תני ישראל בנכרי פטור, ומשמע פטור מן המיתה אבל עובר עליו בלאו, ומשום הכי תנא ברישא לשון איסור, דליתני גבי ישראל מותר, דסבירא ליה כמאן דאמר מותר ממש.

NOTES

penalty even without a warning (see *Ramah* and *Ran*). It has been suggested that a non-Jew is liable for execution, even if he was not properly warned against violating the prohibition prior to the commission of his offense, because the commandments imposed upon non-Jews are all rational obligations, and anyone should know that they are forbidden (see *Margoliyot HaYam*).

HALAKHAH

עַל שֶׁבַע מִצְוֹת בֶּן נֹחַ נֶהֱרָג **A non-Jew is subject to the death penalty for violation of any of the seven Noachide commandments.** "This follows the ruling of Rav Yehudah and the disciples of Rav." (*Rambam, Sefer Shofetim, Hilkhot Melakhim* 9:14.)

עַל הַגָּזֵל בֶּן נֹחַ **Laws of theft for non-Jews.** "A non-Jew is liable to punishment for theft whether he stole from another non-Jew or from a Jew. This includes both open theft (such as purse-snatching) and covert theft (such as house-breaking). It also includes kidnapping, as well as refusal to pay a worker's wages. For all these types of theft a non-Jew is liable to the death penalty. This penalty applies even if the amount stolen is less than a perutah's worth," according to Rav Aḥa bar Ya'akov, Rav Pappa, and Rav Aḥa the son of Rav Ika. (*Rambam, Sefer Shofetim, Hilkhot Melakhim* 9:9.)

TRANSLATION AND COMMENTARY

הָא כָּל הֵיכָא [1]The Gemara has difficulty with this answer: **But surely whenever** the non-Jew **is liable for execution,** the Baraita **states** that liability explicitly, [2]**for an earlier clause** of the Baraita **teaches: "Regarding bloodshed,** the following distinction applies: [3]If **a non-Jew** killed another **non-Jew, or a non-Jew** killed **a Jew,** the killer **is liable** for execution; [4]if **a Jew** killed **a non-Jew, he is exempt** from punishment." Thus, we see that the Baraita does in fact speak in terms of liability and exemption. Hence, when the Baraita states that an act is forbidden, it is precise, meaning that the act is in fact forbidden, but the transgressor is exempt from punishment!

הָתָם הֵיכִי לִיתְנֵי [5]The Gemara resolves this difficulty: **There,** regarding bloodshed, **how should** the Baraita **have been formulated?** [6]**If it had** taught that a non-Jew **is forbidden** to kill another non-Jew or a Jew, **and** a Jew **is permitted** to kill a non-Jew, this would present a difficulty. [7]**For surely it was taught** otherwise in a different Baraita: "Regarding **non-Jews, and shepherds of small cattle** who are assumed to be robbers, since they graze their flocks in other people's pastures — **one does not** have to **raise** them **up** from a pit into which they fell, or rescue them in any other way, **but one** may **not cast** them down into the pit, or actively cause their death in any other way." Thus, we see that a Jew is not permitted to kill a non-Jew, and so regarding bloodshed the other Baraita could only have spoken in terms of liability and exemption. But regarding robbery, the Baraita spoke in terms of the act being forbidden or permitted, for had it spoken in terms of liability and exemption, it would have implied that a Jew is forbidden to steal from a non-Jew, as was explained above.

כַּיּוֹצֵא בּוֹ [8]Regarding the Baraita that was cited above, which stated that a non-Jew is forbidden to steal, rob, take a woman as his prisoner of war, or do something else that is like one of these acts, the Gemara asks: Regarding an act **that is like robbery, what is** it referring to?

[1]וְהָא כָּל הֵיכָא דְּאִית לֵיהּ חִיּוּבָא מִיתְנָא קָתָנֵי, [2]דְּקָתָנֵי רֵישָׁא: "עַל שְׁפִיכוּת דָּמִים, [3]נָכְרִי בְּנָכְרִי וְנָכְרִי בְּיִשְׂרָאֵל, חַיָּיב; [4]יִשְׂרָאֵל בְּנָכְרִי, פָּטוּר". [5]הָתָם הֵיכִי לִיתְנֵי? [6]לִיתְנֵי "אָסוּר" "וּמוּתָּר" — [7]וְהָתַנְיָא: "נָכְרִי וְרוֹעֵי בְּהֵמָה דַקָּה — לֹא מַעֲלִין וְלֹא מוֹרִידִין".
[8]כַּיּוֹצֵא בּוֹ בְּגָזֵל, מַאי הִיא?

LITERAL TRANSLATION

[1]But surely it teaches [that], for wherever he has liability for execution, [2]the first clause teaches: "For bloodshed, [3]a non-Jew to a non-Jew, or a non-Jew to a Jew, he is liable; [4]a Jew to a non-Jew, he is exempt."

[5]There, how should it teach? [6]If it teaches "he is forbidden," and "he is permitted" — [7]but surely it was taught: "A non-Jew and shepherds of small cattle — one does not raise up, nor cast down."

[8]That which is like robbery, what is it?

RASHI

הא כל היכא דאיכא חיוב מיתה מתנא – תנייה בלשון חיוב, ומדנקט הכא לשון איסור שמע מינה דווקא תננהו. **היכי ליתני** – לעולם הכא לאו דוקא איסור נקט, אלא משום סיפא. ודקשיא לך: רישא מדלא נקט נמי לשון איסור – שמע מינה דוקא תני להו – התם לא מצי למיתנא לשון איסור, משום דנבעי למימר ישראל בנכרי מותר, ולא מצי מתני ליה. הכי גרסינן: **הנכרי וכן רועי בהמה דקה ישראל** – שסתמן גזלנים, שמרעים בהמתן בשדות אחרים. **לא מעלין ולא מורידין** – לא מעלין אותם מן הבור להצילם מן המיתה, ולא מורידין אותם לבור להמיתם בידים.

NOTES

לֹא מַעֲלִין וְלֹא מוֹרִידִין **One does not raise up, nor cast down.** Some of the Rishonim note that this statement refers only to non-Jews who violate the seven Noachide commandments. But non-Jews who fulfill the seven Noachide commandments must be rescued just like Jews (see *Meiri*).

HALAKHAH

בֶּן נֹחַ שֶׁהָרַג **A non-Jew who committed murdered.** "A non-Jew who murdered is liable to the death penalty, whether the victim was a Jew or a non-Jew." (*Rambam, Sefer Shofetim, Hilkhot Melakhim* 9:4.)

יִשְׂרָאֵל שֶׁהָרַג נָכְרִי **A Jew who murdered a non-Jew.** "A Jew who murdered a non-Jew is not liable to the death penalty," following the ruling of the *Baraita* here. (*Rambam, Sefer Nezikin, Hilkhot Rotze'ah* 2:11.)

לֹא מַעֲלִין וְלֹא מוֹרִידִין **We do not pull him out [of a pit] and we do not push him in.** "Regarding non-Jews with whom the Jews are not at war — and likewise Jews who shepherd sheep and goats in Eretz Israel and allow their animals to graze in other people's fields (or in Jewish-owned fields outside the Eretz Israel [*Bet Yosef, Sefer Meir Einayim*]) — the law is that one should not do anything to cause their death. However, if one sees that they have fallen into mortal danger of their own accord, one should not try to save them. Some authorities maintain that the correct interpretation is as follows: There is no mitzvah to kill them, but it is permissible to do so (*Bet Yosef, Darkei Moshe, Shakh*). Others maintain that killing them is definitely forbidden (*Maharshal, Taz*). But it is certainly forbidden to kill a non-Jew who observes the seven Noachide commandments (*Meiri*). (*Shulkhan Arukh, Yoreh De'ah* 158; *Ḥoshen Mishpat* 425:5.)

BACKGROUND

פְּרוּטָה Perutah. The perutah was the smallest coin in circulation among the Jews in antiquity. For Halakhic purposes the Sages decreed that the perutah has a certain absolute value, which is that of approximately half a gram of silver. But the term is sometimes used broadly to designate any copper coin of low value. Thus coins known as "perutot" may have been worth more or less than the Halakhically determined value of a perutah.

TRANSLATION AND COMMENTARY

אָמַר [1]**Rav Aḥa bar Ya'akov said: This was only needed** to teach that a non-Jew **working in** someone else's **vineyard** is forbidden to eat the grapes.

פּוֹעֵל בַּכֶּרֶם [2]The Gemara asks: A non-Jew **working in** someone else's **vineyard — when** is he forbidden to eat from the grapes? [3]**If** he was hired to pick grapes, **when** the agricultural **work is being finished,** eating of the grapes should be permitted. A Jew working in the vineyard of another Jew is permitted to eat of the produce at that time, as the verse states (Deuteronomy 23:25): "When you come into your neighbor's vineyard, then you may eat your fill of grapes as you desire," and elsewhere the Rabbis interpret that verse as referring to a worker hired to pick grapes. [4]And **if** he was **not** hired to pick grapes, **when** the agricultural **work is being finished**, meaning that he was hired to hoe or weed the vineyard, [5]eating of the grapes is **outright robbery,** not just something that is like robbery!

אֶלָּא [6]**Rather, Rav Pappa said: This was only needed** to teach that a non-Jew is forbidden to steal even a minute amount of property that is **less than the value of a perutah.**

אִי הָכִי [7]The Gemara asks: **If this** is what the Baraita means, there is a difficulty, for **is** in fact **a non-Jew forbidden** to steal less than a perutah **from a Jew?** [8]**But** surely a Jew **is ready to waive** less than a perutah, and so the act should not be regarded as robbery at all!

נְהִי דְּבָתַר [9]The Gemara answers: **After the fact** a Jew is indeed ready to **waive** less than the value of a perutah that was stolen from him, and so a robber who stole only a minute amount of property is not required to return it. [10]But **at the time** of the robbery, **is** the Jew **not distressed** about his loss?

נָכְרִי בְּנָכְרִי [11]The Gemara asks: But a difficulty still remains, for if a **non-Jew** steals **from** another **non-Jew in a case like that,** [12]**since** non-Jews **are** generally **not ready to waive** anything that was stolen from them, not even less than a perutah, [13]the case should **be** regarded as a case of **outright robbery,** and not just something that is like robbery!

אֶלָּא [14]**Rather, Rav Aḥa the son of Rav Ika said: This was only needed** to teach **about someone who withholds the wages of** his **employee,** which is like robbery, but not outright robbery. The Baraita teaches as follows: Regarding a **non-Jew** who withholds wages **from a non-Jew, or a non-Jew** who withholds wages **from a Jew,** the act **is forbidden.** [15]But regarding **a Jew** who withholds wages **from a non-Jew,** the act **is permitted.**

[1]אָמַר רַב אַחָא בַּר יַעֲקֹב: לֹא נִצְרְכָה אֶלָּא לְפוֹעֵל בַּכֶּרֶם.
[2]פּוֹעֵל בַּכֶּרֶם, [3]אֵימַת? אִי בִּשְׁעַת גְּמַר מְלָאכָה, הֶתֵּירָא הוּא. [4]אִי לָאו בִּשְׁעַת גְּמַר מְלָאכָה, [5]גָּזֵל מְעַלְיָא הוּא!
[6]אֶלָּא, אָמַר רַב פַּפָּא: לֹא נִצְרְכָה אֶלָּא לְפָחוֹת מִשָּׁוֶה פְּרוּטָה.
[7]אִי הָכִי, נָכְרִי בְּיִשְׂרָאֵל, אָסוּר? [8]הָא בַּר מְחִילָה הוּא!
[9]נְהִי דְּבָתַר הָכִי מָחֵיל לֵיהּ, [10]צַעֲרָא בְּשַׁעְתֵּיהּ מִי לֵית לֵיהּ?
[11]נָכְרִי בְּנָכְרִי כַּיּוֹצֵא בָּהֶן, [12]כֵּיוָן דְּלָאו בְּנֵי מְחִילָה נִינְהוּ, [13]גָּזֵל מְעַלְיָא הוּא!
[14]אֶלָּא, אָמַר רַב אַחָא בְּרֵיהּ דְּרַב אִיקָא: לֹא נִצְרְכָה אֶלָּא לְכוֹבֵשׁ שְׂכַר שָׂכִיר. [15]נָכְרִי בְּנָכְרִי, וְנָכְרִי בְּיִשְׂרָאֵל, אָסוּר; [16]יִשְׂרָאֵל בְּנָכְרִי, מוּתָּר.

LITERAL TRANSLATION

[1]Rav Aḥa bar Ya'akov said: It was only needed for a worker in a vineyard.

[2]A worker in a vineyard, when? [3]If at the time of the completion of work, it is permitted. [4]If not at the time of the completion of work, [5]it is outright robbery!

[6]Rather, Rav Pappa said: It was only needed for less than the value of a perutah.

[7]If so, a non-Jew from a Jew, he is forbidden? [8]But he is fit for waiving!

[9]Though afterwards he waives to him, [10]at the time does he not have distress?

[11]A non-Jew from a non-Jew in a case like that, [12]since they are not fit for waiving, [13]it is outright robbery!

[14]Rather, Rav Aḥa the son of Rav Ika said: It was only needed for someone who withholds the wages of an employee. [15]A non-Jew from a non-Jew, and a non-Jew from a Jew, he is forbidden; [16]a Jew from a non-Jew, he is permitted.

RASHI

פועל בכרם — ואוכל מן הענבים. **בשעת גמר מלאכה** — כגון ששכרו לבצור. **התירא הוא** — ואפילו ישראל בישראל, דכתיב (דברים כג) "ואכלת ענבים כנפשך שבעך ואל כליך לא תתן", בשעה שאתה נותן לכליו של בעל הבית אתה אוכל, וברייתא קתני ישראל בנכרי מותר, הא ישראל בישראל אסור, ותו: בנכרי היכי אסור ליה, מי איכא מידי דישראל בישראל שרי ולנכרי אסור?! **אי לאו בשעת גמר מלאכה גזל מעליא הוא** — וגזל תנא ליה רישא. **צערא בשעתא מי לית ליה** — הלכך גזל הוא, אלא שאין בית דין ישראל נזקקין להשיבו, דבתר הכי מחיל ליה. ובישראל בישראל נמי אסור, ומעבר לא עבר דכתיב (ויקרא יט) "לא תגזול" (שם ה) "והשיב את הגזילה" אמידי דהשבון קרי גזל ואידך לא. אבל בנכרי דלאו בר השבון הוא — שכל דינו למיתה, לא נפיק פחות משוה פרוטה מכלל פרוטה, ואפילו מישראל — דמחיל ליה בתר הכי. **נכרי בנכרי כיוצא בו** — בתמיהה, וגבי נכרי בנכרי מוציא פחות משוה פרוטה מכלל פרוטה, וקרי כיוצא בו בגזל ולא גזל ממש. **בכובש שכר שכיר** — דגזל לא הוי אלא בחוטף דבר מיד חבירו, כדאמר בבבא קמא ב"מרובה" (עט,ב) מקרא ד"ויגזול את החנית מיד המצרי". כיוצא בו בגנב נראה בעיני מדלא קבעי לה מאי היא

LITERAL TRANSLATION

[1] That which is like a woman of beautiful appearance, what is it?

[2] When Rav Dimi came, he said in the name of Rabbi Elazar who said in the name of Rabbi Ḥanina: [3] A non-Jew who designated a maidservant for his servant, and had intercourse with her — he is put to death on account of her.

[4] That which is like bloodshed was not taught.

[5] Abaye said: If you find that it was taught, [6] it is Rabbi Yonatan ben Shaul, for it was taught: [7] "Rabbi Yonatan ben Shaul said: Someone who was pursuing his fellow in order to kill him, and he was able to save himself with one of his limbs, but he did not save [himself], [57B] he is put to death on account of him.

[1] כַּיּוֹצֵא בִּיפַת תּוֹאַר, מַאי הִיא? [2] כִּי אֲתָא רַב דִּימִי אָמַר רַבִּי אֶלְעָזָר אָמַר רַבִּי חֲנִינָא: [3] בֶּן נֹחַ שֶׁיִּיחֵד שִׁפְחָה לְעַבְדּוֹ, וּבָא עָלֶיהָ — נֶהֱרָג עָלֶיהָ.

[4] כַּיּוֹצֵא בּוֹ דִּשְׁפִיכוּת דָּמִים לָא תַּנְיָא.

[5] אָמַר אַבַּיֵי: אִי מַשְׁכַּחַתְּ דְּתַנְיָא, [6] רַבִּי יוֹנָתָן בֶּן שָׁאוּל הִיא, דְּתַנְיָא: [7] ״רַבִּי יוֹנָתָן בֶּן שָׁאוּל אוֹמֵר: רוֹדֵף אַחַר חֲבֵירוֹ לְהוֹרְגוֹ, וְיָכוֹל לְהַצִּילוֹ בְּאֶחָד מֵאֵבָרָיו, וְלֹא הִצִּיל — [57B] נֶהֱרָג עָלָיו.

TRANSLATION AND COMMENTARY

כַּיּוֹצֵא [1] The Gemara continues: When the Baraita speaks of something **that is like a beautiful woman** taken as a prisoner of war, **what is** it referring to?

כִּי אֲתָא [2] **When Rav Dimi came** to Babylonia from Eretz Israel, **he said in the name of Rabbi Elazar who said in the name of Rabbi Ḥanina:** [3] If a **non-Jew designated a maidservant for his servant, and** then he himself **had intercourse with her, he is put to death on account of her.**

כַּיּוֹצֵא בּוֹ [4] The Gemara notes: In the clause dealing with robbery, the Baraita taught that a non-Jew is forbidden to rob and steal, or commit an act like them. But in the clause dealing with bloodshed, the Baraita **did not teach** that a non-Jew is liable for bloodshed, and for **that which is like bloodshed,** for there is no act that is like bloodshed and not outright bloodshed.

אָמַר אַבַּיֵי [5] **Abaye said: If you find that** a Baraita **was taught** stating that a non-Jew is liable for bloodshed, and for that which is like bloodshed, [6] know that **it** follows the position of **Rabbi Yonatan ben Shaul, for it was taught** in a Baraita: [7] **"Rabbi Yonatan ben Shaul said:** If **someone was pursuing his fellow** with the intention of **killing him, and** the pursued party **would have been able to save himself** by injuring his pursuer **in one of his limbs, but he did not save himself** in that manner, but rather he killed him, [57B] the killer **is put to death for** killing **him."** This case is like bloodshed, but not actual bloodshed, for the killer acted out of self-defense. Under such circumstances, according to Rabbi Yonatan ben Shaul, a non-Jew is liable for killing another non-Jew, and for killing a Jew, and a Jew is liable for killing a Jew, but a Jew is not liable for killing a non-Jew. According to the Rabbis who disagree with Rabbi Yonatan, there is no liability whatsoever under such circumstances, neither for a Jew nor for a non-Jew, since the act committed is not at all like bloodshed.

RASHI

— לא משכחת ליה ולאו עליה קאי, אלא אגזל ויפת תואר. **נהרג עליו** — משום גזל, ואף על פי שאין זו בעולת בעל דאישות אלא דזנות בעלמא, כחמור ובהמתו, נכרי בישראל — שפחה כנענית שייחד ישראל לעבד עברי, ובא עליה נכרי — נהרג. ישראל בנכרי — מותר. נכרי שייחד שפחה לעבדו ובא ישראל ולקחה בשביה — מותר, דהא אפילו אשתו גמורה מותרת לו, ישראל בישראל — אסור, דהיינו שפחה חרופה שחייבין עליה אשם. **כיוצא בו גבי שפיכות דמים לא תנא** — האי תנא דלעיל, משום דאין לשפיכות דמים שאינו חייב גמור או מותר לגמרי, כגון נרדף שניתן להנצל עצמו בנפשו של רוצח. דאילו שופך דם בשוגג שפיכות דמים גמור הוא אלא רחמנא חס עליה. **ויכול** — הנרדף להציל עצמו באחד מאבריו של רודף, כגון לקטע רגלו. **ולא הציל** — אלא הרגו. **נהרג עליו** — היינו כיוצא בו דשפיכות דמים, דהוי קרוב להתיר ואינו מותר, נכרי בנכרי ונכרי בישראל — חייב, וכן ישראל בישראל. אבל ישראל בנכרי — פטור ואליבא דרבי יונתן. אבל רבנן פליגי עליה ואמרי היתר גמור הוא וליכא כיוצא בו.

CONCEPTS

יְפַת תּוֹאַר **A woman of beautiful appearance.** A non-Jewish female prisoner of war (see Deuteronomy 21:10-14). According to some authorities, a soldier was allowed to engage in sexual relations with such a woman in wartime. Afterwards, if he desired to take her as a wife, she had to shave her head, let her nails grow and undergo a month-long period of mourning in his home. When that period was over, if she decided to convert to Judaism, they could marry. According to other authorities sexual relations with a captive during wartime were forbidden, but the soldier had the right to convert his captive and marry her after the mourning period was concluded.

HALAKHAH

בֶּן נֹחַ שֶׁבָּא עַל שִׁפְחָה נְשׂוּאָה **A non-Jew who had relations with a married female slave.** "If a non-Jew designated a woman as the wife of his slave, and afterwards had relations with her, he is liable to the death penalty for adultery (or, according to *Rashi,* for theft)," following the ruling of Rabbi Ḥannina. (*Rambam, Sefer Shofetim, Hilkhot Melakhim* 9:8.)

רוֹדֵף בְּבֶן נֹחַ **A non-Jew who is attempting to murder someone.** "If one non-Jew was pursuing another in an attempt to murder him, and the intended victim killed the pursuer in self-defense, the law is as follows: If he could have saved himself by wounding the attempted murderer rather than killing him, he himself is guilty of murder and is liable to the death penalty. A Jew under the same circumstances is not liable to judicial execution, but is liable to death at the hands of Heaven." (See *Radbaz, Kesef Mishneh,* and *Leḥem Mishneh.*) (*Rambam, Sefer Shofetim, Hilkhot Melakhim* 9:4.)

TRANSLATION AND COMMENTARY

אַשְׁכַּח [1]**Rabbi Ya'akov bar Aḥa found** the following passage **written in a book of Aggadah in the school of Rav:** [2]**"A non-Jew is put to death on the basis** of a decision given **by a single judge,** [3]and on the basis of testimony given **by a single witness,** and even if he **was not** given a proper **warning** prior to the commission of his offense. [4]He is put to death on the basis of testimony and a decision given **by a man, but not** on the basis of testimony or a decision given **by a woman,** [5]and the man who testified or decided against him can **even** be **a relative.** A Jew can only be put to death by a court of twenty-three judges, and on the basis of the testimony of two male witnesses who are not disqualified from testifying on account of kinship, and after being properly warned against committing the transgression. But none of these rules apply in the case of a non-Jew. [6]**It was said in the name of Rabbi Yishmael:** A non-Jew is put to death **even for** killing a **fetus,** if he struck a pregnant woman, and caused her to miscarry, even though a Jew would be exempt in such a situation."

מְנָהָנֵי מִילֵּי [7]The Gemara asks: **From where are these regulations derived?** What is the Biblical source of these laws? [8]**Rav Yehudah said:** These laws are derived from **the verse** recording God's warning to Noah after he emerged from the ark which **states** (Genesis 9:5): "And surely your blood of your lives will I require; at the hand of every beast will I require it, and at the hand of man; at the hand of every man's brother will I require the life of man." [9]**"And surely your blood of your lives will I require"** — the singular verb *edrosh,* "will I require," [10]teaches that a non-Jew is put to death **even** on the basis of a decision given **by a single judge.** [11]**"At the hand of every beast"** — these words teach that a non-Jew is put to death **even** if he was **not** given **a** proper **warning** prior to the commission of his offense, for man is compared here to a beast, and surely a beast is not fit to receive a warning. [12]**"I will require it, and at the hand of man"** — the singular expression "and at the hand of man" teaches that a non-Jew is put to death **even on** the basis of the testimony of a single witness. [13]**"At the hand of man"** — he is put to death on the basis of testimony and a decision given by a man, [14]**but not** on the basis of testimony or a decision given **by a woman.** [15]**"His brother"** — he is put to death **even** if the witness who testified against him or the judge who decided against him was **a relative.**

[1]אַשְׁכַּח רַבִּי יַעֲקֹב בַּר אַחָא דַּהֲוָה כְּתִיב בְּסֵפֶר אַגַּדְתָּא דְּבֵי רַב: [2]״בֶּן נֹחַ נֶהֱרָג בְּדַיָּין אֶחָד, [3]וּבְעֵד אֶחָד, שֶׁלֹּא בְּהַתְרָאָה, [4]מִפִּי אִישׁ וְלֹא מִפִּי אִשָּׁה, [5]וַאֲפִילּוּ קָרוֹב. [6]מִשּׁוּם רַבִּי יִשְׁמָעֵאל אָמְרוּ: אַף עַל הָעוּבָּרִין״.

[7]מְנָהָנֵי מִילֵּי? [8]אָמַר רַב יְהוּדָה: דְּאָמַר קְרָא: [9]״אַךְ אֶת דִּמְכֶם לְנַפְשֹׁתֵיכֶם אֶדְרֹשׁ״ — [10]אֲפִילּוּ בְּדַיָּין אֶחָד. [11]״מִיַּד כָּל חַיָּה״ — אֲפִילּוּ שֶׁלֹּא בְּהַתְרָאָה. [12]״אֶדְרְשֶׁנּוּ וּמִיַּד הָאָדָם״ — אֲפִילּוּ בְּעֵד אֶחָד. [13]״מִיַּד אִישׁ״ — [14]וְלֹא מִיַּד אִשָּׁה, [15]״אָחִיו״ — אֲפִילּוּ קָרוֹב.

LITERAL TRANSLATION

[1]Rabbi Ya'akov bar Aḥa found that it was written in a book of Aggadah in the school of Rav: [2]"A non-Jew is put to death by one judge, [3]and with one witness, without a warning, [4]from the mouth of a man, but not from the mouth of a woman, [5]and even a relative. [6]In the name of Rabbi Yishmael, they said: Even for fetuses."

[7]From where are these things [derived]? [8]Rav Yehudah said: For the verse states: [9]"And surely your blood of your lives will I require" — [10]even with one judge. [11]"At the hand of every beast" — even without a warning. [12]"I will require it, and at the hand of man" — even with one witness. [13]"At the hand of man" — [14]but not at the hand of a woman. [15]"His brother" — even a relative.

RASHI

מפני איש – על ידי דיין איש או עד איש. אף על העוברין – הכה את האשה ויצאו ילדיה נהרג עליהן, ובישראל עד שיצא לאויר העולם כדתנן במסכת [נדה] (מד,א): תינוק בן יום אחד ההורגו חייב, היכא דקים ליה בגוויה שכלו לו חדשיו ואינו נפל. מיד כל חיה – מיד כל דבר חי.

NOTES

שֶׁלֹּא בְּהַתְרָאָה **Without a warning.** *Bereshit Rabbah* proves that a non-Jew is put to death, even if he was not given a proper warning prior to the commission of his offense, from what God said to Abimelech (Genesis 20:3): "Behold, you are a dead man, because of the woman whom you have taken," even though Abimelech had not been given a

HALAKHAH

בֶּן נֹחַ נֶהֱרָג בְּדַיָּין אֶחָד **A non-Jew is put to death by one judge.** "A non-Jew can be executed on the basis of the testimony of a single witness, and the decision of a single judge, and without having been given a warning prior to the commission of his offense. The witness can even be a close relative of the transgressor. However, neither the witness nor the judge can be a woman." These rulings follow the book of Aggadah found in the academy of Rav. (*Rambam, Sefer Shofetim, Hilkhot Melakhim* 9:14; and see *Radbaz* there.)

אַף עַל הָעוּבָּרִין **Even for fetuses.** "If a non-Jew killed a fetus in its mother's womb, he is liable for the death

[1]"מִשּׁוּם רַבִּי יִשְׁמָעֵאל אָמְרוּ אַף עַל הָעוּבָּרִין". [2]מַאי טַעְמֵיהּ דְּרַבִּי יִשְׁמָעֵאל? [3]דִּכְתִיב: "שֹׁפֵךְ דַּם הָאָדָם בָּאָדָם דָּמוֹ יִשָּׁפֵךְ". [4]אֵיזֶהוּ אָדָם שֶׁהוּא בְּאָדָם? הֱוֵי אוֹמֵר זֶה עוּבָּר שֶׁבִּמְעֵי אִמּוֹ.

[5]וְתַנָּא קַמָּא? [6]תָּנָא דְּבֵי מְנַשֶּׁה הוּא, דְּאָמַר: כָּל מִיתָה הָאֲמוּרָה לִבְנֵי נֹחַ אֵינוֹ אֶלָּא חֶנֶק, [7]וְשָׁדֵי לֵיהּ הַאי "בָּאָדָם" אַסֵּיפֵיהּ דִּקְרָא, [8]וְדָרֵושׁ בֵּיהּ הָכִי: בָּאָדָם דָּמוֹ יִשָּׁפֵךְ. [9]אֵיזֶהוּ שְׁפִיכוּת דָּמִים שֶׁל אָדָם שֶׁהוּא בְּגוּפוֹ שֶׁל אָדָם? [10]הֱוֵי אוֹמֵר זֶה חֶנֶק.

[11]מְתִיב רַב הַמְנוּנָא: וְאִשָּׁה לֹא מְפַּקְּדָה? [12]וְהָכְתִיב: "כִּי יְדַעְתִּיו לְמַעַן אֲשֶׁר יְצַוֶּה וגו׳". [13]הוּא מוֹתִיב לַהּ וְהוּא מְפָרֵק

LITERAL TRANSLATION

[1]"In the name of Rabbi Yishmael, they said: Even for fetuses." [2]What is the reasoning of Rabbi Yishmael? [3]For it is written: "Whoever sheds man's blood by man shall his blood be shed." [4]Who is a man who is inside a man? Say this is a fetus in his mother's womb.

[5]And the first Tanna? [6]He is the Tanna of the school of Menashe, who said: Every execution mentioned regarding non-Jews is strangulation. [7]And he casts this "by man" to the end of the verse, [8]and interprets it as follows: In a man shall his blood be shed. [9]What shedding of man's blood is in a man's body? [10]Say this is strangulation.

[11]Rav Hamnuna objected: And a woman is not commanded? [12]But surely it is written: "For I know him, that he will command, etc."

[13]He raised the objection to it, and he resolved

TRANSLATION AND COMMENTARY

מִשּׁוּם רַבִּי יִשְׁמָעֵאל [1]The passage in the book of Aggadah found in the school of Rav continued: **"It was said in the name of Rabbi Yishmael:** A non-Jew is put to death **even for** the killing of a **fetus."** [2]The Gemara asks: **What is Rabbi Yishmael's reasoning?** [3]The Gemara explains: He derives this law from **the** next **verse** which **states** (Genesis 9:6): **"Whoever sheds man's blood by man** [הָאָדָם בָּאָדָם] **shall his blood be shed."** The words *adam ba'adam* can also be understood as "a man inside a man." [4]**Who is a man who is inside** another **man? Say** that **this** refers to **a fetus inside his mother's womb.**

וְתַנָּא קַמָּא [5]The Gemara asks: **And** how does **the first Tanna** who disagrees with Rabbi Yishmael understand this verse? [6]The Gemara explains: The first Tanna **is the Tanna of the school of Menashe, who said: Every execution mentioned** in the Torah **regarding non-Jews** is death by **strangulation.** [7]That Tanna **casts** the words **"in man** [*ba'adam*]" and joins them **to the end of the verse,** [8]**and** so he **interprets** the verse **as follows: In a man shall his blood be shed.** [9]**What shedding of man's blood is** there **inside a man's body?** [10]**Say** that **this** refers to death by **strangulation,** for when a person is executed by strangulation, there is only internal bleeding.

מְתִיב רַב הַמְנוּנָא [11]**Rav Hamnuna raised an objection: Is a** non-Jewish **woman** really **not commanded** to establish a legal system, as implied by the regulation that she is disqualified from serving as a witness or a judge? [12]**But surely the verse** dealing with Abraham when he still had the status of "a descendant of Noah" (for the Jewish people did not yet exist) **states** (Genesis 18:19): **"For I know him, that he will command** his sons and his household after him, and they shall keep the way of the Lord, to do charity and judgment." The term "household" refers to the women living in his house. Thus, the obligation of establishing a legal system applies to both men and women.

הוּא מוֹתִיב לַהּ [13]The Gemara answers: Rav Hamnuna **raised the objection, and** Rav Hamnuna himself **resolved** his difficulty: The verse states that Abraham would command his sons and his household to do

RASHI

שופך דם האדם באדם – שכתוב האדם, דמו ישפך. זה חנק – דאין דמו יוצא לחוץ. ואשה – בת נח לא מפקדה על הדין.

NOTES

warning before he sinned. *Ramah* explains that this is derived in our Gemara from the analogy drawn between man and beast, "At the hand of every beast will I require it, and at the hand of man." Just as a beast is liable even without a warning, for a warning has no meaning regarding a beast, so too the descendants of Noah are liable even without a warning. Elsewhere, the Rishonim discuss whether it follows from the non-Jew's liability when he was not warned prior to the commission of his offense, that a non-Jew is also liable in a case if he committed his offense unintentionally (see *Margoliyot HaYam*).

זֶה עוּבָּר **This is a fetus.** A Jew is not put to death for the killing of a fetus. He is only liable for the killing of an infant that has been born and is viable. But this cannot serve as an example of a prohibition that is binding upon non-Jews but not upon Jews, for a Jew is indeed forbidden to kill a fetus. He is merely exempt from the death penalty (*Rabbi S. Eiger*).

HALAKHAH

penalty. (A Jew, by contrast, is not liable for the killing of a fetus.)" This follows Rabbi Yishmael, who disagrees with the Tanna of the school of Menashe. (*Rambam, Sefer Shofetim, Hilkhot Melakhim* 9:4.)

TRANSLATION AND COMMENTARY

charity and judgment. [1]**His sons** — the men — he commanded **about judgment,** for they were bound by the obligation to establish a system of laws; [2]and **his household** — the women — he commanded **about charity,** for they were not bound by that obligation.

אָמַר לֵיהּ [3]**Rav Avya the Elder said to Rav Pappa:** If so, **say that a non-Jewish woman who killed** another person **should not be executed** for her crime, [4]**for the verse states** (Genesis 9:5): **"At the hand of man"** — which implies **not at the hand of a woman.**

אָמַר לֵיהּ [5]Rav Pappa **said** to Rav Avya the Elder: **Rav Yehudah said as follows:** The very next verse states (Genesis 9:6): [6]**"Whoever sheds man's blood** by man shall his blood be shed," using the word אָדָם, which applies to both men and women, [7]thus implying that **in all cases** the killer is put to death.

אִימָא בַּת נֹחַ [8]Rav Avya the Elder raised another question: Following this line of reasoning, **we should say that a non-Jewish woman who committed adultery should not be executed** for her offense, [9]**for the verse states** (Genesis 2:24): **"That is why a man leaves his mother and his father,** and cleaves to his wife; and they become one flesh," implying that a man is commanded to cleave to his wife, and not his neighbor's wife, [10]**but a woman** is **not** commanded to cleave to her husband, and not her neighbor's husband!

אָמַר לֵיהּ הָכִי [11]Rav Pappa **said to him: Rav Yehudah said as follows:** That very verse ends: **"And they become one flesh."** [12]After having specified a man, **the verse then mixed** man and woman together, implying that the same law applies to the two of them.

תָּנוּ רַבָּנַן [13]**Our Rabbis taught** the following Baraita: "The verse states (Leviticus 18:6): 'No man [*ish ish*] shall approach to any that is near of kin to him, to uncover her nakedness.' It would have sufficed for the word '*Ish* [man]' to have been written one time. [14]**What did** the Torah mean to **teach by** doubling the word, so that the verse reads '*Ish ish*'? [15]The word is doubled in order **to include non-Jews** in the prohibition, **that they** too **are warned about forbidden sexual relations just like Jews."**

וְהָא מֵהָכָא נָפְקָא [16]The Gemara asks: **But is** this law **learned from here?** [17]Surely it was taught earlier (56b) that the universal prohibition against adultery and incest **is learned from** a verse found **elsewhere** (Genesis 2:16): "And the Lord God commanded the man, saying," [18]the word **"saying"** being a reference to against **forbidden sexual relations!**

לָהּ: [1]בָּנָיו — לְדִין, [2]בֵּיתוֹ — לִצְדָקָה.

[3]אֲמַר לֵיהּ רַב אַוְיָא סָבָא לְרַב פַּפָּא: אֵימָא בַּת נֹחַ שֶׁהָרְגָה לֹא תֵּיהָרֵג, [4]״מִיַּד אִישׁ״ וְלֹא מִיַּד אִשָּׁה כְּתִיב!

[5]אֲמַר לֵיהּ: הָכִי אָמַר רַב יְהוּדָה: [6]״שֹׁפֵךְ דַּם הָאָדָם״ — [7]מִכׇּל מָקוֹם.

[8]אֵימָא בַּת נֹחַ שֶׁזִּינְּתָה לֹא תֵּיהָרֵג, [9]דִּכְתִיב: ״עַל כֵּן יַעֲזׇב אִישׁ״, [10]וְלֹא אִשָּׁה!

[11]אֲמַר לֵיהּ: הָכִי אָמַר רַב יְהוּדָה: ״וְהָיוּ לְבָשָׂר אֶחָד״ — [12]הֲדַר עָרְבִינְהוּ קְרָא.

[13]תָּנוּ רַבָּנַן: ״אִישׁ״. [14]מַה תַּלְמוּד לוֹמַר ״אִישׁ אִישׁ״? [15]לְרַבּוֹת אֶת הַכּוּתִים שֶׁמּוּזְהָרִין עַל הָעֲרָיוֹת כְּיִשְׂרָאֵל.

[16]וְהָא מֵהָכָא נָפְקָא? [17]מֵהָתָם נָפְקָא: [18]״לֵאמֹר״ — זֶה גִּילּוּי עֲרָיוֹת!

LITERAL TRANSLATION

it: [1]His sons — for judgment; [2]his household for charity.

[3]Rav Avya the Elder said to Rav Pappa: Say that a non-Jewess who killed should not be put to death, [4][for] it is written: "At the hand of man," and not at the hand of a woman.

[5]He said to him: Thus said Rav Yehudah: [6]"Whoever sheds man's blood"— [7]in any case.

[8]Say that a non-Jewess who committed adultery should not be put to death, [9]for it is written: "That is why a man leaves his mother and his father," [10]and not a woman!

[11]He said to him: Thus said Rav Yehudah: "And they become one flesh" — [12]the verse then mixed them together.

[13]Our Rabbis taught: "'*Ish.*' [14]What is taught by '*Ish ish*'? [15]To include non-Jews that they are warned about forbidden sexual relations like Jews."

[16]But is this learned from here? [17]It is learned from there: [18]"Saying" — this is forbidden sexual relations.

RASHI

ביתו — היינו נשים. **מה תלמוד לומר איש איש** — ״אל כל שאר בשרו וגו׳״.

NOTES

בֵּיתוֹ — לִצְדָקָה His household — for charity. According to some Rishonim, the word *tzedakah* is used here in the sense of "charity," thus non-Jews are bound by an additional obligation, the obligation to give charity. It is not counted among the seven Noachide laws, because all of those obligations are essentially negative commandments (even the obligation to establish a legal system [see below, 59a]), and the obligation regarding charity is a positive commandment (see *Ramah*).

TRANSLATION AND COMMENTARY

הָתָם בַּעֲרָיוֹת [1]The Gemara answers: **There** the verse forbids a non-Jew from having intercourse **with a Gentile woman who is forbidden** to him, whether because she is related to him within the prohibited degrees of kinship, or because she is married to another man. [2]**And here** the verse forbids a non-Jew from having intercourse **with a Jewish woman who is forbidden** to him because she is another man's wife. [3]**For a later clause** of the Baraita dealing with that verse **teaches: "If** a non-Jew **has intercourse with a Jewish woman who is forbidden** to him, such as another man's wife, [4]**he is judged according to the law applying to a Jew."**

לְמַאי הִלְכְתָא [5]The Gemara asks: **Regarding what law** is a non-Jew who had intercourse with the wife of a Jew judged according to the law applying to a Jew? [6]**Rav Naḥman said in the name of Rabbah bar Avuha:** This ruling **was only needed** to teach us that the non-Jew must be tried before **a Lesser Sanhedrin**, a court composed of twenty-three judges; [7]that he may only be executed on the basis of the testimony **of two witnesses;** [8]**and** that he may only be punished if he had been properly **warned** prior to his commission of his transgression. Ordinarily, a non-Jew may be put to death on the basis of a decision given by a single judge, and on the basis of testimony given by a single witness, and even if he had not been given a proper warning prior to the commission of his offense. If a non-Jew had intercourse with the wife of a Jew, the non-Jew is judged in accordance with the regulations that usually apply only to Jews.

מְגָרַע גָּרַע [9]The Gemara asks: Can it be that the law regarding a non-Jew who had intercourse with a married Jewish woman **is more lenient** than if he had intercourse with a married Gentile? If the non-Jew had intercourse with a married Gentile, he could be executed even on the basis of the decision of a single judge, the testimony of a single witness, and without having received a warning. How then can it be that if he had intercourse with a married Jewess, he is not executed without a lesser Sanhedrin, two witnesses, and a warning?

אֶלָּא [10]**Rather, Rabbi Yoḥanan said:** The Baraita's ruling that a non-Jew who had intercourse with the wife of a Jew is judged according to the law applying to a Jew **was only needed** to teach us **about when the woman was** still only **betrothed** to her husband. [11]**For** a non-Jew **is not liable** for execution if he had intercourse with a non-Jewish betrothed woman. Therefore, the Baraita teaches us that if a non-Jew had intercourse with a betrothed Jewish woman, [12]**we judge him according to the law applying to a Jew.**

[1]הָתָם בַּעֲרָיוֹת דִּידְהוּ, [2]וְהָכָא בַּעֲרָיוֹת דִּידַן. [3]דְּקָתָנֵי סֵיפָא: ״בָּא עַל עֲרָיוֹת יִשְׂרָאֵל, [4]נִידּוֹן בְּדִינֵי יִשְׂרָאֵל״.

[5]לְמַאי הִלְכְתָא? [6]אָמַר רַב נַחְמָן אָמַר רַבָּה בַּר אֲבוּהּ: לָא נִצְרְכָה, אֶלָּא לְעֵדָה [7]וְעֵדִים [8]וְהַתְרָאָה.

[9]מִגְרַע גָּרַע?

[10]אֶלָּא אָמַר רַב יוֹחָנָן: לָא נִצְרְכָה אֶלָּא לְנַעֲרָה הַמְאוֹרָסָה, [11]דִּלְדִידְהוּ לֵית לְהוּ, [12]דְּדָיְינִינַן לְהוּ בְּדִינָא דִּידַן.

LITERAL TRANSLATION

[1]There with their forbidden women, [2]and here with our forbidden women. [3]For the last clause teaches: "[If] he had intercourse with forbidden women who are Jewish, [4]he is judged according to the laws applying to a Jew."

[5]Regarding what law? [6]Rav Naḥman said in the name of Rabbah bar Avuha: It was needed only for a congregation, [7]and witnesses, [8]and a warning.

[9]Is it more lenient?

[10]Rather, Rabbi Yoḥanan said: It was needed only for a betrothed girl, [11]which they do not have, [12]that we judge them according to our law.

RASHI

בעריות דידן — באשת איש ישראל. למאי הלכתא — נדון בדיני ישראל. שצריך עדה ועדים והתראה — כישראל. מגרע גרע — זה הבא על אשת ישראל, מהבא על אשת נכרי שנהרג בעד אחד ובדיין אחד ושלא בהתראה, מגרע גרע לשון קולא ובתמיהה. לא נצרכה — האי דקתני נידון בדיני ישראל. אלא — שבא על נערה המאורסה ישראלית. דלדידהו לית להו — מיתה בנערה המאורסה אלא בבעולת בעל. וגבי ישראל נהרג מריבויא ד״איש איש״, על כרחך האי דקטלוה — משום דאתרביה ב״איש איש״ כישראל, ולגבייהו לאו אשת איש דנחייב קטלא דידהו אלא נידון בסקילה, אבל אין צריך עדה ועדים והתראה דלא גרע מעריות דידהו.

NOTES

לָא נִצְרְכָה אֶלָּא לְנַעֲרָה הַמְאוֹרָסָה **It was only needed for a betrothed girl.** We must be dealing here with a non-Jew

HALAKHAH

לָא נִצְרְכָה אֶלָּא לְנַעֲרָה הַמְאוֹרָסָה **It was only needed for a betrothed girl.** "If a non-Jew had sexual intercourse with a betrothed Jewish woman, he is liable for death by stoning. If he had intercourse with a woman who had entered under the bridal canopy with her husband, but did not yet engage in sexual relations with him, he is liable for death by strangulation," following the Baraita, and Rabbi Yoḥanan and Rav Naḥman bar Yitzḥak. (*Rambam, Sefer Shofetim, Hilkhot Melakhim* 9:7.)

דִּלְדִידְהוּ לֵית לְהוּ **Which they do not have.** "If a non-Jew had sexual intercourse with a non-Jewish married woman, he is liable for death by decapitation. But if he had relations

אֲבָל אֵשֶׁת אִישׁ, בְּדִינָא דִּידְהוּ דָּיְינִינַן לְהוּ? ²וְהָתַנְיָא: "בָּא עַל נַעֲרָה הַמְאוֹרָסָה, נִידּוֹן בִּסְקִילָה; עַל אֵשֶׁת אִישׁ, נִידּוֹן בְּחֶנֶק". ³וְאִי בְּדִינָא דִּידְהוּ, סַיִיף הוּא!

⁴אָמַר רַב נַחְמָן בַּר יִצְחָק: מַאי "אֵשֶׁת אִישׁ" דְּקָתָנֵי? ⁵כְּגוֹן שֶׁנִּכְנְסָה לַחוּפָּה וְלֹא נִבְעֲלָה, ⁶דִּלְדִידְהוּ לֵית לְהוּ, ⁷דָּיְינִינַן לְהוּ בְּדִינָא דִּידַן. ⁸דְּתָנֵי רַבִּי חֲנִינָא: "בְּעוּלַת בַּעַל — יֵשׁ לָהֶן; ⁹נִכְנְסָה לַחוּפָּה, וְלֹא נִבְעֲלָה — אֵין לָהֶן".

¹⁰תַּנְיָא כְּוָותֵיהּ דְּרַבִּי יוֹחָנָן:

LITERAL TRANSLATION

[1]But [regarding] a married woman, we judge them according to their law? [2]But surely it was taught: "[If] he had intercourse with a betrothed girl, he is judged with stoning; with a married woman, he is judged with strangulation." [3]And if according to their law, it is with the sword!

[4]Rav Naḥman bar Yitzḥak said: What is [the meaning of] "a married woman" that was stated? [5]As when she entered under the bridal canopy, but did not engage in intercourse, [6]which they do not have, [7][and so] we judge them according to our law. [8]For Rabbi Ḥanina taught: "A woman who has had intercourse with her husband — they have; [9][a woman who] entered under the bridal canopy, but did not engage in intercourse — they do not have."

[10]It was taught in accordance with Rabbi Yoḥanan:

TRANSLATION AND COMMENTARY

אֲבָל אֵשֶׁת אִישׁ [1]The Gemara asks: **But** does it follow then that if a non-Jew had intercourse with the wife of a Jew who was already **married** to her husband, **we judge him** not according to the law applying to a Jew, but **according to the law applying to non-Jews?** [2]**But surely** this is difficult, for **it was taught** in a Baraita: **"If** a non-Jew **had intercourse with a betrothed** Jewish **woman, he is sentenced to** death by **stoning;** and if he had intercourse **with a married** Jewish **woman, he is sentenced** to death by **strangulation."** [3]If it is true that a non-Jew who had intercourse with a married Jewish woman is judged **according to the law applying to non-Jews,** the non-Jew should be sentenced **to** death **by decapitation,** for as we learned earlier in the chapter (56a), wherever execution is mentioned in the Torah with respect to non-Jews, it refers to decapitation!

אָמַר [4]**Rav Naḥman bar Yitzḥak said: What** does the Baraita mean when **it speaks** here of **"a married woman"**? [5]The Baraita is referring to special circumsances: when the woman **has entered under the bridal canopy** with her husband, **but has not** yet **engaged in** sexual **intercourse** with him. [6]For a non-Jew **is not liable** for execution if he has intercourse with a Gentile woman who has performed the wedding ceremony but has not consumated the marriage. So if a non-Jew has intercourse with a Jewish woman who has already entered under the bridal canopy with her husband, but has not yet consummated the marriage, [7]**we judge him according to the law applying to a Jew.** He is liable to death by strangulation, just like a Jew who was guilty of the same offense. Otherwise he is judged according to the law applying to non-Jews and liable to death by decapitation. [8]This interpretation of the Baraita is in accordance with another Baraita **taught by Rabbi Ḥanina** which states: "If a non-Jew has intercourse with a non-Jewish **woman who has** already **had intercourse with her husband, he is liable** to execution, for the verse states (Genesis 20:3): "You are a dead man, because of the woman whom you have taken, for she has had intercourse with her husband." [9]But if he had intercourse with **a woman who** only **entered under the bridal canopy** with her husband, **but has not** yet **engaged in intercourse** with him, **he is not liable** for execution."

תַּנְיָא כְּוָותֵיהּ [10]A Baraita **was taught in accordance with** the position of **Rabbi Yoḥanan.** He interpreted

RASHI

אבל – בא על אשת איש ישראל בדינא דידהו דיינינן ליה? בתמיה. בא על נערה המאורסה נידון בסקילה – כישראל, דהא בדינא דידהו סייף הוא – דכל מיתת בן נח אינו אלא סייף לרבנן דפליגי אתנא דבי מנשה. נכנסה לחופה ולא נבעלה – בדיני ישראל חנק הוא, כשאר אשת איש. דגבי סקילה כתיב "נערה בתולה מאורסה וגו'" ודרשינן (כתובות מח,א) בתולה ולא בעולה, מאורסה ולא נשואה, ומאי נשואה – אילימא נשואה ונבעלה – מבתולה ולא בעולה נפקא, אלא שנכנסה לחופה ולא נבעלה ומעטה קרא מסקילה וישנה בחנק, דהכל היו בכלל נואף ונואפת ויצאה ארוסה לידון בעצמה וזו שלא יצאה עמדה בכללה. בעולת בעל יש להם – דכתיב (בראשית כ) "והיא בעולת בעל" ולא כתיב "והיא אשת איש", אלמא הנך מת משום בעילתו של בעל – ולא מפני קדושין וחופתו. תניא כוותיה דרבי יוחנן – דאמר: בא על עריות ישראל דקתני, נידון בדיני ישראל – לא מתוקמא אלא בנכנסה לחופה או בנערה המאורסה וכו', דלדידהו לית להו.

NOTES

who had intercourse with the betrothed girl with the girl's consent, for if he raped her, then even if she was betrothed to a non-Jew, he is liable to execution, for he is guilty of robbery (*Binyan Shlomo*).

HALAKHAH

with a non-Jewish betrothed woman, or with one who had entered under the bridal canopy, but had not yet had relations with her husband, he is exempt from the death penalty." (*Rambam, Sefer Shofetim, Hilkhot Melakhim* 9:7.)

TRANSLATION AND COMMENTARY

the Baraita which stated that a non-Jew who has intercourse with the wife of a Jew is judged according to the law applying to a Jew as applying to a woman who was only betrothed to her husband or who has entered under the bridal canopy with him, but has not had sexual intercourse with him. [1]The new Baraita stated: **"Any forbidden** sexual **relationship for which a Jewish court would impose execution** upon a Jew, such as intercourse with one's mother or daughter, **a non-Jew is prohibited** from engaging in. Any forbidden sexual relationship for which **a Jewish court would not impose execution** upon a Jew, meaning sexual sins that are punishable by excision, but not capital punishment, like intercourse with one's sister or aunt, [2]**a non-Jew is not prohibited** from engaging in. [3]**This is the position of Rabbi Meir.** [4]**But the Sages** disagree and **say:** There **are many forbidden relationships for which a Jewish court does not impose execution** upon a Jew, [5]**but a non-Jew is** nevertheless **prohibited** from engaging in them. [6]If the **non-Jew** has **intercourse with a Jewish woman who is forbidden** to him, **he is judged according to the law applying** in such a case **to a Jew.** [7]And **if he has intercourse with a Gentile woman who is forbidden to him, he is judged according to the law applying to non-Jews.** [8]And the **only** case that we **have** in which the non-Jew is judged according to the law applying to a Jew is when he had intercourse with **a betrothed** Jewish **woman."** Since a non-Jew is not liable for intercourse with a betrothed Gentile woman, if he has intercourse with a betrothed Jewish woman, he is judged according to the law applying to a Jew guilty of the same offense. Therefore he is sentenced to death by stoning, as was argued by Rabbi Yoḥanan.

וְנַחְשׁוֹב נַמִי [9]The Gemara asks: **But count also** a non-Jew who had intercourse with **a Jewish woman who has entered under the bridal canopy** with her husband, **but has not** yet **had intercourse** with him! Since a non-Jew would not be liable in the parallel case involving a Gentile woman, here too he should be judged according to the law applying to a Jew, and therefore sentenced to death by strangulation, rather than death by decapitation, the usual mode of execution imposed upon non-Jews. [10]The Gemara answers: The Baraita does not count that case, because the **Tanna** of the Baraita **is the Tanna of the School of Menashe, who said:** [11]**Every execution mentioned** in the Torah **regarding non-Jews is** death by **strangulation.** Thus there is no difference between the law applying to a Jew and the law applying to non-Jews. [12]According to **both,** the offending non-Jew would be liable to death **by strangulation.**

[1]״כָּל עֶרְוָה שֶׁבֵּית דִּין שֶׁל יִשְׂרָאֵל מְמִיתִין עָלֶיהָ, בֶּן נֹחַ מוּזְהַר עָלֶיהָ. [2]אֵין בֵּית דִּין שֶׁל יִשְׂרָאֵל מְמִיתִין עָלֶיהָ — אֵין בֶּן נֹחַ מוּזְהַר עָלֶיהָ, [3]דִּבְרֵי רַבִּי מֵאִיר. [4]וַחֲכָמִים אוֹמְרִים: הַרְבֵּה עֲרָיוֹת יֵשׁ שֶׁאֵין בֵּית דִּין שֶׁל יִשְׂרָאֵל מְמִיתִין עֲלֵיהֶן, [5]וּבֶן נֹחַ מוּזְהַר עֲלֵיהֶן. [6]בָּא עַל עֲרָיוֹת יִשְׂרָאֵל, נִידּוֹן בְּדִינֵי יִשְׂרָאֵל. [7]בָּא עַל עֲרָיוֹת בֶּן נֹחַ, נִידּוֹן בְּדִינֵי בֶּן נֹחַ. [8]וְאָנוּ אֵין לָנוּ אֶלָּא נַעֲרָה הַמְאוֹרָסָה בִּלְבַד״.

[9]וְנַחְשׁוֹב נַמִי נִכְנְסָה לַחוּפָּה וְלֹא נִבְעֲלָה! [10]הַאי תָּנָא תָּנָא דְּבֵי מְנַשֶּׁה הוּא, דְּאָמַר: [11]כָּל מִיתָה הָאֲמוּרָה לִבְנֵי נֹחַ אֵינוֹ אֶלָּא חֶנֶק. [12]אִידִי וְאִידִי חֶנֶק הוּא.

LITERAL TRANSLATION

[1]"Any forbidden sexual relationship for which a Jewish court executes, a non-Jew is warned about it. [2][If] a Jewish court does not execute for it, a non-Jew is not warned about it. [3][These are] the words of Rabbi Meir. [4]And the Sages say: There are many forbidden sexual relationships for which a Jewish court does not execute, [5]but a non-Jew is warned about them. [6][If] he had intercourse with forbidden women who are Jewish, he is judged according to the laws applying to a Jew. [7][If] he had intercourse with forbidden women who are non-Jewish, he is judged according to the laws applying to a non-Jew. [8]And we only have a betrothed girl."

[9]But count also [a woman] who entered under the bridal canopy, but did not have intercourse! [10]This Tanna is the Tanna of the School of Menashe, who said: [11]Every execution mentioned regarding non-Jews is strangulation. [12]This and that are by strangulation.

RASHI

אין בית דין של ישראל ממיתין עליה — כגון חייבי כריתות, אחותו ואחות אביו, ואחות אמו, ואשת אחיו, ואשת אחי אביו, ואחות אשתו. **אין בן נח מוזהר עליה** — כדמפרש לקמן דרבי מאיר אליבא דרבי עקיבא אמרה, דנפקי ליה עריות בבני נח מ״על כן יעזב איש וגו׳״, והתם חייבי מיתות הוא דכתיבי. **הרבה עריות יש** — כגון כל חייבי כריתות בן נח מוזהר עליהם, דלרבנן אתרבו בני נח מ״איש איש״ לכל האמור בפרשה. ורבי מאיר לא דריש ״איש איש״ לרבויי. **בא על עריות ישראל** — עבריות. **עריות בני נח** — נכריות. **ואנו אין לנו** — שיהא בן נח חלוק בין ישראלית לנכרית, אלא נערה המאורסה משום דלדידהו לית להו — קטלינן ליה בקטלא דידן. **אידי ואידי חנק הוא** — דיננו ודיניהן שוין בה.

TRANSLATION AND COMMENTARY

וְסָבַר רַבִּי מֵאִיר [1]The Gemara raises a question about the position of Rabbi Meir cited in the Baraita: **Does Rabbi Meir** really **maintain** that **any forbidden** sexual **relationship for which a Jewish court would impose execution** upon a Jew, [2]**a non-Jew is prohibited** from engaging in? [3]**But surely it was taught** otherwise in the following Baraita: **"A convert** [58A] [4]**whose conception was in an unhallowed condition, but whose birth was in a hallowed condition** (this refers to a convert whose mother conceived him while she was still a Gentile but gave birth to him after converting to Judaism), [5]**has relatives through his mother, but he does not have relatives through his father.** By Torah law, a convert is like a newborn child, and is considered to have no ties to his natural parents or relatives. Nevertheless, the Sages forbade a convert from marrying relatives of his who had themselves converted and who were forbidden to him prior to his conversion by Noachide law, lest the convert think that his conversion reduced his sanctity. Thus, a convert is forbidden to marry maternal relatives, who are forbidden to a non-Jew, but he is permitted to marry paternal relatives, who are permitted to a non-Jew. [6]**How so?** [7]**If** a convert **married his maternal sister,** who had also converted to Judaism, **he must divorce her,** for a non-Jew is forbidden to his maternal sister by Noachide law. [8]But if he married **his paternal sister, he may keep her** as his wife, for a non-Jew is permitted to his paternal sister. [9]If the convert married **his father's maternal sister,** who had also converted to Judaism, **he must divorce her,** even though she is related to him through his father, for a non-Jew is also forbidden to marry his father's maternal sister, as will be explained below. [10]But if he married **his father's paternal sister, he may keep her** as his wife, for a non-Jew is permitted to marry his father's paternal sister. [11]If the convert married **his mother's maternal sister, he must divorce her,** for a non-Jew is forbidden to marry his mother's maternal sister by Noachide law. [12]If the convert married **his mother's paternal sister,** the Tannaim disagree about the law. [13]**Rabbi Meir says:** Even though his aunt is

[1]וְסָבַר רַבִּי מֵאִיר: כָּל עֶרְוָה שֶׁבֵּית דִּין שֶׁל יִשְׂרָאֵל מְמִיתִין עָלֶיהָ, [2]בֶּן נֹחַ מוּזְהַר עָלֶיהָ? [3]וְהָא תַּנְיָא: "גֵּר [58A] [4]שֶׁהָיְתָה הוֹרָתוֹ שֶׁלֹּא בִּקְדוּשָּׁה וְלֵידָתוֹ בִּקְדוּשָּׁה, [5]יֵשׁ לוֹ שְׁאֵר הָאֵם וְאֵין לוֹ שְׁאֵר הָאָב. [6]הָא כֵּיצַד: [7]נָשָׂא אֲחוֹתוֹ מִן הָאֵם, יוֹצִיא; [8]מִן הָאָב, יְקַיֵּים; [9]אֲחוֹת הָאָב מִן הָאֵם, יוֹצִיא; [10]מִן הָאָב, יְקַיֵּים; [11]אֲחוֹת הָאֵם מִן הָאֵם, יוֹצִיא. [12]אֲחוֹת הָאֵם מִן הָאָב, [13]רַבִּי מֵאִיר אוֹמֵר:

LITERAL TRANSLATION

[1]Does Rabbi Meir maintain: Any forbidden relationship for which a Jewish court executes, [2]a non-Jew is warned about it? [3]But surely it was taught: "A convert [58A] [4]whose conception was in an unhallowed condition, but whose birth was in a hallowed condition, [5]has relatives through his mother, but he does not have relatives through his father. [6]How so? [7][If] he married his maternal sister, he must divorce [her]; [8]his paternal [sister], he may keep [her]; [9]his father's maternal sister, he must divorce [her]; [10]his [father's] paternal [sister], he may keep her; [11]his mother's maternal sister, he must divorce [her]. [12]His mother's paternal sister, [13]Rabbi Meir says:

RASHI

שהורתו שלא בקדושה — וכל גר שנתגייר כקטן שנולד עכשיו, בלא אב ואם וקרובים דמי, ואין עליו קורבה מקודם לכן, ומיהו רבנן הוא דגזור עליה בכל האסורות לו (בהיותו נוכרי) משום שלא יאמרו באין מקדושה חמורה לקדושה קלה. הלכך נשא אחותו מן האם שנולדה קודם שנתגיירה אמה, ונתגיירה עם אמה ונשאה זה משגדל — יוציא, דאחותו היא ולא גרע מבן נח, ומדרבנן — שלא יאמרו וכו׳. דקסבר רבי מאיר אחותו מן האם אסורה לבני נח, ואפילו אחות אביו מן האם ואחות אמו מן האב, ויליף לה מ״על כן יעזב איש את אביו ואת אמו״ דאביו — זה אחות אביו, ואמו — זה אחות אמו, כדדריש ליה רבי אליעזר לקמן בשמעתין. **מן האב יקיים** — דלא נאסר איסור אחוה בבני נח אלא מן האם, דכתיב (בראשית כ) ״וגם אמנה אחותי בת אבי היא אך לא בת אמי״ אלמא בת האב שריא להו, ובת האם לא שריא להו. **אחות אביו מן האם יוציא** — כדכתיב (שם ב) ״על כן יעזב איש את אביו״ ודרשינן: את אביו — אחות אביו מן האם. **אחות אם מן האם יוציא** — כדכתיב את אמו — זו אחות אמו מן האם. **רבי מאיר אומר יוציא** — גזירה משום אחותו מן האם, דכיון דשם לד שאר האם כאן, אף על גב דמן האב היא אי שרית ליה אתי למימר: אין לגר אפילו שאר אם ואתי למישרי אפילו אחותו מן

HALAKHAH

איסור עֲרָיוֹת לַגֵּר Forbidden relations for a convert. "A convert is Rabbinically forbidden to have relations with women who are closely related to him through his mother. Thus he is permitted to marry the widow or ex-wife of his paternal half-brother. Likewise he is permitted to marry the widow or ex-wife of his father, his paternal uncle, or his son, even if the father, uncle or son had converted before marrying her. He also is permitted to marry the paternal half-sister of his mother, his own paternal half-sister, or his own daughter, if these women converted. However he is forbidden to marry his maternal half-sister, his mother's maternal half-sister, or the widow or ex-wife of his maternal half-brother, if his half-brother had married her after she converted. If his half-brother had married her while he and his bride were still non-Jews, the convert is permitted to marry her if his half-brother died or divorced her," following the ruling of the Sages in our Baraita. (*Shulḥan Arukh, Yoreh De'ah* 269:3.)

יוֹצִיא. [1]וַחֲכָמִים אוֹמְרִים:
יְקַיֵּים. [2]שֶׁהָיָה רַבִּי מֵאִיר אוֹמֵר:
כָּל עֶרְוָה שֶׁהִיא מִשּׁוּם שְׁאֵר
אֵם יוֹצִיא, [3]מִשּׁוּם שְׁאֵר הָאָב
יְקַיֵּים. [4]וּמוּתָּר בְּאֵשֶׁת אָחִיו,
וּבְאֵשֶׁת אֲחִי אָבִיו, [5]וּשְׁאָר כָּל
עֲרָיוֹת מוּתָּרוֹת לוֹ" — [6]לְאַתוּיֵי
אֵשֶׁת אָבִיו. [7]"נָשָׂא אִשָּׁה
וּבִתָּהּ, [8]כּוֹנֵס אַחַת וּמוֹצִיא
אַחַת. [9]וּלְכַתְּחִילָּה לֹא יִכְנוֹס.
[10]מֵתָה אִשְׁתּוֹ, מוּתָּר בַּחֲמוֹתוֹ".

LITERAL TRANSLATION

He must divorce [her]. [1]And the Sages say: He may keep [her]. [2]For Rabbi Meir would say: Any woman forbidden to him because of a relationship through a mother he must divorce. [3]Because of a relationship through a father he may keep. [4]And he is permitted to his brother's wife, and to his father's brother's wife, [5]and all other forbidden relationships are permitted to him" — [6]to include his father's wife. [7]"[If] he married a woman and her daughter, [8]he keeps one and divorces one. [9]But from the outset, he may not marry [them]. [10][If] his wife died, he is permitted to his mother-in-law."

TRANSLATION AND COMMENTARY

only related to his mother through their common father, the nephew **must** still **divorce her**, for she is related to him through his mother, and if we permit him to keep her as his wife, he might come to marry his own maternal sister, or the maternal sister of his mother or father. [1]**But the Sages** disagree and **say:** The nephew **may keep** his aunt as his wife, for a non-Jew is permitted to marry his mother's paternal sister, and we are not concerned that allowing him to keep her as his wife will lead him to marry maternal relatives who are in fact forbidden to him. [2]**Rabbi Meir says** that he must divorce the woman, for **any woman forbidden to him because of a relationship through his mother,** the convert **must divorce.** [3]But any woman **related to him through his father, he may keep** as his wife. [4]**And he is permitted to the wife of his** deceased **brother,** who had also converted to Judaism, even the wife of his brother through his mother, **and** he is permitted **to the wife of his father's brother** after his death, [5]**and** so too **all other women who are related to him** by marriage **are permitted to him.** A non-Jew is not forbidden to marry relatives by marriage, and so there is no concern that the convert will think that his conversion reduced his sanctity." [6]The Gemara notes that this last clause comes **to include the wife of his** deceased **father,** ruling that even she is permitted to the convert. [7]The Baraita continues: **"If he married a woman and her daughter** who had converted to Judaism together, by Torah law he may keep them both as his wives, for the familial bond between the two was dissolved when they converted. But lest they think that their conversion reduced their sanctity, [8]**he may keep** only **one** of the two women as his wife, **and he must divorce** the **other one.** Regarding all those women that the Baraita said the convert may keep as his wife, this only applies once he has married one of them. [9]**But from the outset, he may not marry** one of those women, lest a Jew who is not a convert marry a woman who is related to him in the same manner. [10]**If his wife** who herself had also converted to

RASHI

האם, וכל שכן אחות אמו ואחות אביו מן האם. **וחכמים אומרים יקיים** — ולא גזרינן, והוא הדין להורתו ולידתו שלא בקדושה, והא דנקט הורתו שלא בקדושה ולידתו בקדושה לא בא למעוטי הורתו ולידתו שלא בקדושה — אלא למעוטי הורתו ולידתו בקדושה, וכיון דדמי ליה לישראל גזר ביה רבי מאיר דילמא אתי לאחלופי בישראל, ואפילו בשאר האב, ואפילו נולדו אותן קרובות בהיותו נכרי. **ומותר באשת אחיו** — ואפילו מאמו ולאחר מיתה, ואפילו נשאה אחיו משנתגייר או נשאה כשהוא נכרי, ומשנתגייר קיימה דאין אשת אח לבני נח, וליכא למיחש שמא יאמרו וכו׳. וכן אשת אחי האב וכן כל הבאות מחמת אישות, דכיון דלשמא יאמרו ליכא למיחש דקסבר לא נאסרו לבני נח, ומשום קורבה נמי ליכא למיחש — דכקטן שנולד דמי. **ושאר כל עריות** — שבאות מחמת אישות מותרות לו. **לאתויי אשת אביו** — אבל כלתו ואחות אשתו ליכא לרבויי, דהא בגר שהיתה לידתו בקדושה קיימא וזה לא היתה לו כלל אשה אלא ביהדות, ולאתויי אחות אשתו נמי לא (צריכא ליה), דהא קתני בהדיא: נשא אשה ובתה — כונס אחת ומוציא אחת, והוא הדין לשתי אחיות. **נשא אשה ובתה** — אשאר גריס קאי, כשנשאם בהיותם כותי ונתגיירו עמו. אי נמי: אהא קאי, ומשום דהך גיורת קאמר, והוא הדין לישראל גמור. **ולבתחילה לא יכנוס** — מפרש ביבמות בפרק "נושאין על האנוסה" (צח,ב) דאהך דאמרן לעיל יקיים — קאמר דלכתחלה לא יכנוס. **מתה אשתו מותר בחמותו** — ואף על פי שקיימה לאשתו משנתגייר, דבן נח לא הוזהר על חמותו דנימא באים מקדושה וכו׳, וחמותו ממש לא

NOTES

מוּתָּר בַּחֲמוֹתוֹ **He is permitted to his mother-in-law.** Elsewhere (*Yevamot* 98b), the Gemara explains that the Sage who says that a convert is permitted to his mother-in-law after his wife's death, agrees with Rabbi Akiva,

HALAKHAH

גֵּר הַנָּשׂוּי לַעֲרָיוֹת **A convert who had already married someone who was forbidden to him.** "If a married couple converted, and she is one of the relatives forbidden to a convert, they need not divorce, unless she is his mother or his mother's sister." (*Shulḥan Arukh, Yoreh De'ah* 269:2)

גֵּר שֶׁנָּשָׂא אִשָּׁה וּבִתָּהּ **A convert who married a woman and her daughter.** "If a convert married a female convert as well as her daughter who was also a convert, he must divorce one of them," following the ruling of our Baraita. (*Shulḥan Arukh, Yoreh De'ah* 269:5.)

קְרוֹבוֹת אִשְׁתּוֹ לְאַחַר מִיתָה **The relatives of his deceased wife.** "If a convert married a female convert and she died,

[1]וְאִיכָּא דְּאָמְרִי: "אָסוּר בַּחֲמוֹתוֹ".

[2]אָמַר רַב יְהוּדָה: לָא קַשְׁיָא. [3]הָא — רַבִּי מֵאִיר אַלִּיבָּא דְּרַבִּי אֱלִיעֶזֶר, [4]וְהָא — רַבִּי מֵאִיר אַלִּיבָּא דְּרַבִּי עֲקִיבָא. [5]דְּתַנְיָא: [6]"'עַל כֵּן יַעֲזָב אִישׁ אֶת אָבִיו וְאֶת אִמּוֹ'. [7]רַבִּי אֱלִיעֶזֶר אוֹמֵר: 'אָבִיו' — אֲחוֹת אָבִיו, [8]'אִמּוֹ' — אֲחוֹת אִמּוֹ. [9]רַבִּי עֲקִיבָא אוֹמֵר: 'אָבִיו' — אֵשֶׁת אָבִיו. [10]'אִמּוֹ' — אִמּוֹ מַמָּשׁ. [11]'וְדָבַק' —

LITERAL TRANSLATION

[1]And there are [some] who say: "He is forbidden to his mother-in-law."

[2]Rav Yehudah said: It is not difficult. [3]This — Rabbi Meir according to Rabbi Eliezer, [4]and this — Rabbi Meir according to Rabbi Akiva. [5]For it was taught: [6]"'That is why a man leaves his father and his mother.' [7]Rabbi Eliezer says: 'His father' — his father's sister. [8]'His mother' — his mother's sister. [9]Rabbi Akiva says: 'His father' — his father's wife. [10]'His mother' — his actual mother. [11]'And he cleaves'

TRANSLATION AND COMMENTARY

Judaism **died, he is** then **permitted to** marry **his mother-in-law." [1]And there are some who say:** "If his wife died, **he is forbidden to** marry **his mother-in-law."** Now we learn from this Baraita, which records the position of Rabbi Meir, that a convert is permitted to marry his father's wife, from which it follows that a non-Jew is also permitted to marry his father's wife. But this is difficult, for a Jew who had intercourse with his father's wife is liable for execution, and in the Baraita cited earlier Rabbi Meir ruled that a forbidden sexual relationship for which a Jewish court would impose execution upon a Jew is also forbidden to a non-Jew. Consequently a non-Jew should also be forbidden to marry his father's wife. Furthermore, this Baraita says that a convert is forbidden to marry his maternal sister, from which it follows that a non-Jew is also forbidden to marry his maternal sister. But this too is difficult, for a Jew who had intercourse with his sister is not liable for execution. Since Rabbi Meir ruled in the earlier Baraita that a forbidden sexual relationship for which a Jewish court would not impose execution is permitted to a non-Jew, a non-Jew should be permitted to marry his maternal sister.

אָמַר רַב יְהוּדָה [2]**Rav Yehudah said: There is** really **no difficulty.** [3]**This** second Baraita **Rabbi Meir** taught **in accordance with** the position of one of his teachers, **Rabbi Eliezer.** [4]**And that** first Baraita **Rabbi Meir** taught **in accordance with** the position of another one of his teachers, **Rabbi Akiva.** [5]**For it was taught** in the following Baraita that Rabbi Eliezer and Rabbi Akiva disagreed about the matter: "The verse states (Genesis 2:24): [6]**'That is why a man leaves his father and his mother,** and cleaves to his wife; and they become one flesh,' teaching that the sexual prohibitions are universal. [7]**Rabbi Eliezer says: 'His father'** — this refers to **his father's sister.** [8]**'His mother'** — this refers to **his mother's sister.** Every man must leave his father's sister and his mother's sister, and all the more so his own sister, and seek a wife elsewhere, for his sister and aunts are forbidden to him. [9]**Rabbi Akiva says: 'His father'** — this refers to **his father's wife.** [10]**'His mother'** — this refers to **his actual mother.** Every man must leave his father's wife and his own mother, and seek a wife elsewhere, for those women are forbidden to him. [11]The words, **'And he cleaves,'** teach that a man may engage in

RASHI

הויא אף על גב דנתגיירו — דגר שנתגייר וכו׳. ואין קורבות זה לזה. **ואיכא דתני אסור בחמותו** — התם מפרש במאי פליגי. קתני מיהת מותר באשת אביו, ואף על פי שבית דין של ישראל ממיתין עליה, וכן בחמותו, וקתני: אסור באחותו, ובאחות אביו ואחות אמו, ואף על פי שאין בית דין של ישראל ממיתין עליהם. **הא רבי מאיר וכו׳** — תלמיד של שניהם היה, כדאמרינן במס׳ ביצה (ג,ב) גבי ליטרא קציעות, רבי מאיר אומר אמר רבי אליעזר: רואין כאילו הן פרודות וכו׳, ובמסכת עירובין בפרק קמא (יג,א) אמר: רבי מאיר שמש את רבי עקיבא, הא דקתני אחותו אסורה לו ואשת אביו מותרת לו רבי מאיר היא משום רבי אליעזר, והאי דקתני חייבי מיתות נאסרו להם ולא חייבי כריתות — רבי מאיר היא אליבא דרבי עקיבא. **על כן יעזב איש את אביו ואת אמו** — לאדם הראשון נאמר. **אחות אביו** — וכל שכן אחותו.

NOTES

who maintains that regarding an ordinary Jew, the prohibition against intercourse with his mother-in-law becomes less stringent after his wife's death, and is no longer punishable by judicial execution. This being the case regarding an ordinary Jew, regarding a convert the prohibition was removed altogether, for in the case of a convert, the prohibition against intercourse with his mother-in-law, even during his wife's lifetime, is only by Rabbinic decree.

HALAKHAH

he is permitted to marry her mother or daughter, for the Rabbinic preventive decree forbidding a convert to marry his wife's relatives applies only when the wife is alive." (*Shulḥan Arukh, Yoreh De'ah* 269:5.)

הָעֲרָיוֹת הָאֲסוּרוֹת לִבְנֵי נֹחַ With whom is a non-Jew forbidden to have relations. "Six catergories are forbidden to a non-Jew: His mother, his step-mother, his mother's sister, a married woman, a male, and an animal."

In general, this follows the ruling of Rabbi Akiva in the Baraita. However, regarding his mother's sister, *Rambam*

TRANSLATION AND COMMENTARY

sexual intercourse with a woman, **but** he may **not** have intercourse with **another man,** for such a union does not result in 'cleaving.' [1]The words, **'To his wife,'** teach that a man may engage in sexual intercourse with his own wife, **but not** with **someone else's wife,** for she is forbidden to him. [2]The words, **'And they become one flesh,'** teach that a man may engage in sexual intercourse with a woman with **whom he may become one flesh,** meaning one with whom he may have a child, [3]**to the exclusion of cattle and beasts with whom he cannot become flesh** and have a child." The first Baraita, in which Rabbi Meir states that any forbidden sexual relationship for which a Jewish court would impose execution upon a Jew is forbidden to a non-Jew, follows the position of Rabbi Akiva, who understands that the words, "his father and his mother," refer to his father's wife and his own mother, intercourse with whom is punishable by execution. And the second Baraita, in which Rabbi Meir maintains that a non-Jew is forbidden to his maternal sister but permitted to his father's wife, follows the position of Rabbi Eliezer, who understands that the words, "his father and his mother," refer to his father's sister and his mother's sister.

אָמַר מָר [4]**It was said above** in the Baraita: **"Rabbi Eliezer says:** [5]**'His father'** — this refers to **his father's sister."** [6]The Gemara asks: **Say** that these words refer to **his actual father,** and that the verse prohibits homosexual intercourse with one's father!

הַיְינוּ ״וְדָבַק״ [7]The Gemara answers: **That is** learned from the words, **'And he cleaves,'** which teach that a man may engage in sexual intercourse with a woman, [8]**but** he may **not** have intercourse with **another man,** including his father.

אֵימָא אֵשֶׁת אָבִיו [9]The Gemara asks: **Say** then that the words, "His father," refer to **his father's wife,** as was argued by Rabbi Akiva!

הַיְינוּ ״בְּאִשְׁתּוֹ״ [10]The Gemara answers: **That is** learned from the words, **'To his wife,'** which teach that a man may engage in sexual intercourse with his own wife, [11]**but not** with **someone else's wife,** including his father's wife.

אֵימָא [12]The Gemara asks: **Say** then that the words, "His father," refer to his father's wife, and prohibit a man from having intercourse with his father's wife even **after** his father's **death** when she is no longer forbidden to him as a married woman, but only because of the blood relationship!

דּוּמְיָא [13]The Gemara answers: It stands to reason that when the Torah spoke of "His father," it was referring to someone who is **similar to** the person referred to by the words **"His mother"**: [14]**Just as** the words **"His mother"** do **not** refer to someone who is forbidden to him **because of marriage,** but rather because of blood relationship, [15]**so too** the words **"His father"** must **not** be referring to someone who is forbidden to him **because of marriage,** but rather because of blood relationship, i.e., his father's sister, and not his father's wife after his death.

LITERAL TRANSLATION

— and not a man. [1]'To his wife' — and not his fellow's wife. [2]'And they become one flesh' — they who become one flesh, [3]to the exclusion of cattle and beasts, who do not become one flesh."

[4]The master said: "Rabbi Eliezer says: [5]'His father' — his father's sister." [6]Say his actual father!

[7]That is [learned from] "And he cleaves" — [8]and not a man.

[9]Say his father's wife!

[10]That is [learned from] "To his wife" — [11]and not his fellow's wife.

[12]Say after death!

[13]Similar to "His mother": [14]Just as "His mother" not because of marriage, [15]so too "His father" not because of marriage.

וְלֹא בְּזָכָר. [1]'בְּאִשְׁתּוֹ' — וְלֹא בְּאֵשֶׁת חֲבֵירוֹ. [2]'וְהָיוּ לְבָשָׂר אֶחָד' — מִי שֶׁנַּעֲשִׂים בָּשָׂר אֶחָד, [3]יָצְאוּ בְּהֵמָה וְחַיָּה, שֶׁאֵין נַעֲשִׂין בָּשָׂר אֶחָד".

[4]אָמַר מָר: "רַבִּי אֱלִיעֶזֶר אוֹמֵר: [5]'אָבִיו' — אֲחוֹת אָבִיו".

[6]אֵימָא: אָבִיו מַמָּשׁ!

[7]הַיְינוּ "וְדָבַק" — [8]וְלֹא בְּזָכָר.

[9]אֵימָא אֵשֶׁת אָבִיו!

[10]הַיְינוּ "בְּאִשְׁתּוֹ" [11]וְלֹא בְּאֵשֶׁת חֲבֵירוֹ.

[12]אֵימָא לְאַחַר מִיתָה!

[13]דּוּמְיָא דְּ"אִמּוֹ": [14]מָה "אִמּוֹ" דְּלָאו אִישׁוּת, [15]אַף "אָבִיו" דְּלָאו אִישׁוּת.

RASHI

ודבק ולא בזכר – דליכא דיבוק, דמתוך שאין הנשכב נהנה אינו נדבק עמו. **מי שנעשה לבשר אחד** – שזרע יוצא מהם, שנעשה בשר האם והאב אחד בו. **יצאו בהמה וחיה** – שאין יולדין מן האדם, הני דרבי עקיבא כולהו חייבי מיתות נינהו, ומינה יליף לכל חייבי מיתות, אבל לרבי אליעזר לית ליה קורבא דאישות, ואית ליה קורבה דאחוה. **אימא לאחר מיתה** – לחייבו על אשת אביו לאחר מיתת אביו, ומשני: דומיא דאמו.

HALAKHAH

relied on other places in the Talmud where it is stated that a non-Jew is punishable for having relations with maternal relatives — a law which is also evident from the relevant passages in Scripture (*Radbaz;* and see *Kesef Mishneh* and *Leḥem Mishneh*). (*Rambam, Sefer Shofetim, Hilkhot Melakhim* 9:5.)

TRANSLATION AND COMMENTARY

אִמּוֹ [1]It was also stated above in the Baraita: "Rabbi Eliezer says: **'His mother'** — this refers to **his mother's sister.**" [2]The Gemara asks: **Say** that these words refer to **his actual mother,** as was argued by Rabbi Akiva!

״הַיְינוּ בְּ״אִשְׁתּוֹ [3]The Gemara answers: **That is** learned from the words, **'To his wife,'** which teach that a man may engage in sexual intercourse with his own wife, [4]**but not** with **someone else's wife,** including his mother, who is his father's wife.

וְאֵימָא [5]The Gemara asks: **Say** then that the words "His mother," refer to his actual mother, and come to prohibit a person from having intercourse with his mother even **after** his father's **death** when she is no longer forbidden to him as a married woman!

״דּוּמְיָא דְ״אָבִיו [6]The Gemara answers: It stands to reason that when the Torah spoke of "His mother," it was referring to someone who is **similar to** the person referred to by the words **"His father"**: [7]**Just as** the words **"His father"** do **not** refer to his **actual** father, but rather to a relative of his father's, [8]**so too** the words **"His mother"** do **not** refer to his **actual mother,** but to a relative of his mother's.

רַבִּי עֲקִיבָא אוֹמֵר [9]The Gemara proceeds to analyze the next portion of the Baraita cited earlier: **"Rabbi Akiva says: 'His father' — this refers to his father's wife."** [10]**But say** that these words refer to **his actual father,** and that the verse prohibits homosexual intercourse with one's father!

״הַיְינוּ ״וְדָבַק [11]The Gemara answers as it had answered above: **That is** learned from the words, **'And he cleaves,'** which teach that a man may engage in sexual intercourse with a woman, [12]**but** he may **not** have intercourse with **another man,** including his father.

אִי הָכִי [13]The Gemara asks: **If so,** then how can you say that the words "His father" refer to **his father's wife?** [14]Surely **that is** learned from the words **'To his wife,'** which teach that a man may engage in sexual intercourse with his own wife, [15]**but not** with **someone else's wife,** including his father's wife.

לְאַחַר מִיתָה [16]The Gemara answers: The verse prohibits a person from having intercourse with his father's wife even **after** his father's **death,** when she is no longer forbidden to him as a married woman, but only on account of the blood relationship.

'אִמּוֹ' [17]It was also stated in the Baraita cited above: "Rabbi Akiva says: **'His mother'** — this refers to **his actual mother."** [18]The Gemara asks: Surely **that** follows from the words **"To his wife,"** which teach that a man may engage in sexual intercourse with his own wife, [19]**but not** with **someone else's wife,** including his mother, who is his father's wife!

[1]״׳אִמּוֹ׳ — אֲחוֹת אִמּוֹ״. [2]וְאֵימָא אִמּוֹ מַמָּשׁ! [3]הַיְינוּ בְּ״אִשְׁתּוֹ״ — [4]וְלֹא בְּאֵשֶׁת חֲבֵירוֹ. [5]וְאֵימָא לְאַחַר מִיתָה! [6]דּוּמְיָא דְ״אָבִיו״: [7]מָה ״אָבִיו״ — דְּלָאו מַמָּשׁ. [8]אַף אִמּוֹ — דְּלָאו מַמָּשׁ. [9]״רַבִּי עֲקִיבָא אוֹמֵר: ׳אָבִיו׳ — אֵשֶׁת אָבִיו״. [10]וְאֵימָא: אָבִיו מַמָּשׁ! [11]הַיְינוּ ״וְדָבַק״ — [12]וְלֹא בְּזָכָר. [13]אִי הָכִי, אֵשֶׁת אָבִיו נַמִי, [14]הַיְינוּ ״בְּאִשְׁתּוֹ״ [15]וְלֹא בְּאֵשֶׁת חֲבֵרוֹ! [16]לְאַחַר מִיתָה. [17]״׳אִמּוֹ׳ — אִמּוֹ מַמָּשׁ״. [18]הַיְינוּ ״בְּאִשְׁתּוֹ״ — [19]וְלֹא בְּאֵשֶׁת חֲבֵרוֹ!

LITERAL TRANSLATION

[1]"'His mother' — his mother's sister." [2]Say his actual mother!

[3]That is [learned from] "To his wife" — [4]and not his fellow's wife.

[5]Say after death!

[6]Similar to "His father": [7]Just as "His father" — not actually, [8]so too "His mother" — not actually.

[9]"Rabbi Akiva says: 'His father' — his father's wife." [10]But say his actual father!

[11]That is [learned from] "And he cleaves" — [12]and not a man.

[13]If so, his father's wife, too, [14]that is [learned from] "To his wife" — [15]and not his fellow's wife!

[16]After death.

[17]"'His mother' — his actual mother." [18]That is [learned from] "To his wife" — [19]and not his fellow's wife!

RASHI

אמו אמו ממש – ולאו היינו אשת חבירו, ובלאחר מיתת אביו נמי ליכא לתרוצה, דהיינו אשת אביו דאוקימנא לאחר מיתה. ומשני: אמו אנוסת אביו דלאו אשתו, ואין כאן אלא משום אמו אפילו בחייו.

HALAKHAH

בֶּן נֹחַ בְּאִמּוֹ וּבְאֵשֶׁת אָבִיו A non-Jew who had relations with his mother or step-mother. "If a non-Jew has relations with his mother, he is liable to the death penalty — even if she was not married to his father, but was only seduced or raped by him. If he had relations with his step-mother, during his father's lifetime or even after his father's death, he is liable to the death penalty," following the ruling of Rabbi Akiva. (*Rambam, Sefer Shofetim, Hilkhot Melakhim* 9:6.)

TRANSLATION AND COMMENTARY

אִמּוֹ [1]The Gemara proposes another possibility: The verse prohibits a man from having intercourse with **his mother who had been raped** or seduced by his father, but was never married to him. In such a case, she is not forbidden to her son as a married woman, but only on account of the blood relationship.

בְּמַאי קָא מִיפַּלְגִי [2]The Gemara asks: **About what** point **do** Rabbi Eliezer and Rabbi Akiva **disagree?** [3]The Gemara explains: **Rabbi Eliezer maintains:** [58B] [4]It stands to reason that the words **"His father"** refer to someone who **is similar to** the person referred to by the words **"His mother,"** [5]**and** that the words **"His mother"** refer to someone who **is similar to** the person referred to by the words **"His father.** These expressions cannot refer to a man's actual father and mother, because the prohibition against intercourse with one's father follows from the words, "And cleaves." Similarly, they cannot refer to relatives forbidden to a man because of marriage, since his mother is not forbidden to him because of marriage, but because of blood relationship. [6]**You** can **only find** a parallelism between the expressions "His father" and "His mother," if you understand that the verse is referring to the parents' **siblings,** i.e., the father's sister and the mother's sister. [7]**And Rabbi Akiva** maintains: **It is preferable to explain** the words "His father" **as referring to his father's wife,** [8]for elsewhere we find that a man's father's wife **is called "his father's nakedness,"** as the verse states (Leviticus 18:8): "The nakedness of your father's wife shall you not uncover; it is your father's nakedness." [9]And we should **exclude** the possibility **of** explaining the words "His father" as referring to **his father's sister,** for elsewhere a man's father's sister **is called "his father's kinswoman,"** as the verse states (Leviticus 18:12): "You shall not uncover the nakedness of your father's sister; she is your father's near kinswoman," [10]**but nowhere is she called "his father's nakedness."**

תָּא שְׁמַע [11]The Gemara tries now presents Biblical support for each of the Tannaitic positions: **Come and hear** what is stated in the verse (Exodus 26:20): **"And Amram took** him **Jocheved his father's sister** to wife." [12]**Does** the verse **not** mean that Jocheved was Amram's **father's sister** even **through their mother,** as well as their father? Since Amram at the time was bound only by Noachide law, it follows that a non-Jew is permitted to marry his father's full sister, as was argued by Rabbi Akiva, and against Rabbi Eliezer!

לֹא [13]The Gemara rejects this proof: **No,** Jocheved was Amram's **father's sister** only **through their father.** Amram's father Kehat and Jocheved had the same father but different mothers. Even Rabbi Eliezer who says that a non-Jew is forbidden to marry his father's sister limits the prohibition to his father's maternal sister, but a non-Jew is in fact permitted to marry his father's half sister, if they were born of different mothers.

[1]אִמּוֹ מְאֲנוּסָתוֹ.
[2]בְּמַאי קָא מִיפַּלְגִי? [3]רַבִּי אֱלִיעֶזֶר סָבַר: [58B] [4]״אָבִיו״ דּוּמְיָא דְ״אִמּוֹ״, [5]וְ״אִמּוֹ״ דּוּמְיָא דְ״אָבִיו״, [6]לָא מַשְׁכַּחַת לָהּ אֶלָּא בְּאַחֲוָוה. [7]וְרַבִּי עֲקִיבָא: מוּטָּב לְאוֹקְמֵיהּ בְּאֵשֶׁת אָבִיו [8]דְּאִיקְּרֵי ״עֶרְוַת אָבִיו״, [9]לְאַפּוּקֵי אֲחוֹת אָבִיו דִּ״שְׁאֵר אָבִיו״ אִיקְּרֵי, [10]״עֶרְוַת אָבִיו״ לָא אִיקְּרֵי.
[11]תָּא שְׁמַע: ״וַיִּקַּח עַמְרָם אֶת יוֹכֶבֶד דֹּדָתוֹ״. [12]מַאי לָאו דּוֹדָתוֹ מִן הָאֵם?
[13]לֹא, דּוֹדָתוֹ מִן הָאָב.

LITERAL TRANSLATION

[1]His mother who was raped.
[2]About what do they disagree? [3]Rabbi Eliezer maintains: [58B] [4]"His father" is similar to "His mother," [5]and "His mother" is similar to "His father." [6]You only find this with a sibling relationship. [7]And Rabbi Akiva: It is better to explain it as [referring to] his father's wife [8]who is called "his father's nakedness," [9]to the exclusion of his father's sister, who is called "his father's near kinswoman," [10][but] is not called "his father's nakedness."
[11]Come [and] hear: "And Amram took Jocheved his father's sister." [12]Is it not his father's sister through [their] mother?
[13]No, his father's sister through [their] father.

RASHI

אביו דומיא דאמו ואמו דומיא דאביו לא משכחת לה אלא באיסור דאחווה — דתרוייהו ממש ליכא למימר, דאם כן היינו ודבק — ולא בזכר, ותרוייהו באישות ליכא למימר, דהא אמו לאו משום אישות, דאם כן היינו אשת אביו, הלכך תרוייהו באחוה. **ורבי עקיבא מוטב לאוקמא באשת אביו** — כמשמעותה דקרא דקרי ליה אביו, דכתיב "יעזב איש את אביו", ואשת אביו אשכחן דקרי בישראל ערות אביו דכתיב (ויקרא יח) "ערות אביך היא", ולאו לאוקמא באחות אביו, דקרא לא משמע הכי — דאחות אביו שאר אביו הוא דאקרי — "ערות אחות אביך לא תגלה כי שאר אביך היא" (שם). **דודתו** — אחות קהת אביו. **מאי לאו** — אחות קהת אף מן האם היתה והותרה לעמרם, אלמא אחות אב מן האם מותרת לו קודם מתן תורה. **לא דודתו מן האב** — אחות קהת מן האב היתה, ולא מן האם, ואחות האב הותרה להם, והא דכתיב "יעזב איש את אביו" ודרשינן: אחות אביו (אביו) — באחותו מן האם קאמר, כדילפינן מ"וגם אמנה אחותי בת אבי היא".

TERMINOLOGY

בְּמַאי קָא מִיפַּלְגִי? About what do they disagree? When the practical difference between two conflicting points of view is clear, but the theoretical basis of the dispute is not, the Talmud may use this expression to inquire into the theoretical issue at the heart of the dispute.

NOTES

אִמּוֹ מְאֲנוּסָתוֹ His mother who was raped. *Tzofnat Pa'ane'aḥ* argues that the Gemara could not have answered that the verse prohibits a person from having intercourse with his mother who had been seduced by his father. The laws regarding seduction do not apply to non-Jews. Thus if a non-Jewish man seduced a woman, she is regarded as his wife, even if he had no intention of taking her in marriage.

TERMINOLOGY

וְתִסְבְּרָא And do you think? The Gemara uses this expression when seeking to refute an argument based on a particular interpretaion of an authoritative (usually Biblical) text, showing that the text upon which the argument is based must anyway (for other reasons) be understood differently or amended.

TRANSLATION AND COMMENTARY

תָּא שְׁמַע [1]The Gemara continues: **Come and hear** what Abraham said to Abimelech about Sarah (Genesis 20:12): **"And yet indeed she is my sister; she is the daughter of my father, but not the daughter of my mother;** and she became my wife." Now this verse seems to be saying that Sarah was permitted to Abraham because she was the daughter of his father, but they had different mothers, [2]and **this implies that** had she been also **the daughter of his mother,** so that they were full brother and sister, she would have been **forbidden** to marry him. Since Abraham at the time was bound only by Noachide law, it follows that a non-Jew is forbidden to his sister with whom he shares the same mother, as was argued by Rabbi Eliezer, and against Rabbi Akiva.

וְתִסְבְּרָא [3]The Gemara rejects this proof as well: **Do you** really **think that** this verse can be understood literally and that Sarah **was** Abraham's **sister?** [4]Surely Sarah **was the daughter of** Abraham's **brother,** for according to tradition, Sarah may be identified with Iscah, the daughter of Haran, Abraham's brother! [5]**Since** the verse can surely not be understood literally, it may be argued that **there is no difference between a** non-Jew's half **sister through their** common **father and** his full **sister through their mother** as well, [6]for in both cases **she is permitted** to marry him, as posited by Rabbi Akiva. [7]And **there** in the incident involving Sarah, when Abraham **said to** Abimelech: "And yet indeed she is my sister; she is the daughter of my father, but not the daughter of my mother," he meant to say as follows: [8]**I am related to her as if she were my sister,** for the daughter of a brother is like a sister, [9]and she is the daughter of my brother **through our** common **father,** Terach, **but not** the daughter of my brother **through a** common **mother,** for Haran and I have different mothers.

תָּא שְׁמַע [10]**Come and hear** a different proof from a Baraita which taught: **"Why did Adam not marry his daughter?** [11]**So that Cain would** be able to **marry his sister** and multiply, **as the verse states** (Psalms 89:3): **'For I have said, The world is built on lovingkindness** [חֶסֶד].' The word *ḥesed*, used here in its usual sense of 'lovingkindness,' is also used in the opposite sense of "disgraceful deed" in connection with the sinful cohabitation of a person with his sister, as the Torah states (Leviticus 20:17): 'And if a man shall take his sister...it is a disgraceful deed [חֶסֶד].' Thus, the verse implies that when the world was first established, Cain was permitted to marry his sister, so that the world could be quickly built up and populated." [12]**But if not for this** special allowance for Cain, he would not have been permitted to marry his sister. [13]Thus a sister **is** indeed **forbidden** to her brother, as argued by Rabbi Eliezer, and against Rabbi Akiva!

[1]תָּא שְׁמַע: ״וְגַם אָמְנָה אֲחֹתִי בַת אָבִי הִיא אַךְ לֹא בַת אִמִּי״. [2]מִכְּלָל דְּבַת הָאֵם אֲסוּרָה! [3]וְתִסְבְּרָא אֲחוֹתוֹ הֲוַאי? [4]בַּת אָחִיו הֲוַאי! [5]וְכֵיוָן דְּהָכִי הוּא — לָא שְׁנָא מִן הָאָב, וְלָא שְׁנָא מִן הָאֵם — [6]שַׁרְיָא. [7]אֶלָּא הָתָם הָכִי קָאָמַר לֵיהּ: [8]קוּרְבָא דְּאָחוֹת אִית לִי בַּהֲדָהּ, [9]מֵאַבָּא וְלָא מֵאִמָּא. [10]תָּא שְׁמַע: ״מִפְּנֵי מָה לֹא נָשָׂא אָדָם אֶת בִּתּוֹ? [11]כְּדֵי שֶׁיִּשָּׂא קַיִן אֶת אֲחוֹתוֹ, שֶׁנֶּאֱמַר: ׳כִּי אָמַרְתִּי עוֹלָם חֶסֶד יִבָּנֶה׳״. [12]הָא לָאו הָכִי, [13]אֲסִירָא!

LITERAL TRANSLATION

[1]Come [and] hear: "And yet indeed she is my sister; she is the daughter of my father, but not the daughter of my mother." [2]This implies that the daughter of one's mother is forbidden!

[3]And do you think that she was his sister? [4]She was the daughter of his brother! [5]And since that is so, there is no difference between [a sister] through [one's] father and [a sister] through [one's] mother — [6]she is permitted. [7]Rather, there he said to him: [8]The relationship of a sister I have with her, [9]through my father, and not through my mother.

[10]Come [and] hear: "Why did Adam not marry his daughter? [11]So that Cain would marry his sister, as it is stated: 'For I have said, The world is built on lovingkindness." [12]But if not for this, [13]she is forbidden!

RASHI

תא שמע וגם אמנה וכו' — מכלל דבת האם אסורה — קשיא לרבי עקיבא. **אחותו הוה** — בתמיהה, הא בת אחיו הוה, וכיון דהכי לא שנא מן האם ולא שנא מן האב שריא ליה. **אלא התם הכי הוה אמר ליה קורבא דאחוה וכו'** — בת אחי מן האב היא ולא מן האם, ולא משום איסורא והתירא קאמר ליה אלא משום לתקוני דיבורא קמא שאמר: אחותי היא, קאמר ליה הכי: אחותי בת אבי היא, דבת אחי בן אבי היא, וקרי לה אחותו — דבני בנים הרי הם כבנים, והרי היא כבת אביו, והאי דקאמר: ״אך לא בת אמי״ לאו משום דאי הוה אחוה מן האם הויא אסורה, אלא משום קושטא דמילתא אמר לו. **חסד יבנה** — תחילתו של עולם נבנה בחסד, שלוה אדם הראשון לגמול חסד את בנו ואסרה לו והתירה לקין, כדי שיבנה העולם והיינו דכתיב (ויקרא כ) ״(כי יקח איש) את אחותו בת אביו חסד הוא״ — מה שהתרתי לקין חסד גמלתי עמו.

NOTES

כְּדֵי שֶׁיִּשָּׂא קַיִן אֶת אֲחוֹתוֹ So that Cain would marry his sister. Some Rishonim understand the Baraita as follows: Why did Adam not marry his daughter who was in fact permitted to him, and then his son Cain could have married the daughter born of that union, for a non-Jew is permitted to marry his paternal sister? The Baraita explains that even

TRANSLATION AND COMMENTARY

כֵּיוָן [1]The Gemara rejects this proof: Rabbi Akiva can say that intercourse with one's sister should indeed have been prohibited to all, but **since it was permitted** to Cain, [2]**it was permitted** for all generations to all non-Jews, and prohibited only for Jews.

אָמַר רַב הוּנָא [3]**Rav Huna said:** Both according to Rabbi Akiva and according to Rabbi Eliezer, **a non-Jew is permitted to** marry **his** own **daughter.** [4]**And if you should ask: Why** then **did Adam not marry his** own **daughter?** — the reason is as follows: [5]**So that Cain would** be able to **marry his sister** and multiply, **as** the verse states: "For I have said, **The world is built on lovingkindness.**"

וְאִיכָּא דְּאָמְרִי [6]The Gemara now cites another version of Rav Huna's statement: **And there are some who say** that **Rav Huna said** as follows: [7]**A non-Jew is forbidden to** marry **his** own **daughter.** [8]**Know** that **this** is true, **for Adam did not marry his daughter.** [9]**But** the Gemara rejects this position, arguing that **this is not so,** for a non-Jew is in fact permitted to marry his own daughter. [10]**There the reason** that Adam did not marry his daughter is **so that Cain would** be able to **marry his sister** and quickly populate the world, [11]**as** the verse states: **"The world is built on lovingkindness."**

אָמַר רַב חִסְדָּא [12]**Rav Ḥisda said:** A non-Jewish **slave** belonging to a Jew **is permitted to** marry **his mother, his daughter,** and all his other relatives, for when he is immersed in a ritual bath following his acquisition, he undergoes a change of status, which among other things obligates him to observe all the Torah's prohibitions and all the positive commandments that are not dependent upon a specific time for their performance. [13]During that period, **he is removed from the category of non-Jew,** so that he no longer has family connections with his natural relatives. [14]But **he has not** yet entered **the category of Jew,** and so the Rabbinic decree regarding a convert — that he is prohibited from having intercourse with a relative who was forbidden to him prior to his conversion, lest he think that his conversion reduced his sanctity — does not apply him. Thus, he is not bound by any of the prohibitions against intercourse with his relatives, neither as a non-Jew, nor as a Jew.

[1]כֵּיוָן דְּאִשְׁתְּרִי, [2]אִשְׁתְּרִי.

[3]אָמַר רַב הוּנָא: נָכְרִי מוּתָּר בְּבִתּוֹ. [4]וְאִם תֹּאמַר: מִפְּנֵי מָה לֹא נָשָׂא אָדָם אֶת בִּתּוֹ? [5]כְּדֵי שֶׁיִּשָּׂא קַיִן אֶת אֲחוֹתוֹ, מִשּׁוּם: "עוֹלָם חֶסֶד יִבָּנֶה".

[6]וְאִיכָּא דְּאָמְרִי: אָמַר רַב הוּנָא: [7]נָכְרִי אָסוּר בְּבִתּוֹ. [8]תֵּדַע, שֶׁלֹּא נָשָׂא אָדָם אֶת בִּתּוֹ. [9]וְלָא הִיא, [10]הָתָם הַיְינוּ טַעְמָא כְּדֵי שֶׁיִּשָּׂא קַיִן אֶת אֲחוֹתוֹ, [11]מִשּׁוּם דְּ"עוֹלָם חֶסֶד יִבָּנֶה".

[12]אָמַר רַב חִסְדָּא: עֶבֶד מוּתָּר בְּאִמּוֹ, וּמוּתָּר בְּבִתּוֹ. [13]יָצָא מִכְּלָל נָכְרִי, [14]וְלִכְלָל יִשְׂרָאֵל לֹא בָּא.

LITERAL TRANSLATION

[1]Since she was permitted, [2]she is permitted.

[3]Rav Huna said: A non-Jew is permitted to his daughter. [4]And if you say: Why did Adam not marry his daughter? [5]So that Cain would marry his sister, because of "The world is built on lovingkindness."'

[6]And there are [some] who say: Rav Huna said: [7]A non-Jew is forbidden to his daughter. [8]Know [this], for Adam did not marry his daughter. [9]But this is not so. [10]There the reason is so that Cain would marry his sister, [11]because of "The world is built on lovingkindness."

[12]Rav Ḥisda said: A slave is permitted to his mother, and he is permitted to his daughter. [13]He left the category of non-Jew, [14]but did not enter the category of Jew.

RASHI

נכרי מותר בבתו – בין לרבי אליעזר בין לרבי עקיבא, דקסבר רב הונא לא ילפינן שאר עריות מהנך דכתיבי בהאי קרא, מדפרט כל הני – שמע מינה דוקא כתבינהו. **עבד כנעני** – של ישראל. **מותר באמו ובבתו** – וכל שכן בשאר עריות של קורבה. **יצא מכלל נכרי** – ופקע שם בן נח מיניה. **ולכלל ישראל לא בא** – דליגזור ליה עליה משום דשמא יאמרו באין מקדושה חמורה לקדושה קלה.

NOTES

though a non-Jew is forbidden to marry his full sister, God granted Cain a special allowance, as the verse states, "For I have said, The world is built on lovingkindness," so that Cain would not have to wait so long before having children (see *Ran* and *Ramah*).

נָכְרִי מוּתָּר בְּבִתּוֹ A non-Jew is permitted to his daughter. The Rishonim ask: If in fact a descendant of Noah is permitted to marry his daughter, why then does the Torah report the incident involving Lot and his daughters in a reproachful manner, as if an offense had been committed? *Ramban* (in his *Commentary to the Torah*) suggests thatwhile according to the strict letter of the law a descendant of Noah is permitted to his daughter, even in those times such a union was regarded as forbidden incest.

עֶבֶד מוּתָּר בְּאִמּוֹ A slave is permitted to his mother. *Meiri* notes that while a slave is not bound by the various prohibitions against intercourse with his relatives, he is bound by the other sexual prohibitions, such as the

HALAKHAH

בֶּן נֹחַ בְּבִתּוֹ A non-Jew and his daughter. "A non-Jew is permitted to marry his daughter. The only relationships forbidden to him are the six which are derived here from Scripture." (*Rambam, Sefer Shofetim, Hilkhot Melakhim* 9:15.)

דִּין עֶבֶד בַּעֲרָיוֹת A non-Jewish slave. "As soon as a non-Jew has immersed in a mikveh in order to acquire the

TRANSLATION AND COMMENTARY

כִּי אֲתָא [1]When Rav Dimi came to Babylonia from Eretz Israel, **he said in the name of Rabbi Elazar who said in the name of Rabbi Ḥanina:** [2]**If a non-Jew designated a maidservant** to marry **his slave, and** then he himself **had intercourse with her,** [3]**he is put to death** because **of her,** for she is regarded as a married woman.

מְאֵימַת [4]The Gemara asks: **From when** is a maidservant who was designated as the wife of a slave regarded as a married woman? [5]**Rav Naḥman said: From when** the other young women in town begin to **refer to her as "So-and-so's girl."**

מְאֵימַת [6]The Gemara asks: **From when is** the maidservant **permitted** to other men? When is she regarded as having broken the tie that bound her to the slave to whom she had been designated? [7]**Rav Huna said: From when she uncovers her head in the market.** Non-Jewish married women were also accustomed to cover their heads when then they went out to the market. By baring her head in public, the maidservant demonstrates that she no longer is tied to the slave to whom she had been designated, and so she is permitted to other men.

אָמַר רַבִּי אֶלְעָזָר [8]**Rabbi Elazar said in the name of Rabbi Ḥanina: If a non-Jew had intercourse with his wife in an unnatural manner** (anal intercourse), **he is liable** for having violated a sexual prohibition, [9]**for the verse states** (Genesis 2:24): 'That is why a man leaves his father and his mother, **and cleaves** to his wife.' This teaches that a man may have intercourse with his wife in the natural manner by way of which he cleaves to her, **but not in an unnatural manner** which does not result in "cleaving."

אָמַר רָבָא [10]**Rava said: Is there something for which a Jew is not liable, but a non-Jew is liable?** Sexual intercourse with one's wife in an unnatural manner is permitted to a Jew. How then can it be forbidden to a non-Jew?

[1]כִּי אֲתָא רַב דִּימִי, אָמַר רַבִּי אֶלְעָזָר אָמַר רַבִּי חֲנִינָא: [2]בֶּן נֹחַ שֶׁיִּיחֵד שִׁפְחָה לְעַבְדּוֹ וּבָא עָלֶיהָ, [3]נֶהֱרַג עָלֶיהָ.
[4]מֵאֵימַת? [5]אָמַר רַב נַחְמָן: מִדְּקָרְאוּ לָהּ "רְבִיתָא דִּפְלָנְיָא".
[6]מֵאֵימַת הַתָּרָתָהּ? — [7]אָמַר רַב הוּנָא: מִשֶּׁפָּרְעָה רֹאשָׁהּ בַּשּׁוּק.
[8]אָמַר רַבִּי אֶלְעָזָר אָמַר רַבִּי חֲנִינָא: בֶּן נֹחַ שֶׁבָּא עַל אִשְׁתּוֹ שֶׁלֹּא כְּדַרְכָּהּ, חַיָּיב, [9]שֶׁנֶּאֱמַר: "וְדָבַק" — וְלֹא שֶׁלֹּא כְּדַרְכָּהּ.
[10]אָמַר רָבָא: מִי אִיכָּא מִידֵּי דְּיִשְׂרָאֵל לָא מִחַיַּיב, וְנָכְרִי מִחַיַּיב?

LITERAL TRANSLATION

[1]When Rav Dimi came, he said in the name of Rabbi Elazar who said in the name of Rabbi Ḥanina: [2][If] a non-Jew designated a maidservant for his slave, and had intercourse with her, [3]he is put to death on account of her.

[4]From when? [5]Rav Naḥman said: From when they call her "So-and-so's girl."

[6]From when is she permitted? [7]Rav Huna said: From when she uncovers her head in the market.

[8]Rabbi Elazar said in the name of Rabbi Ḥanina: [If] a non-Jew had intercourse with his wife in an unnatural manner, he is liable, [9]for it is stated: "And he cleaves" — and not in an unnatural manner.

[10]Rava said: Is there something for which a Jew is not liable, but a non-Jew is liable?

RASHI

מאימת — חשיב ליה מיוחדת לו. **מדרגיל למיקרי ליה** — בנות העיר. **רביתא דפלניא** — ילדתו של פלוני עבד. **מאימת התרתה** — שלא תקרא מיוחדת לו אם תבא להפקיר עלמה. **משתפרע ראשה בשוק** — שהיו רגילות אף הנכריות הנשואות שלא לצאת בראש פרוע. **שלא בדרכה** — אין כאן דבק, שמתוך שאינה נהנית בדבר אינה נדבקת עמו.

NOTES

prohibition against intercourse with a married woman, homosexual intercourse, and bestiality, and he is liable to the death sentence if he violates them.

"וְדָבַק" — וְלֹא שֶׁלֹּא כְּדַרְכָּהּ **And he cleaves — and not in an unnatural manner.** Some suggest that the prohibition derives from the latter part of the verse, "And cleaves to his wife, and they become one flesh," for anal intercourse does not lead to the couple's becoming one flesh with the conception of a child (*Mitzpeh Eitan*).

HALAKHAH

status of non-Jewish slave, he ceases to be a non-Jew but does not become a Jew. Therefore he is permitted to marry any female relative (even his mother)." (*Rambam, Sefer Kedushah, Hilkhot Issurei Bi'ah* 12:11.)

שִׁפְחָה הַנְּשׂוּאָה לְעֶבֶד **A male and a female non-Jewish slave who are married to each other.** "If a non-Jew designated a woman as the wife of his slave, and this fact is known in his place of residence, and she is known as 'so-and-so's woman,' and afterwards the owner of the slave couple had relations with the woman, he is liable to the death penalty for adultery. Under what circumstances does a woman become released from her marriage with the non-Jewish slave? When she stops living with the slave and begins allowing herself to appear in public with uncovered hair, as is the custom of unmarried women." (*Rambam, Sefer Shofetim, Hilkhot Melakhim* 9:8.)

בִּיאָה שֶׁלֹּא כְּדַרְכָּהּ בְּבֶן נֹחַ **A non-Jew who commits sodomy.** "The punishment a non-Jew incurs for having forbidden relations (such as with another man's wife) applies only in the case of normal copulation, but not sodomy (anal copulation)," following the ruling of Rava. (*Rambam, Sefer Shofetim, Hilkhot Melakhim* 9:7.)

TRANSLATION AND COMMENTARY

אֶלָּא אָמַר רָבָא [1]**Rather, Rava said:** This is the what the verse comes to teach us: **If a non-Jew had intercourse with another man's wife in an unnatural manner, he is exempt** from liability. [2]**What is the reason?** The verse states (Genesis 2:24): "That is why a man leaves his father and his mother, and cleaves to his wife." [3]The words, **"To his wife,"** teach that a man may engage in sexual intercourse with his own wife, **but not** with **someone else's wife.** [4]And the words, **"And he cleaves,"** teach that sexual intercourse with another man's wife is only forbidden if it is done in a manner by way of which he cleaves to her, [5]**but not** if it is done **in an unnatural manner** which does not result in cleaving.

אָמַר רַבִּי חֲנִינָא [6]**Rabbi Ḥanina said: If a non-Jew struck a Jew, he is liable for execution,** [7]**as the verse states** about Moses who saw the Egyptian smiting one of his Hebrew brothers (Exodus 2:12): **"And he looked this way and that, and when he saw that there was no man, he slew the Egyptian,** and hid him in the sand."

וְאָמַר רַבִּי חֲנִינָא [8]**And Rabbi Ḥanina said: Someone who strikes the jaw of a Jew is regarded as if he struck,** as it were, **the jaw of the Shekhinah,** [9]**as the verse states** (Proverbs 20:25): **"It is a snare to a man rashly to declare, It is holy** [מוֹקֵשׁ אָדָם יָלַע קֹדֶשׁ]," to which the following homiletical interpretation may be offered: Someone who strikes [*mokesh*] a Jew [who is called *adam*; see Ezekiel 34:31: "But you my flock, the flock of my pasture, are men (*adam*)"] is regarded as if he struck, as it were, the jaw [*yala*] of the Shekhinah [*kodesh*].

מַגְבִּיהַּ עַבְדּוֹ שַׁבָּת [10]The Gemara now cites three statements of Resh Lakish, but first offers **a mnemonic device** by which to remember them: **He raises, his servant, Shabbat.**

אָמַר רֵישׁ לָקִישׁ [11]**Resh Lakish said: Someone who raises his hand against another person, even if he did not** actually **strike him, is called a wicked man,** [12]**as the verse** recording Moses' response to the two Hebrews

[1]אֶלָּא אָמַר רָבָא: בֶּן נֹחַ שֶׁבָּא עַל אֵשֶׁת חֲבֵירוֹ שֶׁלֹּא כְּדַרְכָּהּ, פָּטוּר, [2]מַאי טַעְמָא? — [3]״בְּאִשְׁתּוֹ״ וְלֹא בְּאֵשֶׁת חֲבֵירוֹ, [4]״וְדָבַק״ — [5]וְלֹא שֶׁלֹּא כְּדַרְכָּהּ.

[6]אָמַר רַבִּי חֲנִינָא: נָכְרִי שֶׁהִכָּה אֶת יִשְׂרָאֵל — חַיָּיב מִיתָה, [7]שֶׁנֶּאֱמַר: ״וַיִּפֶן כֹּה וָכֹה וַיַּרְא כִּי אֵין אִישׁ [וַיַּךְ אֶת הַמִּצְרִי] וגו׳״.

[8]וְאָמַר רַבִּי חֲנִינָא: הַסּוֹטֵר לוֹעוֹ שֶׁל יִשְׂרָאֵל כְּאִילּוּ סוֹטֵר לוֹעוֹ שֶׁל שְׁכִינָה, [9]שֶׁנֶּאֱמַר: ״מוֹקֵשׁ אָדָם יָלַע קֹדֶשׁ״.

[10]מַגְבִּיהַּ עַבְדּוֹ שַׁבָּת — סִימָן.

[11]אָמַר רֵישׁ לָקִישׁ: הַמַּגְבִּיהַּ יָדוֹ עַל חֲבֵירוֹ, אַף עַל פִּי שֶׁלֹּא הִכָּהוּ, נִקְרָא רָשָׁע, [12]שֶׁנֶּאֱמַר:

LITERAL TRANSLATION

[1]Rather, Rava said: [If] a non-Jew had intercourse with his fellow's wife in an unnatural manner, he is exempt. [2]What is the reason? [3]"To his wife" — and not his fellow's wife. [4]"And he cleaves" — [5]and not in an unnatural manner.

[6]Rabbi Ḥanina said: [If] a non-Jew struck a Jew, he is liable for execution, [7]as it is stated: "And he looked this way and that, and when he saw that there was no man, [he slew the Egyptian]."

[8]And Rabbi Ḥanina said: Someone who strikes the jaw of a Jew is [regarded] as if he struck the jaw of the Shekhinah, [9]as it stated: "It is a snare to a man rashly to declare, It is holy."

[10]He raises, his servant, Shabbat — a sign.

[11]Resh Lakish said: Someone who raises his hand against his fellow, even if he did not strike him, is called a wicked person, [12]as is stated:

RASHI

באשתו ולא באשת חבירו — שלא אסרה תורה אלא בדביקה. **ויך את המצרי** — משום דהכה איש עברי. **מוקש אדם ילע קדש** — הנוקש את האדם היינו ישראל שקרויין אדם, דכתיב (יחזקאל לד) ״ואתנה צאני צאן מרעיתי אדם אתם״ — אתם קרויין אדם וכו׳. **ילע קודש** — כאלו לועה את הקדש, כלומר כסוטר על לועו. סוטר = מכה.

NOTES

נָכְרִי שֶׁהִכָּה אֶת יִשְׂרָאֵל **If a non-Jew struck a Jew.** According to some Rishonim, this prohibition is subsumed under the category of robbery, for a person who inflicts a wound upon another person's body is regarded as if he had stolen a part of his body from him. According to this, a non-Jew is liable for execution, not only for striking a Jew, but even for striking

HALAKHAH

נָכְרִי שֶׁהִכָּה אֶת יִשְׂרָאֵל **A non-Jew who strikes a Jew.** "A non-Jew who strikes a Jew, even if he inflicts only a minor wound, is liable to death at the hands of Heaven. However, he is not liable to death at the hands of the human court, since the prohibition against striking a Jew is not counted as one of the seven Noachide laws (*Kesef Mishneh, Radbaz*)." (*Rambam, Sefer Shofetim, Hilkhot Melakhim* 10:7.)

הַמַּגְבִּיהַּ יָדוֹ עַל חֲבֵירוֹ **A Jew who strikes another Jew.** "A Jew who raises his hand against a fellow Jew, even if he does not strike him, is termed a wicked person," as stated here by Resh Lakish. Some say that there is an ancient ban which prescribes that a Jew who struck a fellow Jew cannot be counted in a prayer-quorum. Thus if one Jew did strike another he must request a competent authority to release him from this ban." (*Shulḥan Arukh, Ḥoshen Mishpat* 420:1.)

TRANSLATION AND COMMENTARY

whom he saw fighting **states** (Exodus 2:13): **"And he said to the wicked man, Why will you smite** [לָמָּה הַכִּית] **your fellow."** [1]Moses **did not** use the past tense and **say:** ***Lama hikita,*** "Why did you smite your fellow," which would have implied that Moses deemed him a wicked man, because he had already smitten the other one. [2]**But rather** he used the future tense, saying: ***Lama takeh,*** "Why will you smite your fellow." This implies that he had not yet smitten the other, and nevertheless Moses called him a wicked man. Thus someone who raises his hand against another person with the intention of smiting him, [3]**even if he did not** yet actually **strike him,** is already **called a wicked man.**

אָמַר זְעִירִי אָמַר רַבִּי חֲנִינָא [4]**Ze'iri said in the name of Rabbi Ḥanina:** Someone who raises his hand against another person, even if he did not actually smite him, **is called a sinner,** [5]**as the verses state** (I Samuel 2:15-16): "And before they burnt the fat, the priest's lad came, and said to the man that sacrificed, Give some roasting meat for the priest....And if any man said to him, Let them burn first the fat...then he would answer him, No, but you shall give it to me now, **and if not, I will take it by force."** [6]**And the** next **verse states** (verse 17): **"And the sin of the lads was very great** before the Lord." From here we see that the threat to use force is in itself regarded as a very great sin.

רַב הוּנָא אָמַר [7]**Rav Huna said:** He who acts in this manner, regularly raising his hand against others and threatening them with violence — **let his hand be cut off,** [8]**as the verse states** (Job 38:15): **"And the high arm** [= the arm that is lifted up against another person] **shall be broken."**

רַב הוּנָא אָמַר [9]It was related that **Rav Huna** once **ordered the hand** of someone who regularly threatened others with violence **to be cut off.** For, as we learned in the previous chapter (46a), a court may impose extralegal punishments in order to erect a fence around the Torah, and thereby uphold the authority and enforce the observance of the law.

רַבִּי אֶלְעָזָר אוֹמֵר [10]**Rabbi Elazar said:** A violent man like that **has no remedy other than burial,** [11]**as the verse states** (Job 22:8): **"But like the mighty man, who has the earth"** — a man who uses his might and raises his arm against others is fit to die and be buried in the earth.

וְאָמַר רַבִּי אֶלְעָזָר [12]**Rabbi Elazar** offered another interpretation of that same verse, **saying: Land should only be acquired by the mighty,** [13]**as the verse states** (Job 22:8): **"But like the mighty man, who has the earth."** Ownership of land leads to conflict — with neighbors, with robbers, and with others who claim title to the property. Land should therefore only be acquired by the mighty who can withstand all these challenges.

[1]״וַיֹּאמֶר לָרָשָׁע לָמָּה תַכֶּה רֵעֶךָ״. [2]״לָמָּה הִכִּיתָ״ לֹא נֶאֱמַר, [3]אֶלָּא: ״לָמָּה תַכֶּה״, [4]אַף עַל פִּי שֶׁלֹּא הִכָּהוּ נִקְרָא רָשָׁע.

[5]אָמַר זְעִירִי אָמַר רַבִּי חֲנִינָא: נִקְרָא חוֹטֵא, [6]שֶׁנֶּאֱמַר: ״וְאִם לֹא לָקַחְתִּי בְחָזְקָה״. [7]וּכְתִיב: ״וַתְּהִי חַטַּאת הַנְּעָרִים גְּדוֹלָה מְאֹד״.

[8]רַב הוּנָא אָמַר: תִּיקָּצֵץ יָדוֹ, [9]שֶׁנֶּאֱמַר: ״וּזְרוֹעַ רָמָה תִּשָּׁבֵר״.

[10]רַב הוּנָא קַץ יְדָא.

[11]רַבִּי אֶלְעָזָר אוֹמֵר: אֵין לוֹ תַּקָּנָה אֶלָּא קְבוּרָה, [12]שֶׁנֶּאֱמַר: ״וְאִישׁ זְרוֹעַ לוֹ הָאָרֶץ״.

[13]וְאָמַר רַבִּי אֶלְעָזָר: לֹא נִתְּנָה קַרְקַע אֶלָּא לְבַעֲלֵי זְרוֹעוֹת, [14]שֶׁנֶּאֱמַר: ״וְאִישׁ זְרוֹעַ לוֹ הָאָרֶץ״.

LITERAL TRANSLATION

"And he said to the wicked man, Why do you smite your fellow." [1]It is not stated: *"Lama hikita,"* [2]but rather: *"Lama takeh."* [3]Even if he did not smite him he is called a wicked man.

[4]Ze'iri said in the name of Rabbi Ḥanina: He is called a sinner, [5]as it is stated: "And if not, I will take it by force." [6]And it is written: "And the sin of the lads was very great."

[7]Rav Huna said: Let his hand be cut off, [8]as it is stated: "And the high arm shall be broken."

[9]Rav Huna ordered the hand to be cut off.

[10]Rabbi Elazar said: He has no remedy other than burial, [11]as it is stated: "But [like] the mighty man, who has the earth."

[12]And Rabbi Elazar said: The earth was only given to the mighty, [13]as it is stated: "But [like] the mighty man, who has the earth."

RASHI

אם לא לקחתי בחזקה — בבני עלי כתיב, שהיו תופסים בבשר הזבחים, ואמר: אם לא תתן לי אקח בחזקה, דהיינו כמרים ידו — שהיו מגזמין להכות. **וזרוע רמה** — הרגיל לרום ידו על חבירו. **קץ ידא** — מאדם אחד שהיה רגיל להכות את חבירו, וקנסו בכך כדאמר בפרקין דלעיל (מו,א) בית דין היו מכין ועונשין שלא מן התורה לעשות סייג וגדר לדבר. **איש זרוע** — איש שמניף זרוע לו הארץ מתוקנת לקבורה, כלומר ראוי להמיתו ולקוברו. **לא נתנה קרקע** — כלומר אין ראוי לקנות קרקע אלא לבני זרוע, מפני שהתגר רבה על ידי קרקע שבאות בהמות ומפסידות, וגנבים באין וגונבין, ועוררין עליו וצריך שיהא חזק לעמוד כנגדן.

SAGES

זְעִירִי Ze'iri. A second generation Babylonian Amora, Ze'iri was a student of Rav. After his teacher's death, Ze'iri immigrataed to Israel, where he became an outstanding student of Rabbi Yoḥanan. Some scholars maintain that there were two Ze'iris, one of whom was a colleague of Rav. At any rate, Ze'iri is definitely not the same person as the later Amora Rabbi Zera (or Ze'ira, as he is sometimes known in Jerusalem Talmud).

NOTES

another non-Jew. *Ran* rejects this position, and limits Rabbi Ḥanina's statement to a non-Jew who struck a Jew.

TRANSLATION AND COMMENTARY

וְאָמַר רֵישׁ לָקִישׁ [1]**Resh Lakish said: What is the meaning of the verse which states** (Proverbs 12:11): **"He that tills [עֹבֵד] his land shall have plenty of bread"?** [2]**If a person makes himself into a slave [עֶבֶד] towards his land,** and devotes all of his energies to raising his crops, **he shall have plenty of bread.** [3]**And if not, he shall not have plenty of bread.**

וְאָמַר רֵישׁ לָקִישׁ [4]The Gemara now returns to the laws applying to non-Jews: **Resh Lakish said: If a non-Jew ceased working** for a whole day, **he is liable for execution,** [5]**as the verse states** (Genesis 8:22): "While the earth remains, seed time and harvest, and cold and heat, and summer and winter, and **day and night shall not cease."** A Jew is commanded to observe a weekly day of rest, but a non-Jew is forbidden to cease working for an entire day. [6]**And it was stated above** (57a): Wherever the Torah imposed a **prohibition** on non-Jews, the punishment for violating that prohibition **is execution.**

אָמַר רָבִינָא [7]**Ravina said:** Not only is the non-Jew liable for execution if he refrained from working on the Jewish Sabbath, but **even** if he refrained from working on **a Monday** or some other day of the week, he is liable for that same punishment.

וְלִיחַשְׁבָהּ [8]The Gemara objects: If it is so that a non-Jew is commanded to keep working without taking a day of rest, **then** that obligation **should have been counted along with the** other **seven** Noachide laws!

כִּי קָא חָשֵׁיב [9]The Gemara answers: **When** the Sages **counted** the Noachide laws, they only counted **the negative commandments,** [10]but **the positive commandments, they did not count.** And the verse, "Day and night shall not cease," teaches that non-Jews are bound by a positive commandment to continue working without taking a day of rest.

[1]וְאָמַר רֵישׁ לָקִישׁ: מַאי דִּכְתִיב: "עֹבֵד אַדְמָתוֹ יִשְׂבַּע לָחֶם"? [2]אִם עוֹשֶׂה אָדָם עַצְמוֹ כְּעֶבֶד לָאֲדָמָה, יִשְׂבַּע לֶחֶם. [3]וְאִם לָאו, לֹא יִשְׂבַּע לֶחֶם.

[4]וְאָמַר רֵישׁ לָקִישׁ: נָכְרִי שֶׁשָּׁבַת, חַיָּיב מִיתָה, [5]שֶׁנֶּאֱמַר: "וְיוֹם וָלַיְלָה לֹא יִשְׁבֹּתוּ". [6]וְאָמַר מָר: אַזְהָרָה שֶׁלָּהֶן זוֹ הִיא מִיתָתָן.

[7]אָמַר רָבִינָא: אֲפִילּוּ שֵׁנִי בְּשַׁבָּת.

[8]וְלִיחַשְׁבָהּ גַּבֵּי שֶׁבַע מִצְוֹת! [9]— כִּי קָא חָשֵׁיב — שֵׁב וְאַל תַּעֲשֶׂה, [10]קוּם עֲשֵׂה — לָא קָא חָשֵׁיב.

LITERAL TRANSLATION

[1]And Resh Lakish said: What is [the meaning of] that which is written: "He that tills his land shall have plenty of bread"? [2]If a person makes himself like a slave towards the land, he shall have plenty of bread. [3]And if not, he shall not have plenty of bread.

[4]And Resh Lakish said: [If] a non-Jew ceased working, he is liable for execution, [5]for it is stated: "Day and night shall not cease." [6]And the master said: Their warning is their execution.

[7]Ravina said: Even Monday.

[8]Then count it along with the seven laws!

[9]When he counted, the negative commandments (lit., "sit, and refrain from doing"). [10]The positive commandments (lit., "arise, [and] do") — he did not count.

RASHI

כעבד לאדמה — לעסוק בה תמיד לחרישה והשקאה וניכוש ועידור. **נכרי ששבת** — ממלאכתו יום שלם חייב מיתה שנאמר "יום ולילה לא ישבותו" וקא דריש ליה "לא ישבותו" — ממלאכה דאבני אדם נמי קאי, ולא תימא "לא ישבותו" אהך שמת עתים דקרא קאי! כלומר לא יבטלו ולא יפסקו מלהיות. פשיטא לא גרסינן דהא טובא קא משמע לן, דאבני אדם קאי. **אמר רבינא אפילו שני בשבת** — לא תימא שביתה דקאמר ריש לקיש לשום חובה קאמר, דלא לכוון לשבות כגון בשבת שהוא יום שביתה לישראל או אחד בשבת שעובדין בו הנוצרים, אלא מנוחה בעלמא קא אסר להו, שלא יבטלו ממלאכה ואפילו יום שאינו בר שביתה. שני בשבת יומא קמא דלאו יום בר שביתה נקט, והוא הדין דהוה מצי למינקט שלישי ורביעי. **קום עשה לא חשיב** — והאי "לא ישבותו" קום עשה מלאכה היא.

NOTES

עֹבֵד אַדְמָתוֹ **He that tills his land.** *Meiri* understands this homily as a metaphor for the study of Torah: He who tirelessly studies the Torah will reap the rewards of his efforts and understand and know it.

נָכְרִי שֶׁשָּׁבַת **If a non-Jew ceased working.** According to *Ramah,* the prohibition applying to a non-Jew against resting from work falls under the category of robbery, for someone who rests from work fails to fulfill his obligations to the world (*Ramah*). Others argue that a non-Jew who sets aside a day of rest is liable, for he is seen as attempting to create a new religion (*Rambam, Tashbatz*). *Meiri* maintains that a non-Jew may not observe a day of rest, lest he be thought to be a Jew, and other Jews learn from his ways.

HALAKHAH

נָכְרִי שֶׁשָּׁבַת **A non-Jew who observed the Sabbath.** "If a non-Jew established for himself a day of rest once a week, whether on the Jewish Sabbath or any other day, and observed the Jewish laws of the Sabbath on that day, he is liable to the death penalty. The human court should punish him and inform him that he is liable to the death penalty at the hands of Heaven. However the human court does not execute him (*Kesef Mishneh*)." (*Rambam, Sefer Shofetim, Hilkhot Melakhim* 10:9.)

[59A] [1]וְהָא דִּינִין קוּם עֲשֵׂה הוּא, וְקָא חָשֵׁיב! [2]קוּם עֲשֵׂה וְשֵׁב אַל תַּעֲשֶׂה נִינְהוּ.
[3]וְאָמַר רַבִּי יוֹחָנָן: נָכְרִי שֶׁעוֹסֵק בַּתּוֹרָה חַיָּיב מִיתָה, [4]שֶׁנֶּאֱמַר: ״תּוֹרָה צִוָּה לָנוּ מֹשֶׁה מוֹרָשָׁה״ — [5]לָנוּ מוֹרָשָׁה וְלֹא לָהֶם. [6]וְלִיחַשְׁבָהּ גַּבֵּי שֶׁבַע מִצְוֹת! [7]מַאן דְּאָמַר ״מוֹרָשָׁה״ — [8]מִיגְזַל קָא גָּזֵיל לָהּ. [9]מַאן דְּאָמַר ״מְאוֹרָסָה״ — [10]דִּינוֹ כְּנַעֲרָה הַמְאוֹרָסָה, דְּבִסְקִילָה.

LITERAL TRANSLATION

[59A] [1]But surely laws is a positive commandment, and he counts [it]!

[2]It is a positive commandment (lit., "get up [and] do") and a negative commandment (lit., "sit and do nothing").

[3]And Rabbi Yoḥanan said: A non-Jew who engages in Torah is liable for execution, [4]for it is stated: "Moses commanded us a Torah, an inheritance" — [5]for us an inheritance, but not for them.

[6]But let him count it among the seven laws!

[7]He who says "an inheritance" — [8]he steals it. [9]He who says "betrothed" — [10]his law is like a betrothed girl, which is by stoning.

TRANSLATION AND COMMENTARY

[59A] וְהָא דִּינִין [1]The Gemara asks: **But surely** the injunction to establish a system of **laws is a positive commandment, and** nevertheless the Sages **counted it** among the seven Noachide laws!

קוּם עֲשֵׂה [2]The Gemara answers: The injunction to establish a system of laws was counted because it involves both **a positive commandment and a negative commandment:** The positive commandment to execute justice, and the negative commandment to refrain from committing injustice. But the obligation to work without enjoying a day of rest involves only a positive commandment.

וְאָמַר רַבִּי יוֹחָנָן [3]**Rabbi Yoḥanan said: A non-Jew who engages in** the study of **Torah is liable for execution,** [4]**for the verse states** (Deuteronomy 33:4): **"Moses commanded us a Torah, an inheritance** for the congregation of Jacob" — [5]**to us,** the Jewish people, the Torah was given as **an inheritance, but not to them,** the other nations.

וְלִיחַשְׁבָהּ [6]The Gemara objects: If so, **then** that prohibition **should have been counted along with the** other **seven** Noachide laws!

מַאן דְּאָמַר [7]The Gemara answers: The prohibition for a non-Jew to study Torah is subsumed under one of the other Noachide prohibitions. According to one authority, **who says** that we learn that a non-Jew is forbidden to study Torah from the word *morasha,* **"an inheritance"** given solely to Israel, [8]a non-Jew who studies Torah **steals** from the Jewish people, and is therefore guilty of robbery, one of the seven Noachide prohibitions. [9]According to the other authority, **who says** that the prohibition for a non-Jew to study Torah is derived by reading the word *morasha* as *me'orasah,* **"betrothed"** meaning that the Torah is betrothed to the Jewish people, and therefore forbidden to all others, if a non-Jew studies Torah, [10]**his law is similar** to that of a man who has intercourse with **a betrothed girl,** and **is** therefore liable to death **by stoning.** According to this, the prohibition for a non-Jew to engage in Torah study is subsumed under sexual sins, another of the seven Noachide laws.

RASHI

והא דינין קום עשה — משפט הוא, וקא חשיב. **ומשני קום עשה ושב אל תעשה הוא** — קום עשה — משפט, ושב ואל תעשה — עול, אפילו אינו מצוה לעשות משפט והוא יושב ובטל, מוזהר הוא שלא לעשות עול, ואזהרת "לא תעשו עול" (ויקרא יט) אינה קום עשה משפט אלא לחודה קיימא, שב והבטל מלא תעשה עול, אבל אזהרת לא תשבות על כרחיך אינה אלא קום עשה. **מורשה לנו** — ולא להם, ואיכא משום גזל כדמפרש. **מורשה מאורסה** — אמורשה איכא דדרשי בהו גבי עם הארץ בפרק "אלו עוברין" בפסחים (מט,ב). **מיגזל קא גזל לה** — והא קא חשיב גזל, וכן נערה המאורסה דהא בכלל גילוי עריות הוא.

NOTES

נָכְרִי שֶׁעוֹסֵק בַּתּוֹרָה **A non-Jew who engages in Torah.** The Rishonim offer various explanations for this prohibition. According to *Meiri,* a non-Jew is only forbidden to study Torah, if his intention is to gain knowledge in order to vex Jews. But he is permitted to study Torah, if he wishes to gain knowledge in order to fulfill its commandments. (Similarly, *Rambam* permits Christians to study the Bible, because they accept its divine origin, but he forbids Moslems to do the same, because they do not accept the Bible as truth.) Others have added that it cannot be that a person is forbidden to study the truth which will lead him to abandon his false beliefs (*Ḥamre Veḥaye*).

מִיגְזַל קָא גָּזֵיל **He steals it.** It may be asked: In what sense does a non-Jew who engages in the study of Torah steal from the Jewish people? What loss does he cause them? *Rabbi Ya'akov Emden* answers that if the non-Jew successfully resolves a previously unresolved difficulty, he is regarded as stealing that novel explanation from the Torah's Jewish students.

HALAKHAH

נָכְרִי שֶׁעוֹסֵק בַּתּוֹרָה **A non-Jew who engaged in Torah study.** "A non-Jew is only permitted to engage in Torah study in order to learn about the seven Noachide laws. If he studies other laws and commandments he is liable to the death penalty at the hands of Heaven. The human court only punishes and warns him, but does not execute him (see *Kesef Mishneh, Radbaz,* and *Leḥem Mishneh*)." (*Rambam, Sefer Shofetim, Hilkhot Melakhim* 10:9)

TRANSLATION AND COMMENTARY

מֵיתִיבִי [1]**An objection was raised** against Rabbi Yoḥanan from the following Baraita: [2]**"Rabbi Meir said: From where do we know that even a non-Jew who engages in** the study of **Torah is like a High Priest?** [3]**For the verse states** (Leviticus 18:5): "And you shall keep my statutes, and my judgments, **which if a man does, he shall live in them.'** [4]The verse **does not speak** of **'priests, Levites, and Israelites,'** [5]**but rather** says, **'a man,'** which includes non-Jews. [6]**Thus you learn** from here **that even a non-Jew who engages in** the study of **Torah is like a High Priest."** This Baraita seems to contradict Rabbi Yoḥanan's ruling that a non-Jew who studies Torah is liable for the death penalty.

הָתָם בְּשֶׁבַע [7]The Gemara explains: **There** in the Baraita Rabbi Meir is referring to a non-Jew who studies **the seven** Noachide **laws** that non-Jews are obligated to observe. He indeed is worthy of praise. But a non-Jew is forbidden to study the rest of the Torah, as was argued by Rabbi Yoḥanan.

רַבִּי חֲנִינָא בֶּן גַּמְלִיאֵל [8]The Baraita cited at the beginning of the discussion regarding the seven Noachide laws (56a) continues: **"Rabbi Ḥanina ben Gamliel says:** Non-Jews are **also** bound by the prohibition against eating **the blood of a living animal."** [9]**Our Rabbis taught** a related Baraita: "The verse states (Genesis 9:4): **'But flesh with its life, which is its blood, you shall not eat.'** [10]**This is** a reference to the prohibition against eating **the limb of a living animal.** [11]**Rabbi Ḥanina ben Gamliel says:** This verse is **also** the source of the prohibition against eating **the blood of a living animal."**

מַאי טַעְמָא [12]The Gemara asks: **What is the reasoning of Rabbi Ḥanina ben Gamliel?** How may the verse be understood as referring to the prohibition against eating the blood of an animal? The Gemara explains: [13]Rabbi Ḥanina ben Gamliel **reads** the verse as follows: **"But flesh with its life, you shall not eat;** and **its blood with its life, you shall not eat."**

וְרַבָּנַן [14]The Gemara asks: **And** how do **the Sages** who disagree with Rabbi Ḥanina ben Gamliel interpret the words "its blood"? [15]The Gemara explains: **Those** words **come to permit** a non-Jew to eat the limb of a living **crawling creature,** as will be explained below (see 59b).

כַּיּוֹצֵא בַּדָּבָר [16]The Baraita continues with Rabbi Ḥanina ben Gamliel's argument: **"Similarly, you say** that Jews are forbidden to eat the blood of a living animal, for the verse states: (Deuteronomy 12:23): **'Only be**

[1]מֵיתִיבִי: [2]״הָיָה רַבִּי מֵאִיר אוֹמֵר: מִנַּיִין שֶׁאֲפִילּוּ נָכְרִי וְעוֹסֵק בַּתּוֹרָה שֶׁהוּא כְּכֹהֵן גָּדוֹל? [3]שֶׁנֶּאֱמַר: ׳אֲשֶׁר יַעֲשֶׂה אֹתָם הָאָדָם וָחַי בָּהֶם׳, [4]׳כֹּהֲנִים לְוִיִּם וְיִשְׂרְאֵלִים׳ לֹא נֶאֱמַר, [5]אֶלָּא ׳הָאָדָם׳. [6]הָא לָמַדְתָּ: שֶׁאֲפִילּוּ נָכְרִי וְעוֹסֵק בַּתּוֹרָה הֲרֵי הוּא כְּכֹהֵן גָּדוֹל!״
[7]הָתָם בְּשֶׁבַע מִצְוֹת דִּידְהוּ.
[8]״רַבִּי חֲנִינָא בֶּן גַּמְלִיאֵל אוֹמֵר: אַף הַדָּם מִן הַחַי״. [9]תָּנוּ רַבָּנַן: ״׳אַךְ בָּשָׂר בְּנַפְשׁוֹ דָמוֹ לֹא תֹאכֵלוּ׳ — [10]זֶה אֵבֶר מִן הַחַי. [11]רַבִּי חֲנִינָא בֶּן גַּמְלִיאֵל אוֹמֵר: אַף הַדָּם מִן הַחַי״.
[12]מַאי טַעְמָא דְּרַבִּי חֲנִינָא בֶּן גַּמְלִיאֵל? [13]קָרֵי בֵּיהּ: ״בָּשָׂר בְּנַפְשׁוֹ לֹא תֹאכֵל, דָּמוֹ בְּנַפְשׁוֹ לֹא תֹאכֵל״.
[14]וְרַבָּנַן? [15]הַהוּא לְמִישְׁרֵי שְׁרָצִים הוּא דַּאֲתָא.
[16]״כַּיּוֹצֵא בַּדָּבָר אַתָּה אוֹמֵר:

LITERAL TRANSLATION

[1]They raised an objection: [2]"Rabbi Meir said: From where [do we know] that even a non-Jew who engages himself in Torah is like a High Priest? [3]For it is stated: 'Which if a man does, he shall live in them.' [4]'Priests, Levites, and Israelites' is not stated, [5]but rather 'a man.' [6]Thus you have learned that even a non-Jew who engages himself in Torah is like a High Priest!"

[7]There, with their seven laws.

[8]"Rabbi Ḥanina ben Gamliel said: Also the blood of a living animal." [9]Our Rabbis taught: "'But flesh with its life, which is its blood, you shall not eat' — [10]this is a limb of a living animal. [11]Rabbi Ḥanina ben Gamliel says: Also the blood of a living animal."

[12]What is the reason of Rabbi Ḥanina ben Gamliel? [13]He reads it: "But flesh with its life, you shall not eat; its blood with its life, you shall not eat."

[14]And the Sages? [15]That comes to permit crawling creatures.

[16]"Similarly, you say:

RASHI

האדם – רבי מאיר דלית ליה אתם קרויין אדם ולא נכרים קרויין אדם, ורבי שמעון היא דדרש לה במסכת יבמות (סא,א). **בשבע מצות דידהו** – עוסקין בהלכות אותן שבע מצות להיות בקיאין בהן. **בשר** – בעוד נפשו קיימת לא תאכלו זהו אבר מן החי, **ודמו** – לדרשא אחרינא, למשרי אבר מן החי דשרצים, כדלקמן בשמעתין. **כיוצא בדבר אתה אומר** – שאף ישראל הוזהרו על דם מן החי בסיני ומשום חיות, ורבי חנינא קאמר לה.

NOTES

כְּכֹהֵן גָּדוֹל Like a High Priest. Some understand this to mean that a non-Jew who studies the seven Noachide laws which he is obligated to observe deserves to be honored and rewarded financially, just like a High Priest (*Iyyun Ya'akov*).

'רַק חֲזַק לְבִלְתִּי אֲכֹל הַדָּם כִּי הַדָּם הוּא הַנֶּפֶשׁ וגו׳'. [1]'רַק חֲזַק לְבִלְתִּי אֲכֹל הַדָּם' — זֶה אֵבֶר מִן הַחַי, [2]'כִּי הַדָּם הוּא הַנָּפֶשׁ' — זֶה דָּם מִן הַחַי". [3]וְרַבָּנַן? [4]הַהוּא לְדַם הַקָּזָה שֶׁהַנְּשָׁמָה יוֹצְאָה בּוֹ הוּא דַּאֲתָא.

[5]לָמָּה לִי לְמִיכְתַּב לִבְנֵי נֹחַ [6]וְלָמָּה לִי לְמִשְׁנֵי בְּסִינַי? [7]כִּדְרַבִּי יוֹסֵי בְּרַבִּי חֲנִינָא. דְּאָמַר רַבִּי יוֹסֵי בְּרַבִּי חֲנִינָא: [8]כָּל מִצְוָה שֶׁנֶּאֶמְרָה לִבְנֵי נֹחַ וְנִשְׁנֵית בְּסִינַי — [9]לָזֶה וְלָזֶה נֶאֶמְרָה. [10]לִבְנֵי נֹחַ וְלֹא נִשְׁנֵית בְּסִינַי — [11]לְיִשְׂרָאֵל נֶאֶמְרָה וְלֹא

LITERAL TRANSLATION

'Only be sure that you eat not the blood, for the blood is the life.' [1]'Only be sure that you eat not the blood' — this is a limb of a living animal. [2]'For the blood is the life' — this is the blood of a living animal."

[3]And the Sages? [4]That comes for the blood of blood-letting with which life goes out.

[5]Why do I need it to have been written for the descendants of Noah, [6]and why do I need it to have been repeated at Sinai?

[7]Like that of Rabbi Yose the son of Rabbi Ḥanina, for Rabbi Yose the son of Rabbi Ḥanina said: [8]Every commandment which was told to the descendants of Noah and repeated at Sinai — [9]to this and to that was it told. [10]To the descendants of Noah, but not repeated at Sinai — [11]it was told to Israel, but not

TRANSLATION AND COMMENTARY

sure that you eat not the blood, for the blood is the life, and you may not eat the life with the meat.' [1]**'Only be sure that you eat not the blood**...and you may not eat the life with the meat' — **this is** a reference to the prohibition against eating **the limb of a living animal'** — you may not eat the meat while there is still life in the animal. [2]**'For the blood is the life'** — **this is** a reference to the prohibition against eating **the blood of a living animal."**

וְרַבָּנַן [3]The Gemara asks: **And** how do **the Sages** who disagree with Rabbi Ḥanina ben Gamliel interpret this verse? [4]The Gemara explains: **This** verse **comes** to teach that one is forbidden to eat, not only the blood of a slaughtered animal, but even **the blood** which issues from the animal **by way of bloodletting.** This is included in the general prohibition against eating blood, provided that it is blood **with which life goes out.** Elsewhere, the Gemara explains that this refers to the blood which spurts out, to the exclusion of the blood which drips out at the beginning and at the end of the blood-letting procedure.

לָמָּה לִי [5]The Gemara asks: **Why was it necessary** for the prohibition against eating the limb of an animal **to have been written** once **for the descendants of Noah** in the verse (Genesis 9:4): 'But flesh with its life, which is its blood, you shall not eat,' [6]**and** then **repeated** for the Jewish people **at Sinai** in the verse (Deuteronomy 12:23): 'Only be sure that you eat not the blood, for the blood is the life, and you may not eat the life with the meat'?

כִּדְרַבִּי יוֹסֵי בְּרַבִּי חֲנִינָא [7]The Gemara answers: This may be understood **in accordance with** the opinion of **Rabbi Yose the son of Rabbi Ḥanina, for Rabbi Yose the son of Rabbi Ḥanina said:** [8]**Any commandment which was given** first **to the descendants of Noah, and** later **repeated** for the people of Israel **at Sinai,** [9]**was given** both **to** the descendants of Noah **and to** the people of Israel. [10]And any commandment which was given only **to the descendants of Noah, but not repeated** for the people of Israel **at Sinai,** [11]**was given** only to the people of **Israel, and not to the descendants of Noah.**

RASHI

כי הדם הוא הנפש ולא תאכל הנפש עם הבשר בו׳ — כלומר לא תאכל הדם הנזכר בראש המקרא בעוד הנפש עם הבשר. **ורבנן ההוא** — דסמך דם לאזהרת אבר מן החי לא למסרי משום חיות סמכיה, אלא למיסר דם הקזה שהנפש יוצאה בו משום דם הוא דסמכיה, דלא תימא אזהרת דם גבי "וזבחת מבקרך ומצאנך" כתיב (דברים יב) דם שחיטה הוא דהוי דם, אבל דם הקזה לא הוי דם — להכי אקשייה לאבר מן החי, מה אבר מן החי אסור מחמת איסורו — אף דם מן החי מוזהר עלה משום דם, ובלבד שיהא דם הנפש, אבל דם הקזה שאין הנפש יוצאה בו — אינו קרוי דם, אבל איסור חיות לא נזכר בו ולא בשום דם. ובכריתות (כב,א) מפרש: איזהו דם הקזה שהנפש יוצאה בו — מטיפה המשחרת ואילך, משהוא מתחיל לצאת שחור. **למה לי למכתב** — אבר מן החי בסיני ובבני נח, אטו ישראל משום דקבלו תורה יצאו מכלל מצות הראשונות?! בשלמא עבודה זרה וגילוי עריות בסיני למילתייהו נשנית — לפי שלא פרשו כל כך בבני נח על אלו עבירות עונשן עליהם, וכן בעריות לפרש עונשן — אלא אבר מן החי למה לי לאהדורי? **לזה ולזה נאמרה** — כדמפרש לקמן מדנשנית עבודה זרה וגילוי עריות בסיני ואשכחן דאיענש נכרים עלייהו אף לאחר מתן תורה, כדכתיב (דברים יח) "לא ימצא בך מעביר בנו ובתו וגו׳" ו"בגלל התועבות האלה" וכן בעריות (ויקרא יח) "כי את כל התועבות האל" — שמע מיניה כי יהיב קודשא בריך הוא תורה לישראל לא שקלינהו להנך מבני נח, וכדקיימי להו קיימי, וכל שלא נשנית בסיני נאמר לישראל ולא לבני נח מסיני ואילך אף על גב דעד סיני נצטוו עליה, מדלא הדר תנייה בסיני כדאיתא בעבודה זרה וגילוי עריות דאשכחן דאיענוש נכרים עלייהו — שמע מינה ישראל שיצאו לקדושה עמדו באיסורן, אבל נכרים — נטלן מהן, ולקמן פריך: דילמא להכי לא נשנו, דלבני נח הוא דאסירי ולא לישראל! ומשני: ליכא מידי דלישראל שרי ולנכרי אסור, שכשיצאו מכלל בני נח — להתקדש יצאו, ולא להקל עליהם, ולזה ולזה ליכא למימר — דאם כן אמאי אתני עבודה זרה — הילכך על כרחיך אותה שלא נשנית איכה בבני נח, הילכך אם לא נשנית אבר מן החי הוה אמינא נטלוה מבני נח ממתן תורה ואילך.

TRANSLATION AND COMMENTARY

[1]**And** the **only** example that **we have** of a commandment that was given first to the descendants of Noah, but not repeated for the people of Israel at Sinai, is the prohibition against eating **the sciatic nerve,** the nerve running down the back of the hind leg of an animal (see Genesis 32:33). [2]**And** this may also be understood **according to Rabbi Yehudah,** who maintains elsewhere that the prohibition against eating the sciatic nerve was given to the sons of Jacob, who at the time had the status of descendants of Noah. According to Rabbi Yose the son of Rabbi Ḥanina, the prohibition against eating the limb of a living animal had to be repeated at Sinai, even though it had already been given to the descendants of Noah. Had it not been repeated, we would have thought that the prohibition was removed from the descendants of Noah at Sinai and that henceforth it would apply only to the people of Israel. But the prohibition was indeed repeated at Sinai, indicating that it applies both to Jews and to non-Jews.

אָמַר מָר [3]**It was stated above: Any commandment which was given** first **to the descendants of Noah, and** later **repeated** for the people of Israel **at Sinai,** [4]**was given** both **to** the descendants of Noah **and to** the people of Israel. [5]**On the contrary,** it stands to reason that **since** the commandment **was repeated at Sinai,** [6]**it was given** only **to** the people of **Israel, and not to the descendants of Noah.** For if the commandment is binding upon all the descendants of Noah, why would it have to have been repeated specifically for the Jews at Sinai? Surely the obligations imposed upon the descendants of Noah are binding upon the Jewish people as well!

מִדְּאִיתְנֵי [7]The Gemara answers: **Since** the prohibition against **idol worship was repeated** for the people of Israel **at Sinai,** after it was given to the descendants of Noah, [8]**and we find that** God **punished non-Jews for** violating that prohibition even after the Torah was given to Israel — [9]**infer from this that** any commandment which was given first to the descendants of Noah, and later repeated for the people of Israel at Sinai, **was given** both **to** the descendants of Noah **and to** the people of Israel.

לִבְנֵי נֹחַ [10]Rabbi Yose the son of Rabbi Ḥanina also said: Any commandment which was given only **to the descendants of Noah, but not repeated** for the people of Israel **at Sinai,** [11]**was given** only to the people of **Israel, and not to the descendants of Noah.** [12]The Gemara objects: **On the contrary,** it stands to reason that **since** the commandment **was** given to the descendants of Noah, but **not repeated at Sinai,** [13]**it was given** only **to the descendants of Noah, and not to** the people of **Israel!**

לִבְנֵי נֹחַ. [1]וְאָנוּ אֵין לָנוּ אֶלָּא גִּיד הַנָּשֶׁה, [2]וְאַלִּיבָּא דְּרַבִּי יְהוּדָה. [3]אָמַר מָר: כָּל מִצְוָה שֶׁנֶּאֶמְרָה לִבְנֵי נֹחַ וְנִשְׁנֵית בְּסִינַי — [4]לָזֶה וְלָזֶה נֶאֶמְרָה. [5]אַדְּרַבָּה, מִדְּנִשְׁנֵית בְּסִינַי — [6]לְיִשְׂרָאֵל נֶאֶמְרָה וְלֹא לִבְנֵי נֹחַ! [7]מִדְּאִיתְנֵי עֲבוֹדָה זָרָה בְּסִינַי, [8]וְאַשְׁכַּחַן דְּעֲנַשׁ נָכְרִי עִילָּוָוהּ — [9]שְׁמַע מִינָּהּ לָזֶה וְלָזֶה נֶאֶמְרָה. [10]לִבְנֵי נֹחַ וְלֹא נִשְׁנֵית בְּסִינַי — [11]לְיִשְׂרָאֵל נֶאֶמְרָה וְלֹא לִבְנֵי נֹחַ. [12]אַדְּרַבָּה, מִדְּלֹא נִישְׁנֵית בְּסִינַי, [13]לִבְנֵי נֹחַ נֶאֶמְרָה וְלֹא לְיִשְׂרָאֵל!

LITERAL TRANSLATION

to the descendants of Noah. [1]And we only have the sciatic nerve, [2]and according to Rabbi Yehudah.

[3]The master said: Every commandment which was told to the descendants of Noah and repeated at Sinai — [4]to this and to that was it told. [5]On the contrary, since it was repeated at Sinai, [6]it was told to Israel, but not to the descendants of Noah!

[7]Since idol worship was repeated at Sinai, [8]and we find that He punished non-Jews for it — [9]infer from this that it was told to this and to that.

[10]To the descendants of Noah, but not repeated at Sinai — [11]it was told to Israel, but not to the descendants of Noah. [12]On the contrary, since it was not repeated at Sinai, [13]it was told to the sons of Noah, and not to Israel!

RASHI

ואנו אין לנו — אזהרה בבני נח, ולא נשנית בסיני אלא גיד הנשה. **ואליבא דרבי יהודה** — דאמר בפרק ״גיד הנשה״ (חולין ק,ב): מבני יעקב נאסר גיד הנשה, שהיו בני נח קודם מתן תורה. ורבנן פליגי ואמרו: בסיני נאמר ולא להם, אלא שנכתב במקומו, ואחר מתן תורה כתבו משה במקום המעשה, על העתיד, לידע מאיזה טעם נאסר להם. ולרבי יהודה גופיה — לישראל נאמר ולא לשאר בני נח, דהא בני ישראל כתיב. והא דקאמר הכא דאותן העומדות באיסורן לבני נח לעולם הוצרך לשנותן בסיני — לאו משום דאי לא אהדרינהו הוה אמינא נגמר מגיד הנשה דלא נשנית ולישראל נאמר ולא לבני נח, דמהא ליכא למיגמר שהרי לא נאסרה אלא לישראל, ובעוד שהיו בני נח נמי להם נאסר ולא לאחרים, אלא מדלאתני נכרי הוה גמרינן להו. **ואשכחן דאיענוש נכרי עלייהו** — שבע אומות, כדכתיב ״לא ימצא בך מעביר בנו ובתו באש״. **אדרבה מדלא נשנית בסיני אימא לבני נח נאמרה** — לבני יעקב בעוד שהיו בני נח נאסר להם, ולא משבאו לכלל ישראל.

NOTES

אַשְׁכַּחַן דַּעֲנַשׁ נָכְרִי עִילָּוָוהּ **We find that He punished non-Jews for it.** The Rishonim ask: Where do we find that God punished non-Jews for violating the prohibition against idol worship even after the Torah was given to Israel? Some have argued that since the Torah imposes a very severe punishment upon the Canaanites for their idol worship, and that punishment was only administered forty years after the Torah was given to Israel at Sinai, it stands

TRANSLATION AND COMMENTARY

לֵיכָּא [1]The Gemara rejects this argument: This cannot be, for **there is nothing that is permitted to a Jew, but forbidden to a non-Jew.** When the Jews received the Torah at Sinai, they did not shed any of their prior obligations. Rather they assumed further obligations.

וְלָא [2]The Gemara challenges this contention: **But** is it really true that there is **nothing** that is permitted to a Jew, but forbidden to a non Jew? [3]**But surely** there is the allowance concerning **a beautiful woman,** a non-Jewish female prisoner of war. The Torah allows a Jewish soldier to take such a woman. According to some authorities a Jew may engage in sexual relations with her during wartime, and according to others, to convert and marry her as "a concession to the evil inclination." This allowance is limited to Jews, but non-Jews are forbidden to take a woman in war because of their prohibition against robbery, as was explained earlier in the chapter (57a). Thus, we see that there can be something permitted to a Jew, but forbidden to a non-Jew.

הָתָם מִשּׁוּם [4]The Gemara answers: **There** the reason that a Jew is allowed to take a woman in war, and a non-Jew is not allowed to do so is that non-Jews **are not fit for** wars of **conquest.** Jews were commanded to conquer the Land of Israel, but the other nations were not commanded to conquer lands. Since the allowance regarding a woman of beautiful appearance was only given in the context of a war of conquest, it could only have been given to Jews, and not to non-Jews.

וַהֲרֵי [5]The Gemara raises another objection to the contention that there is nothing that is permitted to a Jew, but forbidden to a non-Jew: **But surely** there is robbery **less than the value of a perutah** which is permitted to a Jew, but forbidden to a non-Jew!

הָתָם מִשּׁוּם [6]The Gemara answers: **There** the reason for the distinction between Jews and non-Jews is as follows: Jews are ready to waive less than a perutah, and so for them the act of stealing such a small amount is not regarded as robbery. But non-Jews **are not ready to waive** even the most minute amount, and so for them robbery of less than the value of a perutah is forbidden.

כָּל מִצְוָה [7]We learned above: **Any commandment which was given** first **to the descendants of Noah, and** later **repeated** for the people of Israel **at Sinai,** [8]**was given** both **to** the descendants of Noah **and to** the people of Israel.

[1]לֵיכָּא מִידַּעַם דִּלְיִשְׂרָאֵל שָׁרֵי, וּלְנָכְרִי אָסוּר. [2]וְלָא? [3]וַהֲרֵי יְפַת תּוֹאַר! [4]הָתָם מִשּׁוּם דְּלָאו בְּנֵי כִּיבּוּשׁ נִינְהוּ. [5]וַהֲרֵי פָּחוֹת מִשָּׁוֶה פְּרוּטָה! [6]הָתָם מִשּׁוּם דְּלָאו בְּנֵי מְחִילָה נִינְהוּ. [7]כָּל מִצְוָה שֶׁנֶּאֶמְרָה לִבְנֵי נֹחַ וְנִשְׁנֵית בְּסִינַי [8]לָזֶה וְלָזֶה נֶאֶמְרָה

LITERAL TRANSLATION

[1]There is nothing that is permitted to a Jew, but forbidden to a non-Jew.

[2]But not? [3]But surely [a woman] of beautiful appearance!

[4]There because they are not fit for conquest.

[5]But surely less than the value of a perutah!

[6]There because they are not fit for waiving.

[7]Every commandment which was told to the descendants of Noah and repeated at Sinai — [8]to this and to that was it told.

RASHI

והרי יפת תואר — שאסורה להם, כדאמר לעיל (נז,א). לאו בני כיבוש נינהו — לא נתנה ארץ לכבוש כי אם לישראל, שאף לישראל לא הותר יפת תואר אלא במלחמה על ידי כיבוש. משום דלאו בני מחילה נינהו — שאף ישראל נצטוו על הגזל, אלא שפחות משוה פרוטה אינו נחשב גזל בעיניהם, שעוברין על מדתן שרחמנין הן ומוחלין על דבר קל, אבל בני נח אכזרים הם.

NOTES

to reason that the Canaanites were punished not only for the offenses that they had committed prior to the revelation at Sinai, but also for the offenses that committed afterward (*Rosh;* and see *Ḥamra Veḥaye*).

לֵיכָּא מִידַּעַם דִּלְיִשְׂרָאֵל שָׁרֵי וּלְנָכְרִי אָסוּר **There is nothing that is permitted to a Jew, but forbidden to a non-Jew.** When God chose the Jewish people and sanctified them with greater sanctity, He certainly did not relieve them of any of the universal obligations that apply to all human beings, but rather He imposed additional obligations upon them. Hence there cannot be anything that is forbidden to a non-Jew, but permitted to a Jew (*Ramah*).

לָאו בְּנֵי כִּיבּוּשׁ נִינְהוּ **They are not fit for conquest.** According to *Ḥatam Sofer,* other nations were also given permission to engage in wars of conquest, but only to conquer other lands, and not do dominate over other people. *Tzofnat Pa'ane'aḥ* writes that other nations were also given permission to engage in wars of conquest, so that they could gain legal and monetary possession of other lands. But that authority does not fall under the category of religious obligation, and so it does not include the allowances which were granted to the people of Israel in their wars of conquest.

TRANSLATION AND COMMENTARY

[59B] וַהֲרֵי מִילָה [1]The Gemara asks: **But surely** the commandment regarding **circumcision was told to** Abraham at the time that he was regarded as one of **the descendants of Noah, as the verse states** (Genesis 17:9): **"And you shall keep my covenant,** you, and your seed after you in their generations," [2]**and** then later **repeated** for the people of Israel **at Sinai,** as the verse states (Leviticus. 12:3): **"And on the eighth day, the flesh of the foreskin shall be circumcised,"** [3]and nevertheless that obligation **was given** only **to** the people of **Israel, and not to the descendants of Noah!**

הַהוּא [4]The Gemara answers: The commandment regarding circumcision was not regarded as having been repeated at Sinai, for **that** second verse **comes** not to instruct us to perform circumcision, but rather **to permit** circumcision on **Shabbat,** for the verse emphasizes: [5]**"And on the eighth day,"** the flesh of the foreskin shall be circumcised — **even** if the eighth day falls out **on Shabbat.**

וַהֲרֵי פְּרִיָּה וּרְבִיָּה [6]The Gemara raises another question: **But surely** the commandment to **be fruitful and multiply,** i.e., the obligation of procreation, **was told to the descendants of Noah,** [7]**as the verse states** (Genesis 9:7): **"And as for you, be fruitful and multiply,** bring forth abundantly in the earth, and multiply in it," [8]**and** then later **repeated at Sinai,** as the verse states (Deuteronomy 5:27): **"Go say to them, Return again to your tents."** The Israelites were instructed to return to their wives after being commanded to abstain from sexual realtions in preparation for receiving the Torah. [9]Nevertheless that obligation **was given** only **to** the people of **Israel, and not to the descendants of Noah!**

הַהוּא [10]The Gemara answers: The commandment regarding procreation was not repeated at Sinai, for **that** second verse **comes** not to instruct us to be fruitful, but rather to teach us **that any** prohibited **matter that was passed by a ballot requires another ballot to become permitted** again. Even if a prohibition was explicitly limited in duration, it remains in effect until it is explicitly permitted by an authority equal to the authority who originally instituted the prohibition. In Exodus 19:15, the Torah states: "Be ready by the third day; come not near a woman," and in Deuteronomy 5:27, it states: "Return again to your tents." Even though the injunction not to approach a woman was limited to three days, sexual contact remained forbidden until the Israelites were explicitly told to return to their wives.

אִי הָכִי [11]The Gemara asks: **If so,** then **we can** also **say that all** of the seven Noachide laws **were repeated** at Sinai **for** some special **purpose,** e.g., the prohibition against idol worship was repeated in order to specify

[59B] [1]וַהֲרֵי מִילָה שֶׁנֶּאֶמְרָה לִבְנֵי נֹחַ, דִּכְתִיב: ״וְאַתָּה אֶת בְּרִיתִי תִשְׁמֹר״ [2]וְנִשְׁנֵית בְּסִינַי: ״וּבַיּוֹם הַשְּׁמִינִי יִמּוֹל״, [3]לְיִשְׂרָאֵל נֶאֶמְרָה וְלֹא לִבְנֵי נֹחַ!
[4]הַהוּא לְמִישְׁרֵי שַׁבָּת הוּא דַּאֲתָא: [5]״בַּיּוֹם״ — וַאֲפִילּוּ בַּשַּׁבָּת.
[6]וַהֲרֵי פְּרִיָּה וּרְבִיָּה, שֶׁנֶּאֶמְרָה לִבְנֵי נֹחַ, [7]דִּכְתִיב: ״וְאַתֶּם פְּרוּ וּרְבוּ״, [8]וְנִשְׁנֵית בְּסִינַי: ״לֵךְ אֱמֹר לָהֶם שׁוּבוּ לָכֶם לְאָהֳלֵיכֶם״ — [9]לְיִשְׂרָאֵל נֶאֶמְרָה, וְלֹא לִבְנֵי נֹחַ!
[10]הַהוּא לְכָל דָּבָר שֶׁבְּמִנְיָן צָרִיךְ מִנְיָן אַחֵר לְהַתִּירוֹ הוּא דַּאֲתָא.
[11]אִי הָכִי, כָּל חֲדָא וַחֲדָא נַמִי

LITERAL TRANSLATION

[59B] [1]But surely circumcision which was told to the descendants of Noah, as it is written: "And you shall keep my covenant," [2]and repeated at Sinai: "And on the eighth day, [the flesh of the foreskin] shall be circumcised" — [3]was told to Israel, and not to the descendants of Noah!

[4]That comes to permit Shabbat: [5]"And on the [eighth] day" — even on Shabbat.

[6]But surely being fruitful and multiplying which was told to the descendants of Noah, [7]as it is written: "And as for you, be fruitful and multiply," [8]and repeated at Sinai: "Go say to them, Return again to your tents" — [9]was told to Israel, and not to the descendants of Noah!

[10]That comes for any matter that was passed by a ballot requires another ballot to permit it.

[11]If so, [regarding] each and every one we can

RASHI

והרי מילה — לישראל נאמרה ולא לבני נח, דלא חשבה גבי שבע מצות. **לכל דבר שבמנין** — לא נשנית בסיני אלא מפני שאסר להם תשמיש שלשה ימים קודם מתן תורה, ולאחר שלשה ימים הוצרך להתיר להם, ואף על גב דממילא משתמע התירא דהא שלשה ימים הוא דאסר והרי עברו, אשמעינן קרא לכל דבר הנאסר במנין בית דין אף על פי שקבעו זמן לדבר צריך למנות פעם אחרת להתירו כשעבר הזמן. **אי הכי** — כל שבע מצות שחזרו ונשנו בסיני נימא נמי כל אחת ואחת הוצרכה לשנות על דבר, כגון עבודה זרה לפרש מיתה ועבודות האסורין בה. וכן גלוי עריות לפרש עונשין, ונימא דכולהו לא נשנו ולישראל נאסרו ולא לבני נח.

NOTES

פְּרִיָּה וּרְבִיָּה **Being fruitful and multiplying.** According to the reading of *She'iltot,* the descendants of Noah are indeed bound by the obligation to procreate. According to some authorities, the descendants of Noah are technically exempt from this obligation, but they are bound by the verse (Isaiah 45:18): "He did not create it a waste land, He formed it to be inhabited," which imposes an obligation upon all of mankind to inhabit the world, and not leave it a desolation.

נֵימָא מִשּׁוּם מִילְּתָא אִיתְנֵי! [1]הָכִי קָאָמַר: אַזְהָרָה, מִיהֲדַר וּמִיתְנָא בָּהּ לָמָּה לִי? [2]וְאֵין לָנוּ אֶלָּא גִּיד הַנָּשֶׁה בִּלְבַד, [3]וְאַלִּיבָּא דְּרַבִּי יְהוּדָה! [4]הָנֵי נַמִי לָא אִיתְנֵי! [5]הָנֵי אִיתְנֵי לְשׁוּם מִילְּתָא בְּעָלְמָא; [6]הָא לָא אִיתְנֵי כְּלָל. [7]אִי בָּעֵית אֵימָא: מִילָה מֵעִיקָּרָא לְאַבְרָהָם הוּא דְּקָא מַזְהַר לֵיהּ רַחֲמָנָא: [8]"וְאַתָּה אֶת בְּרִיתִי תִשְׁמֹר אַתָּה וְזַרְעֲךָ אַחֲרֶיךָ לְדֹרֹתָם", [9]אַתָּה וְזַרְעֲךָ — אִין; [10]אִינִישׁ אַחֲרִינָא — לָא. [11]אֶלָּא מֵעַתָּה, בְּנֵי יִשְׁמָעֵאל לִחַיְּיבוּ!

LITERAL TRANSLATION

say that it was repeated for a matter.
[1]He said as follows: A warning, why do I need it to be repeated again?
[2]And we only have the sciatic nerve, [3]and according to Rabbi Yehudah. [4]These too were not repeated!
[5]These were repeated for some matter; [6]this was not repeated at all.
[7]And if you wish, say: [Regarding] circumcision it was from the outset Abraham whom the Torah (lit., "the Merciful") warned: [8]"And you shall keep my covenant, you, and your seed after you for their generations," [9]you and your seed — yes; [10]another person — no.
[11]But now, let the descendants of Yishmael be obligated!

TRANSLATION AND COMMENTARY

the forbidden practices, and the prohibition against incest and adultery was repeated in order to specify the punishment for each offense. Thus, it would follow that none of the seven Noachide laws was repeated at Sinai, and so they were given only to the people of Israel, and not to the descendants of Noah!

הָכִי קָאָמַר [1]The Gemara answers: Rabbi Yose the son of Rabbi Ḥanina meant to **say as follows:** Granted that the seven Noachide laws were repeated at Sinai for some special purpose, but **why was it necessary for the** basic **warnings,** such as "You shall not kill," or "You shall not steal," **to be repeated again,** if not to teach us that those seven laws apply not only to the people of Israel, but also to the descendants of Noah?

וְאֵין לָנוּ [2]It was stated above that Rabbi Yose the son of Rabbi Ḥanina also said: **And** the **only** example that **we have** of a commandment that was given first to the descendants of Noah, but not repeated for the people of Israel at Sinai, is the prohibition against eating **the sciatic nerve,** [3]**and according to Rabbi Yehudah,** who maintains elsewhere that the prohibition against eating the sciatic nerve was given to the sons of Jacob, who at the time had the status of descendants of Noah. The Gemara asks: But surely the commandments that were mentioned above, circumcision and procreation, [4]**were** also **not repeated** at Sinai, for as we explained earlier, they were mentioned again for some special purpose. Thus, other commandments were given to the descendants of Noah and not repeated for the people of Israel at Sinai!

הָנֵי אִיתְנֵי [5]The Gemara answers: Rabbi Yose the son of Rabbi Ḥanina did not count **those** two commandments, circumcision and procreation, because they **were** nevertheless **repeated** at Sinai **for some** special **purpose,** [6]whereas the prohibition against eating the sciatic nerve **was not repeated** there **at all.**

אִי בָּעֵית אֵימָא [7]The Gemara offers a second answer: **And if you wish,** you can **say** that before the revelation of the Torah at Sinai, the commandment of circumcision had not been given to the descendants of Noah, for **regarding circumcision, it was from the outset** only **Abraham** and his descendants **whom the Torah warned,** as the verse states (Genesis 17:9): [8]**"And you shall keep my covenant, you, and your seed after you in their generations"** — [9]**you and your seed** — must **indeed** keep my covenant, [10]but **other people** are **not** required to do so.

אֶלָּא מֵעַתָּה [11]The Gemara asks: **But** if the reason why the commandment of circumcision is binding upon the Jewish people and not the descendants of Noah is not because it was not repeated at Sinai, but rather because it was given only to Abraham and his descendants, **then let the descendants of Yishmael,** who are also descendants of Abraham, **be obligated** to perform circumcision even today!

RASHI

אזהרה מהדר ומתנא בה למה ליה — למהדר ומיכתב אזהרה דידהו — אלא שמע מינה להזהירה לבני נח ולישראל אתא. **הני נמי** — מילה ופריה ורביה, הא לא איתנו — דהא אמרת למילתא הוא דאיתנו. **הא** — דגיד הנשה לא איתנו כלל, ומשום הכי לא חשיב להו בהדיה, ומיהו הנך נמי מן האמורות לבני נח ולא נשנו בסיני הס, ולישראל נאמרו ולא לבני נח מסיני ולהלן. **ואיבעית אימא מילה** — ודאי מסיני נאמרה לעיקר מצותיה. ודקשיא לך: הא אמר רבי יוסי כל שנאמרה לבני נח ונשנית בסיני לזה ולזה נאמרה — הא דלא חשיב ליה לגבי מצות בני נח, משום דמילה לאו לבני נח נאמרה אפילו מקודם סיני — אלא לזרע אברהם לחודיה, והשתא נמי זרע אברהם דהיינו ישראל, הוא דנהיגי בה. **בני ישמעאל ליחייבו** — השתא.

HALAKHAH

מִי נִכְלָל בְּמִצְוַת מִילָה? **Who is included in the commandment of circumcision?** "The commandment of circimcision was given to Abraham and his descendants. Neither the descendants of Ishmael nor the descendants of Esau are included in this commandment, but all the descendants of Jacob are included in it." (*Rambam, Sefer Shofetim, Hilkhot Melakhim* 10:7.)

[1]״כִּי בְיִצְחָק יִקָּרֵא לְךָ זָרַע״.
[2]בְּנֵי עֵשָׂו לִחַיְּיבוּ!
[3]״בְּיִצְחָק״ — וְלֹא כָּל יִצְחָק.
[4]מַתְקִיף לָהּ רַב אוֹשַׁעְיָא: אֶלָּא מֵעַתָּה בְּנֵי קְטוּרָה לָא לִחַיְּיבוּ!
[5]הָאָמַר רַבִּי יוֹסֵי בַּר אָבִין וְאִיתֵימָא רַבִּי יוֹסֵי בַּר חֲנִינָא: [6]״אֶת בְּרִיתִי הֵפַר״ — לְרַבּוֹת בְּנֵי קְטוּרָה.
[7]אָמַר רַב יְהוּדָה אָמַר רַב: אָדָם הָרִאשׁוֹן לֹא הוּתַּר לוֹ בָּשָׂר לַאֲכִילָה, [8]דִּכְתִיב: ״לָכֶם יִהְיֶה לְאָכְלָה. וּלְכָל חַיַּת

LITERAL TRANSLATION

[1]"For in Isaac shall your seed be called."
[2]Let the descendants of Esau be obligated!
[3]"In Isaac" — and not all of Isaac.
[4]Rav Oshaya strongly objected: But now the descendants of Keturah should not be obligated!
[5]Surely Rabbi Yose bar Avin said (and some say [it was] Rabbi Yose bar Ḥanina): [6]"He has broken my covenant" — to include the descendants of Keturah.
[7]Rav Yehudah said in the name of Rav: The first man was not permitted to eat meat, [8]as it is written: "To you it shall be for food. And to every beast

TRANSLATION AND COMMENTARY

כִּי בְיִצְחָק [1]The Gemara answers: The verse states (Genesis 21:12): **"For in Isaac shall your seed be called,"** teaching that only Isaac's descendants are considered Abraham's seed, to the exclusion of the descendants of Yishmael who are not considered Abraham's seed.

בְּנֵי עֵשָׂו לִחַיְּיבוּ [2]The Gemara asks: But then at least **let the descendants of Esau be obligated** to the commandment of circumcision, for they are also Abraham's descendants through Isaac!

״בְּיִצְחָק״ [3]The Gemara answers: Even the descendants of Esau are excluded from this obligation, for the verse states: "For **in Isaac** shall your seed be called" — in part of Isaac shall be called your seed, **but not all of Isaac.**

מַתְקִיף לָהּ [4]**Rav Oshaya strongly objected: But** if the verse "For in Isaac shall your seed be called," restricts the commandment of circumcision to the people of Israel, **then the descendants of** Abraham's other wife, **Keturah, should** also **not be obligated** in circumcision, but we know that the descendants of Keturah are indeed bound by that obligation!

הָאָמַר [5]The Gemara answers: There is a special verse which includes the descendants of Keturah in the obligation of circumcision, as **Rabbi Yose bar Avin said (and some say** that **it was Rabbi Yose bar Ḥanina** who said): The verse which states (Genesis 17:14): "And the uncircumcised manchild the flesh of whose foreskin is not circumcised, that soul shall be cut off from his people; [6]**he has broken my covenant" — includes the descendants of Keturah** in the obligation of circumcision.

אָמַר רַב יְהוּדָה [7]**Rav Yehudah said in the name of Rav:** When **the first man** was created, he **was not permitted to eat meat,** [8]**as the verse states** (Genesis 1:29-30): "And God said, Behold I have given you every herb bearing seed, which is upon the face of all the earth, and every tree, on which is the fruit yielding seed; **to you it shall be for food. And to every beast of the earth,** and to every bird of the air, and to everything that creeps on the earth, wherein there is life, I have given every green herb for food." The green herbs

RASHI

בני קטורה — אותן ששה שנולדו לאברהם, הן עצמן לא לחייבו, ונימא: השתא דלא מל אברהם כל בניו שהיו לו בחייו. **לרבות בני קטורה** — אותם ששה לבדם ולא זרעם, אבל אברהם נצטווה לכל הנולדים לו. **לא הותר בשר באכילה דכתיב הנה נתתי לכם את כל עשב וגו׳** — לכם ולחיות נתתי העשבים והאילנות ואת כל ירק עשב לאכלה, אבל לא חית הארץ נתונה לכם.

NOTES

בְּנֵי עֵשָׂו וּבְנֵי קְטוּרָה **The descendants of Esau and the descendants of Keturah.** The distinction between the descendants of Esau and the descendants of Keturah has been explained as follows: Esau had at first belonged to the house of Abraham, and had the potential of being part of the chosen people, but he rejected that destiny. When he had children from Canaanite wives, the obligations upon the seed of Abraham no longer applied to them, just as they do not apply to the offspring of a Jewish man and a non-Jewish woman. But the descendants of Keturah were from the outset regarded as descendants of Noah, to whom was added the obligation of circumcision, and they remained bound by that obligation for all generations (*Tzofnat Pa'ane'aḥ*).

אָדָם הָרִאשׁוֹן לֹא הוּתַּר לוֹ בָּשָׂר **The first man was not permitted to eat meat.** The authorities disagree about the scope of this prohibition, whether Adam was absolutely forbidden to eat meat, or whether he was only forbidden

HALAKHAH

חִיּוּב בְּנֵי קְטוּרָה בְּמִילָה **The obligation of the sons of Keturah regarding circumcision.** "The sons of Keturah who were born after Isaac are obligated to observe the commandment of circumcision." *Rambam* maintains that this commandment applies not only to them but to all their descendants. Since the descendants of Ishmael intermingled over the generations with the descendants of Keturah, and became the Arabs, all Arabs are obligated to be circumcised on the eighth day. This follows the ruling of Rabbi Yose (*Kesef Mishneh*). However *Rashi* maintains that this commandment applied only to the sons of Keturah, but their descendants are not included in it. (*Rambam, Sefer Shofetim, Hilkhot Melakhim* 10:7.)

הָאָרֶץ״ — [1]וְלֹא חַיַּת הָאָרֶץ לָכֶם. [2]וּכְשֶׁבָּאוּ בְּנֵי נֹחַ הִתִּיר לָהֶם, [3]שֶׁנֶּאֱמַר: ״כְּיֶרֶק עֵשֶׂב נָתַתִּי לָכֶם אֶת כֹּל״. [4]יָכוֹל לֹא יְהֵא אֵבֶר מִן הַחַי נוֹהֵג בּוֹ. [5]תַּלְמוּד לוֹמַר: ״אַךְ בָּשָׂר בְּנַפְשׁוֹ דָמוֹ לֹא תֹאכֵלוּ״. [6]יָכוֹל אַף לִשְׁרָצִים. [7]תַּלְמוּד לוֹמַר: ״אַךְ״.

[8]וּמַאי תַּלְמוּדָא? [9]אָמַר רַב הוּנָא: ״דָמוֹ״ — מִי שֶׁדָּמוֹ חָלוּק מִבְּשָׂרוֹ. [10]יָצְאוּ שְׁרָצִים שֶׁאֵין דָּמָם חָלוּק מִבְּשָׂרָם.

[11]מֵיתִיבִי: ״וּרְדוּ בִּדְגַת הַיָּם״. [12]מַאי לָאו לַאֲכִילָה? [13]לֹא, לִמְלָאכָה.

LITERAL TRANSLATION

of the earth" — [1]and not the beast of the earth for you. [2]And when the descendants of Noah came, he permitted [it] for them, [3]as it is stated: "Even as the green herb have I given you all things." [4]I might have thought the limb of a living animal does not apply to it. [5][Therefore] the Torah states: "But flesh with its life, [which is] its blood, you shall not eat." [6]I might have thought even crawling creatures. [7][Therefore] the Torah states: "But."

[8]And what is the derivation? [9]Rav Huna said: "Its blood" — that whose blood is distinguished from its flesh. [10]Crawling creatures are excluded for their blood is not distinguished from their flesh.

[11]They raised an objection: "And have dominion over the fish of the sea." [12]Is it not for eating?

[13]No, for work.

TRANSLATION AND COMMENTARY

shall be food for you and the rest of the animals, [1]**but the beasts of the earth shall not be** food **for you,** for you are forbidden to eat meat. [2]**But when the descendants of Noah emerged** from the ark after the great flood, God **permitted them** to eat meat, [3]**as the verse states** (Genesis 9:3): "Every moving thing that lives shall be food for you; **even as the green herb have I given you all things."** Since the prohibition against eating meat was removed from the descendants of Noah, [4]**I might have thought** that the prohibition against eating **the limb of a living animal should** also **not apply to** the meat that they were now permitted to eat. [5]**Therefore the Torah states** in the very next verse (Genesis 9:4): **"But flesh with its life, which is its blood, you shall not eat."** You may not eat the flesh of an animal while the animal is still alive. [6]**I might have thought** that the prohibition against eating the limb of a living animal applies **even** to **crawling creatures.** [7]**Therefore the Torah states: "But** flesh with its life," the word "but [אַךְ]" being a restrictive expression which excludes crawling creatures from the prohibition.

וּמַאי תַּלְמוּדָא [8]The Gemara asks: **What is** the basis of **the derivation** that crawling creatures are excluded from the prohibition of eating the limb of a living animal? [9]**Rav Huna said:** This is learned from the words, **"Its blood,"** which are extraneous, since the verse could simply have said: "But flesh with its life, you shall not eat." The words "its blood" teach that the prohibition only applies to **that whose blood is distinguished** for Halakhic purposes **from its flesh,** animals whose blood is regarded as blood, and whose flesh is regarded as flesh. [10]Thus, **crawling creatures are excluded, for their blood is not distinguished** for Halakhic purposes **from their flesh.** The blood of crawling creatures is indeed forbidden to be eaten, but not because of the prohibition against eating blood. Rather it is because of the prohibition against eating crawling creatures, which does not distinguish between the flesh of the crawling creature and its blood.

מֵיתִיבִי [11]**An objection was raised** against Rav's contention that when the world was first created, man was forbidden to eat animal meat: Surely God instructed Adam as follows (Genesis 1:28): "Be fruitful, and multiply, replenish the earth, and subdue it; **and have dominion over the fish of the sea,** and over the birds of the air, and over every living thing that moves on the earth." When God granted man dominion over the fish of the sea, [12]**was it not** that he permitted him **to eat** them?

לֹא, לִמְלָאכָה [13]The Gemara counters this argument: **No,** God meant to permit man **to** do **work** with fish.

RASHI

כירק עשב — שהפקרתי לאדם לאכול, נתתי לכם מעכשיו ״את כל״ — אפילו בהמות וחיות. **יכול אפילו לשרצים** — יהא אבר מן החי אסור להם. **תלמוד לומר אך** — מיעוט, וכל אכין ורקין מעוטין. **מאי תלמודא** — היכי משמע דשרצים ממעטי מיניה, דילמא בהמה וחיה ממעטינן מיניה ולא שרצים?! **אמר רב הונא דמו** — האי ״דמו״ יתירה הוא, דהוה ליה למכתב ״בשר בנפשו לא תאכלו״ דהיינו בעוד שהנפש בו אל תאכלו את בשרו, האי ״בנפשו דמו״ למה לי — וכי לא ידענא דנפש זה הוא הדם?! אלא לומר לך, מי שדמו חלוק מבשרו — שהדם קרוי נפש והבשר בשר, יצאו שרצים שאין דמן חלוק מבשרן שאין דמם קרוי דם. שכשהוזהרו ישראל על הדם לא הוזהרו על דם שרצים משום דם אלא משום שרצים כבשר. והכי אמרינן בכריתות בפרק ״דם שחיטה״ (כא,ב): דם שרצים התרו בו משום שרץ — לוקה, משום דם — אינו לוקה. **בדגת הים** — לאדם הראשון נאמר.

NOTES

to kill an animal for its meat, but if he came across an animal that had died of natural causes, or was killed by another animal, he was indeed permitted to eat it.

TRANSLATION AND COMMENTARY

וְדָגִים [1]The Gemara asks: **But are fish** really **fit for** any type of **work?**

אִין [2]The Gemara answers: **Yes, like that** question posed by the Sage **Rahavah, for Rahavah asked:** [3]If a person tied a cart to **a goat** that was on land **and** to **a mullet** that was in the water, and **drove** the cart with those two animals, **what is the law?** Is he liable for lashes for violating the prohibition against working a team of animals comprising different species? Rahavah's question indicates that it is possible to do certain types of work with fish.

תָּא שְׁמַע [4]The Gemara continues: **Come and hear** what is stated in the continuation of that verse: "And have dominion over the fish of the sea, **and over the birds of the air."** When God granted man dominion over the birds of the air, [5]**was it not** that he permitted him **to eat** them?

לֹא [6]The Gemara rejects this proof: **No,** here too God meant to permit man **to** do **work** with birds.

וְעוֹפוֹת [7]The Gemara asks: **But are birds** really **fit for** any type of **work?**

אִין [8]The Gemara answers: **Yes, like** that which **Rabbah bar Rav Huna asked:** [9]**What is the law according to Rabbi Yose the son of Rabbi Yehudah** when a person **threshes** his grain **using geese or chickens** to do the work? Does the prohibition against muzzling an animal while working apply in this case, or not? According to Rabbi Yose the son of Rabbi Yehudah, an ox is not entitled to eat while it works unless it works with both its forelegs and its hind legs. What is the law regarding geese or chickens which have only two feet? Rabbah bar Rav Huna's question shows that it is possible to do certain types of work with birds.

תָּא שְׁמַע [10]The Gemara raises yet another objection: **Come and** hear what is stated in the continuation of that verse: [11]"And have dominion over the fish of the sea, and over the birds of the air, **and over every living thing that moves on the earth."** Does this not mean that Adam was granted permission to eat the living things that move on the earth?

LITERAL TRANSLATION

[1]But are fish fit for work?

[2]Yes, like that of Rahavah, for Rahavah asked: [3]If he drove with a goat and a mullet, what [is the law]?

[4]Come [and] hear: "And over the birds of the air." [5]Is it not for eating?

[6]No, for work.

[7]But are birds fit for work?

[8]Yes, like Rabbah bar Rav Huna asked: [9][If] he threshed with geese or chickens, according to Rabbi Yose the son of Rabbi Yehudah what [is the law]?

[10]Come [and] hear: [11]"And over every living thing that moves on the earth."

[1]וְדָגִים בְּנֵי מְלָאכָה נִינְהוּ?

[2]אִין, כִּדְרַחֲבָה, דִּבְעֵי רַחֲבָה:

[3]הִנְהִיג בְּעִיזָּא וְשִׁיבּוּטָא, מַאי?

[4]תָּא שְׁמַע: "וּבְעוֹף הַשָּׁמַיִם".

[5]מַאי לָאו לַאֲכִילָה?

[6]לֹא, לִמְלָאכָה.

[7]וְעוֹפוֹת בְּנֵי מְלָאכָה נִינְהוּ?

[8]אִין, כִּדְבָעֵי רַבָּה בַּר רַב הוּנָא:

[9]דָּשׁ בְּאַוָּוזִין וְתַרְנְגוֹלִין, לְרַבִּי יוֹסֵי בְּרַבִּי יְהוּדָה, מַאי?

[10]תָּא שְׁמַע: [11]"וּבְכָל חַיָּה הָרֹמֶשֶׂת עַל הָאָרֶץ"!

RASHI

הנהיג בעיזא ושיבוטא — קשר קרון לדג שבים ולעז ביבשה על שפת הים, ושניהם מנהיגין אותו. מהו — לוקה משום מנהיג בכלאים או לא? חורש בשור ובחמור לאו דוקא, דכל תרי מיני נמי אסירי, בבבא קמא ב"שור שנגח את הפרה". **דש באווזין ותרנגולין לרבי יוסי ברבי יהודה מהו** — ב"השוכר את הפועלים" תנן: היה עושה בידיו אבל לא ברגליו, ברגליו אבל לא בידיו, הרי זה יאכל, כדכתיב "כי תבא בכרם רעך וגו'" בביאת פועל הכתוב מדבר, רבי יוסי ברבי יהודה אומר: אינו אוכל עד שיעשה בידיו וברגליו. וקמבעיא ליה לרבה, דש באווזין ותרנגולין שאין להם אלא רגלים מהו? מי עבר עלייהו משום "לא תחסום שור" או לא, ידיו ורגליו בעינן כשור — וליכא, או דילמא כל כחו כשור בעינן והא איכא, — אלמא בני מלאכה נינהו. **ובכל חיה הרומשת** — ואי לאו לאכילה חיות בני מלאכה נינהו? ומשני ההוא לאתויי נחש ולמלאכה, דנחש בר מלאכה ניהו קודם שנתקלל לילך על גחון.

SAGES

רַחֲבָה Rahavah. A Babylonian Amora of the third generation, Rahavah was a disciple of Rav Yehudah and reported many Halakhic teachings in his name. We also find him quoted in the Talmud in discussions with other Sages of his generations. Rahavah was famous for the precision with which he reported teachings, so that when the Sages wished to express praise for someone's precision they would say he was accurate and precise as "Rahavah of Pumbedita." His two sons, Efah and Avimi, was famous Sages, known as "the sharp-witted scholars of Pumbedita."

NOTES

הִנְהִיג בְּעִיזָּא וְשִׁיבּוּטָא If he drove with a goat and a mullet. The Torah prohibition (Deuteronomy 22:10), "You shall not plow with an ox and an ass together," forbids a person from working any team of animals comprising different species, and not only an ox and an ass. Rahavah asked whether sea creatures are also included in this prohibition, or whether the prohibition only applies to animals that are normally used for work.

דָּשׁ בְּאַוָּוזִין וְתַרְנְגוֹלִין If he threshed with geese or chickens. The Torah prohibition (Deuteronomy 25:4), "You shall not muzzle an ox when it is treading grain," forbids a person from preventing an animal from eating while it is working. Elsewhere, the Gemara discusses the scope of the prohibition, to which animals it applies, and to which types of work. While the prohibition is certainly extended to other animals and other types of work, the verse implies that the prohibition applies only in a case similar to that of threshing with an ox. Rabbah bar Rav Huna was in doubt as to whether this means that the animal must work with all its strength, a condition that is also met by geese and chickens, or whether the prohibition is limited to animals that work with four limbs, thus excluding fowl.

SAGES

רַבִּי שִׁמְעוֹן בֶּן מְנַסְיָא Rabbi Shimon ben Menasya. A fifth-generation Tanna. His father's name, Menasya, is apparently an Aramaic or Hellenized form of the Hebrew מְנַשֶּׁה, Menasheh. Rabbi Shimon ben Menasya was an outstanding disciple of Rabbi Meir. He also studied with other Tannaim, such as Rabbi Shimon bar Yoḥai.

רַבִּי יְהוּדָה בֶּן תֵּימָא Rabbi Yehudah ben Tema. Rabbi Yehudah ben Tema was a Tanna. He was probably one of the Sages present in Yavneh after the destruction of the Second Temple.

LANGUAGE

סַנְדַּלְבּוֹנִים Gems. The source of this word is possibly the Greek σανλαράχη, *sandaraki*, meaning "a red stone." It also may be derived from σαρδονύχιον, *sandonykhion*, meaning "a precious stone."

LITERAL TRANSLATION

[1]That comes to include a snake, [2]as it was taught: "Rabbi Shimon ben Menasya says: Alas, a great helper was lost from the world, for had the snake not been cursed, each and every one of Israel would happen upon two good snakes. [3]One he would send north and one he would send south to bring him precious gems and precious stones and jewels. [4]And furthermore, they would fasten a strap under its tail, and it would remove earth to his garden or his ruin."

[5]They raised an objection: [6]"Rabbi Yehudah ben Tema said: The first man was dining in the garden of Eden, and the ministering angels were roasting meat for him, and filtering wine for him. [7]The snake looked at him, and beheld his honor, and envied him."

[8]There with meat that fell from Heaven.

[9]Is there meat that falls from Heaven?

[10]Yes, like that of Rabbi Shimon ben Ḥalafta who was walking along the road. [11]Certain lions met him who were

[1]הַהוּא לְאַתּוּיֵי נָחָשׁ הוּא דַּאֲתָא. [2]דְּתַנְיָא: "רַבִּי שִׁמְעוֹן בֶּן מְנַסְיָא אוֹמֵר: חֲבָל עַל שַׁמָּשׁ גָּדוֹל שֶׁאָבַד מִן הָעוֹלָם, שֶׁאִלְמָלֵא לֹא נִתְקַלֵּל נָחָשׁ, כָּל אֶחָד וְאֶחָד מִיִּשְׂרָאֵל הָיוּ מִזְדַּמְּנִין לוֹ שְׁנֵי נְחָשִׁים טוֹבִים. [3]אֶחָד מְשַׁגְּרוֹ לַצָּפוֹן וְאֶחָד מְשַׁגְּרוֹ לַדָּרוֹם לְהָבִיא לוֹ סַנְדַּלְבּוֹנִים טוֹבִים וַאֲבָנִים טוֹבוֹת וּמַרְגָּלִיּוֹת. [4]וְלֹא עוֹד אֶלָּא שֶׁמַּפְשִׁילִין רְצוּעָה תַּחַת זְנָבוֹ, וּמוֹצִיא בָּהּ עָפָר לְגִנָּתוֹ וּלְחוּרְבָּתוֹ".

[5]מֵיתִיבִי: [6]"הָיָה רַבִּי יְהוּדָה בֶּן תֵּימָא אוֹמֵר: אָדָם הָרִאשׁוֹן מֵיסֵב בְּגַן עֵדֶן הָיָה, וְהָיוּ מַלְאֲכֵי הַשָּׁרֵת צוֹלִין לוֹ בָּשָׂר, וּמְסַנְּנִין לוֹ יַיִן. [7]הֵצִיץ בּוֹ נָחָשׁ וְרָאָה בִּכְבוֹדוֹ, וְנִתְקַנֵּא בּוֹ!

[8]הָתָם בְּבָשָׂר הַיּוֹרֵד מִן הַשָּׁמַיִם.

[9]מִי אִיכָּא בָּשָׂר הַיּוֹרֵד מִן הַשָּׁמַיִם?

[10]אִין, כִּי הָא דְּרַבִּי שִׁמְעוֹן בֶּן חֲלַפְתָּא הֲוָה קָאָזֵיל בְּאוֹרְחָא. [11]פְּגַעוּ בּוֹ הָנָךְ אַרְיָוָתָא דַּהֲווּ

RASHI

חבל = הפסד, לשון "אהה", כל חבל לשון צער וקבל הוא, כלומר הפסד בא לעולם ויש לקבול על שמש וכו׳. סנדלבונין = שם אבן טוב. צולין לו בשר – אלמא: הותר לו לאכול בהמות וחיות.

TRANSLATION AND COMMENTARY

הַהוּא לְאַתּוּיֵי [1]The Gemara rejects this proof: **That** part of the verse **comes to include a snake** in the allowance of working with animals, for when the snake was first created, it too was fit for work, [2]**as it was taught** in the following Baraita: **"Rabbi Shimon ben Menasya says: Alas, a great helper was lost from the world, for had the snake not been cursed** that it must crawl upon its belly, **every member** of the people **of Israel would happen upon two good snakes.** [3]One snake **he would send north and the other** snake **he would send south to bring him precious gems and precious stones and jewels.** [4]**And furthermore, he would fasten a strap under its tail** like a harness, **and it would carry earth out** of his house **to his garden or his ruin."** Thus, we see that snakes were fit for work when they were first created.

מֵיתִיבִי [5]**Another objection was raised** from a Baraita against the position of Rav that when man was first created, he was forbidden to eat meat: [6]**"Rabbi Yehudah ben Tema said: Adam was dining in the garden of Eden, and the ministering angels were roasting meat for him, and filtering wine for him,** [7]**when the snake looked at him, and beheld the honor** that was being shown him, **and envied him.** Then and there the snake decided to convince Adam to eat the forbidden fruit, so that he would be cast out of the garden of Eden." Thus, the Baraita states explicitly that Adam ate meat while he was still in the garden of Eden, against Rav!

הָתָם [8]The Gemara counters: **There** the Baraita is referring to **meat that fell** miraculously **from Heaven,** which was permitted to Adam.

מִי אִיכָּא [9]The Gemara asks: But **is there** really **meat that falls from Heaven?**

אִין [10]The Gemara answers: **Yes, like that** about which was reported in the incident involving **Rabbi Shimon ben Ḥalafta who was** once **walking along the road,** [11]when **he was met by lions who roared before him**

NOTES

אִלְמָלֵא לֹא נִתְקַלֵּל נָחָשׁ Had the snake not been cursed. From the curses which God cast upon the snake, the Rabbis inferred what the snake would have been like had it not been cursed. Had the snake not been cursed, it could have been sent to the far ends of the world in search of precious stones, and so it was cursed that it would have to crawl on its belly, and not be able to go very far. And had it not been cursed, it could have been used to remove earth from the house, and so it was cursed that it would eat earth (*Maharsha*).

בָּשָׂר הַיּוֹרֵד מִן הַשָּׁמַיִם Meat that fell from Heaven. While it happens occasionally in particularly violent storms that a "rain" of living creatures (frogs, fish, and the like) falls to the ground, those creatures are first sucked up from the ground or from the sea by the wind, and then cast down in another place. Here however we are dealing with a miraculous event, in which special creatures were created and then cast down from Heaven (see *Meiri*).

TRANSLATION AND COMMENTARY

and were about to devour him. Seeking divine assistance, Rabbi Shimon ben Ḥalafta cited a verse (Psalms 104:21), [1]and **said: "The young lions roar after their prey,** and seek their food from God." [2]Two **flanks** of meat miraculously **came down for him** from heaven, **one** of which the lions **ate, and one** of which **they left** uneaten. [3]**He took** the uneaten meat **and brought it** with him **to the academy,** showed it to his colleagues, [4]**and asked about it: Is this a clean thing** which may be eaten, **or an unclean thing** which is forbidden?

אָמְרוּ לֵיהּ [5]His colleagues **said to him:** Surely it is a clean thing, for **no unclean thing falls from Heaven.**

בָּעֵי [6]It was related that **Rabbi Zera asked Rabbi Abbahu: If something that looks like a donkey** miraculously **fell for** a person from Heaven, **what is the law?** Is the meat permitted or forbidden? [7]Rabbi Abbahu **said to him: You howling yarod!** [8]**Surely** the Rabbis already **said** to Rabbi Shimon ben Ḥalafta: **No unclean thing falls from Heaven.** Thus, you are asking about something that does not happen. And if it happened, it would be regarded as a clean thing.

רַבִּי שִׁמְעוֹן אוֹמֵר [9]The Baraita cited earlier at the beginning of the discussion regarding the seven Noachide laws (56a) continues: **"Rabbi Shimon says:** Non-Jews are **also** bound by the prohibition against **sorcery."** [10]The Gemara asks: **What is the reasoning of Rabbi Shimon?** [11]**For the verse states** (Exodus 22:17): [60A] [12]**"You shall not suffer a sorceress to live."** [13]**And the** very next **verse states** (Exodus 22:18): **"Whoever lies with a beast shall surely be put to death."** [14]These two verses appear next to each other to teach us that **whoever is included in** the prohibition, **"Whoever lies with a beast** shall surely be put to death," [15]**is** also **included in** the prohibition, **"You shall not suffer a sorceress** to live." As non-Jews are bound by the prohibition against bestiality, so too they are bound by the prohibition against sorcery.

רַבִּי אֱלְעָזָר אוֹמֵר [16]The Baraita which lists the Noachide laws continues: **"Rabbi Eliezer says:** Non-Jews are **also** bound by the prohibition against **forbidden mixtures.** How so? Non-Jews are permitted to wear garments containing a mixture of wool and linen, and they are also permitted to plant diverse kinds in one area of

קָא נָהֲמִי לְאַפֵּיהּ, [1]אֲמַר: ״הַכְּפִירִים שֹׁאֲגִים לַטָּרֶף״. [2]נְחִיתוּ לֵיהּ תַּרְתֵּי אַטְמָתָא, חֲדָא אֲכַלוּהָ וַחֲדָא שַׁבְקוּהָ. [3]אַיְתְיֵהּ וַאֲתָא לְבֵי מִדְרְשָׁא, [4]בְּעֵי עֲלָהּ: דָּבָר טָמֵא הוּא זֶה אוֹ דָּבָר טָהוֹר? [5]אָמְרוּ לֵיהּ: אֵין דָּבָר טָמֵא יוֹרֵד מִן הַשָּׁמַיִם. [6]בָּעֵי מִינֵּיהּ רַבִּי זֵירָא מֵרַבִּי אַבָּהוּ: יָרְדָה לוֹ דְּמוּת חֲמוֹר, מַהוּ? [7]אֲמַר לֵיהּ: יָארוֹד נָאלָא! [8]הָא אָמְרִי לֵיהּ: אֵין דָּבָר טָמֵא יוֹרֵד מִן הַשָּׁמַיִם. [9]״רַבִּי שִׁמְעוֹן אוֹמֵר: אַף עַל הַכִּישּׁוּף״. [10]מַאי טַעְמֵיהּ דְּרַבִּי שִׁמְעוֹן? [11]דִּכְתִיב: [60A] [12]״מְכַשֵּׁפָה לֹא תְחַיֶּה״. [13]וּכְתִיב: ״כָּל שֹׁכֵב עִם בְּהֵמָה מוֹת יוּמָת״. [14]כָּל שֶׁיֶּשְׁנוֹ בִּכְלָל ״כָּל שֹׁכֵב עִם בְּהֵמָה״ [15]יֶשְׁנוֹ בִּכְלָל ״מְכַשֵּׁפָה לֹא תְחַיֶּה״. [16]״רַבִּי אֱלְעָזָר אוֹמֵר אַף עַל

LITERAL TRANSLATION

roaring before him. [1]He said: "The young lions roar after their prey." [2]Two flanks came down for him, one they ate, and one they left. [3]He brought it and came to the academy, [4][and] asked about it: Is this a clean thing or an unclean thing?

[5]They said to him: No unclean thing falls from Heaven.

[6]Rabbi Zera asked Rabbi Abbahu: [If] something with the appearance of a donkey fell for him, what [is the law]? [7]He said to him: You howling yarod! [8]Surely they said to him: No unclean thing falls from Heaven.

[9]"Rabbi Shimon says: Also for sorcery." [10]What is the reason of Rabbi Shimon? [11]For it is written: [60A] [12]"You shall not suffer a sorceress to live." [13]And it is written: "Whoever lies with a beast shall surely be put to death." [14]Whoever is included in "Whoever lies with a beast" [15]is included in "You shall not suffer a sorceress."

[16]"Rabbi Eliezer says: Also for

RASHI

נהמו לאפיה — לאכלו. **ירדה דמות חמור מהו** — מי אמר: הא ודאי דבר טמא הוא ואסור. **ירוד נאלא** — תנין שוטה. עוף ששמו תנין, והוא שוטה ובוכה ומספיד תמיד. וכל תנין דמקרא מתרגמינן ירודין. **הא אמרו ליה אין דבר טמא יורד מן השמים** — ודבר שאינו הוא, ואם ישנו — טהור הוא. **מכשפה לא תחיה וכל שוכב עם בהמה** — סמוכין הן בפרשת ״ואלה המשפטים״.

BACKGROUND

יָרוֹד **Yarod.** In the Talmud this word refers to a kind of bird (sometimes in place of the word תנה that appears in the Bible). Based on the Biblical context, it is a bird whose call sounds like weeping, a nocturnal bird whose call is a wail.

Some commentators suggest that Rabbi Abbahu called Rabbi Zera by that name because he used to fast a lot, and therefore he compared him to a bird that always appears to be mourning and weeping.

LANGUAGE

נָאלָא **Howling.** This word is apparently based on the root אלה, meaning "to whine or weep." Some authorities believe it means "a fool," as in the phrase נוֹאֲלוּ שָׂרֵי צֹעַן, "the princes of Zoan are fools" (Isaiah 19:13).

NOTES

דְּמוּת חֲמוֹר **Something with the appearance of a donkey.** It has been noted that the same law applies if a kosher animal gave birth to a creature which looks like a non-kosher animal, or lacks the identifying marks of a kosher animal: the young is regarded as a kosher animal (*Rabbi Ya'akov Emden*).

HALAKHAH

אַף עַל הַכִּלְאַיִם **Also for forbidden mixtures.** "According to the oral tradition, non-Jews are forbidden to mate together

הַכִּלְאַיִם״.
[1]מְנָא הָנֵי מִילֵּי? [2]אָמַר שְׁמוּאֵל: דְּאָמַר קְרָא: ״אֶת חֻקֹּתַי תִּשְׁמֹרוּ״ — [3]חוּקִּים שֶׁחָקַקְתִּי לְךָ כְּבָר. [4]״בְּהֶמְתְּךָ לֹא תַרְבִּיעַ כִּלְאַיִם שָׂדְךָ לֹא תִזְרַע כִּלְאַיִם״. [5]מַה בְּהֶמְתְּךָ בְּהַרְבָּעָה, אַף שָׂדְךָ בְּהַרְכָּבָה. [6]מַה בְּהֶמְתְּךָ — בֵּין בָּאָרֶץ בֵּין בְּחוּצָה לָאָרֶץ, [7]אַף שָׂדְךָ — בֵּין בָּאָרֶץ בֵּין בְּחוּצָה לָאָרֶץ. [8]אֶלָּא מֵעַתָּה ״וּשְׁמַרְתֶּם אֶת חֻקֹּתַי וְאֶת מִשְׁפָּטַי״ — [9]חֻקִּים שֶׁחָקַקְתִּי לְךָ כְּבָר!

LITERAL TRANSLATION

forbidden mixtures."

[1]From where are these things [derived]? [2]Shmuel said: For the verse states: "My statutes you shall keep" — [3]statutes which I have already ordained for you. [4]"You shall not let your cattle mate with a diverse kind; you shall not sow your field with mingled seed." [5]Just as your cattle is with mating, so too your field is with grafting. [6]Just as your cattle — whether in Eretz Israel or outside Eretz Israel, [7]so too your field — whether in Eretz Israel or outside Eretz Israel."

[8]If so, "And you shall keep my statutes, and my judgments" [9]statutes which I have already ordained for you!

TRANSLATION AND COMMENTARY

the same field. They are only forbidden to crossbreed different species of animals, and graft different species of trees onto one another."

מְנָא הָנֵי מִילֵּי [1]The Gemara asks: **From where are these laws derived?** What is their Biblical source? [2]**Shmuel said:** This is learned from **the verse** which **states** (Leviticus 19:19): **"My statutes you shall keep;** you shall not let your cattle mate with a diverse kind; you shall not sow your field with mingled seed." When God commanded Israel to avoid forbidden mixtures, He opened in an unusual manner with the words, "My statutes you shall keep." [3]Infer from this that He meant to say: **Statutes which I have already ordained for** the descendants of Noah you shall continue to keep. [4]Those statutes are as follows: **"You shall not let your cattle mate with a diverse kind; you shall not sow your field with mingled seed."** The nature and the scope of the second prohibition mentioned in the verse is derived by analogy from the first prohibition mentioned there. [5]**Just as** the prohibition, "You shall not let **your cattle** mate with a diverse kind," forbids **mating** together animals of different species, **so too** the prohibition, "You shall not sow **your field** with mingled seed," forbids **grafting** different species of trees onto one another, which is similar to mating together animals of different species. However, it does not forbid planting diverse kinds in one area of the same field, or planting other crops in a vineyard, actions which are forbidden to Jews. [6]"And furthermore, **just as** the prohibition, "You shall not let **your cattle** mate with a diverse kind," applies **both in Eretz Israel and outside Eretz Israel,** for it is a personal obligation that is not connected in any way to the land, [7]**so too** the prohibition, "You shall not sow **your field** with mingled seed," applies **both in Eretz Israel and outside Eretz Israel.**

אֶלָּא מֵעַתָּה [8]The Gemara raises an objection: **If so,** then the verse referring to the commandments in general (Leviticus 18:5): **"And you shall keep my statutes, and my judgments,"** should be understood in similar fashion: [9]And you shall keep the **statutes which I have already ordained for** the descendants of Noah. Thus, it should follow that non-Jews are bound by all of the Torah's commandments, just like Jews!

RASHI

את חקתי תשמרו — כשהזהיר ישראל בסיני ״בהמתך לא תרביע וגו׳״ פתח בהו קרא ״את חקותי תשמרו״, מה שלא פתח כן בשאר מקומות — שמע מינה הכי קאמר להו: את חקותי שחקקתי כבר לבני נח תשמרו, ואלו הן: בהמתך לא תרביע כלאים, אבל על חרישת שור וחמור לא הזהרתים. **שדך לא תזרע כלאים** — וזריעה זו אינה זריעה ממש, דלא נצטוו בני נח על כלאי הכרם — אלא שלא להרכיב האילן על שאינו מינו, דלא תזרע דומיא דלא תרביע, מה בהמה בהרבעה דבר המסוייס על דבר המסוייס. **מה בהמה בין בארץ בין בחוץ לארץ** — דחובת הגוף שאינה תלויה בחובת הארץ, נפקא לן בקדושין (לו, א) דנוהגת אפילו בחוץ לארץ. **אלא מעתה ושמרתם את חקותי** — דכתיב בכל התורה כולה — הכי נמי דנצטוו בני נח עליהם.

NOTES

חֻקִּים שֶׁחָקַקְתִּי **Statutes which I had already ordained.** *Tosafot* and other ask: Why are non-Jews not bound by the prohibition against wearing a garment made of a mixture of wool and linen, for surely that prohibition is found in that very same verse beginning with "My statutes you shall keep"? This question may be answered according to the reading of the Jerusalem Talmud: "Statutes which I had ordained in My world." According to that reading, God ordained statutes in His world, setting each species apart from the rest, and commanding that those species remain distinct one from the other. Thus, even non-Jews are forbidden to crossbreed different species of animals, and graft different species of trees onto one another, for that will lead to mixed species. But it does not follow that they

HALAKHAH

animals of different species, and to graft different species of trees onto one another. But they are not subject to judicial execution for the violation of these prohibitions." (*Rambam, Sefer Shofetim, Hilkhot Melakhim* 10:6; and see *Sefer Zeraim, Hilkhot Kilayim* 9:1; 1:5.)

TRANSLATION AND COMMENTARY

הָתָם [1]The Gemara distinguishes between the two verses, noting the difference in word order: **There** the verse states: **"And you shall keep my statutes."** Israel's obligation to keep the statutes precedes the statutes themselves. God commanded the people of Israel: [2]And you shall keep the statutes that I ordain for your **now.** [3]But **here** regarding the prohibition against forbidden mixtures the verse states: **"My statutes you shall keep."** The statutes precede Israel's obligation to observe them. God commanded the people of Israel: [4]My **statutes** which already existed **from the beginning** as an obligation upon the descendants of Noah **you shall** also **keep.**

אָמַר [5]Having completed its discussion regarding the Noachide laws, the Gemara now resumes its analysis of the Mishnah regarding blasphemy: **"Rabbi Yehoshua ben Korḥah said:** Whenever the judges examined the witnesses in a case involving blasphemy, they would discuss the matter with them using a substitute word." [6]**Rav Aḥa bar Ya'akov said:** The blasphemer **is not liable** to the death penalty **unless he cursed a** Divine **Name of Four Letters,** yod, heh, vav and heh, [7]**to the exclusion of** a Divine Name **of** only **Two Letters,** yod and heh, when he is **not liable** to that penalty.

פְּשִׁיטָא [8]The Gemara asks: But surely **this is obvious,** [9]for **we have learned** in the Mishnah: "The witnesses would not repeat the actual words of the blasphemer, but rather they would testify that the blasphemer said: **'May Yose strike Yose,'** substituting the name Yose for the Divine Name." Now since the Mishnah chose the Four Letter Name Yose [יוסי] to substitute for the Divine Name, surely this implies that the blasphemer is only liable if he cursed a Divine Name of Four Letters, similar to the name Yose!

מַהוּ דְּתֵימָא [10]The Gemara rejects this argument: The wording of the Mishnah cannot serve as conclusive proof, for **you might have said** that the Tanna of the Mishnah **merely seized the name** Yose as an example. [11]**Therefore** it was necessary for Rabbi Aḥa bar Ya'akov to **teach us** that the wording of the Mishnah is in fact precise, and the blasphemer is only liable if he cursed a Four-Letter Divine Name.

אִיכָּא דְּאָמְרִי [12]The Gemara cites a slightly different version of the preceding discussion: **There are those who say** that **Rav Aḥa bar Ya'akov said** as follows: [13]**Infer from this** Mishnah **that a** Divine **Name of Four Letters is also a** Divine **Name,** the cursing of which results in liability for blasphemy, and there is no need for the blasphemer to curse a Divine Name of Twelve Letters or a Divine Name of Forty-Two Letters.

1 הָתָם "וּשְׁמַרְתֶּם אֶת חֻקֹּתַי" — 2 דְּהָשְׁתָּא, 3 הָכָא "אֶת חֻקֹּתַי תִּשְׁמֹרוּ" — 4 חֻקִּים דְּמֵעִיקָּרָא תִּשְׁמֹרוּ.

5 "אָמַר רַבִּי יְהוֹשֻׁעַ בֶּן קָרְחָה כו'". 6 אָמַר רַב אַחָא בַּר יַעֲקֹב: אֵינוֹ חַיָּיב עַד שֶׁיְּבָרֵךְ שֵׁם בֶּן אַרְבַּע אוֹתִיּוֹת, 7 לְאַפּוּקֵי בֶּן שְׁתֵּי אוֹתִיּוֹת, דְּלָא.

8 פְּשִׁיטָא. 9 "יַכֶּה יוֹסֵי אֶת יוֹסֵי" תְּנַן!

10 מַהוּ דְּתֵימָא: מִילְּתָא בְּעָלְמָא הוּא דִּנְקַט. 11 קָא מַשְׁמַע לָן.

12 אִיכָּא דְּאָמְרִי: אָמַר רַב אַחָא בַּר יַעֲקֹב: 13 שְׁמַע מִינַּהּ שֵׁם בֶּן אַרְבַּע אוֹתִיּוֹת נַמִי שֵׁם הוּא.

LITERAL TRANSLATION

[1]There, "And you shall keep my statutes" — [2]from now. [3]Here, "My statutes you shall keep" — [4]statutes from the beginning you shall keep.

[5]"Rabbi Yehoshua ben Korḥah said, etc." [6]Rav Aḥa bar Ya'akov said: He is not liable unless he curses a [Divine] Name of Four Letters, [7]to the exclusion of [a Divine Name] of Two Letters, that not.

[8]This is obvious. [9]We have learned: "May Yose strike Yose"!

[10]You might have said: He merely seized a word. [11][Therefore] he teaches us.

[12]There are [those] who say: Rav Aḥa bar Ya'akov said: [13]Infer from this [that] a [Divine] Name of Four Letters is also a [Divine] Name.

RASHI

הכא כתיב את חקותי תשמרו — דהקדים חקים למצות שמירה, דמשמע חקים דמעיקרא. ואף על גב דגבי שביעית ויובל כתיב נמי "את משפטי תעשו ואת חקתי תשמרו" דהקדים נמי חקים למצות שמירה — התם כיון דרישא דקרא כתיב "את משפטי תעשו" — ארחיה למיכתב "ואת חקתי תשמרו". **שם בן ארבע אותיות** — שם הוא, ולא בעינן שם המפורש בן ארבעים ושתים אותיות.

NOTES

should also be forbidden to wear garments made of a mixture of wool and linen, or to sow one field with mingled seed (see *Rabbenu Yonah, Yefeh Enayim*).

HALAKHAH

אֵינוֹ חַיָּיב עַד שֶׁיְּבָרֵךְ שֵׁם בֶּן אַרְבַּע אוֹתִיּוֹת He is not liable unless he curses a Divine Name of Four Letters. "A blasphemer is not liable to death by stoning unless he cursed the Divine Name of Four Letters, the name consisting of the letters alef, dalet, nun, yod, or the name consisting of the letters yod, heh, vav, heh," following Rav Aḥa bar Ya'akov. (*Rambam, Sefer Mada, Hilkhot Avodah Zarah* 2:7.)

TRANSLATION AND COMMENTARY

פְּשִׁיטָא [1]The Gemara asks: But surely **this is obvious,** for **we have learned** in the Mishnah: "The witnesses would not repeat the actual words of the blasphemer, but rather they would testify that the blasphemer had said: [2]**'May Yose strike Yose,'** substituting the name Yose for the divine name." This implies that the blasphemer is liable if he cursed a Divine Name of Four Letters, similar to the name Yose!

מַהוּ דְּתֵימָא [3]The Gemara rejects this argument: Had we only had the Mishnah, **you might have said** that the blasphemer is in fact not liable **unless** he cursed one of the **Great Names** of God, and the Tanna of the Mishnah **merely seized the name** Yose as an example, without having meant to imply that the blasphemer is liable if he cursed a Divine Name of Four Letters. [4]**Therefore** it was necessary for Rabbi Aḥa bar Ya'akov to **teach us** that the wording of the Mishnah is precise, and the blasphemer is in fact liable if he cursed a Divine Name of Four Letters.

נִגְמַר הַדִּין [5]The Mishnah regarding the blasphemer continues: "**If the judgment was concluded** and the judges agreed on a guilty verdict, the judges would ask the witnesses to repeat what they had heard from the blasphemer, using the blasphemer's own words. Upon hearing the actual blasphemy, the judges would stand on their feet, rend their garments in mourning over the desecration of God's name, and never mend them." [6]The Gemara asks: **From where do we know that** the judges must **stand** up when they hear the actual blasphemy? [7]Rabbi Yitzḥak the son of Ammi says: This is learned from **the verse** which **states** (Judges 3:20): [8]**"And Ehud came to him** [Eglon, king of Moab], **and he was sitting in a cool upper chamber, which he was his alone. And Ehud said, I have a message from God to you. So he arose out of his seat."** [9]**Surely the matter** follows by way of a ***kal vaḥomer*****: If Eglon the king of Moab** — [10]**who was a non-Jew, and only knew** God by **a substitute name,** [11]nevertheless **stood** up from his seat when he heard God's name being mentioned, surely then **a Jew** who hears **the Tetragrammaton** being pronounced, [12]must **all the more so** stand up.

קוֹרְעִין [13]The Mishnah relating to blasphemy continues: "Upon hearing the actual blasphemy, the judges would stand on their feet, **rend their garments** in mourning over the desecration of God's name." [14]The Gemara asks: **From where do we know** that the judges must rend their garments when they hear the actual blasphemy? [15]The Gemara answers: This is learned from **the verse** which **states** (II Kings 18:37): **"Then**

[1]פְּשִׁיטָא. [2]"יַכֶּה יוֹסֵי אֶת יוֹסֵי" תְּנַן! [3]מַהוּ דְּתֵימָא: עַד דְּאִיכָּא שֵׁם רַבָּה, וּמִילְּתָא בְּעָלְמָא הוּא דְּנָקַט. [4]קָא מַשְׁמַע לָן.
[5]"נִגְמַר הַדִּין כו'". [6]עוֹמְדִין מְנָלַן? [7]אָמַר רַבִּי יִצְחָק בַּר אַמִּי: דְּאָמַר קְרָא: [8]"וְאֵהוּד בָּא אֵלָיו וְהוּא יֹשֵׁב בַּעֲלִיַּת הַמְּקֵרָה אֲשֶׁר לוֹ לְבַדּוֹ וַיֹּאמֶר אֵהוּד דְּבַר אֱלֹהִים לִי אֵלֶיךָ וַיָּקָם מֵעַל הַכִּסֵּא". [9]וַהֲלֹא דְּבָרִים קַל וָחוֹמֶר: וּמָה עֶגְלוֹן מֶלֶךְ מוֹאָב, [10]שֶׁהוּא נָכְרִי וְלֹא יָדַע אֶלָּא בְּכִינּוּי, [11]עָמַד, יִשְׂרָאֵל וְשֵׁם הַמְּפוֹרָשׁ, [12]עַל אַחַת כַּמָּה וְכַמָּה.
[13]"קוֹרְעִין". [14]מְנָלַן? [15]דִּכְתִיב:

LITERAL TRANSLATION

[1]This is obvious. [2]We have learned: "May Yose strike Yose"!

[3]You might have said: Until there is the Great Name, and he merely seized a word. [4][Therefore] he teaches us.

[5]"If the judgment was concluded, etc." [6]From where do we [know that] they stand? [7]Rabbi Yitzḥak the son of Ammi says: For the verse states: [8]"And Ehud came to him, and he was sitting in a cool upper chamber, which was his alone. And Ehud said, I have a message from God to you. So he arose out of his seat." [9]Surely the matter is a *kal vaḥomer*: If Eglon the king of Moab, [10]who was a non-Jew, and only knew a substitute name, [11]stood, a Jew, and the Tetragrammaton, (lit. "the Explicit Name"), [12]all the more so.

[13]"They rend [their garments]." [14]From where do we [know this]? [15]For it is written:

RASHI

ושם המפורש — כלומר: שם המיוחד.

NOTES

שֵׁם רַבָּה The Great Name. The Rishonim disagree about the meaning of the term "Great Name." Some say that it refers to a special appellation of God consisting of twelve letters. Others say that it refers to an even longer name, a Divine Name consisting of forty-two letters (alluded to in the prayer *Ana beko'aḥ*) (see *Ramah*). Both of these names are esoterically related to the "explicit name" of Four Letters, the Tetragrammaton (yod, heh, vav, heh). These names were known only to a select group of people, and rarely pronounced even in the Temple.

עוֹמְדִין They stand. The judges' obligation to stand up upon upon hearing the actual blasphemy does not appear to be

HALAKHAH

עוֹמְדִין They stand. "When the judges hear the actual blasphemy, they are obligated to stand up on their feet," following the Mishnah. (*Rambam, Sefer Mada, Hilkhot Avodah Zarah* 2:8.)

קוֹרְעִין They rend. "When the judges hear the actual blasphemy, they must rend their garments while standing." (*Rambam,*

CHAPTER SEVEN

TRANSLATION AND COMMENTARY

came Elyakim the son of Hilkiah who was over the household, **and Shevna the scribe, and Jo'ah the son of Asaf the recorder, to Hezekiah with their clothes rent, and told him the words of Ravshakeh."** From here we see that Hezekiah's men had rent their clothes when they heard Ravshakeh's blasphemy, as the verse states (II Kings 19:4): "It may be that the Lord your God will hear all the words of Ravshakeh, whom the king of Ashur his master has sent to blaspheme the living God."

לֹא מְאַחִין [1] We learned in the Mishnah: "Upon hearing the actual blasphemy, the judges would stand on their feet, rend their garments in mourning for the desecration of God's name, **and never mend them."** [2] **From where do we know** that the rent garments may never be mended? [3] **Rabbi Abbahu said:** The law regarding **rending** garments in mourning for the desecration of God's name **is learned** by a *gezerah shavah* **from** another instance of **rending** garments. [4] **Here** regarding those who heard the blasphemous words of Ravshakeh **the verse states** (II Kings 18:37): "Then came Elyakim...**with their clothes rent."** [5] **And elsewhere** regarding the prophet Elijah's ascent to Heaven, **the verse states** (II Kings 2:12): **"And Elisha saw it, and he cried, My father, my father, the chariots of Israel, and their horsemen. And he saw him no more; and he took hold of his own clothes, and rent them in two pieces."** [6] **Since the text states: "And he took hold of his own clothes, and rent them in two,"** [7] **is it not obvious that** the clothes **are** now in **pieces?** [8] **What then does the verse teach** when it adds the apparently superfluous word **"pieces"?** [9] **It teaches that** the clothes **must remain rent** in pieces **forever,** mending them being forbidden.

תָּנוּ רַבָּנָן [10] **Our Rabbis taught** a related Baraita: **"Both someone who heard** the blasphemy with his own ears **and someone who heard** the blasphemy second-hand **from someone who heard** it with his own ears **are obligated to rend their garments** as a sign of mourning for the desecration of God's name.

LITERAL TRANSLATION

"Then came Elyakim the son of Hilkiah [who was over the household], and Shevna the scribe, and Jo'ah the son of Asaf the recorder, to Hezekiah with their clothes rent, and told him the words of Ravshakeh."

[1] "And they do not mend [them]." [2] From where do we [know this]? [3] Rabbi Abbahu said: Rending is learned from rending. [4] It is written here: "With their clothes rent." [5] And it is written there: "And Elisha saw it, and he cried, My father, my father, the chariots of Israel, and their horsemen. And he saw him no more; and he grasped his own clothes, and rent them in two pieces." [6] By deduction from the text, [7] "And rent them in two," do I not know that they are pieces? [8] What then does the verse teach: "Pieces"? [9] It teaches that they remain rent forever.

[10] Our Rabbis taught: "Both someone who hears and someone who hears from someone who heard are obligated

"וַיָּבֹא אֶלְיָקִים בֶּן חִלְקִיָּהוּ [וְגוֹ'] וְשֶׁבְנָא הַסֹּפֵר וְיוֹאָח בֶּן אָסָף הַמַּזְכִּיר אֶל חִזְקִיָּהוּ קְרוּעֵי בְגָדִים וַיַּגִּידוּ לוֹ אֶת דִּבְרֵי רַבְשָׁקֵה".

[1] "לֹא מְאַחִין". [2] מְנָלַן? [3] אָמַר רַבִּי אַבָּהוּ: אָתְיָא קְרִיעָה קְרִיעָה. [4] כְּתִיב הָכָא: "קְרוּעֵי בְגָדִים". [5] וּכְתִיב הָתָם: "וֶאֱלִישָׁע רֹאֶה וְהוּא מְצַעֵק אָבִי אָבִי רֶכֶב יִשְׂרָאֵל וּפָרָשָׁיו וְלֹא רָאָהוּ עוֹד. וַיַּחֲזֵק בִּבְגָדָיו וַיִּקְרָעֵם לִשְׁנַיִם קְרָעִים". [6] מִמַּשְׁמַע שֶׁנֶּאֱמַר, "וַיִּקְרָעֵם לִשְׁנַיִם", [7] אֵינִי יוֹדֵעַ שֶׁהֵן קְרָעִים? [8] וּמָה תַּלְמוּד לוֹמַר: "קְרָעִים"? [9] מְלַמֵּד שֶׁהֵן קְרוּעִים לְעוֹלָם.

[10] תָּנוּ רַבָּנָן: "אֶחָד הַשּׁוֹמֵעַ, וְאֶחָד שׁוֹמֵעַ מִפִּי שׁוֹמֵעַ — חַיָּיב

RASHI

קרועי בגדים — על גדופין שמעו מפי רבשקה, כדכתיב (מלכים ב יט) "אשר שלחו מלך אשור [אדניו] לחרף אלהים חי".

NOTES

connected to their obligation to rend their garments. But rather they are required to stand up in honor of God's name, just as Eglon, the king of Moab, stood up when he heard God's name being mentioned (see *Ḥamra Veḥaye*).

HALAKHAH

Sefer Mada, Hilkhot Avodah Zarah 2:7, *Sefer Shofetim, Hilkhot Evel* 9:7; *Shulḥan Arukh, Yoreh De'ah* 340:1.)

לֹא מְאַחִין **They do not mend them.** "The garments which the judges rent upon hearing blasphemy may be stitched together roughly, but not entirely mended." (Rambam, *Sefer Mada, Hilkhot Avodah Zarah* 2:7, *Sefer Shofetim, Hilkhot Evel* 9:3; *Shulḥan Arukh, Yoreh De'ah* 340:39.)

אֶחָד הַשּׁוֹמֵעַ, וְאֶחָד שׁוֹמֵעַ מִפִּי שׁוֹמֵעַ **Both someone who hears and someone who hears from someone who heard.** "Someone who heard blasphemy, whether he heard the actual blasphemy or he heard it second-hand from someone who heard the actual blasphemy, is required to rend his garments," following the Baraita. But someone who heard blasphemy third-hand (from someone who heard it from someone who heard the actual blasphemy) is not required to rend his garments (*Kesef Mishneh* in the name of the Jerusalem Talmud). (Rambam, *Sefer Mada, Hilkhot Avodah Zarah* 2:10, *Sefer Shofetim, Hilkhot Evel* 9:7; *Shulḥan Arukh, Yoreh De'ah* 340:37.)

לִקְרוֹעַ. [1]וְהָעֵדִים אֵין חַיָּיבִין לִקְרוֹעַ, [2]שֶׁכְּבָר קָרְעוּ בְּשָׁעָה שֶׁשָּׁמְעוּ".

[3]וְכִי קָרְעוּ בְּשָׁעָה שֶׁשָּׁמְעוּ, מַאי הָוֵי: [4]הָא קָא שָׁמְעִי הָשְׁתָּא!

[5]לָא סָלְקָא דַּעֲתָךְ, דִּכְתִיב: "וַיְהִי כִּשְׁמֹעַ הַמֶּלֶךְ חִזְקִיָּהוּ (אֶת דִּבְרֵי רַבְשָׁקֵה) וַיִּקְרַע אֶת בְּגָדָיו". [6]הַמֶּלֶךְ חִזְקִיָּהוּ קָרַע, [7]וְהֵם לֹא קָרְעוּ.

[8]אָמַר רַב יְהוּדָה אָמַר שְׁמוּאֵל: הַשּׁוֹמֵעַ אַזְכָּרָה מִפִּי הַנָּכְרִי אֵינוֹ חַיָּיב לִקְרוֹעַ. [9]וְאִם תֹּאמַר רַבְשָׁקֵה, יִשְׂרָאֵל מוּמָר הָיָה.

[10]וְאָמַר רַב יְהוּדָה אָמַר שְׁמוּאֵל: אֵין קוֹרְעִין אֶלָּא עַל שֵׁם הַמְיוּחָד בִּלְבַד, [11]לְאַפּוּקֵי כִּינּוּי, דְּלָא.

[12]וּפְלִיגִי דְּרַבִּי חִיָּיא בְּתַרְוַיְיהוּ, דְּאָמַר רַבִּי חִיָּיא: [13]הַשּׁוֹמֵעַ

LITERAL TRANSLATION

to rend [their garments]. [1]And the witnesses are not obligated to rend [their garments], [2]for they already rent [their garments] when they heard."

[3]And if they rent [their garments] when they heard, what is there: [4]Surely they hear now!

[5]This cannot enter your mind, for it is written: "And it came to pass, when King Hezekiah heard the words of Ravshakeh, that he rent his clothes." [6]King Hezekiah rent [his clothes], [7]but they did not rend [their clothes].

[8]Rav Yehudah said in the name of Shmuel: Someone who hears a mention [of God's name] by a non-Jew is not obligated to rend [his garments]. [9]And if you say Ravshakeh, he was an apostate Jew.

[10]And Rav Yehudah said in the name of Shmuel: We only rend [garments] for the Tetragrammaton, [11]to the exclusion of substitute names, that not.

[12]And these disagree with Rabbi Ḥiyya about two things, for Rabbi Ḥiyya said: [13]Someone who hears

TRANSLATION AND COMMENTARY

[1]**The witnesses** when they repeat in court the blasphemer's own words **are not obligated to rend their garments,** [2]**for they already rent their garments when they heard** the blasphemer cursing God."

וְכִי קָרְעוּ [3]The Gemara asks: **What** difference does it make **if** the witnesses already **rent their garments when they heard** the blasphemer cursing God? [4]**Surely** when they repeat his blasphemy in court, **they hear** the blasphemy **now** for a second time, and so they should be obligated to rend their garments again!

לָא סָלְקָא דַּעֲתָךְ [5]The Gemara answers: **You cannot** possibly **say that, for the verse states** (II Kings 19:1): **"And it came to pass, when king Hezekiah heard it, that he rent his clothes."** [6]The verse teaches that **King Hezekiah rent his clothes** when he was told of Ravshakeh's blasphemy, [7]**but** his men who reported the blasphemy to him **did not rend their clothes** at that time, for they rent their clothes when they first heard Ravshakeh blaspheming God.

אָמַר רַב יְהוּדָה [8]**Rav Yehudah said in the name of Shmuel: Someone who hears a** blasphemous **mention of God's name by a non-Jew is not obligated to rend his garments.** [9]**And if you say** that the incident involving **Ravshakeh** proves otherwise, Ravshakeh **was** in fact **an apostate Jew.**

וְאָמַר רַב יְהוּדָה [10]**Rav Yehudah said in the name of Shmuel: Someone** who heard the blasphemous utterance of God's name **is only obligated to rend his garments** if the blasphemy involved **the Tetragrammaton.** [11]This **excludes** blasphemy involving one **of the substitute names,** in which case the person who hears the blasphemy is **not** obligated to rend his garments.

וּפְלִיגִי דְּרַבִּי חִיָּיא [12]The Gemara notes: Shmuel, who says that hearing blasphemy uttered by a non-Jew or blasphemy involving one of God's substitute names does not obligate a person to rend his garments, **disagrees with Rabbi Ḥiyya about two matters, for Rabbi Ḥiyya said:** [13]**If someone hears a** blasphemous **mention**

RASHI

והעדים — בשעה שמעידין בפירוש מה ששמעו אין חייבין לקרוע. **הא שמעו השתא** — מפי עצמן. **השומע אזכרה** — ברכת השם, מפי הנכרי אינו חייב לקרוע. **ואם תאמר** — הרי קרעו על רבשקה! — ישראל מומר היה.

NOTES

הַמֶּלֶךְ חִזְקִיָּהוּ קָרַע **King Hezekiah rent.** *Tosafot* and others ask: Why did Hezekiah's men repeat Ravshakeh's blasphemy before Hezekiah? Surely we learned in our Mishnah that even when the witnesses come to court to testify against the blasphemer, they first use substitute names, so as not to repeat the actual blasphemy! Some suggest according to the viewpoint that Ravshakeh was an apostate Jew that the men who reported his words to Hezekiah wished to testify against him, so that if they would later apprehend him, they would be permitted to kill him (see *Maharik, Rosh*). Others argue that Hezekiah rent his garments not because he heard God's name being mentioned in a blasphemous way, but because he heard the contents of Ravshakeh's blasphemy, in which Ravshakeh

HALAKHAH

הָעֵדִים אֵין חַיָּיבִין לִקְרוֹעַ **The witnesses are not obligated to rend their garments.** "The witnesses in a case involving blasphemy are not required to rend their garments when they give their testimony in court, for they already rent their

TRANSLATION AND COMMENTARY

of God's name in these times, he **is not obligated to rend his garments,** [1]**for if you do not say this,** every **garment will be filled with rents.** The courts are no longer authorized to impose capital punishment, and as a result blasphemy has become rampant. The Gemara clarifies Rabbi Ḥiyya's position: [2]**If you say** that Rabbi Ḥiyya is dealing with blasphemy uttered **by a Jew, have Jews become so bold** and irreverent that they blaspheme God so frequently? [3]**Rather, it is obvious** that Rabbi Ḥiyya must be dealing with blasphemy uttered **by a non-Jew.** Now, with which divine name do the non-Jews blaspheme God? [4]**If** you say that they blaspheme God with **the Tetragrammaton,** there is a difficulty, for **did** non-Jews ever **learn** that name? Surely that is a divine name used only by Jews! [5]**Rather, is it not** that the non-Jews blaspheme God using one of His **substitute names?** Thus, Rabbi Ḥiyya says that if today someone hears a non-Jew blaspheming one of God's substitute names, he is not obligated to rend his garments. [6]**And** you may **infer from this** that it is only **in these times** that a person **is not obligated** to rend his garments upon hearing such blasphemy, because blasphemy has become so widespread. [7]**But previously** when blasphemy was infrequent, a person **was** indeed **obligated** to rend his garments, even if the blasphemy was uttered by a non-Jew, and even if it involved one of God's substitute names. [8]The Gemara concludes: Indeed, it is legitimate to **infer from this** that Rabbi Ḥiyya disagrees with Shmuel regarding both of these issues.

הַשֵּׁנִי אוֹמֵר [9]We learned in the Mishnah: **"The second** witness in a case involving blasphemy would not repeat what he had heard from the blasphemer, but rather he **would say: 'I also** heard just **like** the first witness.'" [10]**Resh Lakish said:** It is legitimate to **infer from this** ruling that by Torah law, testimony in the form of **"I also** saw or heard **like** the other witness," [11]**is valid** both **in monetary cases and in capital cases,** [12]**and** that it was **the Sages** who **instituted a higher standard** regarding testimony, and obligated each of the witnesses to state explicitly what he saw or heard. [13]And **here** in a case involving blasphemy **where it is**

LITERAL TRANSLATION

a mention [of God's name] in these times is not obligated to rend [his garments], [1]for if you do not say this, the garment will be filled with rents. From who? [2]If you say from a Jew, are they so bold? [3]Rather, it is obvious from a non-Jew. [4]And if the Tetragrammaton, did they learn [it]? [5]Rather, is it not a substitute name? [6]And infer from this, in these times he is not [obligated], [7]but from the beginning, he was obligated. [8]Infer from this.

[9]"And the second one would say: 'I too like him.'" [10]Resh Lakish said: Infer from this: "I too like him" — [11]is valid in monetary cases and in capital cases. [12]And the Sages made a higher standard, [13]and here because it is not possible,

אַזְכָּרָה בַּזְּמָן הַזֶּה אֵינוֹ חַיָּיב לִקְרוֹעַ, [1]שֶׁאִם אִי אַתָּה אוֹמֵר כֵּן, נִתְמַלֵּא כָּל הַבֶּגֶד קְרָעִים. מִמַּאן? [2]אִילֵימָא מִיִּשְׂרָאֵל, מִי פְּקִירִי כּוּלֵּי הַאי? [3]אֶלָּא פְּשִׁיטָא מִנׇּכְרִי. [4]וְאִי שֵׁם הַמְיוּחָד, מִי גְּמִירִי? [5]אֶלָּא לָאו בְּכִינּוּי? [6]וּשְׁמַע מִינָּהּ, בַּזְּמַן הַזֶּה הוּא דְּלָא, [7]הָא מֵעִיקָּרָא, חַיָּיב. [8]שְׁמַע מִינָּהּ.

[9]״הַשֵּׁנִי אוֹמֵר: ׳אַף אֲנִי כָּמוֹהוּ׳״. [10]אָמַר רֵישׁ לָקִישׁ: שְׁמַע מִינָּהּ: ״אַף אֲנִי כְּמוֹהוּ״ — [11]כָּשֵׁר בְּדִינֵי מָמוֹנוֹת וּבְדִינֵי נְפָשׁוֹת. [12]וּמַעֲלָה הוּא דַּעֲבִיד רַבָּנַן, [13]וְהָכָא כֵּיוָן דְּלֹא אֶפְשָׁר,

RASHI

בזמן הזה — שאנו בגלות ואין אימת בית דין מוטלת עליהם לדון חייבי מיתות. נתמלא כל הבגד קרעים — לפי שהדבר תדיר, לפי שאין מתיראין מבית דין. מי גמירי — נכרי שם המיוחד כל כך שמקללין בו תמיד, דקאמר נתמלא כל הבגד כולו קרעים. אלא לאו בכנוי — תדיר, ובזמן הזה הוא דלא קרעינן משום דנתמלא כל הבגד וכו׳, אבל בזמן בית דין — קורעין על נכרי ואכנוי. ומעלה הוא דעבוד רבנן — בדיני ממונות ודיני נפשות, שהצריכו כל העדים לפרש עדותן. הכא — בברכת השם דלא אפשר לפרש מפני כבוד השם.

NOTES

likened God to the gods of the other countries (II Kings 18:35): "Which of all the gods of the countries, have delivered their country out of my hand, that the Lord should deliver Jerusalem out of my hand?"

HALAKHAH

garments when they heard the blasphemer cursing God." (*Rambam, Sefer Shofetim, Hilkhot Evel* 9:8; *Shulḥan Arukh, Yoreh De'ah* 340:37.)

אַף אֲנִי כָּמוֹהוּ I too like him. "If the first witness offered his testimony, and the second witness said, 'I too saw or heard the same just like the first witness,' this is valid testimony according to Torah law (see *Rama, Shulḥan Arukh, Ḥoshen Mishpat* 28:10). But the Rabbis enacted that each witness must state his testimony explicitly. In a case of blasphemy, where it is preferable not to repeat the blasphemy unnecessarily, we rely on the Torah law and allow the second witness to say, 'I heard the same just like the first witness.'" (*Rambam, Sefer Shofetim, Hilkhot Edut* 20:4.)

[1]אוּקְמוּהָ רַבָּנַן אַדְּאוֹרַיְיתָא. [2]דְּאִי סָלְקָא דַּעֲתָךְ פָּסוּל, [3]הָכָא מִשּׁוּם דְּלָא אֶפְשָׁר קָטְלִינַן לְגַבְרָא? [4]״וְהַשְּׁלִישִׁי אוֹמֵר: ״אַף אֲנִי כָּמוֹהוּ״. [5]סְתָמָא כְּרַבִּי עֲקִיבָא, [6]דְּמַקִּישׁ שְׁלֹשָׁה לִשְׁנַיִם.

[60B] **משנה** [7]הָעוֹבֵד עֲבוֹדָה זָרָה, [8]אֶחָד הָעוֹבֵד, וְאֶחָד הַמְזַבֵּחַ, וְאֶחָד הַמְקַטֵּר, וְאֶחָד הַמְנַסֵּךְ, [9]וְאֶחָד הַמִּשְׁתַּחֲוֶה, וְאֶחָד הַמְקַבְּלוֹ עָלָיו לֶאֱלוֹהַּ,

LITERAL TRANSLATION

[1]the Sages stood it on Torah law. [2]For if it enters your mind [that it is] invalid, [3]here because it is not possible we kill a person?

[4]"And the third one would say: 'I too like him.'" [5]The anonymous [Tanna] is like Rabbi Akiva, [6]who compares three to two.

[60B] MISHNAH [7]Someone who worships an idol, [8]whether he worships, or sacrifices, or burns incense, or offers a libation, [9]or bows, or accepts it upon himself as a god,

TRANSLATION AND COMMENTARY

not possible to do so, for we do not want the blasphemous utterance to be unnecessarily repeated, [1]**the Sages stood** the matter **on Torah law,** and allowed the second witness to say: "I also heard just like the first witness."

[2]Know that this is so, **for if you think** that testimony in that form is **invalid** by Torah law, there is a difficulty. [3]Can it be that **here, because it is not possible** to repeat the blasphemous utterance, **we put** the blasphemer **to death** on the basis of testimony that is not valid by Torah law?

וְהַשְּׁלִישִׁי אוֹמֵר [4]Our Mishnah continues: "If there was **a third** witness, he too **would say: 'I also** heard just **like** the first witness.'" [5]The Gemara notes: **The anonymous Tanna** of our Mishnah **agrees with Rabbi Akiva,** [6]**who compares** a case involving **three** witnesses **to** a case involving **two** witnesses: with two witnesses, if one of the two was found to be closely related to the accused or otherwise disqualified from giving testimony, their testimony is invalid, for there is now only one qualified witness. Similarly with three witnesses, if one of the three was found to be closely related to the accused or to one of the other witnesses or otherwise disqualified from giving testimony, the testimony of all three is invalid, even though there are still two other competent witnesses. The ineligibility of any one witness invalidates the evidence of the whole group. The anonymous Tanna of our Mishnah similarly maintains that just as the first two witnesses must state explicitly what they heard the blasphemer say (either repeating his words, or saying "I also heard just like the first witness"), so too the third witness must state explicitly what he heard the blasphemer say.

[60B] **MISHNAH** הָעוֹבֵד עֲבוֹדָה זָרָה [7]The Torah states (Deuteronomy 17:2-5): "If there be found among you...a man or a woman, who has committed wickedness...and has gone and served other gods and bowed down to them...then shall you bring forth that man or that woman...and you shall stone that man or that woman with stones till they die." Thus, we see that an idolater is liable to death by stoning, as was also taught earlier in the chapter (53a). Our Mishnah clarifies what types of idol worship are punishable by stoning: **Someone who worships an idol** is liable to death by stoning, [8]**whether he worships** the idol, **or offers** it **a sacrifice,** or **burns incense** before it, **or offers** it **a libation** of wine, [9]**or bows down** before it, **or accepts it upon**

RASHI

אוקמוה אדאורייתא — וקטלינן ליה בהאי עדות. דאי סלקא דעתך — בעלמא פסול עד שיפרשו כולם. אטו הכא משום דלא אפשר קטלינן ליה לגברא — בלא העדאת עדים? כרבי עקיבא — במסכת מכות (ה,א) דמקיש שלשה לשנים, דאם נמצא שלישי קרוב או פסול — עדות של כולן בטלין. הלכך בדקינן ליה בהדייהו דאי מתזם או מתכחש — מבטלין לסהדותייהו.

משנה אחד העובד — מפרש בגמרא. אחד המזבח ואחד המקטר וכו׳ — ובגמרא מוקים לה לכולה מתניתין בשאין דרכה של אותה עבודה זרה לעבדה בכך, ואפילו הכי אהנך עבודות מיחייב, כדיליף לה בברייתא. והמקבלו עליו באלוה — ואפילו אמירה בעלמא, כגון האומר לו: אלי אתה, דאיתקש לזביחה, דכתיב (שמות לב) ״וישתחוו לו ויזבחו לו ויאמרו אלה אלהיך ישראל״. לישנא אחרינא: והמקבלו לאלוה — שלא בפניו, והאומר לו אלי אתה — בפניו, ותנא סיפא לגלויי רישא דאי תנא רישא הוה אמינא הני מילי בפניו, אבל שלא בפניו — לא, תנא סיפא בפניו מכלל דרישא שלא בפניו — ואפילו הכי חייב.

NOTES

הַמְקַבְּלוֹ עָלָיו לֶאֱלוֹהַּ, וְהָאוֹמֵר לוֹ: ״אֵלִי אַתָּה״ **Someone who accepts it upon himself as a god, or says to it: "You are my god."** Someone who accepts an idol as a god, or says to the idol: "You are my god," is liable to death by stoning, even though he violated a prohibition that does not involve an action, for the distinction between negative commandments that involve an action, and negative commandments that do not involve an action only applies regarding lashes.

HALAKHAH

הָעוֹבֵד עֲבוֹדָה זָרָה **Someone who worships an idol.** "If someone worships an idol in the usual manner in which other idolaters worship the idol, or if he offers a sacrifice to the idol, or burns incense before it, or offers it a libation of wine, or bows down before it, even if that is not the usual manner in which the idol is served, he is liable to death by stoning." (*Rambam, Sefer Mada, Hilkhot Avodah Zarah* 3:3.)

הַמְקַבְּלוֹ עָלָיו **Someone who accepts it upon himself.** "If someone accepts an idol upon himself as a god, for

TRANSLATION AND COMMENTARY

himself as a god, [1]or says to it: "You are my god." [2]But if he embraces the idol, or kisses it, or sweeps the floor before it, or sprinkles water on the floor before it in order to keep down the dust, or washes the idol, [3]or anoints it with oil, or dresses it, or puts its shoes on, [4]he violates the negative commandment (Exodus 20:5): "You shall not serve them," but those acts of veneration are not punishable by death. [5]If someone takes a vow in an idol's name, denying himself benefit from a certain object or person, or if he swears in the idol's name, [6]he violates the negative commandment (Exodus 23:13): "And make no mention of the name of other gods." [7]If he relieves himself before the idol called Ba'al Pe'or, he is liable to death by stoning, for that is the usual manner in which other idolators worship it. [8]Similarly, if he casts stones on the Roman deity called Marculis, he is liable to death by stoning, for that is the usual manner in which other idolaters worship it.

GEMARA מַאי "אֶחָד הָעוֹבֵד"? [9]The Gemara asks: What does the Mishnah mean when it states that the idol worshipper is liable to death by stoning "whether he worships the idol," or he serves it in any of the ways specified in the Mishnah? Surely all the specific ways of serving the idol mentioned in the Mishnah are forms of worship!

[1]וְהָאוֹמֵר לוֹ: "אֵלִי אַתָּה". [2]אֲבָל הַמְגַפֵּף, וְהַמְנַשֵּׁק, וְהַמְכַבֵּד, וְהַמְרַבֵּץ, וְהַמְרַחֵץ, וְהַסָּךְ, [3]וְהַמַּלְבִּישׁ, וְהַמַּנְעִיל, [4]עוֹבֵר בְּלֹא תַעֲשֶׂה. [5]הַנּוֹדֵר בִּשְׁמוֹ וְהַמְקַיֵּים בִּשְׁמוֹ, [6]עוֹבֵר בְּלֹא תַעֲשֶׂה. [7]הַפּוֹעֵר עַצְמוֹ לְבַעַל פְּעוֹר, זוֹ הִיא עֲבוֹדָתָהּ. [8]הַזּוֹרֵק אֶבֶן לְמַרְקוּלִיס, זוֹ הִיא עֲבוֹדָתָהּ.

גמרא [9]מַאי "אֶחָד הָעוֹבֵד"?

LITERAL TRANSLATION

[1]or says to it: "You are my god." [2]But [if] he embraces, or kisses, or sweeps, or sprinkles, or washes, or anoints, [3]or dresses, or puts on shoes, [4]he violates a negative commandment. [5][If] he takes a vow in its name, or swears in its name, [6]he violates a negative commandment. [7][If] he relieves himself before Ba'al Pe'or, that is its [way of] worship. [8][If] he casts a stone on a Marculis, that is its [way of] worship.

GEMARA [9]What is [meant by] "whether he worships"?

RASHI

אבל המגפף והמנשק – שלא כדרכה. **עובר בלא תעשה** – ד"לא תעבדם" יתירא כתיבי, חד בדברות ראשונות ואחרונות, וחד "לא תשתחוה לאלהיהם ולא תעבדם ולא תעשה כמעשיהם" (שמות כג) – אם אינו ענין לכדרכה. תנהו ענין לשלא כדרכה, אבל מיתה לא מיחייב בשלא כדרכה אלא הני דפרט בהו קרא. **הנודר בשמו** – בלשון נדר: קונם עלי כל פירות שבעולם בשם עבודה זרה פלונית אם ארחץ. **והמקיים בשמו** = שבועה, נשבע מתרגם: מקיים. **עובר בלא תעשה** – "ושם אלהים אחרים לא תזכירו" (שם). **הפוער עצמו** – מתריז רעי בפניו, וזהו עבודתו – וחייב עליו מיתה. **מרקוליס** – מגדדין שלש אבנים אחת מכאן ואחת מכאן ואחת מלמעלה על גביהן וקורין אותם מרקולים, ועובדין אותה בזריקת האבנים.

גמרא מאי אחד העובד – אטו כל הני לאו עובד נינהו.

BACKGROUND

הַמְרַחֵץ **The washer of an idol.**

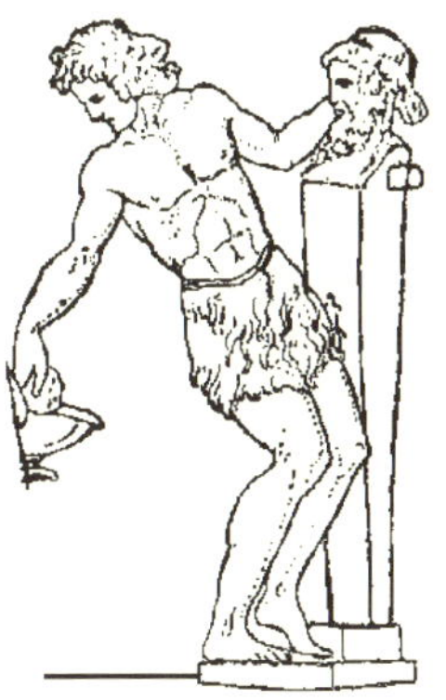

Section of a Roman frieze showing a man washing the statue of Mercury.

מַרְקוּלִיס **Marculis.** This is the name given by the Sages to the Roman god Mercury, known as Hermes in Greek mythology. Among his many attributes he was held to be the patron of roads and journeys. Hence statues of Mercury were often placed at the start of roads, usually unfinished and symbolic figures (a herm, as in the illustration above). Wayfarers used to place stones next to these statues. Sometimes a pile of stones served as a symbol of this god, and every passerby would place a stone on it as an offering.

NOTES

But the death penalty may be imposed for a capital offense, even if the offender violated the prohibition without performing an action (*Arukh LeNer*).

הָאוֹמֵר לוֹ: "אֵלִי אַתָּה" **Someone who says to it: "You are my god."** According to *Rashi*, the Mishnah mentions someone who says to an idol: You are my god, as an example of someone who accepts an idol as a god. *Ramah* argues that it was necessary for the Mishnah to specify that such an offender was liable. Otherwise we might have thought that he is exempt, since that formulation is a statement of fact, not an expression of acceptance of the idol as a god. The wording of that statement is based on the verse (Isaiah 44:17): "Deliver me, for you are my god."

הַנּוֹדֵר בִּשְׁמוֹ וְהַמְקַיֵּים בִּשְׁמוֹ **If he takes a vow in its name, or swears in its name.** Even though the prohibitions against taking a vow and swearing in an idol's name are derived from the verse (Exodus 23:13): "And make no mention of the name of other gods," and so a person is liable as soon as he mentions the idol's name, even if he does not swear or take a vow, the Mishnah teaches us that if a person took a vow or swore in the idol's name, he is not liable to the death penalty, even though what he did is similar to accepting the idol as a god (*Meiri*).

הַמְקַיֵּים בִּשְׁמוֹ **If he swears in its name.** *Ramah* understands that the Mishnah refers to a case where someone forbid another a person from enjoying certain benefit by way of a vow taken in an idol's name, and that other person accepted upon himself to fulfill the vow.

HALAKHAH

example, if he says to an idol, 'You are my god,' he is liable to death by stoning." (*Rambam, Sefer Mada, Hilkhot Avodah Zarah* 3:4.)

הַמְגַפֵּף, וְהַמְנַשֵּׁק **If he embraces, or kisses it.** "If someone embraces an idol, or kisses it, or sweeps the floor before it, or sprinkles water on the floor before it, or washes it, or anoints it with oil, or dresses it, or puts its shoes on, or shows it honor in some other way, he violates the negative commandment, 'You shall not serve them.'" (*Rambam, Sefer Mada, Hilkhot Avodah Zarah* 3:6.)

הַנּוֹדֵר בִּשְׁמוֹ **If he takes a vow in its name.** "If someone takes a vow in the name of an idol, or if he swears in the idol's name, he is liable to be punished by flogging for having violated the negative commandment, 'And make no mention of the name of other gods.'" (*Rambam, Sefer Mada, Hilkhot Avodah Zarah* 5:10.)

[1]אָמַר רַבִּי יִרְמְיָה: הָכִי קָאָמַר: [2]אֶחָד הָעוֹבֵד כְּדַרְכָּהּ, וְאֶחָד הַמְזַבֵּחַ, וְאֶחָד הַמְקַטֵּר, וְאֶחָד הַמְנַסֵּךְ, וְאֶחָד הַמִּשְׁתַּחֲוֶה, [3]וַאֲפִילּוּ שֶׁלֹּא כְּדַרְכָּהּ.
[4]וְלִיחְשׁוֹב נַמִי זוֹרֵק!
[5]אָמַר אַבַּיֵי: זוֹרֵק הַיְינוּ מְנַסֵּךְ, [6]דִּכְתִיב: "בַּל אַסִּיךְ נִסְכֵּיהֶם מִדָּם".
[7]מְנָהָנֵי מִילֵּי? [8]דְּתָנוּ רַבָּנַן: "אִילּוּ נֶאֱמַר 'זֹבֵחַ יָחֳרָם', [9]הָיִיתִי אוֹמֵר: בְּזוֹבֵחַ קָדָשִׁים בַּחוּץ הַכָּתוּב מְדַבֵּר. [10]תַּלְמוּד לוֹמַר: 'לָאֱלֹהִים' — בְּזוֹבֵחַ

LITERAL TRANSLATION

[1]Rabbi Yirmeyah said: He said as follows: [2]Whether he worships it in its usual manner, or sacrifices, or burns incense, or offers a libation, or bows, [3]even if that is not its usual manner.

[4]Then count also someone who sprinkles!

[5]Abaye said: Sprinkling is libating, [6]as it is written: "Their drink offerings of blood will I not offer."

[7]From where are these things [derived]? [8]As our Rabbis taught: "Had it stated: 'He that sacrifices shall be utterly destroyed,' [9]I would have said: The verse is talking about someone who offers sacrifices outside. [10][Therefore] the Torah states: 'To any god' —

TRANSLATION AND COMMENTARY

אָמַר רַבִּי יִרְמְיָה [1]**Rabbi Yirmeyah said:** The Mishnah means to **say as follows:** [2]The idol worshipper is liable to death by stoning **whether he worships** the idol **in the usual manner** in which other idolaters worship that specific idol — **or he offers a sacrifice** to the idol, **or burns incense** before it, **or offers** it **a libation** of wine, **or bows down** before it, [3]**even if that is not the usual manner** in which other idolaters worship that idol, for this is how God is worshipped in the Temple.

וְלִיחְשׁוֹב נַמִי זוֹרֵק [4]The Gemara asks: If so, **then** why not **also count sprinkling** sacrificial blood on the altar among the modes of worship for which the idol worshipper is liable to be executed, even if the particular idol which he worshipped is not usually served in that manner?

אָמַר אַבַּיֵי [5]**Abaye said: Sprinkling** sacrificial blood **is** in fact included in the Mishnah under the heading of **libation,** for we find that the sprinkling of blood can also be referred to as a libation, [6]**as the verse states** (Psalms 16:4): **"Their drink offerings of blood will I not offer."**

מְנָהָנֵי מִילֵּי? [7]The Gemara asks: **From where** do we derive **this regulation** that an idolater is liable to be executed if he served his false god in the same manner in which God is worshipped in the Temple? [8]The Gemara explains: **As our Rabbis taught** in a Baraita: "The verse states (Exodus 22:19): 'He that sacrifices to any god, save to the Lord only, he shall be utterly destroyed.' **Had** the verse **stated** only: **'He that sacrifices shall be utterly destroyed,'** [9]**I might have said** that **the verse is dealing with someone who offered a sacrifice outside** the Temple. We find elsewhere that the Torah forbids the offering of sacrifices outside the Temple, and I might have said that here the Torah teaches that the crime is punishable by execution. [10]**Therefore the Torah added** the words: **'To any god,'** teaching that **the**

RASHI

אחד העובד — כל עבודה, אף גפוף ונשוק, אף דרך בזיון בכדרכה, וחייב מיתה דכתיב "וילך ויעבוד אלהים אחרים" וכתיב בתריה "וסקלתם באבנים". ואזהרתיה מהכא "ופן תדרוש לאלוהיהם לאמר איכה יעבדו הגויים האלה את אלהיהם" וגו׳ (דברים יב) דהיינו בכדרכה. **ואחד המזבח** — אפילו שלא כדרכה בעבודות הללו, כדיליף לקמן דכל עבודות הנעשות בפנים לגבוה חייבין עליה מיתה בעבודה זרה — אפילו שלא כדרכה. **ולחשוב נמי זורק** — דבשלמא מקבל ומוליך לא קשיא לן אף על גב דעבודת פנים הם — דלא אשכחן דלהוו עבודות הנעשות לשם עבודה זרה כדאשכחן הנך, זביחה — "ויזבחו לו" (שמות לב), קטור — "אשר חלב זבחימו יאכלו" (דברים לב), ניסוך — "ישתו יין נסיכם" (שם). ומיהו דם אשכחן בעבודה זרה "בל אסיך נסכיהם מדם", וכיון דגמרינן דכל עבודות פנים חייבין בהם אף שלא כדרכה, נתנייה נמי! **אמר אביי זורק בכלל ניסוך** — דמתניתין, דהא קרא נמי ניסוך קרייה. **מנא הני מילי** — דמחייב בהני עבודות אף בשלא כדרכה. **אילו נאמר זובח יחרם הייתי אומר** — באיזו זביחה בא הכתוב לענוש מיתה — ודאי בזובח קדשים בחוץ קאמר, שמלינו שהזהיר עליהם במקום אחר. ולקמן פריך: הרי כבר פרשו להם עונש אחר "ונכרתה" דכתיב גבי שחוטי חוץ. **תלמוד לומר לאלהים יחרם** — דבא הכתוב לעונשו מיתה, דהאי "יחרם" — לשון מיתה, דכתיב (ויקרא כז) "כל חרם אשר יחרם מן האדם לא יפדה מות יומת", זובח לאלהים — כל אלהים במשמע, ואפילו שלא כדרכה, מדלא כתביה בלשון עבודה עובד לאלהים בזביחה יחרם — שמע מינה אפילו אינה עבודה שלו קאמר. וכל עבודות שבעולם לכדרכה נפקא לן בהו מיתה מ"וילך ויעבוד וגו׳" דמשמע דבר שהוא עבודה לו.

HALAKHAH

הָעוֹבֵד כְּדַרְכָּהּ **He worships it in its usual manner.** "An idol worshipper is only liable if he worships the idol in the usual manner in which other idolaters serve it. This applies to modes of worship other than offering a sacrifice to the idol, burning incense before it, offering it a libation, and bowing down to the idol. But if he served the idol in one of those ways, he is liable even if the idol is not usually served in that manner." (*Rambam, Sefer Mada, Hilkhot Avodah Zarah* 3:3.)

זוֹרֵק **He sprinkles.** "If someone sprinkles sacrificial blood before an idol, he is liable to death by stoning, even if the idol is not usually served in that manner, for the sprinkling of sacrificial blood is treated like a libation of wine." (*Rambam, Sefer Mada, Hilkhot Avodah Zarah* 3:3.)

זוֹבֵחַ קָדָשִׁים בַּחוּץ **Someone who offers sacrifices outside.** "Someone who intentionally offers a sacrifice outside the Temple is liable for excision." (*Rambam, Sefer Avodah, Hilkhot Ma'aseh Korbanot* 18:2.)

TRANSLATION AND COMMENTARY

verse is dealing with someone who offers a sacrifice to an idol. The idolater is liable to be executed no matter which idol he worshipped, even if that particular idol is not usually served through sacrifice. And had the verse stated only: 'He that sacrifices to any god shall be utterly destroyed,' [1]**I would only know** that **someone who offers a sacrifice** to an idol is liable to be executed, even if that is not the idol's usual form of worship. [2]**From where do I know** that **someone who burns incense** before the idol **or offers** it **a libation** of wine is also liable to be executed, even if that particular idol is not usually worshiped that way? [3]Therefore **the Torah states:** 'He that sacrifices to any god, **save to the Lord only,** shall be utterly destroyed.' [4]Thus, the Torah **designated all the modes of worship to the Lord.** Consequently, someone who worshipped an idol the way God is worshipped is liable to be executed, even if that is not how other idolaters usually worship that idol. Elsewhere the Torah states (Deuteronomy 17:2-5): 'If there be found among you...a man or a woman, who has committed wickedness...and has gone and served other gods...then shall you bring forth that man or that woman...and you shall stone that man or that woman with stones till they die.' Now, this ruling seems to imply that an idolater is liable to death by stoning no matter how he served the false god. Yet the Torah states once again: "He that sacrifices to any god, save to the Lord only, shall be utterly destroyed," singling out idol worship through sacrifice. One of the hermeneutic principles for deriving legal rulings from the Torah states: A specific commandment that was included in a generalization, but was specified to teach something, was intended to teach not just about itself, but about the entire generalization. Thus, when the Torah singles out worship through sacrifice, it means to say that the generalization stated elsewhere applies only to worship that is similar to the offering of a sacrifice, which was performed in the inner Temple, like burning of incense and libation of wine. [5]Now, **if** worship through **sacrifice was specified** in order **to teach** that the idolater is liable to be executed if he served the idol in one of the **modes of worship** practiced **in the inner Temple,** [6]**from where do I know to add** that someone who **bowed** down to an idol is also liable to be executed, even if that idol was not usually served in that manner? This does not follow from the general rule regarding idol worship which was modified by the specific rule regarding worship through sacrifice, for bowing down before God is not a mode of worship practiced in the inner Temple. [7]Therefore, **the verse states:** 'If there be found among you...a man or a woman, who has committed wickedness...**and has gone and served other gods and bowed down to them."** [8]**And** the **following** verse states: **'Then shall you bring forth that man** or that woman...and you shall stone that man or that woman with stones till they die.' This teaches that someone who bowed down to

לַעֲבוֹדָה זָרָה הַכָּתוּב מְדַבֵּר. [1]אֵין לִי אֶלָּא בְּזוֹבֵחַ, [2]מְקַטֵּר וּמְנַסֵּךְ מִנַּיִן? [3]תַּלְמוּד לוֹמַר: ׳בִּלְתִּי לַה׳ לְבַדּוֹ׳ — [4]רִיקֵּן הָעֲבוֹדוֹת כּוּלָּן לַשֵּׁם הַמְיוּחָד. [5]לְפִי שֶׁיָּצְאָה זְבִיחָה לִידּוֹן בַּעֲבוֹדוֹת פְּנִים, [6]מְנַּיִין לְרַבּוֹת הִשְׁתַּחֲוָאָה? [7]תַּלְמוּד לוֹמַר: ׳וַיֵּלֶךְ וַיַּעֲבֹד אֱלֹהִים אֲחֵרִים וַיִּשְׁתַּחוּ לָהֶם׳, [8]וּסְמִיךְ לֵיהּ: ׳וְהוֹצֵאתָ אֶת הָאִישׁ הַהוּא

LITERAL TRANSLATION

the verse is talking about someone who sacrifices to an idol. [1]I have only someone who sacrifices. [2]From where [do I have] someone who burns incense or offers a libation? [3]The Torah states: 'Save to the Lord only' — [4]it designated all the [modes of] worship to the Lord (lit., 'the special name [of the Lord]'). [5]Since sacrificing was specified to teach about [modes of] worship in the inner Temple, [6]from where [do I know] to add bowing? [7]The Torah states: 'And he went, and served other gods, and bowed before them.' [8]And following it: 'Then shall you remove that man,

RASHI

בלתי לה׳ לבדו — ריקן ונטל כל העבודות מלעבדה בהן, ונתנן לשם המיוחד משמע דאכל עבודות הראויות לשם קאמר. **לפי שיצאה זביחה** — בפירוש מכלל שאר עבודות שנכללו בכלל ״וילך ויעבוד״, ומדה היא בתורה דדבר שהוא בכלל ויצא מן הכלל ללמד לא ללמד על עצמו יצא — אלא ללמד על הכלל כולו יצא, שאין הכלל הזה מחייב אלא עבודה הדומה לזבוח — שהוא עבודת פנים, ומהשתא לא נפקא לן דליחייב אהשתחואה שלא כדרכה — דלאו עבודה היא בפנים, מניין לרבות השתחואה? הכי גרסינן בסיפרי **תלמוד לומר וילך ויעבוד אלהים אחרים וישתחו להם** — דעל כרחיך לשלא כדרכה קאמר, — דאי דרכה לעבדה בכך — בכלל ״ויעבוד״ הוא.

NOTES

מְקַטֵּר וּמְנַסֵּךְ מִנַּיִן **From where do I have someone who burns incense or offers a libation.** We might have distinguished between slaughtering a sacrifice for an idol and burning incense before it or offering it a libation, because slaughtering a sacrifice involves sacrificial blood and might have been considered a more serious mode of worship than burning incense or offering a libation. Thus we might have thought that someone who burns incense to an idol or offers it a libation is only liable to death by stoning, if that is the usual manner in which other idolaters serve the idol (*Rabbenu Yonah*).

רִיקֵּן הָעֲבוֹדוֹת כּוּלָּן **It designated all the modes of worship to the Lord.** *Ran* explains that the words "Save to the Lord only," teach that any mode of worship in which God is

וגו׳׳. [1]עוֹנֶשׁ — שָׁמַעְנוּ, [2]אַזְהָרָה מִנַּיִין? [3]תַּלְמוּד לוֹמַר: ׳כִּי לֹא תִשְׁתַּחֲוֶה לְאֵל אַחֵר׳. [4]יָכוֹל שֶׁאֲנִי מַרְבֶּה הַמְגַפֵּף וְהַמְנַשֵּׁק וְהַמְנְעִיל. [5]תַּלְמוּד לוֹמַר: ׳זֹבֵחַ׳ — זְבִיחָה בִּכְלָל הָיְתָה. [6]וְלָמָּה יָצְאָה? [7]לְהַקִּישׁ אֵלֶיהָ וְלוֹמַר לְךָ: [8]מַה זְּבִיחָה מְיוּחֶדֶת — שֶׁהִיא עֲבוֹדַת פְּנִים וְחַיָּיבִין עָלֶיהָ מִיתָה, [9]אַף כָּל שֶׁהִיא עֲבוֹדַת פְּנִים — וְחַיָּיבִין עָלֶיהָ מִיתָה, [10]יָצְאָה הִשְׁתַּחֲוָאָה לִידּוֹן בְּעַצְמָהּ, [11]יָצְאָה זְבִיחָה

LITERAL TRANSLATION

etc.' [1]We have heard a punishment. [2]From where the warning? [3]The Torah states: 'For you shall not bow down to another god.' [4]I might have thought to add someone who embraces, kisses, or puts on shoes. [5][Therefore] the Torah states: 'He who sacrifices.' Sacrificing was in the generalization. [6]Why was it specified? [7]To compare to it and tell you: [8]Just as sacrifice is unique — for it is worship in the inner Temple and one is liable to be executed because of it, [9]so too any worship in the inner Temple — and one is liable to be executed because of them. [10]Bowing was specified to teach about itself. [11]Sacrifice was specified

TRANSLATION AND COMMENTARY

an idol is liable for execution, even if that idol is not usually served in that manner (for bowing down to the idol when that is its usual manner of worship is included in 'and has gone and served gods'). [1]**We have heard the punishment** that is imposed upon someone who bowed down to an idol. [2]But **where is the warning** teaching that the act is prohibited? An act is not a punishable criminal offense unless it was laid down in express terms in the Bible. It does not suffice for there to be a provision imposing a specific penalty. Not only must a specific penalty be imposed for the act, but the act itself must first be distinctly prohibited. Where then does the Torah state that bowing down to an idol is forbidden, even if that is not the usual manner of worshipping it? [3]This is learned from **the verse** which **states** (Exodus 34:14): **'For you shall not bow down to another god.'** [4]Now, **I might have thought** that bowing down to the idol was explicitly specified in order **to add** that **someone who embraces** an idol, or **kisses** it, **or puts** its **shoes on** is also liable for execution, even if that idol was not usually worshipped in that manner. For I might have thought that bowing down to the idol was explicitly specified in order to teach about the entire generalization. Just as bowing down to an idol is a respectful way of worshipping it, and someone who bows down to an idol is liable for execution, even if that is not the idol's usual manner of worship, so too embracing the idol, and kissing it, and putting its shoes on, are respectful ways of worshipping the it, and so the idolater who worships the idol in one of these ways should be liable to be executed, even if that is not the idol's usual manner of worship. [5]**Therefore, the Torah states: 'He that sacrifices** to any god, save the Lord only, he shall be utterly destroyed.' **Sacrifice was in the generalization,** as was explained above. If bowing down to an idol was specified in order to teach about the entire generalization, [6]**why** then **was** sacrifice **specified?** Surely all respectful modes of worship were already learned from bowing down to the idol! Rather, sacrifice was specified in order to teach about the entire generalization, that is, [7]**to compare** other modes of worship **to it and teach you:** [8]**Just as sacrifice is** a mode of **worship** practiced **in the inner Temple, and one is liable to be executed** if he served an idol in that manner, even if that is not the idol's usual manner of worship, [9]**so too** regarding **any** other mode of **worship** that is practiced **in the inner Temple, one is liable for execution** for serving an idol in that manner, even if that is not the idol's usual manner of worship. [10]Thus, **bowing** down to an idol **was specified** in order **to teach about itself,** that a person who bowed down to an idol which is usually not served in that manner is liable to be executed, even though bowing is not a mode of worship practiced in the inner Temple. [11]And offering a **sacrifice was** explicitly **specified** in order

RASHI

עונש שמענו — דכתיב ביה ״וסקלתם״ לעיל. **אזהרה מניין תלמוד לומר כי לא תשתחוה לאל אחר** — והאי נמי אם אינו ענין לכדרכה תנהו ענין לשלא כדרכה, וספרים דכתוב בהו ״(כי) לא תשתחוה״ שיבוש הוא, דהא מיתה הכא לא כתיבא. **יכול שאני מרבה וכו׳** — דנימא השתחואה שיצא מן הכלל ללמד על הכלל כולו יצא, דמה השתחואה מיוחד שהיא דרך כבוד וחייב עליה אף שלא כדרכה — אף כל שהוא דרך כבוד כגון אלו חייב. **תלמוד לומר זובח** — ואם השתחואה ללמד על הכלל באתה — למה פרט לך זביחה? — הלא דרך כבוד הוא ומהשתחואה נפקא ליה! — אלא היא באתה ללמד על הכלל; לומר לך: זביחה בכלל היתה ויצאה מן הכלל להקיש לה כל הנכללות עמה, ולומר לך: מה זביחה מיוחדת עבודת פנים, אף כל שהיא עבודת פנים חייבין עליה בחוץ לעבודה זרה. ומשום דהשתחואה לא נפקא לן מהכא לחיובא הוצרכה השתחואה לחזור ולצאת כדי לדון בעצמה לבדה שיתחייבו עליה, ואף על פי שאין חייבין כיוצא בה, ויצאה זביחה ללמד על הכלל כולו.

NOTES

served must be performed for God alone, and not for some other god, even if that other god is not usually worshipped in that manner. The words, "He that sacrifices to any god," are not needed for this derivation. They appear in the verse only because the words, "Save to the Lord only," cannot stand alone without some example of a mode of worship in which God is served.

לִידוֹן עַל הַכְּלָל כּוּלּוֹ.

[1]אָמַר מָר: הָיִיתִי אוֹמֵר בְּזוֹבֵחַ קֳדָשִׁים בַּחוּץ הַכָּתוּב מְדַבֵּר. [2]זוֹבֵחַ קֳדָשִׁים בַּחוּץ כָּרֵת הוּא! [3]סָלְקָא דַּעֲתָךְ אָמִינָא: כִּי אַתְרוּ בֵּיהּ — קְטָלָא, [4]כִּי לָא אַתְרוּ בֵּיהּ — כָּרֵת. [5]קָא מַשְׁמַע לָן. [6]אֲמַר לֵיהּ רָבָא בַּר רַב חָנָן לְאַבַּיֵי: אֵימָא יָצְאָה הִשְׁתַּחֲוָאָה לְלַמֵּד עַל הַכְּלָל כּוּלּוֹ. [7]וְכִי תֵּימָא זוֹבֵחַ לָמָּה לִי — [8]לְגוּפֵיהּ, [9]דִּמְחַשְּׁבִין מֵעֲבוֹדָה לַעֲבוֹדָה.

LITERAL TRANSLATION

to teach about the entire generalization. [1]The master said: "I would have said: The verse is talking about someone who offers sacrifices outside." [2]Someone who offers sacrifices outside is [liable for] excision! [3]It might have entered your mind to say: When they warned him — execution, [4]when they did not warn him — excision. [5][Therefore] it teaches us. [6]Rava bar Rav Ḥanan said to Abaye: Say that bowing was specified to teach about the entire generalization. [7]And if you say: Why do I need someone who sacrifices — [8]for itself, [9]that he can have in mind from one [part of the] service to [another part of the] service.

TRANSLATION AND COMMENTARY

to teach about the entire generalization, that if a person served an idol in a manner that God is worshipped in the inner Temple, he is liable to be executed, even if that is not the idol's usual manner of worship."

אָמַר מָר [1]**It was stated above** in the Baraita: "Had the verse stated only: 'He who sacrifices shall be utterly destroyed,' **I might have said** that **the verse is dealing with someone who offered a sacrifice outside** the Temple." The Gemara asks: How could anybody have thought that someone who offered a sacrifice outside the Temple is liable to be executed? [2]Surely, the Torah states explicitly that **someone who offers a sacrifice outside** the Temple **is liable for excision,** for the verses state (Leviticus 17:8-9): "Whatever man there be of the house of Israel...who offers a burnt offering or sacrifice, and brings it not to the door of the Tent of Meeting, to offer it to the Lord; that man shall be cut off from among his people."

סָלְקָא דַּעֲתָךְ [3]The Gemara explains: **You might have thought to say** that **if** the transgressor **was warned** not to bring a sacrifice outside the Temple, he is punishable by judicial **execution,** [4]and **if he was not given** such **a warning,** he is liable for **excision** at the hand of God. [5]**Therefore** the Baraita **teaches us** that this is not so, for a person who offered a sacrifice outside the Temple is not punishable by judicial execution, even if he was properly warned prior to committing the offense.

אָמַר לֵיהּ [6]**Rava bar Rav Ḥanan said to Abaye:** Why not **say that bowing** down to an idol **was** explicitly **specified** in order **to teach about the entire generalization?** Just as someone who bows down to an idol is liable for execution, even if that is not the idol's usual manner of worship, so too embracing the idol, and kissing it, and putting its shoes on, are respectful ways of worshipping the idol, and the idolater who worships the idol in one of these ways should be liable for execution, even if that is not the idol's usual manner of worship. [7]**And if you** should **say:** If so, **why** then **was it necessary** that **someone who offers a sacrifice** to the false god be mentioned explicitly as being liable to be executed — I will answer: [8]That was necessary **for itself.** It teaches us that a person is liable for offering a sacrifice to an idol, even if he did not slaughter the animal to the idol, but rather he slaughtered the animal for himself, having in mind that he would sprinkle the blood, or burn the animal's fat for an idol. [9]**For an** idolatrous **thought in one part of** the sacrificial **service regarding another part of that service** is indeed a thought for which the idolater can become liable.

RASHI

סלקא דעתך אמינא — האי "יחרם" אתא לאורויי לן דאי אתרו ביה לקטלא וכרת כי לא אתרו ביה הוא, כדלגבי שבת ועבודה זרה ועריות. הכי גרסינן: סלקא דעתך אמינא אתרו ביה קטלא ולא אתרו ביה כרת — קא משמע לן. אימא יצאה לן השתחואה ללמד על הכלל — ומתרבי מגפף ומנשק וכל שהוא דרך כבוד כהשתחואה. וקא קשיא ליה לתנא: אם כן "זובח" למאי אתא? — תיפוק ליה מהשתחואה דהא עבודת כבוד הוא! לגופיה אתא — ולאורויי דאפילו לא שחט שחיטת עצמו לעבודה זרה אלא שוחט לעצמו וחשב בה על מנת לזרוק דמה לעבודה זרה חייב, ואפילו לא זרק. דמחשבין מעבודה לעבודה — כלומר דמחשבה שהוא מחשב בשעת עבודה זו על עבודה אחרת — מחשבה היא להתחייב עליה.

HALAKHAH

מְחַשְּׁבִין מֵעֲבוֹדָה לַעֲבוֹדָה **He can have in mind from one part of the service to another part of the service.** "If someone slaughtered an animal having in mind to sprinkle its blood for an idol, or to burn the animal's fat for an idol, the animal is forbidden for benefit, for we learn the laws regarding improper thoughts involving non-consecrated animals slaughtered outside the Temple from the laws regarding improper thoughts involving consecrated animals slaughtered inside the Temple," following Rabbi Yoḥanan, against Resh Lakish. (*Rambam, Sefer Kedushah, Hilkhot Sheḥitah* 2:15; *Shulḥan Arukh, Yoreh De'ah* 4:1.)

[1]דְּאִיתְּמַר, הַשּׁוֹחֵט בְּהֵמָה לִזְרוֹק דָּמָהּ לַעֲבוֹדָה זָרָה, וּלְהַקְטִיר חֶלְבָּהּ לַעֲבוֹדָה זָרָה, [2]רַבִּי יוֹחָנָן אָמַר: [61A] [3]אֲסוּרָה. [4]וְרֵישׁ לָקִישׁ אָמַר: מוּתֶּרֶת. [5]הָנִיחָא לְרַבִּי יוֹחָנָן. [6]אֶלָּא לְרֵישׁ לָקִישׁ, [7]בָּעֵי קְרָא! [8]מַתְקִיף לָהּ רַב פַּפָּא: [9]וּלְרַבִּי יוֹחָנָן לָא בָּעֵי קְרָא? [10]עַד כָּאן לָא קָא אָסַר רַבִּי יוֹחָנָן אֶלָּא בְּהֵמָה. [11]אֲבָל גַּבְרָא לָא בַּר קְטָלָא הוּא, [12]וַאֲתָא קְרָא לְחַיּוּבֵי גַּבְרָא לִקְטָלָא.

LITERAL TRANSLATION

[1]For it was stated: [If] someone slaughters an animal [intending] to sprinkle its blood for an idol, or to burn its fat for an idol, [2]Rabbi Yoḥanan said: [61A] [3]It is forbidden. [4]And Resh Lakish said: It is permitted.

[5]Granted according to Rabbi Yoḥanan. [6]But according to Resh Lakish, [7]he needs the verse!

[8]Rav Pappa strongly objected: [9]And according to Rabbi Yoḥanan, he does not need the verse? [10]Up to here Rabbi Yoḥanan only forbade the animal. [11]But the man is not liable for execution. [12]And the verse comes to make the man liable for execution.

TRANSLATION AND COMMENTARY

דְּאִיתְּמַר [1]The Gemara continues: **For it was stated** that the Amoraim disagree about the following matter: **If someone slaughtered an animal** for himself, **having in mind to sprinkle its blood for an idol, or** intending **to burn** the animal's **fat for an idol,** [2]**Rabbi Yoḥanan said:** [61A] [3]The animal **is forbidden** for benefit, for benefit may not be derived from sacrifices offered to an idol. Even though the animal was not slaughtered for the idol, and its blood was not sprinkled for the idol, nor was its fat burned for the idol, the animal is still forbidden for benefit. According to Rabbi Yoḥanan, the laws regarding sacrifices offered to an idol are derived from the laws regarding sacrifices offered to God. If, while engaged in bringing a sacrifice to God, a priest expresses his intention of sprinkling the blood of the sacrifice, or burning it on the altar, or eating it after the appropriate time, this intention disqualifies the sacrifice and renders it a *piggul*, an offering disqualified by improper intention. Similarly, an idolatrous thought can render an animal forbidden for benefit. [4]**Resh Lakish** disagreed with Rabbi Yoḥanan and **said:** The animal **is permitted,** for we do not learn the laws regarding idolatry from the laws regarding *piggul*.

הָנִיחָא [5]The Gemara continues: **Granted** that we understand the Baraita cited above **according to Rabbi Yoḥanan**. Rabbi Yoḥanan can also learn from the laws of *piggul* that an idolatrous thought in one part of the sacrificial service regarding another part of the sacrificial service can render the person who brought the sacrifice liable to be executed for having committed idolatry. If his view is accepted, the verse, "He that sacrifices to any god, save to the Lord only, shall be utterly destroyed," is available to teach about the entire generalization: If a person served an idol in a manner that God is worshiped in the inner Temple, he is liable to be executed. [6]**But according to Resh Lakish,** there is a difficulty, for he does not learn the laws regarding idolatry from the laws regarding *piggul*. [7]Thus **he needs the verse,** "He that sacrifices to any god," to teach that an idolatrous thought in one part of the sacrificial service regarding another part of the sacrificial service can render the person who brought the sacrifice liable to be executed for having committed idolatry! Since the verse is needed for that purpose, it is no longer available to teach us about the entire generalization. Thus, according to Resh Lakish, one may say that bowing down to an idol was explicitly specified in order to teach about the entire generalization, and so a person should be liable to be executed if he worshiped an idol by embracing it, or kissing it, or putting on its shoes, even if those are not the usual manners in which the idol is worshiped, as was argued by Rava bar Rav Ḥanan!

מַתְקִיף לָהּ [8]**Rav Pappa strongly objected** to what the Gemara said that according to Rabbi Yoḥanan there is no room for Rava bar Rav Ḥanan's question: [9]Is it true that **Rabbi Yoḥanan does not need the verse,** "He that sacrifices to any god," for some other purpose? [10]But surely **Rabbi Yoḥanan only forbade the animal,** saying that an idolatrous thought in one part of the sacrificial service regarding another part of that service can render the slaughtered animal forbidden for benefit. [11]**But** I might have thought that **the man** who offered the idolatrous sacrifice **is not liable to be executed.** [12]**And** therefore it was necessary for **the verse** to **come** and **teach** us **that the man** who offered the sacrifice and had an idolatrous thought **is** indeed **liable to be executed** for having committed idolatry. Thus, Rava bar Rav Ḥanan's question is valid even according to Rabbi Yoḥanan!

RASHI

אסורה – הבהמה בהנאה, ואף על פי שהשחיטה לאו לעבודה זרה היתה, ואפילו לא זרק דמה לעבודה זרה נאסרה, וילפינן טעמא בשחיטת חולין דגמר לה רבי יוחנן ממחשבת פגול דהויא מעבודה לעבודה, דהשוחט את הזבח על מנת לזרוק את הדם למחר – פיגול. **וריש לקיש אמר מותרת** – לא יליף חוץ מפנים, אין מחשבין מעבודה לעבודה. **הניחא** – הא דמייתר לן זובח ללמד על הכלל, ולא מוקמינן לה האי דרשא לומר שמחשב מעבודה לעבודה. הא ניחא לרבי יוחנן דנפקא ליה לענין איסורי ממחשבת פיגול – איכא למימר דלענין איחויבי גברא נמי מהתם יליף, ועל כרחיך אייתר ליה זובח, אלא לריש לקיש דלא יליף עבודה זרה מפיגול – נימא דהאי זובח להכי הוא דאתא, שמחשבין מעבודה לעבודה.

LITERAL TRANSLATION

[1]מַתְקִיף לָהּ רַב אַחָא בְּרֵיהּ דְּרַב אִיקָא: [2]וּלְרֵישׁ לָקִישׁ מִי בָּעֵי קְרָא? [3]עַד כָּאן לָא קָא שָׁרֵי רֵישׁ לָקִישׁ אֶלָּא בְּהֵמָה. [4]אֲבָל גַּבְרָא בַּר קְטָלָא הוּא, [5]מִידֵּי דַּהֲוָה אַמִּשְׁתַּחֲוֶה לְהַר, [6]דְּהַר מוּתָּר, [7]וְעוֹבְדָהּ בְּסַיִיף.

[8]אֲמַר לֵיהּ רַב אַחָא מִדִּפְתִּי לְרָבִינָא: לְמַאי דְּקָאָמַר לֵיהּ רָבָא בַּר רַב חָנָן לְאַבַּיֵי: אֵימָא יָצְאָה הִשְׁתַּחֲוָאָה לְלַמֵּד עַל הַכְּלָל כּוּלּוֹ, [9]״אֵיכָה יַעַבְדוּ״, [10]לְמַעוֹטֵי מַאי? [11]וְכִי תֵּימָא: לְמַעוֹטֵי הַפּוֹעֵר עַצְמוֹ לַזּוֹבְחִים, [12]מֵהִשְׁתַּחֲוָאָה נָפְקָא. [13]מָה הִשְׁתַּחֲוָאָה דֶּרֶךְ כִּיבּוּד [14]אַף כֹּל דֶּרֶךְ כִּיבּוּד. [15]אֶלָּא, לְמַעוֹטֵי

[1]Rav Aḥa the son of Rav Ika strongly objected: [2]And according to Resh Lakish, does he need the verse? [3]Up to here Resh Lakish only permitted the animal. [4]But the man is liable for execution, [5]like someone who bows down to a mountain, [6]the mountain is permitted, [7]but the one who worshiped it is [put to death] by the sword.

[8]Rav Aḥa of Difti said to Ravina: According to what Rava bar Rav Ḥanan said to Abaye: Say that bowing was specified to teach about the entire generalization, [9]"How did [these nations] serve," [10]to exclude what? [11]And if you say: To exclude someone who relieves himself before [an idol worshiped through] sacrifice, [12]this is learned from bowing. [13]Just as bowing is a respectful manner, [14]so too any respectful manner. [15]Rather, to exclude

TRANSLATION AND COMMENTARY

מַתְקִיף לָהּ [1]**Rav Aḥa the son of Rav Ika strongly objected**, arguing that even according to Resh Lakish there is no difficulty: [2]**Does Resh Lakish** really **need the verse,** "He that sacrifices to any god," to teach that an idolatrous thought in one part of the sacrificial service regarding another part of that service can render the person who brought the sacrifice liable to be executed? [3]But surely **Resh Lakish only permitted the animal,** saying that an idolatrous thought cannot render the sacrificed animal forbidden for benefit. [4]**But the man** who offered the sacrifice **is** indeed **liable to be executed** for idolatry. You might ask: How can it be that the man who offered the sacrifice is put to death for idolatry, and yet the animal which he offered to the idol is still permitted for benefit? [5]I can answer that this is **like someone who bows down** in worship **to a mountain.** [6]In such a case, **the mountain is permitted** for benefit. [7]**But the one who worshiped** the mountain **is put to death by the sword** for idolatry. Here too then the animal is permitted for benefit, but the man who offered the sacrifice is liable to be executed. Thus, it follows that even according to Resh Lakish, the verse, "He that sacrifices to any god," is available to teach about the entire generalization, namely, that if a person served an idol the way God is worshiped in the inner Temple, he is liable to be executed, even if that is not the ordinary way to worship that idol. So Rava bar Rav Ḥanan's question is invalid, both according to Rabbi Yoḥanan and according to Resh Lakish.

אֲמַר לֵיהּ [8]**Rav Aḥa of Difti said to Ravina: According to what Rava bar Rav Ḥanan said to Abaye** that we should **say that bowing** down to an idol **was specified** in order **teach about the entire generalization** that if someone worshiped an idol in a respectful way, he is liable to be executed, even if that is not the idol's usual manner of worship, a question arises: The verse which states (Deuteronomy 12:30): "Take heed to yourself that you be not ensnared into following them, after they are destroyed from before you, and that you inquire not after their gods, saying, [9]**How did these nations serve** their gods," implies that if a person served a false god the way other idolaters worship it, he is liable, but if he served it differently, he is exempt. According to Rava bar Rav Ḥanan who argues that a person is liable for any respectful mode of worship, even if that is not the usual way in which the idol is served, [10]**what** does this verse come **to exclude?** [11]**You might say** that this verse comes **to exclude someone who relieved himself** (in the manner in which Ba'al Pe'or is worshiped) **before an** idol that is usually **worshiped through sacrifice.** [12]However, this is difficult, for we **derive** that ruling **from bowing** down to an idol. [13]**Just as bowing** down to an idol **is a respectful manner** of worshiping the idol, and someone who bows down to an idol is liable to be executed, even if that is not the idol's usual manner of worship, [14]**so too** one is liable to be executed for serving the idol in **any** other **respectful manner.** But if someone served an idol in a way that degrades the idol, he is exempt. [15]**Rather,** the verse, "How did these

RASHI

נכרים העובדין את ההרים — תניא במסכת עבודה זרה (מה,א): ההרים מותרין בהנאה דכתיב "אלהיהם על ההרים", ולא ההרים אלהיהם. **ועובדיהם בסייף** — אף על גב דמחובר לא מתסר, עבודה זרה מיהא הוי, והכא נמי לא בעיא קרא, הואיל ושחיטה צורך זריקה היא והא חשב בשחיטה על מנת לזרוק — הוה ליה כעובד עבודה זרה, דהא זריקה בלא שחיטה לא סגי. הלכך על כרחיך אי השתחואה ללמד על הכלל נפקא ליה לא הוה ליה למיכתב זובח. **איכה יעבדו** — דמשמע כדרכה — אין, שלא כדרכה — לא. **למעוטי מאי** — שלא כדרכה, מאחר דילפינן בהשתחואה דאפילו אינה עבודת פנים מחייב שלא כדרכה, אי נימא למעוטי עבודת בזיון לעבודה זרה שעבודתה דרך כבוד — כגון: פוער עצמו לעבודה זרה שזובחין, למה לי למעוטי מהאי קרא. **הא מהשתחואה נפקא** — שמלמדת על

TRANSLATION AND COMMENTARY

nations serve their gods," must come **to exclude someone who relieved himself before the god Marculis.** [1]**You might have thought** that **since its usual mode of worship is one of degradation,** for people serve Marculis by casting stones upon it, [2]**so too** one is liable for serving Marculis by **any other manner of degradation.** [3]**Therefore,** the verse **teaches us** that a person is only liable if he served an idol in the manner in which other idolaters worship it.

אֶלָּא הָא [4]The Gemara now raises another difficulty according to Rava bar Rav Ḥanan. **Rabbi Elazar said: From where do we know that if someone sacrificed an animal to Marculis,** an idol whose usual mode of worship is one of degradation, **he is liable**? [5]For the verse **states** (Leviticus 17:7): **"And they shall no more offer their sacrifices to the demons."** [6]Now, **if** this verse **does not refer to worship in its usual manner** such as, offering a sacrifice to an idol which is usually worshiped in that way, **for** that is learned from [7]**the verse** which **states** (Deuteronomy 12:30): **"How did these nations serve** their gods," implying that a person is liable for worshiping a false god in the customary way, [8]then **refer** the verse **to worship not in its usual manner.** But according to Rava bar Rav Ḥanan, why is this verse, "And they shall no more offer their sacrifices," necessary? [9]Liability for any type of respectful **worship,** even if it is **not the usual manner** in which the idol is served, **is learned from bowing** down to the idol!

הָתָם בְּזוֹבֵחַ [10]The Gemara answers: **There** Rabbi Elazar is dealing with a person who sacrificed the animal to Marculis, not in devotion to Marculis, but in **defiance** of God and Torah law. The verse, "And they shall no more offer their sacrifices," teaches that such a person transgresses a Torah prohibition.

הַפּוֹעֵר עַצְמוֹ לְמַרְקוּלִיס. [1]סָלְקָא דַּעְתָּךְ אָמִינָא: הוֹאִיל וַעֲבוֹדָתוֹ בְּבִזָּיוֹן הוּא, [2]אַף כֹּל בְּבִזָּיוֹן. [3]קָא מַשְׁמַע לָן. [4]אֶלָּא הָא דְּאָמַר רַבִּי אֱלִיעֶזֶר: מִנַּיִן לְזוֹבֵחַ בְּהֵמָה לְמַרְקוּלִיס שֶׁהוּא חַיָּיב, [5]שֶׁנֶּאֱמַר: "וְלֹא יִזְבְּחוּ עוֹד אֶת זִבְחֵיהֶם לַשְּׂעִירִם". [6]אִם אֵינוֹ עִנְיָן לְכְדַרְכָּהּ, [7]דִּכְתִיב: "אֵיכָה יַעַבְדוּ", [8]תְּנֵיהוּ עִנְיָן לְשֶׁלֹּא כְּדַרְכָּהּ. [9]שֶׁלֹּא כְּדַרְכָּהּ מֵהִשְׁתַּחֲוָאָה נָפְקָא! [10]הָתָם בְּזוֹבֵחַ לְהַכְעִיס.

LITERAL TRANSLATION

someone who relieves himself before Marculis. [1]It might have entered your mind to say: Since its [mode of] worship is by degradation, [2]so too any degradation. [3][Therefore] it teaches us.

[4]But that which Rabbi Elazar said: From where [do we know] that someone who sacrifices an animal to Marculis is liable? [5]For it is stated: "And they shall no more offer their sacrifices to the demons." [6]If it does not refer to [worship] in its [usual] manner, [7]for it is written: "How did [these nations] serve," [8]refer it to [worship] not in its [usual] manner. [9][Worship] not in its [usual] manner is learned from bowing!

[10]There where he sacrifices in defiance.

RASHI

הכלל שאינו חייב אלא דרך כבוד, כהשתחואה. אלא הא דאמר רבי אלעזר מניין לזובח בהמה — שהיא עבודת כבוד למרקוליס שעבודתה בזיון, והוא הדין לפעור, אם איתא לרבה בר רב חנין שהשתחואה מלמדת על הכלל, למה ליה האי קרא להכי? מהשתחואה נפקא! לזובח להכעיס — ואינו מתכוין לקבלו עליו באלוה, ואשמועינן קרא דעובר בלאו.

NOTES

זוֹבֵחַ לְהַכְעִיס **He sacrifices in defiance.** The Rishonim disagree about the meaning of this expression. Our commentary follows *Rabbenu Ḥananel* and others who understand that we are dealing here with a person who sacrificed the animal to Marculis without worshiping him as a god. Rather he sacrificed the animal in order to defy God. *Ramah* suggests that the person sacrificed the animal to Marculis in order to anger and defy Marculis. A special verse, "And they shall no more offer their sacrifices to the demons," was needed to teach us that he is liable in such a case. He did not mean to worship the idol in a respectful manner, but he did relate to it as a god.

HALAKHAH

הַפּוֹעֵר עַצְמוֹ לְמַרְקוּלִיס **Someone who relieves himself before Marculis.** "If someone relieved himself before Marculis, an idol whose usual manner of worship involves casting stones upon it, or if he cast stones upon Pe'or, an idol whose usual manner of worship involves relieving oneself before it, he is exempt, for in neither case did he serve the idol in the usual manner in which other idolaters worship it." (*Rambam, Sefer Mada, Hilkhot Avodah Zarah* 3:2.)

זוֹבֵחַ בְּהֵמָה לְמַרְקוּלִיס **Someone who sacrifices an animal to Marculis.** "If someone offered a sacrifice to an idol whose usual manner of worship does not involve sacrifices (e.g., if he offered a sacrifice to Marculis), he is liable to death by stoning, for he worshiped the idol in the same manner as God is worshiped. If he offered the idol a sacrifice, not because he accepted the idol upon himself as a god, but in order to violate Torah law and defy God, he transgresses a Torah prohibition," following Rabbi Elazar. (*Rambam, Sefer Mada, Hilkhot Avodah Zarah* 3:3.)

TRANSLATION AND COMMENTARY

רַב הַמְנוּנָא [1]It was related that **Rav Hamnuna** once **lost his oxen,** and went out to search for them, [2]**Rabbah met him, and cast** the following two **Mishnayot onto each** other, pointing out the contradiction between them. [3]**We have learned** in our Mishnah: **"Someone who worships an idol** is liable to death by stoning." [4]This implies that if he **worships** the idol, he **is** indeed liable, [5]but if he merely **says** that he intends to worship the idol, he is **not** liable. [6]**But surely we have learned** otherwise in a different Mishnah (below, 67a): **"If someone says:** [7]**'I will worship an idol,'** or **'I will go and worship an idol,'** [8]or **'Let us go and worship an idol,'** he is liable. The verse states (Deuteronomy 13:9): 'You shall not consent to him, nor hearken to him.' This means that once a person consents to commit idolatry, he is liable immediately, even if he did not yet actually do so, and even if he must go somewhere else to do so, so that he might change his mind, and even if he included himself among others who agreed to worship the idol, and he might not commit idolatry if the others decide not to."

אָמַר לֵיהּ [9]Rav Hamnuna **said to** Rabbah: There is no difficulty, for the two Mishnayot are dealing with two different cases. Our Mishnah, which implies that a person is only liable for having committed idolatry when he actually does so, is dealing with a person who **says:** [10]**"I will only accept** the idol **upon myself** as a god **when** I **worship** it, and not before." The other Mishnah, which says that a person is liable as soon as he says that he will worship the idol, is dealing with a person who accepts the idol as a god right away.

רַב יוֹסֵף אָמַר [11]**Rav Yosef said** to Rabbah: **Do you remove** the **Tannaim** and their disputes **from the world?** [12]Surely this matter **is** the subject of **a Tannaitic dispute,** and the two Mishnayot reflect an earlier controversy. **For it was taught** in a Baraita: **"If someone says:** 'I am a god; **come and worship me,'** [13]**Rabbi Meir says: He is liable** for having incited the other person to commit idolatry. [14]**And Rabbi Yehudah** disagrees and **exempts**

[1]רַב הַמְנוּנָא אִירְכַּסוּ לֵיהּ תּוֹרֵי. [2]פְּגַע בֵּיהּ רַבָּה, רְמָא לֵיהּ מַתְנִיתִין אַהֲדָדֵי. [3]תְּנַן: "הָעוֹבֵד עֲבוֹדָה זָרָה", [4]עוֹבֵד — אִין; [5]אוֹמֵר — לֹא. [6]וְהָאֲנַן תְּנַן: "הָאוֹמֵר: [7]'אֶעֱבוֹד', 'אֵלֵךְ וְאֶעֱבוֹד', [8]'נֵלֵךְ וְנַעֲבוֹד'!" [9]אֲמַר לֵיהּ: בְּאוֹמֵר: [10]"אֵינִי מְקַבְּלוֹ עָלַי אֶלָּא בַּעֲבוֹדָה". [11]רַב יוֹסֵף אֲמַר: תַּנָּאֵי שָׁקַלְתְּ מֵעָלְמָא? [12]תַּנָּאֵי הִיא. דְּתַנְיָא "הָאוֹמֵר: 'בּוֹאוּ וְעִבְדוּנִי', [13]רַבִּי מֵאִיר: מְחַיֵּיב. [14]וְרַבִּי יְהוּדָה

LITERAL TRANSLATION

[1]Rav Hamnuna lost his oxen. [2]Rabbah met him, [and] cast the Mishnayot onto each other. [3]We have learned: "Someone who worships an idol." [4]Worships — yes; [5]says — no. [6]But surely we have learned: "Someone who says: [7]'I will worship,' 'I will go and worship,' [8]'Let us go and worship.'"

[9]He said to him: Where he says: [10]"I will accept it upon myself only with worship."

[11]Rav Yosef said: Do you remove Tannaim from the world? [12]It is Tannaim, for it was taught: "[If] someone says: 'Come and worship me,' [13]Rabbi Meir says: He is liable. [14]And Rabbi Yehudah

RASHI

ארכסו ליה תורי — והלך לבקשן. **האומר אעבוד** — משעה שהסיתוהו ונתרצה חייב מיתה, דנפקא לן לקמן מ"לא תאבה ולא תשמע" — הא אבה ושמע חייב מיד. **אלך ואעבוד** — שמחוסר הליכה אף על גב דאיכא למימר אדהכי הדר ביה. **נלך ונעבוד** — אף על פי שכלל עצמו עם אחרים, דאיכא למימר הני אחרים לא אזלי ואיהו נמי לא ליזיל. **אמר ליה** — מתניתין דקתני עובד — אין, אומר — לא. **באומר איני מקבלו עלי** — באלוה. **אלא בעבודה** — "עד שאעבדנו", דכל כמה דלא פלח ליה אין כאן אבה ושמע. וסיפא דמשמע באמירה חייב — בשקבלו עליו אלוהו מיד, דכיון דאמר "אעבוד" מסתמא קבליה עליה באלוה אי לא פירש בהדיא שאינו מקבלו עליו אלא בעבודה. **בואו ועבדוני** — עושה את עצמו עבודה זרה ומסית בני אדם לעבדו. **מחייב** — מיתה כמסית.

NOTES

אִירְכַּסוּ לֵיהּ תּוֹרֵי **He lost his oxen.** The Gemara notes that the discussion between Rav Hamnuna and Rabbah took place while Rav Hamnuna was searching for his lost oxen, in order to teach us how highly Rav Hamnuna regarded Torah study, so that even when threatened with a financial loss, he put his concerns aside, and devoted himself to answering Rabbah's question (*Ramah*).

תַּנָּאֵי שָׁקַלְתְּ מֵעָלְמָא? **Do you remove Tannaim from the world?** This expression is uniquely associated with Rav Yosef. After a contradiction between similar cases is resolved by distinguishing between them, Rav Yosef asks: Did you remove Tannaim from the world, meaning: did you forget that this matter might be the subject of a Tannaitic controversy? In fact it is a Tannaitic controversy, and hence

HALAKHAH

הָאוֹמֵר: 'בּוֹאוּ וְעִבְדוּנִי' **If someone says: 'Come and worship me.'** "If someone incited another person to worship him as a god, and the other person worshiped him, the inciter is liable for stoning. If the other person did not actually worship him, but only agreed to worship him, the inciter is exempt from stoning," following Rabbi Yehudah, against Rabbi Meir. (*Rambam, Sefer Mada, Hilkhot Avodah Zarah* 5:5.)

LITERAL TRANSLATION

exempts [him]." [1]Where they worshiped him, everyone agrees (lit., "the whole world does not differ"), [2]for it is written: "You shall not make for yourself any carved idol." [3]When do they disagree — with mere speech. [4]Rabbi Meir maintains: Speech is something. [5]And Rabbi Yehudah maintains: Speech is not anything.

[6]Rav Yosef later said: It is nothing what I said, for even according to Rabbi Yehudah, he is liable for speech, [7]as we have learned: "Rabbi Yehudah said: He is not liable unless he says: 'I will worship,' 'I will go and worship,' 'Let us go and worship.'" [8]About what do they disagree? [9]They disagree about someone who incites [others to worship] him, and they say to him, "Yes." [10]One Sage maintains: [If] someone incites [others to worship] him, they listen to him, [11]and the "yes" which they said — it is truth.

פּוֹטֵר". [1]הֵיכָא דִּפְלַחוּ, כּוּלֵּי עָלְמָא לָא פְּלִיגִי, [2]דִּכְתִיב: "לֹא תַעֲשֶׂה לְךָ פֶסֶל". [3]כִּי פְּלִיגִי — בְּדִיבּוּרָא בְּעָלְמָא. [4]רַבִּי מֵאִיר סָבַר: דִּיבּוּרָא מִילְּתָא הִיא. [5]וְרַבִּי יְהוּדָה סָבַר: דִּיבּוּרָא לָאו מִילְּתָא הִיא.

[6]הֲדַר אֲמַר רַב יוֹסֵף: לָאו מִילְּתָא הִיא דַּאֲמַרִי. דַּאֲפִילּוּ לְרַבִּי יְהוּדָה בְּדִיבּוּרָא נַמִי חִיּוּבֵי מְחַיֵּיב, [7]דִּתְנַן: "רַבִּי יְהוּדָה אוֹמֵר: לְעוֹלָם אֵינוֹ חַיָּיב עַד שֶׁיֹּאמַר: 'אֶעֱבוֹד', 'אֵלֵךְ וְאֶעֱבוֹד', 'נֵלֵךְ וְנַעֲבוֹד'". [8]בְּמַאי קָמִיפַּלְגִי? [9]בְּמֵסִית לְעַצְמוֹ, וְאָמְרִי לֵיהּ "אִין", קָמִיפַּלְגִי. [10]מָר סָבַר: מֵסִית לְעַצְמוֹ, שָׁמְעִי לֵיהּ, [11]וְ"אִין" דְּקָאָמְרִי לֵיהּ — קוּשְׁטָא הוּא.

RASHI

רבי יהודה אומר לעולם אינו חייב — בשביל דבור בלא מעשה, אלא בניסת לעבודה זרה ואבה ושמע ואמר "אעבוד" אלך ואעבוד, אבל באומר "בואו ועבדוני" — פטור, אלמא טעמא דרבי יהודה במסית אחרים לעצמו טעמא אחרינא הוא, דהא בניסת — חיובי מחייב בדיבורא.

TRANSLATION AND COMMENTARY

him from all liability." [1]The Gemara clarifies the matter that is under dispute: **When** the other person actually **worshiped him, everybody agrees** — both Rabbi Meir and Rabbi Yehudah — that he is liable, [2]**for the verse states** (Exodus 20:4): **"You shall not make for yourself** [לְךָ] **any carved idol,"** and the seemingly superfluous word *lekha*, "yourself," teaches that one is forbidden to make oneself into an idol. [3]Rabbi Meir and Rabbi Yehudah only **disagree** about a person who **merely** agreed **in speech** to worship him. [4]**Rabbi Meir maintains** that **verbal agreement** to commit idolatry **has** Halakhic **significance,** and so the person who incited him to idolatry is liable. [5]**And Rabbi Yehudah maintains** that **verbal agreement** to commit idolatry **has no** Halakhic **significance,** and so the inciter bears no liability. Our Mishnah which implies that a person is only liable after actually worshiping the idol follows the position of Rabbi Meir, and the other Mishnah which says that a person is liable as soon as he says that he is going to worship an idol follows the position of Rabbi Yehudah.

הֲדַר [6]After further consideration, **Rav Yosef later said: What I said** before **is nothing, for even according to Rabbi Yehudah,** a person **can become liable for** idolatry through mere **speech,** [7]**as we have learned** in another Baraita: **"Rabbi Yehudah said:** A person **cannot become liable** for idolatry through mere speech, **unless he says: 'I will worship** an idol,' or **'I will go and worship** an idol,' or **'Let us go and worship** an idol.' But if he says: 'I am an idol; come and worship me,' he is not liable." Thus, we see that Rabbi Meir and Rabbi Yehudah agree that when a person says he will commit idolatry, he is liable. [8]**About what** issue then **do they disagree?** [9]**They disagree about someone who** claims to be a god and **incites others to worship him, and they say to him, "Yes,"** whether or not he is liable for incitement. [10]**One Sage** — Rabbi Meir — **maintains: If someone incites others to worship himself, they listen to him,** [11]**and the "yes" which they said** means that they regard what he said as **the truth,** and accept him as a god. Thus, the inciter is

NOTES

there is no need to differentiate between the two cases! Or else the expression may mean: Do you bring Tannaim from the market, and attribute to them viewpoints which where never expressly stated by them? Or else it may mean: Is it necessary to bring Tannaim from the market? Surely the Tannaim have already clarified this matter (see *Ramah*).

כִּי פְּלִיגִי — בְּדִיבּוּרָא בְּעָלְמָא When do they disagree — with mere speech. The Rishonim disagree about whether we are dealing here with the inciter or the person whom he incited to commit idolatry. According to one viewpoint, the inciter is always liable, whether his listener was swayed or not. The Gemara's discussion revolves around the person who was incited to idol worship, inquiring whether he is liable as soon as he agrees to commit idolatry, or only when he actually worships the idol (see *Tosafot*). Others understand that we are dealing here with the inciter. If he incites another person to worship an idol, he is liable whether or not he influences the other person. But if he incites the other person to worship the inciter himself, there is a reason to say that since his arguments are so far-fetched, they should not be regarded as incitement to idolatry, unless the other person actually worships him (see *Rashi, Ramah*).

LITERAL TRANSLATION

[1]And the other Sage maintains: [If] someone incites [others to worship] him, they do not listen to him, [2][for] they say: [61B] [3]How is he different from us? [4]And the "yes" which they said — [5]they laughed at him.

[6]As for the Mishnayot, [7]here with an individual who was incited [to commit idolatry]; [8]here — with a community that was incited. [9]An individual does not reconsider, and goes astray after him. [10]A community reconsiders, and does not go astray after him.

[11]Rav Yosef said: From where do I say this? [12]For it is written: "You shall not consent to him, nor hearken to him." [13]Thus, if he consented or hearkened, he is liable.

[14]Abaye raised an objection: Is there a difference between a community that was incited and an individual who was incited?

[1]וּמָר סָבַר: מֵסִית לְעַצְמוֹ, לָא שָׁמְעִי לֵיהּ, [2]מֵימַר אָמְרִי: [61B] [3]מַאי שְׁנָא אִיהוּ מִינַּן דִּידַן? [4]וְ״אִין״ דְּקָאָמְרִי — [5]אַחוּכֵי עֲלֵיהּ.

[6]וּמַתְנִיתִין, [7]כָּאן בְּיָחִיד הַנִּיסָּת; [8]כָּאן בְּרַבִּים הַנִּסָּתִים. [9]יָחִיד לָא מִימְלַךְ, וְטָעֵי בַּתְרֵיהּ, [10]רַבִּים מִימְלְכִי וְלָא טָעוּ בַּתְרֵיהּ.

[11]אֲמַר רַב יוֹסֵף: מְנָא אָמִינָא לָהּ? [12]דִּכְתִיב: ״לֹא תֹאבֶה לוֹ וְלֹא תִשְׁמַע אֵלָיו״, [13]הָא אָבָה וְשָׁמַע, חַיָּיב.

[14]אֵיתִיבֵיהּ אַבַּיֵי: מִי שָׁאנֵי בֵּין נִיסָּת דְּרַבִּים לְנִיסָּת יָחִיד?

TRANSLATION AND COMMENTARY

liable. [1]**And the other Sage** — Rabbi Yehudah — **maintains: If someone incites others to worship him, they do not listen to him,** [2]**for they say** to themselves: [61B] [3]**How is he** any **different from us?** [4]**And the "yes" which they said** does not mean that they accepted him as a god, [5]but rather **they were laughing at him.** Thus, the inciter is exempt from all liability.

וּמַתְנִיתִין [6]Rav Yosef continues: **As for the** apparent contradiction between the two **Mishnayot,** this can be resolved as follows: [7]**Here** in the second Mishnah, which says that a person is liable as soon as he says that he is going to worship an idol, we are dealing **with an individual who was incited to commit idolatry.** [8]And **here** in our Mishnah, which implies that a person is only liable if he actually worshiped the idol, we are dealing **with a community that was incited** to worship idols. What is the difference between the two? [9]**An individual** who was enticed to worship an idol **does not** consult with others and **reconsider** his decision before **he** actually **goes astray after** the inciter. Thus, as soon as he says that he will worship the idol, he is regarded as having consented. [10]But **a community** of people who were enticed to worship an idol consult among themselves and **reconsider** their decision, and so they **may not** actually **go astray after** the inciter. Thus, they are not regarded as having consented unless they actually served the idols.

אֲמַר רַב יוֹסֵף [11]**Rav Yosef said: From where do I** know to **say this?** [12]**For the verse** regarding a person who incites another person to commit idolatry **states** (Deuteronomy 13:9): **"You shall not consent to him, nor hearken to him,"** [13]implying that if a person **consented or hearkened** to the other person who came to incite him, **he is liable** immediately, even if he did not yet actually worship the idol.

אֵיתִיבֵיהּ [14]**Abaye raised an objection** to Rav Yosef's distinction: **Is there** really **a difference between a community** of people **who were incited** to commit idolatry **and a** single **individual who was incited** to do the

RASHI

מסית לעצמו — במסית אחרים לעצמו שיעבדוהו, אי הוי מסית או לא. **לא שמעי ליה** — שהרי הוא אדם כמותם, ואפילו הניסתים לשאר צלמי עבודה זרה אין ניסתין לעבוד אדם. **מאי שנא איהו** — להיות אלוה יותר ממני, ו״אין״ דקאמר ליה — אחוכי עליה. **ומתניתין** — דקשיין אהדדי, הכי מתוקמא: רישא דקתני עובד — אין, אומר — לא. **ברבים הניסתים** — דאפילו נתרצו מימלכי והדרי בהו ולא טעו. הלכך לא קרינא ביה אבה ושמע. **וסיפא** דמחייב באבה ושמע — ביחיד הניסת, דכיון דנתרצה לאו דעתיה למהדר, והוא אבה ושמע ורחמנא חייביה.

NOTES

כָּאן בְּיָחִיד הַנִּיסָּת, כָּאן בְּרַבִּים הַנִּסָּתִים **Here with an individual who was incited; here with a community that was incited.** Some of the Rishonim had the opposite reading: "An individual reconsiders; a community does not reconsider." According to this, the Gemara means as follows: An individual who was enticed to worship an idol might consult with others and reconsider his decision before he actually goes astray, and so he is only liable if he actually worshiped the idol. But a community of people who were enticed to worship an idol do not consult with anybody else. Rather they all follow each other and go astray after the inciter. Thus, they are liable as soon as they say that they are going to worship an idol (*Ran*).

HALAKHAH

הַנִּיסָּת **Someone who was incited.** "If someone incited another person to worship an idol, and that other person listened to him and said, 'Yes, let us go and worship the idol,' then even if that other person did not yet actually worship the idol, they are both subject to the penalty of death by stoning." (*Rambam, Sefer Mada, Hilkhot Avodah Zarah* 5:5.)

[1]וְהָתַנְיָא: ״׳כִּי יְסִיתְךָ אָחִיךָ בֶן אִמֶּךָ׳ — [2]אֶחָד יָחִיד הַנִּיסָּת וְאֶחָד רַבִּים הַנִּיסָּתִים, [3]וְהוֹצִיא הַכָּתוּב יָחִיד מִכְּלַל רַבִּים, [4]וְרַבִּים מִכְּלָל יָחִיד. [5]יָחִיד מִכְּלַל רַבִּים, לְהַחְמִיר עַל גּוּפוֹ, [6]וּלְהָקֵל עַל מָמוֹנוֹ. [7]רַבִּים מִכְּלַל יָחִיד — לְהָקֵל עַל גּוּפָם, [8]וּלְהַחְמִיר עַל מָמוֹנָם״. [9]בְּהָא מִילְּתָא, הוּא דְּשָׁאנֵי, [10]אֲבָל בְּכָל מִילֵּי, כִּי הֲדָדֵי נִינְהוּ!

[11]אֶלָּא אֲמַר אַבַּיֵי: [12]כָּאן — בְּנִיסָּת מִפִּי עַצְמוֹ; [13]כָּאן — בְּנִיסָּת מִפִּי אֲחֵרִים. [14]מִפִּי עַצְמוֹ — מִימְּלַךְ, [15]מִפִּי אֲחֵרִים — גָּרֵיר בָּתְרַיְיהוּ.

LITERAL TRANSLATION

[1]But surely it was taught: "'If your brother, the son of your mother, incite you' — [2]both an individual who was incited and a community that was incited. [3]And the verse removed the individual from the rule regarding the community, [4]and the community from the rule regarding the individual. [5]The individual from the rule regarding the community, to be stringent with his body, [6]and to be lenient with his money. [7]The community from the rule regarding the individual — to be lenient with their bodies, [8]and to be stringent with their money." [9]Regarding this matter, they are different, [10]but regarding all [other] matters, they are the same!

[11]Rather, Abaye said: [12]Here — when he was incited by himself; [13]here — when he was incited by others. [14]By himself — he reconsiders. [15]By others — he follows after them.

TRANSLATION AND COMMENTARY

same? [1]**But surely it was taught** in a Baraita: "The verse states (Deuteronomy 13:7): **'If your brother, the son of your mother,** or your son, or your daughter, or the wife of your bosom, or your friend, who is as your own soul, **incite you** secretly, saying, Let us go and serve other gods.' [2]This verse refers to **both an individual who was incited** to commit idolatry **and a community** of people **who were incited** to worship idols. [3]**But the verse removed the individual from the rule regarding the community,** teaching that the individual is not governed by the same law as is the community, [4]**and** it removed **the community from the rule regarding the individual,** teaching that the community is not governed by the same law as is the individual. How so? [5]The Torah removed **the individual from the rule regarding the community to be** more **stringent with** him regarding **his body,** [6]**but** more **lenient with** him regarding **his money.** [7]And it removed **the community from the rule regarding the individual to be** more **lenient with** them regarding **their bodies,** [8]**but** more **stringent with** them regarding **their money.** If an individual committed idolatry, he is liable to death by stoning, the most stringent mode of capital punishment, as the verse states (Deuteronomy 17:3-5): 'And he has gone and served other gods...then shall you bring forth that man...and shall stone that man...with stones until they die.' Nothing need be done, however, to his property. But if an entire city was guilty of idolatry, the inhabitants are liable to die by the less stringent mode of capital punishment, decapitation, as the verse states (Deuteronomy 13:16): 'You shall surely smite the inhabitants of that city with the edge of the sword.' But all the property in the city must be destroyed, and all its buildings razed to the ground, as the verse states (Deuteronomy 13:17): 'And you shall gather all the spoil of it into the midst of the open place of the city, and shall burn with fire both the city and the entire plunder taken in it.'" [9]Now, this Baraita implies that **regarding these matters,** the law applying to an individual who was incited to commit idolatry and the law applying to a community which was incited to do the same **are** indeed **different,** [10]**but regarding all other matters, they are the same!** How then can you rule that an individual who merely said that he will worship an idol is liable, but a community of people are not liable unless they actually do so?

אֶלָּא [11]**Rather, Abaye said:** The contradiction between the two Mishnayot can be resolved in the following manner: [12]**Here** in our Mishnah which implies that the idolater is only liable if he actually worshiped the idol, we are dealing with an idolater who **was incited by himself.** He decided to worship the idol without having been persuaded to do so by anyone else. [13]And **here** in the other Mishnah, which says that the idolater is liable as soon as he says that he is going to worship the false god, we are dealing with an idolater who **was incited by others.** Why is there a difference between the two? [14]If he came to the decision to worship the idol **by himself, he** might still **reconsider** that decision. But if he was incited by others to commit idolatry, [15]he **follows after them** and does not reconsider his decision. Hence he is liable as soon as he says that he will worship the idol.

RASHI

והוציא הכתוב יחיד מכלל רבים — ״וילך ויעבוד וגו׳ וסקלתם״ (דברים יז). **ורבים מכלל יחיד** — לדון בסייף ״הכה תכה״ (שם יג) דעיר הנדחת. **להחמיר על ממונם** — ״ושרפת באש וגו׳״ (שם) אבל יחיד הקל בממונו — שלא גזר עליו לאבדו. **מפי עצמו** — שאין אחר מסיתו.

[1]אָמַר אַבַּיֵי: מְנָא אָמִינָא לָהּ? [2]דִּכְתִיב: "לֹא תֹאבֶה לוֹ וְלֹא תִשְׁמַע אֵלָיו", [3]הָא אָבָה וְשָׁמַע — חַיָּיב.

[4]רָבָא אָמַר: אִידִי וְאִידִי בְּנִיסָּת מִפִּי אֲחֵרִים. [5]הָא דְּאָמַר לֵיהּ: "כָּךְ אוֹכֶלֶת, כָּךְ שׁוֹתָה, כָּךְ מְטִיבָה, כָּךְ מְרִיעָה". [6]הָא, דְּלֹא אָמַר לֵיהּ: "כָּךְ אוֹכֶלֶת, כָּךְ שׁוֹתָה כו׳".

[7]אָמַר רָבָא: מְנָא אָמִינָא לָהּ? [8]דִּכְתִיב: "מֵאֱלֹהֵי הָעַמִּים אֲשֶׁר סְבִיבֹתֵיכֶם הַקְּרֹבִים אֵלֶיךָ וגו׳". [9]מַה לִּי קְרוֹבִים, וּמַה לִּי רְחוֹקִים? [10]הָכִי קָאָמַר לָךְ: [11]מִטִּיבוּתָן שֶׁל קְרוֹבִים אַתָּה לָמֵד מַה טִּיבוּתָן שֶׁל רְחוֹקִים. [12]מַאי לָאו דְּאָמַר לֵיהּ: "כָּךְ אוֹכֶלֶת, כָּךְ שׁוֹתֶה, כָּךְ מְטִיבָה, כָּךְ מְרִיעָה"? [13]שְׁמַע מִינָּהּ.

LITERAL TRANSLATION

[1]Abaye said: From where do I say this? [2]For it is written: "You shall not consent to him, nor hearken to him." [3]Thus, if he consented or hearkened, he is liable.

[4]Rava said: This and that when he was incited by others. [5]This, when he said to him: "Thus it eats, thus it drinks, thus it does good, thus it does bad." [6]This, when he did not say to him: "Thus it eats, thus it drinks, etc."

[7]Rava said: From where do I say this? [8]For it is written: "Of the gods of the people who are round about you, either near to you, etc." [9]What is it to me if they are near, what is it to me if they are far? [10]Thus it says to you: [11]From the nature of those that are near learn what is the nature of those that are far. [12]Is it not what he said to him: "Thus it eats, thus it drinks, thus it does good, thus it does bad"? [13]Infer from this.

TRANSLATION AND COMMENTARY

אָמַר אַבַּיֵי [1]**Abaye said: From where do I know** that if a person was incited by others to idol worship, he is liable as soon as he says that he will worship the idol? [2]This is learned from **the verse** which **states** (Deuteronomy 13:9): **"You shall not consent to him, nor heed him,"** [3]**implying that** if a person **consented or hearkened** to the other person who incited him, **he is liable** immediately, even if he did not yet actually worship the idol.

רָבָא אָמַר [4]**Rava said: Both** Mishnayot deal with a person who **was incited** to idol worship **by others.** [5]**The other** Mishnah, which says that the idolater is liable as soon as he says that he is going to worship the false god, is dealing with an inciter who **said to him: "Thus** the idol **eats, thus it drinks, thus it benefits** those who worship it, and **thus it harms** those who do not worship it." [6]And **our** Mishnah, which rules that the idolater is only liable if he actually worshiped the idol, is dealing with an inciter who **did not say to him: "Thus** the idol **eats, thus it drinks,** thus it benefits those who worship it, and thus it harms those who do not worship it." If the person who was being incited to commit idolatry was not told anything about the idol, he is not liable unless he actually worshiped it, for he might still reconsider his decision.

אָמַר רָבָא [7]**Rava said: From where do I know** that when the Torah imposes liability for consenting to worship an idol, it is referring to a case when the incited party was told the praises of the idol? [8]This follows from **the verse** which **states** (Deuteronomy 13:7-8): "Let us go and serve other gods...**of the gods of the people who are round about you, either near to you,** or far from you." [9]For it may be asked: **What** difference does it make **whether** the people whose gods he wishes to worship **are near or far?** [10]Rather, the verse means to **say to you as follows:** When someone incites another person to commit idolatry, he is likely to speak the praises of the god of a distant, unfamiliar people. [11]Thus the Torah issues the warning: **From the nature of** the gods **that are near** and that you know have no substance, **learn the nature of** the gods **that are far off** that they too have no substance. [12]**Is it not** proven from here that the verse which imposes liability for consenting to worship an idol is dealing with an inciter who **said: "Thus** the idol **eats, thus it drinks, thus it benefits** those who worship it, and **thus it harms** those who do not worship it"? [13]The Gemara concludes: Indeed, it is legitimate to **infer from this** that a person is only liable for consenting to worship an idol, if the inciter praised the idol to him.

RASHI

מנא אמינא לה — דבדבורא ניסת מפי אחרים הוא דמחייב. **הא אבה ושמע** — למסיתו, — חייב. **אידי ואידי בניסת מפי אחרים** — ומשכחת לה דלא נתחייב ניסת משום אבה ושמע, כגון: דלא אמר ליה מסית שבחיה דעבודה זרה "כך אוכלת וכך שותה", דכיון דלא ידע ביה מילתא דשבחיה מהדר קא הדר ביה, ולא אבה ושמע. **מנא אמינא לה** — דכי כתוב אבה ושמע בדאמר ליה "כך אוכלת וכך שותה" משתעי. **דכתיב** — בפרשת מסית "מאלהי העמים אשר סביבותיכם הקרובים אליך או הרחוקים ממך" מה לי קרובים ומה לי רחוקים, ולמה הזכיר קרוב ורחוק — אלא מפני שדרכו של מסית לדבר על עבודה זרה רחוקה שאינו מכיר בה, ומוציא בפיו השקר ואומר "כך אוכלת וכך שותה". לפיכך אני אומר לך הסתכל בעבודות זרות הקרובות לך ותראה שאין בהן ממש, ומהן אתה למד טיבן של רחוקים. אלמא קרא בדאמר ליה "כך אוכלת" כתוב.

NOTES

מִטִּיבוּתָן שֶׁל קְרוֹבִים **From the nature of those that are near.** *Arukh* interprets the term טִיבוּתָן in accordance with the meaning of the word in Aramaic, "report" (= to the Hebrew דִּיבָּה). According to this, the Gemara means: From

¹רַב אַשִׁי אָמַר: סֵיפָא בְּיִשְׂרָאֵל מְשׁוּמָּד.
²רָבִינָא אָמַר: "לֹא זוֹ אַף זוֹ" קָתָנֵי.
³אִיתְּמַר: הָעוֹבֵד עֲבוֹדָה זָרָה מֵאַהֲבָה וּמִיִּרְאָה, ⁴אַבַּיֵי אָמַר: חַיָּיב. ⁵רָבָא אָמַר: פָּטוּר. ⁶אַבַּיֵי אָמַר: חַיָּיב, דְּהָא פְּלַחָהּ. ⁷רָבָא אָמַר: פָּטוּר. ⁸אִי קַבְּלֵיהּ עֲלֵיהּ בֶּאֱלוֹהַּ — אִין, ⁹אִי לָא — לָא.
¹⁰סִימָן עֶבֶ"ד יִשְׁתַּחֲוֶ"ה לְמָשִׁי"חַ.
¹¹וַאֲמַר אַבַּיֵי: מְנָא אָמִינָא לָהּ?

LITERAL TRANSLATION

¹Rav Ashi said: The last clause [deals] with an apostate Jew.

²Ravina said: It teaches "not only this but also this."

³It was stated: Someone who worships an idol from love or from fear, ⁴Abaye said: He is liable. ⁵Rava said: He is exempt. ⁶Abaye said: He is liable, for he worshiped it. ⁷Rava said: He is exempt. ⁸If he accepted it upon himself as a god, yes; ⁹if not, not.

¹⁰A sign: A slave, bows down, to an anointed [High Priest].

¹¹And Abaye said: From where do I say this?

RASHI

רב אשי אמר סיפא — דמחייב באמירה בישראל מומר, דכיון דקבל עליה תו לא הדר ביה, — שהרי הופקר בכך. **רבינא אמר** — לעולם בישראל גמור, וכולה מתניתין בחד טעמא, ותנא רישא עובד וסיפא אומר, ולא זו אף זו קתני, כלומר: ולא עובד בלבד אמרו, אלא אף אומר חייב. **מאהבה ומיראה** — מאהבת אדם ומיראת אדם, ולא חשבה בלבו באלהות. **חייב** — במזיד ובהתראה במיתה, ובשוגג דכסבור מותר לעשות כן — חייב בחטאת. **פטור** — בין במזיד בין בשוגג, דלאו כלום עבד.

TRANSLATION AND COMMENTARY

רַב אַשִׁי אָמַר ¹**Rav Ashi said:** The apparent contradiction between the two Mishnayot can be resolved as follows: **The last clause** of the other Mishnah, which states that a person is liable for idolatry as soon as he consents to serve the idol, refers to **an apostate Jew.** Once such a person consents to serve an idol, he will not reconsider his decision, and so he is liable even if did not yet actually commit idolatry.

רָבִינָא אָמַר ²**Ravina suggested** another way to resolve the contradiction between the two Mishnayot: In fact, both Mishnayot deal with an ordinary Jew who was not known to be an apostate, and they **follow** the stylistic principle of **"not only this but also this."** The first Mishnah teaches the relatively simple case, and the second Mishnah teaches the more complicated case. Not only is the idolater liable if he actually worshiped the idol, but rather he is liable, even if he only said that he was going to worship the idol.

אִיתְּמַר ³**It was stated** that the Amoraim disagree about the following matter: If **someone worshiped an idol from love or fear** of the person who suggested that he worship the idol, and not from any inner conviction as to the idol's divinity, the Amoraim disagree. ⁴**Abaye said** that the idolater **is liable** for such worship. ⁵**Rava** disagreed and **said** that **he is exempt** from all liability. ⁶The Gemara explains: **Abaye said** that the idolater **is liable, for** surely **he worshiped** the idol. ⁷**Rava said: He is exempt** because the primary criterion for liability is whether or not the idolater accepted the idol upon himself as a god. ⁸**If he accepted** the idol **as a god,** he is **indeed** liable; ⁹**if** he did **not** accept the idol as a god, he is **not** liable.

סִימָן ¹⁰Abaye now tries to bring support for his position from various Tannaitic sources. **A mnemonic device** composed of key words taken from each passage is: **A slave, bows down, to an anointed High Priest.**

וַאֲמַר אַבַּיֵי ¹¹**Abaye said: From where do I know** that a person who worshiped an idol from love or fear

NOTES

what you hear reported about those near to you, learn about those far off from you.

מֵאַהֲבָה וּמִיִּרְאָה **From love or fear.** The Rishonim disagree about the meaning of the expressions "from love" and "from fear." Our commentary follows *Rashi* and others, who understand that the Gemara is discussing someone who worshiped an idol from love or fear of the person who suggested that he worship the idol, and not from inner conviction regarding the idol's divinity. According to *Rambam,* the Gemara is dealing with a person who worshiped an idol because he loved its form or beauty, or because of a superstitious fear that it would harm him if he did not worship it. *Meiri* argues with *Rambam,* and insists that anybody who worships an idol because he fears that it would otherwise punish him is guilty of outright idolatry. Some Rishonim understand that we are dealing

HALAKHAH

הָעוֹבֵד עֲבוֹדָה זָרָה מֵאַהֲבָה וּמִיִּרְאָה **Someone who worships an idol from love or fear.** "If someone worshiped an idol out of love or fear, and he accepted the idol as a god, he is liable to death by stoning. But if he worshiped the idol without having accepted it as a god, he is exempt from the death penalty. According to some Rishonim, we are dealing here with a person who worshiped the idol out of love or fear of the person who suggested that he do so (*Rashi, Ra'avad, Hagahot Maimoniyot, Rambam* according to *Rivash*). Others understand that he worshiped the idol out of love or fear of the idol, because he was attracted to it for its physical beauty, or because of his superstitious fears that if he acted otherwise it would harm him (*Rambam* according to *Kesef Mishneh*)." The law follows Rava that he is only liable if he accepted the idol as a god. (*Rambam, Sefer Mada, Hilkhot Avodah Zarah* 3:6.)

TRANSLATION AND COMMENTARY

is liable? [1]**For we have learned** in our Mishnah: **"Someone who worships an idol** is liable to death by stoning, **whether he worships** the idol, or offers it a sacrifice, or burns incense before it, or offers it a libation of wine, or bows down before it, or accepts it upon himself as a god, or says to it: 'You are my god.'" Now, surely offering a sacrifice, burning incense, offering a libation, and the like, are all forms of idol worship. What then does the Mishnah mean when it says: "Whether he worships the idol"? [2]**Is it not** that the Mishnah means to say: Someone who worships an idol is liable to death by stoning, **whether he worships** the idol **from love or fear** of the person who suggested that he worship the idol, even if he is not convinced of the idol's divinity?

וְרָבָא [3]**Rava can say to you: No,** the Mishnah should be understood **as it was explained by Rabbi Yirmeyah:** An idol worshiper is liable to death by stoning no matter how he worships the idol, either the way other idolators worship it, or the way God is worshiped in the Temple. The Mishnah implies nothing about love or fear.

אָמַר אַבַּיֵי [4]Trying another proof, **Abaye said: From where do I know** that a person who worshiped an idol from love or fear is liable? [5]**For it was taught** in the following Baraita: "The verse states (Exodus 20:5): **'You shall not bow down to them.'** [6]The words 'to them' come to teach that it is only **to them** — idols served as gods — that **you may not bow down,** [7]**but you may bow down to a person like yourself** as a sign of acceptance of the other person's authority. Now, had the verse only stated: 'You shall not bow down to them,' [8]**I might have thought** that one is permitted to bow down to a person, **even** if that person is **someone who is worshiped as** in the case of **Haman.** [9]Therefore, **that** same **verse continues: 'And you shall not serve them.'** These apparently superfluous words come to teach that one may not bow down to anything that is served as a god, not even a person." [10]**Now surely Haman was worshiped out of fear,** not because they believed that he was a god, but because the king had commanded them to do so, as the verse states (Esther 3:3): "Then the king's servants, who were in the king's gate, said to Mordecai, Why do you transgress the king's commandment." Yet the Baraita teaches that one may not bow down to a person who is worshiped like Haman. Thus we see that someone who worships an idol from love or fear is indeed liable!

וְרָבָא [11]**Rava** understands that when the Baraita said that a person may not bow down to someone who is worshiped like Haman, it did not mean to forbid bowing from fear. Rather it meant that one may not bow down to a person believing that he is a god. And when it said "like Haman," it meant **like Haman, but not like Haman.** [12]One may not bow to a person **like Haman, who** thought of **himself as a god.** And therefore

[1]דִּתְנַן: "הָעוֹבֵד עֲבוֹדָה זָרָה אֶחָד הָעוֹבֵד כו׳". [2]מַאי לָאו: אֶחָד הָעוֹבֵד מֵאַהֲבָה וּמִיִּרְאָה! [3]וְרָבָא אָמַר לָךְ: לָא, כִּדְמְתָרֵץ רַבִּי יִרְמְיָה.

[4]אֲמַר אַבַּיֵי: מְנָא אָמִינָא לָהּ? [5]דְּתַנְיָא: "'לֹא תִשְׁתַּחֲוֶה לָהֶם'. [6]לָהֶם אִי אַתָּה מִשְׁתַּחֲוֶה, [7]אֲבָל אַתָּה מִשְׁתַּחֲוֶה לְאָדָם כְּמוֹתְךָ. [8]יָכוֹל אֲפִילּוּ נֶעֱבָד כְּהָמָן. [9]תַּלְמוּד לוֹמַר: 'וְלֹא תָעָבְדֵם'". [10]וְהָא הָמָן מִיִּרְאָה הֲוָה נֶעֱבַד.

[11]וְרָבָא: כְּהָמָן, וְלֹא כְּהָמָן. [12]כְּהָמָן, דְּאִיהוּ גּוּפֵיהּ עֲבוֹדָה

LITERAL TRANSLATION

[1]For we have learned: "Someone who worships an idol, whether he worships, etc." [2]Is it not: Whether he worships from love or fear!

[3]And Rava can say to you: No, as Rabbi Yirmeyah explained.

[4]Abaye said: From where do I say this? [5]For it was taught: "'You shall not bow down to them.' [6]To them you may not bow down, [7]but you may bow down to a person like yourself. [8]It might even be someone who is worshiped like Haman. [9]The verse states: 'And you shall not serve them.'" [10]And surely Haman was worshiped from fear!

[11]And Rava: Like Haman, and not like Haman. [12]Like Haman, who himself was

RASHI

אחד העובד – והלא המזבח והמקטיר עובדין הן – אלא הכי קאמר: אחד העובד ואפילו מאהבה ומיראה, ואחד המזבח לשם אלהות, דתנא סיפא לגלויי עליה דרישא דמאהבה ומיראה הוא ואפילו הכי חייב. **כדמתרץ רבי ירמיה** – אחד העובד כל עבודה שהיא דרכה בכך, ואחד המזבח שלא כדרכה. ולעולם רישא וסיפא לשם אלהות. **ולא תעבדם** – יתירא הוא. **נעבד בהמן** – שעשה עצמו עבודה זרה כדאמר במגילה (יט,א). דאי לאו הכי לא הוה מרדכי מתגרה בו והיה כורע ומשתחוה לו. **והא המן** – מיראת המלך הוו פלחי ליה, כדכתיב (אסתר ג) "כי כן צוה לו המלך" – וקתני דלא. **ודלא כהמן** – דקתני יכול אפילו נעבד כהמן לאו למיסר מיראה, אלא למיסר אדם הנעבד לשם עבודה זרה שלא מיראה למסגד ליה בסתמא. **והאי דנקט המן** – משום דעשה עצמו עבודה זרה הוא.

NOTES

here with a person who worshiped an idol under the threat of death (*Ran* in the name of *Rabbi David*). *Ramban* argues that if the person's life was threatened, even Abaye would agree that he is exempt from liability. Therefore, the Gemara must be dealing with a person who worshiped the idol under the threat of financial penalty.

TRANSLATION AND COMMENTARY

someone who bowed down to Haman, as a sign of belief in his divinity, is liable. [1]**But** one is **not** forbidden to bow down to a person **like Haman, for Haman was worshiped from fear,** [2]**and here,** the Baraita forbids bowing to a person, **not from fear,** but from inner conviction that the person is indeed a god.

וַאֲמַר אַבַּיֵי [3]Since the Baraita did not prove his point, **Abaye** tried again and **said: From where do I know** that a person who worshiped an idol from love or fear is liable? [4]**For it was taught** in the following Baraita: "In which case does **a High Priest anointed** with the oil bring a sin-offering for committing **idol worship?** [5]**Rabbi** Yehudah HaNasi **says:** Ordinarily the High Priest is not required to sacrifice a sin-offering if he committed an unwitting transgression because he had forgotten the law, or lacked certain factual information, but only if he sinned as a result of an incorrect Halakhic ruling. However, in the case of idol worship the High Priest is liable even if **he committed an unwitting transgression,** as is any other Jew. [6]**The Sages** disagree and **say:** Even in the case of idol worship, the High Priest is only liable if he sinned because he was **unaware of the law,** meaning that he issued an incorrect Halakhic ruling for himself. [7]**But they** all **agree** — both Rabbi Yehudah HaNasi and the Sages — **that** a High Priest who must bring a sin-offering for inadvertently committing idol worship **is liable for a she-goat** just **like an** ordinary **individual** who inadvertently worshiped an idol, and not a bullock, the usual sin-offering brought by a High Priest. [8]**And they** also all **agree that** a High Priest **does not bring a doubtful guilt-offering,** the sacrifice brought by a

זָרָה. [1]וְלֹא כְּהָמָן, דְּאִילּוּ הָמָן מִיִּרְאָה, [2]וְהָכָא לָאו מִיִּרְאָה. [3]וַאֲמַר אַבַּיֵי: מְנָא אָמִינָא לָהּ? [4]דְּתַנְיָא: "כֹּהֵן מָשִׁיחַ בַּעֲבוֹדָה זָרָה. [5]רַבִּי אוֹמֵר: בְּשִׁגְגַת מַעֲשֶׂה. [6]וַחֲכָמִים אוֹמְרִים: בְּהֶעְלֵם דָּבָר. [7]וְשָׁוִין שֶׁבִּשְׂעִירָה כְּיָחִיד, [8]וְשָׁוִין שֶׁאֵין מֵבִיא

LITERAL TRANSLATION

a god. [1]But not like Haman, for Haman [was worshiped] from fear, [2]and here, not from fear.

[3]And Abaye said: From where do I say this? [4]For it was taught: "An anointed High Priest regarding idol worship. [5]Rabbi says: When [he committed] an unwitting act. [6]And the Sages say: When he was unaware of a matter. [7]And they agree that [he is liable] for a she-goat like an individual. [8]And they agree that he does not bring

RASHI

כהן משוח — בקרבן עבודה זרה. **רבי אומר בשגגת מעשה** — אפילו לא נעלם ממנו איסור עבודה זרה אלא שגג במעשה — חייב, ואף על גב דבשאר מצות אין מביא קרבן האמור בו אלא אם כן נעלמה ממנו הלכה דכתיב (ויקרא ד) גבי חטאת צבור "ונעלם דבר" כגון: הורו בית דין שחלב מותר ועשו על ידי העלמתן, דבפר כהן משוח כתוב (שם) "לאשמת העם" הרי משוח כצבור, אפילו הכי בעבודה זרה שקרבנו שוה לשאר יחידים כדקתני ואזיל, מחייב בשגגת מעשה בלא העלם דבר, ולקמן מפרש האי שגגת מעשה היכי דמי. **וחכמים אומרים** — אף כאן אינו חייב אלא בהעלם דבר, ובהוריות בפרק שני (ז,ב) ילפינן טעמא מקרא. **ושוין שבשעירה ביחיד** — ואפילו לרבנן דלא משוי ליה כשאר יחיד לענין להתחייב בלא העלם דבר, מודים הן שאין קרבנו בעבודה זרה חלוק משאר יחיד שמביא שעירה. דכתיב גבי קרבן עבודה זרה בפרשת שלח לך "ואם נפש אחת" — אחד יחיד ואחד נשיא ואחד משוח משמע. ואף על פי שנשיא ומשוח חלוקין מן היחידים בשאר מצות שהנשיא מביא שעיר זכר ונאכל, וכהן משוח פר ונשרף, והיחיד מביא כשבה או שעירה — בעבודה זרה שוין הן. **ושוין שאינו מביא אשם תלוי** — על שום "לא הודע" שבתורה, משום דגבי אשם תלוי כתיב (ויקרא ה) "על שגגתו אשר שגג", משמע, מי שמביא חטאת על הודע דשגגת מעשה, מביא אשם תלוי על לא הודע, — יצא משוח שאין

NOTES

כֹּהֵן מָשִׁיחַ בַּעֲבוֹדָה זָרָה **An anointed High Priest regarding idol worship.** Special laws apply to the leaders of the Jewish people, such as the king or the High Priest regarding the sin-offerings that they must bring for their unwitting transgressions. An ordinary Jew is liable for a sin-offering if he inadvertently committed a sin punishable by excision, whether his transgression resulted from forgetfulness, inattention, or ignorance. But the bull sacrificed because of an unwitting transgression committed by the community as a whole is only offered for a transgression which resulted from an erroneous Halakhic decision issued by the great Sanhedrin. Similarly, the bull sacrificed as a sin-offering by the High Priest for a transgression other than idol worship is only brought for a transgression which resulted from an erroneous Halakhic decision made by the High Priest himself. Here the Tannaim disagree about the sin-offering brought by the High Priest for idol worship, whether he brings a sin-offering for any unwitting transgression, just like an ordinary individual, or only for a transgression which resulted from his erroneous Halakhic decision.

HALAKHAH

כֹּהֵן מָשִׁיחַ בַּעֲבוֹדָה זָרָה **An anointed High Priest regarding idol worship.** "If the High Priest issued an incorrect Halakhic ruling for himself regarding idol worship, preserving part of the law and abrogating part of the law, and he acted in accordance with his ruling, he must bring a she-goat as a sin-offering. But if he committed an unwitting transgression without having issued an incorrect Halakhic ruling for himself, whether that transgression involved idol worship or some other prohibition, he does not bring a sin-offering," following the Sages. (*Rambam, Sefer Korbanot, Hilkhot Shegagot* 15:3.)

כֹּהֵן מָשִׁיחַ אֵינוֹ מֵבִיא אָשָׁם תָּלוּי **An anointed High Priest does not bring a doubtful guilt-offering.** "If an anointed High Priest was in doubt as to whether he committed a sin

LITERAL TRANSLATION

a doubtful guilt-offering." [1]And this, when [he committed] an unwitting act of idol worship — what is it like? [2]If he thought it was a synagogue, and he bowed to it, [3]surely his heart is to heaven. [4]Rather, he saw a statue, and bowed to it. [5]If he accepted it upon himself as a god, he is an intentional sinner. [62A] [6]And if he did not accept it upon himself as a god, it is not anything. [7]Rather, is it not [when he worshipped] because of love or fear.

[8]And Rava can say to you: No, [9]when he said: It is permitted. [10][When] he said: It is permitted, [11]that is [the same as] when he was unaware of a matter!

אָשָׁם תָּלוּי". [1]הַאי שִׁגְגַת מַעֲשֶׂה דַּעֲבוֹדָה זָרָה הֵיכִי דָּמֵי? [2]אִי קָסָבַר בֵּית הַכְּנֶסֶת הוּא, וְהִשְׁתַּחֲוָה לוֹ, [3]הֲרֵי לִבּוֹ לַשָּׁמַיִם. [4]אֶלָּא, דַּחֲזָא אַנְדְּרְטָא, וְהִשְׁתַּחֲוָה לוֹ. [5]אִי קַבְּלֵיהּ עֲלֵיהּ בֶּאֱלוֹהַּ, מֵזִיד הוּא, [62A] [6]וְאִי לָא קַבְּלֵיהּ עֲלֵיהּ בֶּאֱלוֹהַּ, לֹא כְּלוּם הוּא. [7]אֶלָּא לָאו מֵאַהֲבָה וּמִיִּרְאָה.

[8]וְרָבָא אָמַר לָךְ: לָא, [9]בְּאוֹמֵר: מוּתָּר.

[10]אוֹמֵר: מוּתָּר, [11]הַיְינוּ הֶעְלֵם דָּבָר!

TRANSLATION AND COMMENTARY

person who is uncertain as to whether he committed a sin that requires a sin-offering." [1]Now, **how do you visualize the case where** the High Priest **committed an unwitting transgression involving idol worship** without having been unaware of the law? [2]**If he thought** that **he** was **in a synagogue,** where the worship of God is permitted, **and** it turned out that he was in a heathen temple and that **he** had **bowed down to** an idol, [3]**surely his heart was** directed **to** God in **Heaven,** and so he should be exempt from all liability. [4]**Rather,** it must be that **he saw a statue** of a human figure, not knowing that it was an idol, **and** he **bowed down to it.** [5]But this is difficult, for **if he accepted** the statue **as a god,** surely **he is an intentional sinner,** and therefore not liable for a sin-offering. [62A] [6]And **if he did not accept** the statue **upon himself as a god,** but rather he merely bowed down to the statue as a sign of honor, **he did not commit any** transgression for which he should be liable for a sin-offering. [7]**Rather,** the person bowed down to an idol **from love or fear** of another person, not knowing that bowing down to the idol from love or fear of another person is forbidden. And thus we see that someone who bows down to an idol from love or fear is liable, as argued by Abaye!

וְרָבָא [8]**And Rava can say to you:** In fact, a person who bows down to an idol from love or fear is **not** liable. When the Baraita says that a High Priest who committed an unwitting transgression involving idol worship is liable, [9]it was referring to a High Priest who unknowingly **said** that idol worship **is permitted.**

אוֹמֵר [10]The Gemara challenges this: If the High Priest **said** that idol worship **is permitted,** [11]this **is** precisely **the same as** being **unaware of the law,** and in that case even the Sages agree that the High Priest is liable!

RASHI

מביא חטאת אלא בהעלם דבר, ושמעינן הכא אפילו לרבי דאמר שיש לך קרבן שהמשוח חייב בשגגת מעשה — מודה הוא שאין מביא אשם תלוי. ובמסכת הוריות (שם) יליף מקרא מדכתיב באשם תלוי "שגגתו" "שגגתו" תרי זימני — מי שכל חטאו בשגגה, יצא משוח שאין כל חטאו בשגגה שהרי בשאר מצות צריך העלם דבר. **שגגת מעשה** — בלא העלם דבר היכי דמי? **הרי לבו לשמים** — ולא השתחוה זה לעבודה זרה לא מזיד ולא שוגג הוא, אלא לשמים, שהרי לשמים נתכוין, ואפילו היה יודע שזה הבית עבודה זרה הוא והוא משתחוה בתוכו לשמים — אין כאן עונש, שהרי אף משתחוה לבית הכנסת לא לבית הוא משתחוה אלא למי ששכן שמו עליה. **אלא דחזא אנדרטא וסגיד ליה** — שראה דמות שהיו רגילין לעשות בדמות המלך, והרואה אותו משתחוה לו לכבוד המלך ופעמים שעובדין אותו, וזה ראה אחד שהיה נעבד ולא ידע שהוא נעבד והשתחוה לו. **אי דקבליה עליה באלוה** — שהשתחוה לו לשם עבודה זרה — מזיד הוא. **ואי לא קבליה עליה באלוה** — אלא לכבוד המלך השתחוה לו, לא כלום הוא. דהא לא אכוין לשם עבודה זרה. **אלא לאו** — שעבד עבודה זרה מאהבה ומיראת אדם, כסבור שמותר לעשות, והאי אומר מותר כי האי גוונא דידע ליה לאיסור עבודה זרה בכל עבודות שלה — לאו העלם דבר קרי לה, אף על פי שנעלם ממנו איסור אהבה ויראה, שאין זו מגוף האיסור אלא אם כן נעלם ממנו עיקר עבודה זרה באחת מעבודותיה, כסבור שעבודה זו מותר לה. **ורבא אמר לך** — לא הוי שגגת מעשה הכי, אלא באומר מותר לעבוד עבודה זרה. כסבור אין עבודה זרה בתורה. **אומר מותר היינו העלם דבר** — ובהא אפילו רבנן מודו.

LANGUAGE

אַנְדְּרְטָא **Monument.** This word dirives from the Greek ἀνδριάντος, *andriantos,* meaning "a statue, a human figure."

NOTES

אָשָׁם תָּלוּי **A doubtful guilt-offering.** A doubtful guilt-offering is one of the sub-categories of the guilt-offering (see Leviticus 5:17-19). Such a sacrifice is brought as atonement when a person is unsure whether or not he committed a sin which requires a sin-offering. For example, if a person unwittingly ate blood, he is liable for a sin-offering. But if he is uncertain as to whether what he ate was or was not blood, he must bring a doubtful sin-offering, which atones for his sin until he ascertains that what he ate was indeed blood.

HALAKHAH

that required a sin-offering, he does not bring a doubtful guilt-offering," following the Baraita. (*Rambam, Sefer Korbanot, Hilkhot Shegagot* 15:6.)

TRANSLATION AND COMMENTARY

בְּאוֹמֵר [1]The Gemara explains: When Rava said that the Baraita is referring to a High Priest who said to himself that idol worship is permitted, he meant that the Baraita is referring to a High Priest who **said** to himself that idol worship **is altogether permitted,** thinking that there is no prohibition whatsoever against idol worship. Rabbi Yehudah HaNasi maintains that in such a case the High Priest is liable for a sin-offering, just as an ordinary individual would be liable for a sin-offering. The Sages disagree, and say that even in the case of idol worship, the High Priest is only liable for a sin-offering if he sinned because [2]**he was unaware of the law** and issued an incorrect Halakhic ruling for himself, [3]**preserving part** of the law, **and abrogating part** of it, for example, he might have thought incorrectly that offering a sacrifice or burning incense before an idol is forbidden, but bowing down to it is permitted.

תָּנֵי רַבִּי זַכַּאי [4]**Rabbi Zakkai taught** the following Baraita **before Rabbi Yoḥanan: "If someone** unwittingly **slaughtered a sacrifice** before an idol, **and burned incense** before it, **and offered** it **a libation** of wine, **and bowed down** before it, serving the idol in all four ways **in one period of unawareness,** before realizing that he had sinned, [5]**he is only liable for one sin-offering."** If a person unwittingly violated a prohibition whose willful violation carries the penalty of excision, he is obligated to bring a sin-offering. If he repeated the transgression after having realized that he had sinned, he is obligated to bring a separate offering for each transgression. But if he repeated the same transgression before realizing that he had sinned ("in a single period of unawareness"), he is only obligated to bring a single offering. Slaughtering a sacrifice before an idol, burning incense before it, offering it a wine libation, and bowing down before it, are all included in the same transgression (Exodus 20:5): "You shall not worship them." Thus, if a person served an idol in those various different ways before realizing that he had sinned, he is only liable for one sin-offering.

אֲמַר לֵיהּ [6]Rabbi Yoḥanan **said to** Rabbi Zakkai: **Go out** of the academy, **and teach** that Baraita **outside,** but here in the academy we maintain that someone who worshiped an idol in several different ways before realizing that he had sinned is obligated to bring a separate sin-offering for each transgression.

אָמַר רַבִּי אַבָּא [7]**Rabbi Abba said: That which Rabbi Zakkai said is** [8]in fact **the subject of a dispute between Rabbi Yose and Rabbi Natan,** [9]**for it was taught** in a Baraita: "Even though all forms of labor are forbidden on the Sabbath, as the verse states (Exodus 20:10): 'You shall not do any work,' another verse (Exodus 35:3) singles out kindling a fire and states: 'You shall kindle no fire throughout your habitations on the Sabbath day.' The prohibition against **kindling** a fire on the Sabbath **was singled out** from among all the other categories of labor in order to teach that its transgression is a violation of **a** plain **negative commandment,** and therefore not punishable by stoning or *karet,* the usual punishments for Sabbath desecration. [10]**This is the position of Rabbi Yose.** [11]**Rabbi Natan** disagrees and **says:** The prohibition against kindling a fire on the Sabbath **was singled**

[1]בְּאוֹמֵר: מוּתָּר לְגַמְרֵי. [2]הֶעְלֵם דָּבָר — [3]קִיּוּם מִקְצָת, וּבִיטּוּל מִקְצָת.

[4]תָּנֵי רַבִּי זַכַּאי קַמֵּיהּ דְּרַבִּי יוֹחָנָן: "זִיבֵּחַ, וְקִיטֵּר, וְנִיסֵּךְ, וְהִשְׁתַּחֲוָה בְּהֶעְלֵם אֶחָד, [5]אֵינוֹ חַיָּיב אֶלָּא אַחַת".

[6]אֲמַר לֵיהּ: פּוֹק תְּנֵי לְבָרָא!

[7]אָמַר רַבִּי אַבָּא: הָא דְּאָמַר רַבִּי זַכַּאי, [8]מַחֲלוֹקֶת רַבִּי יוֹסֵי וְרַבִּי נָתָן, [9]דְּתַנְיָא: "הַבְעָרָה לְלָאו יָצְאָה. [10]דִּבְרֵי רַבִּי יוֹסֵי. [11]וְרַבִּי נָתָן אוֹמֵר: לְחַלֵּק

LITERAL TRANSLATION

[1]When he said: It is altogether permitted. [2]When he was unaware of a matter — [3]when he preserved part, and abrogated part.

[4]Rabbi Zakkai taught before Rabbi Yoḥanan: "[If] someone sacrificed, and burned incense, and offered a libation, and bowed down in one period of unawareness, [5]he is only liable for one [sin-offering]."

[6]He said to him: Go out, [and] teach [it] outside!

[7]Rabbi Abba said: That which Rabbi Zakkai said is [8][the subject of] a dispute between Rabbi Yose and Rabbi Natan, [9]for it was taught: "Kindling was specified for a negative commandment. [10][These are] the words of Rabbi Yose. [11]Rabbi Natan says: It was specified

RASHI

ומשני: אומר מותר דקאמינא — היינו דקא עקר לה לגמרי. העלם דבר קיום מקצת ובטול מקצת — כגון יש עבודה זרה בתורה שלא לזבוח ושלא לקטר, אבל המשתחוה מותר. אינו חייב אלא אחת — וכל עבודותיה באזהרה אחת "הן לא תעבדם" (שמות כ) — הלכך אין כאן חלוק חטאות. פוק תני לברא — דטעות הוא, ולקמן מפרש טעמא. הבערה שיצאה מכלל — "לא תעשה כל מלאכה" (שם) דשבת. ללאו יצאה — להוציאה מחומרי שאר מלאכות וללמד עליה שאינה לא בכרת ולא במיתה אלא בלאו. לחלק — לחלוק ולומר לך מה זו מיוחדת שהיא מאבות מלאכות הנעשית במשכן וחייב עליה הכתוב בפני עצמו, שפרט לה לבדה, — אף כל שהוא אב מלאכה אם עשאן בהעלם אחד חייב

TERMINOLOGY

פּוֹק תְּנֵי לְבָרָא **Go out [and] teach it outside.** When a Baraita is rejected as being unauthoritative and hence not binding, the Talmud may use this expression, meaning that the Baraita should have no place in the discussion in the Bet Midrash.

NOTES

לְחַלֵּק יָצְאָה **It was specified to distinguish.** This interpretation of the verse is based on the hermeneutic principle that

יָצְאָה״. [1]לְמַאן דְּאָמַר הַבְעָרָה לְלָאו יָצְאָה, [2]הִשְׁתַּחֲוָאָה נַמִי לְלָאו יָצְאָה. [3]לְמַאן דְּאָמַר הַבְעָרָה לְחַלֵּק יָצְאָה, [4]הִשְׁתַּחֲוָאָה נַמִי לְחַלֵּק יָצְאָה. [5]מַתְקִיף לָהּ רַב יוֹסֵף: [6]דִּילְמָא עַד כָּאן לָא קָאָמַר רַבִּי יוֹסֵי הָתָם הַבְעָרָה לְלָאו יָצְאָה, [7]דְּנָפְקָא לֵיהּ חִילּוּק מְלָאכוֹת מֵ״אַחַת מֵהֵנָּה״, [8]דְּתַנְיָא: ״רַבִּי יוֹסֵי אוֹמֵר: ׳וְעָשָׂה מֵאַחַת מֵהֵנָּה׳ — [9]פְּעָמִים שֶׁחַיָּיב אַחַת

LITERAL TRANSLATION

to distinguish." [1]According to the one who said: Kindling was specified for a negative commandment, [2]bowing was also specified for a negative commandment. [3]According to the one who said: Kindling was specified to distinguish, [4]bowing was also specified to distinguish. [5]Rav Yosef strongly objected: [6]Perhaps Rabbi Yose only stated [his opinion] there [that] kindling was specified for a negative commandment, [7]because he learns the separate treatment of each labor from "Of one of them," [8]as it was taught: "Rabbi Yose says: 'And shall do (of) one of them' — [9]sometimes you are liable for one [act of atonement]

TRANSLATION AND COMMENTARY

out in order **to distinguish** between each category of forbidden labor, so that a person who inadvertently performed different types of labor on the Sabbath requires a separate sin-offering to atone for each type of labor." [1]**According to** Rabbi Yose **who said** that **kindling** a fire on the Sabbath **was singled out** from among all the other categories of labor in order to teach that its transgression is a violation of **a** plain **negative commandment,** and therefore not punishable by stoning or *karet*, [2]**bowing down** to an idol **was also singled out** from among all the other modes of worship by the verse (Exodus 20:5): "You shall not bow down to them," in order to teach that its transgression is a violation of **a** plain **negative commandment,** and therefore not punishable by *karet* or a sin-offering. Thus, in Rabbi Yose's view, there is no verse to teach that if a person inadvertently performed several modes of idol worship, he is liable for a separate sin-offering for each mode of worship. [3]And **according to** Rabbi Natan **who said** that **kindling** a fire on the Sabbath **was singled out** from among all the other categories of labor in order **to distinguish** between each category of forbidden labor, [4]**bowing down** to an idol **was also singled out** from among all the other modes of worship in order **to distinguish** between each mode of idol worship. Thus, in Rabbi Natan's view, a person who unwittingly performed several modes of idol worship is obligated to bring a separate sin-offering for each mode of worship.

מַתְקִיף לָהּ [5]**Rav Yosef strongly objected** to this comparison between the Sabbath and idol worship: [6]**Perhaps Rabbi Yose only stated his opinion there that kindling** a fire on the Sabbath **was singled out** from among all the other categories of labor in order to teach that its transgression is a violation of **a** plain **negative commandment,** [7]**because he derives the separate treatment of each** category of **labor** regarding sin-offerings **from** the words **"Of one of them,"** [8]**as it was taught** in the following Baraita: **"Rabbi Yose says:** The verse states (Leviticus 4:2): 'If a soul shall unwittingly sin against any of the commandments of the Lord concerning things which ought not to be done, **and shall do of one of them**...then let him bring for his sin....' [9]The combination of the singular term מֵאַחַת, 'of one,' and the plural term מֵהֵנָּה, 'of them,' teaches that **sometimes** a person **is liable for a single** sin-offering **for**

RASHI

על כל אחת ואחת. דכל דבר שהיה בכלל ויצא מן הכלל ללמד לא ללמד על עצמו יצא אלא ללמד על הכלל כולו יצא. השתחואה נמי ללאו יצאה — לקמן (סנהדרין סג,א) אמר שלש השתחואות נאמרו באזהרת עבודה זרה, אחת לשלא כדרכה לכדאמרן לעיל אזהרה מניין — תלמוד לומר "לא תשתחוה", ואחת לכדרכה, ואחת לחלק — מה השתחואה מיוחדת מעשה לעצמו וחייב עליה בעצמה, אף כל עבודה ועבודה בשוגג חייב עליה חטאת לעצמה, ותנא דרבי זכאי סבירא ליה כרבי יוסי דההוא השתחואה יתירא לאו לחלק יצאה, אלא ללמד עליה שהיא בלאו ולא בכרת ואין חטאת על שגגתה, ואף על פי שחייבין עליה מיתה דהא גבי סקילה כתיב (דברים יז) "וישתחוו להם" מיהו מכרת ומחטאת אפקה, הלכך לא משכחת קרא בעבודה זרה לחלק. **מאחת מהנה** — גבי חטאת כתיב פעמים שחייב חטאת אחת על כולן, כגון שוגג בשבת כסבור אין היום שבת אבל יודע היה שכל מלאכות שהוא עושה אסורות בשבת — מביא קרבן אחד דחדא שגגה היא. ופעמים שחייב על כל אחד ואחד, כגון שהזיד בשבת ויודע שהוא שבת היום ויש שבת בתורה ושגג במלאכות, שלא היה יודע שהמלאכות הללו אסורות אלא מלאכות אחרות, — חייב על כל אחת ואחת, שיש כאן שגגות הרבה.

NOTES

something that was included in a generalization, but was specified to teach something, was intended to teach not just about itself but about the entire generalization. The Torah states that all work is forbidden on the Sabbath (a generalization), yet it also states that it is forbidden to kindle fire on the Sabbath. From here it may be derived that just as kindling a fire on the Sabbath is independently prohibited, so that someone who kindles a fire on the Sabbath is liable for a separate sin-offering, so, too, each category of forbidden labor is independently prohibited, so that someone who performs different types of labor on the Sabbath during a single period of unawareness is liable for a separate sin-offering for each type of labor that he performed.

BACKGROUND

אָבוֹת וְתוֹלָדוֹת **Principal labors and sub-categories.** The concept of *avot*, "principal categories," and *toledot*, "sub-categories," is found in several areas of Halakhah (see the beginning of tractates *Shabbat* and *Bava Kamma*), such as Sabbath law, impurities, and damages. The *avot* are the primary Halakhic categories — usually specifically mentioned or at least alluded to in the Bible — from which the Sages derived sub-categories. In some cases, the principal categories and the sub-categories differ only as to their source, or in that they are listed separately. In other cases, the principal categories and the sub-categories differ also as to the laws which apply to each.

TRANSLATION AND COMMENTARY

many unwitting transgressions, [1]and **sometimes** he **is liable** for a sin-offering **for each** unwitting transgression **separately.** How so? If a person knew which labors are forbidden on the Sabbath, but he did not know that the day was the Sabbath, and he performed several different categories of labor, he is liable for only a single sin-offering, even though he committed several transgressions, for his ignorance was confined to a single item of information, the day of the week. Conversely, if he knew that it was the Sabbath, but he did not know which categories of labor are forbidden, and he performed several different categories of labor, he is liable for a sin-offering for each category of labor that he had performed, for his ignorance related to each category of labor." [2]**And Rabbi Yonatan** clarified Rabbis Yose's position and **said: What is the reasoning of Rabbi Yose?** [3]**For the verse states: "And shall do of one of them."** [4]Instead of using the word **"one,"** it uses the restrictive expression **"of one,"** [5]and instead of using the word **"them,"** it uses the restrictive expression **"of them."** Thus, the verse imposes liability for a sin-offering for "one," for "of one," for "them," and for "of them." The combination of the two expressions, "of one" and "of them," [6]teaches that he is liable for **one** sin-offering **for many** transgressions, [7]**and many** sin-offerings **for one** prohibition. [8]The Gemara explains: The word **"one"** teaches that a person is liable for a sin-offering if he violated the Sabbath and completed the labor which he had intended to perform. [9]For example, he wrote the name **Shimon** as intended writing being one of the labors forbidden on the Sabbath. [10]The expression **"of one,"** which may be interpreted as "part of one," teaches that a person is liable for Sabbath desecration, even if he did not complete the labor which he intended to perform. [11]For example, he meant to write the name Shimon (שִׁמְעוֹן), but only completed the first two letters of the name, and wrote **Shem** (שֵׁם), which is in itself a full name. [12]The word **"them"** teaches that a person is liable for a sin-offering if he performed any one of the thirty-nine **principal labors.** [13]The expression **"of them,"** which may be interpreted as "of that which is similar to them," teaches that he is liable for a sin-offering if he performed any of the **sub-categories** of those principal labors. The combination of the two expressions, "of onc" and "of them," [14]teaches that a person is sometimes liable for **one** prohibition **many** sin-offerings. [15]For example, if **he knew** that it was **the Sabbath, but he did not know** which **labors** are forbidden on that day, and he performed several different categories of labor. [16]That combination of

עַל כּוּלָּן, [1]פְּעָמִים שֶׁחַיָּיב עַל כָּל אַחַת וְאַחַת". [2]וְאָמַר רַבִּי יוֹנָתָן: מַאי טַעְמָא דְּרַבִּי יוֹסֵי? [3]דִּכְתִיב: "וְעָשָׂה מֵאַחַת מֵהֵנָּה". [4]"אַחַת מֵאַחַת, [5]הֵנָּה מֵהֵנָּה. [6]אַחַת שֶׁהִיא הֵנָּה, [7]וְהֵנָּה שֶׁהִיא אַחַת". [8]"אַחַת" — [9]שִׁמְעוֹן, [10]"מֵאַחַת" — [11]שֵׁם מִשִּׁמְעוֹן. [12]"הֵנָּה" — אָבוֹת; [13]"מֵהֵנָּה" — תּוֹלְדוֹת. [14]אַחַת שֶׁהִיא הֵנָּה — [15]זְדוֹן שַׁבָּת, וּשְׁגָגוֹת מְלָאכוֹת. [16]הֵנָּה

LITERAL TRANSLATION

for all of them, [1]sometimes you are liable for each one separately." [2]And Rabbi Yonatan said: What is the reason of Rabbi Yose? [3]For it is written: "And shall do (of) one of them." [4]One, of one, [5]them, of them. [6]One which is them, [7]and them which is one. [8]"One" — [9]Shimon; [10]"of one" — [11]Shem of Shimon. [12]"Them" — principal labors; [13]"of them" — sub-categories. [14]One which is them — [15]intentional violation regarding the Sabbath, and unintentional violation regarding the labors. [16]Them

RASHI

רבי יונתן — מפרש טעמא דרבי יוסי היכי משמע ליה האי מהאי קרא. ועשה מאחת מהנה — הוה ליה למכתב, "ועשה אחת מהנה", אי נמי: "ועשה מהנה", אי נמי: "ועשה אחת" ולישתוק. מדכתבינהו הכי — שמע מינה למדרש כל חד וחד לחודיה לחייבו על אחת, ועל מאחת, כלומר מקצת העבירה, על הנה ועל מהנה, כדמפרש: הנה — אבות, מהנה — תולדות, ולמדרשינהו נמי כי הדדי הכי מדסמכי להדדי. אחת שהיא הנה — כלומר פעמים שהוא חייב על מצוה אחת חטאות הרבה, והנה שהיא אחת — פעמים שאינו חייב אלא אחת על מצות הרבה. והכי משמע: מאחת — מחייב הנה, מהנה — מחייב אחת, מדכתיב מ׳ יתירא. והשתא מפרש לה: אחת — כשעשה עבירה שלימה, שנתכוין לכתוב שמעון וכתבו כולו. מאחת — על מקצתו נמי מחייב, כגון נתכוין לכתוב שמעון ולא כתב אלא שתי אותיות — חייב. ולהכי נקט שמעון משום דשתי אותיות ראשונות הוו להו שם במקום אחר, כגון שם בן נח. והוא הדין גד מגדיאל, דן מדניאל. אבל נתכוין לכתוב שם אחר כגון נפתלי ולא כתב ממנו אלא שתי אותיות — לא מיחייב, שאין כאן מלאכה בשום מקום. מהנה תולדות — דנפקא לן מדדמי להו לאבות, והיינו "מהנה", כלומר: מן הדומות להם. אחת שהיא הנה — דאמרן לעיל פעמים שמתחייב על כל אחת ואחת, דהיינו על אחת הנה — על מצוה אחת כמה חטאות, כגון עושה מלאכות הרבה בזדון שבת ושגגות מלאכות כדפרישית לעיל, דיש כאן שגגות הרבה.

HALAKHAH

זְדוֹן שַׁבָּת, וּשְׁגָגוֹת מְלָאכוֹת **Intentional violation regarding the Sabbath, and unintentional violation regarding the labors.** "If someone knew that it was the Sabbath, but he was ignorant of the law, for example, he did not know that the labors he was performing were forbidden, or he knew that they were forbidden, but he did not know that they bear the penalty of excision, he is liable for a separate sin-offering for each different category of labor

TRANSLATION AND COMMENTARY

expressions also teaches that a person is sometimes liable for **many** transgressions only **one** sin-offering. [1]For example, **he did not know** that it was **the Sabbath, but he knew** that **the labors** that he was performing were forbidden on that day. Rabbi Yose treated each category of labor separately, inferring from the verse, "And shall do of one of them." Thus he can understand the verse, "You shall kindle no fire," as teaching that the prohibition against kindling a fire on the Sabbath is a plain negative commandment, and therefore not punishable by stoning or *karet*. [2]**But here** regarding idol worship, Rabbi Yose **does not derive the separate treatment of each mode** of worship regarding sin-offerings **from anywhere else,** [3]so perhaps **everybody agrees that bowing down** to an idol **was singled out** from among all the other modes of worship in order **to distinguish** between the modes of idol worship, so that a person who unwittingly performed several modes of idol worship is obligated to sacrifice a separate sin-offering for each mode of worship.

חִילּוּק מְלָאכוֹת [4]The Gemara asks: Why do we not **also learn that each mode of idol worship should be treated separately** regarding sin-offerings from the verse, **"of one of them"**? That verse does not refer specifically to the Sabbath, but rather it refers in general to prohibitions for whose inadvertent transgression one brings a sin-offering. Just as we interpret the verse regarding the Sabbath, so we should interpret the verse regarding idol worship as follows: [5]The word **"one"** teaches that a person is liable for a sin-offering if he completed a single mode of idol worship. [6]For example, he might have **slaughtered** an animal for an idol, cutting both its windpipe and esophagus. [7]The expression **"of one"** teaches that a person is liable for idol worship, even if he did not complete the mode of worship. For example, he might have slaughtered an animal for an idol, [8]cutting through only **one** of its **organs,** either its windpipe or its esophagus. [9]The word **"them"** teaches that a person is liable for a sin-offering if he performed any of the **principal modes** of idol worship: [10]**Slaughtering** an animal for an idol, **burning incense** before it, **offering** it **a** wine-**libation, or bowing down** before it. [11]The expression **"of them"** teaches that a person is liable for a sin-offering if he performed any of the **sub-categories** of those principal modes of worship. [12]For example, he might have **broken a stick in front of** the idol which is usually worshiped that way, for breaking a stick in front of an idol is a sub-category of slaughtering an animal for it. [13]The combination of expressions, "of one" and "of them," teaches that a person is sometimes liable for the violation of **one** prohibition **many**

שֶׁהִיא אַחַת — [1]שִׁגְגַת שַׁבָּת, וּזְדוֹן מְלָאכוֹת. [2]אֲבָל הָכָא, דְּלָא נָפְקָא לֵיהּ חִילּוּק מְלָאכוֹת מִדּוּכְתָּא אַחֲרִיתִי — [3]דְּכוּלֵּי עָלְמָא הִשְׁתַּחֲוָאָה לְחַלֵּק יָצְאָה. [4]חִילּוּק מְלָאכוֹת דַּעֲבוֹדָה זָרָה נַמִי תֵּיפּוּק לֵיהּ מֵ״אַחַת מֵהֵנָּה״: [5]״אַחַת״ — [6]זְבִיחָה, [7]״מֵאַחַת״ — [8]סִימָן אֶחָד, [9]״הֵנָּה״ — אָבוֹת: [10]זִיבּוּחַ, קִיטּוּר, נִיסּוּךְ, וְהִשְׁתַּחֲוָאָה. [11]״מֵהֵנָּה״ — תּוֹלָדוֹת: [12]שָׁבַר מַקֵּל לְפָנֶיהָ. [13]אַחַת שֶׁהִיא הֵנָּה

LITERAL TRANSLATION

which is one — [1]unintentional violation regarding the Sabbath, and intentional violation regarding the labors. [2]But here, where he does not derive the separate treatment of each labor from another place, [3]everybody agrees (lit., "the whole world") [that] bowing down was specified to distinguish.

[4]Learn also the separate treatment of each labor regarding idol worship from "of one of them": [5]"One" — [6]sacrificing; [7]"of one" — [8]one organ; [9]"them" — principal modes [of worship]: [10]Sacrificing, burning incense, offering a libation, and bowing. [11]Of them" — subcategories: [12]If he broke a stick in front of it. [13]One which is them

RASHI

שגגת שבת וזדון מלאכות — יודע שמלאכות הללו אסורות בשבת, אבל כסבור אין שבת היום — כולה חדא שגגה היא. דכולי עלמא לחלק יצאה — דהכל מודים דכל היוצא מן הכלל ללמד על הכלל כלו יצא, אי לא נפקא לן מדוכתא אחריתי, ומשום הכי אמר ליה פוק תני לברא. דאפילו לרבי יוסי חייב על כל אחת ואחת. תיפוק לי מאחת מהנה — לרבי אבא פריך, נהי דמתניתין רבי יוסי היא דהשתחואה ללאו יצאה — מיהו תיפוק לן דחייב על כל אחת ואחת "מהנה" כדנפקא ליה לרבי יוסי בשבת, דהא האי קרא גבי חטאת סתמא כתיב ונדרשיה נמי בעבודה זרה הכי, אחת ועשה אחת — שעשה עבודה שלימה כגון זבח, מאחת ועשה מאחת — כגון שחט סימן אחד לעבודה זרה, דאשכחן ליה הכשר גבי חטאת העוף בפנים. שבר מקל לפניה — לשם עבודה זרה, דדמי לשחיטה ששובר מפרקתה. וכגון דדרכה לעובדה במקל כדאמרינן במסכת עבודה זרה בפרק "רבי ישמעאל" (נא,א): עבודה זרה שעובדין אותה במקל, שבר מקל לפניה — חייב. אחת שהיא הנה — פעמים שהוא חייב על עבודה אחת חטאות הרבה, כגון שעבד עבודות הרבה.

HALAKHAH

that he performed." (*Rambam, Sefer Korbanot, Hilkhot Shegagot* 7:3.)

שִׁגְגַת שַׁבָּת, וּזְדוֹן מְלָאכוֹת Unintentional violation regarding the Sabbath, and intentional violation regarding the labors. "If someone knew the laws of Sabbath, but forgot that it was the Sabbath, then even if he performed many different labors, he is liable for only one sin-offering." (*Rambam, Sefer Korbanot, Hilkhot Shegagot* 7:2.)

TRANSLATION AND COMMENTARY

sin-offerings. [1]For example, he might have **known** that there was a prohibition **regarding idol worship, but he did not know** which **modes of worship** are forbidden, and he performed several modes of worship. [2]That combination of expressions also teaches that a person is sometimes liable for the commission of **many** transgressions only **one** sin-offering. [3]For example, he might **not have known** that the worship of a certain statue was considered **idol worship, but he knew that the** various **modes of idol worship** that he was performing were forbidden.

הַאי [4]The Gemara objects: How can you argue that the verse also refers to idol worship? **How can you visualize a case when someone did not know** that the worship of a certain statue was considered **idol worship,** but he knew that the various modes of idol worship that he was performing were forbidden? [5]**If** a person **thought** that **he was** in **a synagogue,** where worship of God is permitted, **and** it turned out that he was in a heathen temple and that **he** had **bowed down to** an idol, [6]**surely his heart was** directed **to** God in **heaven,** and so he should be exempt from all liability. [7]**Rather,** the person must have **seen a statue** of a human figure, not knowing that it was an idol, **and** he **bowed down to it.** [8]But this is difficult, for **if he accepted** the statue **upon himself** as a god, [9]surely **he is an intentional sinner,** and therefore not liable for a sin-offering. [10]And **if he did not accept** the statue **upon himself** as a god, but rather he merely bowed down to the statue as a sign of honor, [11]**he did not commit any** transgression for which he should be liable for a sin-offering.

אֶלָּא [12]**Rather,** it must be that the person bowed down to an idol **out of love or fear** of another person, not knowing that bowing down to the idol out of love or fear of another person is forbidden. [13]Now, **this is well according to Abaye, who said** above **that** in such a case, **he is liable** for a sin-offering. [14]**But according to Rava, who said** above **that** in such a case, **he is exempt** from bringing a sin-offering, **what is there to say?** [15]**Rather,** the person must have **thought that** idol worship **is permitted** altogether. The verse teaches that even if he committed many transgressions under the false impression that idol worship is permitted altogether, he is liable for only one sin-offering. The Gemara now asks: But this too is difficult, for if this is what the verse teaches, [16]we should be able to **resolve** the question **which Rava asked of Rav Naḥman:**

— [1]זְדוֹן עֲבוֹדָה זָרָה וְשִׁגְגַת עֲבוֹדוֹת. [2]הֲנָּה שֶׁהִיא אַחַת — [3]שִׁגְגַת עֲבוֹדָה זָרָה, וּזְדוֹן עֲבוֹדוֹת.

[4]הַאי שִׁגְגַת עֲבוֹדָה זָרָה, הֵיכִי דָּמֵי? [5]אִי קָסָבַר בֵּית הַכְּנֶסֶת הוּא וְהִשְׁתַּחֲוָה לוֹ, [6]הֲרֵי לִבּוֹ לַשָּׁמַיִם. [7]אֶלָּא דַּחֲזָא אַנְדַּרְטָא וְסָגֵיד לֵיהּ. [8]אִי קַבְּלֵיהּ עֲלֵיהּ, [9]מֵזִיד הוּא. [10]אִי לָא קַבְּלֵיהּ עֲלֵיהּ, [11]לֹא כְּלוּם הוּא.

[12]אֶלָּא, מֵאַהֲבָה וּמִיִּרְאָה. [13]הָנִיחָא לְאַבַּיֵי, דְּאָמַר חַיָּיב. [14]אֶלָּא לְרָבָא, דְּאָמַר פָּטוּר, מַאי אִיכָּא לְמֵימַר? [15]אֶלָּא, בְּאוֹמֵר מוּתָּר. [16]תִּפְשׁוֹט דִּבְעָא

LITERAL TRANSLATION

— [1]intentional violation regarding idol worship, and unintentional violation regarding the [modes of] worship. [2]Them which is one — [3]unintentional violation regarding idol worship, and intentional violation regarding the [modes of] worship.

[4]This unintentional violation regarding idol worship, what is it like? [5]If he thought it was a synagogue, and he bowed down to it, [6]surely his heart is to heaven. [7]Rather, he saw a statue, and bowed down to it. [8]If he accepted it upon himself, [9]he is an intentional sinner. [10]If he did not accept it upon himself, [11]it is nothing.

[12]Rather, from love or fear. [13]This is well according to Abaye, who said that he is liable. [14]But according to Rava, who said that he is exempt, what is there to say? [15]Rather, when he said it is permitted. [16]Resolve

RASHI

בזדון עבודה זרה ושגגת עבודות — דיודע שעבודה זרה אסורה בזבוח, אבל כסבור שמותר לקטר ולנסך ולהשתחוות. **האי שגגת עבודה זרה היכי דמי?** — כלומר היכי מתוקם קרא בעבודה זרה, הא לא משכחת לה שגגת עבודה זרה בזדון עבודות, הלכך לא נפקא לן בעבודה זרה חלוק מלאכות מהכא. **אלא מאהבה ומיראה** — יודע שאסורה עבודה זרה בעבודות הללו, אבל שגג בכך, כסבור שאין עבודה זרה בתורה מאהבה ומיראת אדם, והוי כשגגת עבודה זרה וזדון עבודות דמחייב חדא. **אלא באומר מותר** — כסבור אין עבודה זרה בתורה, ונהי דלא הוי שגגת עבודה זרה וזדון עבודות אלא שגגת זה וזה, מיהו קרא דקאמר הנה שהיא אחת בהכי מוקים לה.

HALAKHAH

שִׁגְגַת עֲבוֹדָה זָרָה **Unintentional violation regarding idol worship.** "If someone bowed down to an idol, and offered it a libation, and burned incense before it, and offered it a sacrifice, all in one period of unawareness, he is liable for four sin-offerings. This ruling applies if he knew that it was forbidden to worship that idol, but he did not know that those modes of worship were forbidden. But if he knew that those modes of worship were forbidden, but he did not know that it was forbidden to worship that particular idol, he is liable for only one sin-offering," following Rabbi Yoḥanan, against Rabbi Zakkai. (*Rambam, Sefer Korbanot, Hilkhot Shegagot* 7:1.)

מִינֵּיהּ רָבָא מֵרַב נַחְמָן: [1]הֶעְלֵם זֶה וְזֶה בְּיָדוֹ, מַהוּ? [2]תִּיפְשׁוֹט דְּאֵינוֹ חַיָּיב אֶלָּא אַחַת!
[3]הָא לָא קַשְׁיָא, [4]וְתִפְשׁוֹט.
[5]וּמִי מָצֵית מוֹקְמַתְּ לְהָנֵי קְרָאֵי בַּעֲבוֹדָה זָרָה, [6]דְּאִילּוּ הָכָא כְּתִיב בְּמָשִׁיחַ פַּר, וּבְנָשִׂיא שָׂעִיר, וּבְיָחִיד כִּשְׂבָּה וּשְׂעִירָה, [7]וְאִילּוּ בַּעֲבוֹדָה זָרָה, תְּנַן: [8]״וְשָׁוִין שֶׁבִּשְׂעִירָה כְּיָחִיד״.
[9]וְתוּ לָא מִידֵּי.
[10]כִּי אֲתָא רַב שְׁמוּאֵל בַּר יְהוּדָה אָמַר: [62B] [11]הָכִי תְּנָא קַמֵּיהּ: ״חוֹמֶר בַּשַּׁבָּת מִשְּׁאָר מִצְוֹת, [12]חוֹמֶר בִּשְׁאָר מִצְוֹת מִבַּשַּׁבָּת. [13]חוֹמֶר בַּשַּׁבָּת —

TRANSLATION AND COMMENTARY

[1]If a person **was unaware of** both **this and that,** meaning that he performed a number of forbidden labors on the Sabbath, knowing neither that it was the Sabbath nor that those labors are forbidden, **what is the law?** Is he liable for only one sin-offering, like someone who does not know what day it is and performs several forbidden labors on the Sabbath, or is he liable for a sin-offering for each labor, like someone who performs several forbidden labors on the Sabbath, not knowing that those labors are forbidden? If this is what the verse comes to teach, why then was Rava's question left unresolved? Just as when a person committed several idolatrous acts under the false impression that idol worship is permitted altogether, he is liable for only a single sin-offering, so too if he performed several forbidden labors, not knowing that it was the Sabbath, nor that those labors are forbidden, [2]**he should be liable for only one** sin-offering!

הָא לָא קַשְׁיָא [3]The Gemara responds: **This is not difficult.** [4]Indeed, we can **resolve** Rava's question from here.

וּמִי מָצֵית [5]The Gemara objects: **But can you** really **explain this verse,** "And shall do of one of them," **as referring to idol worship?** [6]But surely **here** in the passage containing that verse **it states that an anointed High Priest** brings **a bullock** as his sin-offering for his unwitting transgression, **the king** brings **a goat, and an** ordinary **individual** brings **a lamb or a she-goat,** [7]**whereas regarding** the unwitting commission of **idol worship, it was taught** earlier in a Baraita: [8]**"And** all **agree** that a High Priest who unwittingly committed idol worship is obligated to bring **a she-goat** as his sin-offering just **like an** ordinary **individual."** Thus, it follows that the verse, "And shall do of one of them," cannot be referring to the unwitting commission of idol worship.

וְתוּ לָא מִידֵּי [9]The discussion is concluded: There is **nothing more** to say about the matter, for it has been demonstrated that the verse, "And shall do of one of them," cannot refer to idol worship, and so we cannot learn from that verse that each mode of idol worship should be treated separately regarding sin-offerings. Thus, the objection raised by Rav Yosef earlier in the passage stands.

כִּי אֲתָא [10]The Gemara continues: **When Rav Shmuel bar Yehudah came** to Babylonia from Eretz Israel, **he said:** [62B] [11]Rabbi Zakkai **taught** a Baraita **before** Rabbi Yoḥanan **as follows: "There is a stringency regarding the Sabbath greater than the rest of the** Torah's **commandments,** [12]**and** there is **a stringency regarding the rest of the** Torah's **commandments greater than the Sabbath.** How so? [13]**There is a stringency regarding the Sabbath**

LITERAL TRANSLATION

that which Rava asked of Rav Naḥman: [1]If he had unawareness of this and that in his hand, what [is the law]? [2]Resolve that he is liable only for one!

[3]This is not difficult, [4]and resolve it.

[5]But can you explain these verses as [referring to] idol worship, [6]for here is written regarding the anointed [High Priest] a bullock, and regarding the king a goat, and regarding an individual a lamb or a she-goat, [7]whereas regarding idol worship, we have learned: [8]"And they agree that [he is liable for] a she-goat like an individual."

[9]And nothing more.

[10]When Rav Shmuel bar Yehudah came, he said: [62B] [11]Thus, he taught before him: "There is a stringency regarding the Sabbath more than the rest of the commandments, [12][and] a stringency regarding the rest of the commandments more than the Sabbath. [13]There is a stringency regarding the Sabbath,

RASHI

דבעא מיניה רבא מרב נחמן – במסכת שבת פרק "כלל גדול" (ע,ב). להני קראי – האי "אחת" והאי "הנה". ואילו בעבודה זרה תניא (תנן) – לעיל ושוין רבי וחכמים שכהן משיח בשעירה כיחיד. ותו לא מידי – ליכא לשנויי מידי, הלכך לא נפקא לן חלוק מלאכות בעבודה זרה מהכא אלא מהשתחואה כאתקפתא דרב יוסף, והא דרבי זכאי דפטר לה בחדא נפקא (לקמן סג) מ"לא תעבדם" – הכתוב עשאן עבודה אחת. הכי תנא קמיה – רבי זכאי קמיה דרבי יוחנן. חומר בשבת וכו' – לקמן מפרש לה.

SAGES

רַב שְׁמוּאֵל בַּר יְהוּדָה **Rav Shmuel bar Yehudah.** A Babylonian Amora of the third generation, Rav Shmuel bar Yehudah was a disciple and close friend of the famous Amora Rav Yehudah (bar Yeḥezkel). Rav Shmuel came from a family of proselytes and reached prominence as a Rabbinic scholar. He visited Eretz Israel and studied with Rabbi Yoḥanan and Rabbi Elazar in Tiberias, and transmitted to Babylonia many rulings of the Palestinian Amoraim. Abaye was one of his disciples.

HALAKHAH

הֶעְלֵם זֶה וְזֶה בְּיָדוֹ **If he had unawareness of this and that in his hand.** "If someone forgot that it was the Sabbath, and he also did not know that the labors he was performing were forbidden, he is liable for only one sin-offering," in accordance with the answer given to Rava's question. (*Rambam, Sefer Korbanot, Hilkhot Shegagot* 7:4.)

SAGES

רַבִּי אַמִּי Rabbi Ammi. A Palestinian Amora of the third generation, Rabbi Ammi (bar Natan) was a priest and a close friend of Rabbi Assi. They studied with ;the greatest Sages of Eretz Israel and were especially close disciples of Rabbi Yoḥanan. Rabbi Ammi also studied with Rabbi Yoḥanan's greatest students. In the Jerusalem Talmud he is commonly known as Rabbi Immi.

After Rabbi Yoḥanan's death Rabbi Ammi was appointed head of the Tiberias Yeshiva. The Sages of Babylonia also consulted him about Halakhic problems. He is widely quoted in both the Babylonian and the Jerusalem Talmud. Rabbi Ammi seems to have lived to a great age, and even the Sages of the fourth generation in Babylonia used to send him their questions.

[1] שֶׁהַשַּׁבָּת עָשָׂה שְׁתַּיִם בְּהֶעְלֵם אֶחָד — [2] חַיָּיב עַל כָּל אַחַת וְאַחַת, [3] מַה שֶּׁאֵין כֵּן בִּשְׁאָר מִצְוֹת. [4] חוֹמֶר בִּשְׁאָר מִצְוֹת — [5] שֶׁבִּשְׁאָר מִצְוֹת שָׁגַג בְּלֹא מִתְכַּוֵּין — חַיָּיב, [6] מַה שֶּׁאֵין כֵּן בַּשַּׁבָּת.

[7] אָמַר מָר: ״חוֹמֶר בַּשַּׁבָּת שֶׁהַשַּׁבָּת עָשָׂה שְׁתַּיִם כו׳״. [8] הֵיכִי דָּמֵי? [9] אִילֵימָא דְּעָבַד קְצִירָה וּטְחִינָה, [10] דִּכְוָותָהּ גַּבֵּי שְׁאָר מִצְוֹת, דְּאָכַל חֵלֶב וְדָם. [11] הָכָא תַּרְתֵּי מִיחַיַּיב, [12] וְהָכָא תַּרְתֵּי מִיחַיַּיב! [13] אֶלָּא, גַּבֵּי שְׁאָר מִצְוֹת דְּאֵינוֹ חַיָּיב אֶלָּא אַחַת הֵיכִי דָּמֵי? [14] דְּאָכַל חֵלֶב וְחֵלֶב, [15] דִּכְוָותָהּ גַּבֵּי שַׁבָּת דְּעָבַד קְצִירָה וּקְצִירָה. [16] הָכָא חֲדָא מִיחַיַּיב, [17] וְהָכָא חֲדָא

LITERAL TRANSLATION

[1] for regarding the Sabbath, [if] someone did two in one period of unawareness, [2] he is liable for each one, [3] which is not so regarding the rest of the commandments. [4] There is a stringency regarding the rest of the commandments, [5] for regarding the rest of the commandments, [if] someone unwittingly sinned without intention, he is liable, [6] which is not so regarding the Sabbath.

[7] The master said: "There is a stringency regarding the Sabbath, for regarding the Sabbath, [if] someone did two, etc." [8] What is it like? [9] If you say that he performed reaping and grinding, [10] the corresponding case regarding the rest of the commandments is eating fat and blood. [11] Here he is liable for two, [12] and here he is liable for two! [13] Rather, regarding the rest of the commandments, when he is only liable for one, what is it like? [14] [If you say] when he ate fat and fat, [15] the corresponding case regarding the Sabbath is when he performed reaping and reaping. [16] Here he is liable for one, [17] and here he

TRANSLATION AND COMMENTARY

greater than the rest of the Torah's commandments, [1] **for regarding the Sabbath, if someone** inadvertently **performed two** forbidden labors **in one period of unawareness,** performing the second forbidden labor before realizing that he had sinned the first time, [2] **he is liable** for a separate sin-offering **for each** forbidden act, [3] **which is not so regarding the rest of the** Torah's **commandments.** [4] And **there is a stringency regarding the rest of the** Torah's **commandments** greater than the Sabbath, [5] **for regarding the rest of the** Torah's **commandments, if someone unwittingly sinned without intention, he is liable** for a sin-offering, [6] **which is not so regarding the Sabbath,** as will be explained below.

אָמַר מָר [7] It was said above in the Baraita: **"There is a stringency regarding the Sabbath** greater than the rest of the Torah's commandments, **for regarding the Sabbath, if someone** inadvertently **performed two** forbidden labors in one period of unawareness, he is liable for a separate sin-offering for each one that he had performed, which is not the case regarding the rest of the Torah's commandments." The Gemara wishes to clarify the meaning of this statement: [8] **How do you visualize the case?** [9] **If you say that** the Baraita is referring to a person who **performed** two different principal labors on the Sabbath, such **reaping and grinding,** [10] **the corresponding example regarding the rest of the** Torah's **commandments is eating** two different prohibited foods, such as **fat and blood.** [11] But this is difficult, for **here** regarding the Sabbath **he is liable for two** sin-offerings, [12] **and here** too regarding the rest of the Torah's commandments, **he is liable for two** sin-offerings! [13] **Rather, regarding the rest of the** Torah's **commandments, how do you visualize** a case **where he** performs two transgressions and **is liable for only one** sin-offering? [14] **If you say** that the Baraita is referring to the eating of forbidden **fat and** then eating more **fat,** all in the same period of unawareness, [15] **the corresponding case regarding the Sabbath would be reaping and** then **reaping again,** all in the same period of unawareness. [16] But this too is difficult, for **here** regarding the rest of the Torah's commandments **he is liable for** only **one** sin-offering, [17] **and here** regarding the Sabbath **he is also liable for** only **one** sin-offering! Thus, it seems that there is no special stringency regarding the number of sin-offerings for multiple violations of the Sabbath in relation to the number of sin-offerings brought for multiple violations of the rest of the

RASHI

שגג בלא מתכוין — לא נתכוין למלאכה זו אלא לדבר אחר ועלתה בידו מלאכה זו. קצירה וטחינה — דאיכא שמות מחולקין, ומשום הכי חייב שתים. חלב וחלב — שני זיתים בשני ימים ולא נודע לו בנתיים שחטא — אינו חייב אלא אחת, כדפרש טעמא לקמן.

NOTES

קְצִירָה וּטְחִינָה — חֵלֶב וְדָם **Reaping and grinding — fat and blood.** It may be asked: How can the Gemara compare reaping and grinding on the Sabbath to eating fat and blood? Although reaping and grinding on the Sabbath require separate sin-offerings, they are both violations of the same law, whereas eating fat and blood are two totally separate prohibitions! It might be suggested that since the prohibitions against eating fat and blood are recorded in the same verse, they might be regarded as one category of prohibition (*Arukh LeNer*).

[1]מִיחַיַּיב! [1]וְהַיְינוּ דְּאָמַר לֵיהּ: פּוּק תְּנִי לְבָרָא!

[2]מַאי קוּשְׁיָא? [3]דִּילְמָא לְעוֹלָם אֵימָא לָךְ דְּעָבַד קְצִירָה וּטְחִינָה. [4]מַה שֶּׁאֵין כֵּן בִּשְׁאָר מִצְוֹת — [5]אֲתָאן לַעֲבוֹדָה זָרָה, כִּדְרַבִּי אַמִי, [6]דְּאָמַר רַבִּי אַמִי: זִיבֵּחַ וְקִיטֵּר וְנִיסֵּךְ בְּהֶעְלֵם אֶחָד [7]אֵינוֹ חַיָּיב אֶלָּא אַחַת.

[8]לָא מִיתּוֹקְמָא לֵיהּ בַּעֲבוֹדָה זָרָה, [9]דְּקָתָנֵי סֵיפָא: "חוֹמֶר בִּשְׁאָר מִצְוֹת, [10]שֶׁבִּשְׁאָר מִצְוֹת שָׁגַג בְּלֹא מִתְכַּוֵּין, חַיָּיב". [11]שׁוֹגֵג בְּלֹא מִתְכַּוֵּין בַּעֲבוֹדָה זָרָה, הֵיכִי דָּמֵי? [12]אִי דְּקָסָבַר בֵּית הַכְּנֶסֶת הוּא, וְהִשְׁתַּחֲוָה לוֹ, [13]הֲרֵי לִבּוֹ לַשָּׁמַיִם! [14]אֶלָּא דַּחֲזָא אַנְדַּרְטָא, וְסָגִיד לֵיהּ, [15]אִי קַבְּלֵיהּ עֲלֵיהּ בֶּאֱלוֹהַּ, מֵזִיד הוּא. [16]וְאִי לָא קַבְּלֵיהּ עֲלֵיהּ,

LITERAL TRANSLATION

is liable for one! [1]And that is what he said to him: Go out [and] teach outside!

[2]What is the difficulty? [3]Perhaps in fact I can say to you when he performed reaping and grinding. [4]Which is not so regarding the rest of the commandments — [5]we have come to idol worship, like that of Rabbi Ammi. [6]For Rabbi Ammi said: [If] someone sacrificed, and burned incense, and offered a libation in one period of unawareness, [7]he is only liable for one [sin-offering].

[8]You cannot explain it as referring to idol worship, [9]for the last clause teaches: "There is a stringency regarding the rest of the commandments, [10]for regarding the rest of the commandments, [if] someone unwittingly sinned without intention, he is liable." [11]Sinning unwittingly without intention regarding idol worship, what is it like? [12]If he thinks it is a synagogue, and he bowed down to it, [13]surely his heart is to Heaven! [14]Rather, he saw a statue, and bowed down to it. [15]If he accepted it upon himself as a god, he is an intentional sinner. [16]If he did not accept it upon himself,

TRANSLATION AND COMMENTARY

Torah's commandments. [1]**And that is why** Rabbi Yoḥanan **said to** Rabbi Zakkai: **Go out** of the academy, **and teach** that Baraita **outside,** for that Baraita is not fit to be brought inside.

מַאי קוּשְׁיָא [2]The Gemara asks in astonishment: **What was** Rabbi Yoḥanan's **difficulty** that he rejected the Baraita taught by Rabbi Zakkai? [3]**Perhaps in fact I can say to you** that the Baraita refers to a person who **performed** two different principal labors on the Sabbath, such as **reaping and grinding.** And regarding that which the Baraita states: [4]**"Which is not the case regarding the rest of the** Torah's **commandments,"** [5]**we have come to** transgressions involving **idol worship, as** was argued by **Rabbi Ammi.** [6]**For Rabbi Ammi said: If someone** unwittingly **slaughtered a sacrifice** before an idol, **and burned incense** before it, **and offered** it **a libation** of wine, serving the idol in these three ways **in one period of unawareness,** before realizing that he had sinned, [7]**he is only liable for one sin-offering.** Here the Sabbath prohibitions are greater than those concerning idol worship. For regarding the Sabbath, a person is liable for a separate sin-offering for each labor that he had inadvertently performed, but regarding idol worship, he is not liable for a separate sin-offering for each mode of worship in which he served the idol.

לָא מִיתּוֹקְמָא לֵיהּ [8]The Gemara rejects this interpretation of the Baraita: **You cannot explain** the Baraita **as referring to idol worship,** [9]**for the next clause teaches: "There is a stringency regarding the rest of the** Torah's **commandments,** [10]**for regarding the rest of the** Torah's **commandments, if someone unwittingly sinned without intention, he is liable** for a sin-offering, which is not the case regarding the Sabbath." [11]The Gemara first clarifies the meaning of this statement: **How do you visualize** an instance of **sinning unwittingly and without intention regarding idol worship?** [12]**If** you say that the Baraita is referring to a person who **thought** that **he was** in **a synagogue,** where worship of God is permitted, **and** he was in a heathen temple and **bowed to** an idol, there is a difficulty, [13]for **surely his heart was** directed **to** God in **Heaven,** and so he was exempt from all liability! [14]**Rather,** the Baraita must be dealing with a person who **saw a statue** of a human figure, not knowing that it was an idol, **and** he **bowed to it.** [15]But this too is difficult, for **if he accepted** the statue **upon himself as a god,** surely **he is an intentional sinner,** and therefore not liable for a sin-offering. [16]And **if he did not accept** the statue **upon himself** as a god, but he bowed to

RASHI

שבשאר מצות שגג בלא מתכוין — בחלבין ובעריות איכא למתוקמא — כגון חלב המהותך לפניו וכסבור רוק הוא ובלעו, דלא מתכוין לאכילה אלא מתעסק בדבר אחר, בבליעת רוק. והיכי דמי שוגג גמור — כסבור שומן הוא ואכלו, דנתכוין לאכילה. אבל זה לא שוגג הוא ואפילו הכי חייב, כדאמרן לקמן בשמעתין — שכן נהנה, מה שאין כן בשבת, כגון נתכוין להגביה את התלוש וחתך את המחובר — פטור, שנאמר (ויקרא ד) "אשר חטא בה" — עד שיתכוין למלאכה זו, פרט למתעסק בדבר אחר ועלתה בידו מלאכה זו. ומיהו מתעסק ועלה בידו אכילת חלבים או עריות — חייב, שכבר נהנה. אבל בעבודה זרה ליכא לאוקומא. והיכי דמי שגג בלא מתכוין — אי נימא וכו'. **הרי לבו לשמים** — ולשמים נתכוין והשתחוה, ואין כאן עבירה כלל לא שוגג ולא מזיד.

TRANSLATION AND COMMENTARY

it as a sign of honor, **he did not commit any** transgression for which he should be liable for a sin-offering. [1]**Rather,** the Baraita must be dealing with a person who bowed to an idol **from love or fear** of someone else, not knowing that such an act is forbidden. [2]Now, **this is well according to Abaye, who said** earlier **that** in such a case **he is liable** for a sin-offering. [3]**But according to Rava, who said that he is exempt, what is there to say?**

אֶלָּא בְּאוֹמֵר [4]**Rather,** continues the Gemara, the Baraita must be dealing with a person who **thought that** idol worship **is permitted** altogether, ruling that he is liable for a sin-offering, [5]**which is not so regarding the Sabbath,** for **he would be exempt altogether.** [6]But this too is difficult, for **Rava only asked Rav Naḥman about** a person who **was unaware of** both **this and that,** meaning that he performed a number of forbidden labors on the Sabbath, knowing neither that it was the Sabbath, nor that those labors are forbidden. [7]Rava wanted to know **whether he is liable for one** sin-offering, **or for two** or more sin-offerings, one for each labor that he had performed. [8]**But** that **he should be exempt altogether** from liability for a sin-offering — **there is no one who said that!** You cannot argue that when the Baraita speaks of the rest of the Torah's commandments, it is referring to the prohibition against idol worship, for then you cannot explain the second clause of the Baraita.

מַאי קוּשְׁיָא [9]The Gemara rebuts this objection: **What is the difficulty?** [10]**Perhaps in fact I can say to you that the first clause refers to** the greater stringency of Sabbath laws in comparison to that of **idol worship and the next clause refers to** the greater stringency of **the rest of the** Torah's **commandments,** other than the prohibition against idol worship, in comparison to that concerning the Sabbath. And we can explain the Baraita as follows: The rest of the Torah's commandments are more stringent than those of the Sabbath, for regarding the rest of the Torah's commandments, [11]if **someone unwittingly sinned without intention,** [12]and **he thought that** what was in his mouth **was** only **spittle, and** so **he swallowed it,** and it turned out that it was forbidden fat that he had eaten, he is liable for a sin-offering. [13]**This is not so regarding the Sabbath,** for **he is exempt** from a sin-offering for similar unintentional violation of the Sabbath. [14]For example, **if** a person **had intended to lift up something which was detached** from the ground, which is a permissible act, [15]**but** instead **he** inadvertently **cut off** a plant **which was** still **attached** to the ground, which is forbidden because of the prohibition against reaping, **he is exempt** from bringing a sin-offering, for a person is not liable for violating the Sabbath with an unintended labor. [16]This is **in accordance with what Rav Naḥman said in the name of Shmuel, who said:** [17]**If a**

לֹא כְּלוּם הִיא. [1]אֶלָּא, מֵאַהֲבָה וּמִיִּרְאָה. [2]הָנִיחָא לְאַבַּיֵי דְּאָמַר חַיָּיב. [3]אֶלָּא לְרָבָא, דְּאָמַר פָּטוּר, מַאי אִיכָּא לְמֵימַר? [4]אֶלָּא בְּאוֹמֵר מוּתָּר. [5]מַה שֶּׁאֵין כֵּן בַּשַּׁבָּת, דְּפָטוּר לְגַמְרֵי. [6]עַד כָּאן לָא בְּעָא מִינֵּיהּ רָבָא מֵרַב נַחְמָן הֶעְלֵם זֶה וָזֶה, [7]אֶלָּא אִי לְחַיּוּבֵי חֲדָא, אִי לְחַיּוּבֵי תַּרְתֵּי. [8]פָּטוּר לְגַמְרֵי, לֵיכָּא לְמַאן דְּאָמַר!

[9]מַאי קוּשְׁיָא? [10]דִּלְמָא לְעוֹלָם אֵימָא לָךְ רֵישָׁא בַּעֲבוֹדָה זָרָה וְסֵיפָא בִּשְׁאָר מִצְוֹת. [11]וְשָׁגַג בְּלֹא מִתְכַּוֵּין — [12]דְּקָסָבַר: רוֹק הוּא, וּבוֹלְעוֹ. [13]מַה שֶּׁאֵין כֵּן בַּשַּׁבָּת, דְּפָטוּר — [14]שֶׁנִּתְכַּוֵּין לְהַגְבִּיהַּ אֶת הַתָּלוּשׁ [15]וְחָתַךְ אֶת הַמְחוּבָּר פָּטוּר. [16]וְכִדְרַב נַחְמָן אָמַר שְׁמוּאֵל, דְּאָמַר: [17]הַמִּתְעַסֵּק

LITERAL TRANSLATION

it is nothing. [1]Rather, from love or fear. [2]This is well according to Abaye, who said that he is liable. [3]But according to Rava, who said that he is exempt, what is there to say?

[4]Rather, when he said it is permitted. [5]Which is not so regarding the Sabbath, for he is exempt altogether. [6]Up to now, Rava only asked Rav Naḥman [about] having unawareness of this and that, [7]whether to make him liable for one, or to make him liable for two. [8][But] to exempt him altogether, there is no one who said [that]!

[9]What is the difficulty? [10]Perhaps in fact I can say to you [that] the first clause refers to idol worship and the last clause refers to the rest of the commandments. [11]And sinning unwittingly without intention — [12]that he thought it was spittle, and he swallowed it. [13]Which is not so on the Sabbath, for he is exempt — [14]when he intended to lift up that which was detached, [15]and he cut that was attached, [in which case] he is exempt. [16]Like what Rav Naḥman said in the name of Shmuel, who said: [17]If a person acted

RASHI

אלא — שוגג בלא מתכוין, כגון מאהבה ומיראה, ולא נתכוין לעבודה זרה אלא לאהבת האיש ושגג, — כסבור מותר לעשות כן. אלא באומר מותר — דאמר אין עבודה זרה בתורה, וכיון דלא הוזכרה לו מעולם אין מתכוין קרי ליה. המתעסק

NOTES

הַמִּתְעַסֵּק בַּחֲלָבִים **If a person acted unawares regarding fats.** The difficulty has been raised: It appears that two separate

בַּחֲלָבִים וּבַעֲרָיוֹת — [1]חַיָּיב, שֶׁכֵּן נֶהֱנָה. [2]הַמִּתְעַסֵּק בַּשַּׁבָּת פָּטוּר. [3]מְלֶאכֶת מַחֲשֶׁבֶת אָסְרָה תּוֹרָה.

[4]רַבִּי יוֹחָנָן לְטַעֲמֵיהּ, [5]דְּלָא מוֹקֵים מַתְנִיתָא רֵישָׁא בְּחַד טַעְמָא [6]וְסֵיפָא בְּחַד טַעְמָא, [7]דְּאָמַר רַבִּי יוֹחָנָן: "מַאן דִּמְתַרְגֵּם לִי 'חָבִית' אַלִּיבָּא דְּחַד תַּנָּא, [8]מוֹבִילְנָא מָאנֵיהּ בַּתְרֵיהּ לְבֵי מַסּוּתָא".

LITERAL TRANSLATION

unawares regarding fats and forbidden sexual relations, [1]he is liable, for he benefitted. [2]If a person acted unawares on the Sabbath, he is exempt. [3]The Torah forbade purposeful labor.

[4]Rabbi Yoḥanan follows his own opinion, [5]not to explain the first clause with one reason, [6]and the last clause with another reason, [7]for Rabbi Yoḥanan said: "[If] anyone can explain to me [the Mishnah about] 'a barrel' according to one Tanna, [8]I will carry his clothing after him to the bath house."

TRANSLATION AND COMMENTARY

person acted unawares regarding fats and forbidden sexual relations — he ate forbidden fat or engaged in forbidden sexual relations without having intended to do the prohibited act, [1]**he is liable** for a sin-offering, **for he benefitted** from it. [2]But **if a person acted unawares regarding the Sabbath** — he performed a forbidden labor without having intended to do the prohibited act, **he is exempt** from bringing a sin-offering. [3]**The Torah** only **forbade purposeful labor** on the Sabbath, and labor that was performed unintentionally is not regarded as purposeful. Thus, the Baraita cited by Rabbi Zakkai can indeed be reconciled with the law, and so there is no reason for Rabbi Yoḥanan to reject it.

רַבִּי יוֹחָנָן [4]The Gemara explains: When **Rabbi Yoḥanan** rejected the Baraita, he **was following his own opinion** [5]that it is preferable **not to explain the first clause** of a Mishnah or a Baraita **as referring to one case,** [6]**and the next clause** of that same Mishnah or Baraita **as referring to another case.** Rather one should explain the entire Mishnah or Baraita consistently. [7]**For Rabbi Yoḥanan said: "If anyone can explain to me the Mishnah about a barrel** (*Bava Metzia* 41a) in such a way that it can possibly have been written **according to one Tanna,** and we will not have to interpret the two halves of the Mishnah as reflecting two differing schools of thought, [8]**I will** honor him by treating him as a disciple treats his teacher, by **carrying his clothing after him to the bathhouse."**

RASHI

בחלבים ובעריות — כשעלה בידו חלבים ועריות היה מתעסק ולא נתכוין לכך. כל מתעסק קרי ליה שאינו מתכוין בדבר זה כלל. **שכן נהנה** — הלכך חייב בכוונה. **מלאכת מחשבת** — שחשב לעשות זאת. **רבי יוחנן** — דאמר ליה פוק תני לברא, ולא אוקים רישא בעבודה זרה וסיפא בשאר מלות, אזיל לטעמיה דלא מוקים רישא בחד טעמא וסיפא בחד טעמא. **דאמר רבי יוחנן** — בבבא מציעא בפרק "המפקיד". **מאן דמתרגם לי חבית אליבא דחד תנא בו׳** — דקתני התם: המפקיד חבית אצל חברו ולא ייחדו לה הבעלים מקום וטלטלה ונשברה, אם מתוך ידו נשברה, לצרכו — חייב, לצרכה — פטור. אם משהניחה נשברה, בין לצרכה בין לצרכו — פטור. ייחדו לה הבעלים מקום וטלטלה ונשברה בין מתוך ידו בין משהניחה, לצרכו — חייב, לצרכה — פטור. ופריך התם: מני? רבי ישמעאל היא דאמר: לא בעינן דעת בעלים, דתניא: הגונב טלה מן העדר וסלע מן הכיס למקום שגנב יחזיר, דברי רבי ישמעאל. רבי עקיבא אומר: צריך דעת בעלים. אי רבי ישמעאל מאי איריא לא ייחדו, אפילו ייחדו נמי! לא מבעיא קאמר, לא מיבעיא ייחדו דמקומה הוא, אלא אפילו לא ייחדו דלאו מקומה הוא לא בעיא דעת בעלים. סיפא אתאן לרבי עקיבא. אי רבי עקיבא מאי איריא ייחדו, אפילו לא ייחדו נמי! לא מבעיא קאמר, לא מבעיא לא ייחדו דלאו מקומה הוא, אלא אפילו ייחדו נמי דמקומה הוא בעינן דעת בעלים, רישא רבי ישמעאל וסיפא רבי עקיבא, ואילו הוה בעי לאוקמא רישא בשהניחה במקומה הראשון וסיפא בשהניחה במקום שאינה מקומה כדמוקי לה אמוראי התם, הוי מצי לאוקומיה כולה כרבי ישמעאל. ואמר רבי יוחנן — מאן דמתרגם וכו׳ דלא הוה בעי לאוקמיה רישא בחד טעמא וסיפא בחד טעמא. **מסותא** = מרחץ, כמו מסחותה, "וירחץ" מתרגמינן (והסחי).

NOTES

rationales are offered here regarding the law that if a person acted unawares regarding fats or forbidden sexual relations, he is liable for a sin-offering. First, the sinner derived pleasure from his transgression; and second, except for the Sabbath violator, a person is liable for his transgression, even if it was committed unawares. *Ḥamra Vehaye* suggests that there are two types of acting unawares. A person might intend to do a certain permissible act which is similar to a forbidden act, and by mistake he might perform the forbidden act and so be liable, because the act was performed with prior intention. Alternatively, a person might commit a transgression without having intended to do any act whatsoever, in which case he is liable only because of the benefit which he derived from his transgression.

אַלִּיבָּא דְּחַד תַּנָּא **According to one Tanna.** When the Amoraim analyze a particular Mishnah or Baraita, they often find an internal contradiction. Sometimes the contradiction

HALAKHAH

הַמִּתְעַסֵּק בַּחֲלָבִים וּבַעֲרָיוֹת **If a person acted unawares regarding fats and forbidden sexual relations.** "If a person sinned unawares regarding forbidden sexual relations or forbidden foods, engaging in forbidden sexual relations without intending to do a prohibited act or eating forbidden fat thinking that he was swallowing spittle, he is liable for a sin-offering," following Rav Naḥman. (*Rambam, Sefer Korbanot, Hilkhot Shegagot* 2:7.)

הַמִּתְעַסֵּק בַּשַּׁבָּת **If a person acted unawares regarding the Sabbath.** "If a person intended to do something that was

[1]גּוּפָא: [63A] [2]אָמַר רַבִּי אַמִי: זִיבֵּחַ, וְקִיטֵּר, וְנִיסֵּךְ בְּהֶעְלֵם אֶחָד, [3]אֵינוֹ חַיָּיב אֶלָּא אַחַת. [4]אָמַר אַבַּיֵי: מַאי טַעְמָא דְּרַבִּי אַמִי? [5]אָמַר קְרָא: "לֹא תָעָבְדֵם". [6]הַכָּתוּב עֲשָׂאָן כּוּלָּן עֲבוֹדָה אַחַת.

[7]וּמִי אָמַר אַבַּיֵי הָכִי? [8]וְהָאָמַר אַבַּיֵי: שָׁלֹשׁ הִשְׁתַּחֲוָאוֹת בַּעֲבוֹדָה זָרָה לָמָּה? [9]אַחַת לִכְדַרְכָּהּ, [10]וְאַחַת שֶׁלֹּא כְּדַרְכָּהּ, [11]וְאַחַת לְחַלֵּק!

LITERAL TRANSLATION

[1]The thing itself: [63A] [2]Rabbi Ammi said: [If] someone sacrificed, and burned incense, and offered a libation in one period of unawareness, [3]he is only liable for one [sin-offering]. [4]Abaye said: What is the reason of Rabbi Ammi? [5]The verse states: "You shall not serve them." [6]The verse made them all one service.

[7]But did Abaye say thus? [8]But surely Abaye said: Why are there three [instances of] bowing down regarding idol worship? [9]One for in its manner, [10]and one for not in its manner, [11]and one to distinguish.

TRANSLATION AND COMMENTARY

גּוּפָא [1]The Gemara now **returns to a subject** which it had mentioned above in passing: [63A] [2]**Rabbi Ammi said: If someone** unwittingly **slaughtered a sacrifice** before an idol, **and burned incense** before it, **and offered** it **a libation** of wine, serving the idol in these three ways **in one period of unawareness,** [3](before realizing that he had sinned), **he is only liable for one sin-offering.** [4]**Abaye said: What is the reasoning of Rabbi Ammi?** Why does Rabbi Ammi not say that bowing down to an idol was singled out by the verse (Exodus 20:5): "You shall not bow down to them," in order to distinguish among the modes of idol worship, so that a person who unwittingly worshipped an idol in different ways is obligated to bring a separate sin-offering for each one? [5]Abaye explains: That **verse states: "You shall not serve them,"** [6]**treating all** modes of idol worship **as one** manner of **service.**

וּמִי [7]The Gemara asks: **But did Abaye** really agree with Rabbi Ammi and **say** that if someone served an idol in several ways, he is only liable for a single sin-offering? [8]**But surely Abaye said: Why** does the Torah mention **three times** the prohibition of **bowing down to an idol?** Once (Exodus 20:5): "You shall not bow to them"; a second time (Exodus 23:24): "You shall not bow to their gods"; and a third time (Exodus 34:14): "You shall not bow to another god." [9]**One** instance of the prohibition teaches that one may not bow to an idol if that is **the usual manner** in which that idol is served. [10]**The second** instance teaches that one may not bow to an idol even if that is **not the usual manner** in which the idol is worshiped. [11]And **the third** instance singles out the prohibition of bowing to an idol in order **to distinguish** among the ways of idol worship, so that a person who inadvertently worshiped an idol in more than one way is obligated to bring a separate sin-offering for each way. Thus, we see that Abaye's position is different from that of Rabbi Ammi!

RASHI

הכי גרסינן: אמר רבי אמי זיבח וקיטר וניסך בהעלם אחד וכו׳ — ולא גרסינן: "והשתחוה" דהשתחואה לאו בכלל שאר עבודות היא, דעל כרחך לית ליה לרבי אמי השתחואה לחלק יצאה — מדקאמר אינו חייב אלא אחת. מאי טעמא דרבי אמי — דלית ליה השתחואה לחלק יצאה. לא תעבדם — כללן כולן כאחד ו"לא תעבדם" יתירי כתיבי, ודרשינן חד מינייהו להכי. מי אמר אביי — כרבי אמי דאינו חייב אלא אחת. שלש השתחואות — "לא תשתחוה להם" דעשרת הדברות (שמות כ) "כי לא תשתחוה לאל אחר" (שם לד) "לא תשתחוה לאלהיהם" (שם כג). והשתחואה דדברות אחרונות לא חשיב, דאהדורי קא מהדר ליה משה לישראל מה ששמע בסיני. אחת לבדרכה וכו׳ — דאי כתיב חדא הוה אמינא לא אסר אלא בעבודה זרה דדרך עבודתה בהשתחואה.

NOTES

can be resolved by a slight emendation, or by adding a word or a clause. Or else the different parts of the Mishnah can be interpreted as referring to different cases. A common method of reconciling such contradictions is by assigning the different parts to different authorities, attributing the first half of the Tannaitic source to one Tanna, and the second half to a second Tanna who maintains a contradictory view. Some Amoraim regularly adopted this method, but Rabbi Yoḥanan preferred not to interpret the two halves of a Mishnah or Baraita as reflecting two differing schools of thought.

שָׁלֹשׁ הִשְׁתַּחֲוָאוֹת Three instances of bowing down. *Rashi* notes that the prohibition against bowing to an idol is in fact mentioned in the Bible more than three times. *Ramah* explains that those other instances of bowing do not teach that there is a prohibition against bowing to an idol, but rather they are the words of Moses who warns Israel against violating the prohibition.

רַבִּי אַמִי וְאַבַּיֵי Rabbi Ammi and Abaye. It has been suggested that Abaye interprets the prohibition against bowing to an idol by the hermeneutic rule that something that was included in a generalization, but was specified to

HALAKHAH

permitted on the Sabbath, such as lifting something that was detached from the ground, but he inadvertently did something that was forbidden on the Sabbath, such as cutting a plant which was still attached to the ground, he is not liable for a sin-offering, for regarding the Sabbath, the Torah only forbade purposeful labor." (*Rambam Sefer Korbanot, Hilkhot Shegagot* 2:7; *Sefer Zemanim, Hilkhot Shabbat* 1:8.)

[1] לְדְבָרָיו דְּרַבִּי אַמִּי קָאָמַר, וְלֵיהּ לָא סְבִירָא לֵיהּ.
[2] גּוּפָא: [3] אָמַר אַבַּיֵי: שָׁלֹשׁ הִשְׁתַּחֲוָאוֹת בַּעֲבוֹדָה זָרָה לָמָּה? [4] אַחַת לִכְדַרְכָּהּ, [5] וְאַחַת שֶׁלֹּא כְּדַרְכָּהּ, [6] וְאַחַת לְחַלֵּק.
[7] לִכְדַרְכָּהּ מֵ"אֵיכָה יַעַבְדוּ הַגּוֹיִם הָאֵלֶּה", נָפְקָא!
[8] אֶלָּא: אַחַת כְּדַרְכָּהּ, [9] וְשֶׁלֹּא כְּדַרְכָּהּ, [10] וְאַחַת לְשֶׁלֹּא כְּדַרְכָּהּ, [11] וְאַחַת לְחַלֵּק.

LITERAL TRANSLATION

[1] He was speaking according to the words of Rabbi Ammi, but he does not agree with him.

[2] The thing itself: [3] Abaye said: Why are there three [instances of] bowing down regarding idol worship? [4] One for in its manner, [5] and one for not in its manner, [6] and one to distinguish. [7] For in its manner is derived from: "How did these nations serve their gods"!

[8] Rather: One for in its manner, [9] and not in its manner, [10] and one for not in its manner, [11] and one to distinguish.

TRANSLATION AND COMMENTARY

לְדְבָרָיו [1] The Gemara answers: Indeed, when Abaye said that the verse, "You shall not serve them," teaches that all modes of idol worship are treated as one, **he was speaking according to position of Rabbi Ammi, but he** personally **does not agree with him,** for he himself maintains that the Torah distinguishes between the various modes of idol worship.

גּוּפָא [2] The Gemara now **returns to the subject** which it had just mentioned: [3] **Abaye said: Why** does the Torah mention **three times** the prohibition of **bowing down to an idol?** [4] **One** instance teaches that one may not bow down to an idol if that is **the usual manner** in which the idol is worshiped. [5] **The second** instance teaches that one may not bow down to an idol even if that is **not the usual manner of worshiping it.** [6] And **the third** instance singles out the prohibition of bowing down to an idol in order **to distinguish** among the ways of idol worship. The Gemara asks: But surely there is no need for a special verse to teach us that one may not bow down to an idol if that is the usual manner of worshiping it. [7] The prohibition against worshiping an idol **in the usual manner is derived from** the verse (Deuteronomy 12:30): "Take heed to yourself that you inquire not after their gods, saying, **How did these nations serve their gods**"!

אֶלָּא [8] The Gemara answers: **Rather,** you should say as follows: **One** instance of the prohibition teaches that one may not bow to an idol when this is similar to **the usual manner** of worshiping it, [9] **but not** precisely **the manner** in which that idol is served, such as when the usual manner of serving the idol is a respectful mode of worship that is similar to bowing to the idol, such as burning incense before the idol or offering it a libation, but not actually bowing down to the idol. [10] **The second** instance of the prohibition teaches that one may not bow to an idol even if that is **not** even similar to **the usual manner** of worshiping it, such as when the idol's usual manner of worship is one of degradation, as in the case of Ba'al Pe'or or Marculis. [11] And **the third** instance of the prohibition singles out the prohibition of bowing to an idol in order **to distinguish** among the ways of idol worship, so that a person who inadvertently worshiped an idol in different ways must bring a separate sin-offering for each way.

RASHI

לדבריו דרבי אמי קאמר — אביי להך דרשה ד"לא תעבדם", אבל אביי לא סבירא ליה ומוקים לה ללאוי יתירי. ורבי אמי מוקי להך השתחואה לומר ללאו יצאה. **לכדרכה ושלא כדרכה** — שהשתחואה היא להך עבודה זרה כדרכה ושלא כדרכה, כגון שדרכה לעבוד דרך כבוד ולא בהשתחואה, ואי כתיב חד לא הוה מרבינן אלא כי האי גונא — אבל משתחוה לפעור לא, כתב רחמנא השתחואה יתירא שניה לשלא כדרכה, כגון פעור ומרקולים שעבודתה בבזיון. והא דאמר רבי אלעזר לעיל (סא,א) זובח למרקולים — חייב מ"לא יזבחו", ואף על גב דחד קרא יתירא הוא דאיכא, ולא מוקים לה בזובח למקטריה דעבודתו דרך כבוד — דסבר כיון דגלי בהשתחואה קל וחומר בזביחה, מיהו כולה מילתא לא ילפינן מהשתחואה — דאם כן הוה מרבינן כל עבודות כבוד אף על גב דלאו עבודת פנים, לכך יצאה זביחה לומר שלא חייבה אלא עבודות פנים.

NOTES

teach something, was intended to teach not just about itself but about the entire generalization. Thus, the prohibition against bowing down to an idol was singled out in order to teach that a person who inadvertently performed several modes of idol worship is obligated to bring a separate sin-offering for each mode of worship. Rabbi Ammi, on the other hand, interprets the prohibition against bowing to an idol by the hermeneutic rule that something that was included in a generalization but specified as something new, can only be returned to its generalization when the Torah does so. Thus, the specific prohibition against bowing to an idol does not teach us anything about the general prohibition against idol worship (*Rosh*).

אַחַת לִכְדַרְכָּהּ, וְאַחַת שֶׁלֹּא כְּדַרְכָּהּ **For in its manner and not in its manner.** Our commentary follows *Rashi,* who understands that this refers to a case where the usual manner of serving the idol is a respectful mode of worship that is similar to bowing to the idol, such as burning incense before the idol or offering it a libation, but not actually bowing to the idol. *Rabbenu Ḥananel* (cited by *Ramah*) suggests that this refers to a case where the usual manner of serving the idol is by way of bowing before it, and someone bowed to it, but in an unusual way, by kneeling, for example, rather than prostrating himself.

[1] ״הַמְקַבְּלוֹ עָלָיו בֶּאֱלוֹהַּ, הָאוֹמֵר לוֹ: ׳אֵלִי אַתָּה׳״. [2] אָמַר רַב נַחְמָן, אָמַר רַבָּה בַּר אֲבוּהּ אָמַר רַב: [3] כֵּיוָן שֶׁאָמַר לוֹ: ״אֵלִי אַתָּה״, חַיָּיב.
[4] לְמַאי? [5] אִי לִקְטָלָא, [6] מַתְנִיתִין הִיא! [7] אֶלָּא, [8] לְקָרְבָּן.
[9] וַאֲפִילּוּ לְרַבָּנַן? [10] וְהָתַנְיָא: ״אֵינוֹ חַיָּיב אֶלָּא עַל דָּבָר שֶׁיֵּשׁ בּוֹ מַעֲשֶׂה, כְּגוֹן זִיבּוּחַ וְקִיטּוּר וְנִיסּוּךְ וְהִשְׁתַּחֲוָאָה״. [11] וְאָמַר רֵישׁ לָקִישׁ: מַאן תְּנָא הִשְׁתַּחֲוָאָה? [12] רַבִּי עֲקִיבָא הִיא, דְּאָמַר: לָא בָּעֵינַן מַעֲשֶׂה. [13] מִכְּלָל דְּרַבָּנַן סָבְרִי בָּעֵינַן מַעֲשֶׂה!
[14] כִּי קָאָמַר רַב נַמִי לְרַבִּי עֲקִיבָא קָאָמַר.

LITERAL TRANSLATION

[1] "Someone who accepts it upon himself as a god, or says to it: 'You are my god.'" [2] Rav Naḥman said in the name of Rabbah bar Avuha who said in the name of Rav: [3] Since he said to it: "You are my god," he is liable.

[4] For what? [5] If for execution, [6] that is our Mishnah! [7] Rather, [8] for a sacrifice.

[9] Even according to the Rabbis? [10] But surely it was taught: "He is only liable for something that involves an action, like sacrificing, burning incense, libation, or bowing down." [11] And Resh Lakish said: Who taught bowing down? [12] It is Rabbi Akiva, who said: We do not need an action. [13] This implies that the Rabbis maintain that we need an action!

[14] When Rav said it, he also said it according to Rabbi Akiva.

RASHI

כיון דאמר אלי אתה חייב – אף על גב דלא פלחה. לקרבן – אם שגג. ואפילו לרבנן – בתמיה, דפליגי רבנן בכריתות (ז,א) במגדף עליה דרבי עקיבא, דאמרי: מגדף אינו מביא קרבן, דבעינן מעשה. והתניא אינו חייב אלא על דבר שיש בו מעשה – דגבי חטאת כתיב (ויקרא ד) "ועשה אחת מכל מצות ה׳. רבי עקיבא היא דאמר דלא בעינן מעשה גמור – דמגדף מחייב משום מעשה זוטא, דעקימת שפתיו הוה מעשה. והכא נמי כפיפת קומתו הויא מעשה. והאי דקתני אינו חייב אלא על דבר שיש בו מעשה – לאפוקי הרהורא דלא מחייב עלה.

TRANSLATION AND COMMENTARY

הַמְקַבְּלוֹ עָלָיו [1] Our Mishnah lists among those who are liable to death by stoning **"someone who accepts** an idol **upon himself as a god, or says to it: 'You are my god.'"** [2] **Rav Naḥman said in the name of Rabbah bar Avuha who said in the name of Rav:** [3] **If** a person **said to** an idol: **"You are my god," he is liable,** even if he did not actually worship it.

לְמַאי [4] The Gemara asks: **Regarding what** did Rav say that if a person said to an idol: "You are my god," he is liable? [5] **If** he meant to say that a person who willfully sinned and accepted an idol as a god is liable **for execution,** there is a difficulty, [6] for **that is** precisely what **our Mishnah** states, and there would have been no reason for Rav to repeat that ruling. [7] **Rather,** it must be that Rav teaches that if a person unwittingly accepted an idol as a god, [8] he is liable **for a sin-offering.**

וַאֲפִילּוּ לְרַבָּנַן [9] The Gemara asks: Did Rav say this **even according to** the opinion of **the Rabbis** who argue against Rabbi Akiva, and say that a blasphemer is not liable for a sin-offering, because his transgression does not involve an action (*Keritut* 4a)? [10] **But surely it was taught** in a Baraita: "Someone who inadvertently worshiped an idol **is only liable** for a sin-offering if he served the idol **in a manner that involves an action,** such as **slaughtering a sacrifice** to it, **burning incense** before it, **offering** it **a libation, or bowing** before it." [11] And commenting on this Baraita, **Resh Lakish said: Who taught** that a person is liable for a sin-offering for inadvertently **bowing** to an idol? [12] This Baraita follows **Rabbi Akiva, who said:** In order to be liable for a sin-offering, **it is not necessary** for a person to commit a transgression that involves **a** major physical **action.** Just as a blasphemer is liable for a sin-offering, even though he only moves his lips, so too someone who bows to an idol is liable for a sin-offering, even though he only bends his body. [13] Now **this implies that the Rabbis** who disagree with Rabbi Akiva maintain that someone who bows to an idol is not liable for a sin-offering, for in order to be liable for a sin-offering, **it is necessary** for a person to commit a transgression that involves **a** major physical **action.** If bowing to an idol is not considered a major physical action that can make a person liable for a sin-offering, then all the more so saying to an idol: "You are my god," should not be considered a major physical action that can make a person liable for a sin-offering!

כִּי קָאָמַר [14] The Gemara explains: **When Rav said** that if a person says to an idol: "You are my god," he is liable for a sin-offering, **he said it according to Rabbi Akiva,** but according to the Rabbis, the offender would indeed be exempt from a sin-offering.

HALAKHAH

אֵינוֹ חַיָּיב אֶלָּא עַל דָּבָר שֶׁיֵּשׁ בּוֹ מַעֲשֶׂה **He is only liable for something that involves an action.** "If someone inadvertently accepted an idol as a god, he is exempt from a sin-offering, for his transgression did not involve an action," following the Baraita and the Gemara. (*Rambam, Sefer Korbanot, Hilkhot Shegagot* 1:1-2.)

[1]לְרַבִּי עֲקִיבָא פְּשִׁיטָא, הַיְינוּ מְגַדֵּף!
[2]מַהוּ דְּתֵימָא: עַד כָּאן לֹא מְחַיֵּיב רַבִּי עֲקִיבָא קָרְבָּן אֶלָּא בִּמְגַדֵּף, [3]דִּכְתִיב בֵּיהּ כָּרֵת, [4]אֲבָל הָכָא דְּלָא כְּתִיב בֵּיהּ כָּרֵת, [5]אֵימָא לָא. [6]קָא מַשְׁמַע לָן דְּאִתַּקּוֹשֵׁי אִתְקוּשׁ. [7]דִּכְתִיב: "וַיִּשְׁתַּחֲווּ לוֹ וַיִּזְבְּחוּ לוֹ וַיֹּאמְרוּ וגו׳".
[8]אָמַר רַבִּי יוֹחָנָן: אִלְמָלֵא וי"ו שֶׁבְּ׳הֶעֱלוּךָ׳ [9]נִתְחַיְּיבוּ שׂוֹנְאֵיהֶם שֶׁל יִשְׂרָאֵל כְּלָיָיה.
[10]כְּתַנָּאֵי: [11]"אֲחֵרִים אוֹמְרִים: אִלְמָלֵא וי"ו שֶׁבְּ׳הֶעֱלוּךָ׳, [12]נִתְחַיְּיבוּ שׂוֹנְאֵיהֶם שֶׁל יִשְׂרָאֵל כְּלָיָיה. [13]אָמַר לוֹ רַבִּי שִׁמְעוֹן בֶּן יוֹחַאי: וַהֲלֹא כָּל הַמְשַׁתֵּף שֵׁם שָׁמַיִם וְדָבָר אַחֵר

LITERAL TRANSLATION

[1]According to Rabbi Akiva, it is obvious, [for] that is [like] a blasphemer!

[2]Lest you say: Until now Rabbi Akiva only imposed a sacrifice upon a blasphemer, [3]regarding whom is written excision, [4]but here regarding whom excision is not written, [5]say not. [6][Therefore] he teaches that they are compared, [7]for it is written: "And they bowed down to it, and sacrificed to it, and said, etc."

[8]Rabbi Yoḥanan said: Were it not for the *vav* in *he'elukha,* [9]the enemies of Israel would have been liable for destruction.

[10]Like the Tannaim: [11]"The others say: Were it not for the *vav* in *he'elukhah,* [12]the enemies of Israel would have been liable for destruction. [13]Rabbi Shimon ben Yohai said: But surely anyone who combines the name of heaven with something else

RASHI

מגדף – מברך את השם. אתקושי אתקוש – אלי אתה בזביחה דכתיב "וישתחוו לו ויזבחו לו ויאמרו אלה אלהיך ישראל". אלמלא וי"ו שבהעלוך – דהא לא כפרו בהקדוש ברוך הוא לגמרי, שהרי שתפוהו בדבר אחר.

TRANSLATION AND COMMENTARY

לְרַבִּי עֲקִיבָא [1]The Gemara asks: But **according to Rabbi Akiva, it is obvious** that a person who says to an idol: "You are my god," is liable for a sin-offering, **for he is** just **like a blasphemer!** Just as in the case of blasphemy, the transgressor is liable for a sin-offering, even though he only moved his lips, so too in the case of a person who says to an idol: "You are my god," the transgressor should be liable for a sin-offering, even though he only moved his lips!

מַהוּ דְּתֵימָא [2]The Gemara answers: Nevertheless it was necessary for Rav to teach us that a person who says to an idol: "You are my god," is liable for a sin-offering, for otherwise **you might have said** that **Rabbi Akiva only imposed a sin-offering upon a blasphemer,** [3]**regarding whom the verse states** explicitly that if he sinned willfully, he is liable for **excision,** as the verse states (Numbers 15:30): "That person blasphemes the Lord, and that soul shall be cut off from among his people." [4]**But here, the verse does not state** explicitly that if someone intentionally says to an idol, "you are my god", he is liable for **excision.** [5]Therefore you might have **said** that he is **not** liable for a sin-offering for saying it unintentionally. [6]**Therefore** Rav **teaches that** the prohibition against sacrificing to an idol and the prohibition against saying to an idol: "You are my god," **may be compared** one to the other. [7]**For the verse states** (Exodus 32:8): "They made a molten calf, **and bowed down to it, and sacrificed to it, and said,** These are your gods, O Israel, which brought you up out of the land of Egypt." Just as someone who inadvertently sacrifices to an idol is liable for a sin-offering, so too someone who inadvertently says to an idol: "You are my god," is liable for a sin-offering.

אָמַר רַבִּי יוֹחָנָן [8]Having cited the verse, "And they have said, These are your gods, O Israel, which have brought you up [*he'elukha*] out of the land of Egypt," the Gemara continues: **Rabbi Yohanan said: Were it not for the** letter **vav in** the word ***he'elukha,*** "have brought you up," [9]**the people of Israel** (euphemistically referred to here by the expression, "the enemies of Israel") **would have been liable for** immediate **destruction.** The letter vav in the word *he'elukha* [הֶעֱלוּךָ] shows that the verb is a plural form. Thus, when the people of Israel worshipped the golden calf, and said, "These are your gods, which brought you up out of the land of Egypt," they did not deny God altogether. Rather they recognized that God had taken them out of Egypt, and only made the golden calf His partner.

כְּתַנָּאֵי [10]This matter is the subject of a **Tannaitic dispute,** for we have learned in a Baraita: [11]**"The other** Sages **say: Were it not for the** letter **vav in** the word ***he'elukha,*** "which have brought you up," [12]**the people of Israel would have been liable for** immediate **destruction.** [13]**Rabbi Shimon ben Yohai said: But surely anyone who combines the name of heaven with something else** and attributes divinity to that other object **will be**

NOTES

הַמְשַׁתֵּף שֵׁם שָׁמַיִם **Someone who combines the name of heaven.** *Ramah* understands that according to Rabbi Shimon ben Yohai combining the name of Heaven with something else and attributing divinity to that other object

HALAKHAH

כָּל הַמְשַׁתֵּף שֵׁם שָׁמַיִם **Anyone who combines the name of Heaven.** "It is forbidden to swear by something else together

נֶעֱקָר מִן הָעוֹלָם, [1]שֶׁנֶּאֱמַר: ׳בִּלְתִּי לַה׳ לְבַדּוֹ׳! [2]אֶלָּא מַה תַּלְמוּד לוֹמַר: ׳אֲשֶׁר הֶעֱלוּךָ׳? [3]שֶׁאִיווּ אֱלוֹהוּת הַרְבֵּה״.

[4]״אֲבָל הַמְגַפֵּף, וְהַמְנַשֵּׁק, הַמְכַבֵּד, וְהַמְרַבֵּץ כו׳״. [5]כִּי אֲתָא רַב דִּימִי, אָמַר רַבִּי אֶלְעָזָר: [6]עַל כּוּלָּם לוֹקֶה, חוּץ מֵהַנּוֹדֵר בִּשְׁמוֹ, וְהַמְקַיֵּים בִּשְׁמוֹ.

[7]מַאי שְׁנָא הַנּוֹדֵר בִּשְׁמוֹ וְהַמְקַיֵּים בִּשְׁמוֹ דְּלָא לָקֵי — [8]מִשּׁוּם דַּהֲוָה לֵיהּ לָאו שֶׁאֵין בּוֹ מַעֲשֶׂה. [9]הָנֵי נַמִי לָאו שֶׁבִּכְלָלוֹת הוּא, [10]וְאֵין לוֹקִין

LITERAL TRANSLATION

is uprooted from the world, [1]for it is stated: 'Save to the Lord only'! [2]What then is taught by the verse: 'Which have brought you up'? [3]That they yearned for many gods."

[4]"But [if] he embraces, or kisses, or sweeps, or sprinkles, etc." [5]When Rav Dimi came, he said in the name of Rabbi Elazar: [6]For all of them he is flogged, except for someone who takes a vow in its name, or swears in its name.

[7]What is different about someone who takes a vow in its name, or swears in its name that he is not flogged — [8]because it is a prohibition that does not involve an action. [9]These too are [forbidden by] a prohibition [stated] in general terms, [10]and one is not flogged

TRANSLATION AND COMMENTARY

uprooted from the world, [1]**for the verse states** (Exodus 22:19): 'He that sacrifices to any god, **save to the Lord only,** he shall be utterly destroyed.' Had then the people of Israel worshiped God together with the golden calf, they would indeed have been liable for immediate destruction. [2]**What then is taught by the verse:** 'These are your gods, of Israel, **which brought you up** out of the land of Egypt?' [3]The plural form of the word *he'elukha* teaches that the Israelites in the wilderness **yearned** to worship, not only the golden calf, but also **many** other **gods."**

אֲבָל [4]We have learned in our Mishnah: **"But if** a person **embraces** an idol, **or kisses** it, **or sweeps** the floor before it, **or sprinkles** water on the floor before it in order to keep down the dust, or washes the idol, or anoints it with oil, or dresses it, or puts its shoes on, he violates the negative commandment (Exodus 20:5): 'You shall not serve them,' but those acts of veneration are not punishable by death. If someone takes a vow in an idol's name, denying himself benefit from a certain object or person, or if he swears in the idol's name, he violates the negative commandment (Exodus 23:13): 'And make no mention of the name of other gods.'" [5]**When Rav Dimi came** to Babylonia from Eretz Israel, **he said in the name of Rabbi Elazar:** [6]**For any** offense categorized by the Mishnah as a violation of a negative commandment a person **is flogged, except for someone who takes a vow in** an idol's **name, or swears in its name.**

מַאי [7]The Gemara asks: **What is different about someone who takes a vow in** an idol's **name, or swears in its name, that he is not flogged?** You might say that the transgressor is not flogged, [8]**because** he violated **a prohibition that does not involve an action** ("And make no mention of the name of other gods"), and a Torah prohibition which is transgressed by thought or speech, but which does not involve a physical act is not punishable by flogging. [9]But this is difficult, for **these** other offenses **too** — embracing an idol, kissing it, sweeping the floor before it, and the like — **are forbidden by a prohibition which was stated in general terms** (a general prohibition which forbids actions of different kinds — in this case, "You shall not serve them"), [10]and

RASHI

שאיוו לאלוהות הרבה — אף לאלוהות אחרים וקבלו עליהם. **אבל המגפף וכו׳ עובר בלא תעשה** — "ולא תלכו אחרי אלהים אחרים" (ירמיהו כה), אי נמי: "אל תפנו אל האלילים" (ויקרא יט), וכגון שאין דרכן בכך. **הנודר בשמו** — "ושם אלהים אחרים לא תזכירו". **המקיים** — הנשבע, דמתרגמינן "קיים". **לאו שבכללות** — דכולהו משתמעי בחד קרא.

NOTES

is worse than denying God altogether. *Rabbenu Yonah* disagrees and says that even according to Rabbi Shimon ben Yoḥai, denying God altogether is worse than combining Him with something else.

בִּלְתִּי לַה׳ לְבַדּוֹ Save to the Lord only. Elsewhere (in the *Mekhilta*), Rabbi Shimon ben Yoḥai derives the prohibition against combining the name of Heaven with something else from what is stated with regard to the Samaritans (II Kings 17:33): "They feared the Lord, and served their own gods, after the manner of the nations of the countries from which they were carried away."

לָאו שֶׁבִּכְלָלוֹת A prohibition stated in general terms. Our commentary follows *Rashi* and others who explain that embracing an idol, kissing it, sweeping the floor before it, and the like, are forbidden by the prohibition, "You shall not serve them," but those offenses are not punishable by flogging, for they are forbidden by a prohibition that is stated in general terms. The Rishonim ask: There is a major

HALAKHAH

with God's name. Anybody who combines something else with God's name in an oath is uprooted from the world," following Rabbi Shimon ben Yoḥai. (*Rambam, Sefer Hafla'ah, Hilkhot Shevuot* 11:2.)

לָאו שֶׁבִּכְלָלוֹת A prohibition stated in general terms. "Someone who violates a prohibition stated in general

TRANSLATION AND COMMENTARY

there is a rule that **one is not flogged for** the violation of **a prohibition which was stated in general terms!** [1]**For it was taught** in a Baraita: **"From where do we know that someone who eats of an animal before it is completely dead that he violates a negative commandment?** [2]This is learned from **the verse** which **states** (Leviticus 19:26): **'You shall not eat anything with the blood'** — you shall not eat an animal while it is still holding on to its life, which is sometimes referred to as its blood. [3]**Another explanation** of the verse: **'You shall not eat anything with the blood,'** [4]teaches that **you shall not eat of the meat** of a sacrificial animal, **while the** animal's **blood is still in the bowl** out of which the sprinkling is done. Priests are only permitted to eat their portion of the sacrifice after the blood has been sprinkled upon the altar. [5]**Rabbi Dosa says: From where do we know that a mourner's meal is not offered to** the relatives of **those executed by the court,** the way such a meal is usually offered to the relatives of the deceased? [6]This is learned from **the verse** which **states: 'You shall not eat anything with the blood'** — you shall not eat a mourner's meal for the blood of those liable for judicial execution. [7]**Rabbi Akiva says: From where**

עַל לָאו שֶׁבִּכְלָלוֹת! [1]דְּתַנְיָא: "מִנַּיִן לְאוֹכֵל מִן הַבְּהֵמָה קוֹדֶם שֶׁתֵּצֵא נַפְשָׁהּ שֶׁהוּא בְּלֹא תַּעֲשֶׂה? [2]תַּלְמוּד לוֹמַר: 'לֹא תֹאכְלוּ עַל הַדָּם'. [3]דָּבָר אַחֵר: 'לֹא תֹאכְלוּ עַל הַדָּם' — [4]לֹא תֹאכְלוּ בָּשָׂר, וַעֲדַיִן דָּם בַּמִּזְרָק. [5]רַבִּי דוֹסָא אוֹמֵר: מִנַּיִן שֶׁאֵין מַבְרִין עַל הֲרוּגֵי בֵית דִּין? [6]תַּלְמוּד לוֹמַר: 'לֹא תֹאכְלוּ עַל הַדָּם'. [7]רַבִּי עֲקִיבָא אוֹמֵר:

LITERAL TRANSLATION

for a prohibition [stated] in general terms! [1]For it was taught: "From where [do we know] that someone who eats of an animal before its life departs that he [violates] a negative commandment? [2]The verse states: 'You shall not eat anything with the blood.' [3]Another explanation: 'You shall not eat anything with the blood' — [4]you shall not eat of the meat, while the blood is still in the bowl. [5]Rabbi Dosa says: From where [do we know] that we do not offer the mourner's meal for those executed by the court? [6]The verse states: 'You shall not eat anything with the blood.' [7]Rabbi Akiva says:

RASHI

ועדיין הדם במזרק – הקרבנות. שאין מברין – את האבלים ברחבה, כדרך שמברין את האבלים בסעודה ראשונה משל אחרים, כדאמרינן במועד קטן (כז,ב). על הדם – על הנרצח, ומסברא מוקמינן לה אהרוגי בית דין שנהרגין על עונש שלא ינהגו בהם כבוד משום כפרה.

SAGES

רַבִּי דוֹסָא **Rabbi Dosa (ben Horkinas).** Rabbi Dosa ben Horkinas seems to have been a contemporary of Rabban Yoḥanan ben Zakkai and is said to have known the leading scholars of the generation of Yavneh (Rabbi Eliezer and Rabbi Yehoshua) when they were still in their infancy. It is probable that in the period during which the Sanhedrin convened in Yavneh, Rabbi Dosa was no longer active and did not take part in its sessions. But his opinion's were still influential at that time. We know that he lived to a most advanced age and was very wealthy. Rabbi Dosa was one of the senior Sages of Bet Hillel, although he had a younger brother, Yonatan, who was one of the heads of Bet Shammai. It seems that references in the Mishnah to Rabbi Dosa without a patronymic are to Rabbi Dosa ben Horkinas.

NOTES

difference between this prohibition and the classic case of a prohibition stated in general terms, "You shall not eat anything with the blood." There a single verse contains several particular prohibitions of different kinds, among them the prohibition against eating an animal before it is completely dead, the prohibition against eating a sacrificial animal before its blood has been sprinkled on the altar, the prohibition forbidding judges who have condemned a man to death from eating food on the day of his execution, and others. But here the verse, "You shall not serve them," contains only one prohibition — the prohibition against serving an idol in a respectful manner that is not the usual manner in which other idolaters serve it, and that prohibition is a prohibition stated in general terms only because it can be violated in a variety of ways. *Ran* suggests that here too the verse, "You shall not serve them," contains prohibitions of different kinds, for it forbids worshiping an idol in the usual manner, and it forbids worshiping an idol in the manner in which God is served, even if that is not the usual manner in which the idol is worshiped, and it forbids worshiping an idol in any respectful manner even if that is not the usual manner in which other idolaters serve it. *Ramban* argues that the prohibition against embracing an idol, kissing it, and the like, is (Deuteronomy 6:14): "You shall not go after other gods." That is a prohibition stated in general terms, for it also forbids fearing the idol, showing it respect, swearing in its name, and consulting it about the future.

HALAKHAH

terms, such as one that forbids actions of different kinds, like, 'You shall not eat anything with the blood' — is not subject to the penalty of lashes." (*Rambam, Sefer Shofetim, Hilkhot Sanhedrin* 18:2-3.)

אוֹכֵל מִן הַבְּהֵמָה קוֹדֶם שֶׁתֵּצֵא נַפְשָׁהּ **Someone who eats of an animal before its life departs.** "Someone who eats the meat of a slaughtered animal while the animal is still moving convulsively and not yet completely dead violates the prohibition, 'You shall not eat anything with the blood.'" (*Shulḥan Arukh, Yoreh De'ah* 27:1.)

לֹא תֹאכְלוּ בָּשָׂר, וַעֲדַיִן דָּם בַּמִּזְרָק **You shall not eat of the meat, while the blood is still in the bowl.** "Someone who eats the meat of a sacrificial animal in the size of an olive, even the meat of a sacrifice of lesser holiness, before its blood is thrown on the altar, is subject to the penalty of lashes, for he violates the prohibition (Deuteronomy 12:17): 'You may not eat within your gates,' as is explained in tractate *Makkot*. He is not subject to lashes for violating the prohibition: 'You shall not eat anything with the blood,' for that is a prohibition stated in general terms for which there are no lashes." (*Rambam, Sefer Avodah, Hilkhot Ma'aseh HaKorbanot* 11:4.)

אֵין מַבְרִין עַל הֲרוּגֵי בֵית דִּין **We do not offer the mourner's meal for those executed by the court.** "A mourner's meal

מִנַּיִן לְסַנְהֶדְרִין שֶׁהָרְגוּ אֶת הַנֶּפֶשׁ שֶׁאֵין טוֹעֲמִין כְּלוּם כָּל אוֹתוֹ הַיּוֹם? [1]תַּלְמוּד לוֹמַר: ׳לֹא תֹאכְלוּ עַל הַדָּם׳״. [2]אָמַר רַבִּי יוֹחָנָן: אַזְהָרָה לְבֵן סוֹרֵר וּמוֹרֶה מִנַּיִן? [3]תַּלְמוּד לוֹמַר: ״לֹא תֹאכְלוּ עַל הַדָּם״. [4]וְאָמַר רַבִּי אָבִין בַּר חִיָּיא וְאִיתֵימָא רַבִּי אָבִין בַּר כָּהֲנָא: [5]עַל כּוּלָּם אֵינוֹ לוֹקֶה, [6]מִשּׁוּם דַּהֲוָה לֵיהּ לָאו שֶׁבִּכְלָלוֹת.

[7]אֶלָּא, כִּי אֲתָא רָבִין אָמַר רַבִּי אֶלְעָזָר: [8]עַל כּוּלָּן אֵינוֹ לוֹקֶה [9]חוּץ מִן הַנּוֹדֵר בִּשְׁמוֹ וְהַמְקַיֵּים בִּשְׁמוֹ.

[10]מַאי שְׁנָא אַהָנָךְ דְּלָא לָקֵי — [11]דַּהֲוָה לֵיהּ לָאו שֶׁבִּכְלָלוֹת. [12]הָנֵי נַמִי לָאו שֶׁאֵין בּוֹ מַעֲשֶׂה נִינְהוּ!

LITERAL TRANSLATION

From where [do we know] that a Sanhedrin which put a person to death may not eat anything all that day? [1]The verse states: 'You shall not eat anything with the blood.'" [2]Rabbi Yoḥanan said: From where [do we know] a warning for a stubborn and rebellious son? [3]The verse states: "You shall not eat anything with the blood." [4]And Rabbi Avin bar Ḥiyya said, and some say [it was] Rabbi Avin bar Kahana: [5]For none of them is he flogged, [6]for it is a prohibition [stated] in general terms.

[7]Rather, when Ravin came he said in the name of Rabbi Elazar: [8]For none of them is he flogged, [9]except for someone who takes a vow in its name, or swears in its name.

[10]What is different about those that he is not flogged — [11]because it is a prohibition stated in general terms. [12]These too are [forbidden by] a prohibition that does not involve an action!

TRANSLATION AND COMMENTARY

do we know that the judges of **a Sanhedrin which condemned a man to death may not eat anything all that day** of his execution? [1]This is learned from **the verse** which **states: 'You shall not eat anything with the blood'** — you shall not eat anything on the day that you send a man to his death. [2]**Rabbi Yoḥanan added: From where do we learn the warning for a stubborn and rebellious son,** a boy between the age of thirteen and thirteen and three months who steals money from his parents to eat a gluttonous meal of meat and wine in the company of worthless men? The punishment for which the boy is liable is derived from the verse (Deuteronomy 21:21): "And all the men of his city shall stone him with stones," but where is the boy warned against performing such acts? [3]This is learned from **the verse** which **states: "You shall not eat anything with the blood"** — you shall not eat anything which will make you liable for your blood. [4]**And Rabbi Avin bar Ḥiyya said, and some say** that **it was Rabbi Avin bar Kahana** who said: [5]**For none of** these offenses **is** the transgressor **flogged,** [6]**for** the prohibition, "You shall not eat anything with the blood," **is a prohibition which was stated in general terms,** and one is not flogged for the violation of a prohibition which was stated in general terms! And so there is a difficulty with the distinction proposed by Rav Dimi in the name of Rabbi Elazar!

אֶלָּא [7]**Rather, when Ravin came** to Babylonia from Eretz Israel, **he said in the name of Rabbi Elazar** as follows: [8]**For none of** the offenses categorized by the Mishnah as violations of a negative commandment **is** a person **flogged,** [9]**except for someone who takes a vow in** an idol's **name, or swears in its name.**

מַאי שְׁנָא [10]The Gemara asks: **What is different about those** offenses — embracing an idol, kissing it, sweeping the floor before it, and the like — **that** the transgressor **is not flogged?** If you say that the transgressor is not flogged, [11]**because** he violated **a prohibition which is stated in general terms** ("You shall not serve them"), there is a difficulty. [12]**These** other offenses **too** — taking a vow in an idol's name, and swearing in its name — **are forbidden by a prohibition that does not involve an action** ("And make no mention of the name of other gods"), and a prohibition whose violation does not involve a physical act is not punishable by flogging! And so there is also a difficulty with the distinction proposed by Ravin in the name of Rabbi Elazar!

RASHI

לבן סורר ומורה — דלא ענש אלא אם כן הזהיר, והיכן הזהיר? ״לא תאכלו על הדם״ — לא תאכלו אכילה שתהרגהו עליה. **לאו שבכללות** — דכל הני משמע מיניה.

HALAKHAH

is not offered to the relatives of those executed by the court, because of the prohibition, 'You shall not eat anything with the blood,' following Rabbi Dosa. (*Rambam, Sefer Shofetim, Hilkhot Sanhedrin* 13:4.)

סַנְהֶדְרִין שֶׁהָרְגוּ אֶת הַנֶּפֶשׁ שֶׁאֵין טוֹעֲמִין כְּלוּם A Sanhedrin which put a person to death may not eat anything. "A Sanhedrin which condemned a man to death may not eat anything all that day of his execution, because of the prohibition, 'You shall not eat anything with the blood,'" following Rabbi Akiva. (*Rambam, Sefer Shofetim, Hilkhot Sanhedrin* 13:4.)

אַזְהָרָה לְבֵן סוֹרֵר וּמוֹרֶה A warning for a stubborn and rebellious son. "The warning for a stubborn and rebellious son is learned from the verse: 'You shall not eat anything with the blood' — you shall not eat anything which will lead to bloodshed," following Rabbi Yoḥanan. (*Rambam, Sefer Shofetim, Hilkhot Mamrim* 7:1.)

עַל כּוּלָּן אֵינוֹ לוֹקֶה For none of them is he flogged. "If someone served an idol in a respectful manner that was neither the usual manner in which that idol is served, nor

TRANSLATION AND COMMENTARY

הָהוּא כְּרַבִּי יְהוּדָה [1]The Gemara answers: Rabbi Elazar issued his ruling **in accordance with** the position of **Rabbi Yehudah who said:** [2]**One is** indeed **flogged for** the violation of **a prohibition that does not involve an action.** [3]**For it was taught** in a Baraita: "The verse states (Exodus 12:10): **"'And you shall let nothing of it** [the Paschal sacrifice] **remain until the morning;** and that which remains of it until the morning you shall burn with fire.' [4]**The verse comes and imposes the positive commandment,** 'And that which remains of it until the morning you shall burn with fire,' **after** having imposed **the negative commandment,** 'And you shall let nothing of it remain until the morning,' [63B] in order **to teach that one is not flogged for** the violation of the negative commandment. Lashes are not administered for violating a prohibition if the violation can be rectified by the fulfillment of a positive commandment. [5]**This is the position of Rabbi Yehudah.** [6]**Rabbi Ya'akov says: It is not for this reason** that lashes are not administered for violating the prohibition against leaving the Paschal sacrifice after it is permitted to be eaten. [7]**But rather** lashes are not administered for the violation of that prohibition, **because it is a prohibition that does not involve an action.** [8]**And any prohibition that does not involve an action is not punishable by flogging."** Since Rabbi Yehudah offers a different reason as to why lashes are not administered for leaving the Paschal sacrifice uneaten, [9]this **implies that Rabbi Yehudah maintains that** a prohibition that does not involve an action **is** indeed **punishable by flogging.** Thus in his view, a person who takes a vow in an idol's name or swears in its name is also liable for flogging, even though he performs no physical act.

הַנּוֹדֵר בִּשְׁמוֹ [10]We have learned in our Mishnah: **"If** someone **takes a vow in** an idol's **name, or** if he **swears in** the idol's **name, he violates a negative commandment."** [11]The Gemara asks: **From where do we know** that **someone who takes a vow in** an idol's **name, or swears in its name,** violates a negative

[1]הָהוּא כְּרַבִּי יְהוּדָה, דְּאָמַר: [2]לָאו שֶׁאֵין בּוֹ מַעֲשֶׂה לוֹקִין עָלָיו. [3]דְּתַנְיָא: "'לֹא תוֹתִירוּ מִמֶּנּוּ עַד בֹּקֶר' — [4]בָּא הַכָּתוּב לִיתֵּן עֲשֵׂה אַחַר לֹא תַּעֲשֶׂה, [63B] לוֹמַר שֶׁאֵין לוֹקִין עָלָיו. [5]דִּבְרֵי רַבִּי יְהוּדָה. [6]רַבִּי יַעֲקֹב אוֹמֵר: לֹא מִן הַשֵּׁם הוּא זֶה, [7]אֶלָּא מִשּׁוּם דַּהֲוָה לֵיהּ לָאו שֶׁאֵין בּוֹ מַעֲשֶׂה. [8]וְכָל לָאו שֶׁאֵין בּוֹ מַעֲשֶׂה אֵין לוֹקִין עָלָיו". [9]מִכְּלָל דְּרַבִּי יְהוּדָה סָבַר לוֹקִין עָלָיו.

[10]"הַנּוֹדֵר בִּשְׁמוֹ, וְהַמְקַיֵּים בִּשְׁמוֹ, הֲרֵי זֶה בְּלֹא תַּעֲשֶׂה". [11]הַנּוֹדֵר בִּשְׁמוֹ, וְהַמְקַיֵּים בִּשְׁמוֹ,

LITERAL TRANSLATION

[1]That is in accordance with Rabbi Yehudah who said: [2]One is flogged for a prohibition that does not involve an action. [3]For it was taught: "'And you shall let nothing of it remain until the morning' — [4]the verse comes to give a positive commandment after a negative commandment, [63B] to teach that one is not flogged for it. [5]These are the words of Rabbi Yehudah. [6]Rabbi Ya'akov says: It is not for [this] reason. (lit., "name"). [7]But rather because it is a prohibition that does not involve an action. [8]And any prohibition that does not involve an action, one is not flogged for it." [9]This implies that Rabbi Yehudah maintains that one is flogged for it. [10]"[If] he takes a vow in its name, or swears in its name, he violates a negative commandment." [11]From where do we know about someone who takes a vow in its name, or swears in its name?

RASHI

לומר שאין לוקין עליו — דמשמע שזה עונשו של לאו, שאם הותירו — ישרפנו ויפטר. לא מן השם הוא זה — כלומר טעם זה אינו מן העיקר.

NOTES

הַנּוֹדֵר בִּשְׁמוֹ, וְהַמְקַיֵּים בִּשְׁמוֹ **If he takes a vow in its name, or swears in its name.** It may be asked: If there exists already a prohibition against mentioning the name of an idol, why is a special verse needed to forbid taking a vow or swearing by the name of an idol? *Rabbenu Yonah* suggests that the prohibitions against taking a vow and swearing by the name of an idol apply even to a person who takes a vow or swears by the name of an idol without mentioning its name, as when he says that he is swearing by the god of the Philistines.

HALAKHAH

a manner in which God is served, he violated the prohibition, 'You shall not serve them,' but he is not subject to the penalty of lashes, for those modes of worship are not specified explicitly, but only included in a general prohibition." (*Rambam, Sefer Mada, Hilkhot Avodah Zarah* 3:6.)

לָאו שֶׁאֵין בּוֹ מַעֲשֶׂה **A negative commandment that does not involve an action.** "Someone who violates a Torah prohibition that does not involve an action is not liable for flogging (except for one who curses another or himself using the name of God; one who swears falsely; and one who attempts to substitute another animal for a sacrificial animal)," following Rabbi Ya'akov. (*Rambam, Sefer Shofetim, Hilkhot Sanhedrin* 18:2.)

מְנָלַן? [1]דְּתַנְיָא: [2]״׳וְשֵׁם אֱלֹהִים אֲחֵרִים לֹא תַזְכִּירוּ׳ — [3]שֶׁלֹּא יֹאמַר אָדָם לַחֲבֵירוֹ: ׳שְׁמוֹר לִי בְּצַד עֲבוֹדָה זָרָה פְּלוֹנִית׳. [4]׳לֹא יִשָּׁמַע עַל פִּיךָ׳ — [5]שֶׁלֹּא יִדּוֹר בִּשְׁמוֹ, וְלֹא יְקַיֵּים בִּשְׁמוֹ, וְלֹא יִגְרוֹם לַאֲחֵרִים שֶׁיִּדְּרוּ בִּשְׁמוֹ, וְשֶׁיְּקַיְּימוּ בִּשְׁמוֹ. [6]דָּבָר אַחֵר: ׳לֹא יִשָּׁמַע עַל פִּיךָ׳ — [7]אַזְהָרָה לְמֵסִית וּלְמַדִּיחַ״. [8]מֵסִית, [9]בְּהֶדְיָא כְּתִיב בֵּיהּ: ״וְכָל יִשְׂרָאֵל יִשְׁמְעוּ וְיִרָאוּ וגו׳״! [10]אֶלָּא: אַזְהָרָה לְמַדִּיחַ. [11]״וְלֹא יִגְרוֹם לַאֲחֵרִים שֶׁיִּדְּרוּ בִּשְׁמוֹ וְשֶׁיְּקַיְּימוּ בִּשְׁמוֹ״. [12]מְסַיְּיעָא לֵיהּ לַאֲבוּהּ דִּשְׁמוּאֵל, דְּאָמַר אֲבוּהּ דִּשְׁמוּאֵל: [13]אָסוּר לְאָדָם שֶׁיַּעֲשֶׂה שׁוּתָּפוּת עִם הַנָּכְרִי,

LITERAL TRANSLATION

[1]For it was taught: [2]"'And you shall not mention the name of other gods' — [3]that a person should not say to someone else: 'Wait for me next to such-and-such idol.' [4]'Neither let it be heard out of your mouth' — [5]that he should not take a vow in its name, or swear in its name, nor cause others to take a vow in its name, or swear in its name. [6]Another explanation: 'Neither let it be heard out of your mouth' — [7]a warning to one who incites [an individual to idolatry] and one who incites [a community to idolatry]." [8]Regarding one who incites [an individual to idolatry], [9]it is explicitly written: "And all of Israel shall hear, and fear"! [10]Rather, a warning to one who incites [a community to idolatry]. [11]"That he should not cause others to take a vow in its name, or swear in its name." [12]This supports the father of Shmuel, for the father of Shmuel said: [13]A person is forbidden to form a partnership with a non-Jew,

TRANSLATION AND COMMENTARY

commandment? [1]The Gemara answers: **As it was taught** in the Baraita: "The verse states (Exodus 23:13): 'And you shall make no mention of the name of other gods; neither let it be heard out of your mouth.' The first part of the verse, [2]**'And you shall make no mention of the name of other gods,'** [3]teaches **that a person should not say to someone else: 'Wait for me next to such-and-such idol.'** [4]The second part of the verse, **'Neither let it be heard out of your mouth,'** [5]teaches **that a person may not take a vow in** an idol's name, **or swear in its name, nor** may he **cause others,** non-Jews, **to take a vow in** the idol's **name, or swear in its name.** [6]**Another explanation:** The second part of the verse, **'Neither let it be heard out of your mouth,'** [7]serves as **a warning against inciting others, whether an individual or a community, to worship idols.** The Torah passage dealing with the inciter (Deuteronomy 13:7-12) prescribes the punishment of stoning for this most serious offense, but the prohibition against incitement is derived from the verse, 'Neither let it be heard out of your mouth.'"

מֵסִית [8]The Gemara asks: **Regarding one who incites an individual to idolatry,** why is it necessary to derive his warning from this verse? [9]Surely **it is stated explicitly** (Deuteronomy 13:12): **"And all of Israel shall hear, and fear,** and shall do no more any such wickedness as this is among you." The words, "And shall do no more," teach that inciting an individual to idol worship is forbidden! [10]**Rather,** the Baraita means that the verse, "Neither let it be heard out of your mouth," serves as **a warning against inciting a community to worship idols,** for it is not stated anywhere else that such conduct is forbidden.

וְלֹא [11]It was taught in the Baraita: "The words, 'Neither let it be heard out of your mouth,' teach not only that a person may not take a vow or swear in an idol's name, but also that **he may not cause others,** non-Jews, **to take a vow in** an idol's **name, or swear in its name."** [12]The Gemara notes that **this supports** what **Shmuel's father said, for Shmuel's father said:** [13]**A Jew is forbidden to enter into a** business **partnership**

RASHI

שמור לי — המתן. **לא יגרום לאחרים** — לנכרים, ״וכל ישראל ישמעו ויראו ולא יוסיפו לעשות עוד כדבר הרע הזה בקרבך״.

NOTES

לֹא יִשָּׁמַע עַל פִּיךָ Neither let it be heard out of your mouth. According to the understanding that the verse, "Neither let it be heard out of your mouth [עַל פִּיךָ]," teaches that one may not cause others to take a vow in an idol's name, the words *al pikha* must be understood as *al yedei pikha*, "because of your mouth," meaning, because of you.

HALAKHAH

שֶׁלֹּא יֹאמַר אָדָם לַחֲבֵירוֹ: ׳שְׁמוֹר לִי בְּצַד עֲבוֹדָה זָרָה פְּלוֹנִית׳ That a person should not say to someone else: Wait for me next to such-and-such idol. "One may not mention the name of an idol. For example, one may not say to another person: 'Wait for me next to such-and-such idol.' One may also not make a non-Jew take an oath in the name of his idol." (*Rambam, Sefer Mada, Hilkhot Avodah Zarah* 5:10-11.)

אָסוּר לְאָדָם שֶׁיַּעֲשֶׂה שׁוּתָּפוּת עִם הַנָּכְרִי A person is forbidden to form a partnership with a non-Jew. "One must take care not to enter into a business partnership with a non-Jew, lest the non-Jew become liable for an oath to

TRANSLATION AND COMMENTARY

with a non-Jew, lest they come to a disagreement, and the non-Jew **become liable for an oath to him, and he swear by his idol,** [1]**and the Torah said: "Neither let it be heard out of your mouth,"** which forbids a Jew not only to swear by an idol himself, but even to cause a non-Jew to utter an oath by an idol's name.

כִּי אֲתָא [2]The Gemara relates that **when Ulla came** from Eretz Israel to Babylonia, **he spent the night in** a place called **Kalnevo.** [3]Upon meeting him, **Rava asked** Ulla: **"Where did the master spend the night?"** [4]Ulla **explained:** "I spent the night **in Kalnevo."** [5]Rava **said to him: "Surely,** that place is named after an idol, and **the verse states: 'And you shall make no mention of the name of other gods.'"** [6]Ulla **explained** his behavior **to** Rava: "I follow the position of Rabbi Yoḥanan, [7]for **Rabbi Yoḥanan said as follows:** [8]**Any idol that is mentioned** by name **in the Bible may be mentioned** by name **by us.** But the names of other idols that are not found in the Bible may indeed not be mentioned." [9]Rava asked: **"And where is** Kalnevo **mentioned** in the Bible?" [10]Ulla answered: **As the verse states** (Isaiah 46:1): **'Bel bows down, Nevo stoops.'"**

וְאִי לָא [11]The Gemara asks: **And if** the name of an idol **is not** explicitly **mentioned** in the Bible, is it **not** permitted to mention that idol's name? [12]**Rav Mesharsheya raised an objection** against this conclusion from a Mishnah regarding a *zav,* a man suffering from gonorrhea. A man becomes ritually impure as a result of the secretion of a white, pus-like discharge from his penis. A man who has such a discharge on one occasion becomes ritually impure for one day, like one who has emitted semen. If he experiences a second discharge on the same or the following day, he contracts the more severe ritual impurity of a *zav,* lasting seven days. A third discharge experienced within the next twenty-four hours obligates him to bring a sacrifice as part of his purification process. The Mishnah deals with a *zav* who had a prolonged initial discharge (*Zavim* 1:5): [13]**"If** a man **experienced one discharge that was as prolonged as three** discharges, meaning that it continued for as long **as** it takes to

שֶׁמָּא יִתְחַיֵּיב לוֹ שְׁבוּעָה, וְנִשְׁבַּע בַּעֲבוֹדָה זָרָה שֶׁלּוֹ, [1]וְהַתּוֹרָה אָמְרָה "לֹא יִשָּׁמַע עַל פִּיךָ". [2]כִּי אֲתָא עוּלָּא, בָּת בְּקַלְנְבוֹ. [3]אֲמַר לֵיהּ רָבָא: "וְהֵיכָא בָּת מָר"? [4]אֲמַר לֵיהּ: "בְּקַלְנְבוֹ". [5]אֲמַר לֵיהּ: "וְהָכְתִיב: 'וְשֵׁם אֱלֹהִים אֲחֵרִים לֹא תַזְכִּירוּ'"! [6]אֲמַר לֵיהּ: [7]"הָכִי אָמַר רַבִּי יוֹחָנָן: [8]כָּל עֲבוֹדָה זָרָה הַכְּתוּבָה בַּתּוֹרָה, מוּתָּר לְהַזְכִּיר שְׁמָהּ". [9]"וְהָא הֵיכָא כְּתִיבָא"? [10]"דִּכְתִיב: 'כָּרַע בֵּל, קֹרֵס נְבוֹ'". [11]וְאִי לָא כְּתִיבָא — לָא? [12]מְתִיב רַב מְשָׁרְשְׁיָא: [13]"רָאָה אַחַת מְרוּבָּה כְּשָׁלֹשׁ, שֶׁהִיא

LITERAL TRANSLATION

lest he become liable for an oath to him, and he swear by his idol, [1]and the Torah said: "Neither let it be heard out of your mouth."

[2]When Ulla came, he spent the night in Kalnevo. [3]Rava said to him: "And where did the master spend the night?" [4]He said to him: "In Kalnevo." [5]He said to him: "But surely it is written: 'And you shall make no mention of the name of other gods!'" [6]He said to him: [7]"Thus said Rabbi Yoḥanan: [8][Regarding] any idol that is written in the Torah, it is permissible to mention its name." [9]"And where is it written?" [10]"For it is written: 'Bel bows down, Nevo stoops.'"

[11]And if it is not written — not? [12]Rav Mesharsheya objected: [13]"If he sighted one [discharge] that is as prolonged as three, as

RASHI

בת בקלנבו — לן באותה עיר, והיא נקראת על שם עבודה זרה שבה. **ראה אחת מרובה כשלש** — זב שראה ראיה ארוכה, שהוא שופע כשלש ראיות שנעשה בהן זב גמור, שהוא כמגדיון לשילה — כשיעור מהלך מאותה עבודה זרה ששמה גדיון עד שילה, שהן שתי טבילות ושני ספוגין. שכן נתנו חכמים שיעור בין ראיה לראיה כדי לטבול ולהסתפג באלונטית. דהיינו בין ראיה ראשונה לשניה טבילה וספוג, וכן בין שניה לשלישית.

NOTES

עֲבוֹדָה זָרָה הַכְּתוּבָה בַּתּוֹרָה **Any idol that is written in the Torah.** *She'iltot* explains that since one is permitted to mention the name of an idol that is written in the Torah while studying the Torah passage containing that name, one may mention that name in other contexts as well. *Meiri* adds that in the context of Torah study, one may mention the name of any idol, even one that is not mentioned in the Torah.

רָאָה אַחַת מְרוּבָּה **If he sighted one discharge that is prolonged.** A man suffering from gonorrhea who experiences

HALAKHAH

him, and he swear by his idol, and the Jew then violate the prohibition, 'Neither let it be heard out of your mouth,'" following Shmuel's father. *Rema* (in the name of *Tosafot*) adds that today we are lenient about this prohibition, because most non-Jews believe in God and swear in His name, and even if they combine God's name with something else, that is not forbidden to non-Jews. (*Shulḥan Arukh, Oraḥ Ḥayyim* 156:1.)

עֲבוֹדָה זָרָה הַכְּתוּבָה בַּתּוֹרָה **Any idol that is written in the Torah.** "One is permitted to mention the name of an idol that is mentioned by name in the Bible," following Rabbi Yoḥanan. (*Rambam, Sefer Mada, Hilkhot Avodah Zarah* 5:11.)

רָאָה אַחַת מְרוּבָּה **If he sighted one discharge that is as prolonged.** "If a man experienced one pus-like discharge

BACKGROUND

כְּמִגַּדְיוֹן לְשִׁילֹה As from Gadyon to Shiloh. The reading כְּמִגַּדְיוֹן לְשִׁלּוֹחַ, "as from Gadyon to Siloam" is found in many sources and is apparently the basic version. The commentators explain that Gadyon was the name of a place in the walls of Jerusalem where a statue was placed during Greek rule. The distance from the wall to the Siloam spring was apparently 150 cubits (about seventy-five meters).

TRANSLATION AND COMMENTARY

walk **from Gadyon** (a place named after an idol) **to Shiloh,** [1]**which is the time required for twice immersing** oneself in water **and twice drying** oneself **off** (=the time required for walking a hundred cubits), [2]the man **is** regarded as **a full-fledged** *zav* who must bring a sacrifice as part of his purification process. Now, the Mishnah refers to Gadyon, even though that is the name of an idol, and that idol is not mentioned anywhere in the Bible!

אָמַר רָבִינָא [3]**Ravina said:** This is not difficult, for the idol **Gad is also mentioned** in the Bible, [4]**as the verse states** (Isaiah 65:11): **"That set out a table for Gad."**

אָמַר רַב נַחְמָן [5]**Rav Naḥman said: All mockery is forbidden, except for mockery concerning an idol which is permitted,** [6]**as the verses state** (Isaiah 46:1-2): **"Bel bows down, Nevo stoops. They stoop, they bow down together, they could not deliver the burden."** Rav Naḥman understands that the verse is mocking the idols Bel and Nevo, who bow down and stoop in order to relieve themselves. [7]**And similarly the verses state** (Hosea 10:4-5): **"They have spoken...The inhabitants of Samaria shall fear because of the calves of Bat Aven; for its people shall mourn over it, and its priests that rejoiced on it, for its glory, because it is departed from it."** [8]**Read not** the word כְּבוֹדוֹ as *kevodo,* **"its glory,"** [9]**but rather** read it as if it were written כְּבֵידוֹ, *keveido,* **"its weight."** According to this reading, the verse mockingly refers to the idol's weight, the feces which depart from it.

אָמַר רַבִּי יִצְחָק [10]**Rabbi Yitzḥak said: What is the meaning of the verse which states** (Hosea 13:2): **"And now they sin more and more, and have made for themselves molten images of their silver, and idols according to**

כְּמִגַּדְיוֹן לְשִׁילֹה, [1]שֶׁהֵן שְׁתֵּי טְבִילוֹת וּשְׁנֵי סְפוּגִין, [2]הֲרֵי זֶה זָב גָּמוּר״!

[3]אָמַר רָבִינָא: גַּד נַמִי מִכְתַּב כְּתִיב, [4]דִּכְתִיב: ״הָעֹרְכִים לַגַּד שֻׁלְחָן״.

[5]אָמַר רַב נַחְמָן: כָּל לֵיצָנוּתָא אֲסִירָא, חוּץ מִלֵּיצָנוּתָא דַּעֲבוֹדָה זָרָה, דְּשַׁרְיָא. [6]דִּכְתִיב: ״כָּרַע בֵּל קֹרֵס נְבוֹ...קָרְסוּ כָרְעוּ יַחְדָּו לֹא יָכְלוּ מַלֵּט מַשָּׂא״. [7]וּכְתִיב: ״דִּבְּרוּ לְעֶגְלוֹת בֵּית אָוֶן יָגוּרוּ שְׁכַן שֹׁמְרוֹן כִּי אָבַל עָלָיו עַמּוֹ וּכְמָרָיו עָלָיו יָגִילוּ עַל כְּבוֹדוֹ כִּי גָלָה מִמֶּנּוּ״. [8]אַל תִּקְרֵי ״כְּבוֹדוֹ״, [9]אֶלָּא ״כְּבֵידוֹ״.

[10]אָמַר רַבִּי יִצְחָק: מַאי דִּכְתִיב: ״וְעַתָּה יוֹסִפוּ לַחֲטֹא וַיַּעֲשׂוּ לָהֶם מַסֵּכָה מִכַּסְפָּם כִּתְבוּנָם

LITERAL TRANSLATION

from Gadyon to Shiloh, [1]which is [the time required for] twice immersing and twice getting dry, [2]he is a full-fledged *zav*!"

[3]Ravina said: Gad is also written, [4]for it is written: "That set out a table for Gad."

[5]Rav Naḥman said: All mockery is forbidden, except for mockery concerning an idol which is permitted, [6]as it is written: "Bel bows down, Nevo stoops. They stoop, they bow down together, they could not deliver the burden." [7]And it is written: "They have spoken... The inhabitants of Samaria shall fear because of the calves of Bat Aven; for its people shall mourn over it, and its priests that rejoiced on it, for its glory, because it is departed from it." [8]Read not "its glory," [9]but rather "its weight."

[10]Rabbi Yitzḥak said: What is [the meaning of] that which is written: "And now they sin more, and have made for themselves molten images of their silver, and idols according to their understanding,

RASHI

קרס = נתרז, כלומר כרע על ברכיו ונתרז, דהיינו ליצנותא דאישתעי ביה קרא "לא יוכלו מלט משא" הרעי שבנקביהם לא יוכלו לסבול ונתרז. לעגלות בית און – על עגלים שבבית אל. יגורו שכן שומרון – ידאגו שוכני שומרון. כי אבל עליו עמו – שיטלם סנחריב וילך לו. וכמריו – שהיו נושאין אותו. עליו יגילו – ששמחים על כובד משא שגלה מהם. אלא כבידו – משא עגבותיו וריעי שבהן, ואף על גב דלאו בעלי חיים נינהו ואין להם ריעי משתעי בהו קרא לשון גנאי.

NOTES

three discharges of a white, pus-like discharge from his penis is a full-fledged *zav.* There is no minimal amount of discharge, nor must the three discharges be experienced on separate days, as is the case with a *zavah,* a woman who experiences a flow of menstrual-type blood on three consecutive days during a time of the month when she does not ordinarily menstruate. Thus, a man who experiences one prolonged discharge is regarded as if he experienced two or three discharges, depending on the duration of the discharge.

HALAKHAH

that was as prolonged as three discharges, lasting for the time required for twice immersing oneself in water and twice drying oneself off, he is regarded as having experienced three discharges, and is therefore a full-fledged *zav* who is liable for a sacrifice when he comes to purify himself," following the Mishnah. (*Rambam, Sefer Korbanot, Hilkhot Meḥusarei Kaparah* 2:10.)

לֵיצָנוּתָא דַּעֲבוֹדָה זָרָה Mockery concerning an idol. "Mockery concerning an idol is permitted," following Rav Naḥman. (*Shulḥan Arukh, Yoreh De'ah* 147:5.)

TRANSLATION AND COMMENTARY

their understanding, all of it the work of craftsmen; they say of them, Let the men who sacrifice kiss calves." [1] **What is meant by** the words **"and idols according to their understanding"?** Rabbi Yitzḥak understands the word כִּתְבוּנָם (translated here as "according to their understanding") as if it were written כתבניתם, "according to their image." [2] The verse **teaches that every one formed an image of his idol, and put it in his pocket,** and carried it around him with him wherever he went. [3] **Whenever he remembered** the idol, **he would take** the miniature **out of his bosom, and embrace and kiss it.**

מַאי [4] **What is meant by** the end of that verse, **"Let the men who sacrifice kiss calves"?** [5] **Rabbi Yitzḥak said: The priests would set their eyes on those with money,** and devise a plot in order to take the money. [6] They would **starve the calves** which were worshipped as idols, **and** then **form an image of** the rich men's **figures, and place them next to** the hungry animals' food **troughs, and** then **take** the animals **out** to eat. Having been conditioned to associate the images of the rich men with feeding time, [7] **when** the animals **saw** those rich men in the flesh, **they would run after them, and lick them,** as if to say: "Feed us." [8] The priests **would** then **say** to each of the rich men: "It is obvious that **the idol desires you.** [9] **Come, and sacrifice yourself to it."** The priest would succeed to the estates of the rich men who agreed to offer themselves as sacrifices, and take their money for themselves.

אָמַר רָבָא [10] **Rava said: Does this** explanation fit in with the words: **"Let the men who sacrifice kiss calves,"** which imply that the men who offered sacrifices would kiss the calves, and not that the calves would kiss the men? According to Rabbi Yitzḥak's explanation, [11] the verse **should have been** formulated differently, so that it reads: **"The calves will kiss to sacrifice a man."**

אֶלָּא [12] **Rather, Rava said:** The words, "Let the men who sacrifice kiss calves," should be understood as follows: If **someone sacrificed his son to an idol,** [13] the priest **would say to him:** "Surely you have **offered** the idol **a great present.** Thus, you have earned the right to **come and kiss it."**

אָמַר רַב יְהוּדָה [14] **Rav Yehudah said in the name of Rav:** Regarding the nations which the Assyrians settled in Samaria, the verses state (II Kings 17:30-31): "And the men of Bavel made Sukkot-benot, and the men of Kut made Nergal, and the men of Ḥamat made Ashima, and the Avvim made Nivhan and Tartak, and the Sefarvim burnt their sons in fire to Adrammelech, and Anammelech, god of Sefarvayim."

עֲצַבִּים וגו׳״. [1] מַאי ״כִּתְבוּנָם עֲצַבִּים״? [2] מְלַמֵּד שֶׁכָּל אֶחָד וְאֶחָד עָשָׂה דְּמוּת יִרְאָתוֹ, וּמַנִּיחָהּ בְּכִיסוֹ. [3] בְּשָׁעָה שֶׁזּוֹכְרָהּ, מוֹצִיאָהּ מִתּוֹךְ חֵיקוֹ, וּמְחַבְּקָהּ, וּמְנַשְּׁקָהּ.

[4] מַאי ״זֹבְחֵי אָדָם עֲגָלִים יִשָּׁקוּן״? [5] אָמַר רַבִּי יִצְחָק דְּבֵי רַבִּי אַמֵּי: שֶׁהָיוּ כּוֹמָרִים נוֹתְנִים עֵינֵיהֶם בְּבַעֲלֵי מָמוֹן, [6] וּמַרְעִיבִים אֶת הָעֲגָלִים, וְעוֹשִׂין דְּמוּת עֲצַבִּים, וּמַעֲמִידִין בְּצַד אֲבוּסֵיהֶן, וּמוֹצִיאִין אוֹתָן לַחוּץ. [7] כֵּיוָן שֶׁרָאוּ אוֹתָן, רָצִין אַחֲרֵיהֶן, וּמְמַשְׁמְשִׁין בָּהֶן. [8] אוֹמְרִים לוֹ: ״עֲבוֹדָה זָרָה חָפֵץ בְּךָ״. [9] יָבֹא, וְיִזְבַּח עַצְמוֹ לוֹ.

[10] אָמַר רָבָא: הַאי ״זֹבְחֵי אָדָם עֲגָלִים יִשָּׁקוּן״? [11] ״עֲגָלִים יִשָּׁקוּן לִזְבֹּחַ אָדָם״ מִיבָּעֵי לֵיהּ!

[12] אֶלָּא, אָמַר רָבָא: כָּל הַזּוֹבֵחַ אֶת בְּנוֹ לַעֲבוֹדָה זָרָה, [13] אָמַר לוֹ: ״דּוֹרוֹן גָּדוֹל הִקְרִיב לוֹ. יָבֹא וְיִשַּׁק לוֹ״.

[14] אָמַר רַב יְהוּדָה אָמַר רַב:

LITERAL TRANSLATION

etc." [1] What is [meant by] "and idols according to their understanding"? [2] This teaches that every one formed an image of his idol, and put it in his pocket. [3] When he remembered it, he took it out of his bosom, and embraced it, and kissed it.

[4] What is [meant by] "Let the men who sacrifice kiss calves"? [5] Rabbi Yitzḥak said: The priests would set their eyes on those with money, [6] and starve the calves, and form an image of their figures, and place them next to their troughs, and take them out. [7] When they saw them, they would run after them, and lick them. [8] They would say to him: "The idol desires you. [9] Let him come, and sacrifice himself to it."

[10] Rava said: Is this "Let the men who sacrifice kiss calves"? [11] It should have been "The calves will kiss to sacrifice a man"!

[12] Rather, Rava said: Whoever sacrificed his son to an idol, [13] he would say to him: "He offered it a great present. Let him come and kiss it."

[14] Rav Yehudah said in the name of Rav:

RASHI

מרעיבים את העגלים – בעלי חיים שהיו עובדין אותן והיו מרעיבין אותן, ועושין דמות צלמיהם של בעלי ממון, כלומר דמות דיוקנם, ומעמידין אותן בצד אבוסיהן של עגלים. ומחמת שהיו רואין את הדמות תמיד היו מכירין אותן ורצין אחריהם וממשמשין בהן כלומר: האכילנו. ואומרין להם הכומרים: עבודה זרה חפץ בך וכו׳. **זבחי אדם** – משמע אותן שזבחו האדם. **עגלים ישקון** – לאחר מכאן לעגלים ישקון. **ישקון לזבוח אדם מבעי ליה** – להם הם הכומרים אומרים: עגלים הללו נושקין אתכם לזבוח עצמכם להם.

LANGUAGE

דורון **Present.** This derives from the Greek δῶρον, *doron*, meaning "a gift, an offering."

LANGUAGE

סֻכּוֹת בְּנוֹת Sukkot-benot. Some commentators connect this phrase with סִכּוּת (*Sikkut*), the name of a god (and perhaps the name of a planet), mentioned in Amos 5:26.

נֵרְגַל Nergal. This is the name of the Assyrian god of war. The rooster (תַּרְנְגוֹל, *tarnegol,* in Hebrew) was Nergal's sacred bird and symbol.

סַלָמַנְדְּרָא Salamander. This word is derived from the Greek σαλαμάνδρα, *salamandra.* It refers to the lizard known as a salamander, which was supposed to be able to resist fire.

TRANSLATION AND COMMENTARY

[1]**"And the men of Bavel made Sukkot-benot."** [2]**And what idol is that?** [3]An idol in the form of **a hen.** [4]**"And the men of Kut made Nergal."** [5]**And what idol is** that? [6]An idol in the form of **a rooster.** [7]**"And the men of Hamat made Ashima."** [8]**And what idol is that?** An idol in the form of **a bald goat.** [9]**"And the Avvim made Nivhan and Tartak."** [10]**And what idols are they?** [11]Idols in the form of **a dog and an ass.** [12]**"And the Sefarvim burnt their sons in fire to Adrammelech, and Anammelech, god of Sefarvayim."** [13]**And what idols are they?** [14]Idols in the form of **a mule and a horse.** [15]The idol in the form of a mule was called **Adrammelech, because** a mule **honors** (*adar*) **its master** (*melech*) when it carries **his burden.** [16]**And** the idol in the form of a horse was called **Anammelech, because** a horse **answers** (*ani*) and assists **its master** (*melech*) when he goes out to **battle.** [17]The Gemara adds: **So too regarding Hezekiah the king of Judah, his father,** Aḥaz, **wished to do the same thing to him,** (II Kings 16:3): "But [Aḥaz] walked in the way of the kings of Israel, and even made his son pass through the fire, according to the abominations of the nations, whom the Lord cast out from before the children of Israel," and we do not find that Aḥaz had any other sons besides Hezekiah. [18]**But** Hezekiah was not harmed by the fire, because his **mother anointed him with the blood of a salamander**

אָמַר רַב יְהוּדָה [19]**Rav Yehudah said in the name of Rav:** The people of **Israel knew** very well **that idols have no substance,** and they did not worship them out of inner conviction. [20]**They only worshiped idols in order to permit** themselves to engage **in forbidden sexual relations in public,** for many idolatrous rites involved sexual practices that are forbidden by Torah law.

[1]״וְאַנְשֵׁי בָבֶל עָשׂוּ אֶת סֻכּוֹת בְּנוֹת״. [2]וּמַאי נִיהוּ? [3]תַּרְנְגוֹלֶת. [4]״וְאַנְשֵׁי כוּת עָשׂוּ אֶת נֵרְגַל״. [5]וּמַאי נִיהוּ? [6]תַּרְנְגוֹל. [7]״וְאַנְשֵׁי חֲמָת עָשׂוּ אֶת אֲשִׁימָא״. [8]וּמַאי נִיהוּ? [9]בַּרְחָא קַרְחָא, [10]״וְהָעַוִּים עָשׂוּ אֶת נִבְחַן וְאֶת תַּרְתָּק״. [11]וּמַאי נִיהוּ? [12]כֶּלֶב וַחֲמוֹר. [13]״וְהַסְפַרְוִים שֹׂרְפִים אֶת בְּנֵיהֶם וְאֶת בְּנוֹתֵיהֶם בָּאֵשׁ לְאַדְרַמֶּלֶךְ, וַעֲנַמֶּלֶךְ אֱלֹהֵי סְפַרְוָיִם״, [14]וּמַאי נִיהוּ? [15]הַפֶּרֶד וְהַסּוּס. [16]אַדְרַמֶּלֶךְ — דְּאַדַּר לֵיהּ לְמָרֵיהּ בְּטְעִינָה. [17]וַעֲנַמֶּלֶךְ — דְּעָנֵי לֵיהּ לְמָרֵיהּ בִּקְרָבָא. [18]אַף חִזְקִיָּה מֶלֶךְ יְהוּדָה בִּיקֵּשׁ אָבִיו לַעֲשׂוֹת לוֹ כֵּן, [19]אֶלָּא שֶׁסָּכַתּוֹ אִמּוֹ סַלָמַנְדְּרָא.

[20]אָמַר רַב יְהוּדָה אָמַר רַב: יוֹדְעִין הָיוּ יִשְׂרָאֵל בַּעֲבוֹדָה זָרָה שֶׁאֵין בָּהּ מַמָּשׁ, [21]וְלֹא עָבְדוּ עֲבוֹדָה זָרָה אֶלָּא לְהַתִּיר לָהֶם עֲרָיוֹת בְּפַרְהֶסְיָא.

LITERAL TRANSLATION

[1]"And the men of Bavel made Sukkot-benot." [2]And what is it? [3]A hen. [4]"And the men of Kut made Nergal." [5]And what is it? [6]A rooster. [7]"And the men of Hamat made Ashima." [8]And what it it? [9]A bald goat. [10]"And the Avvim made Nivhan and Tartak." [11]And what are they? [12]A dog and an ass. [13]"And the Sefarvim burn their sons in fire to Adrammelech, and Anammelech, god of Sefarvayim." [14]And what are they? [15]A mule and a horse. [16]Adrammelech — that which honors its master with [his] burden. [17]And Anammelech — that which answers its master in battle. [18]So too regarding Hezekiah the king of Judah, his father wished to do the same thing to him, [19]but his mother anointed him with [the blood of] a salamander.

[20]Rav Yehudah said in the name of Rav: Israel knew that idols have have no substance, [21]and they only worshiped idols in order to permit forbidden sexual relations in public.

RASHI

ואנשי בבל עשו את סכות בנות — פסוק אחד בספר מלכים באותן אומות שהושיב סנחריב בשומרון ובעריה, ועשו להם עבודה זרה. **תרנגולת** — לדמות תרנגולת היו עובדין, ובלשונם קורין לתרנגולת סוכות בנות. **ברחא קרחא** = עז, ברחא קרוי כל צאן, והעז קרי ליה קרחא, על שם שאין לו צמר כל כך. **נבחן** — כלב נובח. **דאדר ליה למריה** — מהדר את אדוניו ומכבדו, שמשליך עליו משאו. שהיה צריך לטעון על צוארו. אדר מלך — מהדר את מלכו, כלומר את אדוניו. **לעשות לו כן** — לשורפו באש כמו הספרוים. **סלמנדרא** — חיה קטנה שיוצאה מתנור שהאש בוערת בו שבע שנים, והסך מדמה אין האור שולט בו. ובאחז מצינו כתוב (מלכים ב׳ טז) ״גם את בנו העביר באש״ ולא מצינו לו בן אלא חזקיהו. **אלא להתיר להם עריות בפרהסיא** — שהיה יצרן תקפן על עריות, אמרו: נפרוק כל עול תורה מעלינו ואל יוכיחונו על העריות. אבל על עבודה זרה לא תקפן יצרן.

NOTES

סֻכּוֹת בְּנוֹת Sukkot-benot. *Arukh* interprets the term Sukkot-benot [סֻכּוֹת-בְּנוֹת] as referring to a hen which shades [סוֹכֶכֶת] over her young [בָּנֶיהָ]. Others understand the word Sukkot [סֻכּוֹת] as the feminine form of שֶׂכְוִי, "rooster."

נִבְחַן Nivhan. In the Biblical text, we find Nivhaz [נִבְחַז], which is understood as referring to a dog which barks [נוֹבֵחַ] and displays [from the word חֲזוּת] its teeth (*Radak*), or which barks [נוֹבֵחַ] when it sees a stranger [זָר] (*Rabbi Ya'akov Emden).*

דְּאַדַּר לֵיהּ לְמָרֵיהּ That which honors its master. According to *Radak,* the idol in the form of a mule was called Adrammelech, because a mule carries [*adar*] his master's [*melech*] burden.

[1]מְתִיב רַב מְשַׁרְשְׁיָא ״כִּזְכֹּר בְּנֵיהֶם מִזְבְּחוֹתָם וגו׳״, [2]וְאָמַר רַבִּי אֶלְעָזָר: כְּאָדָם שֶׁיֵּשׁ לוֹ גַּעְגּוּעִין עַל בְּנוֹ!

[3]בָּתַר דַּאֲבִיקוּ בֵּיהּ.

[4]תָּא שְׁמַע: ״׳וְנָתַתִּי פִּגְרֵיכֶם עַל פִּגְרֵי גִלּוּלֵיכֶם׳. [5]אָמַר, אֵלִיָּהוּ הַצַּדִּיק הָיָה מְחַזֵּר עַל תְּפוּחֵי רָעָב שֶׁבִּירוּשָׁלַיִם, [6]פַּעַם אַחַת מָצָא תִּינוֹק שֶׁהָיָה תָּפוּחַ וּמוּטָּל בְּאַשְׁפָּה. [7]אָמַר לוֹ: מֵאֵיזֶה מִשְׁפָּחָה אַתָּה? [8]אָמַר לוֹ: ׳מִמִּשְׁפָּחָה פְּלוֹנִית אֲנִי׳. [9]אָמַר לוֹ: ׳כְּלוּם נִשְׁתַּיֵּיר מֵאוֹתָהּ מִשְׁפָּחָה׳? [10]אָמַר לוֹ: ׳לָאו, חוּץ מִמֶּנִּי׳. [11]אָמַר לוֹ: ׳אִם אֲנִי מְלַמֶּדְךָ דָּבָר שֶׁאַתָּה חַי בּוֹ אַתָּה לָמֵד׳? [12]אָמַר לוֹ: ׳הֵן׳. [13]אָמַר לוֹ: ׳אֱמוֹר בְּכָל יוֹם: ״שְׁמַע יִשְׂרָאֵל ה׳ אֱלֹהֵינוּ ה׳ אֶחָד״׳. [14]אָמַר לוֹ: [64A] [15]׳הַס, שֶׁלֹּא לְהַזְכִּיר בְּשֵׁם ה׳׳, [16]שֶׁלֹּא לִימְּדוֹ אָבִיו וְאִמּוֹ. [17]מִיָּד הוֹצִיא יִרְאָתוֹ מֵחֵיקוֹ, וּמְחַבְּקָהּ וּמְנַשְּׁקָהּ, עַד שֶׁנִּבְקְעָה כְּרֵיסוֹ [18]וְנָפְלָה יִרְאָתוֹ לָאָרֶץ וְנָפַל הוּא עָלֶיהָ. [19]לְקַיֵּים מַה שֶּׁנֶּאֱמַר: ״וְנָתַתִּי אֶת פִּגְרֵיכֶם עַל פִּגְרֵי גִּלּוּלֵיכֶם״!

[20]בָּתַר דַּאֲבִיקוּ בֵּיהּ.

LITERAL TRANSLATION

[1]Rav Mesharshaya objected: "As they remember their children, etc." [2]And Rabbi Elazar said: Like a person who has yearnings for his son.

[3]After they cleaved to it.

[4]Come [and] hear: "'And I will cast your carcasses upon the carcasses of your idols.' [5]He said: Elijah the righteous one went around visiting those bloated by starvation in Jerusalem. [6]Once he found a a child that was bloated and cast upon a dunghill. [7]He said to him: 'From which family are you?' [8]He said to him: 'I am from such-and-such family.' [9]He said to him: 'Is anyone left from that family?' [10]He said to him: 'Nobody, except for me.' [11]He said to him: 'If I teach you something through which you will live, will you learn it?' [12]He said to him: 'Yes.' [13]He said to him: 'Say every day: "Hear, O Israel, the Lord is our God, the Lord is one."' [14]He said to him: [64A] [15]'Be silent, not to mention the name of the Lord,' [16]for his father and mother did not teach him. [17]Immediately, he took his idol out of his bosom, and embraced it, and kissed it, until his stomach split open, [18]and his idol fell to the ground, and he fell upon it, [19]to fulfill what was said: 'And I will cast your carcasses upon the carcasses of your idols.'"

[20]After they cleaved to it.

TRANSLATION AND COMMENTARY

מְתִיב [1]**Rav Mesharshaya raised an objection:** But surely the verse states (Jeremiah 17:2): **"As they remember their children,** so they remember their altars and their asherim by the green trees upon the high hills." [2]**And Rabbi Elazar said:** The verse means to say that **just as a person yearns for his son,** so the people of Israel yearn for their idols.

בָּתַר דַּאֲבִיקוּ בֵּיהּ [3]The Gemara answers: That verse refers to the time **after** the people of Israel **had cleaved to** their idols, and started to believe in them. But at the beginning they were not attracted to those idols out of inner conviction, but out of lust to engage in forbidden sexual relationships.

תָּא שְׁמַע [4]**Come and hear** what was taught in the following Baraita: "The verse states (Leviticus 26:30): **'And I will cast your carcasses upon the carcasses of your idols.'** [5]The Sages **said** that **Elijah the righteous** prophet **went around visiting those languishing with starvation in Jerusalem.** [6]**Once he found a child that was languishing** with starvation **and cast** out **upon a dunghill.** [7]Elijah **asked** the child: **'From which family do** you come?' [8]The child **said to him: 'I come from such-and-such family.'** [9]Elijah then **asked him: 'Is** there **anyone** else **left from that** entire **family?'** [10]The child **answered: 'Nobody** is left, **except for me.'** [11]Elijah **asked him: 'If I teach you something that can save your life, will you learn it?'** [12]The child **answered: 'Yes.'** [13]Elijah **said to him: 'Say every day** (Deuteronomy 6:4): **"Hear, O Israel, the Lord is our God, the Lord is one."'** [14]The child **said to him:** [64A] [15]**'Be silent,** and **mention not the name of the Lord,'** [16]for the child did not want even to hear God's name, because **his father and mother had never taught it to him.** [17]**Immediately,** the child **took his idol out of his bosom, and embraced and kissed it, until his stomach split open** because of his hunger. [18]**The idol** then **fell to the ground, and** the child **fell upon it,** [19]**fulfilling the verse which states** (Leviticus 26:30): **'And I will cast your carcasses upon the carcasses of your idols.'"** This story shows that the sinners of Israel were deeply connected to their idols, against Rava!

בָּתַר דַּאֲבִיקוּ בֵּיהּ [20]The Gemara answers as it had answered above: This incident took place **after** the people of Israel **had** already **cleaved to** their idols, for they came to believe in them. But they were initially attracted to them because idolatry permitted them sexual license.

RASHI

כזכור בניהם מזבחותם — משמע שהיו להם געגועין עליהם, כאדם שיש לו געגועין על בנו, ונזכרו נאנת. והכי משמע: כזכור בניהם דומה להם זכירת מזבחותם ואשריהם. **בתר דאביקו ביה** = אחר שנתקשרו בהן מעלמן, תקפה חיבתן עליהן. **תפוחי רעב** — כמו נפוחי. **הס** = שתוק, כמו (במדבר יג) ״ויהס כלב״ — השתיקם.

LANGUAGE

בַּיָּא בַּיָּא Woe, woe. This expression is an exclamation, taken from the Greek βία. It is used here in the sense of "injustice, oppression, coercion."

TRANSLATION AND COMMENTARY

תָּא שְׁמַע [1]**Come and hear** another proof against Rava: The verse describing the penitential rites which were observed during the days of Ezra and Nehemiah states (Nehemiah 9:4): **"And they cried with a loud voice to the Lord their God."** [2]It may be asked: **What did they say** when they cried out to God? [3]**Rav Yehudah said, and some say** that **it was Rabbi Yonatan** who said: They said as follows: **"Woe, woe!** [4]**This** — the passion for idolatry — **is what caused the Temple to be destroyed, and the sanctuary to be burned, and the righteous men to be killed, and** the people of **Israel to be exiled from their land,** [5]**and still it dances among us,** tempting us to transgress the prohibitions against idol worship! [6]**Did You not instill within us** the passion for idolatry **so that we should receive a reward for** overcoming **it?** [7]**We do not want** the passion for idolatry, **and we do not want** to receive **a reward** for overcoming it!" Since the leaders of Israel prayed to God for control over the people's passion for idolatry, it follows that when they sinned and worshiped idols, they really believed in them, against Rava.

בָּתַר דַּאֲבִיקוּ בֵּיהּ [8]Once again the Gemara answers: This too occurred **after** the people of Israel **had cleaved to** their idols. But at first they worshiped the idols out of their lust to engage in forbidden sexual relations.

יָתְבוּ תְּלָתָא [9]The Gemara continues to describe what happened when the leaders of Israel asked to be freed from the passion for idolatry. **They spent** the next **three days in fast, and prayed for mercy** from Heaven.[10] Then **a note fell from Heaven on which was written** the word **"Truth,"** which indicated that God had acceded to their request.

אָמַר רַבִּי חֲנִינָא [11]Regarding this, **Rabbi Ḥanina noted: Infer from this** that **the seal of the Holy One, blessed be He, is "Truth."**

נְפַק כְּגוּרְיָא [12]The Gemara continues the story: After the note fell from Heaven, a **fire in the form of a young lion came out of the Holy of Holies.** [13]**The Prophet** Zechariah **said to** the people of **Israel: "This is the passion for idolatry** which led you astray to idol worship." [14]**While they were** trying to **seize** the

[1]תָּא שְׁמַע: ״וַיִּזְעֲקוּ בְּקוֹל גָּדוֹל אֶל ה׳ אֱלֹהֵיהֶם״. [2]מַאי אֲמוּר? [3]אָמַר רַב יְהוּדָה וְאִיתֵּימָא רַב יוֹנָתָן: בַּיָּא בַּיָּא! [4]הַיְינוּ דְּאַחְרְבֵיהּ לְבֵיתָא, וְקַלְיָא לְהֵיכָלָא, וְקַטְלִינְהוּ לְצַדִּיקֵי, וְאַגְלִינְהוּ לְיִשְׂרָאֵל מֵאַרְעֲיְיהוּ, [5]וַעֲדַיִין הוּא מְרַקֵּד בֵּינַן. [6]כְּלוּם יְהַבְתֵּיהּ לָן אֶלָּא לְקַבּוּלֵי בֵּיהּ אַגְרָא? [7]לָא אִיהוּ בָּעֵינַן וְלָא אַגְרֵיהּ בָּעֵינַן!

[8]בָּתַר דַּאֲבִיקוּ בֵּיהּ.

[9]יָתְבוּ תְּלָתָא יוֹמָא בְּתַעֲנִיתָא, בְּעוּ רַחֲמֵי. [10]נְפַל לְהוּ פִּיתְקָא מֵרְקִיעָא, דַּהֲוָה כְּתִיב בָּהּ ״אֱמֶת״.

[11]אָמַר רַבִּי חֲנִינָא: שְׁמַע מִינָּהּ: חוֹתָמוֹ שֶׁל הַקָּדוֹשׁ בָּרוּךְ הוּא ״אֱמֶת״.

[12]נְפַק כְּגוּרְיָא דְּנוּרָא מִבֵּית קָדְשֵׁי הַקֳּדָשִׁים. [13]אָמַר לְהוּ נָבִיא לְיִשְׂרָאֵל: ״הַיְינוּ יִצְרָא דַּעֲבוֹדָה זָרָה״. [14]בַּהֲדֵי דְּקָתָפְסִי

LITERAL TRANSLATION

[1]Come [and] hear: "And they cried with a loud voice to the Lord their God." [2]What did they say? [3]Rav Yehudah said, and some say [it was] Rabbi Yonatan: "Woe, woe! [4]This is what destroyed the Temple, and burned the sanctuary, and killed the righteous men, and exiled Israel from their land, [5]and still it dances among us! [6]Did You not give it to us so that we should receive a reward for it? [7]We do not want it, and we do not want its reward!"

[8]After they cleaved to it.

[9]They spent three days in fast, [and] prayed for mercy. [10]A note fell for them from Heaven on which was written: "Truth."

[11]Rabbi Ḥanina said: Infer from this: The seal of the Holy One, blessed be He, is "Truth."

[12]Fire in the form of a young lion went out of the Holy of Holies. [13]The Prophet said to Israel: "This is the passion for idolatry." [14]While they were seizing

RASHI

ויצעקו בני ישראל בקול גדול – באנשי כנסת הגדולה כתיב. **בייא בייא** = בלשון ארמי הוי לשון גנוח וצעקה, כמו ״אהה״ בלשון הקודש. **היינו האי דחרביה לביתיה** – למקדשו. **ובעו רחמי** – היו מבקשים רחמים שימסר בידם יצר הרע של עבודה זרה. **לקבולי ביה אגרא** – לכוף את יצרנו ולקבל שכר על כך. **לא איהו בעינן וכו׳** – אלמא יצר תקפן. **יתבי תלתא יומין וכו׳** – מלתיה דרב יהודה מסיק. **אמת** – משמע: מסכים אני עמהם בתקנה זו, שטוב הדבר לסלקו. **חותמו של הקדוש ברוך הוא אמת** – שהמלך נאות ומסכים עם עבדיו, חותם עמהם בתקנתם את חותמו. **בגוריא** – ארי קטן.

NOTES

הַיְינוּ יִצְרָא דַּעֲבוֹדָה זָרָה This is the passion for idolatry. According to *Ramah,* Israel's request to be freed from the passion for idolatry occurred in a prophetic vision. The story serves as a metaphorical description of the spiritual development of the people of Israel during the Second Temple period. During the First Temple period, the people of Israel were avid idolaters, and sexually licentious, but the Second Temple period saw a major change in both these areas.

לֵיהּ, אִישְׁתְּמִיט בִּינִיתָא מִינֵּיהּ, [1]וַאֲזַל קָלֵיהּ בְּאַרְבַּע מְאָה פַּרְסֵי. [2]אָמְרוּ: ״הֵיכִי נֶיעֱבַד? [3]דִּילְמָא מִשְׁמַיָּא מְרַחֲמִי עֲלֵיהּ״? [4]אֲמַר לְהוּ נָבִיא: ״שַׁדְיוּהוּ בְּדוּדָא דְּאַבָרָא, וְכַסְּיוּהּ בַּאֲבָרָא, דְּשָׁאֵיף קָלֵיהּ. [5]דִּכְתִיב: ״וַיֹּאמֶר זֹאת הָרִשְׁעָה וַיַּשְׁלֵךְ אוֹתָהּ אֶל תּוֹךְ הָאֵיפָה וַיַּשְׁלֵךְ אֶת הָאֶבֶן הָעוֹפֶרֶת אֶל פִּיהָ״. [6]אָמְרִי: ״הוֹאִיל וְעֵת רָצוֹן הוּא נִיבְעֵי רַחֲמֵי אַיִּצְרָא דַּעֲבֵירָה״. [7]בְּעוּ רַחֲמֵי, אִימְּסַר בִּידַיְיהוּ. [8]חֲבָשׁוּהוּ תְּלָתָא יוֹמֵי. [9]אִיבְעוּ בֵּיעֲתָא בַּת יוֹמָא לְחוֹלֶה, וְלָא אַשְׁכָּחוּ. [10]אֲמַרוּ: ״הֵיכִי נַעֲבִיד? [11]נִיבְעֵי פַּלְגָא, [12]פַּלְגָא מֵרְקִיעָא לָא יָהֲבִי״. [13]כַּחֲלִינְהוּ לְעֵינֵיהּ. [14]אַהֲנֵי בֵּיהּ דְּלָא אִיגְּרֵי אִינִישׁ בִּקְרוֹבָתֵיהּ.

[15]אָמַר רַב יְהוּדָה אָמַר רַב: מַעֲשֶׂה בְּנָכְרִית אַחַת שֶׁהָיְתָה חוֹלָה בְּיוֹתֵר, [16]אָמְרָה: ״אִם תַּעֲמוֹד הַהִיא אִשָּׁה מֵחוֹלְיָהּ, תֵּלֵךְ וְתַעֲבוֹד לְכָל עֲבוֹדָה זָרָה

LITERAL TRANSLATION

it, a hair fell from it, [1]and its voice went four hundred Persian miles. [2]They said: "What should we do? [3]Perhaps from Heaven they will have mercy upon it." [4]The Prophet said to them: "Cast it into a lead caldron, and cover it with lead, so that it absorb its voice." [5]As it is written: "And he said, This is wickedness. And he cast her into the midst of the ephah measure, and he cast the lead cover over the mouth of it." [6]They said: "Since it is a time of grace, let us ask for mercy regarding the passion for sin." [7]They prayed for mercy, and it was given over into their hands. [8]They imprisoned it for three days. [9]They needed a fresh egg for a sick person, but they could not find [one]. [10]They said: "What shall we do? [11]If we ask for half, [12]Heaven does not give half." [13]They blinded its eyes. [14]It helped that a person is not tempted by his relatives.

[15]Rav Yehudah said in the name of Rav: It once happened that a certain non-Jewish woman was very ill, [16][and] she said: "If that woman recovers from her illness, she will go and serve every idol

TRANSLATION AND COMMENTARY

fiery figure and gain control over it, **a** single **hair became detached from it,** [1]**and** the figure's **cry** of pain **went out four hundred Persian miles.** [2]The people **asked: "What should we do** now? [3]If we try to kill it, **Heaven might have mercy upon it.** [4]**The Prophet** Zechariah then **said to them: "Cast** the passion for idolatry **into a lead caldron, and cover it with lead, so that it will absorb its voice,** and not let it be heard." [5]**As the verse states** (Zechariah 5:8): **"And he said, This is wickedness. And he cast her into the midst of the ephah measure, and he cast the lead cover over the mouth of it."** And thus the people of Israel rid themselves of the passion for idolatry. [6]The people then **said: "Since it is a time of grace, let us** also **ask for mercy regarding the passion for** sexual **sins."** [7]And so **they prayed for mercy, and** the passion for sexual sins **was given over into their hands.** [8]**They imprisoned it for three days,** and sexual passion disappeared. [9]At that point, **they needed a fresh egg for a sick person, but they could not find one,** for even animals had stopped mating, and chickens ceased to lay eggs. [10]The people **said: "What should we do now?** [11]**If we ask for** sexual lust not to be altogether obliterated, but only reduced by **half,** [12]**Heaven does not do** things **halfway."** [13]And so, instead of killing sexual passion, **they blinded its eyes.** [14]**That helped** insofar as **a man was no** longer **tempted** to have sexual intercourse **with** one of **his relatives,** even though he might still be tempted to have sexual intercourse with a married woman or one who is menstruating.

אָמַר רַב יְהוּדָה [15]**Rav Yehudah said in the name of Rav: It once happened that a certain non-Jewish woman was very ill,** [16]**and she said** about herself: **"If that woman recovers from her illness, may she go and serve every idol** that she finds **in the world."**

RASHI

בינתא – שער. דודא דאברא – קלחת של עופרת. אברא שאיף קליה – שואף את הקול ומעכבו לצאת יותר מכל כלי מתכות. זאת הרשעה – זהו יצר הרע, ובנבואת זכריה כתיב, שהיה בתחילת בית שני. דעבירה – של עריות. חבשוה תלתא יומין וכו׳ – ומתוך כך פסק חמום הזכרים מלהוליד והנקבות מלילד. איבעו ביעתא בת יומא ולא אשתכח – נתבקשה ביצה שנולדה בו ביום. ולא אשתכח – שאפילו אותן שהיו גמורות קודם לכן פסקו מלצאת. לבעו פלגא – שלא יהא שולט במקום עבירה, כדי שלא יהא תובע עריות. כחלינהו לעיניה – סמו עיניו בכחול. אהני ביה – הך תקנתא פורתא, דלא איגרי בקריבתה באמו ובאחותו, אבל מתגרה הוא באשת איש ונדה.

NOTES

פַּלְגָא מֵרְקִיעָא **Heaven does not give half.** *Ramah* understands that the people wished to cut the creature representing sexual desire into two, but they could not present such a request, for no such creature exists in Heaven.

מַעֲשֶׂה בְּנָכְרִית **It once happened that a certain non-Jewish woman.** *Maharsha* suggests that this story expresses the same idea that was stated above that the people of Israel did not worship idols out of inner conviction, but because it allowed them to engage in sexual practices that are forbidden by Torah law. Here, too, it is stated that the people of Israel attached themselves to Baal Peor the way an air-tight lid is attached to a pot, and as is explained elsewhere, all because of the daughters of Moab.

LANGUAGE (RASHI)

בדל״ש* should apparently be written בליט״ש, *bletes*, meaning "beet leaves."

LANGUAGE

סַבְטָא **Sabta**. This appears to be a short form of Σαββάτιος, *Sabatios*, the Greek form of the Hebrew name Shabbtai.

אָלָס **Alas**. This appears to be a form of the Greek name Ἰόλλας, *Iolas*.

TRANSLATION AND COMMENTARY

[1]The woman eventually **recovered** from her illness, and went out to fulfill her vow, **and served every idol in the world.** [2]**When she got to Peor, she asked the priests** who served it: **"How does one serve this idol?"** [3]The priests **said to** the woman: **"One eats beets, and drinks beer, and** then goes out and **has diarrhea before it."** After hearing the disgraceful manner in which Peor is worshiped, [4]the woman **said** to herself: **"It would be better for that woman to be stricken** once again **with her illness, and not serve an idol in that manner."** [5]Rav Yehudah preached: But **You, O house of Israel, are not like that** woman. Regarding your forefathers who worshiped Peor, the verse states (Numbers 25:5): [6]"Slay every one his men **that have attached themselves** [הַנִּצְמָדִים] **to Ba'al Peor."** [7]The word *nitzmadim* implies that the people cleaved to Peor **the way an airtight lid** (צָמִיד פָּתִיל) is attached to a pot. But Israel's connection to God was far less strong, as the verse states (Deuteronomy 4:4): [8]**"But you were attached** [הַדְּבֵקִים] **to the Lord your God."** [9]Israel was stuck to God the way **two dates are stuck together** — easily separated.

בְּמַתְנִיתָא תָּנָא [10]Just the opposite **was taught in** the following **Baraita:** "Regarding those who worshiped Peor, the verse states (Numbers 25:5): **'That have attached themselves** [הַנִּצְמָדִים] **to Baal Peor.'** [11]The word *hanitzmadim* implies that they were **like a bracelet** (*tzamid*) **on the hand of a woman,** close to the idol, but not cleaving to it. And regarding those who remained faithful to God, the verse states (Deuteronomy 4:4): [12]**"But you were attached** [הַדְּבֵקִים] **to the Lord your God.'** [13]The word *hadevekim* implies a much more intimate connection than the word *hanitzmadim,* for the people of Israel **actually cleaved** to God."

תָּנוּ רַבָּנַן [14]**Our Rabbis taught** another Baraita regarding Baal Peor: **"It once happened that** a certain Jewish man named **Sabta ben Alas hired out his ass** and his services as its driver **to a certain non-Jewish woman.** [15]**When she arrived** at the temple in which **Peor** was worshiped, the woman **said to** Sabta: **'Wait until I go in,** worship, **and come out.'** [16]**After she came out,** Sabta **said to her: 'You too wait for me until I go in and come out.'** [17]Surprised by the request, the woman **said to him: 'Are you not a Jew?** Why then do you wish to go in and worship the idol?' [18]Sabta **said to her: 'What concern is it of yours** why I wish to go in?' [19]**He**

שֶׁבָּעוֹלָם״. [1]עָמְדָה וְעָבְדָה לְכָל עֲבוֹדָה זָרָה שֶׁבָּעוֹלָם. [2]כֵּיוָן שֶׁהִגִּיעַ לַפְּעוֹר, שָׁאֲלָה לַכּוֹמָרִים: ״בַּמָּה עוֹבְדִין לָזוֹ״? [3]אָמְרוּ לָהּ: ״אוֹכְלִין תְּרָדִין, וְשׁוֹתִין שֵׁכָר, וּמַתְרִיזִין בְּפָנֶיהָ״. [4]אָמְרָה: ״מוּטָב שֶׁתַּחֲזוֹר הַהוּא אִשָּׁה לְחוֹלְיָהּ, וְלֹא תַּעֲבוֹד עֲבוֹדָה זָרָה בְּכָךְ״. [5]אַתֶּם בֵּית יִשְׂרָאֵל אֵינָן כֵּן. [6]״הַנִּצְמָדִים לְבַעַל פְּעוֹר״ — [7]כְּצָמִיד פָּתִיל. [8]״וְאַתֶּם הַדְּבֵקִים בַּה׳ אֱלֹהֵיכֶם״ — [9]כִּשְׁתֵּי תְמָרוֹת הַדְּבוּקוֹת זוֹ בָּזוֹ.

[10]בְּמַתְנִיתָא תָּנָא: ״׳הַנִּצְמָדִים לְבַעַל פְּעוֹר׳ — [11]כְּצָמִיד עַל יְדֵי אִשָּׁה. [12]׳וְאַתֶּם הַדְּבֵקִים בַּה׳ אֱלֹהֵיכֶם׳ — [13]דְּבוּקִים מַמָּשׁ״.

[14]תָּנוּ רַבָּנַן: ״מַעֲשֶׂה בְּסַבְטָא בֶּן אָלָס שֶׁהִשְׂכִּיר חֲמוֹרוֹ לְנָכְרִית אַחַת. [15]כֵּיוָן שֶׁהִגִּיעָה לַפְּעוֹר, אָמְרָה לוֹ: ׳הַמְתֵּן עַד שֶׁאֶכָּנֵס וְאֵצֵא׳. [16]לְאַחַר שֶׁיָּצְאָה, אָמַר לָהּ: ׳אַף אַתְּ הַמְתִּינִי עַד שֶׁאֶכָּנֵס וְאֵצֵא׳. [17]אָמְרָה לוֹ: ׳וְלֹא יְהוּדִי אַתָּה׳? [18]אָמַר לָהּ: ׳וּמַאי אִיכְפַּת לִיךְ׳? [19]נִכְנַס,

LITERAL TRANSLATION

in the world." [1]She recovered and served every idol in the world. [2]When she got to Peor, she asked the priests: "How does one serve this?" [3]They said to her: "One eats beets, and drinks beer, and has diarrhea before it." [4]She said: "It would be better for that woman to return to her illness, and not serve an idol in that manner." [5]You, O house of Israel, are not like that. [6]"That have attached themselves to Baal Peor" — [7]like an air-tight lid. [8]"But you that did cleave unto the Lord your God" — [9]like two dates that are stuck together.

[10]It was taught in a Baraita: "'That have attached themselves to Baal Peor' — [11]like a bracelet on the hand of a woman. [12]'But you that did cleave unto the Lord your God' — [13]actually attached."

[14]Our Rabbis taught: "It once happened that Sabta ben Alas hired out his ass to a certain non-Jewish woman. [15]When she got to Peor, she said to him: 'Wait until I go in and come out.' [16]After she came out, he said to her: 'You too wait for me until I go in and come out.' [17]She said to him: 'Are you not a Jew?' [18]He said to her: 'What concern is that of yours?' [19]He went in,

RASHI

תרדין = *בלד״ש בלעז ומשלשלין את המעים, וכן שכר חדש. אתם בית ישראל אינן כן — רב יהודה קאמר לה למדרשיה לקרא. הנצמדים לבעל פעור — כלומר: אבל אבותם לא השיבו זאת על לבם שעבודה זרה מגונה היא מכל עבודה זרה שבעולם, ונצמדו ואדבקו בה כצמיד פתיל המוקף על פי כלי שממרחין אותו בשעוה יפה, ואל המקום לא היו נצמדים אלא דבוקים כתמרות המדובקות, שדבוקות ואינן דבוקות. במתניתא תנא — שכא הוא אצלם דדבוק משמע מחובר טפי מנצמד, צמידין אינן מחוברין ונמשכין וזזין אילך ואילך, דבוק — משמע יפה יפה. סבטאי — שם יהודי הוא. בן אלס — בסמך,

TRANSLATION AND COMMENTARY

went in to the temple, **relieved himself before** the idol, **and** then **wiped himself with** the idol's **nose,** intending to treat the idol as disgracefully as possible. [1]**But** his intention was misconstrued for **the priests** of Baal Peor **praised him, saying: 'Never** before **did a person serve** Peor **in such** a praiseworthy **manner.'"**

הַפּוֹעֵר עַצְמוֹ [2]In conclusion: **If someone relieved himself before** the idol called **Baal Peor, that is** the usual manner in which other idolaters **worship** it, and so he is liable for idol worship, **even if he** did not mean to worship the idol, but rather he **meant to treat it disgracefully.** [3]Similarly, **if someone cast a stone on** the Roman deity called **Marculis, that is** the usual manner in which other idolaters **worship** it, and so he is liable for idol worship, **even if he** did not mean to worship the idol, but rather **he intended to stone it.**

רַב מְנַשֶּׁה [4]It was related that **Rav Menasheh was going to** a place called **Bei Torta.** [5]When he passed a certain pile of stones, people **said to him: "There is an idol that stands here** under the stones." [6]**He took a lump** of earth **and threw it at** the pile of stones, intending to add further disgrace to the idol buried there. [7]The people then **said to him: "It is a Marculis** that is buried under those stones, and stoning the idol is the usual manner in which other idolaters worship it." [8]Rav Menasheh **said to them: "We have learned** in the Mishnah: **'If someone casts a stone before a Marculis** (the word Marculis being preceded by a lamed, which is used here in the sense of "before"), that is the usual manner in which other idolaters worship it, and so he is liable.' A careful reading of the Mishnah suggests that only someone who casts a stone before the idol as a form of worship is liable, but someone who casts a stone upon a Marculis in order to disgrace it is exempt." [9]Rav Menasheh **went and asked in the academy** about the correct reading of the Mishnah. [10]The Sages **said to him: "We have learned** in the Mishnah: **'If someone casts a stone on a Marculis** (the word Marculis being preceded by a bet, which is used here in the sense of "upon"), that is the usual manner in which other idolaters worship it, and so he is liable,' which implies that a person is liable for casting a stone upon a Marculis, [11]**even if he intended to** disgrace and **stone it."** [12]Rav Menasheh **said to** the Sages: "In that case,

פָּעַר בְּפָנָיו, וְקִינַּח בְּחוֹטְמוֹ, [1]וְהָיוּ כּוּמָרִין מְקַלְּסִין לוֹ, וְאוֹמְרִים: 'מֵעוֹלָם לֹא הָיָה אָדָם שֶׁעֲבָדוֹ לָזוֹ בְּכָךְ'". [2]הַפּוֹעֵר עַצְמוֹ לְבַעַל פְּעוֹר, הֲרֵי זֶה עֲבוֹדָתוֹ, אַף עַל גַּב דְּמִיכַּוֵּין לְבִיזּוּי. [3]הַזּוֹרֵק אֶבֶן לְמַרְקוּלִיס, זוֹ הִיא עֲבוֹדָתוֹ, אַף עַל גַּב דְּמִיכַּוֵּין לְמִירְגְּמֵיהּ.

[4]רַב מְנַשֶּׁה הֲוָה קָאָזֵיל לְבֵי תּוֹרְתָא. [5]אֲמַרוּ לוֹ: "עֲבוֹדָה זָרָה הִיא דְּקָאֵי הָכָא". [6]שְׁקַל פִּיסָּא שְׁדָא בֵּיהּ. [7]אֲמַרוּ לוֹ: "מַרְקוּלִיס הִיא". [8]אֲמַר לְהוּ: "'הַזּוֹרֵק אֶבֶן לְמַרְקוּלִיס' תְּנַן". [9]אֲתָא שְׁאַל בֵּי מִדְרָשָׁא. [10]אֲמַרוּ לוֹ: "'הַזּוֹרֵק אֶבֶן בְּמַרְקוּלִיס' תְּנַן, [11]אַף עַל גַּב דְּמִיכַּוֵּין לְמִירְגְּמֵיהּ". [12]אֲמַר

LITERAL TRANSLATION

relieved himself before it, and wiped himself with its nose, [1]and the priests praised him, and said: 'Never did a person serve it in that manner.'"

[2][If] someone relieves himself before Baal Peor, that is its [way of] worship, even if he means to treat it disgracefully. [3][If] someone casts a stone on a Marculis, that is its [way of] worship, even if he intends to stone it.

[4]Rav Menasheh was going to Bei Torta. [5]They said to him: "It is an idol which stands here." [6]He took a lump and threw it at it. [7]They said to him: "It is a Marculis." [8]He said to them: "We have learned: 'If someone casts a stone before a Marculis.'" [9]He went [and] asked in the academy. [10]They said to him: "We have learned: 'If someone casts a stone on a Marculis; [11]even if he intends to stone it." [12]He said

RASHI

ושם מקום הוא. וקינח בחוטמו — של פעור. מקלסין = משבחין. ואף על גב דמכוין לבזויי — חייב קרבן על שגגתו, ואם התרו בו — חייב מיתה. לבי תורתא — מקום. פיסא = *בלשט״א בלעז. מרקוליס הוא — זה וזהו עבודתו. למרקוליס תנן — לפניו לכבדו, ואני זרקתי להכות בגופו. במרקוליס — עצמו, להכותו.

LANGUAGE (RASHI)

בלשט״א* should apparently be written בלישט״א, *bleste,* which is Old French for "a clod of earth."

NOTES

דְּמִיכַּוֵּין לְבִיזּוּי **He means to treat it disgracefully.** According to *Ran,* this ruling only applies to a person who accepts Baal Peor as a god. If such a person relieved himself before the idol, even if he did not mean to worship it at the time, but rather to treat it disgracefully, because he was temporarily angry with it, he is liable, for he worshiped the idol in the usual way.

HALAKHAH

הֲרֵי זֶה עֲבוֹדָתוֹ, אַף עַל גַּב דְּמִיכַּוֵּין לְבִיזּוּי **That is its way of worship, even if he means to treat it disgracefully.** "If someone worshiped an idol the way other idolaters worship it, then even if he meant to treat the idol disgracefully, he is liable for a sin-offering for his unintentional transgression." (*Rambam, Sefer Mada, Hilkhot Avodah Zarah* 3:5.)

לְהוּ: ״אֵיזֵיל אִישְׁקְלָהּ״. [1]אָמְרוּ לוֹ: ״אֶחָד הַנּוֹטְלָהּ וְאֶחָד הַנּוֹתְנָהּ חַיָּיב״. [2]כָּל חֲדָא וַחֲדָא רַוְוחָא לַחֲבֵירְתָּהּ שָׁבֵיק.

משנה [3]הַנּוֹתֵן מִזַּרְעוֹ לַמּוֹלֶךְ אֵינוֹ חַיָּיב עַד שֶׁיִּמְסוֹר לַמּוֹלֶךְ, וְיַעֲבִיר בָּאֵשׁ. [4]מָסַר לַמּוֹלֶךְ, וְלֹא הֶעֱבִיר בָּאֵשׁ, [5]הֶעֱבִיר בָּאֵשׁ, וְלֹא מָסַר לַמּוֹלֶךְ, [6]אֵינוֹ חַיָּיב עַד שֶׁיִּמְסוֹר לַמּוֹלֶךְ וְיַעֲבִיר בָּאֵשׁ.

גמרא [7]קָתָנֵי עֲבוֹדָה זָרָה, [8]וְקָתָנֵי מוֹלֶךְ.

[9]אָמַר רַבִּי אָבִין: תְּנַן כְּמַאן דְּאָמַר: מוֹלֶךְ לָאו עֲבוֹדָה זָרָה הִיא. [10]דְּתַנְיָא: ״אֶחָד לַמּוֹלֶךְ וְאֶחָד לִשְׁאָר עֲבוֹדָה זָרָה, חַיָּיב.

LITERAL TRANSLATION

to them: "I will go [and] remove it." [1]They said to him: "Both he who removes [a stone] and he who places [a stone] is liable." [2]Each and every one makes room for another.

MISHNAH [3]Someone who gives of his seed to Molech is not liable until he hands [him] over to Molech, and passes [him] through fire. [4][If] he handed [him] over to Molech, but did not pass [him] through fire, [5][or if] he passed [him] through fire, but did not hand [him] over to Molech, [6]he is not liable until he hands [him] over to Molech, and passes [him] through fire.

GEMARA [7]It teaches idolatry, [8]and it teaches Molech.

[9]Rabbi Avin said: We have learned in accordance with the one who said: Molech is not idolatry. [10]For it was taught: "Whether to Molech or to other idols, he is liable.

TRANSLATION AND COMMENTARY

I will go and remove the lump of earth which I threw upon the pile of stones." [1]The Sages **said to him:** "Leave it be, for **both someone who removes a stone** from the pile of stones cast upon a Marculis, **and someone who places a stone** on that pile, **is liable** for having committed idolatry." The Gemara explains why removing a stone from the pile is forbidden: [2]**Each** stone that is removed **makes room for another** to take its place.

MISHNAH הַנּוֹתֵן מִזַּרְעוֹ [3]**Someone who offers his child to Molech,** the fire-god of the Canaanites, **is not liable** to death by stoning, **unless he hands** the child **over to** the priests that serve **Molech, and** also **passes** the child **through fire.** [4]If the father **handed** his child **over to** the priests that serve **Molech, but did not** also **pass him through fire,** [5]**or if he passed** the child **through fire, but did not** also **hand him over** to the priests that serve **Molech,** [6]**he is not liable** to death by stoning, **until he hands** the child **over to** the priests that serve **Molech, and** also **passes** the child **through fire,** as was explained above.

GEMARA קָתָנֵי עֲבוֹדָה זָרָה [7]The Gemara notes that the Mishnah above (60b) **teaches** the various ways through which a person becomes liable for practicing **idolatry,** [8]**and** here it teaches the way through which a person becomes liable for serving **Molech,** implying that serving Molech is not regarded as idol worship. Thus someone who offers a sacrifice to Molech, or burns incense before it, would not be liable, nor would he be liable if he passed his child through fire before some other idol.

אָמַר רַבִּי אָבִין [9]**Rabbi Avin said:** This implies that **our Mishnah was taught in accordance with the** authority **who said** that serving **Molech is not** regarded as practicing **idolatry,** but rather it is a separate prohibition. [10]**For it was taught** in a Baraita that the Tannaim disagree about the matter: **"Whether** a person handed his child over and passed him through a fire **to Molech or** he handed him over and passed him through fire **to another idol, he is liable,** for when the Torah formulated the prohibition, it singled out Molech

RASHI

ואישקליה – אף על גב שכבר עבד ואין הָשָבון לדבר, קא בעי לאשקליה כדי שלא תתנאה בעבודה שלו. **רווחא לחבירתה שביק** – מפנה לה מקום לזורקים.

משנה שימסור למולך – מוסרו ביד משרתי עבודה זרה. **ויעביר באש** – בגמרא מפרש היכי הוו עבדי, וילפי מקראי דתרווייהו בעינן.

גמרא קתני – מתניתין (נג,א) בחייבי סקילה, עבודה זרה באנפי נפשה ״העובד עבודה זרה״, וקתני ״מולך״ – אלמא מולך לאו בכלל עבודה זרה. ונפקא מינה דאם זבח וקטר לפניו – פטור, אי נמי: העביר מזרעו לשאר עבודה זרה ואין דרכה בכך – לא מחייב, דמולך דוקא כתוב, ששמו מולך. **אחד למולך ואחד לשאר עבודה זרה** – העביר זרעו חייב, קסבר מולך נמי עבודה זרה הוא, ולא איצטריך לאזהורי עלה בכדרכה, דמ״איכה יעבדו״ (דברים יב) נפקא. אלא לומר לך שאם עשה שלא כדרכה – חייב.

NOTES

מוֹלֶךְ לָאו עֲבוֹדָה זָרָה **Molech is not idolatry.** Those who say that serving Molech is not idol worship understand it as a magical act or a superstitious practice whose apparent purpose is to bring a person good luck and blessing. Even

HALAKHAH

הַנּוֹתֵן מִזַּרְעוֹ לַמּוֹלֶךְ **Someone who gives of his seed to Molech.** "Someone who offers his child to Molech, is not liable to death by stoning or for excision, unless he hands the child over to the priests that serve Molech, and unless he passes the child on foot through a fire. But if he handed the child over, but did not pass him through the fire, or if he handed him over, but did not pass him through the fire in the usual manner of passing a child through a fire to Molech, he is exempt," following the Mishnah. (*Rambam, Sefer Mada, Hilkhot Avodah Zarah* 6:4.)

[1]רַבִּי אֶלְעָזָר בְּרַבִּי שִׁמְעוֹן אוֹמֵר: לַמּוֹלֶךְ, חַיָּיב, [2]שֶׁלֹּא לַמּוֹלֶךְ, פָּטוּר״.

[3]אָמַר אַבַּיֵי: רַבִּי אֶלְעָזָר בְּרַבִּי שִׁמְעוֹן וְרַבִּי חֲנִינָא בֶּן אַנְטִיגְנוֹס אָמְרוּ דָּבָר אֶחָד. [4]רַבִּי אֶלְעָזָר בְּרַבִּי שִׁמְעוֹן — הָא דַּאֲמָרַן. [5]רַבִּי חֲנִינָא בֶּן אַנְטִיגְנוֹס, [6]דְּתַנְיָא: ״רַבִּי חֲנִינָא בֶּן אַנְטִיגְנוֹס אוֹמֵר: מִפְּנֵי מָה תָּפְסָה תּוֹרָה לְשׁוֹן ׳מוֹלֶךְ׳? [7]כָּל שֶׁהִמְלִיכוּהוּ עֲלֵיהֶם, אֲפִילּוּ צְרוֹר, וַאֲפִילּוּ קֵיסָם״.

[8]רָבָא אָמַר: מוֹלֶךְ עֲרַאי אִיכָּא בֵּינַיְיהוּ.

[64B] [9]אָמַר רַבִּי יַנַּאי: אֵינוֹ חַיָּיב עַד שֶׁיִּמְסְרֶנּוּ לְכוֹמָרִין, [10]שֶׁנֶּאֱמַר: ״וּמִזַּרְעֲךָ לֹא תִתֵּן לְהַעֲבִיר לַמֹּלֶךְ״.

LITERAL TRANSLATION

[1]Rabbi Elazar the son of Rabbi Shimon said: To Molech, he is liable. [2]Not to Molech, he is exempt."

[3]Abaye said: Rabbi Elazar the son of Rabbi Shimon and Rabbi Ḥanina ben Antigonus said the same thing. [4]Rabbi Elazar the son of Rabbi Shimon — that which we said. [5]Rabbi Ḥanina ben Antigonus, [6]as it was taught: "Rabbi Ḥanina ben Antigonus says: Why did the Torah use the expression 'Molech'? [7]Whatever people make their ruler, even a stone, and even a piece of wood."

[8]Rava said: There is [a difference] between them regarding an improvised Molech.

[64B] [9]Rabbi Yannai said: He is not liable until he hands him over to the priests, [10]as it is said: "And you shall not give of your seed to pass to Molech."

RASHI

שלא למולך פטור — דמולך דווקא כתיבי, שדרכה בכך. ולא משום עבודה זרה אזהר עליו, דהא מ״איכה יעבדו״ נפקא, אלא חוק הוא להם והתורה הקפיד על חוק זה בסקילה, לפיכך הוצרך לכתוב. כל שהמליכו עליהם — שקרא שמו מולך. רבא אמר — לא אמרו דבר אחד, דמולך עראי איכא בינייהו, כגון צרור וקיסם שאינו ראוי לכך, וזה לפי שעה המליכוהו עליו להעביר לו בנו זה. לרבי אלעזר ברבי שמעון לא מחייב אלא במולך קבוע וצא. רבי ינאי — לפרושי ״עד שימסור״ דמתניתין אתא, למימר דהך מסירה למשרתי עבודה זרה קאמר. לא תתן להעביר — לא תתן לאחרים להעביר, וסתמא דמילתא שמשין שלה קא מעבירין לה. הכי גרסינן: תניא נמי הכי,

TRANSLATION AND COMMENTARY

as an example. [1]**Rabbi Elazar the son of Rabbi Shimon** disagreed and **said:** If he handed his child over and passed him through fire **to Molech, he is liable.** [2]But if it was **not to Molech,** but to some other idol, **he is exempt,** for serving Molech is a separate prohibition."

אָמַר אַבַּיֵי [3]**Abaye said: Rabbi Elazar the son of Rabbi Shimon and Rabbi Ḥanina ben Antigonus said the same thing** regarding this matter. How so? [4]**Rabbi Elazar the son of Rabbi Shimon — that which we** have just **said.** [5]And we find that **Rabbi Ḥanina ben Antigonus** said the same thing, [6]**for it was taught** in a Baraita: **"Rabbi Ḥanina ben Antigonus says: Why did the Torah use the expression 'Molech'?** [7]To teach that the prohibition against passing one's child through fire applies to **whatever people make as their ruler** (*melekh*), and call Molech, **even a stone, and even a piece of wood."** Rabbi Elazar, the son of Rabbi Shimon and Rabbi Ḥanina ben Antigonus appear to agree that there is a specific prohibition against serving Molech, but, as Rava explains, they differ about the definition of Molech.

רָבָא אָמַר [8]**Rava said: There is a difference between** their views **regarding an improvised Molech,** such as a stone or a piece of wood. According to Rabbi Ḥanina ben Antigonus, a person is liable even if he passed his child through fire to any idol which people accepted as their temporary ruler and passed their children through fire before it. But according to Rabbi Elazar the son of Rabbi Shimon, he is only liable if he passed his child through fire to a permanent Molech.

[64B] אָמַר רַבִּי יַנַּאי [9]**Rabbi Yannai said:** A person **is not liable** for offering his child to Molech **unless he handed him over to the priests** who serve it, [10]**as the verse states** (Leviticus 18:21): **"And you shall not give of your seed to pass to Molech,"** implying that giving is the prohibited action.

NOTES

though serving Molech does not involve the worship of an idol, the Torah nevertheless forbade the practice with a very severe prohibition (*Ramah, Ran,* and others).

אֲפִילּוּ צְרוֹר, וַאֲפִילּוּ קֵיסָם **Even a stone, even a piece of wood.** Some suggest that this means that the prohibition against passing one's child through a fire to Molech applies even in a case where he heated up a stone until it was fiery hot, or burned a stick and made coals, and then passed his child over to Molech (*Meiri*).

עַד שֶׁיִּמְסְרֶנּוּ לְכוֹמָרִין **Until he hands him over to the priests.** According to *Rashi,* he who serves Molech hands his child over to the priests who serve it, and they — the priests — pass the child through the fire. *Rambam* and others disagree and say that the father hands the child over to the priests who serve as Molech's representatives, and after they hand him back, the father himself passes the child through the fire.

HALAKHAH

שֶׁלֹּא לַמּוֹלֶךְ, פָּטוּר **Not to Molech, he is exempt.** "If someone passes his child through fire to some idol other than Molech, he is exempt," following Rabbi Elazar the son of Rabbi Shimon, who is supported by the anonymous Mishnah. (*Rambam, Sefer Mada, Hilkhot Avodah Zarah* 6:3.)

SAGES

רַבִּי אֶלְעָזָר בְּרַבִּי שִׁמְעוֹן **Rabbi Elazar the son of Rabbi Shimon.** The contemporary of Rabbi Yehudah HaNasi, Rabbi Elazar the son of Rabbi Shimon was a distinguished scholar, like his father, Rabbi Shimon bar Yoḥai. Rabbi Elazar's remarkable personality was the subject of numerous anecdotes. When Rabbi Shimon bar Yoḥai, who was strongly opposed to Roman rule, was betrayed to the Roman authorities by informers, Rabbi Elazar fled with his father and lived with him in a cave for thirteen years. There the two subsisted on the barest essentials and spent their time studying Torah. During this period, Rabbi Elazar learned almost everything he knew from his father, who was his principal teacher (although Rabbi Elazar occasionally disagreed with his father's Halakhic decisions). Rabbi Elazar also studied with other scholars of his father's generation, e.g., Rabbi Yehudah, Rabbi Elazar (ben Shammua), and Rabbi Meir.

Later, Rabbi Elazar was forced to accept the unpopular position of a law enforcement officer, and his acceptance of the post aroused opposition among the Sages. His spiritual independence led to friction between him and various other Rabbis, and to cooler relations with Rabbi Yehudah HaNasi, who was his boyhood friend.

Nevertheless, all acknowledged his personal piety, asceticism, and greatness in Torah knowledge. His father, Rabbi Shimon, considered him one of the most pious people of all time, and he was apparently considered exceptionally pious by the common people as well. Rabbi Elazar is also one of the most prominent figures in the Zohar. When he died, he was eulogized for his great achievement as a student of the Torah, both written and oral, as a preacher, and as a composer of liturgical poetry. The Gemara tells us that he was buried next to his father's grave in Meron.

Rabbi Elazar's teachings are quoted explicitly in several places in the Mishnah, while many other rulings of his apparently entered the Mishnah anonymously. Rabbi Elazar was therefore referred to as "Rabbi Elazar the son of Rabbi Shimon — the Anonymous Ruler" (סְתִימְתָּאָה). Some of his teachings — which were also quoted by the early Amoraim — are cited in the Tosefta and in the Halakhic Midrashim.

TRANSLATION AND COMMENTARY

תַּנְיָא נַמִי הָכִי [1]**The same thing was also taught** in the following Baraita: **"I might have thought that if** a father **passed** his child through a fire, **but did not hand him over** to the priests that serve Molech, **he is** nevertheless **liable.** [2]**Therefore, the verse states** (Leviticus 18:21): 'And **you shall not give** of your seed to pass to Molech.' [3]**If he handed** the child **over to** the priests that serve **Molech, but did not pass him** through a fire, **I might have thought that he is** nevertheless **liable.** [4]**Therefore, the verse states:** 'And you shall not give of your seed **to pass** to Molech.' [5]**If he handed** the child **over, and passed him** through fire, **but not to Molech,** but rather to some other idol, **I might have thought that he is** nevertheless **liable.** [6]**Therefore, the verse states:** 'And you shall not give of your seed to pass **to Molech.** [7]**If he handed** the child **over, and passed him to Molech, but** did **not** pass him **through fire, I might have thought that he is** nevertheless **liable.** [8]**Here the verse states: 'To pass,'** [9]**and below the verse states** (Deuteronomy 18:10): **'There must not be found among you anyone who passes his son or his daughter through the fire.'** [10]**Just as below** the verse refers to passing **through fire, so too here** the verse refers to passing **through fire.** [11]**And just as here** the verse refers to passing to **Molech, so too below** the verse refers to passing to **Molech."**

אָמַר [12]**Rav Aḥa the son of Rava said: If** a person **passed all his children** through a fire to Molech, **he is exempt** from liability, [13]**for the verse states** (Leviticus 18:21): "And you shall not give **of your seed** to pass to Molech." "Of your seed" — [14]**and not all your seed.**

[1]תַּנְיָא נַמִי הָכִי: ״יָכוֹל הֶעֱבִיר וְלֹא מָסַר, יְהֵא חַיָּיב. [2]תַּלְמוּד לוֹמַר: ׳לֹא תִתֵּן׳. [3]מָסַר לַמּוֹלֶךְ, וְלֹא הֶעֱבִיר, יָכוֹל יְהֵא חַיָּיב. [4]תַּלְמוּד לוֹמַר: ׳לְהַעֲבִיר׳. [5]מָסַר, וְהֶעֱבִיר שֶׁלֹּא לַמּוֹלֶךְ, יָכוֹל יְהֵא חַיָּיב. [6]תַּלְמוּד לוֹמַר: ׳לַמֹּלֶךְ׳. [7]מָסַר, וְהֶעֱבִיר לַמּוֹלֶךְ, וְלֹא בָּאֵשׁ, יָכוֹל יְהֵא חַיָּיב. [8]נֶאֱמַר כָּאן: ׳לְהַעֲבִיר׳, [9]וְנֶאֱמַר לְהַלָּן: ׳לֹא יִמָּצֵא בְךָ מַעֲבִיר בְּנוֹ וּבִתּוֹ בָּאֵשׁ׳, [10]מַה לְּהַלָּן בָּאֵשׁ, אַף כָּאן בָּאֵשׁ, [11]וּמַה כָּאן מוֹלֶךְ, אַף לְהַלָּן מוֹלֶךְ״. [12]אָמַר רַב אַחָא בְּרֵיהּ דְּרָבָא: הֶעֱבִיר כָּל זַרְעוֹ, פָּטוּר, [13]שֶׁנֶּאֱמַר: ״מִזַּרְעֲךָ״, [14]וְלֹא כָּל זַרְעֲךָ.

LITERAL TRANSLATION

[1]It was also taught thus: "I might have thought [that if] he passed [him] but did not hand [him] over, he is liable. [2][Therefore], the verse states: 'You shall not give.' [3][If] he handed [him] over to Molech, but did not pass [him], I might have thought that he is liable. [4][Therefore], the verse states: 'To pass.' [5][If] he handed [him] over, and passed [him] not to Molech, I might have thought that he is liable. [6][Therefore], the verse states: 'To Molech.' [7][If] he handed [him] over, and passed [him] to Molech, but not through fire, I might have thought that he is liable. [8]It is stated here: 'To pass,' [9]and it is stated below: 'There must not be found among you anyone who passes his son or his daughter through the fire.' [10]Just as below through fire, so too here through fire. [11]And just as here Molech, so too below Molech."

[12]Rav Aḥa the son of Rava said: [If] he passed all his seed, he is exempt, [13]for it is said: "Of your seed," [14]and not all your seed.

RASHI

יכול העביר ולא מסר כו׳. ולא גרסינן בברייתא ברישא ״ומזרעך לא תתן״, דתו לא יכול למיתני יכול העביר ולא מסר, דהאי ״לא תתן״ מסירה משמע. אלא הכי קתני: יכול העביר ולא מסר יהא חייב ותיפוק ליה מ״לא ימצא בך מעביר בנו ובתו באש״ דלא כתיבא מסירה — תלמוד לומר ״לא תתן״ ״להעביר״, פירש לך הכתוב על העברה שאינה אלא דרך נתינה. לא תתן להעביר — משמע ליה לתנא נתינה הבאה לכלל העברה, ולא משמע ליה נתינה על מנת להעביר לחיוביה על נתינה לחודה. מסר והעביר — לעבודה זרה אחרת, שלא למולך, יכול יהא חייב?

NOTES

הֶעֱבִיר כָּל זַרְעוֹ **If he passed all his seed.** Various explanations have been offered for what would appear to be an astonishing law, for if a person is liable for passing some of his children through a fire to Molech, surely he should be liable for passing all of his children through the fire! While it is true that punishment may not be inflicted on the basis of a law that was inferred through a *kal vaḥomer* argument, the matter needs explanation. It has been suggested that the prohibition depends upon the practices of the idol worshipers, who customarily offered only one child to Molech. Thus someone who offers all of his children to Molech is not guilty of committing an idolatrous practice (*Ran, Rash* the son of *Rashbatz,* and others). *Maharal* explains the rationale behind the idolatrous practice: The idolater offered his child as a token of thanksgiving for the gifts which he thought that the idol had

HALAKHAH

הֶעֱבִיר כָּל זַרְעוֹ **If he passed all his seed.** "If someone passed all his children through a fire to Molech, without leaving any out, he is exempt," following Rav Aḥa the son of Rava. (*Rambam, Sefer Mada, Hilkhot Avodah Zarah* 6:4.)

[1]בָּעֵי רַב אַשִׁי: הֶעֱבִירוֹ סוּמָא, מַהוּ? [2]יָשֵׁן, מַהוּ? [3]בֶּן בְּנוֹ וּבֶן בִּתּוֹ, מַהוּ?

[4]תִּפְשׁוֹט מִיהָא חֲדָא, [5]דְּתַנְיָא: ״׳כִּי מִזַּרְעוֹ נָתַן לַמֹּלֶךְ׳. [6]מַה תַּלְמוּד לוֹמַר? [7]לְפִי שֶׁנֶּאֱמַר: ׳לֹא יִמָּצֵא בְךָ מַעֲבִיר בְּנוֹ וּבִתּוֹ בָּאֵשׁ׳, [8]אֵין לִי אֶלָּא בְּנוֹ וּבִתּוֹ. [9]בֶּן בְּנוֹ וּבֶן בִּתּוֹ מִנַּיִן? [10]תַּלְמוּד לוֹמַר: ׳בְּתִתּוֹ מִזַּרְעוֹ׳״.

[11]״תָּנָא פְּתַח בְּ״כִּי מִזַּרְעוֹ״, [12]וְסָלֵיק ״בְּתִתּוֹ מִזַּרְעוֹ״!

[13]דְּרָשָׁה אַחֲרִינָא הוּא: ״׳זַרְעוֹ׳. [14]אֵין לִי אֶלָּא זֶרַע כָּשֵׁר. [15]זֶרַע

LITERAL TRANSLATION

[1]Rav Ashi asked: [If] he passed him blind, what [is the law]? [2]Asleep, what [is the law]? [3]The son of his son, or the son of his daughter, what [is the law]?

[4]Resolve at least one, [5]for it was taught: "'Because he has given of his seed to Molech.' [6]What does the verse teach? [7]Since it is stated: 'There must not be found among you anyone who passes his son or his daughter through the fire,' [8]I only have his son and his daughter. [9]From where [do I know about] the son of his son and the son of his daughter? [10][Therefore], the verse states: 'When he gives of his seed.'"

[11]The Tanna opened with "Because [he has given] of his seed," [12]and concludes with "When he gives of his seed"!

[13]It is a different exposition: "'His seed.' [14]I only have fit seed. [15]From where [do I know about]

TRANSLATION AND COMMENTARY

בָּעֵי רַב אַשִׁי [1]**Rav Ashi asked** a series of questions: If a person **passed** a **blind** child through a fire to Molech, **what is the law?** [2]And similarly, if he passed a **sleeping** child through a fire to Molech, **what is the law?** Is it necessary for the child to be able to pass through the fire on his own, in which case the father would not be liable for a blind or sleeping child, or is that not necessary? [3]If a person passed **the son of his son or the son of his daughter** through a fire to Molech, **what is the law?** Is he only liable for his own son or daughter, or is he even liable for a grandchild?

תִּפְשׁוֹט מִיהָא חֲדָא [4]The Gemara answers: We can **resolve at least one** of these questions, the question regarding a grandchild, [5]**for it was taught** in a Baraita: "The verse states (Leviticus 20:3): **'Because he has given of his seed to Molech.'** [6]**What do** the seemingly superfluous words in **this verse** come to **teach?** [7]**Since** another **verse states** (Deuteronomy 18:10): **'There must not be found among you anyone who passes his son or his daughter to pass through the fire,'** [8]**I only** know that a person is liable if he passes **his** own **son** or **daughter** through a fire to Molech. [9]**From where do I know** that a person is liable even for **the son of his son and the son of his daughter?** [10]**Therefore, the verse states** (Leviticus 20:4): **'When he gives of his seed,'** the words 'his seed' include a grandchild."

תָּנָא פְּתַח [11]The Gemara raises a question regarding this Baraita: **The Tanna** of the Baraita **opened with** a question regarding the verse, **"Because he has given of his seed,"** [12]**and concludes with** a proof based on a different verse, **"When he gives of his seed"!** One would have expected the Tanna to prove that a person is liable for passing his grandchild through a fire to Molech from the verse, "Because he has given of his seed."

דְּרָשָׁה אַחֲרִינָא [13]The Baraita cites the verse, "When he gives of his seed," as part of **a different exposition,** which is missing: "The verse speaks of **"His seed."** [14]From this **I would only know** that a person is liable for his **fit seed,** his children born from a legal marriage. [15]**From where do I know** that one is liable even

RASHI

העבירו – לבנו סומא או ישן, מי הוה דרך העברה בכך בכהאי גוונא, דאינו יכול לעבור בעצמו אם היה רוצה. **פשוט מיהא** – מתניתין. **חדא** – מהנך שאלות דבן בנו, ובן בתו כבנו. **כי מזרעו נתן למולך מה תלמוד לומר** – פשיטא דהאי כרת על כן נכתב, דהא במעביר למולך כתיב (ויקרא כ) ״ואני אתן את פני וגו׳״ ולעיל מיניה כתיב ״ואשר יתן מזרעו למולך מות יומת״. **תלמוד לומר בתתו מזרעו** – קרא אחרינא הוא, ולא זה שהתחיל התנא לדרוש. ופרכינן: תנא פתח לדרוש ״כי מזרעו נתן למולך״ ובסוף דבריו סיים: תלמוד לומר ״בתתו מזרעו״?! ומשני: דרשה אחריתי דרש מ״בתתו מזרעו״. דרשה קמייתא דבן בנו ובן בתו מ״כי מזרעו״ נפקא ליה, והדר תנא: זרעו פסול מנין, שהיה לו ממזר והעבירו – תלמוד לומר ב״תתו מזרעו״. ״ואם העלם יעלימו וגו׳״ ולא היה צריך למכתב ״בתתו מזרעו״ דהא במעביר מזרעו משתעי, אלא להך דרשה.

NOTES

bestowed upon him. Thus, he offered only a part of what he thought he had received. Others have suggested that a person who offered all of his children to Molech is not liable for the death penalty, because he committed such a heinous offense that even the death penalty cannot bring him atonement (*Smag;* see also *Maharsha*).

HALAKHAH

הֶעֱבִירוֹ סוּמָא אוֹ יָשֵׁן **If he passed him blind or asleep.** "If someone passed his child through a fire to Molech, and the child was blind or asleep, he is exempt," for these issues were not resolved in the Gemara, and when there is a doubt about a capital matter, we opt for leniency. (*Rambam, Sefer Mada, Hilkhot Avodah Zarah* 6:5)

זֶרַע פָּסוּל **Unfit seed.** "A person is liable for passing his descendant through a fire to Molech, whether the child was

פְּסוּל מִנַּיִן? [1]תַּלְמוּד לוֹמַר: ״בְּתִתּוֹ מִזַּרְעוֹ״.״

[2]אָמַר רַב יְהוּדָה: אֵינוֹ חַיָּיב עַד שֶׁיַּעֲבִירֶנּוּ דֶּרֶךְ הַעֲבָרָה.

[3]הֵיכִי דָּמֵי?

[4]אָמַר אַבַּיֵי: שְׁרָגָא דִּלְבְנֵי בְּמִצְעֵי, [5]נוּרָא מֵהַאי גִּיסָא, וְנוּרָא מֵהַאי גִּיסָא.

[6]רָבָא אָמַר: כְּמַשְׁוַורְתָּא דְּפוּרַיָּא.

[7]תַּנְיָא כְּוָותֵיהּ דְּרָבָא: ״אֵינוֹ חַיָּיב עַד שֶׁיַּעֲבִירֶנּוּ דֶּרֶךְ עֲבָרָה. [8]הֶעֱבִירָהּ בָּרֶגֶל, פָּטוּר. [9]וְאֵינוֹ חַיָּיב אֶלָּא עַל יוֹצְאֵי יְרֵיכוֹ. [10]הָא כֵּיצַד? [11]בְּנוֹ וּבִתּוֹ — חַיָּיב. [12]אָבִיו, וְאִמּוֹ, אָחִיו, וַאֲחוֹתוֹ — פָּטוּר. [13]הֶעֱבִיר עַצְמוֹ, פָּטוּר. [14]וְרַבִּי אֶלְעָזָר

LITERAL TRANSLATION

unfit seed? [1][Therefore], the verse states: 'When he gives of his seed.'"

[2]Rav Yehudah said: He is not liable until he passes him in the manner of passing. [3]How do you visualize the case?

[4]Abaye said: A row of bricks in the middle, [5]fire on this side, and fire on that side.

[6]Rava said: Like the leaping on Purim.

[7]It was taught in accordance with Rava: "He is not liable until he passes him in the manner of passing. [8]If he passed him on foot, he is exempt. [9]And he is only liable for those who issue from his loins. [10]How so? [11]His son or his daughter — he is liable. [12]His father, or his mother, his brother, or his sister — he is exempt. [13]If he passed himself, he is exempt. [14]And Rabbi Elazar

TRANSLATION AND COMMENTARY

for **unfit seed,** born through an adulterous or incestuous relationship? [1]**Therefore, the verse states: 'When he gives of his seed,'** which includes even children who are not fit.'"

אָמַר רַב יְהוּדָה [2]**Rav Yehudah said:** A person **is not liable** for offering his child to Molech, **unless he passed him** through a fire **in the** usual **manner of passing** a child through a fire to Molech.

הֵיכִי דָּמֵי [3]The Gemara asks: **How do you visualize the** usual **way** of passing a child through fire to Molech?

אָמַר אַבַּיֵי [4]**Abaye said:** A **row of bricks** would be set up **in the middle,** [5]**a fire** was lit **on this side** of the bricks, **and** another **fire** was lit **on the** other **side** of the bricks, and the father would pass between the two bonfires walking on the bricks with his child.

רָבָא אָמַר [6]**Rava said:** The father would not walk with his child between two bonfires, but rather he would leap with his child over a fire, **in the manner that** children **leap** over a fire **on Purim.** On Purim, a fire would be lit in a pit, and children would entertain themselves by jumping over the fire from one side of the pit to the other. In similar fashion, a child would be passed through a fire to Molech.

תַּנְיָא כְּוָותֵיהּ [7]A Baraita **was taught in accordance with** the position of **Rava:** "A person **is not liable** for offering his child to Molech, **unless he passed him** through a fire **in the** usual **manner of passing** a child through a fire to Molech. [8]**If he passed him** through the fire walking **on foot** between two fires, **he is exempt** from liability, for the usual manner of passing through a fire to Molech is by way of leaping over the fire. [9]**And he is only liable for those who issue from his loins.** [10]How so? [11]If passed **his son or daughter** through a fire to Molech, **he is liable.** [12]But if he passed through a fire **his father, mother, brother, or sister,** or anybody else who did not issue from his loins, **he is exempt.** [13]And similarly, **if** a person **passed himself** through a fire to Molech, **he is exempt.** [14]**Rabbi Elazar the son of Rabbi Shimon** disagrees and **says** that a person who

RASHI

דרך העברה – שלא שינה מן החוק אלא כדרך מנהג העברת המולך. שרגא דלבני – שורת לבנים גבוה, לבנה על גבי לבנה, והאש מכאן ומכאן ומעבירין עליו ואינו שורפו, מדקתני לקמן: המעביר עצמו פטור, אלמא לאחר העברה הוא חי. והא דאמרינן (סנהדרין סג,ב) גבי חזקיה שסכתו אמו סלמנדרא – לאו למולך היה אלא לאלהי ספרוים, דהתם שריפה כתיב. רבא אמר כמשוורתא דפוריא – אינו מעבירו ברגליו אלא קופץ ברגליו כדרך שהתינוקות קופצין בימי הפורים, שהיתה חפירה בארץ והאש בוער בו והוא קופץ משפה לשפה. דרך העברתו – עבודתו של מולך. העבירו ברגל פטור – אלמא דרך עבודתו בקפיצה.

LANGUAGE

שְׁרָגָא A row. The Aramaic root שרג means "to arrange" (and so too the parallel root in Arabic). שְׁרָגָא דִּלְבְנֵי is therefore "an array of bricks."

BACKGROUND

כְּמַשְׁוַורְתָּא דְּפוּרַיָּא Leaping on Purim. The Geonim report that in Babylonia it was customary for young people to make an effigy of Haman out of wood and rags, and burn it on Purim. A ring would be suspended over the fire, and people would jump from side to side over the fire for amusement and celebration.

NOTES

כְּמַשְׁוַורְתָּא דְּפוּרַיָּא **Like the leaping on Purim.** The Rishonim disagree whether the child offered to Molech was merely passed through a fire as a symbolic rite, or whether he was actually burned to death. According to *Rashi,* the child was

HALAKHAH

fit or unfit, whether a son or a daughter, or any one of their descendants." (*Rambam, Sefer Mada, Hilkhot Avodah Zarah* 6:5.)

דֶּרֶךְ הַעֲבָרָה **In the manner of passing.** "A person who passed his child through a fire to Molech is only liable if he passed him in the usual manner of passing a child through a fire to Molech, by carrying him on foot from one side to the other between two fires," following Rava, against Abaye (see *Leḥem Mishneh, Kesef Mishneh*). (*Rambam, Sefer Mada, Hilkhot Avodah Zarah* 6:3.)

אֵינוֹ חַיָּיב אֶלָּא עַל יוֹצְאֵי יְרֵיכוֹ **He is only liable for those who issue from his loins.** "If someone passed his brother, or sister, or father, or himself, through a fire to Molech, he is exempt," following the anonymous first Tanna of the Mishnah. (*Rambam, Sefer Mada, Hilkhot Avodah Zarah* 6:5.)

TRANSLATION AND COMMENTARY

passed himself through a fire to Molech **is liable.** [1]**Whether** a person passed his child through a fire **to Molech or** he passed him through fire **to another idol, he is liable.** [2]**Rabbi Elazar the son of Rabbi Shimon** disagrees and **says:** If he passed the child through fire **to Molech, he is liable.** [3]But if it was **not to Molech,** but to some other idol, **he is exempt."**

אָמַר עוּלָּא [4]**Ulla said: What is the reasoning of Rabbi Elazar the son of Rabbi Shimon** who says that a person who passes himself through a fire to Molech is liable? [5]**The verse states** (Deuteronomy 18:10): **"There must not be found among you** anyone who passes his son or his daughter through the fire." [6]The words **"among you,"** come to include even **you yourself.**

וְרַבָּנַן לָא דָּרְשִׁי [7]The Gemara asks: Does it follow from this that **the Sages do not interpret** the expression, **"among you,"** in the sense of "you yourself"? [8]**But surely we have learned** otherwise in a Mishnah (*Bava Metzia* 33a): "If a person finds two lost objects, one **his own lost object and** the other **a lost object belonging to his father,** and he cannot take care of both at the same time, [9]**his own** lost object **takes precedence."** [10]**And** when we learned that Mishnah **we said: What is the reason** that a person's own lost object takes precedence? [11]**And Rav Yehudah said:** This is learned from **the verse** which **states** (Deuteronomy 15:4): **"Except that there shall be no poor among you."** The superfluous words "among you" teach that a person must avoid becoming a pauper. [12]Hence, a person's **own** financial needs **come before those of all other men.** Thus, we see that even the Rabbis interpret the words "among you," in the sense of "you yourself."

וְהָתָם מֵ״אֶפֶס״ [13]The Gemara answers: **There** the derivation is not from the words "among you," but rather **from** the word **"except."** That word is a restrictive term which teaches that a person must see to it that he does not become a pauper.

אָמַר [14]**Rabbi Yose the son of Rabbi Ḥanina said: Why** was it necessary for the Torah to mention the divine

בְּרַבִּי שִׁמְעוֹן מְחַיֵּיב. [1]אֶחָד לַמּוֹלֶךְ וְאֶחָד לִשְׁאָר עֲבוֹדָה זָרָה חַיָּיב. [2]רַבִּי אֶלְעָזָר בְּרַבִּי שִׁמְעוֹן אוֹמֵר: לַמּוֹלֶךְ, חַיָּיב, [3]שֶׁלֹּא לַמּוֹלֶךְ פָּטוּר״.
[4]אָמַר עוּלָּא: מַאי טַעְמָא דְּרַבִּי אֶלְעָזָר בְּרַבִּי שִׁמְעוֹן? [5]אָמַר קְרָא: ״לֹא יִמָּצֵא בְךָ״, [6]״בְךָ״ — בְּעַצְמְךָ.
[7]וְרַבָּנַן לָא דָּרְשִׁי ״בְּךָ״? [8]וְהָתְנַן: ״אֲבֵידָתוֹ וַאֲבֵידַת אָבִיו, [9]שֶׁלּוֹ קוֹדֶמֶת״. [10]וְאָמְרִינַן: מַאי טַעְמָא? [11]וְאָמַר רַב יְהוּדָה: אָמַר קְרָא: ״אֶפֶס כִּי לֹא יִהְיֶה בְּךָ אֶבְיוֹן״, [12]שֶׁלּוֹ קוֹדֶמֶת לְשֶׁל כָּל אָדָם.
[13]וְהָתָם מֵ״אֶפֶס״.
[14]אָמַר רַבִּי יוֹסֵי בְּרַבִּי חֲנִינָא:

LITERAL TRANSLATION

the son of Rabbi Shimon says he is liable. [1]Whether to Molech or to other idols, he is liable. [2]Rabbi Elazar the son of Rabbi Shimon says: To Molech, he is liable. [3]Not to Molech, he is exempt."

[4]Ulla said: What is the reason of Rabbi Elazar the son of Rabbi Shimon? [5]The verse states: "There must not be found among you." [6]"Among you"— you yourself.

[7]And the Sages do not interpret "among you"? [8]But surely we have learned: "His own lost object, and his father's lost object — [9]his own takes precedence." [10]And we said: What is the reason? [11]And Rav Yehudah said: the verse states, "Except that there shall be no poor among you," — [12]his own comes before that of every man.

[13]There from "except."

[14]Rabbi Yose the son of Rabbi Ḥanina said:

RASHI

מאי טעמא דרבי אלעזר — במעביר עצמו. **ורבנן לא דרשי בך** — בתמיה לאזהרה, למשמע מינה אזהרת עצמו. **לא יהיה בך אביון** — הזהר בעצמך שלא תבא לידי עניות. נימא ההוא סתמא דלא כרבנן. **התם מאפס כי לא יהיה בך אביון** — דאי לאו לאזהרה אתא אלא להבטחה שמבטיחם שלא יהיה בהם אביונים — נכתוב ״לא יהיה בך אביון״. מדכתיב ״אפס״ — לאזהרה אתא, כלומר: אפס וחדל וכלה עניות ממך. ״אפס״ לשון חדלה וכליה, כמו (בראשית מז) ״כי אפס כסף״.

NOTES

not actually burned, but rather he would walk on a row of bricks that was set up between two bonfires, or else jump over a fire that was lit in a pit. Some of the Geonim understand that the child would walk on the bricks or jump over the fire over and over again until he tired and fell into the fire. Others suggest that there was no rule about the matter, and that sometimes the child would be burned, and sometimes he would be saved from burning (*Rabbenu Yehonatan*).

HALAKHAH

אֲבֵידָתוֹ וַאֲבֵידַת אָבִיו **His own lost object, and his father's lost object.** "If a person finds his own lost object and a lost object belonging to his father (or master), his own lost object takes precedence," following the Mishnah cited here. (*Shulḥan Arukh, Ḥoshen Mishpat* 264:1.)

LITERAL TRANSLATION

Three excisions regarding idol worship, why? [1]One for in its manner, [2]and one for not in its manner, [3]and one for Molech.

[4]And according to the one who says [that] Molech is idol worship, [5]why do I need the excision regarding Molech?

[6]For someone who passes his son not in its manner.

[7]And according to the one who says [that] *megadef* is idol worship, [8]why do I need the excision regarding *megadef*?

[9]For that which was taught: [10]"'Shall utterly be cut off.' [11]'Cut off'— in this world. [12]'Utterly'— in the world to come. [13][These are] the words of Rabbi Akiva. [14]Rabbi Yishmael said to him: But surely it was already

שָׁלֹשׁ כְּרִיתוֹת בַּעֲבוֹדָה זָרָה לָמָּה? [1]אַחַת לִכְדַרְכָּהּ, [2]וְאַחַת לְשֶׁלֹּא כְּדַרְכָּהּ, [3]וְאַחַת לַמּוֹלֶךְ.

[4]וּלְמַאן דְּאָמַר מוֹלֶךְ עֲבוֹדָה זָרָה הִיא, [5]כָּרֵת בַּמּוֹלֶךְ לָמָּה לִי?

[6]לְמַעֲבִיר בְּנוֹ שֶׁלֹּא כְּדַרְכָּהּ.

[7]וּלְמַאן דְּאָמַר, מְגַדֵּף עֲבוֹדָה זָרָה הִיא, [8]כָּרֵת בִּמְגַדֵּף לָמָּה לִי?

[9]לִכְדְתַנְיָא: [10]"'הִכָּרֵת תִּכָּרֵת', [11]'הִכָּרֵת' — בָּעוֹלָם הַזֶּה. [12]'תִּכָּרֵת' — לָעוֹלָם הַבָּא. [13]דִּבְרֵי רַבִּי עֲקִיבָא. [14]אָמַר לוֹ רַבִּי יִשְׁמָעֵאל: וַהֲלֹא כְּבָר

TRANSLATION AND COMMENTARY

punishment of **excision three times with regard to idol worship** — (Leviticus 20:3): "And I will set My face against that man, and will cut him off from among his people, because he has given of his seed to Molech"; (Leviticus 20:5): "Then I will set My face against that man, and against his family, and will cut him off, and all that go astray after him, going astray after Molech, from among their people"; and (Numbers 15:30-31): "That person blasphemes the Lord, and that soul shall be cut off from among his people. Because he has despised the word of the Lord, and has broken his commandment, that soul shall utterly be utterly cut off." [1]**One** mention of excision is needed **for** someone who worships an idol **in the usual manner;** [2]**one** mention of excision is needed **for** someone who worships an idol in the way that God is served, even if that is **not** the usual **manner;** [3]**and one** mention of excision is needed **for** someone who passes his child through fire to **Molech.**

וּלְמַאן דְּאָמַר [4]The Gemara asks: **According to the** authority **who says that** passing a child through fire to **Molech is** a form of **idol worship,** [5]**why is it necessary** to make separate mention of **excision regarding Molech?**

לְמַעֲבִיר [6]The Gemara answers: According to that opinion, the third mention of excision teaches that **someone who passes his son** through fire to some other idol is liable for excision, even if that is **not** the usual **manner** of worshiping that idol.

וּלְמַאן דְּאָמַר [7]Bringing in a related subject, the Gemara asks: **According to the** authority **who says that** the *megadef* mentioned in Numbers 15:30 refers not to someone who blasphemes God, but to someone who is guilty of **idol worship,** [8]**why is it necessary** to make separate mention of **excision regarding a** *megadef?*

לִכְדְתַנְיָא [9]The Gemara answers: The excision mentioned with regard to a *megadef* was necessary to teach us that excision involves both premature death in this world and the soul's being cut off in the world to come, **as it was taught** in a Baraita: "When the Torah describes the punishment of the *megadef,* it uses the double verb form (Numbers 15:31): [10]'That soul **shall utterly be cut off** — *hikaret tikaret* (הִכָּרֵת תִּכָּרֵת).' That apparent superfluity comes to teach that a person who is liable for excision will be cut off in two worlds: [11]**'Cut off'** (*hikaret*) — **in this world,** by dying prematurely or suddenly, [12]**'Utterly'** (*tikaret*) — **in the world to come.** [13]**This is the position of Rabbi Akiva.** [14]**Rabbi Yishmael said to him: But surely**

RASHI

שלש כריתות בעבודה זרה — תרתי גבי מולך ב"קדושים תהיו": "ואני אתן את פני באיש ההוא והכרתי אותו מקרב עמו", "ושמתי אני את פני באיש ההוא ובמשפחתו והכרתי אותו ואת כל הזונים וגו'" (ונתתי את פני וגו'). ואי נמי: סבירא ליה דמולך לאו עבודה זרה הוא, מכל מקום קרי ליה עבודה זרה. והשלישית ב"שלח לך אנשים": "כי דבר ה' בזה ואת מצותו הפר הכרת תכרת הנפש ההיא וגו'" ותניא לקמן באלו שאין להם חלק לעולם הבא: "דבר ה' בזה" — זה דבור ראשון שנאמר בסיני, והוא עבודה זרה. והא דכתיב "הכרת תכרת". חדא חשיב ליה, כדמפרש לקמן: דברה תורה כלשון בני אדם. "את ה' הוא מגדף ונכרתה" — לקמן מפרש. **אחת שלא כדרכה** — כרת יתירא גבי מולך, אם אינו ענין לו תנהו ענין לזבוח וקטור ונסוך והשתחואה שהוא חייב עליהם אף שלא כדרכה. **ואחת למולך** — דאף על פי שדרכן בכך, מיבעי ליה למכתבה באפי נפשיה, דמולך לאו עבודה זרה הוא, והקפידה תורה עליו. **ולמאן דאמר מולך עבודה זרה הוא** — והוי בכלל כדרכה, דכל שאר עבודות מ"איכה יעבדו" נפקא, בא הכתוב לחייב עליו אף בשאר עבודה זרה שאין דרכו בכך, שלא מצינו אלא זבוח וקטור ונסוך והשתחואה. **ולמאן דאמר** — בכריתות: מגדף זה העובד עבודה זרה — כגון משורר לעבודה זרה. **כרת דכתיב במגדף למה לי** — אחרי שדרכה בכך. ופלוגתא היא בכריתות (ז,א) איכא למאן דאמר מגדף היינו מברך את השם. **לכדתניא** — כדמוקים ליה רבי ישמעאל, אחד לעולם הזה ואחד לעולם הבא. **והלא כבר נאמר ונכרתה** — באותה פרשה עצמה גבי מגדף. ורבי עקיבא סבירא ליה מגדף היינו מברך את השם, כדאמר בכריתות. ועולם הבא לא נפקא ליה בעבודה זרה אלא מ"הכרת תכרת". ורבי ישמעאל לאו לרבי עקיבא פריך: והלא כבר נאמר "ונכרתה" — דהא רבי עקיבא במברך את השם מוקים לה. אלא טעמא דנפשיה

TRANSLATION AND COMMENTARY

the previous **verse stated** (Numbers 15:30): [1] 'And that soul **shall be cut off** (*venikhretah*) from among his people.' If each reference to 'cutting off' in the expression *hikaret tikaret* refers to another world, then the word *venikhretah* should also refer to a separate world, but that is difficult, [2] for **are there** in fact **three** different **worlds?** [3] **Rather,** the first instance of 'cutting off' — 'And that soul **shall be cut off** (*venikhretah*)' [4] teaches that a person who is liable for excision will be cut off **in this world.** [5] The second instance, 'That soul shall be **cut off** (*hikaret*),' teaches that he will also be cut off **in the world to come.** [6] The third instance, '**Utterly** (*tikaret*),' does not come to add anything, for **the Torah spoke in the language of men,** and the double verb form has no special significance."

[65A] **MISHNAH** בַּעַל אוֹב [7] We learned earlier in the chapter (53a) that a *ba'al ov* ("medium") and a *yid'oni* ("wizard") are liable to death by stoning. **The** type of medium known as a ***ba'al ov* is the *pitom* who** makes the dead **speak from his armpit.** [8] **And the** wizard, known as a ***yid'oni*, is one who** makes the dead **speak** through a bone which he places **in his mouth.** [9] The *ba'al ov* and *yid'oni* **are** liable to be executed **by stoning,** as the verse states (Leviticus 20:27): "A man or a woman that is a medium or a wizard, shall surely be put to death; they shall stone them with stones; their blood shall be upon them." [10] **Someone who asks** the *ba'al ov* or the *yid'oni* to tell the future **violates a negative commandment,** as the verse states (Leviticus 19:31): "You shall not turn to mediums or wizards, nor seek to be defiled by them; I am the Lord your God."

נֶאֱמַר: [1] 'וְנִכְרְתָה'. [2] וְכִי שְׁלשָׁה עוֹלָמִים יֵשׁ? [3] אֶלָּא: 'וְנִכְרְתָה' — [4] בָּעוֹלָם הַזֶּה, [5] 'הִכָּרֵת' — לָעוֹלָם הַבָּא, [6] 'תִּכָּרֵת' — דִּבְּרָה תּוֹרָה כִּלְשׁוֹן בְּנֵי אָדָם".

[65A] **מִשְׁנָה** [7] בַּעַל אוֹב — זֶה פִּיתוֹם הַמְדַבֵּר מִשֶּׁחְיוֹ, [8] וְיִדְּעוֹנִי — זֶה הַמְדַבֵּר בְּפִיו. [9] הֲרֵי אֵלּוּ בִּסְקִילָה, [10] וְהַנִּשְׁאָל בָּהֶם בְּאַזְהָרָה.

LITERAL TRANSLATION

stated: [1] 'Shall be cut off.' [2] Are there three worlds? [3] Rather, 'Shall be cut off'— [4] in this world. [5] 'Cut off'— in the world to come. [6] 'Utterly' — the Torah spoke in the language of men."

[65A] **MISHNAH** [7] A *ba'al ov* — that is the *pitom* who speaks from his armpit. [8] And the *yid'oni* — that is the one who speaks with his mouth. [9] They are [executed] by stoning, [10] and he who asks of them [violates] a negative commandment (lit., "a warning").

RASHI

קאמר: והלא כבר נאמר "ונכרתה" ואנא סבירא ליה דבעבודה זרה כתיבא. וכי שלשה עולמות יש וכו' — ודומה לו ב"שחיטת חולין": והלא במוקדשין האומר רגלה של זו עולה — כולה עולה! דהא פרכא לאו לכשנגדו פריך, דאיהו סבירא ליה אפילו במוקדשין — דאין כולה עולה. אלא טעמא דנפשיה אמר, בפרק [בהמה המקשה] (חולין סט,א).
משנה פיתום — שם המכשף. המדבר משחיו — מעלה את המת מן הארץ ומושיב לו בשחיו תחת זרועותיו ומדבר משחי = *איישל"ה בלעז בית שחי. ידעוני המדבר בפיו — כדמפרש בגמרא. חיה אחת יש ששמה ידוע, ומכניס ממנה עצם לתוך פיו והעצם מדבר מאליו על ידי כשפים. הרי אלו בסקילה — כדכתיב (ויקרא כ) "באבן ירגמו אותם". והנשאל בהם — שבא ושואל בהם להגיד לו דבר העתיד, כגון שאול. באזהרה — ד"אל תפנו אל האובות" (שם יט). ואזהרה דמכשפות גופיה מ"לא ימצא בך וגו' וחובר חבר ושואל אוב וידעוני" (דברים יח).

LANGUAGE

פִּיתוֹם ***Pitom*** ("medium"). This word is derived from the Greek πυθων, *python,* meaning "a medium, someone who told the future under the influence of drugs or the like."

LANGUAGE (RASHI)

איישל"א* From the Old French *aiesele*, meaning "armpit."

NOTES

וְכִי שְׁלשָׁה עוֹלָמִים יֵשׁ? Are there three worlds? *Rashi* explains that Rabbi Yishmael's question is not directed at Rabbi Akiva, for according to Rabbi Akiva, the *megadef* mentioned in Numbers 15:30 refers not to someone who is guilty of idol worship, but to someone who blasphemes God, and so the word *venikhretah* teaches that the blasphemer is liable for excision. Rather, Rabbi Yishmael poses a rhetorical question in order to clarify his own position. *Ramah* suggests that Rabbi Yishmael was not familiar with Rabbi Akiva's position regarding the *megadef* mentioned in the Torah, and so his question can indeed be understood as having been directed at Rabbi Akiva.

הַמְדַבֵּר מִשֶּׁחְיוֹ Who speaks from his armpit. Some have the reading: "And one who speaks from his armpit." According to this there are two types of *ov*: the *pitom,* who takes a human skull, burns incense before it, asks it questions about the future, and it answers; and one who makes the dead speak in a low voice from his armpit (*Bertinoro*).

הֲרֵי אֵלּוּ בִּסְקִילָה They are executed by stoning. The Mishnah mentions that the *ba'al ov* and the *yid'oni* are executed by stoning, even though that was already stated earlier in the chapter, because it wishes to add here that someone who consults a *ba'al ov* or a *yid'oni* about his future violates an ordinary negative commandment, and is therefore not liable for execution (*Ḥamra Veḥaye*).

הַנִּשְׁאָל בָּהֶם He who asks of them. Even though the passive form נִשְׁאָל should mean "he who is asked," the word

HALAKHAH

בַּעַל אוֹב וְיִדְּעוֹנִי A *ba'al* and a *yid'oni*. "Someone who intentionally acted in the manner of an *ov* or a *yid'oni* is liable for excision, and if he was properly warned and there are witnesses, he is subject to death by stoning." (*Rambam, Sefer Mada, Hilkhot Avodah Zarah* 6:1.)

הַנִּשְׁאָל בְּאוֹב וְיִדְּעוֹנִי He who asks of an *ov* and a *yid'oni*. "It is forbidden to consult with an *ov* or a *yid'oni*. Someone who consults with an *ov* or a *yid'oni* violates a negative commandment, and is subject to lashes by Rabbinic decree (for his transgression does not involve an action). If he

TRANSLATION AND COMMENTARY

GEMARA מַאי [1]Tractate *Keritot* opens with a list of thirty-six transgressions, the intentional violation of which is punishable by excision, and the unintentional violation of which obligates the offender to bring a sin-offering. The list includes a *ba'al ov,* but not a *yid'oni.* The Gemara therefore asks: **What is the difference that here** regarding those liable to death by stoning, the Mishnah **mentions** both **the** ***ba'al ov*** **and the** ***yid'oni,*** [2]whereas in tractate *Keritot* **regarding** those liable for **excision,** the Mishnah **mentions** only **the** ***ba'al ov,*** **and leaves out the** ***yid'oni?***

רַבִּי יוֹחָנָן [3]**Rabbi Yoḥanan said:** The *yid'oni* was not listed separately among those liable for excision and a sin-offering, **because the two of them** — the *ba'al ov* and the *yid'oni* — **are included in the same negative commandment** (Leviticus 19:31): "You shall not turn to mediums [*ha'ovot*] or wizards [*hayid'onim*], nor seek to be defiled by them; I am the Lord your God." Thus, if someone inadvertently acted in the manner of a *ba'al ov,* and then, before he realized that he had sinned, he inadvertently acted in the manner of a *yid'oni,* he is liable for only a single sin-offering. If a person commits a number of transgressions in a single period of unawareness, he must bring a sin-offering for each negative commandment that he violated. This Mishnah in *Keritot* could not have listed the *yid'oni* separately, for it teaches us how many different sin-offerings a person can bring for transgressions that he committed in a single period of unawareness.

רֵישׁ לָקִישׁ [4]**Resh Lakish said:** The ***yid'oni*** was not listed in tractate *Keritot,* [5]**for** his transgression — making the dead speak through a bone — **does not involve a** physical **act,** and a person is only liable for a sin-offering if he violated a prohibition whose transgression involves a physical act.

LITERAL TRANSLATION

GEMARA [1]What is the difference that here it teaches *ba'al ov* and *yid'oni,* [2]and what is the difference that regarding excision it teaches *ba'al ov,* and leaves out *yid'oni?*

[3]Rabbi Yoḥanan said: Since the two of them were stated in one negative commandment.

[4]Resh Lakish said: *Yid'oni* — [5]since it does not involve an action.

גמרא [1]מַאי שְׁנָא הָכָא דְּקָתָנֵי בַּעַל אוֹב וְיִדְּעוֹנִי, [2]וּמַאי שְׁנָא גַּבֵּי כְּרֵיתוֹת דְּקָתָנֵי בַּעַל אוֹב, וְשַׁיְּירֵיהּ לְיִדְּעוֹנִי?

[3]רַבִּי יוֹחָנָן אָמַר: הוֹאִיל וּשְׁנֵיהֶן בְּלָאו אֶחָד נֶאֱמְרוּ.

[4]רֵישׁ לָקִישׁ אָמַר: יִדְּעוֹנִי — [5]לְפִי שֶׁאֵין בּוֹ מַעֲשֶׂה.

RASHI

גמרא — בכריתות קא חשיב לכל כריתות שבתורה שחייבין עליהן על שגגתן חטאת, ותנן (שם ב,א) בעל אוב ולא תנא ידעוני. **הואיל ושניהם בלאו אחד נאמרו** — בלאו ד"אל תפנו אל האובות ואל הידעונים" ואם עשה שניהם בהעלם אחד אינו חייב אלא חטאת אחת. שהלאוין מחלקין לחטאות כדכתיב (ויקרא ד) "אשר לא תעשינה" דהיינו דברים שהן בלא תעשה, וסמיך ליה "או הודע אליו" — אלמא חטאת אלאוין קיימי, והני, אף על גב דכי עבד לחד מינייהו באפי נפשיה מיחייב, דהא לאו אתרווייהו קאי — לא תני להו לתרווייהו התם, דכי תנינא התם מידי דמחייב אכל חד וחד כי עביד להו כי הדדי הוא דתנינן. כדאמרינן התם ברישא דגמרא דפרקין: מנינא למה לי? שאם עשאן כולם בהעלם אחת חייב על כל אחת ואחת, הלכך לא מצי למתני שלשים ושבע כריתות לחייבו שלשים ושבע חטאות. והא דנקט "הואיל ושניהם בלאו אחד נאמרו", ולא נקט: הואיל ושניהם בכרת אחת נאמרו, — משום דחלוק חטאות אינו תלוי בחלוק כריתות, דהא מפטם שמן המשחה וסך משמן המשחה, משום דאיכא שני לאוין "על בשר אדם לא ייסך" "ובמתכנתו לא תעשו כמוהו" (שמות ל) — אף על גב דאין בשניהם אלא כרת אחת, כדכתיב (שם) "איש אשר ירקח כמוהו ואשר יתן ממנו על זר ונכרת מעמיו" אמרינן התם דכי עביד להו בשוגג בהדדי — מיחייב על כל אחת ואחת. **ריש לקיש אמר ידעוני** — להכי לא תנינא לה להתם, משום דאפילו כי עביד לה באפי נפשיה לאו בר קרבן הוא, לפי שאין בו מעשה, וחטאת אינה באה אלא על המעשה דכתיב "ועשה אחת". אבל בעל אוב צריך להקים בזרועותיו כדלקמן, והקשת זרועותיו חשיב ליה מעשה. אבל הכנסת העצם ידעוני אינו מדבר בשעת מעשה, אלא לאחר המעשה שהוא בפיו מדבר העצם מאליו.

NOTES

is used here in the active sense, "he who asks." Similarly we find (I Samuel 20:28): "David earnestly asked leave of me [נִשְׁאֹל דָּוִד מֵעִמָּדִי]" (*Torat Ḥayyim*). Moreover, a person who comes to consult with a medium or a wizard sometimes takes an active role in the wizardry, so that he too can be regarded as having been asked about the future (*Oneg Yom Tov*).

HALAKHAH

acted in accordance with what he was told by the *ov* or the *yid'oni,* he is liable for lashes by Torah law." (*Rambam, Sefer Mada, Hilkhot Avodah Zarah* 11:14.)

הוֹאִיל בְּלָאו אֶחָד **Since they were stated in the same negative commandment.** "A *ba'al ov* and a *yid'oni* are each independently liable for a sin-offering," following Rabbi Yoḥanan against Resh Lakish. (*Rambam, Sefer Mada, Hilkhot Avodah Zarah* 6:1-2; *Sefer Korbanot, Hilkhot Shegagot* 1:4.)

TRANSLATION AND COMMENTARY

וְרַבִּי יוֹחָנָן [1]The Gemara notes: According to Resh Lakish, we understand why the Mishnah in *Keritot* mentioned the *ba'al ov*, and not the *yid'oni*, for according to Resh Lakish, a *yid'oni* is never liable for a sin-offering. But according to **Rabbi Yoḥanan** — who maintains that a *yid'oni* is liable for a sin-offering, but he was not mentioned in the Mishnah in *Keritot*, because a person who acted as both a *ba'al ov* and a *yid'oni* is only liable for a single sin-offering — [2]**what is the difference** between the two **that** the Mishnah **chose** to count **the *ba'al ov*,** and not the *yid'oni*?

מִשּׁוּם [3]The Gemara answers: The Mishnah counted the *ba'al ov*, and not the *yid'oni*, **because** all **the verses** which mention the *ba'al ov* and the *yid'oni* **mention** the *ba'al ov* **first.**

וְרֵישׁ לָקִישׁ [4]The Gemara now asks: **What is the reason that Resh Lakish did not say like Rabbi Yoḥanan** that the *yid'oni* was not mentioned in *Keritot* because a person who acted as both a *ba'al ov* and a *yid'oni* is only liable for a single sin-offering?

אָמַר [5]**Rav Pappa said:** Resh Lakish did not say like Rabbi Yoḥanan, because the Torah **separated** between the *ba'al ov* and the *yid'oni* **regarding the execution** that is imposed for the intentional violation of these prohibitions, for the verse states (Leviticus 20:27): "A man also or woman that is a medium [*ov*] or a wizard [*yid'oni*], shall surely be put to death," using the disjunctive term "or" [the word אוֹ], rather than the conjunctive vav. If a person committed two transgressions in a single period of unawareness, and the Torah distinguished between the two regarding execution, he is liable for two sin-offerings. Thus, it follows that if a *yid'oni* were ever liable for a sin-offering, then a person who acted in the manner of a *ba'al ov* and in the manner of a *yid'oni* in a single period of unawareness would be liable for two sin-offerings. Since the Mishnah in *Keritot* did not count the *yid'oni*, argues Resh Lakish, it must be that a *yid'oni* is never liable for a sin-offering, because his transgression does not involve a physical act.

וְרַבִּי יוֹחָנָן [6]The Gemara asks: And how does **Rabbi Yoḥanan** counter this argument? [7]The Gemara explains: Rabbi Yoḥanan maintains that if the Torah **distinguishes** between two transgressions **regarding the negative commandment** under which each is included, that **is regarded as a distinction** which obligates the offender to bring two separate sin-offerings for the unwitting commission of the two transgressions. [8]But if the Torah only **distinguishes** between the two transgressions **regarding the execution** that is imposed for the intentional violation of the prohibitions, that **is not regarded as a distinction** which obligates the offender to bring two separate sin-offerings for the unwitting commission of the two transgressions.

וְרַבִּי יוֹחָנָן [9]The Gemara asks: **And what is the reason that Rabbi Yoḥanan did not say like Resh Lakish** that the *yid'oni* was not mentioned in *Keritot*, because his transgression does not involve a physical act, and so he is not liable for a sin-offering?

אָמַר לָךְ [10]The Gemara answers: Rabbi Yoḥanan **can say to you** that **the Mishnah in** tractate *Keritot* **follows** the position of **Rabbi Akiva,** [11]**who said** that in order for a person to be liable for a sin-offering, **it is not necessary** to perform **a** physical **act.** According to Rabbi Akiva, a person who unwittingly violates the

---

[1]וְרַבִּי יוֹחָנָן, [2]מַאי שְׁנָא בַּעַל אוֹב דְּנָקַט?

[3]מִשּׁוּם דִּפְתַח בֵּיהּ קְרָא.

[4]וְרֵישׁ לָקִישׁ, מַאי טַעְמָא לֹא אָמַר כְּרַבִּי יוֹחָנָן?

[5]אָמַר רַב פַּפָּא: חֲלוּקִין הֵן בְּמִיתָה.

[6]וְרַבִּי יוֹחָנָן: [7]חֲלוּקָה דְּלָאו שְׁמָהּ חֲלוּקָה, [8]דְּמִיתָה לֹא שְׁמָהּ חֲלוּקָה.

[9]וְרַבִּי יוֹחָנָן, מַאי טַעְמָא לֹא אָמַר כְּרֵישׁ לָקִישׁ?

[10]אָמַר לָךְ: מַתְנִיתִין דִּכְרִיתוֹת רַבִּי עֲקִיבָא הִיא, [11]דְּאָמַר:

LITERAL TRANSLATION

[1]And Rabbi Yoḥanan, [2]what is the difference that it seized the *ba'al ov*?

[3]Because the verse opened with him.

[4]And Resh Lakish, what is the reason that he did not say like Rabbi Yoḥanan?

[5]Rav Pappa said: They are distinguished regarding execution.

[6]And Rabbi Yoḥanan: [7]A distinction regarding the negative commandment is called (lit., "its name is") a distinction. [8][A distinction] regarding execution is not called a distinction.

[9]And Rabbi Yoḥanan, what is the reason that he did not say like Resh Lakish?

[10]He can say to you: The Mishnah in *Keritot* [follows] Rabbi Akiva, [11]who said:

RASHI

ורבי יוחנן — דאמר ידעוני באפי נפשיה בר קרבן הוא, והאי דשייריה — משום דלא מיחייב תרתי עלייהו. מאי שנא בעל אוב דנקט — תנא למתנייה ושייריה לידעוני, ולא נקט ידעוני ולשייריה לבעל אוב. משום דפתח ביה קרא — בכל דוכתי אוב כתיב ברישא. חלוקין הן במיתה — כשפירש סקילתן חלקן הכתוב, "כי יהיה בהן אוב או ידעוני מות יומתו באבן ירגמו אותם דמיהם בם" ולא כתיב "וידעוני" — הלכך אי הוה ידעוני בר קרבן הוה מיחייב עליה נמי כי עביד ליה בהדי אוב. מאי טעמא לא אמר כריש לקיש — דפטר ליה לגמרי מקרבן? הא ודאי בעינן מעשה! רבי עקיבא היא — דקא חשיב מגדף בההוא מניינא, ופליגי רבנן עליה במגדף משום דאין בו מעשה. הלכך לרבי עקיבא מחייב עליה, ולא שיירה אלא משום דלא מחייב תרתי אתרוייהו.

TRANSLATION AND COMMENTARY

prohibition against blasphemy is liable for a sin-offering, and blasphemy does not involve a physical act. Thus, a *yid'oni* is also liable for a sin-offering, and the Mishnah in *Keritot* did not mention a *yid'oni* because a person who acted as both a *ba'al ov* and a *yid'oni* is only liable for a single sin-offering.

וְרֵישׁ לָקִישׁ [1]The Gemara asks: **And** how does **Resh Lakish** counter this argument? [2]The Gemara explains: Resh Lakish maintains that while **Rabbi Akiva does not require a major** physical **act**, [3]**he does** however **require** at least **a minor** physical **act,** and the transgression committed by the *yid'oni* does not involve even a minor physical act.

מְגַדֵּף [4]The Gemara objects: But surely Rabbi Akiva obligates **a blasphemer** to bring a sin-offering! [5]**What** physical **act** does his transgression involve? [6]The Gemara explains: **The movement of his lips** as he utters the blasphemy **is** considered **an action** for which he must bring a sin-offering. But in the case of a *yid'oni,* the offender does not even move his lips.

בַּעַל אוֹב [7]The Gemara asks: Regarding **a *ba'al ov*, what** physical **act** does his transgression involve? [8]The Gemara answers: When the *ba'al ov* raises up the dead, he **knocks his arms** together in order to produce a sound, and that **is** considered **an action** which obligates him to bring a sin-offering.

וַאֲפִילּוּ לְרַבָּנַן [9]The Gemara asks: Does Resh Lakish say that the *ba'al ov's* knocking together of his arms is regarded as an action **even according to the Sages** who disagree with Rabbi Akiva and require a major physical act? [10]**But surely it was taught** as follows in a Baraita: "Someone who inadvertently worshiped an idol **is only liable** for a sin-offering if he served the idol **in a manner that involves an action,** such as **slaughtering a sacrifice** to it, **burning incense** before it, **offering** it **a libation, or bowing down** before it." [11]Commenting on this Baraita, **Resh Lakish said: Who taught** that a person is liable for a sin-offering for inadvertently **bowing down** to an idol? [12]This Baraita follows **Rabbi Akiva, who said:** In order to be liable for a sin-offering, **it is not necessary** for a person to perform **a** major physical **act**. [13]**And Rabbi Yoḥanan said: You can even say** that this Baraita **follows** the position of **the Sages** who disagree with Rabbi Akiva, [14]for **the bending of** the idolater's **body** as he bows down before the idol **is considered a** major physical **act.** [15]**Now** the following question may be raised **according to Resh Lakish: If the Sages** who disagree with Rabbi Akiva say that **the bending of the** idolater's **body is not considered a** major physical **act,** [16]**is** it possible that **the knocking together of the *ba'al ov's* arms is considered a** major physical **act**?

לָא בָּעֵינַן מַעֲשֶׂה. [1]וְרֵישׁ לָקִישׁ, [2]נְהִי דְּלָא בָּעֵי רַבִּי עֲקִיבָא מַעֲשֶׂה רַבָּה, [3]מַעֲשֶׂה זוּטָא בָּעֵי. [4]מְגַדֵּף, [5]מַאי מַעֲשֶׂה אִיכָּא? [6]עֲקִימַת שְׂפָתָיו הָוֵי מַעֲשֶׂה. [7]בַּעַל אוֹב, מַאי מַעֲשֶׂה אִיכָּא? [8]הַקָּשַׁת זְרוֹעוֹתָיו הָוֵי מַעֲשֶׂה. [9]וַאֲפִילּוּ לְרַבָּנַן? [10]וְהָתַנְיָא: "אֵינוֹ חַיָּיב אֶלָּא עַל דָּבָר שֶׁיֵּשׁ בּוֹ מַעֲשֶׂה, כְּגוֹן זִיבּוּחַ, קִיטּוּר, וְנִיסּוּךְ, וְהִשְׁתַּחֲוָאָה". [11]וְאָמַר רֵישׁ לָקִישׁ: מַאן תָּנָא הִשְׁתַּחֲוָאָה? [12]רַבִּי עֲקִיבָא הִיא, דְּאָמַר: לָא בָּעֵינַן מַעֲשֶׂה. [13]וְרַבִּי יוֹחָנָן אָמַר: אֲפִילּוּ תֵּימָא רַבָּנַן. [14]כְּפִיפַת קוֹמָתוֹ לְרַבָּנַן הָוֵי מַעֲשֶׂה. [15]הַשְׁתָּא לְרֵישׁ לָקִישׁ כְּפִיפַת קוֹמָתוֹ לְרַבָּנַן לָא הָוֵי מַעֲשֶׂה, [16]הַקָּשַׁת זְרוֹעוֹתָיו דְּבַעַל אוֹב הָוֵי מַעֲשֶׂה?

LITERAL TRANSLATION

We do not need an action.

[1]And Resh Lakish: [2]While Rabbi Akiva does not require a major action, [3]he requires a minor action.

[4]A blasphemer, [5]what action is there? [6]The movement (lit., "twisting") of his lips is an action.

[7]A *ba'al ov,* what action is there? [8]The knocking of his arms is an action.

[9]And even according to the Sages? [10]But surely it was taught: "He is not liable except for something involving an action, like sacrificing, burning incense, libation, or bowing down." [11]And Resh Lakish said: Who taught bowing down? [12]It is Rabbi Akiva, who said: We do not need an action. [13]And Rabbi Yoḥanan said: You can even say [it is] the Sages. [14]The bending of his body according to the Sages is an action. [15]Now according to Resh Lakish, [if] the bending of the body according to the Sages is not an action, [16]is the knocking together of the arms of the *ba'al ov* an action?

RASHI

עקימת שפתיו – שעוקמין ומנענעין כשהוא מדבר, חשיב ליה רבי עקיבא מעשה, אבל ידעוני אפילו עקימת שפתים ליכא. ואפילו לרבנן – קאמר ריש לקיש דהוה מעשה? בתמיהה. כלומר, מדלא פליגי רבנן עליה התם אלא במגדף, אבל בבעל אוב מודו – אלמא הקשת זרועותיו דבעל אוב הוי מעשה. אינו חייב – קרבן על שגגתן. מאן תנא השתחואה – לענין קרבן. רבי עקיבא היא דאמר לא בעינן מעשה – רבה, אלא מעשה זוטא.

HALAKHAH

כְּפִיפַת קוֹמָתוֹ **The bending of his body.** "Someone who bows down before an idol is liable for excision, and if he did so unwittingly, he must bring a sin-offering." (*Rambam, Sefer Korbanot, Hilkhot Shegagot* 7:1.)

1 כִּי קָאָמַר רֵישׁ לָקִישׁ נַמִּי לְרַבִּי עֲקִיבָא, 2 אֲבָל לְרַבָּנַן — לָא. 3 אִי הָכִי, 4 יָצָא מְגַדֵּף וּבַעַל אוֹב מִיבָּעֵי לֵיהּ!

5 אֶלָּא, אָמַר עוּלָּא: 6 בִּמְקַטֵּר לְשֵׁד.

7 אָמַר לֵיהּ רָבָא: מְקַטֵּר לְשֵׁד — עוֹבֵד עֲבוֹדָה זָרָה הוּא!

8 אֶלָּא, אָמַר רָבָא: 9 בִּמְקַטֵּר לְחַבֵּר.

10 אָמַר לֵיהּ אַבַּיֵי: הַמְקַטֵּר לְחַבֵּר חוֹבֵר חֶבֶר הוּא. 11 אִין, וְהַתּוֹרָה אָמְרָה: חוֹבֵר זֶה בִּסְקִילָה.

LITERAL TRANSLATION

1 When Resh Lakish said [that], it was also according to Rabbi Akiva, 2 but according to the Sages — not. 3 If so, it should have said: 4 To the exclusion of the blasphemer and the *ba'al ov*!

5 Rather, Ulla said: 6 Where he burns incense to a spirit.

7 Rava said to him: Someone who burns incense to a spirit is guilty of idol worship!

8 Rather, Rava said: 9 Where he burns incense for purposes of charming.

10 Abaye said to him: Someone who burns incense for purposes of charming is a charmer. 11 Yes, and the Torah said: This charmer is liable to death by stoning.

RASHI

כי אמר ריש לקיש — דהקשת זרועותיו לבעל אוב הוי מעשה — לרבי עקיבא קאמר. אי הכי — מתניתין דקתני התם במילתא דרבנן יצא מגדף שאינו מחייב על שגגתו חטאת לפי שאין בו מעשה. וגבי חטאת כתיב "תורה אחת יהיה לכם לעושה בשגגה" ואי הכי יצא מגדף ובעל אוב מבעיא ליה. במקטר לשד — בעל אוב דקתני בכריתות דמודו ביה רבנן — בהכי עסקינן: שמקטר לפני השד הממונה על אותו דבר, דהוי מעשה גמור. עובד עבודה זרה הוא — ועובד עבודה זרה הא קתני לה התם. ומשני: במקטר לחבר — אינו מקטר לשם אלהות, אלא על ידי הקטרה נעשה המכשפות לחבר השדים לכאן. חובר חבר הוא — ואינו אלא בלאו. והתורה אמרה חבר כגון זה בסקילה — תירוץ הוא, מאחר שמחבר את השדים במזיד אמרה התורה שיהא בסקילה — וכל שזדונו חייב מיתה על שגגתו מביא קרבן. דכי אמרינן חובר חבר אינו אלא באזהרה — זה המחבר חיות ובהמות נחשים ועקרבים למקום אחד על ידי לחשים.

TRANSLATION AND COMMENTARY

כִּי קָאָמַר 1 The Gemara answers: **When Resh Lakish said** the *ba'al ov's* knocking together of his arms is considered a physical act, **it was also** only **according to** the position of **Rabbi Akiva,** who ruled that a minor physical act suffices. 2 **But according to the Sages,** who disagree with Rabbi Akiva, and require a major physical act, the *ba'al ov's* knocking together of his arms is **not** considered a physical act which leads to liability for a sin-offering.

אִי הָכִי 3 The Gemara asks: **If** it is **so** that according to the Rabbis the ***ba'al ov's*** transgression does not involve a physical act, rather than saying that, according to the Rabbis, the verse (Numbers 15:29): "You shall have one Torah for him who *acts* unwittingly," excludes the blasphemer, the Mishnah in *Keritot* **should have said** that those words 4 **exclude** both **the blasphemer and the *ba'al ov*.** Neither is liable for a sin-offering, for neither of them is guilty of a transgression involving a physical act!

אֶלָּא 5 **Rather, Ulla said:** When the Mishnah in *Keritot* says that a *ba'al ov* is liable for a sin-offering even according to the Sages, 6 it is talking about a *ba'al ov* who **burns incense to a spirit** so that it help him raise up the dead, for that is surely considered a major physical act.

אָמַר לֵיהּ רָבָא 7 **Rava said to** Ulla: This is difficult, for **someone who burns incense to a spirit is guilty of idol worship,** and the Mishnah in *Keritot* already said that an idol worshiper is liable for a sin-offering!

אֶלָּא 8 **Rather, Rava said:** When the Mishnah says that a *ba'al ov* is liable for a sin-offering even according to the Rabbis, 9 it is talking about the *ba'al ov* who **burns incense** to spirits, not as a rite of worship, but **for purposes of enchantment,** to assemble them.

אָמַר לֵיהּ אַבַּיֵי 10 **Abaye said to** Rava: This too is difficult, for **someone who burns incense** to spirits **to assemble them is** considered **a charmer,** who transgresses an ordinary negative commandment (see Deuteronomy 18:11), the unintentional violation of which does not obligate the offender to bring a sin-offering. 11 Rava said to Abaye: **Yes, but the Torah said** that **this** type of **charmer** who charms spirits rather than animals, **is liable to** death by **stoning,** if his transgression was intentional. Thus he is liable for a sin-offering, if his transgression was unintentional.

BACKGROUND

חוֹבֵר חֶבֶר **A charmer.** According to *Rambam,* a charmer is a charlatan who foolishly believes that his incantations and magical practices are effective. If the charmer performed some act in addition to what he said, he is liable for lashes by Torah law. If he only recited his incantation, and did not even move a finger, he is only liable for lashes by Rabbinic decree. And similarly, someone who consults with a charmer and believes that his charms are effective, is liable for lashes by Rabbinic decree, for he participates in the charmer's foolishness. According to others, a charmer is indeed capable of charming animals, and so he is only subject to lashes by Torah law if he succeeds in placing animals under his spell.

HALAKHAH

מְקַטֵּר לְשֵׁד **He burns incense to a spirit.** "Someone who burns incense to a spirit for purposes of charming is guilty of idolatry and liable to execution by stoning." (*Shulhan Arukh, Yoreh De'ah* 179:19.)

חוֹבֵר חֶבֶר **A charmer.** "Someone who employs magical incantations to join together living creatures violates the prohibition against acting in the manner of a charmer. If he performs some act in addition to saying words, he is liable for lashes by Torah law. If he does not perform any act, he is subject to lashes by Rabbinic decree. A person may not employ such incantations, even to prevent creatures from causing him harm, unless he is in mortal danger." (*Rambam, Sefer Mada, Hilkhot Avodah Zarah* 11:10-11; *Shulhan Arukh, Yoreh De'ah* 179:65,69.)

[1]תָּנוּ רַבָּנַן: ״׳חֹבֵר חֶבֶר׳ — [2]אֶחָד חֶבֶר גָּדוֹל וְאֶחָד חֶבֶר קָטָן, וַאֲפִילּוּ נְחָשִׁים וַעֲקְרַבִּים.
[3]אָמַר אַבַּיֵי: הִלְכָּךְ, הַאי מַאן דְּצָמֵיד זִיבּוּרָא וַעֲקְרַבָּא, [4]אַף עַל גַּב דְּקָא מִיכַּוֵּין דְּלָא לִיזְקוּ — אָסוּר.
[5]וְרַבִּי יוֹחָנָן, מַאי שְׁנָא דִּכְפִיפַת קוֹמָתוֹ לְרַבָּנַן הָוֵי מַעֲשֶׂה, [6]וַעֲקִימַת שְׂפָתָיו לֹא הָוֵי מַעֲשֶׂה?
[7]אָמַר רָבָא: שָׁאנֵי מְגַדֵּף, הוֹאִיל וְיֶשְׁנוֹ בַּלֵּב.
[65B] [8]מְתִיב רַבִּי זֵירָא; [9]״יָצְאוּ עֵדִים זוֹמְמִין שֶׁאֵין בָּהֶן מַעֲשֶׂה״. [10]וְאַמַּאי? [11]הָא לֵיתַנְהוּ בַּלֵּב!
[12]אָמַר רָבָא: שָׁאנֵי עֵדִים זוֹמְמִין הוֹאִיל וְיֶשְׁנוֹ בְּקוֹל.
[13]וְקוֹל לְרַבִּי יוֹחָנָן לָאו מַעֲשֶׂה

LITERAL TRANSLATION

[1]Our Rabbis taught: "'A charmer' — [2]whether he charms large [animals], or he charms small [animals], and even snakes or scorpions."

[3]Abaye said: Therefore, someone who joins a wasp and a scorpion, [4]even if he has in mind that they not harm him — it is forbidden.

[5]And Rabbi Yoḥanan, what is the difference that the bending of his body according to the Rabbis is an action, [6]and the movement of (lit., "curving") his lips is not an action?

[7]Rava said: A blasphemer is different, since it is in the heart.

[65B] [8]Rabbi Zera objected: [9]"False conspiring witnesses were excluded, because they do not involve an action." [10]But why? [11]Surely they are not in the heart.

[12]Rava said: False conspiring witnesses are different, since it is in the voice.

[13]And a voice according to Rabbi Yoḥanan is not regarded as an action?

TRANSLATION AND COMMENTARY

תָּנוּ רַבָּנַן [1]**Our Rabbis taught** the following Baraita: "The prohibition against being **'a charmer'** (Deuteronomy 18:11), [2]applies **whether he charms large animals, or he charms small animals, and even** if he charms **snakes or scorpions."**

אָמַר אַבַּיֵי [3]**Abaye said: Therefore,** if **someone** employs magic to **join** together **a wasp and a scorpion,** to make them harm each other, [4]**even if he has in mind that they not harm him, it is forbidden,** because of the prohibition against being "a charmer."

וְרַבִּי יוֹחָנָן [5]The Gemara raises a question: According to **Rabbi Yoḥanan: What is the difference according to the Rabbis** between the idolater's **bending his body** as he bows down before his idol **and** the blasphemer's **moving his lips** as he utters his blasphemy. [6]Why is the former **considered a** major physical **act** that obligates the idolater to bring a sin-offering for his transgression, whereas the latter **is not considered** a major physical **act** for which the blasphemer is liable for a sin-offering?

אָמַר רָבָא [7]**Rava said: A blasphemer is different, because** he is only liable if he actually means to curse God, and so his transgression transpires primarily **in his heart.** But the idolater who bows down to his idol commits his transgression with a physical act.

[65B] מְתִיב רַבִּי זֵירָא [8]**Rabbi Zera raised an objection** from a Baraita dealing with sin-offerings: "The verse (Leviticus 4:2): 'And shall do one of them,' teaches that a sin-offering is only brought for a transgression involving a physical act. [9]This **excludes false, conspiring witnesses,** teaching that they are not liable for a sin-offering, **because** their transgression **does not involve** a physical **act."** [10]**But why** should false, conspiring witnesses be excluded from having to bring a sin-offering? False, conspiring witnesses sin with their speech, and the movement of their lips should be considered an action that obligates them to bring a sin-offering. [11]**Surely they are not** included among those whose transgression transpires primarily **in the heart** without involving any action, for they are liable for what they say, and not for what they think.

אָמַר רָבָא [12]**Rava said: False, conspiring witnesses are different, because** they are liable for the testimony which they sound **with their voices.**

וְקוֹל לְרַבִּי יוֹחָנָן [13]The Gemara asks: But is it really true that the sounding of **a voice is not regarded as**

RASHI

אחד חבר גדל — מאסף חיות ובהמות גדולות. **חבר קטן** — מחבר שקצים ורמשים. **ואפילו נחשים ועקרבים** — לגרותן זה בזה, או למקום מדבר שלא ימצאו ביישוב ויזיקו. **אסור** — וכגון שאין רצין אחריו, שאין כאן משום פקוח נפש. **הואיל וישנו בלב** — עיקר חיוב הבא עליו תלוי בלב, שמתכוין לברך השם, שאפילו מברך את השם כל היום ואין בלבו כלפי מעלה, אלא שהעלה את השם לדבר אחר ומכנהו בשם המיוחד ומקללו — אינו מתחייב. **מתיב רבי זירא יצאו עדים זוממין** — אגל חטאת היא שנויה בתורת כהנים, גבי פר כהן משיח: אחר שראינו דברים שהן כעובד עבודה זרה ודברים שאינן כעובד עבודה זרה, למה נאמרה עובד עבודה זרה — לומר לך: מה עבודה זרה מיוחדת שחייבין על זדונה כרת ועל שגגתה חטאת, אף כל שחייבין וכו׳. אי מה עבודה זרה מיוחדת שחייבין עליה מיתת בית דין אף אני מרבה חייבי מיתות בית דין, ואת מי אני מרבה — מקלל לאביו ומסית ועדים זוממין? תלמוד לומר ״ועשה״ יצאו עדים זוממין שאין בהם מעשה. ואמאי לא הויא עקימת שפתיו מעשה הא לא תליא בכונת הלב. הכי גרסינן: **אמר רבא שאני עדים זוממין הואיל וישנן בקול** — עיקר חיובן בשמיעת קולם לפני בית דין הוא בא, וקול לית ביה ממש, הלכך הוי כמגדף דתלוי בלב.

TRANSLATION AND COMMENTARY

a physical **act according to Rabbi Yoḥanan?** [1]**But surely it was stated** that the Amoraim disagree about the following matter: **If someone** figuratively **muzzled** an animal by frightening **it with his voice,** shouting at it whenever it was about to eat, [2]**or if someone drove** a pair of animals of different species **by using his voice,** causing them to move, but without actually touching the animals or the yoke, [3]**Rabbi Yoḥanan said:** In both cases **he is liable** to be flogged, the usual punishment for the violation of an ordinary negative precept. In the first case, he violates the law stated in Deuteronomy 25:4: "You shall not muzzle the ox, when he treads out the corn". In the second case, he is guilty of driving together two animals of different species (see Deuteronomy 22:10: "You shall not plow with an ox and an ass together"). [4]**Resh Lakish** disagreed and **said:** In both cases, **he is exempt** from punishment. The Gemara explains the reasoning behind this difference of opinion: [5]**Rabbi Yoḥanan said** that **he is liable, because** he maintains that **the movement of the lips** when a person speaks **is** considered **an action.** There is a general rule that punishment is not administered for the transgression of a Torah prohibition unless the transgression involves a physical act. According to Rabbi Yoḥanan, speech qualifies as an act punishable by lashes. [6]**Resh Lakish,** however, **said** that **he is exempt, because** he maintains that the mere **use of one's voice is not** considered **an action.** Thus, we see that Rabbi Yoḥanan maintains that speech is regarded as an action, and so it follows that false conspiring witness should indeed be liable for a sin-offering.

אֶלָּא אָמַר רָבָא [7]**Rather, Rava said: False, conspiring witnesses are different, because** their liability depends upon **what they** claim to **have seen.** Even if speech is an action, seeing is certainly not an action, so the giving of false testimony does not involve a physical act.

תָּנוּ רַבָּנַן [8]**Our Rabbis taught** a related Baraita: **"A *ba'al ov* is someone who** raises up the dead and makes him **speak from between the joints** of his body **or from between his elbows,** i.e., from his armpit. [9]**A *yid'oni***

הוּא? [1]וְהָא אִיתְּמַר: חֲסָמָהּ בְּקוֹל [2]וְהִנְהִיגָהּ בְּקוֹל, [3]רַבִּי יוֹחָנָן אָמַר: חַיָּיב. [4]וְרֵישׁ לָקִישׁ אָמַר: פָּטוּר. [5]רַבִּי יוֹחָנָן אָמַר: חַיָּיב, עֲקִימַת פִּיו הָוֵי מַעֲשֶׂה. [6]רֵישׁ לָקִישׁ אָמַר: פָּטוּר, עֲקִימַת פִּיו לָא הָוֵי מַעֲשֶׂה. [7]אֶלָּא אָמַר רָבָא: שָׁאנֵי עֵדִים זוֹמְמִין, הוֹאִיל וְיֶשְׁנָן בִּרְאִיָּה. [8]תָּנוּ רַבָּנַן: "בַּעַל אוֹב — זֶה הַמְדַבֵּר בֵּין הַפְּרָקִים וּמִבֵּין אַצִּילֵי יָדָיו. [9]יִדְּעוֹנִי — זֶה

LITERAL TRANSLATION

[1]But surely it was stated: [If] he muzzled it with [his] voice, [2]or [if] he drove it with [his] voice, [3]Rabbi Yoḥanan said: He is liable. [4]And Resh Lakish said: He is exempt. [5]Rabbi Yoḥanan said: He is liable, [because] the movement (lit., "curving") of his mouth is an action. [6]Resh Lakish said: He is exempt, [because] the movement of his mouth is not an action.

[7]Rather, Rava said: False conspiring witnesses are different, since they are with vision.

[8]Our Rabbis taught: "A *ba'al ov* — that is the one who speaks [from] between his joints or [from] between his elbows. [9]A *yid'oni* — that

RASHI

חסמה בקול — לפרה דשה, וכשרוצה לאכול חסמה בקולו. **והנהיגה בקול** — מנהג בכלאים דחייב משום "לא תחרוש בשור ובחמור" (דברים כב). **בראייה** — עיקר חיובא בא על ידי הראייה, שמעידין שראו, וראיה לית בה מעשה. **מבין הפרקים** — מעלה את המת ויושב לו באחד מבין פרקי העצמות של מכשף, כגון על פרקי אצבעותיו או על פרקי ברכיו.

NOTES

הוֹאִיל וְיֶשְׁנָן בִּרְאִיָּה **Since they are with vision.** Our commentary follows *Rashi* and others who had the reading בִּרְאִיָּה, "with vision." But most of the Geonim and Rishonim had the reading בְּאִיָּה or בְּאִין, Aramaic terms for "yes." According to that reading, the passage must be understood in an altogether different manner. Rava distinguishes here between sounds which can be made without moving one's lips and sounds which can only be made by moving one's lips. Words can be uttered without moving one's lips, particularly if one avoids the labials — *bet, vav, mem,* and *peh.* A witness can offer his testimony without moving his lips, for after the first witness gives his testimony, we can ask the second witness if that is the way the event occurred, and he can answer אִיָּה or אִין, "yes." Since a false, conspiring witness can become liable for testimony offered in this manner — without moving his lips, it follows that

HALAKHAH

חֲסָמָהּ בְּקוֹל וְהִנְהִיגָהּ בְּקוֹל **If he muzzled it with his voice, or if he drove it with his voice.** "If someone prevents an animal from eating by speaking to it, or if he drives a pair of animals of different species by speaking to them, he is liable for flogging," following Rabbi Yoḥanan who maintains that even speech is considered an act that is liable for punishment. (*Shulḥan Arukh, Ḥoshen Mishpat* 338:3; *Yoreh De'ah* 297:11.)

בַּעַל אוֹב וְיִדְּעוֹנִי ***Ba'al ov* and *yid'oni.*** "A *ba'al ov* burns incense, waves a myrtle branch, and whispers in a low tone, so that the person who came to consult with him thinks that someone else is speaking with him and answering his questions from below the ground. Or else he takes a skull, burns incense before it, and whispers in such a way that the other person thinks that a voice is answering him from under the *ba'al ov's* armpit. A *yid'oni*

הַמַּנִּיחַ עֶצֶם יָדוּעַ בְּפִיו, וְהוּא מְדַבֵּר מֵאֵלָיו״.
[1]מֵיתִיבִי: ״וְהָיָה כְּאוֹב מֵאֶרֶץ קוֹלֵךְ״. [2]מַאי לָאו דְּמִשְׁתָּעֵי כִּי אוֹרְחֵיהּ?
[3]לָא, דְּסָלֵיק וְיָתֵיב בֵּין הַפְּרָקִים וּמִשְׁתָּעֵי.
[4]תָּא שְׁמַע: ״וַתֹּאמֶר הָאִשָּׁה אֶל שָׁאוּל אֱלֹהִים רָאִיתִי עֹלִים מִן הָאָרֶץ״. [5]מַאי לָאו דְּמִשְׁתָּעֵי כִּי אוֹרְחֵיהּ?
[6]לָא, דְּיָתֵיב בֵּין הַפְּרָקִים וּמִשְׁתָּעֵי.
[7]תָּנוּ רַבָּנַן: ״בַּעַל אוֹב, אֶחָד הַמַּעֲלֶה בִּזְכוּרוֹ וְאֶחָד הַנִּשְׁאָל בְּגוּלְגּוֹלֶת. [8]מַה בֵּין זֶה לָזֶה? [9]מַעֲלֶה בִּזְכוּרוֹ אֵינוֹ עוֹלֶה כְּדַרְכּוֹ, וְאֵינוֹ עוֹלֶה בַּשַּׁבָּת. [10]נִשְׁאָל בְּגוּלְגּוֹלֶת, עוֹלֶה כְּדַרְכּוֹ, וְעוֹלֶה בַּשַּׁבָּת״.

TRANSLATION AND COMMENTARY

is someone who places the bone of a certain animal called **a** ***yadu'a*** **into his mouth, and** the bone **speaks by itself."**

מֵיתִיבִי [1]**An objection was raised** from the verse (Isaiah 29:4): **"And your voice shall be, as of a medium** [*ke'ov*], **out of the ground."** [2]**Does this not** imply that in the case of an *ov,* the dead **speaks in the usual manner,** from the ground, and not from his armpit or any other part of the medium's body?

לָא [3]The Gemara answers: **No,** the verse means to say that the dead person **rises** from his grave **and sits between the joints** of the *ba'al ov's* body **and speaks,** and his voice is low because he is no longer among the living.

תָּא שְׁמַע [4]The Gemara now raises another objection: **Come and hear** what is stated in the verse dealing with the medium with whom Saul consulted (I Samuel 28:13): **"And the woman said to Saul, I saw a godlike man rising out of the earth."** [5]**Does this not** imply that in the case of an *ov,* the dead **speaks in the usual manner,** i.e., the *ov* makes the dead speak from the grave?

לָא [6]The Gemara answers: **No,** here, too, the verse means to say that the dead person **rises** from his grave **and sits between the joints** of the *ba'al ov's* body, **and speaks.**

תָּנוּ רַבָּנַן [7]**Our Rabbis taught** another Baraita dealing with a *ba'al ov*: "A person is liable as **a** ***ba'al ov,*** **whether he raises** the dead **with a** magical **incantation, or he consults** with a **skull** that is lying before him. [8]**What is** the difference **between this** type of *ba'al ov* **and that** one? [9]**If** the *ba'al ov* **raises** the dead **with a** magical **incantation,** the dead person **does not rise** up **in his usual manner,** but rather upside down, **and** furthermore **he does not rise** up **on the Sabbath.** [10]But **if** the *ba'al ov* **consults** with **the skull, he rises** up **in his usual manner, and he rises** up even **on the Sabbath."**

LITERAL TRANSLATION

is the one who places the bone of a *yadu'a* in his mouth, and it speaks by itself."

[1]They raised an objection: "And your voice shall be, as of a medium, out of the ground." [2]Is it not that it speaks in its usual manner?

[3]No. That he rises and sits between the joints and speaks.

[4]Come [and] hear: "And the woman said to Saul, I saw a godlike man rising out of the earth." [5]Is it not that it spoke in its usual manner?

[6]No. That he rose and sat between the joints and spoke.

[7]Our Rabbis taught: "A *Ba'al ov,* whether he raises him with an incantation, or he consults a skull. [8]What is between this and that? [9][If] he raises him with an incantation, he does not rise in his usual manner, and he does not rise on the Sabbath. [10][If] he consults a skull, he rises in his usual manner, and he rises on the Sabbath."

RASHI

ידוע – שם חיה. כי אורחיה – מתוך קברו, ומתוך כך קולו נמוך. לא דסליק ויתיב בין הפרקים – ומיהו קולו נמוך לפי שאין בו חיותא. בזכורו – מעלה ומושיב את המת על זכרותו. בגולגולת – המוטלת מן המת לארץ ועונה מה ששואלין אותו על ידי כישוף. אינו עולה בדרכו – אלא רגליו למעלה. עולה בדרכו – ולא סליק למיתב בין הפרקים.

BACKGROUND

זְכוּרוֹ **Incantation.** *Tosafot* write that this is the name of a type of sorcerer in Aramaic, and it is not connected at all with זַכְרוּת, the male organ, as *Rashi* suggests. Others have suggested that it derives from the Akkadian *zakaru,* meaning "to curse, to enchant."

NOTES

the movement of the witness's lips is not an integral part of his transgression, and so his offense is regarded as a transgression that does not involve an action (*Geonim, Rif, Ra'avad, Ramah, Ran,* and others).

הַמַּנִּיחַ עֶצֶם יָדוּעַ **One who places the bone of a** ***yadu'a.*** According to most Rishonim, a *yadu'a* is a certain type of beast. *Rambam* understands that it is a type of bird.

נִשְׁאָל בְּגוּלְגֹּלֶת **He consults a skull.** Some of the Geonim suggest that the word גּוּלְגּוֹלֶת, translated here as "skull," be understood in the sense of גַּלְגַּל, "sphere," according to which the Gemara is referring to someone who divines with a stone or crystal ball.

HALAKHAH

takes the bone of a bird called a *yadu'a,* places it in his mouth, burns incense, and does other things until he falls to the ground in a trance and speaks of matters that will occur in the future." (*Rambam, Sefer Mada, Hilkhot Avodah Zarah* 6:1-2.)

TRANSLATION AND COMMENTARY

עוֹלֶה [1]The Gemara asks: How can the Baraita say that if the *ba'al ov* consults with the skull, **he rises** up in the usual manner? [2]**To where does he rise?** [3]**Surely** the skull is already **lying** there **in front of him!**

אֶלָּא [4]**Rather, say** as follows: If the *ba'al ov* consults with the skull, the dead person **answers in his usual manner,** and not from between the joints of the *ba'al ov's* body, [5]**and he answers** even **on the Sabbath.**

וְאַף שְׁאֵלָה זוֹ [6]Having stated that a dead person does not rise up on the Sabbath, the Gemara now relates that **the wicked Turnusrufus,** the Roman commander in Eretz Israel in the days of the Hadrianic persecutions, **also asked Rabbi Akiva this question.** [7]**He said to him: "What is special about this day,** the Sabbath, **over other days,** that you treat it differently?" [8]Rabbi Akiva turned the question around and **said to him: "And what is special about this man** — you, Turnusrufus — **over other men,** that you are their commander?" [9]Turnusrufus **explained:** "**My master** — the Roman emperor — **desired** that I be commander." [10]Rabbi Akiva responded with a similar argument: "Regarding **the Sabbath too, my Master** — God in Heaven — **desired** that it be sanctified." [11]Turnusrufus **said to him: "I mean** to **ask you** as **follows: Who says that now it is the Sabbath?"** [12]Rabbi Akiva **said to him:** "First, **the Sambatyon river** which flows six days of the week and rests on the seventh day **proves** which day is the Sabbath. [13]Second, a ***ba'al ov*** who can raise up the dead six days of the week, but not on the seventh, **proves** which day is the Sabbath. [14]And third, **the grave of your father** which issues smoke six days of the week, because your father is burning in Gehinom, **proves** which day is the Sabbath. Your father's grave [15]**does not issue smoke on the Sabbath,** because even the sinners in Gehinom are allowed to rest on the Sabbath." [16]Turnusrufus **said to him: "You have disgraced** my father, **you have** publicly **humiliated him, and you have cursed him** by saying that he is burning in Gehinom."

שׁוֹאֵל אוֹב [17]The Gemara raises another problem: The *sho'el ov* that is mentioned in the verse (Deuteronomy 18:11) appears to be **the same as the "necromancer"** [*doresh el hametim*] that is mentioned in that very same verse!

[1]עוֹלֶה? [2]לְהֵיכָא סָלֵיק? [3]הָא קַמֵּיהּ מַנַּח!

[4]אֶלָּא, אֵימָא: עוֹנֶה כְּדַרְכּוֹ, [5]וְעוֹנֶה בַּשַּׁבָּת.

[6]וְאַף שְׁאֵלָה זוֹ שָׁאַל טוּרְנוּסְרוּפוּס הָרָשָׁע אֶת רַבִּי עֲקִיבָא. [7]אָמַר לוֹ: "וּמַה יּוֹם מִיּוֹמַיִם"? [8]אָמַר לוֹ: "וּמַה גֶּבֶר מִגּוּבְרִין"? [9]אָמַר לֵיהּ: "דְּמָרֵי צָבֵי". [10]"שַׁבָּת נַמִי, דְּמָרֵי צָבֵי". [11]אֲמַר לֵיהּ: "הָכִי קָאָמִינָא לָךְ: מִי יֵימַר דְּהָאִידָנָא שַׁבְּתָא"? [12]אָמַר לוֹ: "נְהַר סַבַּטְיוֹן יוֹכִיחַ, [13]בַּעַל אוֹב יוֹכִיחַ, [14]קִבְרוֹ שֶׁל אָבִיו יוֹכִיחַ, [15]שֶׁאֵין מַעֲלֶה עָשָׁן בַּשַּׁבָּת". [16]אָמַר לוֹ: "בִּיזִיתוֹ, בִּיַּישְׁתּוֹ, וְקִילַּלְתּוֹ".

[17]שׁוֹאֵל אוֹב, הַיְינוּ "וְדֹרֵשׁ אֶל הַמֵּתִים"!

LITERAL TRANSLATION

[1]He rises! [2]To where does he rise? [3]Surely he lies in front of him!

[4]Rather, say: He answers in his usual manner, [5]and he answers on the Sabbath.

[6]And this question too the wicked Turnusrufus asked Rabbi Akiva. [7]He said to him: "And what is [special about] this day over [other] days?" [8]He said to him: "And what is [special about] this man over [other] men?" [9]He said to him: "My master desired it." [10]"The Sabbath too, my Master desired it." [11]He said to him: "Thus I say to you: Who says that now it is the Sabbath?" [12]He said to him: "The Sambatyon river will prove [it]. [13]*Ba'al ov* will prove it. [14]The grave of his father will prove it, [15]for it does not issue smoke on the Sabbath." [16]He said to him: "You disgraced him, you humiliated him, and you cursed him."

[17]*Sho'el ov* — that is a "necromancer"!

RASHI

מה היום מיומים — למה תחשב יום שבת יותר משאר ימים. **ומה גבר מגוברין** — מה לאיש כמוך להיות שר וגדול מכל אנשים. **דמרי צבי** — אדני חפץ לגדלני, המלך קיסר המשילני. **שבת נמי דמרי צבי** — הקדוש ברוך הוא חפץ והזהיר על כבודו. **דמי יימר דהאידנא שבתא היא** — ודילמא אחד משאר ימים הוא שבת. **נהר סבטיון יוכיח** — נהר אחד של אבנים, ובכל ימות השבת שוטף והולך, וביום השבת שוקט ונח. **בעל אוב יוכיח** — שאינו עולה בשבת. **קברו של אביו** — דטורנוסרופוס כל ימות השבת היה מעלה עשן שהיה נדון ונשרף, ובשבת פושעי גיהנם שובתין. **ביזיתו ביישתו קללתו** — הך קללה אינה אלא גדוף, וכן היה לשונם כמו (מלכים א ב) "קללה נמרצת" שלא היה שם קללה אלא גדוף. **היינו דורש אל המתים** — ולמה נכתבו שניהם במקום אחד?

LANGUAGE

טוּרְנוּסְרוּפוּס Turnusrufus. This name comes from the Greek τυραννος, *Tyrannos*, "a tyrant." The real name of the Roman governor was Tineus Rufus, but he was given the pejorative nickname of Turnus because of his tyranny. Apparently the behavior of this governor was one of the reasons leading to the Bar Kokhba revolt.

סַבַּטְיוֹן Sambatyon. This derives from the Greek Σαββάτιον, *sabation*, meaning sabbatical, pertaining to the Sabbath. This river, also called Sambatyon, appears often in Midrashim and Aggadah folk tales. It is also mentioned by Josephus, who claims that such a stream existed in the mountains of Lebanon, and by the Roman author Pliny. Since some legends state that the ten lost tribes of Israel are across the Sambatyon, it has been identified with a river in the Caucasus mountains or in Afghanistan.

NOTES

וְאַף שְׁאֵלָה זוֹ And this question too. The word "too" is used here, because as we learn from the Midrash, Turnusrufus asked Rabbi Akiva a number of questions, this being one of them (*Ri Berlin*).

TRANSLATION AND COMMENTARY

דּוֹרֵשׁ לְמֵתִים [1]The Gemara explains: **The necromancer** mentioned in that verse refers to somebody altogether different, **as it was taught** in a Baraita: [2]"The verse which mentions **'a necromancer'** refers to **someone who** undergoes privations and **fasts and goes and sleeps in a cemetery so that an unclean spirit might rest upon him,** and he can hear what the dead are saying. [3]**When Rabbi Akiva reached this verse, he would cry** and say: [4]**If someone** undergoes privations and **fasts so that an unclean spirit might rest upon him,** and he succeeds, [5]and **the unclean spirit** indeed **rests upon him,** [6]then it stands to reason that **if someone** undergoes privations and **fasts so that a clean spirit** — a prophetic spirit — **might rest upon him,** [7]**all the more so,** should he succeed, and a clean spirit should rest upon him. [8]**But what can I do, for our sins are responsible for** the fact that a clean and holy spirit does not rest upon us, [9]**as the verse states** (Isaiah 59:2): **'But your iniquities have made a separation between you and your God,** and your sins have hid his face from you, that he will not hear.'"

אָמַר רָבָא [10]Commenting on this verse, **Rava said: If the righteous people wanted, they could create the world, as the verse states: "But your iniquities have made a separation** between you and your God." It is only man's sins that separate him from God.

רָבָא בְּרָא גַּבְרָא [11]To illustrate, the Gemara relates that **Rava** once **created a person,** after having studied the Book of Creation and learned to combine the letters of the divine name. [12]Rava **sent** his creation **to Rabbi Zera.** [13]Rabbi Zera **talked to him, but he was unable to answer,** for he was missing the faculty of speech. [14]Rabbi Zera **said to him: "You were created by** one of **the** Torah **scholars** who mastered the secrets of creation. **Return to your dust."**

[1]דּוֹרֵשׁ לְמֵתִים, כִּדְתַנְיָא: [2]"'וְדֹרֵשׁ אֶל הַמֵּתִים' — זֶה הַמַּרְעִיב עַצְמוֹ וְהוֹלֵךְ וְלָן בְּבֵית הַקְּבָרוֹת כְּדֵי שֶׁתִּשְׁרֶה עָלָיו רוּחַ טוּמְאָה. [3]וּכְשֶׁהָיָה רַבִּי עֲקִיבָא מַגִּיעַ לְמִקְרָא זֶה הָיָה בּוֹכֶה, [4]וּמָה הַמַּרְעִיב עַצְמוֹ כְּדֵי שֶׁתִּשְׁרֶה עָלָיו רוּחַ טוּמְאָה — [5]שׁוֹרָה עָלָיו רוּחַ טוּמְאָה, [6]הַמַּרְעִיב עַצְמוֹ כְּדֵי שֶׁתִּשְׁרֶה עָלָיו רוּחַ טָהֳרָה, [7]עַל אַחַת כַּמָּה וְכַמָּה. [8]אֲבָל מָה אֶעֱשֶׂה שֶׁעֲוֹנוֹתֵינוּ גָּרְמוּ לָנוּ, [9]שֶׁנֶּאֱמַר: 'כִּי [אִם] עֲוֹנוֹתֵיכֶם הָיוּ מַבְדִּלִים בֵּינֵיכֶם לְבֵין אֱלֹהֵיכֶם'".

[10]אָמַר רָבָא: אִי בָּעוּ צַדִּיקֵי בָּרוּ עָלְמָא, שֶׁנֶּאֱמַר: "כִּי עֲוֹנוֹתֵיכֶם הָיוּ מַבְדִּלִים וגו'".

[11]רָבָא בְּרָא גַּבְרָא, [12]שְׁדַרֵיהּ לְקַמֵּיהּ דְּרַבִּי זֵירָא. [13]הֲוָה קָא מִשְׁתָּעֵי בַּהֲדֵיהּ, וְלָא הֲוָה קָא מַהֲדַר לֵיהּ. [14]אֲמַר לֵיהּ: "מִן חַבְרַיָּא אַתְּ, הֲדַר לְעַפְרָיךְ".

LITERAL TRANSLATION

[1]A necromancer, as it was taught: [2]"'And a necromancer' — that is one who starves himself and goes and sleeps in a cemetery so that an unclean spirit might rest upon him. [3]And when Rabbi Akiva would reach this verse, he would cry. [4]If someone who starves himself so that an unclean spirit might rest upon him, [5]an unclean spirit rests upon him, [6]someone who starves himself so that a clean spirit might rest upon him, [7]all the more so. [8]But what can I do, for our sins have caused us, [9]as it is stated: 'But your iniquities have made a separation between you and your God.'"

[10]Rava said: If the righteous people wanted, they could create the world, as it is stated: "But your iniquities have made a separation, etc."

[11]Rava created a person, [12][and] sent him before Rabbi Zera. [13]He talked to him, but he did not answer. [14]He said to him: "You are [a creation of] the scholars. Return to your dust."

RASHI

שתשרה רוח טומאה עליו — שד של בית הקברות יהא אוהבו ומסייעו בכשפיו. **המרעיב עצמו כדי שתשרה עליו רוח טהרה** — נבואת שכינה. **על אחת כמה וכמה** — שהיא המדה נותנת שעל ידי תענית ובקשה תשרה עליו שכינה, דהא מדה טובה יתירה על מדת פורענות, ואנו צועקין על כך ואין אנו נענין, אבל מה אעשה וכו'. **אי בעו צדיקי** — להיות נקיים מכל עון. **הוו ברו עלמא שנאמר כי אם עונותיכם היו מבדילים** — הא אם לא היו בהם עונות אין כאן הבדלה. **ברא גברא** — על ידי ספר יצירה שלמדו צרוף אותיות של שם. **ולא היה מהדר ליה** — שלא היה בו דבור. **מן חבריא** — הנבראים על ידי החברים אתה.

NOTES

עֲוֹנוֹתֵיכֶם הָיוּ מַבְדִּלִים **But your iniquities have made a separation.** *Ramah* explains that were it not for man's sins, the righteous could ask for whatever they wanted, and God would fulfill their every request, even creating for them a new world. It is only because of man's sins that a separation was erected between God and the righteous, so that he no longer listens to all their prayers.

HALAKHAH

דּוֹרֵשׁ לְמֵתִים **Necromancer.** "A necromancer who fasts and sleeps in a cemetery so that an unclean spirit will rest upon him and the dead will appear to him and answer his questions is liable for lashes." (*Shulḥan Arukh, Yoreh De'ah* 179:13.)

TRANSLATION AND COMMENTARY

רַב חֲנִינָא [1]It was further related that **Rav Ḥanina and Rav Oshaya would sit every Friday and engage in the study of the Book of Creation.** [2]These two scholars **would create for themselves a third-grown calf, and eat it.**

תָּנוּ רַבָּנַן [3]**Our Rabbis taught** the following Baraita: "Among the practitioners of magic and divination, the Torah mentions the *'me'onen'* (Deuteronomy 18:10). [4]**Rabbi Shimon says: That is someone who passes seven kinds of semen** from seven different animals **over his eyes** for magical purposes. [5]**The Sages say:** The *me'onen* **is someone who captures** other people's **eyes,** deluding them by optical deception into thinking that he is endowed with magical powers. [6]**Rabbi Akiva says:** The *me'onen* **is someone who calculates the times and hours,** [7]**and says: Today is a good** day **to embark** on a journey. [8]**Tomorrow is a good** day **to purchase** merchandise. [9]**The year before the Sabbatical year the wheat is usually good.** [10]**Pulses that are uprooted,** rather than cut, **do not go bad** or rot."

תָּנוּ רַבָּנַן [11]**Our Rabbis taught** another Baraita: "Among the practitioners of magic and divination, the Torah mentions the *'menaḥesh,'* the diviner who predicts a person's fortune based on an omen. [12]The *menaḥesh* **is someone who says** that certain

[1]רַב חֲנִינָא וְרַב אוֹשַׁעְיָא הֲווּ יָתְבִי כָּל מַעֲלֵי שַׁבְּתָא וְעָסְקִי בְּסֵפֶר יְצִירָה, [2]וּמִיבְרוּ לְהוּ עִיגְלָא תִּילְתָּא, וְאָכְלִי לֵיהּ. [3]תָּנוּ רַבָּנַן: "'מְעוֹנֵן'. [4]רַבִּי שִׁמְעוֹן אוֹמֵר: זֶה הַמַּעֲבִיר שִׁבְעָה מִינֵי זְכוּר עַל הָעַיִן. [5]וַחֲכָמִים אוֹמְרִים: זֶה הָאוֹחֵז אֶת הָעֵינַיִם. [6]רַבִּי עֲקִיבָא אוֹמֵר: זֶה הַמְחַשֵּׁב עִתִּים וְשָׁעוֹת, [7]וְאוֹמֵר: הַיּוֹם יָפֶה לָצֵאת. [8]לְמָחָר יָפֶה לִיקַּח. [9]לִמוּדֵי עַרְבֵי שְׁבִיעִיּוֹת חִטִּין יָפוֹת. [10]עִיקּוּרֵי קִטְנִיּוֹת מִהְיוֹת רָעוֹת". [11]תָּנוּ רַבָּנַן: "'מְנַחֵשׁ'. [12]זֶה

LITERAL TRANSLATION

[1]Rav Ḥanina and Rav Oshaya sat every Friday and engaged in [the study of] the Book of Creation, [2]and they created for themselves a third-grown calf, and ate it.

[3]Our Rabbis taught: "'*Me'onen.*' [4]Rabbi Shimon says: That is the one who passes seven kinds of semen over his eye. [5]And the Sages say: That is the one who captures the eyes. [6]Rabbi Akiva says: That is the one who calculates the times and hours, [7]and says: Today is good to go out. [8]Tomorrow is good to purchase. [9]Usually [in] the year before the Sabbatical year the wheat is good. [10]Uprooted pulses do not go bad."

[11]Our Rabbis taught: "'*Menaḥesh.*' [12]That is

RASHI

עיגלא תילתא – גדול כאלו הגיע לשליש שניו וגמרה גדילתו, דהכי שביחי ומעלי למיכל, כמו (בבא מציעא סח,א) ומגדלין אותן עד שיהו משולשין. לישנא אחרינא – שהיה טוב ובעל טעם כאילו הוא שליש לבטן. **שבעה מיני זכור** – שכבת זרע משבע בריות, ומעביר על עיניו ועושה כשפים. **אוחז את העינים** – אוחז וסוגר עיני הבריות ומראה להם כאילו עושה דברים של פלא, והוא אינו עושה כלום. **המחשב עתים ושעות** – לשון מעונן כמו בעל עונות, שמבחין את עונה ואומר היום יפה לצאת לדרך ויצליח, למחר יפה ליקח מקח וישתכר בו הלוקחו. **למודי ערבי שביעיות** – כלומר, ערב שביעית למדין ורגילין להיות חטין יפות. **עקרי קטניות מהיות רעות** – כלומר, העוקר קטנית ואינו קוצרן שוב אינן מתליעות ואין מרקיבות.

NOTES

עִיגְלָא תִּילְתָּא **A third-grown calf.** This Aramaic expression is equivalent to the Hebrew עֶגְלָה שְׁלִישִׁיָּה. Some say that Rav Ḥanina and Rav Oshaya would create for themselves a calf whose meat was as tasty as that of a calf which is its mother's third-born. Or else they created for themselves a calf that had already reached the size of a three-year old calf (*Geonim, Ramah*).

עִיקּוּרֵי קִטְנִיּוֹת מִהְיוֹת רָעוֹת **Uprooted pulses do not go bad.** *Arukh* understands this to mean that uprooting some of the pulses is a good sign for the rest of the pulses that they

HALAKHAH

מְעוֹנֵן ***Me'onen.*** "A *me'onen* is one who calculates the time and hours, and says that a certain day, or month, or year, is good or bad for a certain activity. Anyone who conducts himself in accordance with what he was told by a *me'onen,* is liable for lashes," following Rabbi Akiva (who does not disagree with the Sages, but only adds to them, or perhaps all agree with him; *Kesef Mishneh*). (*Rambam, Sefer Mada, Hilkhot Avodah Zarah* 11:8.)

הָאוֹחֵז אֶת הָעֵינַיִם **One who captures the eyes.** "Someone who performs an optical illusion, and makes people think that he performed magic, is considered a *me'onen,* and is liable for lashes. There is a contradiction between two of *Rambam's* rulings, for in one place he says that someone who performs an optical illusion is liable for lashes, and in a second place he say that such a person is exempt. Some suggest that *Rambam* means that he is exempt from lashes for sorcery, but liable for lashes for being a *me'onen*; (see *Kesef Mishneh* and *Leḥem Mishneh*). Some distinguish between an optical illusion involving foretelling the future, which is punishable by lashes, and an optical illusion involving magic, which is not punishable by lashes (*Leḥem Mishneh*). *Rambam's* grandson, *Rabbi Yehoshua* (cited by *Kesef Mishneh*), distinguishes between an optical illusion which resembles a supernatural act, which is punishable by lashes, and an optical illusion which appears like a perfectly natural act, which is not punishable by lashes." (*Rambam, Sefer Mada, Hilkhot Avodah Zarah* 11:9;15; *Shulḥan Arukh, Yoreh De'ah* 179:15.)

מְנַחֵשׁ ***Menaḥesh.*** "A *menaḥesh* is one who predicts the future based on an omen, such as someone whose bread

הָאוֹמֵר: [1]'פִּתּוֹ נָפְלָה מִפִּיו', 'מַקְלוֹ נָפְלָה מִיָּדוֹ', 'בְּנוֹ קוֹרֵא לוֹ מֵאַחֲרָיו', 'עוֹרֵב קוֹרֵא לוֹ', 'צְבִי הִפְסִיקוֹ בַּדֶּרֶךְ', 'נָחָשׁ מִימִינוֹ', וְ'שׁוּעָל מִשְּׂמֹאלוֹ', [66A] [2]'אַל תַּתְחִיל בִּי', [3]'שַׁחֲרִית הוּא', [4]'רֹאשׁ חוֹדֶשׁ הוּא' [5]'מוֹצָאֵי שַׁבָּת הוּא'״

[6]תָּנוּ רַבָּנַן: ״'לֹא תְנַחֲשׁוּ וְלֹא תְעוֹנֵנוּ' [7]כְּגוֹן אֵלּוּ הַמְנַחֲשִׁים בְּחוּלְדָּה, בְּעוֹפוֹת וּבְדָגִים״.

משנה [8]הַמְחַלֵּל אֶת הַשַּׁבָּת בְּדָבָר שֶׁחַיָּיבִין עַל זְדוֹנוֹ כָּרֵת [9]וְעַל שִׁגְגָתוֹ חַטָּאת.

גמרא [10]מִכְּלָל דְּאִיכָּא מִידֵּי דְּחִילּוּל שַׁבָּת הָוֵי, [11]וְאֵין חַיָּיבִין לֹא עַל שִׁגְגָתוֹ חַטָּאת, [12]וְלֹא עַל זְדוֹנוֹ כָּרֵת, [13]מַאי

LITERAL TRANSLATION

the one who says: [1]'His bread fell from his mouth,' 'his staff fell from his hand,' 'his son calls him from behind,' 'a raven calls him,' 'a deer caused him to stop on the road,' 'a snake on his right, or a fox on his left,' [66A] [2]'do not start with me,' [3]'it is morning,' [4]'it is the New Moon,' [5]'it is Saturday night.'"

[6]Our Rabbis taught: "'You shall not divine, nor observe times,' — [7]like those who divine with a weasel, with birds, or with fish."

MISHNAH [8]Someone who desecrates the Sabbath [by doing] something for which intentional violation is liable for excision [9]and for which unintentional violation [is liable for] a sin-offering.

GEMARA [10]This implies that there is something that is a desecration of the Sabbath, [11]but one is not liable for a sin-offering for its unintentional violation, [12]nor for excision for its intentional violation. [13]What is

TRANSLATION AND COMMENTARY

omens portend evil. [1]For example: **'His bread fell from his mouth,' 'his staff fell from his hand,' 'his son calls him from behind,' 'a raven calls him,' 'a deer caused him to stop on the road,' 'a snake on his right, or a fox on his left.'** [66A] [2]Or else, the *menaḥesh* says to someone who comes to collect money from him: **'Do not start with me** for that is an evil omen,' [3]**'it is morning,** and it portends evil to start the day with a payment,' [4]**'it is the New Moon,** and it is a bad sign to start the month with a loss,' [5]**'it is Saturday night,** and I do not wish to begin the week losing money.'"

תָּנוּ רַבָּנַן [6]**Our Rabbis taught** a related Baraita: "The verse states (Leviticus 19:26): **'You shall not divine, nor observe times.'** [7]This refers to **those who,** before embarking on a journey or starting an activity, **divine** evil or good fortune **with a weasel, with birds, or with fish."**

MISHNAH הַמְחַלֵּל אֶת הַשַּׁבָּת [8]We learned earlier in the chapter (53a) that **someone who desecrates the Sabbath** is liable to death by stoning. The Sabbath desecrator is only put to death if he was properly warned not to desecrate the Sabbath, and there were two witnesses to his offense. He is only put to death if he desecrated the Sabbath in such a way that, had he **intentionally violated** the Sabbath law without a proper warning, or not in the presence of two witnesses, **he would have been liable for excision,** [9]**and** had he **unintentionally violated** the law, **he would have been liable for a sin-offering.**

GEMARA מִכְּלָל [10]The Gemara notes: The Mishnah's formulation **implies that there is a Sabbath desecration,** [11]regarding which the offender **is not liable for a sin-offering if he committed** the offense **unintentionally,** [12]**nor** is he liable **for excision if he committed** the offense **intentionally.** Otherwise there would be no reason for the Mishnah to specify that a person is only punishable by stoning for Sabbath desecration, if he committed an offense for which one could become liable for excision and a sin-offering. [13]The Gemara asks:

RASHI

פתו נפלה מפיו – צריך לדאג היום מהיזק. **נחש בא מימינו או שועל משמאלו** – סימן רע הוא לו. **צבי הפסיקו** – שהיה הולך ממזרח למערב, והצבי הולך מצפון לדרום, והפסיק דרכו. **אל תתחיל בי** – כשבא הגבאי לגבות מס ממנו או קיצת העיר, אומר לו: בבקשה ממך אל תתחיל בי להיות ראשון בדבר הפסד, שסימן רע הוא לו. **שחרית הוא** – שהיה תובע ממנו חוב, אמר לו: שחרית הוא, ולא אתחיל תחלת מעשה היום בפירעון. **ראש חדש הוא** – המתן לי עד מחר. **מוצאי שבת הוא** – ראשון לימי השבוע. **המנחשין** – כשיוצאין לדרך או כשמתחילין בשום דבר. **משנה המחלל את השבת** – דחשיב ליה תנא בנסקלין, כגון שחללו במלאכה גמורה. **שחייבין על זדונו כרת ועל שגגתו חטאת** – כגון דבר שיש בו מעשה ומלאכת מחשבת, ולא המתעסק.

NOTES

will not go bad. *Ramah* explains that in years when pulses are uprooted and thus cease to be (מְהֵיוֹת), the wheat crop will go bad. *Yalkut* has the reading: מְחֵיוֹת רָעוֹת, "wild animals." Uprooted pulses are an effective deterrent against wild animals.

HALAKHAH

fell from his mouth, or whose staff fell from his hand, and he says that those are bad signs for the future. Anyone who conducts himself in accordance with such an omen is liable for lashes." (*Rambam, Sefer Mada, Hilkhot Avodah Zarah* 11:4; *Shulḥan Arukh, Yoreh De'ah* 179:3.)

לֹא תְנַחֲשׁוּ **You shall not divine.** "One is forbidden to rely on omens, or to divine with a weasel, birds, the stars, or the like." (*Shulḥan Arukh, Yoreh De'ah* 179:3.)

הַמְחַלֵּל אֶת הַשַּׁבָּת **Someone who desecrates the Sabbath.** "If someone desecrated the Sabbath by performing a

TRANSLATION AND COMMENTARY

What is that case? [1]The Gemara explains: One example is crossing the **Sabbath limit,** the distance that a person is permitted to walk on the Sabbath, **and according to Rabbi Akiva,** who maintains that in addition to the Rabbinical ordinance restricting movement to 2,000 cubits past the city limits, there is a Sabbath limit by Torah law, which is approximately 12 miles in every direction. Going past this limit is forbidden by Torah law, but the transgressor is not liable to death by stoning, for excision, or a sin-offering, for those are only imposed upon someone who performs one of the thirty-nine forbidden labors. [2]Another example is **kindling** a fire on the Sabbath, **and according to Rabbi Yose,** who maintains that the prohibition against kindling a fire on the Sabbath was singled out from the other categories of labor (in Exodus 35:3) in order to teach that its transgression is a violation of a plain negative commandment, and therefore not punishable by stoning or excision, the usual punishments for Sabbath desecration.

MISHNAH הַמְקַלֵּל אָבִיו וְאִמּוֹ [3]If **someone cursed his father or his mother,** he **is not liable** to death by stoning **unless he cursed them** using **the Divine Name.** [4]**If he cursed them with** one of God's **substitute names, Rabbi Meir says** that **he is liable,** [5]**but the Sages** say that he is **exempt.**

GEMARA מַאן חֲכָמִים? [6]The Gemara asks: **Who are the Sages** who exempt the son if he cursed his parents with one of God's substitute names? [7]The Gemara answers: **It is** the opinion of **Rabbi Menahem the son of Rabbi Yose.** [8]**For it was taught** in a Baraita: **"Rabbi Menahem the son of Rabbi Yose says:** The verse states (Leviticus 24:16): 'And he who blasphemes the name of the Lord, shall surely be put to death; and all the congregation shall certainly stone him, both the stranger, and he that is born in the land, [9]**when he blasphemes**

LITERAL TRANSLATION

it? [1]Sabbath limits, and according to Rabbi Akiva. [2]Kindling, and according to Rabbi Yose.

MISHNAH [3]Someone who curses his father or his mother is not liable until he curses them with the [Divine] Name. [4][If] he cursed them with a substitute name, Rabbi Meir [says he] is liable, [5]and the Sages exempt [him].

GEMARA [6]Who are the Sages? [7]It is Rabbi Menahem the son of Rabbi Yose. [8]For it was taught: "Rabbi Menahem the son of Rabbi Yose says: [9]'When he blasphemes the name [of the Lord], he shall be put to death.'

הִיא? [1]תְּחוּמִין, וְאַלִּיבָּא דְּרַבִּי עֲקִיבָא. [2]הַבְעָרָה, וְאַלִּיבָּא דְּרַבִּי יוֹסֵי.

מִשְׁנָה [3]הַמְקַלֵּל אָבִיו וְאִמּוֹ אֵינוֹ חַיָּיב עַד שֶׁיְּקַלְּלֵם בְּשֵׁם. [4]קִלְּלָם בְּכִנּוּי, רַבִּי מֵאִיר מְחַיֵּיב [5]וַחֲכָמִים פּוֹטְרִין.

גְּמָרָא [6]מַאן חֲכָמִים? [7]רַבִּי מְנַחֵם בְּרַבִּי יוֹסֵי הוּא. [8]דְּתַנְיָא: "רַבִּי מְנַחֵם בְּרַבִּי יוֹסֵי אוֹמֵר: [9]'בְּנָקְבוֹ שֵׁם יוּמָת'.

RASHI

גמרא תחומין ואליבא דרבי עקיבא – דיליף להו מקראי במסכת סוטה (כז,ב). הבערה ואליבא דרבי יוסי – דאמר ללאו יצאת. ורבי עקיבא מודה נמי בתחומים דאין חייבים עליהם כרת, דתנן (שבת עג,א): אבות מלאכות ארבעים חסר אחת, ולא פליג רבי עקיבא.

משנה עד שיקללם בשם – שיקלל בשמות הגמורין. קללם בכנוי – כגון "שדי" "צבאות" "חנון" "רחום".

גמרא בנקבו יומת – היה לו לכתוב, מה תלמוד לומר "שם"? אם אינו ענין לו, דהא כתיב "ונוקב שם". תנהו ענין למקלל אביו ואמו. ורבי מנחם לא סבירא ליה הא דדרשינן לעיל (נו,א) מהאי קרא: עד שיברך שם בשם, ואפילו לא ברך שם בשם אלא "יתברך יוסי", רבי מנחם ברבי יוסי מחייב עליה.

NOTES

קִלְּלָם בְּכִנּוּי **With a substitute name.** The Rishonim disagree about the meaning of the expressions "the divine name" and "substitute names" as they are used in our Mishnah. It would appear from *Rashi* that a person is only subject to the death penalty for cursing his parents if he cursed them with one of God's special names, such as the Tetragrammaton, or the name spelled alef, dalet, nun, yod. But if he cursed them with another name, even a name included among the seven names that may not be erased, he is exempt. According to *Ramah,* he is only liable if he cursed them with the Tetragrammaton. All other names are regarded as "substitute names," for which he is not liable. *Rambam* maintains that a person is liable to the death penalty if he cursed his parents with any one of the seven Divine Names that may not be erased. But if he cursed them with one of the "substitute names," that is to say, with an attribute, like the Merciful, or the Gracious, he is exempt.

בְּנָקְבוֹ שֵׁם יוּמָת **When he blasphemes the name of the Lord, he shall be put to death.** Even though that verse deals with the blasphemer, and not with someone who curses his parents, the fact that the verse juxtaposes the words, "the name of the Lord," to the words, "he shall be put to death," teaches that in all cases of cursing, a person is only subject to the death penalty if he curses with the Divine Name (*Ran*).

HALAKHAH

forbidden labor, and he had received a warning, and there are witnesses to his offense, he is liable to death by stoning." (*Rambam, Sefer Zemanim, Hilkhot Shabbat* 1:1.)

הַמְקַלֵּל אָבִיו וְאִמּוֹ **Someone who curses his father or his mother.** "If someone cursed his father or his mother using the Divine Name, he is liable to death by stoning. But if he cursed them with one of God's substitute names, he is exempt from stoning," following the Sages. He is however liable to flogging for cursing anyone. (*Rambam, Sefer Shofetim, Hilkhot Mamrim* 5:2; *Shulhan Arukh, Yoreh De'ah* 241:1.)

LANGUAGE

אַנְדְּרוֹגִינוּס **Hermaphrodite.** This derives from the Greek ἀνδρόγυνος *androgynos*, meaning "male and female." The term refers to a person with both male and female sexual organs.

BACKGROUND

טוּמְטוּם, וְאַנְדְּרוֹגִינוּס **A person whose genitals are hidden, and a hermaphrodite.** A *tumtum* is someone whose sexual organs from birth are concealed or are so undeveloped that it is impossible to determine whether the person is male or female. An *androginos* is a person with both male and female reproductive organs. The *tumtum* and the *androginos* are similar, in that it cannot be said with certainty whether they are male or female. The Sages debated whether they were to be given the status of a man or of a woman or were to be considered as a separate, intermediate category.

LITERAL TRANSLATION

[1]Why does the verse state 'name'? [2]To teach about someone who curses his father or his mother that he is not liable until he curses them with the [Divine] Name."

[3]Our Rabbis taught: "'*Ish.*' [4]What is taught by '*Ish ish*'? [5]To include a daughter, a person whose genitals are hidden, and a hermaphrodite. [6]'That curses his father and his mother.' [7]I have only his father and his mother. [8]From where [do I know] his father without his mother, [or] his mother without his father? [9]The verse teaches: 'His father and his mother he has cursed; his blood shall be upon him,' [10][implying that] his father he has cursed,

[1]מַה תַּלְמוּד לוֹמַר ׳שֵׁם׳ [2]לִימֵּד עַל מְקַלֵּל אָבִיו וְאִמּוֹ שֶׁאֵינוֹ חַיָּיב עַד שֶׁיְּקַלְּלֵם בַּשֵּׁם״.

[3]תָּנוּ רַבָּנַן: ״׳אִישׁ׳. [4]מַה תַּלְמוּד לוֹמַר ׳אִישׁ אִישׁ׳? [5]לְרַבּוֹת בַּת, טוּמְטוּם, וְאַנְדְּרוֹגִינוּס. [6]׳אֲשֶׁר יְקַלֵּל אֶת אָבִיו וְאֶת אִמּוֹ׳. [7]אֵין לִי אֶלָּא אָבִיו וְאִמּוֹ, [8]אָבִיו שֶׁלֹּא אִמּוֹ, אִמּוֹ שֶׁלֹּא אָבִיו מִנַּיִין? [9]תַּלְמוּד לוֹמַר: ׳אָבִיו וְאִמּוֹ קִלֵּל דָּמָיו בּוֹ׳, [10]אָבִיו קִילֵּל,

TRANSLATION AND COMMENTARY

the name of the Lord, shall be put to death.' [1]**Why does the verse mention** 'the **name** of the Lord' a second time? If those extraneous words are not needed regarding someone who blasphemes God, refer them to someone who curses his parents. [2]Those words **teach that someone who cursed his father or his mother is not liable** to death by stoning **unless he cursed them with the Divine Name,** but if he cursed them with one of God's substitute names, he is exempt."

תָּנוּ רַבָּנַן [3]**Our Rabbis taught** the following Baraita regarding someone who curses his parents: "The verse states (Leviticus 20:9): 'For everyone [*ish ish*] that curses his father or his mother shall surely be put to death; his father and his mother he has cursed; his blood shall be upon him.' It would have sufficed for the word '*ish* [man]' to have been written once. [4]**What did** the Torah mean to **teach by** doubling the word, so that the verse reads **'*Ish ish*'** [5]This was meant **to include a daughter, a person whose genitals are hidden** from birth, or are so undeveloped that it is impossible to determine its gender, **and a hermaphrodite** who has both male and female reproductive organs. Doubling the word *ish* teaches that they are included in the prohibition against cursing one's parents. The wording of the verse allows for the interpretation: [6]'For everyone **that curses his father and** [וְאֶת] **his mother.'** [7]If only the first part of the verse had been stated, **I would know only** that the son is liable if he curses both **his father *and* his mother,** implying that there is no liability for cursing only one parent. [8]**From where** do I know that he is also punished if he curses **his father without his mother, or his mother without his father?** [9]**The** latter part of the **verse states: 'His father and his mother he has cursed; his blood shall be upon him.'** Since in the first half of the verse the word 'curses' appears next to the word 'father,' whereas in the second half of the verse the word 'cursed' appears next to the word 'mother,' [10]**it may be inferred that** a person is liable whether **he cursed his father,** or **he cursed**

RASHI

איש איש כי יקלל וגו׳ לרבות בת – שקללה, או טומטום שקלל. אין לי אלא אביו ואמו – כאחד. אביו שלא אמו ואמו שלא אביו מניין תלמוד לומר אביו ואמו קלל – כלומר סמך קללה בראש המקרא לאביו, ובסופו סמך לאמו.

NOTES

לְרַבּוֹת בַּת **To include a daughter.** It may be asked: Why was a special word needed to teach that even a daughter is liable for cursing her parents? Surely there is a rule that all the Torah's prohibitions and punishments apply equally to men and women! It may be answered that this rule means only that the masculine verbal forms that are used throughout the Torah should not be understood as restricting the Torah's commandments to men. But if the Torah specifies that a certain commandment applies to a man, as when it uses the term *ish,* that commandment does not apply to a woman unless there is an extraneous word which includes women in the commandment (*Ran*).

טוּמְטוּם, וְאַנְדְּרוֹגִינוּס **A person whose genitals are hidden, and a hermaphrodite.** The question has been raised: A doubt exists regarding a person whose genitals are hidden from view and a hermaphrodite, whether they are males or females. Once it has been established that both men and women are included in the prohibition against cursing one's parents, why is a special word still necessary to teach us that a person whose genitals are hidden and a hermaphrodite are included in the prohibition? *Ran* argues that indeed this was not necessary, and a person whose genitals are hidden and a hermaphrodite were mentioned here merely out of habit. It has also been suggested that it was necessary to mention them here according to the opinion that a person whose genitals are hidden and a hermaphrodite are not doubtful males or females, but a separate gender (*Melo HaRo'im*).

HALAKHAH

טוּמְטוּם, וְאַנְדְּרוֹגִינוּס **A person whose genitals are hidden, and a hermaphrodite.** "The prohibition against cursing a parent applies both to a son and a daughter, and even to a person whose genitals are hidden or undeveloped, and a hermaphrodite who has both male and female reproductive organs." (*Rambam, Sefer Shofetim, Hilkhot Mamrim* 5:1.)

אָבִיו קִילֵּל, אִמּוֹ קִילֵּל **His father he has cursed, his mother he has cursed.** "A person is liable for cursing a parent,

TRANSLATION AND COMMENTARY

his mother. [1]**This is the viewpoint of Rabbi Yoshiyah.** [2]But **Rabbi Yonatan** disagrees and **says:** The second half of the verse is not needed to teach us that someone is liable if he cursed only one of his parents, because that ruling can be derived from the wording of the first half of the verse. [3]A formulation such as 'his father and his mother' **means the two of them together and it means each one separately,** [4]**unless the verse** in the Torah **specifically uses** the expression **'together.'** According to Rabbi Yonatan, a copulative vav may indicate conjunction, meaning 'and,' but it may also indicate disjunction, meaning 'or,' unless there is explicit proof from the rest of the verse that it must be understood in the conjunctive sense."

מוֹת יוּמָת [5]The Baraita continues: "The words, **'he shall surely be put to death,'** teach that the son who cursed one of his parents is executed **by stoning.** [6]**You say** that the verse refers to death **by stoning, but might it not be** that the verse refers to **one of the** other modes of **execution mentioned in the Torah?** The meaning of 'he shall surely be put to death' is learned by way of a *gezerah shavah:* [7]**Here the verse states: 'His blood shall be upon them,'** [8]**and below** regarding a medium and a wizard, **the verse states** (Leviticus 20:27): **'Their blood shall be upon them.'** [9]**Just as below,** the medium and the wizard are liable to death **by stoning,** as the verse states explicitly: [10]'They shall stone them with stones,' **so too here,** the offending son is liable to death **by stoning.** [11]**We have heard the punishment** that is imposed upon someone who cursed one of his parents. [12]But **where is the warning** teaching that the act is prohibited? An act is not a punishable criminal offense unless the Bible both states that it is prohibited and also specifies a penalty for it. Where then does the Torah state that a son is forbidden to curse his father and mother? [13]This is learned from **the verse** which **states** (Exodus 22:27): **'You shall not curse the judges,** nor curse the ruler of your people.'"

אִם הָיָה אָבִיו דַּיָּין [14]The Baraita explains how this verse teaches that a person is forbidden to curse his parent. **"If his father was a judge,** [15]surely **he is included in** the prohibition, **'You shall not curse the judges.'** [16]**And if his father was a ruler,** [17]surely **he is included in** the prohibition, **'Nor curse the ruler of your**

אִמּוֹ קִילֵּל. [1]דִּבְרֵי רַבִּי יֹאשִׁיָּה. [2]רַבִּי יוֹנָתָן אוֹמֵר: [3]מַשְׁמַע שְׁנֵיהֶן כְּאֶחָד, וּמַשְׁמַע אֶחָד בִּפְנֵי עַצְמוֹ, [4]עַד שֶׁיִּפְרוֹט לְךָ הַכָּתוּב 'יַחְדָּו'".

[5]"'מוֹת יוּמָת' — בִּסְקִילָה. [6]אַתָּה אוֹמֵר בִּסְקִילָה, אוֹ אֵינוֹ אֶלָּא בְּאַחַת מִכָּל מִיתוֹת הָאֲמוּרוֹת בַּתּוֹרָה? [7]נֶאֱמַר כָּאן: 'דָּמָיו בּוֹ', [8]וְנֶאֱמַר לְהַלָּן: 'דְּמֵיהֶם בָּם'. [9]מַה לְּהַלָּן — בִּסְקִילָה, [10]אַף כָּאן — בִּסְקִילָה. [11]עוֹנֶשׁ שָׁמַעְנוּ. [12]אַזְהָרָה מִנַּיִין? [13]תַּלְמוּד לוֹמַר: 'אֱלֹהִים לֹא תְקַלֵּל וגו''".

[14]אִם הָיָה אָבִיו דַּיָּין, [15]הֲרֵי הוּא בִּכְלָל 'אֱלֹהִים לֹא תְקַלֵּל'. [16]וְאִם הָיָה אָבִיו נָשִׂיא, הֲרֵי הוּא בִּכְלָל [17]'וְנָשִׂיא בְעַמְּךָ לֹא תָאֹר'.

LITERAL TRANSLATION

his mother he has cursed. [1][These are] the words of Rabbi Yoshiyah. [2]Rabbi Yonatan says: [3]It means the two of them together, and it means [each] one separately, [4]unless the verse specifies to you 'together.'"

[5]"'[He] shall surely be put to death' — by stoning. [6]You say by stoning, but might it not be by one of all the executions mentioned in the Torah? [7]It is stated here: 'His blood shall be upon him.' [8]And it is stated below: 'Their blood shall be upon them.' [9]Just as below — by stoning, [10]so too here — by stoning. [11]We have heard the punishment. [12]From where the warning? [13]The verse states: 'You shall not curse the judges, etc.'"

[14]"If his father was a judge, [15]he is included in 'You shall not curse the judges.' [16]And if his father was a ruler, [17]he is included in 'Nor curse the ruler of your people.'

RASHI

רבי יונתן אומר – מתחלת המקרא משמע את אביו ואת אמו, דאף על גב דוי"ו מוסיף על ענין ראשון משמע נמי אחד מהם, עד שיפרט לך הכתוב יחדיו. כדרך שהוצרך לפרוט בכלאים שכתוב בו (דברים כב) "לא תחרוש בשור ובחמור" ופרט בו "יחדיו", שלא תאמר אסור לחרוש בשור לבדו ובחמור לבדו. ו"אביו ואמו קלל" דסיפא דריש ליה רבי יונתן לקמן ב"אלו הן הנחנקין": לרבות את המקלל לאחר מיתה. **מה להלן בסקילה** – דכתיב "באבן ירגמו אותם".

HALAKHAH

whether he cursed his mother or he cursed his father." (*Rambam, Sefer Shofetim, Hilkhot Mamrim* 6:2; *Shulḥan Arukh, Yoreh De'ah* 241:1.)

וְאִם הָיָה אָבִיו נָשִׂיא If his father was a ruler. "If someone curses a judge, he violates the prohibition, 'You shall not curse the judges.' And so too if someone curses the king or the head of the Sanhedrin, he violates the prohibition, 'Nor curse the ruler of your people.' Whoever curses any Jew violates the prohibition, 'You shall not curse a deaf man.'" (*Rambam, Sefer Shofetim, Hilkhot Sanhedrin* 26:1-2; *Shulḥan Arukh, Ḥoshen Mishpat* 27:1.)

TRANSLATION AND COMMENTARY

people.' [1]From where do I know about someone who is neither a judge, nor a ruler, that his son is forbidden to curse him? [2]You can say as follows: You can construct a generalization based on these two special cases, that of the judge and that of the ruler. If we take the two special prohibitions together, we can derive the prohibition against cursing a parent. [3]For the unique aspect of the ruler is not like the unique aspect of the judge, and even so one is forbidden to curse a ruler, [4]and the unique aspect of the judge is not like the unique aspect of the ruler, and even so one is forbidden to curse a judge. How so? [5]The unique aspect of the judge is not like the unique aspect of the ruler, [6]for surely regarding a judge you are commanded to accept his rulings on legal matters. [7]This is not like the unique aspect of the ruler, for you are not commanded to accept his rulings on legal matters. [8]And the unique aspect of the ruler is not like the unique aspect of the judge, [9]for regarding a ruler you are commanded not to rebel against him when he orders you to do something. [10]This is not like the unique aspect of the judge, for you are not commanded not to rebel against him. Hence the underlying factor on which the two prohibitions are based is neither the obligation to accept the judge's rulings, nor that of refraining from rebelling against the ruler's orders. [11]The common factor between the two — the judge and the ruler — is that they are both from your people — fit members of the people of Israel — [12]and you are warned against cursing them. [13]Likewise I will include in the prohibition your father who is also from your people, [14]and so you are warned against cursing him. But an objection may be raised. Even if we take the two prohibitions together, we cannot derive the prohibition against cursing one's parent, [15]for there is another common factor in the two. [16]Perhaps their elevated rank causes them to be treated differently. Thus, only the cursing of high ranking Jews might be prohibited. [17]Therefore, the verse states (Leviticus 19:14): 'You shall not curse a deaf man, nor put a stumbling block before the blind.' [18]Here

[1]אֵינוֹ לֹא דַּיָּין וְלֹא נָשִׂיא מִנַּיִין? [2]אָמַרְתָּ: הֲרֵי אַתָּה דָּן בִּנְיַן אָב מִשְּׁנֵיהֶן: [3]לֹא רְאִי נָשִׂיא כִּרְאִי דַּיָּין, [4]וְלֹא רְאִי דַּיָּין כִּרְאִי נָשִׂיא. [5]לֹא רְאִי דַּיָּין כִּרְאִי נָשִׂיא, [6]שֶׁהֲרֵי דַּיָּין אַתָּה מְצוּוֶּה עַל הוֹרָאָתוֹ. [7]כִּרְאִי נָשִׂיא, שֶׁאִי אַתָּה מְצוּוֶּה עַל הוֹרָאָתוֹ. [8]וְלֹא רְאִי נָשִׂיא כִּרְאִי דַּיָּין, [9]שֶׁהַנָּשִׂיא אַתָּה מְצוּוֶּה עַל הַמְרָאֲתוֹ. [10]כִּרְאִי דַּיָּין, שֶׁאִי אַתָּה מְצוּוֶּה עַל הַמְרָאֲתוֹ. [11]הַצַּד הַשָּׁוֶה שֶׁבָּהֶם שֶׁהֵן בְּעַמְּךָ, [12]וְאַתָּה מוּזְהַר עַל קִלְלָתָן. [13]אַף אֲנִי אָבִיא אָבִיךָ, שֶׁבְּעַמְּךָ, [14]וְאַתָּה מוּזְהַר עַל קִלְלָתוֹ. [15]מַה לְּהַצַּד הַשָּׁוֶה שֶׁבָּהֶן, [16]שֶׁכֵּן גְּדוּלָּתָן גָּרְמָה לָהֶן! [17]תַּלְמוּד לוֹמַר: 'לֹא תְקַלֵּל חֵרֵשׁ' — [18]בְּאוּמְלָלִים

LITERAL TRANSLATION

[1]From where [do I know about someone who] is neither a judge, nor a ruler? [2]You say: You construct a generalization from the two of them: [3]The characteristic of the ruler is not like the characteristic of the judge, [4]and the characteristic of the judge is not like the characteristic of the ruler. [5]The characteristic of the judge is not like the characteristic of the ruler, [6]for surely [regarding] a judge you are commanded about his ruling. [7]Like the characteristic of the ruler, for you are not commanded about his ruling. [8]And the characteristic of the ruler is not like the characteristic of the judge, [9]for [regarding] a ruler you are commanded about rebelling against him. [10]Like the characteristic of the judge, for you are not commanded about rebelling against him. [11]The common factor between them is that they are from your people, [12]and you warned about cursing them. [13]So too I will bring your father who is from your people, [14]and you are warned about cursing him. [15]What is [special] about the common factor in them [16][is that] their high rank caused them! [17]The verse states: 'You shall not curse a deaf man' — [18]Scripture speaks about the most miserable

RASHI

בנין אב משניהם – דמחד מינייהו לא אתיא, דאיכא למיפרך: מה לדיין שכן אתה מצווה וחייב מיתה על הוראתו, שנאמר (דברים יז) "ושמרת לעשות ככל אשר יורוך והאיש אשר יעשה בזדון לבלתי וגו'". ובנשיא איכא למיפרך: שכן אתה חייב מיתה על המראתו, שלא למרוד בצוויו ולהמרות את פיו, שנאמר ביהושע "כל איש אשר ימרה את פיך וגו'". **לא ראי דיין כראי נשיא** – לא ראיה של זה, צד חמור שנאמר בדיין, ישנה בנשיא, אפילו הכי הוזהר על הנשיא. **שהן בעמך** – עושין מעשה עמך. **באומללים** – בשפלים, כמו "היהודים האמללים" בספר עזרא (נחמיה ג).

NOTES

שֶׁכֵּן גְּדוּלָּתָן גָּרְמָה Their high rank caused them. Even though a son is obligated to honor and fear his father, the Torah did not grant a father high rank in relationship to those who are not his children, as it did to a judge and a ruler (*Ramah*).

HALAKHAH

לֹא תְקַלֵּל חֵרֵשׁ You shall not curse a deaf man. "The verse, 'You shall not curse a deaf man,' teaches that one is

TRANSLATION AND COMMENTARY

Scripture speaks about the humblest among your people, teaching that the prohibition against cursing another person applies to all Jews. But another objection may be raised. [1]Perhaps **a deaf person is special in that his deafness causes him** to be treated differently. This objection can be refuted: [2]The prohibition that applies to **a ruler and a judge proves** that the decisive factor in the case of a deaf person is not his deafness or low status. For a ruler and a judge are among the elevated of the people, and yet one is forbidden to curse them. [3]Again the objection is raised: Perhaps **a ruler and a judge are special because of high rank.** [4]This argument can be refuted: The prohibition that applies to **a deaf man proves** that the decisive factor regarding a ruler and a judge is not their high rank. [5]Thus, we see that **the argument is circular.** The prohibition against cursing a parent cannot be derived from the prohibition against cursing a ruler or a judge, for it can be argued that they are unique in that they enjoy an elevated status. Nor can it be derived from the prohibition against cursing a deaf man, for it can be argued that a deaf person is unique in that he is among the lowest of the people. But if we take all the prohibitions together, we can derive the prohibition against cursing a parent. [6]For **the** unique **aspect** of the ruler and the judge **is not like the** unique **aspect** of the deaf person, **and the** unique **aspect** of the deaf person **is not like the** unique **aspect** of the ruler and the judge. [7]**The common factor among them all is that they are** all **from your people** — fit members of the people of Israel — [8]**and you are warned against cursing them.** [9]**Likewise, I will include** in the prohibition **your father who is** also **from your people,** [10]**and** so **you are warned against cursing him.** But one final objection may be raised: [11]**There is** another **common factor:** The ruler, the judge, and the deaf person **are** each **unusual** in some way. Thus, the prohibition against cursing another person might not apply to ordinary people. [12]**Rather,** the prohibition against cursing one's parent is derived as follows: **If** it is **so** that the prohibition is limited to those of elevated status and those of low status, **the Torah should have mentioned either a judge and a deaf man,** [13]**or a ruler and a deaf man.** That would have sufficed to teach me that one is forbidden to curse people of high and low rank. [14]**Why** then **was it necessary** to mention **a judge** as well? [15]Rather, **if** the verse that mentions a judge **is not relevant for itself,** [16]**refer it to** a person's **father** that he too is included in the prohibition."

שֶׁבְּעַמְּךָ הַכָּתוּב מְדַבֵּר. [1]מַה
לְחֵרֵשׁ, שֶׁכֵּן חֲרִישָׁתוֹ גָּרְמָה לוֹ!
[2]נָשִׂיא וְדַיָּין יוֹכִיחוּ. [3]מַה
לְנָשִׂיא וְדַיָּין, שֶׁכֵּן גְּדוּלָּתָן
גָּרְמָה לָהֶן! [4]חֵרֵשׁ יוֹכִיחַ. [5]וְחָזַר
הַדִּין, [6]לֹא רְאִי זֶה כִּרְאִי זֶה,
וְלֹא רְאִי זֶה כִּרְאִי זֶה. [7]הַצַּד
הַשָּׁוֶה שֶׁבָּהֶן: שֶׁהֵן בְּעַמְּךָ,
[8]וְאַתָּה מוּזְהַר עַל קִלְלָתָן —
[9]אַף אֲנִי אָבִיא אָבִיךָ, שֶׁבְּעַמְּךָ,
[10]וְאַתָּה מוּזְהַר עַל קִלְלָתוֹ.
[11]מַה לַּצַּד הַשָּׁוֶה שֶׁבָּהֶן, שֶׁכֵּן
מְשׁוּנִּין. [12]אֶלָּא, אִם כֵּן, נִכְתּוֹב
קְרָא אוֹ אֱלֹהִים וְחֵרֵשׁ, [13]אוֹ
נָשִׂיא וְחֵרֵשׁ. [14]אֱלֹהִים לָמָּה
לִי? [15]אִם אֵינוֹ עִנְיָן לְגוּפוֹ,
[16]תְּנֵהוּ עִנְיָן לְאָבִיו".

LITERAL TRANSLATION

among your people. [1]What is [special] about a deaf man [is that] his deafness causes him! [2]A ruler and a judge will prove [it]. [3]What is [special] about a ruler and a judge [is that] that their high rank causes them! [4]A deaf man will prove [it]. [5]And the argument is circular (lit., "returns"). [6]This characteristic is not like that characteristic, and that characteristic is not like this characteristic. [7]The common factor between them is that they are among your people, [8]and you are warned about cursing them. [9]So too I will bring your father who is from your people, [10]and you are warned about cursing him. [11]What is [special] about the common factor in them [is that] they are unusual! [12]Rather, if so, let the verse write either judge and deaf man, [13]or ruler and deaf man. [14]Why do I [need] a judge? [15]If it is not relevant for itself, [16]refer it to his father."

RASHI

חרשותו גרמה לו – מתוך שהוא שפל הזהיר עליו הכתוב שלא תבזהו ולא תצערהו, מפני שנותן צרתו על לבו ומיצר על שפלותו. שכן משונין – משאר בני אדם, אלו לאמללות ואלו לגדולה. וקיימא לן בשחיטת חולין (קטו,ב): כל מה הצד פרכינן כל דהוא, כגון שכן משונין, דאינו צד חמור. דאי צד חמור פריך לאו פירכא היא דאביו נמי אית ביה צד חמור – שהוקש כבודו לכבוד המקום. הכי גרסינן: אם כן נכתוב אלהים וחרש או נשיא וחרש – פירוש: אלא לא אתיא אביו בבנין אב אלא ב"אם אינו ענין" – נכתוב אלהים וחרש וניתי נשיא בהצד השוה: לא ראי דיין שהוא גדול שאתה מצווה על הוראתו כראי חרש שאי אתה מצווה על הוראתו, ולא ראי חרש ששפלותו גרמה לו כראי דיין שאין שפלותו גרמה לו, הצד השוה שבהן – שהן בעמך, אף אני אביא נשיא. והכא ליכא למיפרך שכן משונין, דהא נשיא נמי משונה הוא. או נשיא וחרש – וניתי דיין מינייהו.

HALAKHAH

forbidden to curse any other Jew, including a parent. The violation of this prohibition is punishable by flogging." (*Rambam, Sefer Shofetim, Hilkhot Sanhedrin* 26:1-2; *Hilkhot Mamrim* 5:4.)

[1]הָנִיחָא לְמַאן דְּאָמַר אֱלֹהִים חוֹל. [2]אֶלָּא לְמַאן דְּאָמַר קוֹדֶשׁ, [3]מַאי אִיכָּא לְמֵימַר? [4]דְּתַנְיָא: "׳אֱלֹהִים׳ — חוֹל. [5]דִּבְרֵי רַבִּי יִשְׁמָעֵאל. [6]רַבִּי עֲקִיבָא אוֹמֵר: ׳אֱלֹהִים׳ — קוֹדֶשׁ". [7]וְתַנְיָא: "רַבִּי אֱלִיעֶזֶר בֶּן יַעֲקֹב אוֹמֵר: [8]אַזְהָרָה לַמְבָרֵךְ אֶת הַשֵּׁם מִנַּיִין? [9]תַּלְמוּד לוֹמַר: ׳אֱלֹהִים לֹא תְקַלֵּל׳".

[10]לְמַאן דְּאָמַר אֱלֹהִים חוֹל, גָּמַר קוֹדֶשׁ מֵחוֹל, [11]לְמַאן דְּאָמַר אֱלֹהִים קוֹדֶשׁ, גָּמְרִינַן חוֹל מִקּוֹדֶשׁ.

[12]בִּשְׁלָמָא לְמַאן דְּאָמַר אֱלֹהִים חוֹל, [13]גָּמַר קוֹדֶשׁ מֵחוֹל. [14]אֶלָּא לְמַאן דְּאָמַר אֱלֹהִים קוֹדֶשׁ, [15]גָּמַר חוֹל מִקּוֹדֶשׁ? [16]דִּילְמָא אַקּוֹדֶשׁ אַזְהַר, אַחוֹל לָא אַזְהַר!

LITERAL TRANSLATION

[1]This is well according to the one who says [that] *elohim* is secular. [2]But according to the one who says [that *elohim*] is holy, [3]what is there to say? [4]For it was taught: "'*Elohim*' — secular. [5][These are] the words of Rabbi Yishmael. [6]Rabbi Akiva says: '*Elohim*' — holy." [7]And it was taught: "Rabbi Eliezer ben Ya'akov says: [8]A warning against cursing (lit., "blessing") the [Divine] Name, from where? [9]The verse states: 'You shall not curse God.'"

[10]According to the one who says [that] *elohim* is secular, he learns the holy from the secular. [11]According to the one who says [that] *elohim* is holy, we learn the secular from the holy.

[12]Granted according to the one who says [that] *elohim* is secular, [13]he learns the holy from the secular. [14]But according to the one who says [that] *elohim* is holy, [15]does he learn the secular from the holy? [16]Perhaps it warned about the holy, [but] did not warn about the secular!

TRANSLATION AND COMMENTARY

הָנִיחָא [1]The Gemara raises a question: All **this is well according to the** Tanna **who says that** the word ***elohim*** in the verse (Exodus 22:27): "You shall not curse *elohim*, nor curse the ruler of your people," **is secular** and refers to human judges. According to that viewpoint, the verse is superfluous, for the prohibition against cursing a judge could have been derived from the prohibitions against cursing a ruler and a deaf person, and so it can serve as the source for the prohibition against cursing a parent. [2]**But according to the** Tanna **who says that** the word *elohim* in that verse **is holy,** and that it refers to God, [3]**what is there to say?** According to that viewpoint, the verse is not superfluous, for it teaches that cursing God is forbidden. [4]**For it was taught** in a Baraita: "The verse states (Exodus 22:27): 'You shall not curse *elohim*.' Here in this verse the word **'*elohim*'** is **secular,** and it refers to a human judge; [5]**this is the viewpoint of Rabbi Yishmael.** [6]**Rabbi Akiva** disagrees and **says:** The word **'*elohim*'** as used here is **holy,** and it refers to God." [7]**And it was taught** in a second Baraita: **"Rabbi Eliezer ben Ya'akov says:** [8]**Where is the warning** teaching **that cursing the Divine Name** is prohibited? [9]This is derived from **the verse** which **states** [Exodus 22:7]: **'You shall not curse God** [*elohim*].'"

לְמַאן [10]The Gemara explains: **The** Tanna **who says that** the word ***elohim*** **is** used here in a **secular** sense **must learn the holy from the secular,** that is to say, he must learn that one is forbidden to curse God from the prohibition against cursing a judge, for there is no other verse prohibiting the cursing of God. [11]So too then **the** Tanna **who says that** the word ***elohim*** in this verse **is holy** can **learn the secular from the holy,** that is to say, he can learn that one is forbidden to curse a judge from the prohibition against cursing God. This interpretation makes the second half of the verse, "Nor curse the ruler of your people," superfluous, for we could have derived that prohibition from those against cursing a judge and a deaf person. And so the verse, "Nor curse the ruler of your people," can serve as the source for the prohibition against cursing a parent.

בִּשְׁלָמָא [12]The Gemara objects to this argument: **Granted according to the** Tanna **who says that** the word ***elohim*** in this verse **is secular,** [13]**he** can **learn the holy from the secular.** [14]**But according to the** Tanna **who says that** the word ***elohim*** in this verse **is holy,** [15]**can he learn the secular from the holy?** [16]Surely that argument can be refuted, for **perhaps** the Torah **prohibits cursing** God, **but does not prohibit** cursing **the secular** human judge! Thus, the verse, "Nor curse the ruler of your people," is not superfluous and cannot serve as the source for the prohibition against cursing a parent.

RASHI

אלהים חול — דהא אלהים דהכא חול הוא, ולאזהרת דיין אתא. **אלא למאן דאמר קודש** — וכאן הזהיר על ברכת השם, מאי איכא למימר? אין כאן קרא יתירא. ומשני: מאן דאמר אלהים חול, על כרחיך גמר קודש מחול, דהא לא אשכחן אזהרה לברכת השם אלא מהכא. הלכך מאן דאמר קודש גמר נמי חול מקודש, ויש כאן אזהרה לדיין דיליף לה מאזהרה דקדש, וקסלקא דעתך במה מצינו גמר, ומשום הכי פריך: דילמא אקודש הזהיר, אחול לא הזהיר.

HALAKHAH

אֱלֹהִים — קוֹדֶשׁ *Elohim* — holy. According to *Kesef Mishneh* (*Hilkhot Mamrim* 5:4), *Rambam* rules that this instance of the word *elohim* is holy, for the law is in accordance with Rabbi Akiva. Another source suggests that *Rambam* rules that this instance of the word *elohim* is secular (see *Kesef Mishneh, Hilkhot Sanhedrin* 26:1). Regarding

[1]אִם כֵּן, לִכְתּוֹב קְרָא: "לֹא תָקֵל". [66B] [2]מַאי "לֹא תְקַלֵּל"? [3]שְׁמַע מִינָּהּ תַּרְתֵּי.

משנה [4]הַבָּא עַל נַעֲרָה הַמְאוֹרָסָה — אֵינוֹ חַיָּיב עַד שֶׁתְּהֵא נַעֲרָה, [5]בְּתוּלָה, מְאוֹרָסָה, וְהִיא בְּבֵית אָבִיהָ. [6]בָּאוּ עָלֶיהָ שְׁנַיִם, הָרִאשׁוֹן בִּסְקִילָה, [7]וְהַשֵּׁנִי בְּחֶנֶק.

גמרא [8]תָּנוּ רַבָּנַן: [9]"'נַעֲרָה' וְלֹא בּוֹגֶרֶת. [10]'בְּתוּלָה' וְלֹא

LITERAL TRANSLATION

[1]If so, let the verse write: *"Lo takel."*

[66B] [2]What is *"lo tekalel?"* [3]Infer from this two.

MISHNAH [4]Someone who has intercourse with a betrothed girl is not liable unless she is a *na'arah,* [5]a virgin, betrothed, and she is in her father's house. [6][If] two people had intercourse with her, the first one [is put to death] by stoning, [7]and the second one by strangulation.

GEMARA [8]Our Rabbis taught: [9]"'A *na'arah*' — and not one who has come of age. [10]'A virgin' — and not

TRANSLATION AND COMMENTARY

אִם כֵּן [1]The Gemara resolves the difficulty: **If** it were **so** that the verse, "You shall not curse *elohim,"* only teaches the prohibition against cursing God, then **the verse should have been formulated** as follows: *"Elohim lo takel* [תָּקֵל, with one *kuf*]," meaning: you shall not disgrace God. We would understand from this that cursing God is forbidden.

[66B] מַאי "לֹא תְקַלֵּל" [2]**What** then does the Torah mean to teach when it writes: *"Elohim* **lo tekalel** תְקַלֵּל, with two *lameds*]"? [3]**Infer from this** that the verse prohibits **two** types of cursing, cursing God and cursing a judge, who can also be referred to by the term *elohim.* Since the verse forbids the cursing of a judge, it was unnecessary for it to continue with a prohibition against cursing a ruler. Thus, the verse, "Nor curse the ruler of your people," is superfluous, and it can serve as the source for the prohibition against cursing a parent.

MISHNAH הַבָּא [4]We learned earlier in the chapter (53a) that a man who had sexual intercourse with a betrothed girl is liable to death by stoning, as the verse states (Deuteronomy 22:23-24): "If a *na'arah* that is a virgin is betrothed to a man, and a man finds her in the city, and lies with her; then you shall bring them both out to the gate of that city, and you shall stone them with stones that they die." Our Mishnah teaches that if **a man had** sexual **intercourse with a betrothed girl,** he **is not liable** to death by stoning **unless** the girl **was a** *na'arah* (a young woman between the age of twelve and twelve-and-a-half years old, who has reached puberty, as evidenced by her having grown at least two pubic hairs), [5]**a virgin,** only **betrothed** to her husband, but not yet married to him, **and** still living **in her father's house.** [6]**If two** different **people had** sexual **intercourse with** such a girl, **the first is put to death by stoning,** for he had intercourse with a betrothed girl who was still a virgin, [7]**but the second** is put to death **by strangulation,** for she was no longer a virgin.

GEMARA תָּנוּ רַבָּנַן [8]**Our Rabbis taught** a Baraita which elaborates on our Mishnah: "The verse states (Deuteronomy 22:23): 'If a *na'arah* that is a virgin is betrothed to a man, and a man finds her in the city, and lies with her, then you shall bring them both out to the gate of that city, and you shall stone them with stones that they die.' This text teaches us that adultery is punishable by stoning only if the offense was committed by 'a *na'arah* that is a virgin' who is 'betrothed.' A precise reading of the verse leads to the following conclusions: [9]A man who commits adultery with **'a *na'arah*'** is subject to the penalty of stoning, **but not** someone who commits adultery with a girl **who has come of age,** at twelve-and-a-half. [10]A man

RASHI

לא תקלל – שתי קללות במשמע. ו"אלהים" נמי שתי לשונות יש בו, הלכך לא תקלל דרשינן אתרווייהו.

משנה אינו חייב – סקילה. עד שתהא נערה – אבל קטנה שקדשה אביה – הבא עליה בקטנותה אינו בסקילה. ופלוגתא דתנאי היא, איכא למאן דאמר בחנק, ואיכא למאן דאמר פטור לגמרי. בתולה – ולא בעולה. מאורסה – ולא נשואה, ואפילו נכנסה לחופה ולא נבעלה, דקרינא ביה בתולה מיהו לא קרינא ביה מאורסה. והיא בבית אביה – למעוטי מסרה האב לשלוחי הבעל וזינתה בדרך. באו עליה שנים – ועדיין היא בתולה, כגון שבאו עליה שלא כדרכה. הראשון בסקילה – ד"משכבי אשה" כתיב (ויקרא יח). והשני בחנק – דבעולה היא. והא סתמא רבי היא, דאמר שלא כדרכה נפקא ליה מכלל בתולה לקמן.

גמרא תנו רבנן נערה ולא בוגרת – אקרא קאי "כי תהיה נערה בתולה מאורסה וגו'" (דברים כב) וסקילה כתיבא התם. נערה – משתביא שתי שערות עד שירבה שחור על הלבן, ואין בין נערות לבגרות אלא ששה חדשים בלבד.

HALAKHAH

the laws governing a Torah scroll, *Keset HaSofer* maintains that this instance of the word *elohim* is holy. *Meir Einei Soferim* maintains that the matter is in doubt whether the word is holy or secular.

הַבָּא עַל נַעֲרָה הַמְאוֹרָסָה **Someone who has intercourse with a betrothed girl.** "If a man had sexual intercourse with a betrothed girl who was still a virgin and had not yet been handed over to her bridegroom's agents for marriage, he is liable to death by stoning. If she was a willing partner, she too is liable to death by stoning." (*Rambam, Sefer Kedushah, Hilkhot Issurei Bi'ah* 3:4.)

בּוֹגֶרֶת **One who has come of age.** "If a man had sexual intercourse with a betrothed girl who had already come of age (at twelve-and-a-half), he is liable to death by

TRANSLATION AND COMMENTARY

with **'a virgin'** is subject to the penalty of stoning, **but not** someone who commits adultery with a girl who was **not a virgin** at the time of the offense. [1]A man who commits adultery with a girl who was only **'betrothed'** to her husband is subject to stoning, **but not** a man who commits adultery with a girl who was already **married** at the time of the transgression. Another verse states (Deuteronomy 22:21): 'The men of the city shall stone her to death, because she has done a shameful thing in Israel to commit adultery [2]**in her father's house.'** This verse teaches us that the penalty of stoning is imposed only if she committed the offense while she was still in her father's house. [3]This **excludes** adultery after **her father** had **handled her over to her bridegroom's agents.** For then she is executed by strangulation, because she has the status of a married woman."

אָמַר [4]**Rav Yehudah said in the name of Rav:** Our Mishnah, which states that a man who had sexual intercourse with a betrothed girl is not liable to death by stoning unless she was a *na'arah*, implying that he is not liable to death by stoning if she was a minor, [5]**follows the position of Rabbi Meir.** If a *na'arah* was seduced or raped, the seducer or the rapist must pay the girl's father a fine of fifty silver shekalim (see Exodus 22:15-16; Deuteronomy 22:28-29). Elsewhere, Rabbi Meir states that this fine is only paid if the girl was a *na'arah,* but not if she was a minor. Just as there Rabbi Meir maintains that the fine is limited to a *na'arah,* so too here he maintains that the penalty of stoning in the case of adultery involving a young girl is limited to a *na'arah.* [6]**But the Sages** who disagree with Rabbi Meir about the fine paid by the seducer or the rapist, also disagree with Rabbi Meir about the penalty of stoning imposed in the case of adultery. They **say:** [7]When the Torah imposed the penalty of stoning in the case of adultery involving **a betrothed *na'arah,*** [8]it meant **to include even a minor.** The Torah meant only to exclude a girl who has reached legal majority at the age of twelve-and-a-half.

אֲמַר לֵיהּ [9]**Rav Aḥa of Difti said to Ravina: How do you know that our Mishnah follows** the viewpoint of **Rabbi Meir,** [10]**and** that when it speaks about a *na'arah,* it means **to exclude even a minor?** [11]**Perhaps** the Mishnah **follows** the viewpoint of **the Sages** who disagree with Rabbi Meir, [12]**and** means **to exclude a girl who has come of age, and nothing more!**

LITERAL TRANSLATION

a woman who has had sexual relations. [1]'Betrothed' — and not married. [2]'In her father's house' — [3]to exclude if the father has delivered [his daughter] to the husband's agents."

[4]Rav Yehudah said in the name of Rav: [5]This [ruling] is the words of Rabbi Meir. [6]But the Sages say: [7]A betrothed *na'arah* — [8]even a minor is included.

[9]Rav Aḥa of Difti said to Ravina: From where [do you know] that our Mishnah is Rabbi Meir, [10]and also to the exclusion of a minor? [11]Perhaps it is the Rabbis, [12]and to the exclusion of one who has come of age, and nothing more!

בְּעוּלָה. [1]'מְאוֹרָסָה' וְלֹא נְשׂוּאָה. [2]'בְּבֵית אָבִיהָ' — [3]פְּרָט לְשֶׁמָּסַר הָאָב לִשְׁלוּחֵי הַבַּעַל".

[4]אָמַר רַב יְהוּדָה אָמַר רַב: [5]זוֹ דִּבְרֵי רַבִּי מֵאִיר. [6]אֲבָל חֲכָמִים אוֹמְרִים: [7]נַעֲרָה הַמְאוֹרָסָה — [8]אֲפִילּוּ קְטַנָּה בְּמַשְׁמָע.

[9]אֲמַר לֵיהּ רַב אַחָא מִדִּפְתִּי לְרָבִינָא: מִמַּאי דְּמַתְנִיתִין רַבִּי מֵאִיר הִיא, [10]וּלְמַעוֹטֵי קְטַנָּה נַמִי? [11]דִּילְמָא רַבָּנַן הִיא, [12]וּלְמַעוֹטֵי בּוֹגֶרֶת, וְתוּ לֹא!

RASHI

בית אביה – בפרשת מוציא שם רע כתיב (שם) "לזנות בית אביה" והתם נמי סקילה כתיבא. **זו דברי רבי מאיר** – אמתניתין קאי, דקתני: עד שתהא נערה, ומשמע – למעוטי קטנה, זו דברי רבי מאיר, דאמר בכתובות ב"אלו נערות" (כט,א): קטנה אין לה קנס חמשים כסף דנערה דוקא כתיב ולא קטנה, הלכך גבי נערה המאורסה אין קטנה במשמע. **אבל חכמים** – שנחלקו עליו ואמרו: יש קנס במקום מכר, חולקין עליו אף כאן ואומרים: קטנה ארוסה – בסקילה, ולא מיעט הכתוב אלא בוגרת. **דילמא** – למעוטי בוגרת ותו לא אתא למעוטי מידי.

HALAKHAH

strangulation." (*Rambam, Sefer Kedushah, Hilkhot Issurei Bi'ah* 3:4.)

מָסַר הָאָב לִשְׁלוּחֵי הַבַּעַל **The father handed his daughter over to the husband's agents.** "A betrothed girl whom her father had already handed over to her bridegroom's agents (and all the more so a girl who had already entered under the bridal canopy) is treated like a married woman, so that if another man had sexual intercourse with her, he is liable to death by strangulation." (*Rambam, Sefer Kedushah, Hilkhot Issurei Bi'ah* 3:4.)

אֲפִילּוּ קְטַנָּה בְּמַשְׁמָע **Even a minor is included.** "If a man had sexual intercourse with a betrothed minor, he is liable to death by stoning, and she is exempt from punishment," following the Sages. (*Rambam, Sefer Kedushah, Hilkhot Issurei Bi'ah* 3:5.)

¹אֲמַר לֵיהּ: הַאי ״אֵינוֹ חַיָּיב עַד שֶׁתְּהֵא נַעֲרָה, בְּתוּלָה, מְאוֹרָסָה״? ²״אֵינוֹ חַיָּיב אֶלָּא עַל נַעֲרָה בְּתוּלָה מְאוֹרָסָה״ מִיבָּעֵי לֵיהּ, ³וְתוּ לָא מִידֵּי!

⁴בְּעָא מִינֵּיהּ רַבִּי יַעֲקֹב בַּר אַדָּא מֵרַב: בָּא עַל הַקְּטַנָּה מְאוֹרָסָה, ⁵לְרַבִּי מֵאִיר מַהוּ? ⁶לְגַמְרֵי מַמְעִיט לֵיהּ, ⁷אוֹ מִסְּקִילָה מַמְעִיט לֵיהּ?

⁸אֲמַר לֵיהּ: מִסְתַּבְּרָא, מִסְּקִילָה מְמַעֵט לֵיהּ.

⁹וְהָכְתִיב ״וּמֵתוּ גַּם שְׁנֵיהֶם״ — ¹⁰עַד שֶׁיְּהוּ שְׁנֵיהֶן שָׁוִין!

¹¹שָׁתֵיק רַב.

¹²אָמַר שְׁמוּאֵל: מַאי טַעְמָא שָׁתֵיק רַב? ¹³וְנֵימָא לֵיהּ: ¹⁴״וּמֵת הָאִישׁ אֲשֶׁר שָׁכַב עִמָּהּ

LITERAL TRANSLATION

¹He said to him: Is that "He is not liable unless she is a *na'arah,* a virgin, [and] betrothed"? ²It should have said: "Hc is only liable for a *na'arah,* a virgin [and] one who is betrothed"! ³And nothing more.

⁴Rabbi Ya'akov bar Adda asked Rav: [If] someone has intercourse with a betrothed minor, ⁵what [is the law] according to Rabbi Meir? ⁶Does he totally exclude him, ⁷or does he exclude him from stoning?

⁸He said to him: It stands to reason that he excluded him from stoning.

⁹But surely it is written: "Then they shall both of them die" — ¹⁰until the two of them are the same!

¹¹Rav was silent.

¹²Shmuel said: What is the reason that Rav was silent? ¹³Let him say to him: ¹⁴"Then only the man that lay with her

TRANSLATION AND COMMENTARY

אֲמַר לֵיהּ ¹Ravina **said to** Rav Aḥa of Difti: **Is that** the meaning of **"he is not liable** for stoning **unless** the girl **was a *na'arah*, a virgin, and** only **betrothed** to her husband, and not yet married to him"? Surely that formulation — the words עַד שֶׁתְּהֵא, translated here as "unless," but literally meaning "until" — implies that his liability does not begin until she becomes a *na'arah.* If the Mishnah meant only to exclude a girl who has come of age, ²**it should have been formulated** as follows: **"He is only liable** to death by stoning if he had intercourse with a girl who is **a *na'arah*, a virgin, and betrothed,** but not yet married." ³The Gemara concludes: **And** there is **nothing more** to say about the matter, for surely our Mishnah was taught in accordance with the viewpoint of Rabbi Meir.

בְּעָא מִינֵּיהּ ⁴**Rabbi Ya'akov bar Adda asked Rav: If a man had** sexual **intercourse with a betrothed minor,** ⁵**what is the law according to Rabbi Meir** who excludes him from the penalty of stoning? The Gemara explains the two sides of the question: ⁶**Does** Rabbi Meir **totally exclude him** from liability and exempt him from punishment? ⁷**Or does** Rabbi Meir only **exclude him from stoning,** leaving him liable to execution by strangulation?

אֲמַר לֵיהּ ⁸Rav **said to** Rabbi Ya'akov bar Adda: **It stands to reason that** Rabbi Meir only **excluded him from** the penalty of **stoning,** but he is still subject to the penalty of strangulation.

וְהָכְתִיב ⁹Rav Ya'akov bar Adda asked Rav: **But surely the verse states** (Deuteronomy 22:22): "If a man be found lying with a woman married to a man, **then they shall both of them die,** both the man that lay with the woman, and the woman," ¹⁰implying that punishment may not be imposed for adultery **unless the two** partners to the offense **are** punished **equally!** The girl in our case is not subject to the death penalty, for she is only a minor and therefore not liable for punishment. How then can her lover be put to death?

שָׁתֵיק רַב ¹¹The Gemara notes that **Rav remained silent,** and did not counter the argument put forward by Rav Ya'akov bar Adda.

אָמַר ¹²**Shmuel said: What is the reason that Rav remained silent?** ¹³**He should have said to him:** But surely another verse states (Deuteronomy 22:25): "But if a man finds a betrothed girl in the field, and the man forces her, and lies with her, ¹⁴**then only the man that lay with her shall die,** but to the girl you shall do

BACKGROUND

שָׁתֵיק רַב **Rav was silent.** We frequently find in the Talmud that when an objection was raised against Rav, he remained silent. Often in such cases, we find other sages adducing proofs in support of Rav's viewpoint, and also that Rav did not retract. Two explanations have been offered for this phenomenon: Sometimes Rav remained silent because he did not attach importance to the objection raised against him. At other times, Rav did not answer because he had a strong tradition regarding the correctness of his position, so that even if he was unable to answer an objection raised against him, he would not question the truth of his view.

RASHI

אמר ליה — אם כן האי עד שתהא נערה, האי לישנא משמע בהדיא למעוטי קטנה, דהכי משמע: אינו חייב בקטנותה עד שתגדיל ותהא נערה, ולא למעוטי בוגרת לחודא אתא — הכי איבעיא ליה למתני: אינו חייב אלא על נערה בתולה וכו׳. ותו לא מידי — אין עוד להקניט בדבר, דודאי מתניתין רבי מאיר היא. לרבי מאיר — דאוקמה למתניתין דממעט קטנה אליביה. לגמרי קא ממעט ליה — דפטרינן ליה לגברא ממיתה הואיל והיא פטורה דלאו בת עונשין היא, ולא קרינן בהו ״ומתו גם שניהם״ דכתיב גבי שוכב עם אשה בעולת בעל. או דילמא מסקילה ממעט ליה — אבל חנק מחייבי. שתיק — רב. ונימא ליה ומת האיש השוכב עם האשה לבדו — במאורסה כתיב ״ואם בשדה ימצא האיש את הנערה המאורסה והחזיק בה האיש ושכב עמה ומת האיש אשר שכב עמה לבדו״ למה לי, אילימא למעוטי לדידה הא

NOTES

וּמֵתוּ גַּם שְׁנֵיהֶם **Then they shall both of them die.** *Ramban* argues that the real proof-text regarding this matter is the verse which deals with a betrothed *na'arah* (Deuteronomy 22:24): "And you shall bring them both out to the gate of that city," and not the verse cited here in the Gemara which deals with the adultery committed by a married woman.

HALAKHAH

אֲשֶׁר שָׁכַב עִמָּהּ לְבַדּוֹ **That lay with her shall die.** "Regarding all forbidden sexual relations, if one partner was

BACKGROUND

מַעֲשֵׂה חִידּוּדִים **Frottage.** There are various different readings and explanations of this expression. Our commentary follows *Rashi* and others who understand that the Gemara is referring here to a case where the man stimulates himself against the woman's body from the outside without penetrating her. Others had the reading: מַעֲשֵׂה הֵירוֹדֵס (or מַעֲשֵׂה הוֹרְדוּס), and understand the expression to mean "an act of Herod," meaning intercourse with a dead woman.

לְבַדּוֹ״!

[1] כְּתַנָּאֵי: [2] ״׳וּמֵתוּ גַּם שְׁנֵיהֶם׳ — עַד שֶׁיְּהוּ שְׁנֵיהֶן שָׁוִין. [3] דִּבְרֵי רַבִּי יֹאשִׁיָּה. [4] רַבִּי יוֹנָתָן אוֹמֵר: ׳וּמֵת הָאִישׁ אֲשֶׁר שָׁכַב עִמָּהּ לְבַדּוֹ׳״.

[5] וְאִידָךְ, [6] הַהִיא ״וּמֵתוּ גַּם שְׁנֵיהֶם״ מַאי דָּרֵישׁ בֵּיהּ?

[7] אָמַר רָבָא: לְמַעוֹטֵי מַעֲשֵׂה חִידּוּדִים.

[8] וְאִידָךְ — [9] מַעֲשֵׂה חִידּוּדִים לָאו כְּלוּם הִיא.

[10] וְאִידָךְ, [11] הַאי ״לְבַדּוֹ״ מַאי דָּרֵישׁ בֵּיהּ?

[12] כִּדְתַנְיָא: ״בָּאוּ עָלֶיהָ עֲשָׂרָה בְּנֵי אָדָם וַעֲדַיִין הִיא בְּתוּלָה,

TRANSLATION AND COMMENTARY

nothing"! Thus we have a case where one partner in an adulterous relationship is put to death, and not the other. So too then we can say that a man who had sexual intercourse with a betrothed minor, the girl is exempt from all liability, but the man is subject to the penalty of strangulation.

כְּתַנָּאֵי [1] The Gemara notes that this matter is the subject of **a Tannaitic dispute,** for it was taught in a Baraita: "The verse dealing with adultery involving a married woman states (Deuteronomy 22:25): [2] **'Then they shall both of them die,'** teaching that punishment may not be imposed for adultery **unless the two** partners to the offense **are** punished **equally.** [3] **This is the position of Rabbi Yoshiyah.** [4] **Rabbi Yonatan** disagrees and **says:** Another verse dealing with rape states (Deuteronomy 22:25): **'Then only the man that lay with her shall die.'**

וְאִידָךְ [5] The Gemara asks: **The other** Tanna — Rabbi Yonatan, who maintains that the death penalty may be imposed upon one partner, and not the other — [6] **how does he interpret** the verse: **"Then they shall both of them die"?**

אָמַר רָבָא [7] **Rava said:** According to Rabbi Yonatan, that verse **excludes** a man who obtains **sexual gratification by frottage.** The words, "they shall both," teach that in such a case both parties are exempt from punishment, for punishment is only imposed when the man and the woman achieve gratification in equal measure.

וְאִידָךְ [8] The Gemara asks: **And** how does **the other** Tanna — Rabbi Yoshiyah — counter this argument? The Gemara explains: [9] Rabbi Yoshiyah maintains that obtaining sexual **gratification by frottage is nothing** at all, meaning that it does not have the legal significance of full sexual intercourse.

וְאִידָךְ [10] The Gemara asks: **The other** Tanna — Rabbi Yonatan, who maintains that the death penalty may not be imposed upon only one partner of an adulterous relationship — [11] **how does he interpret** the verse, "Then **only** the man that lay with her shall die"?

כִּדְתַנְיָא [12] The Gemara answers: Rabbi Yonatan needs that verse for what **was taught** in the following Baraita: **"If ten men had** sexual **intercourse with** a betrothed girl, **and she remained a virgin,** meaning that all

LITERAL TRANSLATION

shall die"!

[1] Like the Tannaim: [2] "'Then they shall both of them die' — until the two of them are the same. [3] [These are] the words of Rabbi Yoshiyah. [4] Rabbi Yonatan says: 'Then only the man that lay with her shall die.'"

[5] And the other one, [6] that "Then they shall both of them die" — how does he interpret it?

[7] Rava said: To exclude frottage.

[8] And the other one — [9] frottage is nothing.

[10] And the other one, [11] that "[Then] only [the man that lay with her shall die]" — how does he interpret it?

[12] As it was taught: "[If] ten men had intercourse with her, and she is still a virgin,

RASHI

כתיב ״ולנערה לא תעשה דבר״ — אלא להביא את הבא על הקטנה מדעתה, ואף על גב דפטור דידה לאו משום אונס — אלא משום קטנות דאיהי לאו בת עונשין לגמרי, איהו מיהא מיחייב. **שניהם שוין** — שני בני עונשין. **למעוטי מעשה חדודין** — מחדד ומקשה אברו בבשרה מבחוץ, דהוא נהנה והיא אינה נהנית, להכי כתיב ״שניהם״ שיהיו שניהם שוין נהנין. ומיהו שלא כדרכה אף על גב דהיא אינה נהנית — מ״משכבי אשה״ איתרבאי לחיובא. **לא כלום הוא** — ולא איצטריך למעוטי. ואיכא דאמרי מעשה הורדוס (בבא בתרא ג,ב), שהטמינה שבע שנים בדבש. **ועדיין היא בתולה** — שבאו כולם שלא כדרכה.

HALAKHAH

an adult, and the other was still a minor (though old enough for his or her sexual act to be regarded as sexual intercourse), the adult is liable, and the minor is exempt." (*Rambam, Sefer Kedushah, Hilkhot Issurei Bi'ah* 1:18.)

מַעֲשֵׂה חִידּוּדִים **Frottage.** "If someone engaged in sexual contact with a woman who is forbidden to him in a manner other than actual sexual intercourse, he is exempt from the death penalty, but liable for lashes for having engaged in activity that leads to forbidden sexual intercourse." (*Rambam, Sefer Kedushah, Hilkhot Issurei Bi'ah* 21:1.)

בָּאוּ עָלֶיהָ עֲשָׂרָה בְּנֵי אָדָם **If ten men had intercourse with her.** "If ten men engaged in vaginal intercourse with a betrothed girl, the first is liable to death by stoning, and all the others are liable to death by strangulation. If all ten engaged in anal intercourse, so that girl's hymen remained intact, they are all liable to death by stoning," following the Sages against Rabbi Yehudah HaNasi. (*Rambam, Sefer Kedushah, Hilkhot Issurei Bi'ah* 3:6.)

TRANSLATION AND COMMENTARY

ten engaged in anal intercourse, so that her hymen remained intact, **they are all put to death by stoning.** [1]**Rabbi** Yehudah HaNasi disagrees and **says: The first one is put to death by stoning,** for he had intercourse with a betrothed girl who was still a virgin, **but all** the rest **of them** are put to death **by strangulation,** for the verse states (Deuteronomy 22:25): 'Then only the man that lay with her shall die.' The word 'only' teaches that only one man is put to death for this offense by way of stoning and all the rest are executed by strangulation."

תָּנוּ רַבָּנַן [2]**Our Rabbis taught** the following Baraita: "The verse states (Leviticus 21:9): **'And the daughter of a priest, if she profanes** [תֵחֵל] **herself by playing the harlot,** she profanes her father; she shall be burnt with fire.' [3]**Rabbi** Yehudah HaNasi **says:** The word תֵחֵל (translated here as 'profane') is used here in the sense of **beginning** (as will be explained below). [4]**And similarly the verse states** (Deuteronomy 22:25): **'Then only the man that lay with her shall die.'"**

מַאי קָאָמַר? [5]The Gemara is puzzled by this cryptic remark: **What did** Rabbi Yehudah HaNasi mean to **say?** [6]**Rav Huna the son of Rav Yehoshua said: Rabbi** Yehudah HaNasi **agrees with Rabbi Yishmael, who said:** [7]Only **the betrothed** daughter of a priest who committed adultery **goes out for burning, but not the married** daughter of a priest. The married daughter of a priest who committed adultery is liable to death by strangulation, like any other married Jewish woman. [8]**And** Rabbi Yehudah HaNasi **said** here **as follows: If** the priest's daughter's **first** act of sexual **intercourse was adulterous,** meaning that if she committed adultery while betrothed, **she is put to death by burning.** [9]But for **any other** act of adulterous intercourse after marriage, she is put to death **by strangulation.** [10]And **what** did Rabbi Yehudah HaNasi mean when he said "**And similarly** the verse states: 'Then only the man that lay with her shall die'"? [11]Rav Huna the son of Rav Yehoshua explains that Rabbi Yehudah HaNasi meant that the law here regarding the daughter of a priest is **like** the law **there** regarding a betrothed girl who was raped. [12]**Just as there** regarding a betrothed girl who was raped, **the verse deals with** the girl's **first** act of sexual **intercourse,** during her betrothal, [13]**so** too **also here** regarding a priest's daughter, **the verse deals with** the girl's **first** act of sexual **intercourse,** during her betrothal. In such a case she is executed by burning. But the married daughter of a priest who committed adultery is executed by strangulation.

אֲמַר לֵיהּ [14]**Rav Bevai bar Abaye said to** Rav Huna the son of Rav Yehoshua: Our **Master did not say like that.** [15]The Gemara notes: **And who is** "Our Master"? [16]It is **Rav Yosef.** Rav Yosef explained Rabbi Yehudah HaNasi's cryptic remark as follows: [17]**Rabbi** Yehudah Ḥanasi **agrees with Rabbi Meir, who said:** If a priest's

כּוּלָּם בִּסְקִילָה. [1]רַבִּי אוֹמֵר: הָרִאשׁוֹן בִּסְקִילָה, וְכוּלָּן בְּחֶנֶק. [2]תָּנוּ רַבָּנַן: "'וּבַת אִישׁ כֹּהֵן כִּי תֵחֵל לִזְנוֹת'. [3]רַבִּי אוֹמֵר: תְּחִילָּה. [4]וְכֵן הוּא אוֹמֵר: 'וּמֵת הָאִישׁ אֲשֶׁר שָׁכַב עִמָּהּ לְבַדּוֹ'". [5]מַאי קָאָמַר? [6]אָמַר רַב הוּנָא בְּרֵיהּ דְּרַב יְהוֹשֻׁעַ: רַבִּי כְּרַבִּי יִשְׁמָעֵאל סְבִירָא לֵיהּ, דְּאָמַר: [7]אֲרוּסָה יָצְאָה לִשְׂרֵיפָה, וְלֹא נְשׂוּאָה. [8]וְהָכִי קָאָמַר: אִם תְּחִילַּת בִּיאָה בִּזְנוּת — בִּשְׂרֵיפָה. [9]אִידָךְ — בְּחֶנֶק. [10]מַאי "וְכֵן"? [11]כִּי הָתָם. [12]מַה הָתָם, בִּתְחִילַּת בִּיאָה קָמִשְׁתָּעֵי קְרָא, [13]הָכָא נַמִי, בִּתְחִילַּת בִּיאָה קָמִשְׁתָּעֵי קְרָא.
[14]אֲמַר לֵיהּ רַב בֵּיבָי בַּר אַבַּיֵי: מָר לָא הָכִי אָמַר. [15]וּמַנּוּ? [16]רַב יוֹסֵף. [17]רַבִּי כְּרַבִּי מֵאִיר סְבִירָא

LITERAL TRANSLATION

they are all [put to death] by stoning. [1]Rabbi says: The first one [is put to death] by stoning, and all of them by strangulation."

[2]Our Rabbis taught: "'And the daughter of a priest, if she profanes herself by playing the harlot.' [3]Rabbi says: Beginning. [4]And similarly it states: 'Then only the man that lay with her shall die.'"

[5]What did he say? [6]Rav Huna the son of Rav Yehoshua said: Rabbi agrees with Rabbi Yishmael, who said: [7]A betrothed woman goes out for burning, but not a married woman. [8]And he said as follows: If her first intercourse was adulterous, [she is put to death] by way of burning. [9]Any other — by strangulation. [10]What is "And similarly"? [11]Like there. [12]Just as there, the verse deals with the first intercourse, [13]so also here, the verse deals with the first intercourse.

[14]Rav Bevai bar Abaye said to him: Master did not say like that. [15]And who is he? [16]Rav Yosef. [17]Rabbi agrees with Rabbi Meir,

RASHI

וכולן בחנק – דגבי סקילה לבדו כתיב, וקרא יתירא הוא למעוטי כי האי גוונא, דאף על גב דקרינא ביה בתולה אין בסקילה אלא אחד מהם – אותו ששכב עמה לבדו, דהיינו ראשון, שביאתו היתה יחידית. רבי אומר – "כי תחל" – לשון תחלה, ולקמיה מפרש לה. דרבי ישמעאל – בריש פירקין. אם תחלת ביאתה בזנות – שזו היא ביאה ראשונה שנבעלה. כי התם – מה מצינו בנערה המאורסה שיצאה מחנק לסקילה, ולא יצאה אלא בביאה ראשונה וכתיב "לבדו" למעוטי שני. אף בת כהן לא נשתנית מיתתה אלא בביאה ראשונה, הלכך בנערה בתולה והיא ארוסה הכתוב מדבר. ברבי מאיר סבירא ליה – דאמר בת כהן נשואה לכשר – בשריפה, אבל נשאת לאחד מן הפסולין שנתחללה משעת נשואין –

TRANSLATION AND COMMENTARY

daughter was married to someone who was qualified to marry her, and she committed adultery, she is executed by burning. [1]But **if** the priest's daughter **was married to someone who was disqualified** from marrying her, such as a mamzer or a *natin,* and she committed adultery, **she is executed by strangulation.** [2]**And** Rabbi Yehudah HaNasi **said** here **as follows:** If the priest's daughter's **first** act of **profanation is through adultery, she is put to death by burning.** [3]But in **any other** case, meaning that she had profaned herself by marrying a person who was disqualified from marrying her, and now she commits adultery, she is put to death **by strangulation.**

[4]And **what** did Rabbi Yehudah HaNasi mean when he said **"And similarly** the verse states: 'Then only the man that lay with her shall die'"? Regarding the priest's daughter, the verse insists that her adultery be her first act of profanation. But regarding the betrothed girl who was raped, the verse insists that the girl's rape be her first act of sexual intercourse!

[67A] סִימָנָא בְּעָלְמָא [5]Rav Bevai bar Abaye explains that Rabbi Yehudah HaNasi cited the verse, "Then only the man who lay with her shall die," as **a mere sign** that the other verse, "If she profanes herself by playing the harlot," deals with a beginning. Just as one verse deals with the girl's first act of sexual intercourse, the other verse deals with her first act of profanation.

לֵיהּ, דְּאָמַר: [1]נִשֵּׂאת לְאֶחָד מִן הַפְּסוּלִין, מִיתָתָהּ בְּחֶנֶק. [2]וְהָכִי קָאָמַר: אִם תְּחִילַּת אַחֲלָתָהּ בִּזְנוּת, בִּשְׂרֵיפָה. [3]וְאִידָךְ — בְּחֶנֶק. [4]וּמַאי ״וְכֵן״?

[67A] [5]סִימָנָא בְּעָלְמָא.

מִשְׁנָה [6]הַמֵּסִית — [7]זֶה הֶדְיוֹט. [8]וְהַמֵּסִית אֶת הַהֶדְיוֹט. [9]אָמַר: ״יֵשׁ יִרְאָה בְּמָקוֹם פְּלוֹנִי. [10]כָּךְ אוֹכֶלֶת, כָּךְ שׁוֹתָה, כָּךְ מְטִיבָה, כָּךְ מְרִיעָה״.

LITERAL TRANSLATION

who said: [1]If she was married to one of those who are disqualified, her execution is by strangulation. [2]And he said as follows: If her first profanation is through adultery, [she is put to death] by way of burning. [3]Any other — by strangulation. [4]And what is "And similarly"?

[67A] [5]A mere sign.

MISHNAH [6]An inciter — [7]that is a common person, [8]and someone who incites a common person. [9]He said: "There is an idol in such-and-such place. [10]Thus it eats, thus it drinks, thus it does good, thus it does bad."

RASHI

שוב אינה אלא בחנק. והאי תחלה דקאמר רבי, הכי קאמר: אם זו תחלת חילולה — בשריפה, ואם לאו — בחנק. ומאי וכן — הכא לא קפיד אלא אתחלת חלול, ולא אתחלת ביאה, והתם אתחלת ביאה נמי קפיד. סימנא בעלמא — ובתחילת שום דבר הכתוב מדבר, דתחלת חלול מיהא הוה.

משנה המסית זה הדיוט — מסית דחשבינן ליה בנסקלין. זה הדיוט שהסית. אבל נביא שהסית אינו בסקילה אלא בחנק, כדמפרש בגמרא. המסית את ההדיוט — הוא דבסקילה, אבל מסית את הרבים כגון עיר הנדחת — בחנק, כדמפרש בגמרא. והא ליכא למידק: אבל מסית את הנביא בחנק, דלא מצינו חלוק בין מסית את הנביא למסית את ההדיוט, אבל מצינו חלוק בין נביא שהסית, להדיוט שהסית. דהדיוט שהסית כתיב (דברים יג) ״וסקלתו באבנים״, ובנביא כתיב (שם) ״והנביא ההוא או חולם החלום ההוא יומת״ ומיתה האמורה בתורה סתם אינה אלא חנק.

MISHNAH הַמֵּסִית [6]We learned earlier in the chapter (53a) that someone who incites another person to worship idols is liable for death by stoning, as the verses state (Deuteronomy 13:7-11): "If your brother...entices you secretly, saying, let us go and serve other gods....You shall not consent to him, nor heed him; nor shall your eye pity, nor shall you spare, nor shall you conceal him. But you shall surely kill him....And you shall stone him to death with stones, because he has sought to draw you away from the Lord your God, who brought you out of the land of Egypt, from the house of bondage." Our Mishnah teaches that when the Torah speaks of **an inciter** who is liable to death by stoning, [7]it is referring to **an ordinary person** who incites another Jew to idolatry, and not to a Prophet who leads people astray to serve false gods, for a false prophet is liable to death by strangulation (as will be explained in the Gemara). [8]**And** furthermore, when it speaks of an inciter who is liable to death by stoning, it is referring to **someone who incites an ordinary person** to idol worship, not to someone who incites an entire community to worship idols. What is considered incitement to idol worship? [9]For example, if someone **said** to another person: **"There is a** certain **idol in such-and-such place.** [10]**Thus** the idol **eats, thus it drinks, thus it benefits** those who worship it, and **thus it harms** those who do not worship it."

NOTES

כָּךְ אוֹכֶלֶת **Thus it eats.** *Meiri* understands this as follows: Thus the idol feeds those who worship it, and thus it gives drink to those who worship it, and thus it benefits its worshipers, and thus it harms those who do not worship it.

HALAKHAH

הַמֵּסִית **The inciter.** "Someone who incites another Jew to commit idol worship is subject to death by stoning, even if neither one actually worshiped the idol. The inciter is liable whether he was an ordinary person or a prophet, and whether the incited party was a man or a woman, a single individual or a number of individuals." (*Rambam, Sefer Mada, Hilkhot Avodah Zarah* 5:1.)

TRANSLATION AND COMMENTARY

כָּל חַיָּיבֵי מִיתוֹת [1]The verse which states (Deuteronomy 13:9): "Nor shall your eye pity, nor shall you spare [the inciter]," teaches that the inciter may be deprived of certain legal benefits ordinarily conferred on suspects in capital cases. The general rule **regarding those who are liable for** judicial **execution by Torah law** is that **we do not conceal witnesses** to entrap the suspect. [2]This rule applies to all those who are suspected of a capital offense, **except for** the inciter. [3]**If** the inciter approached **two people** together and **said to** them, 'Let us go and worship an idol,' [4]those two people **may serve as witnesses** and testify against him, and a prior warning is not necessary as is ordinarily required in capital cases. [5]Rather **they** may **bring him to court, and he is stoned** on the basis of their testimony. [6]**If** the inciter **spoke** his words of incitement **to** only **one person,** so that there is only a single witness, he cannot be convicted and put to death. [7]However, a person who heard the words of incitement may **say** to the inciter: **"I have friends who are interested in** idol worship; come and tell them what you told me." [8]**If** the inciter **is cunning, and** says that he **cannot speak before** his friends, [9]the court may **hide witnesses behind a fence** [10]**and** the person to whom he spoke then **says to him: "Repeat** for me **what you had said** earlier, for we are **alone,** and nobody else can hear you." [11]If the inciter **repeats** his words, [12]his interlocator **says to him: "How can we abandon our God in Heaven, and go and worship** idols made of **wood and stones?"** [13]If the inciter shows remorse and **retracts** what he had said, **that is good.**

[1]כָּל חַיָּיבֵי מִיתוֹת שֶׁבַּתּוֹרָה אֵין מַכְמִינִין עֲלֵיהֶם, [2]חוּץ מִזּוֹ. [3]אָמַר לִשְׁנַיִם, [4]הֵן עֵדָיו, [5]וּמְבִיאִין אוֹתוֹ לְבֵית דִּין, וְסוֹקְלִין אוֹתוֹ. [6]אָמַר לְאֶחָד, [7]הוּא אוֹמֵר: "יֵשׁ לִי חֲבֵירִים רוֹצִים בְּכָךְ". [8]אִם הָיָה עָרוּם, וְאֵינוֹ יָכוֹל לְדַבֵּר בִּפְנֵיהֶם, [9]מַכְמִינִין לוֹ עֵדִים אֲחוֹרֵי הַגָּדֵר, [10]וְהוּא אוֹמֵר לוֹ: "אֱמוֹר מַה שֶּׁאָמַרְתָּ בְּיִחוּד"! [11]וְהַלָּה אוֹמֵר לוֹ, [12]וְהוּא אוֹמֵר לוֹ: "הֵיאַךְ נַנִּיחַ אֶת אֱלֹהֵינוּ שֶׁבַּשָּׁמַיִם וְנֵלֵךְ וְנַעֲבוֹד עֵצִים וַאֲבָנִים"? [13]אִם חוֹזֵר בּוֹ, הֲרֵי

LITERAL TRANSLATION

[1][Regarding] all those who are liable for execution in the Torah, we do not conceal [witnesses], [2]except for this one. [3][If] he said to two [people], [4]they are his witnesses, [5]and they bring him to court, and stone him. [6][If] he said to one [person], [7]he says: "I have friends who desire that." [8]If he was cunning, and cannot speak before them, [9]they hide witnesses behind a fence, [10]and he says to him: "Say what you said in privacy," [11]and that one says to him, [12]and he says to him: "How can we abandon our God in Heaven, and go and worship wood and stones?" [13]If he retracts, that

RASHI

אמר לשנים — יחד, הן עצמן נעשו עדים ואין צריכין להתרות בו כשאר חייבי מיתות, אלא מביאין אותו לבית דין דכתיב (שם) "לא תחמול ולא תכסה עליו". **אמר לאחד הוא אומר יש לי חברים רוצים בכך** — הניסת צריך להשיבו "יש לי חברים רוצים בכך, בא ואמור לי בפניהם". **ואם היה המסית ערום ואינו יכול לדבר בפניהם** — כלומר, אומר: "איני יכול לפרסם הדבר מפני יראת בית דין". **מכמינין לו** — דמתרגמינן "וארב לו" וכמן ליה (דברים יט), מעמידין ליה מארבין אחורי הגדר לשמוע דבריו. **ביחוד** — כלומר אין איש עכשיו עמנו ויכול אתה לומר מה שאמרת לי.

NOTES

אָמַר לִשְׁנַיִם....אָמַר לְאֶחָד If he said to two people....If he said to one person. According to some authorities, there is no difference between an inciter who approached two people and one who approached only one person. In both cases the inciter must be given a chance to retract. However, most Rishonim distinguish between the two cases and say that the inciter is given the chance to retract only if he approached just one person. Some explain that if the inciter approached one person, he can claim that he was testing his interlocutor, and so he must be given the chance to retract. But if he approached two people, he cannot put forward such an argument and does not deserve the chance to retract (*Ḥayyim Shenayim Yeshalem*). Others explain that if the inciter approached two people, he is not given the chance to retract, because we cannot rely on his retraction. It might stem from his fear that the two people will testify against him. But if the inciter approached only one person, he must be given the opportunity to retract, for their is no reason to doubt the sincerity of his retraction (*Ramah*).

אֱמוֹר מַה שֶּׁאָמַרְתָּ בְּיִחוּד Say what you said in privacy. *Rashash* understands this to mean: "Say what you said clearly." The person whom the inciter had incited to idol worship must offer him the opportunity to clarify what he had said, to show whether he really meant it.

HALAKHAH

אָמַר לִשְׁנַיִם, הֵן עֵדָיו If he said to two people, they are his witnesses. "If someone incited two other people to commit idol worship, those two people may serve as witnesses and testify against him." (*Rambam, Sefer Mada, Hilkhot Avodah Zarah* 5:2.)

מַכְמִינִין לוֹ עֵדִים They hide witnesses. "Someone who incites another person to commit idol worship may be put to death without a warning prior to the commission of his offense. It is also permissible to conceal witnesses to entrap a suspected inciter, and even to trick him into committing his offense in the presence of the hidden witnesses." (*Rambam, Sefer Shofetim, Hilkhot Sanhedrin* 11:5.)

TRANSLATION AND COMMENTARY

[1] **And if he says: "It is our obligation** to worship idols, **it is good for us** to engage in idol worship," [2] the witnesses **standing behind the fence** may **bring him to court, and he is stoned.**

הָאוֹמֵר [3] If **someone says** to another person: **"I will worship** an idol," or **"I will go and worship** an idol," or **"Let us go and worship** an idol," or **"I will sacrifice** to an idol," [4] or **"I will go and sacrifice** to an idol," or **"Let us go and sacrifice** to an idol," [5] or **"I will burn incense** before an idol," or **"I will go and burn incense** before an idol," or **"Let us go and burn incense** before an idol," [6] or **"I will offer a libation** to an idol," or **"I will go and offer a libation** to an idol," or **"Let us go and offer a libation** to an idol," [7] or **"I will bow down** before an idol," or **"I will go and bow down** before an idol," or **"Let us go and bow down** before an idol" — in every one of these cases, he is regarded as an inciter and is liable to death by stoning.

GEMARA הַמֵּסִית [8] We have learned in our Mishnah: "When the Torah speaks of **an inciter** who is liable to death by stoning, it is referring to **an ordinary person** who incites another person to idolatry." A careful reading of the Mishnah leads to the following conclusion: [9] **The reason** that the inciter is subject to the penalty of stoning **is that he is an ordinary person.** [10] **But** if he claimed to be **a prophet,** he is not subject to the penalty of stoning, but rather he is liable to death **by strangulation,** as the verse states (Deuteronomy 13:6): "And that prophet, or that dreamer of dreams, shall be put to death." Wherever the Torah speaks of execution without mentioning the method, it refers to death by strangulation.

וְהַמֵּסִית [11] We also learned in our Mishnah: "The inciter who is liable to death by stoning is **someone who incites an ordinary person** to idol worship." [12] This formulation implies that **the reason** that the inciter is subject to the penalty of stoning **is that he incited an individual. But** if he incited **a community** to worship an idol, he is liable to death **by strangulation.**

מַתְנִיתִין מַנִּי [13] The Gemara asks: **According to which** Tanna was **our Mishnah** taught? [14] The Gemara answers: Our Mishnah follows the viewpoint of **Rabbi Shimon, as it was taught** in a Baraita: [15] **"A prophet who enticed** an individual to commit idolatry is subject to death **by stoning,** just like an ordinary

זֶה מוּטָּב. [1] וְאִם אָמַר: "כָּךְ הִיא חוֹבָתֵנוּ, כָּךְ יָפֶה לָנוּ", [2] הָעוֹמְדִין מֵאֲחוֹרֵי הַגָּדֵר מְבִיאִין אוֹתוֹ לְבֵית דִּין, וְסוֹקְלִין אוֹתוֹ.

[3] הָאוֹמֵר: "אֶעֱבוֹד", "אֵלֵךְ וְאֶעֱבוֹד", "נֵלֵךְ וְנַעֲבוֹד", [4] "אֲזַבֵּחַ", "אֵלֵךְ וַאֲזַבֵּחַ", "נֵלֵךְ וּנְזַבֵּחַ", [5] "אַקְטִיר", "אֵלֵךְ וְאַקְטִיר", "נֵלֵךְ וְנַקְטִיר", [6] "אֲנַסֵּךְ", "אֵלֵךְ וַאֲנַסֵּךְ", "נֵלֵךְ וּנְנַסֵּךְ", [7] "אֶשְׁתַּחֲוֶה", "אֵלֵךְ וְאֶשְׁתַּחֲוֶה", "נֵלֵךְ וְנִשְׁתַּחֲוֶה".

גמרא [8] "הַמֵּסִית — זֶה הֶדְיוֹט". [9] טַעְמָא דְּהֶדְיוֹט. [10] הָא נָבִיא — בְּחֶנֶק.

[11] "וְהַמֵּסִית אֶת הַהֶדְיוֹט". [12] טַעְמָא דְּיָחִיד, הָא רַבִּים — בְּחֶנֶק.

[13] מַתְנִיתִין מַנִּי? [14] רַבִּי שִׁמְעוֹן הִיא, דְּתַנְיָא: [15] "נָבִיא שֶׁהִדִּיחַ

LITERAL TRANSLATION

is good. [1] And if he says: "That is our obligation, that is good for us," [2] those who are standing behind the fence bring him to court, and stone him.

[3] Someone who says: "I will worship," "I will go and worship," "Let us go and worship," [4] "I will sacrifice," "I will go and sacrifice," Let us go and sacrifice," [5] "I will burn incense," "I will go and burn incense," "Let us go and burn incense," [6] "I will offer a libation," "I will go and offer a libation," "Let us go and offer a libation," [7] "I will bow down," "I will go and bow down," "Let us go and bow down."

GEMARA [8] "An inciter — that is a common person." [9] The reason is that he is a common person. [10] But a prophet — by strangulation.

[11] "And someone who incites a common person." [12] The reason is that [he incites] an individual, but a community — by strangulation.

[13] Our Mishnah is like whom? [14] It is Rabbi Shimon, for it was taught: [15] "A prophet who incited —

RASHI

האומר אעבוד וכו׳ — באחת מכל הלשונות הללו הוי מסית וחייב. **גמרא הא נביא** — אם מסית זה נביא, שהיה מתנבא בשם הקדוש ברוך הוא לעבוד עבודה זרה. **טעמא** — דמסית את ההדיוט כלומר את היחיד, הא אם מסית את הרבים כגון אנשי עיר הנדחת — לאו בסקילה הוא אלא בחנק, דהא ליכא למידק, דהא דקתני **והמסית את ההדיוט** — למעוטי מסית את הנביא קאמר, דלא אשכחן תנא דמפליג בין מסית את הנביא למסית את ההדיוט. אבל בין נביא המסית להדיוט המסית אשכחן חלוק, כדמפרש ואזיל. **טעמא דרבי שמעון ורבנן** — מפרש ב״אלו הן הנחנקין״.

HALAKHAH

"אֶעֱבוֹד", "נֵלֵךְ וְנַעֲבוֹד" **"I will worship," "let us go and worship."** "Whether the inciter spoke in the singular, e.g., 'I will worship an idol,' or he spoke in the plural, e.g., 'Let us go and worship an idol,' he is liable to death by stoning." (*Rambam, Sefer Mada, Hilkhot Avodah Zarah* 5:2.)

נָבִיא שֶׁהִדִּיחַ **A prophet who seduced.** "If a prophet incited another person to commit idolatry, he is liable to death by stoning, just like an ordinary person," following the Sages,

[1] רַבִּי שִׁמְעוֹן — בִּסְקִילָה. אוֹמֵר: בְּחֶנֶק. [2] מַדִּיחֵי עִיר הַנִּדַּחַת — בִּסְקִילָה. [3] רַבִּי שִׁמְעוֹן אוֹמֵר: בְּחֶנֶק". [4] אֵימָא סֵיפָא: [5] "הַמַּדִּיחַ — זֶה הָאוֹמֵר: 'נֵלֵךְ וְנַעֲבוֹד עֲבוֹדָה זָרָה'". [6] וְאָמַר רַב יְהוּדָה אָמַר רַב: מַדִּיחֵי עִיר הַנִּדַּחַת שָׁנוּ. [7] אֲתָאָן לְרַבָּנַן. [8] רֵישָׁא רַבִּי שִׁמְעוֹן, [9] וְסֵיפָא רַבָּנַן. [10] רָבִינָא אָמַר: כּוּלָּהּ רַבָּנַן הִיא. [11] "וְלֹא זוֹ אַף זוֹ" קָתָנֵי.

LITERAL TRANSLATION

by stoning. [1] Rabbi Shimon says: By strangulation. [2] The inciters of an idolatrous condemned city — by stoning. [3] Rabbi Shimon say: By strangulation." [4] Say the last clause: [5] "The inciter — that is someone who says: 'Let us go and worship idols.'" [6] And Rav Yehudah said in the name of Rav: They taught about the inciters of an idolatrous city. [7] We have come to the Sages. [8] The first clause is Rabbi Shimon, [9] and the last clause is the Sages. [10] Ravina said: The entire [Mishnah] is the Sages. [11] And it teaches "not [only] this, [but] also this."

TRANSLATION AND COMMENTARY

person. [1] **Rabbi Shimon says:** A prophet who enticed an individual to commit idolatry is subject to death **by strangulation.** [2] **The inciters of an idolatrous city** are subject to the penalty of death **by stoning,** just like the inciter of a single individual. [3] **Rabbi Shimon say:** The inciters of a condemned city are subject to death **by strangulation."** Our Mishnah, which implies that a prophet who enticed an individual to commit idolatry and an ordinary person who incited a community to worship idols are not subject to stoning, but to strangulation, seems to follow the position of Rabbi Shimon against the Sages (the anonymous first Tanna of the Baraita).

אֵימָא סֵיפָא [4] The Gemara points out a difficulty: **Consider the next Mishnah,** which seems to follow the position of the Sages who disagree with Rabbi Shimon: [5] **"The inciter** mentioned earlier in the chapter (53a) among those liable to death by stoning **is someone who says** to the community at large: **'Let us go and worship idols.'"** [6] **And Rav Yehudah said in the name of Rav: The inciters of a condemned city were meant** here. [7] Thus, **we have come to** the position of **the Sages** who maintain that the inciters of a condemned city are subject to stoning. [8] This forces us to the difficult conclusion that **the first Mishnah follows** the position of **Rabbi Shimon,** [9] **and the next Mishnah follows** the position of **the Sages.**

רָבִינָא אָמַר [10] **Ravina said: The entire** Mishnah — our Mishnah and the following one — **follows** the position of **the Sages,** who disagree with Rabbi Shimon. When the Mishnah says that someone who incites an individual to idol worship, it does not mean that the inciters of a condemned city are not liable for the same penalty. Rather the Mishnah teaches first that someone who incites an individual to idol worship is liable to death by stoning, and then it adds that the seducers of a condemned city are subject to the same punishment. It cannot be argued that the Mishnah should have taught only that the inciters of a condemned city are subject to stoning, and we would have known that someone who incites an individual is also liable for that punishment, [11] for the Mishnah **was written** according to the stylistic convention called **"not only this, but also this."** Using this convention, a Mishnah begins by mentioning a simple, relatively obvious matter, and from there it proceeds to a more complicated matter. Thus, the Mishnah teaches that not only is someone who incites a single individual subject to the penalty of death by stoning, but even the inciters of a condemned city are subject to that same punishment.

RASHI

מדיחי עיר הנדחת שנו — במשנתנו זאת, ואשמועינן סיפא דמדיח דרישא במדיח עיר הנדחת קאמר, והכי קאמר: המדיח דתנן לעיל (נג,א) בהדי נסקלין — זה האומר לרבים נלך ונעבוד עבודה זרה. **רבינא אמר** גרס, ולא גרסינן "אמר רבינא", דאיהו ורב פפא לא פליגי, אלא מר מתרץ חדא, ומר מתרץ חדא, ולא פליגי, דהא בתרי מילי אוקימנא לרישא כרבי שמעון, ואתו הנך אמוראי לתרוצה כרבנן. והכי פירושה: רבינא תרצה לחדא ואמר: רישא נמי רבנן, והמסית את ההדיוט לאו למעוטי מסית את הרבים אתא, אלא תרוייהו תנא להו, תנא רישא מסית את היחיד, והדר תנא סיפא המדיח זה האומר לרבים נלך ונעבוד עבודה זרה. **ולא זו אף זו קתני** — כלומר, אי קשיא לך: ליתני מסית את הרבים ולא ליתני מסית את היחיד, דהא פשיטא דכולהו מודו בה דבסקילה — אורחא לתנא למתני הכי, תנא מילתא ברישא דפשיטא ליה, והדר תנא רבותא: ולא זו דמסית יחיד בלבד בסקילה, אלא אף זו דמסית רבים בסקילה, ודלא כרבי שמעון, ורב פפא אתא אף לתרוצי לדקתני "המסית זה הדיוט" — לאו למעוטי נביא המסית קתני, אלא כל המסיתים קרי הדיוטות משום הכמנה, כלומר, מסית הדיוט ושוטה הוא, ומדת הקלין נוהג בו, שמקילין בחייו, שכל חייבי מיתות צריכין התראה וזה נהרג בהכמנה.

HALAKHAH

against the minority opinion of Rabbi Shimon. (*Rambam, Sefer Mada, Hilkhot Avodah Zarah* 5:1.)

מַדִּיחֵי עִיר הַנִּדַּחַת **The inciters of a condemned city.** "Those who incited the inhabitants of an entire city to commit idolatry are liable to death by stoning," following the Sages, and against Rabbi Shimon. (*Rambam, Sefer Mada, Hilkhot Avodah Zarah* 4:1.)

BACKGROUND

סְטָדָא **Setada.** Christian censors as well as popular tradition identified "ben Setada" and "ben Pandera" with Jesus of Nazareth because of the similarity of several aspects of the two stories. However, *Tosafot* regarded this identification as being impossible because of the chronology. Some modern commentators believe that this is the name of a sorcerer who came from Egypt, who was mentioned by Josephus.

LANGUAGE

פַּנְדֵּירָא **Pandera.** "Pandera" might be derived from the Greek name Πανδαρος, *pandaros*, or else from the nickname Πανθηρ, *panter*, meaning "a panther." Both names were rather common at the time among the Roman soldiers.

[1]רַב פַּפָּא אָמַר: כִּי קָתָנֵי "מֵסִית" — זֶה הֶדְיוֹט" — [2]לְהַכְמָנָה. [3]דְּתַנְיָא: "וּשְׁאָר כָּל חַיָּיבֵי מִיתוֹת שֶׁבַּתּוֹרָה אֵין מַכְמִינִין עֲלֵיהֶן, [4]חוּץ מִזּוֹ. [5]כֵּיצַד עוֹשִׂין לוֹ? [6]מַדְלִיקִין לוֹ אֶת הַנֵּר בַּבַּיִת הַפְּנִימִי, [7]וּמוֹשִׁיבִין לוֹ עֵדִים בַּבַּיִת הַחִיצוֹן, [8]כְּדֵי שֶׁיְּהוּ הֵן רוֹאִין אוֹתוֹ, וְשׁוֹמְעִין אֶת קוֹלוֹ, וְהוּא אֵינוֹ רוֹאֶה אוֹתָן. [9]וְהַלָּה אוֹמֵר לוֹ: 'אֱמוֹר מַה שֶּׁאָמַרְתָּ לִי בְּיִחוּד', [10]וְהוּא אוֹמֵר לוֹ, [11]וְהַלָּה אוֹמֵר לוֹ: 'הֵיאַךְ נַנִּיחַ אֶת אֱלֹהֵינוּ שֶׁבַּשָּׁמַיִם, וְנַעֲבוֹד עֲבוֹדָה זָרָה'? [12]אִם חוֹזֵר בּוֹ, מוּטָב. [13]וְאִם אָמַר: 'כָּךְ הִיא חוֹבָתֵנוּ, וְכָךְ יָפֶה לָנוּ', [14]הָעֵדִים שֶׁשּׁוֹמְעִין מִבַּחוּץ מְבִיאִין אוֹתוֹ לְבֵית דִּין, וְסוֹקְלִין אוֹתוֹ. [15]וְכֵן עָשׂוּ לְבֶן סְטָדָא בְּלוּד, [16]וּתְלָאוּהוּ בְּעֶרֶב הַפֶּסַח".
[17]בֶּן סְטָדָא? [18]בֶּן פַּנְדֵּירָא הוּא!
[19]אָמַר רַב חִסְדָּא: בַּעַל — סְטָדָא, [20]בּוֹעֵל — פַּנְדֵּירָא.

LITERAL TRANSLATION

[1]Rav Pappa said: When it taught "An inciter — that is a common person" — [2]for concealing [witnesses]. [3]As it was taught: "[Regarding] all those who are liable for execution in the Torah, we do not conceal [witnesses], [4]except for this one. [5]What do they do to him? [6]They light a candle for him in an inner room, [7]and plant witnesses in the outer room, [8]so that they can see him, and hear his voice, but he cannot see them. [9]And that one says to him: 'Say what you said to me in privacy,' [10]and he says to him, [11]and that one says to him: 'How can we abandon our God in Heaven, and worship an idol?' [12]If he retracts, that is good. [13]And if he says: 'That is our obligation, and that is good for us,' [14]the witnesses who hear him from outside bring him to court, and stone him. [15]And thus they did to the son of Setada in Lod, [16]and they hanged him on the eve of Passover."

[17][Was he] the son of Setada? [18]He was the son of Pandera!

[19]Rav Ḥisda said: The husband was Setada, [20]the lover was Pandera.

RASHI

בבית הפנימי — בחדרי חדרים, לפי שהוא ירא לדבר בגלוי. **הן רואין אותו** — לאור הנר שעמו, דאי לא מצי חזו ליה לא מצי מסהדי עליה לחיוביה קטלא, ואף על גב דשמעי קליה, דמצי למימר: לא הואי אנא. **ושומעין קולו** — שהוא אומר דברי הסתה. **בעל סטדא** — בעל אמו סטדא שמו.

TRANSLATION AND COMMENTARY

רַב פַּפָּא אָמַר [1]**Rav Pappa said: When** the Mishnah **taught** that the inciter is a *"hedyot"*, it did not mean, as we have so far understood it, that when the Torah speaks of **an inciter** who is liable for the penalty of stoning, it refers to **an ordinary person** who incites someone to idolatry, to the exclusion of a prophet who leads people astray to serve false gods — the position of Rabbi Shimon against the Sages. Rather the Mishnah follows the position of the Sages, and teaches that an inciter is regarded as a *"hedyot"* — a fool — [2]**regarding the concealing of witnesses.** The inciter is treated as a fool, who has little regard for his own life, and so the court may conceal witnesses in order to entrap him. [3]**As it was taught** in the following Baraita: "The general rule **regarding those who are liable for** judicial **execution by Torah law** is that **we do not conceal witnesses** in order to entrap the suspect. [4]This rule applies to all suspects **except for** the inciter, for in the case of a person who is suspected of incitement to idolatry, the court may intentionally hide witnesses in order to apprehend the offender, as will be explained below. [5]**What do they do to him?** [6]**They light a candle for him in an inner room** where he will be more likely to speak openly, [7]**and they plant witnesses in the outer room** which remains in darkness, [8]so the witnesses **can see** the inciter, **and hear his voice, but he cannot see them.** [9]**And** the person to whom he had spoken **says to him: 'Repeat** for me **what you had said** earlier, for we are **alone.'** [10]If the inciter **repeats** his words of incitement, [11]his interlocutor **says to him: 'How can we abandon our God in Heaven,** and go **and worship an idol?'** [12]**If** the inciter shows remorse and **retracts** what he had said, **that is good.** [13]**And if he says: 'It is our obligation** to worship idols, **and it is good for us,'** [14]**the witnesses who hear him from outside** may **bring him to court, and** he is **stoned.** [15]It was related that **this** is precisely what **they did to** the well-known inciter, **the son of Setada in** the city of **Lod,** [16]**who was hanged** for his crimes **on the eve of Passover."**

בֶּן סְטָדָא [17]The Gemara raises a question about this anecdote: Was the inciter **the son of Setada?** [18]But surely we know that he was **the son of Pandera!**

אָמַר רַב חִסְדָּא [19]**Rav Ḥisda said: The husband** of the inciter's mother **was** named **Setada,** and so the inciter was known as the son of Setada. [20]But **her lover** who was in fact the inciter's father, **was** named **Pandera,** and so the inciter was also known as the son of Pandera.

NOTES

זֶה הֶדְיוֹט — לְהַכְמָנָה **That is a common person — for concealing witnesses.** Some understand from this that neither a prophet who incited an individual, nor an ordinary person who seduced a community is regarded as a *hedyot,*

TRANSLATION AND COMMENTARY

בַּעַל פַּפּוֹס בֶּן יְהוּדָה [1]The Gemara does not accept this resolution of the difficulty: But surely it is known that **the** mother's **husband was** named **Pappos the son of Yehudah!**

אֶלָּא אִמּוֹ סְטָדָא [2]The Gemara answers: **Rather,** the inciter's **mother was** named **Setada,** and his father was named Pandera. Thus, the inciter was known as the son of Setada, and also as the son of Pandera.

אִמּוֹ מִרְיָם מְגַדְּלָא [3]The Gemara quickly rejects this answer: But surely it is known that the inciter's **mother was** named **Miryam the woman's hair-dresser!**

כִּדְאָמְרִי בְּפוּמְבְּדִיתָא [4]The Gemara explains: Setada is not a proper name, but rather a fitting description of the inciter's mother. **As** the people **say in Pumbedita** about a promiscuous woman: [5]**That one strayed** (*setat da*) **from her husband.**

MISHNAH הַמֵּדִיחַ [6]We learned earlier in the chapter (53a) that an inciter is liable to death by stoning. Our Mishnah teaches that **an inciter is someone who says** to the community at large: [7]**"Let us go and worship idols."**

הַמְכַשֵּׁף [8]We also learned earlier in the chapter that **a sorcerer** is liable to death by stoning. [9]Our Mishnah teaches that only someone **who** actually **performs an act** of magic **is liable** to death by stoning, [10]**but not someone who deceives** other people into thinking that he is endowed with magical powers. [11]**Rabbi Akiva said in the name of Rabbi Yehoshua: Two** people might **gather** together the **gourds** in a field using magic. [12]**One** might **gather** the gourds **and be exempt** from the penalty of stoning, [13]**and one** might **gather** the gourds **and be liable** to stoning. [14]**The one who** actually **performs an act** of magic to gather the gourds **is liable** to death by stoning, [15]whereas **the one who** deceives people, making them think that he employed magic to gather the gourds **is exempt.**

[1]בַּעַל פַּפּוֹס בֶּן יְהוּדָה הוּא! [2]אֶלָּא, אִמּוֹ סְטָדָא. [3]אִמּוֹ מִרְיָם מְגַדְּלָא נְשַׂיָּא הֲוַאי! [4]כִּדְאָמְרִי בְּפוּמְבְּדִיתָא: [5]סְטַת דָּא מִבַּעֲלָהּ.

משנה [6]הַמֵּדִיחַ — זֶה הָאוֹמֵר: [7]"נֵלֵךְ וְנַעֲבוֹד עֲבוֹדָה זָרָה".

[8]הַמְכַשֵּׁף, [9]הָעוֹשֶׂה מַעֲשֶׂה חַיָּיב, [10]וְלֹא הָאוֹחֵז אֶת הָעֵינַיִם. [11]רַבִּי עֲקִיבָא אוֹמֵר מִשּׁוּם רַבִּי יְהוֹשֻׁעַ: שְׁנַיִם לוֹקְטִין קִשּׁוּאִין, [12]אֶחָד לוֹקֵט פָּטוּר, [13]וְאֶחָד לוֹקֵט חַיָּיב. [14]הָעוֹשֶׂה מַעֲשֶׂה חַיָּיב, [15]הָאוֹחֵז אֶת הָעֵינַיִם פָּטוּר.

LITERAL TRANSLATION

[1]The husband was Pappos the son of Yehudah!

[2]Rather, his mother was Setada.

[3]His mother was Miryam the woman's hair-dresser!

[4]As they say in Pumbedita: [5]That one strayed from her husband.

MISHNAH [6]The inciter — that is someone who says: [7]"Let us go and worship idols."

[8]The sorcerer, [9]who performs an act is liable, [10]but not someone who performs an illusion (lit., "captures the eyes"). [11]Rabbi Akiva said in the name of Rabbi Yehoshua: Two gather gourds, [12]one gathers, [and is] exempt, [13]and one gathers, [and is] liable. [14]The one who performs an act is liable. [15]The one who captures the eyes is exempt.

RASHI

סטת דא — על שם שזינתה קרי לה הכי.

משנה המדיח זה האומר וכו׳ — בגמרא מוקים לה במדיח עיר הנדחת. העושה מעשה — ממש, בסקילה. ולא האוחז את העינים — מראה לבריות כאילו הוא עושה, ואינו עושה כלום. שנים מלקטין קשואין — במכשפות לפניו, אחד מהן לוקט וחייב, וחברו לוקט ופטור. העושה מעשה — שסיתה כאן שדה קשואין ולקטה ממש בכשפים — חייב. האוחז את העינים — מראה לנו כאילו התקבצו כולם במקום אחד, והקשואין לא זזין ממקומן — פטור.

NOTES

a fool. Therefore these transgressors cannot be convicted without proper warning (*Tzofnat Pa'ane'aḥ*).

הָאוֹחֵז אֶת הָעֵינַיִם **Someone who deceives.** *Tiferet Yisrael* distinguishes between a person who creates an optical illusion with magic and a person who creates an optical illusion with a sleight of hand or some other trick. In the first case, the person is exempt from liability, but forbidden nonetheless to act in that manner, whereas in the second case, he is permitted to act in that manner.

HALAKHAH

הַמְכַשֵּׁף **The sorcerer.** "A sorcerer is liable to death by stoning, provided that he actually performed an act of magic. But if he merely performed an optical illusion, he is only subject to lashes by Rabbinic decree. According to *Kesef Mishneh,* such a person is also subject to lashes by Torah law for having violated the prohibition against acting like a *me'onen.* Alternatively, a person who uses an optical illusion to make it appear as if he had performed a supernatural act is subject to lashes by Torah law. But if the optical illusion appears like a perfectly natural act, he is exempt from lashes by Torah law." (*Rambam, Sefer Mada, Hilkhot Avodah Zarah* 11:15.)

TRANSLATION AND COMMENTARY

GEMARA אָמַר רַב יְהוּדָה [1]**Rav Yehudah said in the name of Rav: The inciters of a condemned city were meant here.**

הַמְכַשֵּׁף [2]We learned in our Mishnah: **"The sorcerer** who is liable to death by stoning is someone **who** actually **performs an act** of magic, and not just an optical illusion." [3]**Our Rabbis taught** a related Baraita: "Even though the verse states (Exodus 22:17): 'You shall not let **a sorceress** live,' anyone who practices sorcery, [4]**whether a man or a woman,** is subject to the death penalty. [5]**If so, why does the verse state:** 'You shall not let **a sorceress** live'? [6]**Because most women are familiar with sorcery,** so there was special reason to warn them against it. [7]**By what** mode of **execution** is a sorcereress put to death? [8]**Rabbi Yose the Galilean says: Here the verse states** (Exodus 22:17): [9]**'You shall not let a sorceress live.'** [10]**And below** regarding the conquest of the seven Canaanite nations **the verse states** (Deuteronomy 20:16): **'You shall not let a soul live.'** [11]**Just as there,** the Canaanites were put to death **by the sword,** as the verse states (Numbers 21:24): 'And Israel smote them with the edge of the sword,' [12]**so too here,** the sorceress is put to death **by the sword.** [13]**Rabbi Akiva says: Here the verse states: 'You shall not let a sorceress live.'** [14]**And below** regarding those who cross the bounds that were to be set up around Mount Sinai, **the verse states** (Exodus 19:13): 'No hand shall touch him, but he shall surely be stoned, or shot; **whether it be beast or man, it shall not live.'** [15]**Just as there,** the violation of the prohibition against approaching the mountain was punishable **by stoning,** [16]**so too here** the violation of the prohibition against sorcery is punishable **by stoning.** [17]**Rabbi Yose said to him: 'I learned** the meaning of the verse, **"You shall not let live** (*lo teḥayeh*),' [18]by way of analogy **from** the verse, **"You shall not let live** (*lo teḥayeh*)," [19]**and you learned** the meaning of the verse, **"You shall not let live** (*lo teḥayeh*),' by way of analogy **from** the verse **"it shall not live** (*lo yiḥyeh*)."' [20]**Rabbi Akiva said to him: 'I learned** the punishment applying to **a Jew** who violated the prohibition against sorcery **from** the punishment applying to **a Jew** who violated the prohibtion against approaching the mountain. [21]**Regarding** Jews, **Scripture stated many** different **modes of execution.** Thus if "it shall not live" means death by stoning, "You shall not suffer to live," showed also mean death by stoning. [22]**You,** on the other hand, **learned** the

גמרא [1]אָמַר רַב יְהוּדָה אָמַר רַב: מְדִיחֵי עִיר הַנִּדַּחַת שָׁנוּ כָּאן.

[2]״הַמְכַשֵּׁף זֶה הָעוֹשֶׂה מַעֲשֶׂה וכו׳״. [3]תָּנוּ רַבָּנַן: ״׳מְכַשֵּׁפָה׳ — [4]אֶחָד הָאִישׁ וְאֶחָד הָאִשָּׁה. [5]אִם כֵּן, מַה תַּלְמוּד לוֹמַר: ׳מְכַשֵּׁפָה׳? [6]מִפְּנֵי שֶׁרוֹב נָשִׁים מְצוּיוֹת בִּכְשָׁפִים. [7]מִיתָתָן, בַּמֶּה? [8]רַבִּי יוֹסֵי הַגְּלִילִי אוֹמֵר: נֶאֱמַר כָּאן: [9]׳מְכַשֵּׁפָה לֹא תְחַיֶּה׳, [10]וְנֶאֱמַר לְהַלָּן: ׳לֹא תְחַיֶּה כָּל נְשָׁמָה׳. [11]מַה לְהַלָּן בְּסַיִיף [12]אַף כָּאן בְּסַיִיף. [13]רַבִּי עֲקִיבָא אוֹמֵר: נֶאֱמַר כָּאן: ׳מְכַשֵּׁפָה לֹא תְחַיֶּה׳. [14]וְנֶאֱמַר לְהַלָּן: ״אִם בְּהֵמָה אִם אִישׁ לֹא יִחְיֶה׳. [15]מַה לְהַלָּן בִּסְקִילָה, [16]אַף כָּאן בִּסְקִילָה. [17]אָמַר לוֹ רַבִּי יוֹסֵי: ׳אֲנִי דַּנְתִּי ״לֹא תְחַיֶּה״ [18]מִ״לֹּא תְחַיֶּה״, [19]וְאַתָּה דַּנְתָּ ״לֹא תְחַיֶּה״ מִ״לֹּא יִחְיֶה״׳! [20]אָמַר לוֹ רַבִּי עֲקִיבָא: ׳אֲנִי דַּנְתִּי יִשְׂרָאֵל מִיִּשְׂרָאֵל, [21]שֶׁרִיבָּה בָּהֶן הַכָּתוּב מִיתוֹת הַרְבֵּה, [22]וְאַתָּה דַּנְתָּ

LITERAL TRANSLATION

GEMARA [1]Rav Yehudah said in the name of Rav: They taught here about the inciters of an idolatrous city.

[2]"The sorcerer, who performs an act, etc." [3]Our Rabbis taught: "'A sorceress' — [4]whether a man or a woman. [5]If so, why does the verse state: 'A sorceress'? [6]Because most women are familiar with sorcery. [7]Their execution, by what? [8]Rabbi Yose the Galilean says: It is stated here: [9]'You shall not let a sorceress live.' [10]And it is stated below: 'You shall not let a soul live.' [11]Just as there by the sword, [12]so too here by the sword. [13]Rabbi Akiva says: It is stated here: 'You shall not let a sorceress live.' [14]And it is stated below: 'Whether it be beast or man, it shall not live.' [15]Just as there by stoning, [16]so too here by stoning. [17]Rabbi Yose said to him: 'I learned "You shall not let live," [18]from "You shall not let live," [19]and you learned "You shall not let live," from "it shall not live."' [20]Rabbi Akiva said to him: 'I learned a Jew from a Jew, [21]regarding whom Scripture stated many [modes of] execution, [22]and you learned

RASHI

גמרא **מכשפה אחד האיש ואחד האשה** — דהא גבי אוב וידעוני דמכשפים הם לא חלק בין איש לאשה דכתיב (ויקרא כ) ״איש או אשה״. **לא תחיה כל נשמה** — בשבע אומות כתיב. **מה להלן בסייף** — דכתיב סיחון ועוג ״ויכהו ישראל לפי חרב״ (במדבר כא). **מה להלן** — בסיני. **בסקילה** — דכתיב (שמות יט): ״כי סקול יסקל או ירה יירה״. **שריבה בהן הכתוב מיתות הרבה** — ומצינו בסיני שנאמרה בהן סקילה.

HALAKHAH

מִיתָתָן, בַּמֶּה? **Their execution, by what?** "A sorcerer is liable to death by stoning," following Rabbi Akiva, whose opinion is law when he disagrees with a colleague, and Abaye. (*Rambam, Sefer Mada, Hilkhot Avodah Zarah* 11:15.)

TRANSLATION AND COMMENTARY

punishment applying to **a Jew** who violated the prohibition against sorcery **from** what is stated regarding the **non-Jews** who did not recognize the Israelite conquest of the Land of Israel. [1]But **regarding** non-Jews **Scripture only stated** [67B] **one mode of execution,** for whenever a non-Jew is liable for execution, he is put to death by way of the sword. Thus, while "You shall not let a soul live," means that the Canaanites are put to death by the sword, this teaches us nothing about the meaning of the verse, "You shall not let a sorceress live." [2]**Ben Azzai says:** The mode of execution administered to a sorceress is derived from a different source. [3]**The verse states** (Exodus 22:17): **'You shall not let a sorceress live.'** [4]**And the** next **verse states** (Exodus 22:18): **'Whoever cohabits with a beast shall surely be put to death.'** [5]**The matter** of a sorceress **was placed next to** the matter of cohabiting with a beast to teach us that **just as someone who cohabits with a beast** is executed **by stoning,** (as we learned earlier in the chapter, 54b), [6]**so too a sorcerer** or sorceress is executed **by stoning.** [7]**Rabbi Yehudah said to** Ben Azzai: Are you suggesting that merely **because the matter** of a sorceress **was placed next** to the matter of cohabiting with a beast, **we should remove** sorcery from the offenses that are punishable by one of the less severe modes of execution, and say that the sorcerer is liable **to** death by **stoning,** the most severe mode of execution? [8]**Rather,** the punishment imposed upon a sorcerer is learned as follows: **An *ov* and a *yid'oni* were included in the general category of sorcerers,** about whom the Torah states that they shall not be allowed to live. [9]**So why were** the *ov* and the *yid'oni* **singled out** and banned by specific prohibitions? [10]**To compare** all sorcerers **to them, and to teach you** by way of a *binyan av*, an interpretation based on induction from one case, where certain details are specified, to other analogous cases, where those details are not given. [11]**Just as an *ov* and a *yid'oni*** are put to death **by stoning,** as is stated explicitly in the verse (Leviticus 20:27): 'A man also or woman that is a medium or a wizard, shall surely be put to death; they shall stone them with stones,' [12]**so too a sorcerer** is put to death **by stoning,"** though this is not stated explicitly.

יִשְׂרָאֵל מִנָּכְרִים, [1]שֶׁלֹּא רִיבָּה בָּהֶן הַכָּתוּב אֶלָּא [67B] מִיתָה אַחַת. [2]בֶּן עַזַּאי אוֹמֵר: [3]נֶאֱמַר: 'מְכַשֵּׁפָה לֹא תְחַיֶּה', [4]וְנֶאֱמַר: 'כָּל שֹׁכֵב עִם בְּהֵמָה מוֹת יוּמָת'. [5]סָמְכוּ עִנְיָן לוֹ: מַה שּׁוֹכֵב עִם בְּהֵמָה — בִּסְקִילָה, [6]אַף מְכַשֵּׁף — בִּסְקִילָה. [7]אָמַר לוֹ רַבִּי יְהוּדָה: וְכִי מִפְּנֵי שֶׁסָּמְכוּ עִנְיָן לוֹ, נוֹצִיא לָזֶה בִּסְקִילָה? [8]אֶלָּא, אוֹב וְיִדְּעוֹנִי בִּכְלַל מְכַשְּׁפִים הָיוּ, [9]וְלָמָּה יָצְאוּ? [10]לְהַקִּישׁ עֲלֵיהֶן, וְלוֹמַר לְךָ: [11]מָה אוֹב וְיִדְּעוֹנִי בִּסְקִילָה, [12]אַף מְכַשֵּׁף בִּסְקִילָה".

LITERAL TRANSLATION

a Jew from non-Jews, [1]regarding whom Scripture only stated [67B] one [mode of] execution. [2]Ben Azzai says: [3]It is stated: 'You shall not let a sorceress live.' [4]And it is stated: 'Whoever cohabits with a beast shall surely be put to death.' [5]They juxtaposed the matter to it: Just as someone who cohabits with a beast — by stoning, [6]so too a sorcerer — by stoning. [7]Rabbi Yehudah said to him: Because they juxtaposed the matter to it, we should take that one out for stoning? [8]Rather, an *ov* and a *yid'oni* were included in the general category of sorcerers. [9]So why were they specified? [10]To compare to them, and say to you: [11]Just as an *ov* and a *yid'oni* — by stoning, [12]"so too a sorcerer — by stoning."

RASHI

מיתה אחת — כל מיתה האמורה לבני נח אינו אלא סייף. **סמכו ענין לו** — סמך ענין המכשף לשוכב עם בהמה. **ענין** — פרשה. **שוכב עם בהמה בסקילה** — הא ילפינן לה בהאי פרקין מ"דמיהם בם", דכתיב בם בפרשת "קדושים תהיו" וגמרינן לה מאוב וידעוני דכתיב בהו "באבן ירגמו אותם דמיהם בם" (ויקרא כ). **רבי יהודה** — לא דריש סמוכין. **נוציא** — את זה מדין מיתות קלות לסקילה החמורה מכולן? **אלא** — מכלל ופרט אתה למד בו סקילה. **בכלל** — כל המכשפים היו, וכבר חייב בהן הכתוב מיתה, כדכתיב "לא תחיה". **למה יצאו?** להזכירן בעצמן ולכתוב בהן סקילה — **להקיש** להם את הכלל, וזו מדה בתורה, כל דבר שהיה בכלל ויצא מן הכלל וכו׳.

NOTES

מִפְּנֵי שֶׁסָּמְכוּ Because they juxtaposed. Rabbi Yehudah's opposition to the exegetical principle of juxtaposition was not limited to this case which involves capital punishment, but rather he opposed in general deriving Halakhic conclusions from the fact that two verses appear next to each other. But even Rabbi Yehudah agreed that the principle is valid regarding the verses found in the Book of Deuteronomy.

וְלָמָּה יָצְאוּ? לְהַקִּישׁ Why were they specified? To compare. The question has been raised: Why not invoke here a different exegetical principle: "Something that was included in a generalization but was specified as something new, cannot be returned to its generalization until the Torah explicitly returns it to its generalization"? According to that rule, we cannot extend the new law to the generalization, and so we should not be able to apply the punishment of stoning stated with regard to an *ov* and a *yid'oni* to the entire category of sorcerers! It has been suggested that the punishment of stoning cannot be regarded as "something new," for that refers to a law which contradicts another law taught regarding a generalization. Rather, it is regarded as a specific law which was taught in a particular case, and can therefore be applied by way of induction to the entire generalization (*Tiferet Shlomo*).

LANGUAGE

פָּמַלְיָא Household, family. This word derives from the Latin *familia*, meaning "a household staff of servants and attendants." It was used in place of the Biblical expression צְבָא הַשָּׁמַיִם, "Heavenly host."

TRANSLATION AND COMMENTARY

לְרַבִּי יְהוּדָה [1]The Gemara raises a problem: **Also according to Rabbi Yehudah,** there is a difficulty, for the prohibitions against **an *ov* and a *yid'oni*** should **be** regarded as **two verses that come as one** to teach the same thing. Ordinarily, a *binyan av* may be derived from a law stated in connection with one case in the Torah. However, if such a law appears in connection with two or more cases in the Torah, these cases constitute "two verses that come as one," [2]**and whenever two verses come as one** to teach the same thing **they cannot teach** us anything about analogous cases, that is to say, the method of *binyan av* may not be employed. This is because a law that had to be mentioned in two different places cannot be a general rule, but must instead be an exceptional case. The Torah specifies the punishment of death by stoning regarding both the *ov* and the *yid'oni.* Since the penalty of stoning was specified with respect to two particular types of sorcerers, it cannot be generalized.

אָמַר רַבִּי זְכַרְיָה [3]**Rabbi Zekhariyah said: This means that Rabbi Yehudah** disagrees about the use of the hermeneutic principle of *binyan av.* He **maintains that two verses that come as one** to teach the same law can in fact **teach** us the law in analogous cases.

אָמַר רַבִּי יוֹחָנָן [4]**Rabbi Yoḥanan said: Why are** sorcerers **called *kashafim*?** [5]That term may be understood as an abbreviation of the words *makhḥishin pamaliyah shel ma'alah* — **they deny the power of the Heavenly household,** for they defy divine decrees, and impose death upon those who were decreed to live.

אֵין עוֹד מִלְּבַדּוֹ [6]The verse states (Deuteronomy 4:35): "To you it was shown, that you might know that the Lord He is God; **there is none else beside Him."** [7]**Rabbi Ḥanina said:** This verse teaches that **even sorcerers** cannot do anything that contradicts God's will.

הַהִיא [8]It was related that **a certain woman tried to collect dust from under the feet of Rabbi Ḥanina** and use it in an act of sorcery directed against him. [9]Rabbi Ḥanina **said to her: "If you** think that you will **succeed** in practicing your sorcery against me, **go** right ahead **and try.** For **the verse states:** [10]**'There is none else beside Him.'** Whatever happens is God's will."

אִינִי [11]The Gemara asks: **Is it** really **so** that sorcerers can do nothing to defy the will of God? [12]**But surely**

[1]לְרַבִּי יְהוּדָה נַמִי, לֶיהֱווּ אוֹב וְיִדְּעוֹנִי שְׁנֵי כְּתוּבִים הַבָּאִים כְּאֶחָד, [2]וְכָל שְׁנֵי כְתוּבִין הַבָּאִין כְּאֶחָד, אֵין מְלַמְּדִין!
[3]אָמַר רַבִּי זְכַרְיָה: עֲדָא אָמְרָה קָסָבַר רַבִּי יְהוּדָה שְׁנֵי כְתוּבִין הַבָּאִין כְּאֶחָד מְלַמְּדִין.
[4]אָמַר רַבִּי יוֹחָנָן: לָמָּה נִקְרָא שְׁמָן מְכַשְּׁפִים? [5]שֶׁמַּכְחִישִׁין פָּמַלְיָא שֶׁל מַעְלָה.
[6]"אֵין עוֹד מִלְּבַדּוֹ". [7]אָמַר רַבִּי חֲנִינָא: אֲפִילּוּ לִדְבַר כְּשָׁפִים.
[8]הַהִיא אִיתְּתָא דַּהֲוַת קָא מְהַדְּרָא לְמִשְׁקַל עַפְרָא מִתּוֹתֵי כַּרְעֵיהּ דְּרַבִּי חֲנִינָא. [9]אֲמַר לָהּ: אִי מִסְתַּיַּיעַת, זִילִי עֲבִידִי. [10]'אֵין עוֹד מִלְּבַדּוֹ' כְּתִיב.
[11]אִינִי? [12]וְהָאָמַר רַבִּי יוֹחָנָן:

LITERAL TRANSLATION

[1]According to Rabbi Yehudah also, let *ov* and *yid'oni* be two verses that come together, [2]and whenever two verses come together, they do not teach!

[3]Rabbi Zekhariyah said: This means [that] Rabbi Yehudah maintains [that] two verses that come together teach.

[4]Rabbi Yoḥanan said: Why is their name called *kashafim*? [5]Because they lessen the power of the Heavenly household.

[6]"There is none else beside Him." [7]Rabbi Ḥanina said: Even matters of sorcery.

[8][There was] a certain woman who tried to take the dust from under the feet of Rabbi Ḥanina. [9]He said to her: "If you succeed, go and do [it]. [10]It is written: 'There is none else beside Him.'"

[11]Is it so? [12]But surely Rabbi Yoḥanan said:

RASHI

שני כתובין — הוה ליה למכתב חד, או אוב, או ידעוני, ולשתוק. **עדא אמרה** — כמו הדא אמרה, זאת אומרת. **קסבר רבי יהודה וכו'** — ובכל דוכתי דאמר אלא למאן דאמר מלמדין מאי איכא למימר — רבי יהודה היא, ומהכא ילפינן. **כשפים** = נוטריקון כחש פמליא של מעלה, שעל מי שנגזר לחיות ממיתין. **אפילו כשפים** — אין בהן כח לפני גזרתו, שאין כח מלבדו. **מתותי ברעיה** — לעשות לו מכשפות. **אם מסתייע** — מילתיך, אם את מצלחת לעשות לי מְכַשְּׁפוּת — עשי. **אין עוד מלבדו כתיב** — ואם המקום חפץ בי לא תוכלי להרע, ואם תוכלי מאתו יצא ואני מקבלן.

NOTES

מַכְחִישִׁין They lessen. Some understand the word מַכְחִישִׁין as "contradict." Sorcerers contradict the Heavenly household, for decrees are issued in Heaven, and sorcerers deny them. Others understand מַכְחִישִׁין as "weaken." Sorcerers weaken the decrees issued in Heaven, turning a good decree into an evil one (*Ramah*). *Rabbenu Ḥananel* explains that a sorcerer does not actually weaken a Heavenly decree, for without divine approval, his magic would not have any effect. Rather, the sorcerer makes it appear as if he were weakening the decree issued in Heaven.

לָמָּה נִקְרָא שְׁמָן מְכַשְּׁפִים? [1]שֶׁמַּכְחִישִׁין פָּמַלְיָא שֶׁל מַעְלָה! [2]שָׁאנֵי רַבִּי חֲנִינָא דִּנְפִישׁ זְכוּתֵיהּ.

[3]אָמַר רַבִּי אַיְיבוּ בַּר נַגְרִי אָמַר רַבִּי חִיָּיא בַּר אַבָּא: [4]"בְּלָטֵיהֶם" — אֵלּוּ מַעֲשֵׂה שֵׁדִים. [5]"בְּלַהֲטֵיהֶם" — אֵלּוּ מַעֲשֵׂה כְּשָׁפִים, [6]וְכֵן הוּא אוֹמֵר: "וְאֵת לַהַט הַחֶרֶב הַמִּתְהַפֶּכֶת".

[7]אָמַר אַבָּיֵי: דְּקָפֵיד אַמָּנָא — שֵׁד. [8]דְּלָא קָפֵיד אַמָּנָא — כְּשָׁפִים.

[9]אָמַר אַבָּיֵי: הִלְכוֹת כְּשָׁפִים כְּהִלְכוֹת שַׁבָּת. [10]יֵשׁ מֵהֶן בִּסְקִילָה, [11]וְיֵשׁ מֵהֶן פָּטוּר אֲבָל אָסוּר, [12]וְיֵשׁ מֵהֶן מוּתָּר לְכַתְּחִלָּה. [13]הָעוֹשֶׂה מַעֲשֶׂה —

LITERAL TRANSLATION

Why is their name called *kashafim*? [1]Because they lessen the power of the Heavenly household. [2]Rabbi Ḥanina is different, because his merits are many.

[3]Rabbi Aivo bar Nagri said in the name of Rabbi Ḥiyya bar Abba: [4]*"Belateihem"* — those are acts of spirits. [5]*"Belahateihem"* — those are acts of sorcery. [6]And similarly it says: "And the bright blade of a revolving sword."

[7]Abaye said: Someone who is particular about a utensil — a spirit. [8][Someone] who is not particular about a utensil — sorcery.

[9]Abaye said: The laws of sorcery are like the laws of the Sabbath. [10]There are among them [acts punishable] by stoning; [11]there are among them [acts that are] exempt but forbidden; [12]and there are among them [acts that are] permitted from the outset. [13]Someone who performs an act —

TRANSLATION AND COMMENTARY

Rabbi Yoḥanan said: Why are sorcerers **called** *kashafim*? [1]**Because they deny the power of the Heavenly household,** and they do have power to do damage.

שָׁאנֵי רַבִּי חֲנִינָא [2]The Gemara answers: **Rabbi Ḥanina is different** from ordinary people, **for he has many merits,** which protect him from sorcerers.

אָמַר [3]**Rabbi Aivo bar Nagri said in the name of Rabbi Ḥiyya bar Abba:** When the Torah speaks about the secret arts practiced by Pharaoh's magicians, it sometimes (see Exodus 7:22) uses the word *belateihem* [בְּלָטֵיהֶם, without a heh], and elsewhere (see Exodus 7:11) it uses the word *belahateihem* [בְּלַהֲטֵיהֶם, with a heh]. [4]When it uses the word **"belateihem,"** it refers to magical **acts** performed with the help **of spirits,** hidden [see Ruth 3:7: "And she came covertly (בלט)"] and invisible beings. [5]And when it uses the word **"belahateihem,"** it refers to **acts of sorcery** performed by the magicians themselves. [6]**And similarly the verse says** (Genesis 3:24): **"And the bright** [לַהַט] **blade of a whirling sword,"** which implies that the sword whirled on its own, without the help of any spirits, just as the magicians perform their *lahatim*, without the help of any spirits.

אָמַר אַבָּיֵי [7]**Abaye said: Someone who is particular about the utensil** with which he performs his magical acts performs his magic with the help of **a spirit.** [8]**Someone who is not particular about the utensil** with which he performs his magic, performs **sorcery** without the help of spirits.

אָמַר אַבָּיֵי [9]**Abaye said: The laws of sorcery are similar to the laws of the Sabbath.** Magical acts are divided into three categories corresponding to the three categories of Sabbath labors. Certain Sabbath labors are punishable by stoning, others are exempt from judicial punishment but nevertheless forbidden by Rabbinic decree, and yet others are totally permitted from the outset. [10]Similarly **certain** magical acts are punishable **by stoning,** [11]others magical acts are **exempt** from judicial punishment, **but** nevertheless **forbidden** by Rabbinic decree, [12]**and** yet others are **permitted from the outset.** How so? [13]**Someone who** actually **performs an act** of magic

RASHI

דנפיש זכותיה — ומסרי נפשיה משמיא לאצוליה. **בלטיהם** — כמו (רות ג) "ותבא (בלט)" — בסתר. **זה מעשה שדים** — שנסתרים ואינן נראין. כל מקום שנאמר "בלטיהם" היו החרטומין עושין בלחשיהם על ידי שדים. **בלהטיהם אלו מעשה כשפים** — שאינו עושה על ידי שדים אלא מעצמו. **להט החרב המתהפכת לשמור את דרך עץ החיים** — ומתהפכת מאליה ודומה לכשפים, (ולא) [שלא] על ידי שדים היתה מתהפכת, אלא מאליה, וקרי ליה להט. **דקפיד אמנא שד** — מי שמקפיד על הכלי שאינו יכול לעשות דבר בלא כלי הראוי לאותו דבר, כגון שרי בוהן שצריכין סכין שקתו שחור, ושרי כוס שצריכין כוס של זכוכית. **דלא קפיד אמנא** — שבכל כלי היה עושה. **בהלכות שבת** — דמלאכות בסקילה, ושבות פטור אבל אסור. ולידת צבי וצפור שנכנסת לו תחת כנפיו יושב ומשמרו עד שתחשך, ומפיס מורסא להוציא ממנה לחה, הכי איתא בפרק "רבי אליעזר דאורג" (קז,א), וכן צד נחש במתעסק בו שלא ישכו אותו — מותר לכתחילה, הכא נמי העושה מעשה ממש — בסקילה.

NOTES

לָטֵיהֶם — לַהֲטֵיהֶם *Lateihem — lahateihem.* Some Rishonim (*Arukh, Ramah*) had the opposite reading: "*Belateihem* — those are the acts of sorcery. *Belahateihem* — those are the acts of spirits. And similarly it says: 'And the bright [*lahat*]

HALAKHAH

הָעוֹשֶׂה מַעֲשֶׂה....הָאוֹחֵז אֶת הָעֵינַיִם **Someone who performs an act....Someone who captures the eyes.** "A sorcerer who

LANGUAGE (RASHI)

מוקיי״ר* From the Old French *mochier*, meaning "to wipe the nose, to wipe."

אסקד״א** This should apparently be אישקייל״א. From the Old French *eschiele*, meaning "a small bell."

LANGUAGE

טַבְלָא A drum. This is similar to the Arabic طبل, and also the Greek τυβαλα, both of which apparently derive from a Persian or Parthian word.

BACKGROUND

טַבְלָא A drum.

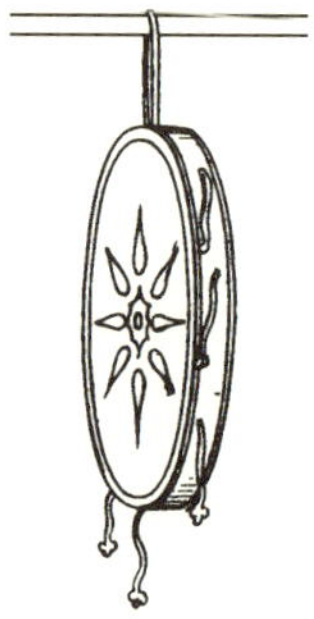

A small drum from the Talmudic period.

Sometimes small bells were attached to it, as with a tambourine.

TRANSLATION AND COMMENTARY

is subject to death **by stoning.** [1]**Someone who deludes** other people into thinking that he is endowed with magical powers when he is not, [2]**is exempt** from punishment, **but** nevertheless **forbidden** to do such a thing. [3]The magical acts which are totally **permitted from the outset** are **like** those performed by **Rav Ḥanina and Rav Oshaya,** [4]who would sit **every Friday** and **engage in the study of the laws of creation.** [5]These two scholars **would** recombine the letters of God's name and **create for themselves a third-grown calf, and eat it.** Such acts are permitted, because they are not actually performed by way of magic, but rather by way of God's holy name.

אָמַר רַב אַשִׁי [6]**Rav Ashi said:** I once **saw Karna's father blow his nose,** [7]**and** make it appear as if he were **casting bundles of silk from his nostrils.**

וַיֹּאמְרוּ [8]Having made reference above to Pharaoh's magicians, the Gemara continues: the Torah states (Exodus 8:15): **"And the magicians said to Pharaoh, This is the finger of God."** Pharaoh's magicians were able to replicate the first two plagues, that of blood and the frogs, but they could not repeat the third plague and bring forth lice. Thus they concluded that the plague of lice was an act of God, and not sorcery. [9]**Rabbi Eliezer said: From** this story **we see that a** demonic **spirit cannot create a creature smaller than a barleycorn.**

אָמַר רַב פַּפָּא [10]**Rav Pappa said: By God!** [11]A spirit **cannot even create** a creature **the size of a camel,** for it cannot create anything at all. Rather than create anything, a spirit gathers elements together from different places. [12]Large creatures, like camels, **it can gather** together from different places. [13]**But** small creatures, like lice, **it cannot gather** together from different places.

אָמַר לֵיהּ [14]**Rav said to Rabbi Ḥiyya: "I myself saw a certain Arab take a sword, and cut up a camel, and**

בִּסְקִילָה. [1]הָאוֹחֵז אֶת הָעֵינַיִם — [2]פָּטוּר אֲבָל אָסוּר. [3]מוּתָּר לְכַתְּחִלָּה — כְּדְרַב חֲנִינָא וְרַב אוֹשַׁעְיָא. [4]כָּל מַעֲלֵי שַׁבְּתָא הָווּ עָסְקִי בְּהִלְכוֹת יְצִירָה, [5]וּמִיבְרֵי לְהוּ עִיגְלָא תִּילְתָּא, וְאָכְלִי לֵיהּ. [6]אֲמַר רַב אַשִׁי: חֲזֵינָא לֵיהּ לַאֲבוּהּ דְּקַרְנָא דְּנָפֵיץ, [7]וְשָׁדֵי כְּרִיכֵי דְּשִׁירָאֵי מִנְּחִירֵיהּ. [8]"וַיֹּאמְרוּ הַחַרְטֻמִּם אֶל פַּרְעֹה אֶצְבַּע אֱלֹהִים הִיא". [9]אָמַר רַבִּי אֱלִיעֶזֶר: מִיכָּן שֶׁאֵין הַשֵּׁד יָכוֹל לִבְראוֹת בְּרִיָּה פָּחוֹת מִכַּשְּׂעוֹרָה. [10]רַב פַּפָּא אֲמַר: הָאֱלֹהִים! [11]אֲפִילּוּ כְּגַמְלָא נַמִי לָא מָצֵי בָּרֵי. [12]הַאי — מִיכְנִיף לֵיהּ; [13]וְהַאי — לָא מִיכְנִיף לֵיהּ. [14]אֲמַר לֵיהּ רַב לְרַבִּי חִיָּיא: "דִּידִי חֲזִי לִי הַהוּא טַיָּיעָא דְּשַׁקְלֵיהּ לְסַפְסֵירָא, וְגַיְּידֵיהּ לְגַמְלָא, וּטְרַף לֵיהּ בְּטַבְלָא,

LITERAL TRANSLATION

by stoning. [1]Someone who captures the eyes — [2]exempt but forbidden. [3]Permitted from the outset — like Rav Ḥanina and Rav Oshaya, [4][who] every Friday engaged in [the study of] the laws of creation, [5]and they created for themselves a third-grown calf, and ate it.

[6]Rav Ashi said: I saw that Karna's father blew [his nose], [7]and cast bundles of silk from his nostrils.

[8]"And the magicians said to Pharaoh, This is the finger of God." [9]Rabbi Eliezer said: From here [we see] that a spirit cannot create a creature less than [the size of] a barleycorn.

[10]Rav Pappa said: By God! [11]Even like a camel it cannot create. [12]This — it can gather; [13]but this — it cannot gather.

[14]Rav said to Rabbi Ḥiyya: "I myself saw a certain Arab who took a sword, and cut up a camel, and beat on a drum,

RASHI

האוחז את העינים — מראה כאילו עושה, ואינו עושה כלום, פטור — אבל אסור. **עסקי בהלכות יצירה** — וממילא אברו להו עגלא תילתא על ידי שהיו מצרפים אותיות השם שבהם נברא העולם. ואין כאן משום מכשפות, דמעשה הקדוש ברוך הוא הן, על ידי שם קדושה שלו הוא. **אבוה דקרנא** — מכשף היה. **מנפץ** — חוטמו בכח, *מוקיי״ר בלעז, לקנח האף, למחוט. **ושדי בריכי דשיראי מנחיריו** — משליך חתיכות של מעילים. **אצבע אלהים היא** — מכה זו של כנים לא על ידי מכשפות באה אלא על פי הקדוש ברוך הוא, דאין לחרטומים יכולת בה. **לא מצי ברי** — אין יכול לברוא אפילו בריה גדולה, אלא כשהשד צריך לבריות גדולות הוא מאסף ומביא מן ההפקר. **האי מיכניף ליה** — בריות גדולות נוחים לקבלם ולאספם יחד, אליו, אבל בריה קטנה אינה נאספת, שאין בה כח לבא ממקום רחוק. **הכי גרסינן: אמר לו רב לרבי חייא** — ולא גרסינן איני. **טייעא** — סוחר ערבי. **שקל ספסירא וגיידיה לגמליה** — נטל חרב וחתך גמל לאברים, גיידיה = כמו: ראוהו מגוייד דפרק בתרא דיבמות (קכ,ב). **וטרף ליה בטבלא וקם** — קשקש לו בזוג — **אסקד״א בלעז, פעמון קטן, ועמד על רגליו.

NOTES

blade of a revolving sword." *Arukh* understands this proof-text as follows: A spirit [*lahat*] changes form and color, just like the bright [*lahat*] blade of a revolving sword.

HALAKHAH

actually performs an act of magic is liable to death by stoning, but someone who by optical illusion makes people think that he had performed an act of magic, when he did not, is only subject to lashes by Rabbinic decree." (*Rambam, Sefer Mada, Hilkhot Avodah Zarah* 11:15.)

הִלְכוֹת יְצִירָה The laws of creation. "It is permitted to perform supernatural acts by way of Divine Names, the Book of Creation, or the like. Some authorities say that it

TRANSLATION AND COMMENTARY

then afterwards he **beat on a drum, and** the animal **stood up** again and lived." [1]Rabbi Ḥiyya **said to him: "After** the camel supposedly came back to life, did you find on the ground any **traces of the blood or excretions** which must have issued from the animal when it was being cut up? [2]**Rather,** the whole event **was an optical illusion."**

זְעֵירִי [3]It was related that **Ze'iri** once **came to Alexandria in Egypt,** where **he bought an ass.** [4]**When he came to give** the animal **water to drink,** the charm **was broken,** the animal disappeared, [5]**and there stood** before him **the plank of a bridge.** Ze'iri then returned to the person who had sold him the animal and demanded his money back. [6]The seller **said to him: "Were you not** the great Torah sage **Ze'iri, I would not return** the purchase money **to you.** [7]**Does anyone buy something here** in Egypt, a land known for sorcery, **and not examine it with water** prior to taking possession?"

יַנַּאי [8]It was further related that **Yannai** once **came to a certain inn,** [9]and **said to** the proprietors: **"Give me** some **water to drink."** [10]He was **offered a mixture of water and flour.** As the woman who was serving him the drink approached him, [11]**he saw that her lips were moving** and immediately suspected that she was a sorceress uttering an incantation. [12]**He threw a little of** the water to the ground, **and** the water **became scorpions,** confirming his suspicions. Knowing himself how to cast a spell, Yannai pretended to drink the water that had been served him and [13]**said to** the proprietors of the inn: **"I drank from your** drink; so I ask that **you too drink from mine,"** putting a spell on it. [14]**He** then **gave** water to the woman who had served him **to drink, and she turned into an ass** because of his spell. [15]**He rode** upon the ass, **and went** with her **to the market.** [16]But **another woman came and released** her from the spell, [17]so people **saw him riding on a woman in the market.**

וְקָם״. [1]אֲמַר לֵיהּ: ״לְבָתַר הָכִי,
דָּם וּפַרְתָּא מִי הֲוַאי? [2]אֶלָּא,
הַהִיא אֲחִיזַת עֵינַיִם הֲוָה.
[3]זְעֵירִי אִיקְלַע לַאֲלֶכְסַנְדְּרִיָּא
שֶׁל מִצְרַיִם. זְבַן חֲמָרָא. [4]כִּי
מְטָא לְאַשְׁקוּיֵיהּ מַיָּא — פְּשַׁר,
[5]וְקָם גַּמְלָא דוּסְקַנִיתָא. [6]אֲמַרוּ
לֵיהּ: ״אִי לָאו זְעֵירִי אַתְּ —
לָא הֲוָה מְהַדְּרִינַן לָךְ. [7]מִי
אִיכָּא דְזָבֵין מִידֵּי הָכָא וְלָא
בָּדֵיק לֵיהּ אַמַּיָּא״?
[8]יַנַּאי אִיקְלַע לְהַהוּא
אוּשְׁפִּיזָא. [9]אֲמַר לְהוּ: ״אַשְׁקְיַין
מַיָּא״! [10]קְרִיבוּ שַׁתִּיתָא. [11]חֲזָא
דְּקָא מְרַחֲשַׁן שִׂפְוָותָהּ, [12]שְׁדָא
פּוּרְתָּא מִינֵּיהּ, הָווּ עַקְרַבֵּי.
[13]אֲמַר לְהוּ: ״אֲנָא שְׁתַאי
מִדִּידְכוּ: אַתּוּן נַמִי שְׁתוּ
מִדִּידִי.״ [14]אַשְׁקְיָיהּ, הֲוַאי
חֲמָרָא. [15]רַכְבָהּ, סְלֵיק לְשׁוּקָא.
[16]אֲתָא חֲבֶרְתָּהּ פַּשְׁרָה לָהּ.
[17]חַזְיֵיהּ דְּרָכֵיב וְקָאֵי אַאִיתְּתָא
בְּשׁוּקָא.

LITERAL TRANSLATION

and it stood up." [1]He said to him: "Afterwards, were there [traces of] blood and excretions? [2]Rather, that was a capturing of the eyes."

[3]Ze'iri came to Alexandria in Egypt. He bought an ass. [4]When he came to give it water to drink, [the charm] was broken, [5]and it became a plank of a bridge. [6]They said to him: "Were you not Ze'iri, I would not return [it] to you. [7]Is there someone who buys something here, and does not examine it with water?"

[8]Yannai came to a certain inn. [9]He said to them: "Give me water to drink." [10]They offered him water which was mixed with flour. [11]He saw that her lips were moving, [12]he threw a little of it, [and] it became scorpions. [13]He said to them: "I drank from yours; you too drink from mine." [14]He gave her to drink, [and] she became an ass. [15]He rode her, and went to the market. [16]Another woman came and released her. [17]They saw him riding on a woman in the market.

RASHI

אמר לו – רבי חייא לרב. **לבתר הכי דם ופרתא מי הוה** – אחר שעמד הגמל כלום נמלאת שם לכלוך מן הדם והפרש? **ההוא אחיזת עינים הוה** – ולא מגוייד הוא, שאינו יכול להחיות המת. **פשר** – נמס המכשפות, כל מילי מכשפות נבדקין על מים חיים ונמוחין. **קם גמלא דסקוניתא** – נעשה החמור של גשר, שעשו תחלה את הדף חמור. גמלא = גשר, סקוניתא = מין עץ הוא. **איכא דזבין מידעם הכא וכו׳** – כלומר יש לוקח בעיר הזאת שמוחזקת בכשפים שום סחורה ואינו בודקה על המים? **ינאי איקלע לההיא אושיפזא** – ולא גרסינן רבי ינאי, דלאו איניש מעליא הוא – שעשה כשפים. **שתיתא** – קמח טרוף במים. **חזייה דמרחשן שפוותה** – ראה ינאי האשה המביאה לו המשקה שהיו שפתיה נעות, הכיר שכשפנית היא. **שדא פורתא** – מן המשקה לארץ, ונעשו עקרבים. **אנא שתאי מדידכו** – לא גלה להם הדבר שהבין בדבר, והראה עצמו כאילו שתה. **הואי חמרא** – האשה נעשית חמור. **רכבה** – ינאי, וסליק בשוקא. **פשרא לה** – מיחת את הכשפים וחזרה לקדמותה.

LANGUAGE

דוּסְקַנִיתָא **A plank of a bridge.** This is apparently an abridged form of דְּאוּסְקַנִיתָא, "the name of a kind of tree, or something made from wood." Similarly we have חַסְקְנִיאֲתָא, apparently the name of a kind of tree, or a wooden bridge.

HALAKHAH

is preferable not to use Divine Names in that manner, except in order to save a community, or to sanctify God's name, or for some other great need (see *Levush, Shakh*)." (*Shulḥan Arukh, Yoreh De'ah* 179:15.)

LANGUAGE

קִינוֹף **Curtained couch.** This apparently derives from the Greek κωνωπειον, *konopeion*, meaning "a bed surrounded by curtains."

טְרַקְלִין **Reception room.** This word derives from the Greek τρικλινον, *trikhlinon*, basically meaning "a room with three beds to lie on," but its meaning was expanded to refer to a salon or large guest room.

BACKGROUND

טְרַקְלִין **Reception room.**

A Roman salon during the Mishnaic period.

TRANSLATION AND COMMENTARY

וַתַּעַל הַצְפַרְדֵּעַ [1]Having made reference to the plague of frogs, the Gemara continues: The verse states (Exodus 8:2): **"And the frog came up, and covered the land of Egypt,"** referring to the frog in the singular. [2]**Rabbi Elazar: There was** at first only **one frog, and it bred, and filled all the land of Egypt** with frogs.

כְּתַנָּאֵי [3]This understanding of the plague of frogs is the subject of a dispute among **the Tannaim,** for it was taught in a Baraita: [4]**"Rabbi Akiva says: There was** at first only **one frog,** and it bred, **and** eventually **filled up all the land of Egypt** with frogs. [5]**Rabbi Elazar ben Azaryah** disagreed and **said** to him: **"Akiva!** [6]**What have you** to do **with Aggadah?** [7]**Cease from your** homiletical **interpretations, and go** back **to leprous spots and tents.** Halakhah is your field! [8]As for the plague of frogs, **there was** at first only **one frog,** [9]and **it croaked to** all the other frogs in the world, **and they** all **came** to Egypt."

אָמַר רַבִּי עֲקִיבָא [10]We learned in the Mishnah: **"Rabbi Akiva said** in the name of Rabbi Yehoshua: Two people might gather together the cucumbers in a field using magic. One might gather the cucumbers and be exempt from the penalty of stoning, and one might gather the cucumbers and be liable to stoning."

[68A] וְהָא רַבִּי עֲקִיבָא [11]The Gemara asks: **But did Rabbi Akiva** really **learn** about magic involving cucumbers **from Rabbi Yehoshua?** [12]**But surely it was taught** otherwise in the following Baraita: **"When Rabbi Eliezer became ill, Rabbi Akiva and his colleagues went in to visit with him.** [13]Rabbi Eliezer **was seated** inside **on his curtained couch, and they were seated** outside **in his reception room,** waiting to be ushered in. [14]**That day** happened to **be a Friday,** and the Sabbath was approaching, **and Horkanus,** Rabbi Eliezer's **son, went in** to his father **to remove his phylacteries,** which may not be worn on the Sabbath.

[1]"וַתַּעַל הַצְפַרְדֵּעַ וַתְּכַס אֶת אֶרֶץ מִצְרָיִם", [2]אָמַר רַבִּי אֶלְעָזָר: צְפַרְדֵּעַ אַחַת הָיְתָה, הִשְׁרִיצָה וּמִלְאָה כָּל אֶרֶץ מִצְרַיִם.

[3]כְּתַנָּאֵי: [4]"רַבִּי עֲקִיבָא אוֹמֵר: צְפַרְדֵּעַ אַחַת הָיְתָה, וּמִלְאָה כָּל אֶרֶץ מִצְרַיִם. [5]אָמַר לוֹ רַבִּי אֶלְעָזָר בֶּן עֲזַרְיָה: 'עֲקִיבָא, [6]מַה לְּךָ אֵצֶל הַגָּדָה, [7]כַּלֵּה מִדַּבְּרוֹתֶיךָ, וְלֵךְ אֵצֶל נְגָעִים וְאֳהָלוֹת! [8]צְפַרְדֵּעַ אַחַת הָיְתָה. [9]שָׁרְקָה לָהֶם וְהֵם בָּאוּ'".

[10]"אָמַר רַבִּי עֲקִיבָא כו'".

[68A] [11]וְהָא רַבִּי עֲקִיבָא מֵרַבִּי יְהוֹשֻׁעַ גְּמִיר לָהּ? [12]וְהָתַנְיָא: "כְּשֶׁחָלָה רַבִּי אֱלִיעֶזֶר נִכְנְסוּ רַבִּי עֲקִיבָא וַחֲבֵירָיו לְבַקְּרוֹ. [13]הוּא יוֹשֵׁב בְּקִינוֹף שֶׁלּוֹ, וְהֵן יוֹשְׁבִין בִּטְרַקְלִין שֶׁלּוֹ. [14]וְאוֹתוֹ הַיּוֹם עֶרֶב שַׁבָּת הָיָה, וְנִכְנַס הוּרְקָנוֹס בְּנוֹ לַחֲלוֹץ תְּפִלָּיו.

LITERAL TRANSLATION

[1]"And the frog came up, and covered the land of Egypt." [2]Rabbi Elazar: There was one frog, and it bred, and filled up all the land of Egypt.

[3]Like the Tannaim: [4]"Rabbi Akiva says: There was one frog, and it filled up all the land of Egypt. [5]Rabbi Elazar ben Azaryah said: 'Akiva! [6]What have you [to do] with Aggadah? [7]Cease from your interpretations, and go to leprous spots and tents! [8]There was one frog. [9]It croaked to them, and they came.'"

[10]"Rabbi Akiva said, etc."

[68A] [11]But did Rabbi Akiva learn this from Rabbi Yehoshua? [12]But surely it was taught: "When Rabbi Eliezer became ill, Rabbi Akiva and his colleagues went in to visit him. [13]He was seated on his curtained couch, and they were seated in his reception room. [14]And that day was Friday, and Horkanus his son went in to remove his phylacteries.

RASHI

הצפרדע – אחת משמע. **השריצה** – ממעיה ויצאו ולדות. **מדברותיך** – מנע מדבריך, ופנה להלכות נגעים ואהלות שהן חמורים ובהם אתה מחודד, ולא בהגדה. **שרקה להם** – ושמעו קולה כל הצפרדעים שבעולם והם באו. **והא** – מילתא דלקיטת קשואין. **רבי עקיבא מרבי יהושע גמר לה** – בתמיה. **קינוף** – ארבעה עמודים וכילה פרוסה עליהם, כדאמרינן בסוכה (י,א). **לחלוץ תפיליו** – של אביו, דקסבר שבת לאו זמן תפילין הוא, ואסור להניחן שמא יצא בהן לרשות הרבים.

NOTES

וַתַּעַל הַצְפַרְדֵּעַ **And the frog came up.** *Rabbi Tzvi Ḥayyot* explains the connection between the homiletical discussion regarding the plague of frogs and the previous passage. Earlier in the discussion, Rav Pappa had argued that a spirit cannot create anything at all. All that it can do is gather creatures together from different places. The Gemara now supports this argument from what the Torah states regarding the plague of frogs. God said to Moses (Exodus 7:28): "And the river shall bring [וְשָׁרַץ] forth frogs in swarms," using the word *vesharatz*, the same word that is used in the story of creation found in Genesis. But regarding Pharaoh's magicians (Exodus 8:3), the verse states: "And the magicians did so with their secret arts, and brought up frogs on the land of Egypt," implying that they did not create them, but only gathered them from various different places. The Gemara therefore brings the dispute between Rabbi Akiva and Rabbi Elazar ben Azaryah on the matter of how the frogs filled the land.

לַחֲלוֹץ תְּפִלָּיו **To remove his phylacteries.** *Tosafot* argue that on Friday afternoon a person may indeed first remove his phylacteries, and only then light the Sabbath candles. Horkanus became involved in caring for his ailing father,

TRANSLATION AND COMMENTARY

[1]But Rabbi Eliezer **rebuked him, and** Horkanus **left** his room **feeling reprimanded.** [2]Horkanus **said to his** father's **colleagues** in the reception room: **'It seems to me that my father's mind is no** longer **clear.'** [3]Hearing what his son was saying about him, Rabbi Eliezer called out to his colleagues and **said to them:** 'It is my son's **mind and that of his mother that are confused.** [4]**How do they put off** worrying about **a prohibition** whose violation is **punishable by stoning, and involve themselves in** something that is only **a Rabbinic prohibition?** Instead of worrying about my wearing phylacteries on the Sabbath which is only forbidden by Rabbinic decree, they should be taking care of the Sabbath candles and arranging the food that it remain warm during the Sabbath, to avoid violating the Sabbath by lighting a fire or cooking. [5]**When the Sages saw** from Rabbi Eliezer's words **that his mind was** perfectly **clear,** [6]**they went in** to see him, **and sat** down **before him at a distance of four cubits.** Rabbi Eliezer had been excommunicated when he refused to accept the majority opinion regarding the 'oven of Akhnai' (see *Bava Metzia* 59b), and it is prohibited to stand or sit within four cubits of a person who is excommunicated. [7]Rabbi Eliezer **said to them: 'Why have you come?'** Not wishing to say that they expected him to die shortly, [8]**they said to him: 'We have come to learn Torah** from you.' [9]Rabbi Eliezer **said to them:** 'If so, then **up until now, why have you not come** to learn Torah from me?' [10]**They said to him:** 'Up until now, **we did not have the time** to come.' [11]Rabbi Eliezer **said to them: 'I would be surprised if** you people **die a natural death,'** predicting that they would be tortured to death by the Roman authorities. [12]**Rabbi Akiva said to him: 'What** will be the mode of **my death?'** [13]Rabbi Eliezer **said to him: 'Your death will be** even **more severe than** that of the others, for you were my closest disciple, and still you did not come to learn Torah from me.' [14]Rabbi Eliezer then **took his two arms, and**

[1]גָּעַר בּוֹ וְיָצָא בִּנְזִיפָה. [2]אָמַר לָהֶן לַחֲבֵירָיו: ׳כִּמְדוּמֶּה אֲנִי שֶׁדַּעְתּוֹ שֶׁל אַבָּא נִטְרְפָה׳. [3]אָמַר לָהֶן: ׳דַּעְתּוֹ וְדַעַת אִמּוֹ נִטְרְפָה. [4]הֵיאַךְ מַנִּיחִין אִיסּוּר סְקִילָה, וְעוֹסְקִין בְּאִיסּוּר שְׁבוּת׳? [5]כֵּיוָן שֶׁרָאוּ חֲכָמִים שֶׁדַּעְתּוֹ מְיוּשֶּׁבֶת עָלָיו, [6]נִכְנְסוּ וְיָשְׁבוּ לְפָנָיו מֵרָחוֹק אַרְבַּע אַמּוֹת. [7]אָמַר לָהֶם: ׳לָמָּה בָּאתֶם׳? [8]אָמְרוּ לוֹ: ׳לִלְמוֹד תּוֹרָה בָּאנוּ׳. [9]אָמַר לָהֶם: ׳וְעַד עַכְשָׁיו, לָמָּה לֹא בָּאתֶם׳? [10]אָמְרוּ לוֹ: ׳לֹא הָיָה לָנוּ פְּנַאי׳. [11]אָמַר לָהֶן: ׳תָּמֵיהַּ אֲנִי אִם יָמוּתוּ מִיתַת עַצְמָן׳. [12]אָמַר לוֹ רַבִּי עֲקִיבָא: ׳שֶׁלִּי, מַהוּ׳? [13]אָמַר לוֹ: ׳שֶׁלְּךָ קָשָׁה מִשֶּׁלָּהֶן׳. [14]נָטַל שְׁתֵּי זְרוֹעוֹתָיו, וְהִנִּיחָן

LITERAL TRANSLATION

[1]He rebuked him and he went out feeling reprimanded. [2]He said to his colleagues: 'It seems to me that my father's mind is confused.' [3]He said to them: 'His mind and the mind of his mother are confused. [4]How do they ignore a prohibition punishable by stoning, and involve themselves in a Rabbinic prohibition?' [5]When the Sages saw that his mind was clear (lit., 'settled'), [6]they went in and sat before him at a distance of four cubits. [7]He said to them: 'Why have you come?' [8]They said to him: 'We have come to learn Torah.' [9]He said to them: 'And until now, why have you not come?' [10]They said to him: 'We did not have the time.' [11]He said to them: 'I would be surprised if they die a natural death.' [12]Rabbi Akiva said to him: 'My [death], what is it?' [13]He said to him: 'Yours is more severe than theirs.' [14]He took his two arms, and placed them

RASHI

שדעתו של אבא נטרפה – וקרוב הוא למות, שאילו היתה דעתו מיושבת היה חולץ תפיליו. **איסור סקילה** – הדלקת הנר והטמנת חמין, **ועוסקין** בדבר שאינו אלא איסור שבות, דמניח תפילין בשבת אין כאן איסור מלאכה, ואפילו יצא לרשות הרבים, דהא דרך מלבוש הוא ותכשיטין הוא לו בחול. **ברחוק ארבע אמות** – מפני הנדוי, שברכוהו במחלוקת תנורו של עכנאי, בבבא מציעא (נט,ב). **שלו מהו** – במה תהא מיתתו. **שלך קשה משלהן** – מפני שלבך פתוח כאולם, ואילו שמשתני היית למד תורה הרבה. **נטל** – רבי אליעזר שתי זרועותיו.

NOTES

although the Sabbath was quickly approaching. So his father reprimanded him for bothering with his phylacteries, when he should have been lighting the Sabbath candles, so as not to violate a Torah prohibition.

דַּעְתּוֹ וְדַעַת אִמּוֹ His mind and the mind of his mother. Rabbi Eliezer mentioned Horkanus' mother, because the woman of the house is responsible for the Sabbath candles, and she had not yet lit them (*Ramah*).

נִכְנְסוּ וְיָשְׁבוּ לְפָנָיו They went in and sat before him. The real reason that Rabbi Akiva and his colleagues had avoided Rabbi Eliezer was that Rabbi Eliezer had been excommunicated for rejecting the majority opinion regarding the "oven of Akhnai." But they offered a different excuse, so as not to embarrass him. Rabbi Eliezer was nevertheless angry with them, for while a person may not stand or sit within four cubits of an excommunicated person, he may indeed learn Torah from him (*Ramah*).

שֶׁלְּךָ קָשָׁה מִשֶּׁלָּהֶן Yours is more severe than theirs. Some Rishonim explain that Rabbi Eliezer told Rabbi Akiva that his death would be even more severe than that of his colleagues, because he was more righteous than they, and God is particular with His most pious servants even about

TRANSLATION AND COMMENTARY

placed them across his heart, and said: [1]**'Woe to you, my two arms, which are like two Torah scrolls that are rolled up,** so that the text cannot be seen and studied. The Torah that is within me will be lost forever after I die. because you stayed away from me. [2]**I have learned a lot of Torah** in the course of my life, **and I have** also **taught a lot of Torah.** [3]**I have learned much of Torah, but I did not diminish of my masters'** wisdom, [4]**even as much as a dog which laps** water **out of the sea.** [5]**I have taught much Torah, and my disciples have only diminished me,** [6]**the way a brush** diminishes the paint each time that it is inserted **into the tube.** I have taught only a little that I have learned. [7]**And furthermore, I have taught three hundred laws regarding an intense bright** leprous **spot,** [8]**and nobody has ever asked me about them,** for I have never had a disciple who really understood me. [9]**And furthermore, I have taught three hundred laws (and some say** that it was **three thousand laws** that he had taught) **regarding the planting of cucumbers** by magic, [10]**and nobody has ever asked me about them, except for Akiva ben Yosef.** [11]**Once,** Akiva **and I were walking along the road,** [12]when **he said to me: "O Master, teach me about planting cucumbers** by magic." [13]**I said** only **one thing, and the entire field was** magically **filled with cucumbers.** [14]Akiva then **said to me: "O Master, you have taught me about planting** cucumbers. [15]**Teach me** now how to **uproot them** by magic." [16]Again, **I said** only **one thing, and all** the cucumbers **were** magically **gathered in one place.'**

עַל לִבּוֹ, אָמַר: [1]אוֹי לָכֶם, שְׁתֵּי זְרוֹעוֹתַיי, שֶׁהֵן כִּשְׁתֵּי סִפְרֵי תוֹרָה שֶׁנִּגְלָלִין. [2]הַרְבֵּה תוֹרָה לָמַדְתִּי, וְהַרְבֵּה תוֹרָה לִימַּדְתִּי. [3]הַרְבֵּה תוֹרָה לָמַדְתִּי, וְלֹא חִסַּרְתִּי מֵרַבּוֹתַי, [4]אֲפִילּוּ כְּכֶלֶב הַמְלַקֵּק מִן הַיָּם. [5]הַרְבֵּה תוֹרָה לִימַּדְתִּי, [6]וְלֹא חִסְּרוּנִי תַּלְמִידַי אֶלָּא כְּמִכְחוֹל בַּשְּׁפוֹפֶרֶת. [7]וְלֹא עוֹד, אֶלָּא שֶׁאֲנִי שׁוֹנֶה שְׁלֹשׁ מֵאוֹת הֲלָכוֹת בְּבַהֶרֶת עַזָּה, [8]וְלֹא הָיָה אָדָם שׁוֹאֲלֵנִי בָּהֶן דָּבָר מֵעוֹלָם. [9]וְלֹא עוֹד, אֶלָּא שֶׁאֲנִי שׁוֹנֶה שְׁלֹשׁ מֵאוֹת הֲלָכוֹת, וְאָמְרִי לָהּ שְׁלֹשֶׁת אֲלָפִים הֲלָכוֹת, בִּנְטִיעַת קִשּׁוּאִין, [10]וְלֹא הָיָה אָדָם שׁוֹאֲלֵנִי בָּהֶן דָּבָר מֵעוֹלָם, חוּץ מֵעֲקִיבָא בֶּן יוֹסֵף. [11]פַּעַם אַחַת, אֲנִי וְהוּא מְהַלְּכִין הָיִינוּ בַּדֶּרֶךְ. [12]אָמַר לִי: "רַבִּי, לַמְּדֵנִי בִּנְטִיעַת קִשּׁוּאִין". [13]אָמַרְתִּי דָּבָר אֶחָד נִתְמַלְּאָה כָּל הַשָּׂדֶה קִשּׁוּאִין. [14]אָמַר לִי: "רַבִּי, לִמַּדְתַּנִי נְטִיעָתָן — [15]לַמְּדֵנִי עֲקִירָתָן". [16]אָמַרְתִּי דָּבָר אֶחָד, נִתְקַבְּצוּ כּוּלָּן לְמָקוֹם אֶחָד'.

LITERAL TRANSLATION

on his heart, [and] said: [1]'Woe to you, my two arms, which are like two Torah scrolls that are rolled. [2]I have learned much Torah, and I have taught much Torah. [3]I have learned a lot of Torah, but I did not diminish of my masters, [4]even like a dog which laps out of the sea. [5]I have taught a lot of Torah, [6]and my disciples have only diminished of me like a brush in a tube. [7]And furthermore, I teach three hundred laws regarding an intense bright spot, [8]and there was no man who ever asked me about them. [9]And furthermore, I teach three hundred laws (and some say, three thousand laws) regarding the planting of cucumbers, [10]and there was no man who ever asked me about them, except for Akiva ben Yosef. [11]Once, he and I were walking along the road. [12]He said to me: "O Master, teach me about the planting of cucumbers." [13]I said one thing, [and] the entire field was filled with cucumbers. [14]He said to me: "O Master, you have taught me about their planting. [15]Teach me about their uprooting." [16]I said one thing, [and] they were all gathered in one place.'

RASHI

שנגללין — כשגוללין ספר תורה והכתב מכוסה — כך תתעלם ותתכסה תורה שבלבי כשאמות, לפי שלא שמשוני ולמדו ממני. **ולא חסרתי מרבותי ככלב המלקק מן הים** — לפי חכמתם שהיתה גדולה אין תלמודי עולה לחסרם ולקבל מהם חכמה אלא מעט ככלב המלקק מן הים, וכן תלמידי לא חסרוני ולא קבלו מחכמתי לחסר את יתרון חכמתי מהם אפילו כמו שמחסר המכחול בשפופרת בטבול אחד. **ולא חסרתי** — כלומר לא חסרתים מחכמתם ממה שהיו מתחילה גדולים יותר ממני וגם עתה גדולים הם ממני, לפי שלא למדתי מחכמתם כי אם מעט מהם. **שפופרת** — קנה שנותנין בה כחול קיסם של עץ או של כסף שתוחבין מכחול בתוכו ומטבלו בכחול ומוציאו. **בבהרת עזה** — בהלכות מראות נגעים. **בנטיעת קשואים** — הלכות מיני כשפים שעל ידיהם נתמלא כל השדה קשואים.

NOTES

the most minute infractions. Others argue that Rabbi Akiva was the sharpest among his contemporaries, so he would have benefited most from studying with Rabbi Eliezer (*Ramah*). It has also been pointed out that Rabbi Akiva said that someone who does not properly attend to a Torah scholar is liable to death at the hand of Heaven, and so it was his absence that upset Rabbi Eliezer the most (see *Margaliyot HaYam*).

כְּכֶלֶב...כְּמִכְחוֹל **Like a dog...like a brush.** Rabbi Eliezer spoke about himself in the most modest fashion, comparing himself to a dog who laps water out of the sea. But regarding his disciples, he used the more respectful metaphor, that of the paintbrush and the tube (*Maharsha*).

TRANSLATION AND COMMENTARY

[1]The Sages who came to visit Rabbi Eliezer **said to him: 'What is the law** regarding **a** leather **ball** that is filled with wool or rags, **or a shoemaker's last** (a leather form filled with wool or rags upon which a shoemaker fashions shoes), **or a** leather **amulet** that is filled with a written text or herbs, **or a** leather **bag in which jewels** are bound up, **or** a leather pouch encasing **a small weight?'** Elsewhere, the Rabbi Eliezer and the Sages disagree about these and similar items. According to the Sages, these items do not contract ritual impurity, because a leather utensil can only contract ritual impurity if it can serve as a receptacle, and these items which are permanently filled are not regarded as receptacles. Rabbi Eliezer disagrees and says that they do contract ritual impurity, because even a utensil which is permanently filled is regarded as a receptacle. If a filled leather utensil was ripped open, the Sages agree that it is regarded as a receptacle, and therefore it contracts ritual impurity, but they disagree with Rabbi Eliezer about how the ritually impure utensil must be immersed in a mikveh. According to the Sages, the filling must be removed before the utensil is immersed. Otherwise it would stand between the utensil and the water of the mikveh. Rabbi Eliezer disagrees and says that the utensil may be immersed as it is, because the utensil and its filling are regarded as a single vessel, and so the filling does not stand between the utensil and the water of the mikveh. The Sages who came to visit Rabbi Eliezer before he died asked him whether he had changed his position on these matters. [2]Rabbi Eliezer **said to them:** 'I still maintain that filled leather utensils **can contract ritual impurity, and** that they may be immersed in a mikveh for **purification as they are** without removing the filling.' The Sages asked Rabbi Eliezer one additional question: [3]'**What is the law regarding shoes** that are ready to be worn, but which are still **on the shoemaker's last?'** Elsewhere, Rabbi Eliezer disagrees with the Sages about this matter as well. According to the Sages, they can contract ritual impurity, because they are regarded as a finished utensil, since even a non-professional can remove them from the shoemaker's form. Rabbi Eliezer disagrees and says that while they are on the shoemaker's last they are not regarded as finished utensils, and therefore they do not contract ritual impurity. The Sages who came to visit Rabbi Eliezer wanted to know whether Rabbi Eliezer's position on the matter had changed. [4]Rabbi Eliezer **said to them:** 'I still maintain that the shoes are **ritually pure.'** [5]**And his soul departed in purity,** as he was uttering the words 'ritually pure.' [6]**Rabbi Yehoshua stood up on his feet, and said: 'The ban** which had been placed on Rabbi Eliezer **has been rescinded, the ban** which

[1]אָמְרוּ לוֹ: ׳הַכַּדּוּר, וְהָאִמּוּס, וְהַקָּמֵיעַ, וּצְרוֹר הַמַּרְגָּלִיּוֹת, וּמִשְׁקוֹלֶת קְטַנָּה, מַהוּ׳? [2]אָמַר לָהֶן: ׳הֵן טְמֵאִין, וְטָהֳרָתָן בְּמַה שֶּׁהֵן׳. [3]׳מִנְעָל שֶׁעַל גַּבֵּי הָאִמּוּס, מַהוּ׳? [4]אָמַר לָהֶן: ׳הוּא טָהוֹר׳. [5]וְיָצְאָה נִשְׁמָתוֹ בְּטָהֳרָה. [6]עָמַד רַבִּי יְהוֹשֻׁעַ עַל רַגְלָיו, וְאָמַר: ׳הוּתַּר הַנֶּדֶר,

LITERAL TRANSLATION

[1]They said to him: 'A ball, and a shoemaker's last, and an amulet, a bag of jewels, and a small weight, what [is the law]?' [2]He said to them: 'They are ritually impure, and their purification is as they are.' '[3]The shoe that is on the shoemaker's last, what [is the law]?' [4]He said to them: 'It is ritually pure.' [5]And his soul departed in purity. [6]Rabbi Yehoshua stood on his feet, and said: 'The vow is annulled,

RASHI

אימר לו הכדור והאימוס וכו׳ — כדור = *פלוט״ה מחופה עור ומלאה מתוכו צמר של איל כדוחק. וכן אימוס שלהם של עור היה, כעין מנעל וממולא מתוכו שער ופיו תפור, וכו היו עושין המנעלים כמו שעושין הרצענין שלנו בדפוס של עץ. **הקמיע** — של עור וממולא מתוכו, ותלאהו בצואר לנוי. **משקולת קטנה** — כעין אונקיא שעושין מעופרת ומחפין אותה בעור כדי שלא תחסר, אבל משקולת גדולה אין דרכה לחפותה בעור. **וצרור המרגלית** — תופרין המרגלית בעור ותולין אותו בצואר בהמה לרפואה. **מהו** — לפי שנחלקו באלו רבי אליעזר וחכמים בסדר טהרות (כלים פרק כג) וחכמים אומרים אינן מקבלין טומאה, לפי שכלי עור אין מקבל טומאה אלא אם כן יש לו בית קיבול דהא איתקש לשק, והני הואיל וקבולן נעשית למלאותן מלוי בתוכו עולמית לא שמיה קבול. ורבי אליעזר אומר מקבל טומאה, דבית קיבול העשוי למלאות שמיה קבול, ועוד נחלקו בכדור ובאימוס שנקרעו ונראה חלל שלהם, דמודו רבנן דמקבלי טומאה דהא איכא בית קיבול, ופליגי לענין טבילה, שחכמים אומרים מה שבתוכו חוצץ, ורבי אליעזר אומר מה שבתוכו אינו חוצץ, דכולי חד כלי הוא. ובשעת פטירתו היו רוצין לידע אם חזר בו ושאלוהו: מה אתה אומר באותן שני המחלוקות? אמר להם: טמאים אפילו שלמים והטומאה נוגעת מבחוץ. **וטהרתן במה שהן** — כלומר אם נקרעו שחכמים מודים שמקבלין טומאה וחלוקין עלי לומר שהמלוי חוצץ, ועומד אני בדברי שהמלוי אינו חוצץ — שמטבילין כמות שהן. **מנעל שעל גבי אימוס מהו** — שאף בו נחלקו בתוספתא דטהרות, חכמים אומרין הואיל ואינו מחוסר מלאכה הצריכה אומן, שהדיוט יכול לסלקו מעל האימוס כבר שם כלי עליו — וטמא, ורבי אליעזר מטהר שעדיין לא נגמרה מלאכתו. **הותר הנדר** — שברכוהו.

BACKGROUND

אִמּוּס A last for shoes.

Shoemakers and a shoemaker's last from the Mishnaic period.

As described in the Mishnah, this refers to a form made of leather stuffed with small pieces of cloth. As today, there were also lasts made of wood.

The word apparently derives from the Semitic root אם meaning "a basis, a primary form."

LANGUAGE (RASHI)

פלוט״א* From the Old French *pelote*, meaning "a ball."

NOTES

טָהֳרָתָן בְּמַה שֶּׁהֵן Their purification is as they are. *Ramah* has a different reading: טָהֳרָתָן בְּמַשֶּׁהוּ, "their purification is with the most minute amount." The Baraita means to say that such utensils, if they are chipped even the slightest amount, are no longer considered utensils, and so they are automatically considered ritually pure.

TRANSLATION AND COMMENTARY

had been placed on Rabbi Eliezer **has been rescinded.'** [1]Rabbi Akiva was not present when Rabbi Eliezer died, but **on Saturday night he met up** with the funeral entourage as it was proceeding **from Caesaria to Lod.** [2]**He beat his flesh** in grief **until his blood flowed to the ground.** [3]He then **opened his eulogy** as those who came to pay their condolences stood **in a line.** Citing the words of Elisha which he spoke as Elijah ascended to heaven (II Kings 2:12), [4]Rabbi Akiva **said: '"My father, my father, the chariots of Israel, and their horsemen."** [5]**I have many coins, but I have no money-changer to sort them.** I still have many questions, but now that Rabbi Eliezer is dead, nobody can answer them.'" [6]**This** story **implies that** Rabbi Akiva learned the laws of planting cucumbers by magic **from Rabbi Eliezer,** and not from Rabbi Yehoshua!

גְּמָרָהּ [7]The Gemara explains: First Rabbi Akiva **learned** these matters **from Rabbi Eliezer, but he did not** fully **understand** them. [8]**Then he learned** them again **from Rabbi Yehoshua, and he explained them to him.**

הֵיכִי עָבֵיד הָכִי [9]The Gemara asks: **How did** Rabbi Eliezer **act in the way** described in the Baraita, planting and uprooting cucumbers by magic? [10]**But surely we have learned** in our Mishnah: **"Someone who performs an act** of magic to bring the cucumbers together **is liable** to be executed by stoning."

לְהִתְלַמֵּד שָׁאנֵי [11]The Gemara answers: Performing acts of magic in order **to learn** how they are done **is different,** and permitted. Here Rabbi Eliezer planted and uprooted the cucumbers so that Rabbi Akiva could learn how that is done. [12]**As the Sage said:** The Torah states (Deuteronomy 18:9-10): **"You shall not learn to do** after the abominations of those nations. There must not be found among you anyone who passes his son or his daughter through a fire, or that uses divination, a soothsayer, or an enchanter, or a sorcerer." [53]These verses teach that **you may not learn** how to perform acts of magic in

הוּתַּר הַנֶּדֶר׳! [1]לְמוֹצָאֵי שַׁבָּת פָּגַע בּוֹ רַבִּי עֲקִיבָא מִן קֵסָרִי לְלוֹד. [2]הָיָה מַכֶּה בִּבְשָׂרוֹ עַד שֶׁדָּמוֹ שׁוֹתֵת לָאָרֶץ. [3]פָּתַח עָלָיו בַּשּׁוּרָה, [4]וְאָמַר: ׳״אָבִי, אָבִי, רֶכֶב יִשְׂרָאֵל, וּפָרָשָׁיו״. [5]הַרְבֵּה מָעוֹת יֵשׁ לִי, וְאֵין לִי שׁוּלְחָנִי לְהַרְצוֹתָן׳״. [6]אַלְמָא, מֵרַבִּי אֱלִיעֶזֶר גְּמָרָהּ!

[7]גְּמָרָהּ מֵרַבִּי אֱלִיעֶזֶר, וְלָא סְבָרָהּ. [8]הֲדַר גְּמָרָהּ מֵרַבִּי יְהוֹשֻׁעַ וְאַסְבְּרָהּ נִיהֲלֵיהּ.

[9]הֵיכִי עָבֵיד הָכִי? [10]וְהָאֲנַן תְּנַן: ״הָעוֹשֶׂה מַעֲשֶׂה חַיָּיב״!

[11]לְהִתְלַמֵּד שָׁאנֵי. [12]דְּאָמַר מָר: ״לֹא תִלְמַד לַעֲשׂוֹת״. [13]לַעֲשׂוֹת

LITERAL TRANSLATION

the vow is annulled!' [1]Saturday night, Rabbi Akiva met him between Caesaria and Lod. [2]He beat his flesh until his blood flowed to the ground. [3]He opened [his eulogy] about him in the line, [4]and said: '"My father, my father, the chariots of Israel, and their horsemen." [5]I have many coins, but I have no money-changer to sort them.'" [6]This implies that he learned from Rabbi Eliezer!

[7]He learned it from Rabbi Eliezer, but he did not understand it. [8]Then he learned it from Rabbi Yehoshua, and he explained it to him.

[9]How did he act in that way? [10]But surely we have learned: "The one who performs an act is liable."

[11]To learn is different. [12]As the master said: "You shall not learn to do." [13]To do

RASHI

בין קסרי ללוד — שהיו נושאין את מטתו מקסרי ללוד. **פתח עליו בשורה** — שהיו עושין שורה סביבות המטה להספד. **הרבה מעות יש לי** — להחליף. **ואין לי שולחני להרצותן** — כלומר: הרבה שאלות יש לי לשאול, ואין למי לשאול. **היכי עביד** — רבי אליעזר הכי, שעשה מעשה בנטיעת קשואין? **להתלמד** — בפני רבי עקיבא, הוא דעבד רבי אליעזר.

הדרן עלך ארבע מיתות

NOTES

הָיָה מַכֶּה בִּבְשָׂרוֹ **He beat his flesh.** The Rishonim ask: How could Rabbi Akiva have beat himself until he was bleeding? Surely the verse states (Leviticus 19:28): "You shall not make any cuttings in your flesh for the dead"? Some answer: Inflicting a wound upon oneself is only forbidden in the presence of the corpse. But if the corpse is not present, it is permitted. Others suggest that the prohibition is restricted to cutting the flesh. But beating one's flesh until it bleeds is permitted. Yet others explain that a person is forbidden to inflict a wound upon himself in his distress over another person's passing, but he is permitted to inflict such a wound in his distress over the Torah that was lost (see *Tosafot, Meiri*).

HALAKHAH

לְהִתְלַמֵּד שָׁאנֵי **To learn is different.** "A judge appointed to the Sanhedrin should be knowledgeable in matters of magic, in order to judge a person accused of sorcery or the like. Thus, apparently, a person is permitted to study the arts of magic in order to understand them, as long as he does not actually perform any acts of magic." (*Rambam, Sefer Shofetim, Hilkhot Sanhedrin* 2:1.)

TRANSLATION AND COMMENTARY

order **to do** them. [1] **But you may learn** them **in order to understand** them yourself **and teach** them to others.

אִי אַתָּה לָמֵד, [1] אֲבָל אַתָּה לָמֵד לְהָבִין וּלְהוֹרוֹת.

הדרן עלך ארבע מיתות

LITERAL TRANSLATION

you may not learn, [1] but you may learn in order to understand and teach.

NOTES

אֲבָל אַתָּה לָמֵד לְהָבִין וּלְהוֹרוֹת **But you may learn in order to understand and teach.** The Sages studied sorcery by way of traditions that were transmitted from generation to generation. Even after capital punishment was no longer administered, traditions regarding sorcery continued to be transmitted in certain families. These matters were studied so that the Sanhedrin would be capable of distinguishing between actual sorcery and deception, and thus be able to pass judgment in cases involving sorcerers. Moreover, it was necessary to understand these matters in order to evaluate a person who performs what appears to be a miracle as proof that he is a Prophet, to decide whether he is a true Prophet or merely a sorcerer (*Rav Hai Gaon*).

Conclusion to Chapter Seven

Conclusion to Chapter Seven

This chapter clarified the four methods of judicial execution, and the order of their severity was determined: Stoning, burning, decapitation, and strangulation. Most of the discussion in the chapter centered on transgressions punishable by stoning (aside from the rebellious son, to which a separate chapter will be devoted). The source of each law in the Torah was ascertained as well as the detailed laws according to which a death sentence is imposed.

In the course of discussing these transgressions, which are among the most severe crimes in Torah law, two other topics were included which do not appear outwardly to be connected to the subject of this chapter, but they are connected to its essential significance. The discussion of severe sins and the various methods of execution led to the need to construct a method for evaluating the importance of the various commandments and deciding which are the most severe and important. The need for clarifying this is not merely theoretical. At all times the practical question exists: what should a person do if he is forced to violate a severe commandment, whether by a person who forces him to commit the transgression, or by an illness that requires him to violate the Torah? The basic discussion of the transgressions which a person must be killed (or to die) rather than commit is found in this chapter, though it is also mentioned elsewhere in the Talmud. The conclusion is that a person is permitted to violate all of the laws of the Torah under compulsion, except for three especially strict prohibitions: that against idolatry, which is the denial of the essence of the Jewish faith; that against the spilling of blood; and that against incest and adultery. This permission to violate the Torah applies only when the compulsion derives from an illness or from the need to comply with the arbitrary orders or needs of another person. However, when there is religious persecution, and the authorities seek to make all the Jews convert, every Jew must give up his life rather than violate even the slightest commandment, one which is not punishable by judicial execution or lashes.

Another discussion which sheds general light on Jewish law is that of the Noachide laws. Tractate Sanhedrin deals with the entire structure of a state. Hence the Torah cannot ignore the existence of non-Jews living in it, or who are subject to its laws in another way. Moreover, Judaism has a principled approach and understanding of the religious and moral obligations of a human being as such (called, formally, a son of Noah, meaning, any human being).

In comparison to the many and severe commandments incumbent upon the Jews, it was necessary to determine which commandments apply universally or in one form or another to all human beings, and which apply only to the Jewish people, as a "kingdom of priests and holy nation." The Halakhic conclusion regarding this subject is that there are basic commandments which obligate all human beings, and there exists a universal system of law, trial, and judgment.

Usually one speaks of the Seven Noachide laws, which include the prohibitions against idolatry, the spilling of blood, forbidden sexual relations, cursing God, theft, and eating from a living animal. There is also a commandment to establish a legal system so as to institute an orderly way of life. These commandments, including their detailed prescriptions and additional commandments (which, according to one source, are thirty in number) are explained in this chapter. They are the basis of a universal human religion according to Judaism.

List of Sources

List of Sources

Aḥaronim, lit., "the last," meaning Rabbinic authorities from the time of the publication of Rabbi Yosef Caro's code of Halakhah, *Shulḥan Arukh* (1555).

Arba'ah Turim, code of Halakhah by Rabbi Ya'akov ben Asher, b. Germany, active in Spain (c. 1270-1343).

Arukh, Talmudic dictionary, by Rabbi Natan of Rome, 11th century.

Arukh LeNer, novellae on the Talmud by Rabbi Ben Tzion Ya'akov Etlinger, Germany (1798-1871).

Baḥ (Bayit Ḥadash), commentary on *Arba'ah Turim,* by Rabbi Yoel Sirkes, Poland (1561-1640).

Be'er HaGolah, commentary on unusual Aggadic passages in the Talmud by Rabbi Yehudah Loew ben Betzalel of Prague (1525-1609).

Bereshit Rabbah, Midrash on the Book of Genesis.

Bertinoro, Ovadyah, 15th century commentator on the Mishnah.

Bet Yosef, Halakhic commentary on *Arba'ah Turim* by Rabbi Yosef Caro (1488-1575), which is the basis of his authoritative Halakhic code, *Shulḥan Arukh.*

Birkei Yosef, novellae on *Shulḥan Arukh* by Rabbi Ḥayyim Yosef David Azulai, Israel and Italy (1724-1807).

Darkhei Moshe, commentary on *Tur* by Rabbi Moshe ben Isserles, Poland (1525-1572).

Ein Ya'akov, collection of Aggadot from the Babylonian Talmud by Rabbi Ya'akov ben Shlomo Ḥabib, Spain and Salonika (c. 1445-1515).

Even HaEzer, section of *Shulḥan Arukh* dealing with marriage, divorce, and related topics.

Geonim, heads of the academies of Sura and Pumbedita in Babylonia from the late 6th century to the mid-11th century.

Hagahot Maimoniyot, commentary on *Mishneh Torah,* by Rabbi Meir HaKohen, Germany, 14th century.

Hagahot Ram Arak, novellae on the Talmud by Rabbi Meir Arak, Poland, early 20th century.

Hagahot Ri Pik Berlin, Rabbi Yeshayahu Pik Berlin, Talmudic scholar, Breslau (1725-1799).

Halakhot Gedolot, a code of Halakhic decisions written in the Geonic period. This work has been ascribed to Sherira Gaon, Rav Hai Gaon, Rav Yehudah Gaon and Rabbi Shimon Kayyara.

Ḥamra Veḥaye, novellae on tractate *Sanhedrin,* by Rabbi Ḥayyim Benevisti, Turkey, 17th century.

Hayyim Shenayim Yeshalem, novellae on *Sanhedrin,* by Rabbi Shmuel Vital.

Ḥokhmat Manoaḥ, commentary on the Talmud by Rabbi Manoaḥ ben Shemaryah, Poland, 16th century.

Ḥoshen Mishpat, section of *Shulḥan Arukh* dealing with civil and criminal law.

Imrei Tzvi, novellae of the Talmud by Rabbi Tzvi Kohen, Vilna, 19th century.

Iyyun Ya'akov, commentary on *Ein Ya'akov,* by Rabbi Ya'akov bar Yosef Riesher, Prague, Poland, and France (d. 1733).

Keli Yakar, commentary on the Torah by Rabbi Shlomo Efrayim of Luntshitz, Poland (d. 1619)

Keneset HaGedolah (see *Shayarei Keneset HaGedolah*).

Kesef Mishneh, commentary on *Mishneh Torah,* by Rabbi Yosef Caro, author of *Shulḥan Arukh.*

Keset HaSofer, laws regarding the writing of Torah scrolls and mezuzahs, by Rabbi Shlomo Ganzfried, Hungary (19th century).

Ketzot HaḤoshen, novellae on *Shulḥan Arukh, Ḥoshen Mishpat,* by Rabbi Aryeh Leib Heller, Galicia (1754?-183).

Kos Yeshuot, novellae on the Talmud by Rabbi Shmuel HaKohen Shatin, Germany (d. 1719).

Leḥem Mishneh, commentary on the *Mishneh Torah,* by Rabbi Avraham di Boton, Salonica (1560-1609).

Lekaḥ Tov, Midrashim and commentary on the Torah by Rabbi Tuvyah the son of Rabbi Eliezer, Bulgaria (11th century).

Levush, abbreviation of *Levush Mordekhai,* Halakhic code by Rabbi Mordekhai Yaffe, Poland (1530-1612).

Magen Avraham, commentary on *Shulḥan Arukh, Oraḥ Hayyim,* by Rabbi Avraham HaLevi Gombiner, Poland (d. 1683).

Maggid Mishneh, commentary on *Mishneh Torah,* by Rabbi Vidal de Tolosa, Spain, 14th century.

Maharal, Rabbi Yehudah Loew ben Betzalel of Prague (1525-1631). Novellae on the Talmud.

Maharam Schiff, novellae on the Talmud by Rabbi Meir ben Ya'akov HaKohen Schiff (1605-1641), Frankfurt, Germany.

Maharik, Rabbi Yosef Kolon, France and Italy (c. 1420-1480). Responsa literature.

Maharsha, Rabbi Shmuel Eliezer ben Yehudah HaLevi Edels, Poland (1555-1631). Novellae on the Talmud.

Maharshal, Rabbi Shlomo ben Yeḥiel Luria, Poland (1510-1573). Novellae on the Talmud.

Maharshashakh, Rabbi Shmuel Shotten, Germany (17th century). Novellae on the Talmud.

Margoliyot HaYam, novellae on tractate *Sanhedrin* by Rabbi Reuben Margoliyot, Poland, 20th century.

Megaleh Amukot, Kabbalistic commentary on the Torah by Rabbi Natan Shapiro, Poland (1585-1633).

Meir Einei Soferim, laws regarding the writing of Torah scrolls, mezuzahs, and bills of divorce, by Rabbi David Krosik.

Meiri, commentary on the Talmud (called *Bet HaBeḥirah*), by Rabbi Menaḥem ben Shlomo, Provence (1249-1316).

Mekhilta, Halakhic Midrash on the Book of Exodus.

Melekhet Shlomo, commentary on the Mishnah by Rabbi Shlomo Adeni, Yemen and Israel (1567-1626).

Melo HaRo'im, commentary on the Talmud by Rabbi Ya'akov Tzvi Yolles, Poland (c. 1778-1825).

Menorat HaMa'or, Anthology of Midrashim, by Rabbi Yitzḥak Abohav (15th century).

Midrash Shir HaShirim Rabbah, Midrash on the Song of Songs.

Midrash Tanḥuma, see *Tanḥuma.*

Mishneh LeMelekh, commentary on *Mishneh Torah* by Rabbi Yehudah ben Shmuel Rosanes, Turkey (1657-1727).

Mishnah Berurah, commentary on *Shulḥan Arukh, Oraḥ Ḥayyim,* by Rabbi Yisrael Meir HaKohen, Poland (1837-1933).

Mitzpeh Eitan, glosses on the Talmud by Rabbi Avraham Maskileison, Byelorussia (1788-1848).

Nimmukei Yosef, commentary on *Hilkhot HaRif,* by Rabbi Yosef Ḥaviva, Spain, early 15th century.

Oraḥ Ḥayyim, section of *Shulḥan Arukh* dealing with daily religious observances, prayers, and the laws of the Sabbath and Festivals.

Pirkei DeRabbi Eliezer, Aggadic Midrash on the Torah.

Pitḥei Teshuvah, compilation of responsa literature on *Shulḥan Arukh* by Rabbi Avraham Tzvi Eisenstadt, Russia (1812-1868).

Ra'avad, Rabbi Avraham ben David, commentator and Halakhic authority. Wrote comments on *Mishneh Torah.* Provence (c. 1125-1198?).

Rabbenu Ḥananel (ben Ḥushiel), commentator on the Talmud, North Africa (990-1055).

Rabbenu Meshulam, French Tosafist, 12th century.

Rabbenu Sa'adya Gaon, scholar and author, Egypt and Sura, Babylonia (882-942).

Rabbenu Shimshon of Sens, Tosafist, France and Eretz Israel (late 12th-early 13th century).

Rabbenu Tam, commentator on the Talmud, Tosafist, France (1100-1171).

Rabbenu Yehonatan of Lunel, Yehonatan ben David HaKohen of Lunel, Provence, Talmudic scholar (c.1135-after 1210).

Rabbenu Yonah, see *Talmidei Rabbenu Yonah.*

Rabbenu Zeraḥyah HaLevi, author of *HaMa'or,* commentary on *Hilkhot HaRif.* Spain, 12th century.

Rabbi David Bonfil (Bonfied), commentary on tractate *Sanhedrin* by Rabbi David Bonfil (Bonfied), France, 11th century.

Rabbi David Pardo, novellae on the Talmud, Italy, 18th century.

Rabbi E. M. Horowitz, Rabbi Elazar Moshe Horowitz, novellae on the Talmud, Pinsk (19th century).

Rabbi Issac Ḥaver, novellae on the Talmud by Rabbi Issac Ḥaver, Poland, 18th century.

Rabbi Tzvi Ḥayyot (Chajes), Galician Rabbi, 19th century.

Rabbi Ya'akov Emden, Talmudist and Halakhic authority, Germany (1697-1776).

Rabbi Yehudah Almandri, author of commentary on *Rif,* tractate *Sanhedrin,* Syria, 13th century.

Rabbi Yeshayahu Pik Berlin, Talmudic scholar, Breslau (1725-1799).

Rabbi Yitzḥak Ibn Giyyat, Halakhist, Bible commentator and liturgical poet, Spain (1038-1089).

Rabbi Yosef of Jerusalem, French Tosafist of the twelfth and thirteenth centuries, France and Eretz Israel.

Rabbi Yoshiyah Pinto, Eretz Israel and Syria (1565-1648). Commentary on *Ein Ya'akov.*

Rabbi Zeraḥyah ben Yitzḥak HaLevi, Spain, 12th century. Author of *HaMa'or,* Halakhic commentary on *Hilkhot HaRif.*

Radak, Rabbi David Kimḥi, grammarian and Bible commentator, Narbonne, Provence (1160?-1235?).

Radbaz, Rabbi David ben Shlomo Avi Zimra, Spain, Egypt, Eretz Israel, and North Africa (1479-1574). Commentary on *Mishneh Torah.*

Raḥ, Rabbenu Ḥananel (ben Ḥushiel), commentator on the Talmud, North Africa (990-1055).

Ramah, novellae on the Talmud by Rabbi Meir ben Todros HaLevi Abulafiya, Spain (c. 1170-1244). See *Yad Ramah.*

Rambam, Rabbi Moshe ben Maimon, Rabbi and philosopher, known also as Maimonides. Author of *Mishneh Torah,* Spain and Egypt (1135-1204).

Ramban, Rabbi Moshe ben Naḥman, commentator on Bible and Talmud, known also as Naḥmanides, Spain and Eretz Israel (1194-1270).

Ran, Rabbi Nissim ben Reuven Gerondi, Spanish Talmudist (1310?-1375?).

Rash, Rabbi Shimshon ben Avraham, Tosafist, commentator on the Mishnah, Sens (late 12th- early 13th century).

Rashash, Rabbi Shmuel ben Yosef Shtrashun, Lithuanian Talmud scholar (1794-1872).

Rashba, Rabbi Shlomo ben Avraham Adret, Spanish Rabbi famous for his commentaries on the Talmud and his responsa (c. 1235-c.1314).

Rashbam, Rabbi Shmuel ben Meir, commentator on the Talmud, France (1085-1158).

Rashi, Rabbi Shlomo ben Yitzḥak, the paramount commentator on the Bible and the Talmud, France (1040-1105).

Rav Aha of Sabha, author of *She'iltot,* Babylonia, 8th century.

Rav Hai Gaon, Babylonian Rabbi, head of Pumbedita Yeshivah, 10th century.

Rav Natronai Gaon, of the Sura Yeshivah, 9th century.

Rav Sherira Gaon, of the Pumbedita Yeshivah, 10th century.

Rav Tzemaḥ Gaon, Tzemaḥ ben Ḥayyim, Gaon of Sura (889-895).

Rema, Rabbi Moshe ben Yisrael Isserles, Halakhic authority, Poland (1525-1572).

Responsa of Ḥatam Sofer, responsa literature by Rabbi Moshe Sofer (Schreiber), Pressburg (1763-1839).

Ri, Rabbi Yitzḥak ben Shmuel of Dampierre, Tosafist, France (died c. 1185).

Ri Almandri, Rabbi Yehudah Almandri. Author of commentary on *Rif,* tractate *Sanhedrin,* Syria, 13th century.

Ri Migash, Rabbi Yosef Ibn Migash, commentator on the Talmud, Spain (1077-1141).

Ri Yolles, Rabbi Ya'akov Tzvi Yolles, Talmudic scholar, Poland (c. 1778-1825).

Rif, Rabbi Yitzḥak Alfasi, Halakhist, author of *Hilkhot HaRif,* North Africa (1013-1103).

Rishonim, lit., "the first," meaning Rabbinic authorities active between the end of the Geonic period (mid-11th century) and the publication of *Shulḥan Arukh* (1555).

Ritva, novellae and commentary on the Talmud by Rabbi Yom Tov ben Avraham Ishbili, Spain (c. 1250-1330).

Riva, Rabbenu Yitzḥak ben Asher, Tosafist, novellae on tractate *Sanhedrin.*

Rosh, Rabbi Asher ben Yeḥiel, also known as Asheri, commentator and Halakhist, German and Spain (c. 1250-1327).

Sanhedrei Ketanah, novellae on tractate *Sanhedrin* by Rabbi Avraham Yehoshua Bornstein, Russia, 19th century.

Sefer Meir Einayim, see *Sma.*

Shakh (Siftei Kohen), commentary on the *Shulḥan Arukh* by Rabbi Shabbetai ben Meir HaKohen, Lithuania (1621-1662).

Shayarei Keneset HaGedolah, a Halakhic work by Rabbi Ḥayyim Benevisti, Turkey, 17th century.

Shelah (Shenei Luḥot HaBrit), an extensive work on Halakhah, ethics and Kabbalah by Rabbi Yeshayahu ben Avraham HaLevi Horowitz. Prague, Poland and Eretz Israel (c. 1565-1630).

She'eilot U'Teshuvot HaMibit, Responsa literature of Rabbi Moshe of Tirani, Sefad (1500-1580).

Shemot Rabbah, Midrash on the Book of Exodus.

Shulḥan Arukh, code of Halakhah by Rabbi Yosef Caro, b. Spain, active in Eretz Israel (1488-1575).

Sifrei, Halakhic Midrash on the Books of Numbers and Deuteronomy.

Sma, (Sefer Meirat Einaim), commentary on *Shulḥan Arukh, Ḥoshen Mishpat,* by Rabbi Yehoshua Falk Katz, Poland (c. 1550-1614).

Smag, (Sefer Mitzvot Gedolot), an extensive work on the positive and negative commandments by Rabbi Moshe ben Ya'akov of Coucy, 13th century.

Talmid Rabbenu Peretz, commentary on the Talmud by the school of Rabbi Peretz of Corbiel, France (13th century)

Talmidei Rabbenu Yonah, commentary on *Hilkhot HaRif* by the school of Rabbi Yonah of Gerondi, Spain (1190-1263).

Tanḥuma, Midrash on the Five Books of Moses.

Tashbatz, Respona literature of Rabbi Shimon ben Tzemaḥ Duran, Spain and Algeria (1361-1444).

Taz, abbreviation for *Turei Zahav.* See *Turei Zahav.*

Tiferet Yisrael, commentary on the Mishnah, by Rabbi Yisrael Lipshitz, Germany (1782-1860).

Torat Ḥayyim, novellae on the Talmud by Rabbi Avraham Ḥayyim Shor, Galicia (d. 1632).

Tosafot, collection of commentaries and novellae on the Talmud, expanding on Rashi's commentary, by the French-German Tosafists (12th and 13th centuries).

Tosafot Ḥadashim, commentary on the Mishnah by Rabbi Shimshon Bloch, Hamburg, Germany (d. 1737).

Tosefot Hokhmei Angli'a, collection of novellae on the Talmud by English Tosafists (13th century).

Tosefot Rabbenu Peretz, Tosefot of the school of Rabbi Peretz ben Eliyahu of Corbeil (d. 1295).

Tosefot Rosh, an edition based on *Tosefot Sens* by the *Rosh,* Rabbi Asher ben Yeḥiel, Germany and Spain (c. 1250-1327).

Tosefot Yom Tov, commentary on the Mishnah by Rabbi Yom Tov Lipman HaLevi Heller, Prague and Poland (1579-1654).

Tur, abbreviation of *Arba'ah Turim,* Halakhic code by Rabbi Ya'akov ben Asher, b. Germany, active in Spain (c. 1270-1343).

Tzofnat Pa'ane'aḥ, novellae and commentaries by Rabbi Yosef Rozin, Lithuania (1858-1936).

Yad Malakhi, a work on Talmudic and Halakhic methodology, by Rabbi Malakhi ben Ya'akov HaKohen, Italy (died c. 1785).

Yafeh Mar'eh, commentary on the Midrash by Rabbi Shmuel Yaffe, Turkey, 16th century.

Yalkut (see *Yalkut Shimoni*).

Yalkut Shimoni, Aggadic Midrash on the Bible.

Yefeh Enayim, cross-references and notes to the Jerusalem Talmud, by Rabbi Yeshayahu Pik Berlin, Breslau (1725-1799).

Yoreh De'ah, section of *Shulḥan Arukh* dealing mainly with dietary laws, interest, ritual purity, and mourning.

About the Type

This book was set in Leawood, a contemporary typeface designed by Leslie Usherwood. His staff completed the design upon Usherwood's death in 1984. It is a friendly, inviting face that goes particularly well with sans serif type.